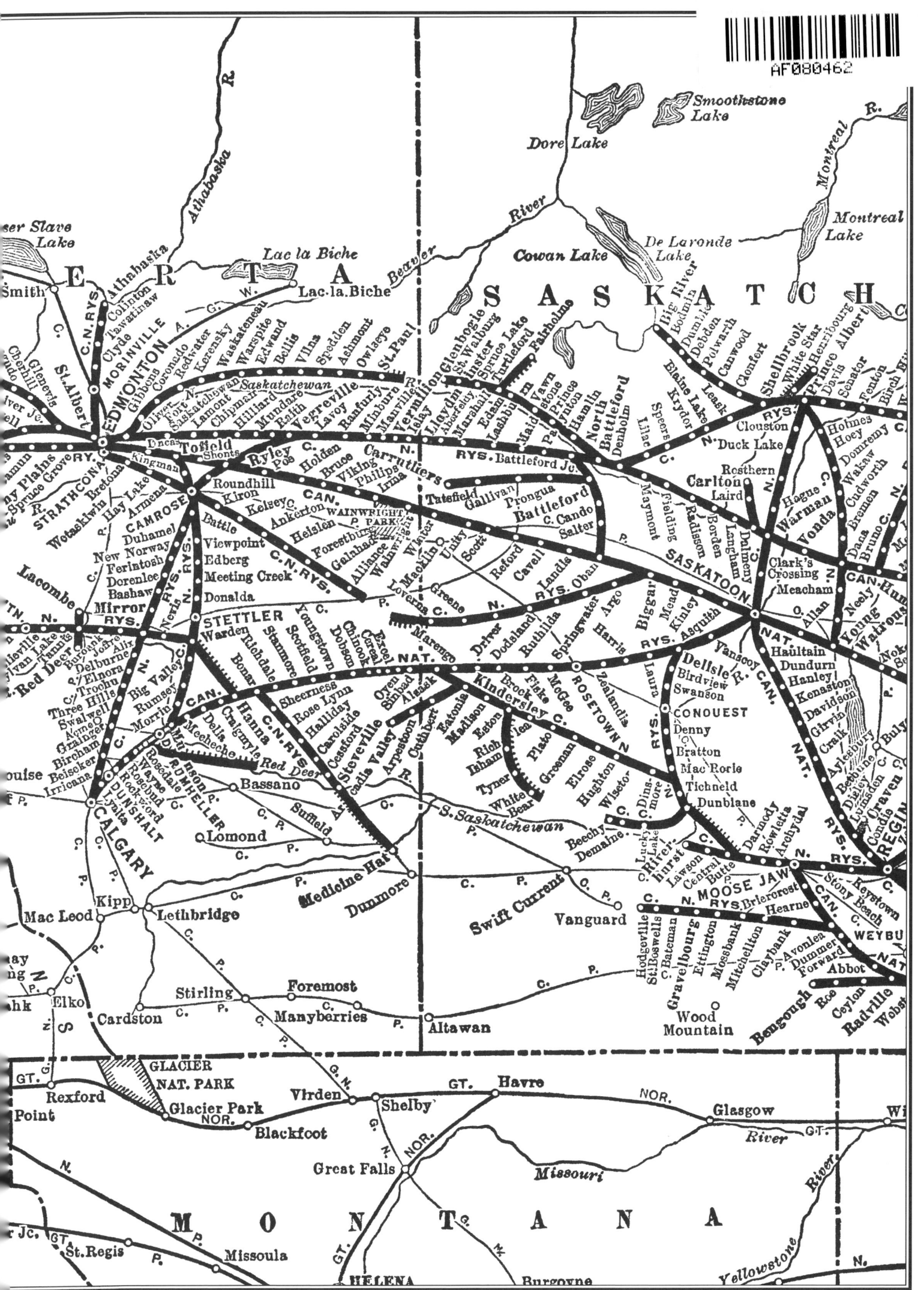

—Map excerpted from a Rand McNally map dated March 1925, reproduced in the March 1928 issue of the OFFICIAL RAILWAY EQUIPMENT REGISTER

Canadian National's Western Stations

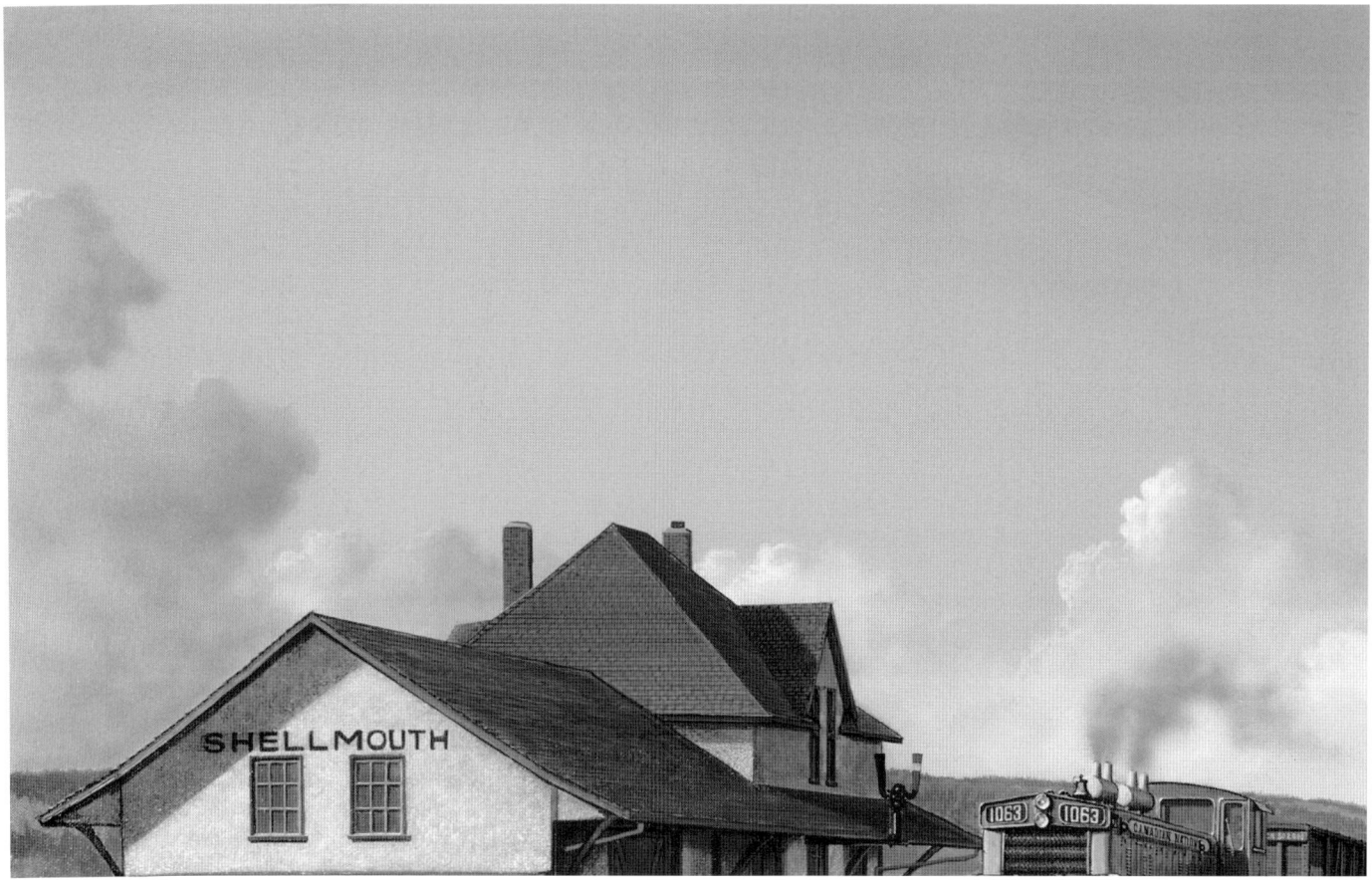

Shellmouth, Manitoba (ORIGINAL PAINTING BY MAX JACQUIARD)

By Charles W. Bohi and Leslie S. Kozma

A **Railfare** Book

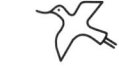

Fitzhenry & Whiteside

The extensive involvement of, support and assistance from, the CN Lines Special Interest Group in the preparation and production of this book is acknowledged.

Canadian National's Western Stations
Copyright © 2002 Fitzhenry & Whiteside

All rights reserved. No part of this book may be reproduced in any manner without the express written consent from the publisher, except in the case of brief excerpts in critical reviews and articles. All inquiries should be addressed to:

Fitzhenry and Whiteside Limited
195 Allstate Parkway
Markham, Ontario L3R 4T8

In the United States:
121 Harvard Avenue, Suite 2
Allston, Massachusetts 02134

www.fitzhenry.ca godwit@fitzhenry.ca

Fitzhenry & Whiteside acknowledges with thanks the Canada Council for the Arts, the Government of Canada through its Book Publishing Industry Development Program, and the Ontario Arts Council for their support of our publishing program.

10 9 8 7 6 5 4 3 2 1

National Library of Canada Cataloguing in Publication

Bohi, Charles W., 1940-
   Canadian National's western stations / Charles Bohi and Leslie Kozma.

Includes bibliographical references and index.
ISBN 1-55041-632-4

1. Railroad stations – Canada, Western. I. Kozma, Leslie S II. Title.

TF302.C3B64 2002   385.3'14'09712   C2002-902682-2

United States Publisher Cataloging-in-Publication

Bohi, Charles W., 1940-
Canadian National's Western stations / by Charles Bohi ; Leslie Kozma. – 1st ed.
[176] p. : ill., photos., maps ; cm.
Includes bibliographical references and index.
ISBN 1-55041-632-4
1. Railroad stations – Canada, Western. 2. Canadian National Railways. I. Kozma, Leslie. II. Title.
385/.314/ 09712 21 CIP TF302.C2.B63 2002

Book Design by Ian Cranstone
Cover Design by Darrell McCalla
Cover image: *Shellmouth, Manitoba* from an original painting by Max Jacquiard
Printed and bound in Canada

Contents

Preface..4

Section I
Historical Perspective..7
Shelters, Portable Stations and Temporary Stations.....................................14
Combination Station and Section Houses..22
Combination Stations..24
Passenger Stations...36

Section II
Exterior Colour Schemes..47

Section III
Rosters..65
Roster I: Listed Alphabetically by Province..66
Roster II: Listed by Subdivision..101
Roster III: Listed by Type..123
Roster IV: Summary of Stations Constructed by Type................................145
Selected Plans..147

Index..159

The following abbreviations are used in this volume:

- C&E — Calgary and Edmonton Railway
- CNR — Canadian National Railways
- CNoR — Canadian Northern Railway
- CPR — Canadian Pacific Railway
- DW&P — Duluth Winnipeg and Pacific Railway
- GTP — Grand Trunk Pacific Railway
- MRM — Midland Railway of Manitoba
- NPR — Northern Pacific Railway
- NTR — National Transcontinental Railway
- QLL&S — Qu'Appelle Long Lake and Saskatchewan Railway

Preface

"Such visible symbolic objects as railroad stations are markers of a simpler, more comfortable time (at least in our minds), and stations now have a cultural or historic meaning separate from there original function… The passage of time creates this new meaning."

John P. Hankey, "*Visionaries or Fools? Time Will Tell,*" LOCOMOTIVE & RAILWAY PRESERVATION (September-October 1993), page 54

MUCH TIME HAS PASSED SINCE CHARLES Bohi's pioneering effort, CANADIAN NATIONAL'S WESTERN DEPOTS, was published in 1977. Until about the early 1980s there was still ample opportunity to photograph western depots on their original sites. Since then, railways have undergone a major transformation. Regrettably, most of this change has not been kind to western Canada's railway stations. True, the federal government's Heritage Railway Station Protection Act (1987) culminated in the designation of many significant depots as historical resources and gained for them some measure of protection from alteration and demolition.

But at this writing, relatively few depots remain on their original locations. Most of those acquired by local heritage groups have been either fenced off or moved back from the tracks for liability reasons. Only a handful of these buildings has been restored to their former glory. Those remaining in railway service or awaiting disposition are, for the most part, in very poor physical condition. Railways can no longer justify or afford to keep these aging buildings from withering away. In this context, the future looks grim. In the "helter-skelter" of the today's global economy, it appears that younger generations have had little time to recognize or understand the former important role of the depot as the centre of life in the West. In many ways this is also an indictment of the education system, but that is another story.

On a more positive note, a hard-core group of individuals throughout the country has shown considerable interest in railway stations. Scholarship about Canadian stations has proliferated. Groups such as the Canadian Northern Society and the CANADIAN STATION NEWS have collected and disseminated valuable information about these depots, much of it used in preservation efforts.

When Al Lill and Stafford Swain of *CN LINES* suggested an update to CANADIAN NATIONAL'S WESTERN DEPOTS, the authors jumped at the opportunity. Important new information had come to light since the original book. Further, technology has made the compilation of works of this scope significantly less onerous.

This update is intended to complement rather than replace the original, seminal work. The most significant changes are in the rosters, where considerable data has been added. The only other serious shortcoming of the original volume—the lack of historical photographs—has also been addressed. And finally, technology has made it feasible to discuss the station colour schemes used by CNR.

Still, the preparation of this update to CANADIAN NATIONAL'S WESTERN DEPOTS was a major undertaking, very much a collaborative project. While the authors appreciate the efforts of all who assisted, the following individuals deserve special recognition:

—Al Lill and Stafford Swain of *CN LINES* and David Henderson of Railfare Enterprises for their initiative in suggesting this update, providing the means to publish it and their unending support;
—Ian Cranstone for his professional skill and flair in laying out this book;
—Max Jacquiard for his evocative cover artwork;
—Keith Ewart, who has spent the last decade or so relentlessly hunting down the disposition of every station in Saskatchewan;
—David Capelazo and Peter Bowers for their assistance with the colour section;
—Daryl Adair, George Bergson, Dr. George H. Buck, Jack V. Deragon, Herb Dixon,

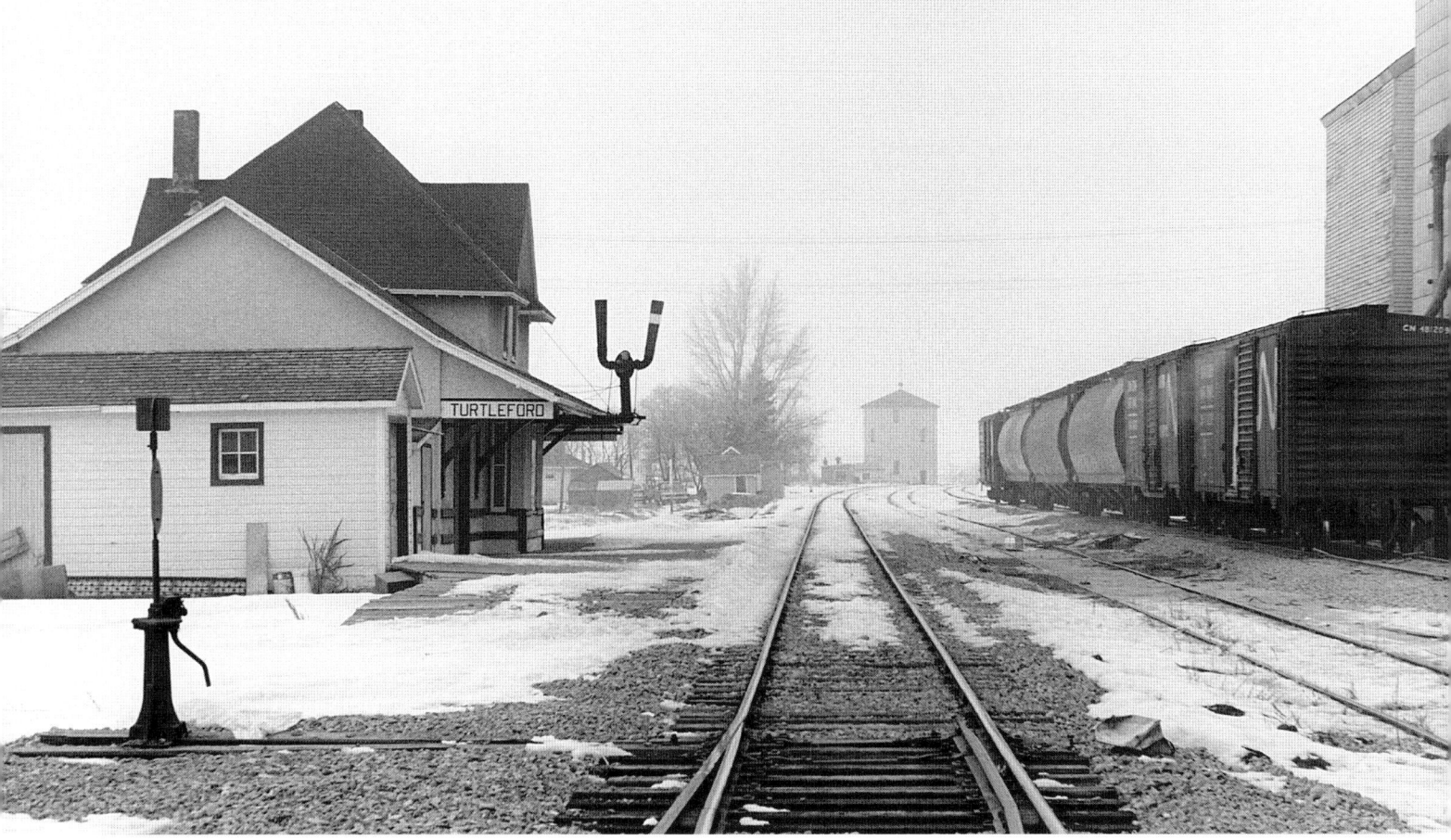

CNoR Turtleford, Saskatchewan (CHARLES W. BOHI PHOTO), 1981

Even as late as 1981, branch line points like Turtleford, Saskatchewan had depots with active train order offices. In the distance was the water tank, another vanishing railway landmark. The combination of boxcars and cylindrical hoppers being loaded at the local elevator is yet another indicator of change. The Canadian Northern 3rd Class station built in 1914 is now a museum but, regrettably, the water tank was demolished. This was the end of steel until 1922 when the line was extended to St. Walburg. The proposed through connection with the Oliver Branch to Edmonton was never made.

David Else, Fred Fowler (F-G-F), Hilt Friesen, the late Dick George, Alf Goodall, Tim Green, Tom Hanson, Eric L. Johnson, Robert Kirkham, David Koshman, Frank Korvemaker, Tom Hanson, William Linley, David Monaghan, Ernie Moorhouse, Steve Ondic, Antony Pacey, Al Paterson, Lorne Perry, Sonny Potiuk, Glenn Roemer, John A. Rushton (J-A-R), Robert Sandusky, Dave Savage, Dave Shaw, Dirk Septer, Derek Sim, Shawn I. Smith, Len Stroh and Brian West for sharing their insights and personal photographs and for their assistance and encouragement;

—The staffs of the B.C. Archives and Record Service (Victoria), Bulkley Valley Historical & Museum Society (Smithers, B.C.), Canadian Northern Society (Big Valley, Alberta), City of Edmonton Archives, Glenbow Archives (Calgary), Manitoba Provincial Archives (Winnipeg), Moose Jaw Public Library, National Archives of Canada (Ottawa), National Museum of Science and Technology (Ottawa), Northern Pacific Railway Historical Association (Blaine, Minnesota), Provincial Archives of Alberta (Edmonton), Saskatchewan Archives Board (Regina and Saskatoon), Saskatoon Public Library, Visualarity Communications (Montreal), Valley Museum & Archives (McBride, B.C.) and the Western Canadian Pictorial Index (Winnipeg) for providing data and for preserving and making available photographs and other materials from their vast collections.

The merits of this work are due in no small part to the efforts made by these individuals and organizations. Any errors of fact, interpretation or omission are the responsibility of the authors.

Charles W. Bohi   *Leslie S. Kozma*
White River Jct., Vermont   *Edmonton, Alberta*

WHAT'S IN A NAME?

When the authors and publishers were first thinking about the title of this book, it was helpful to consider how customs, and nomenclature, differ on each side of the Canada/U.S.A. border. What's known as a "railway" in Canada is almost universally referred to as a "railroad" in U.S.A. And in Canada, folks would almost universally say "I'm going down to the station, to meet Mom", while the "railroad depot" was where our American friends said they'd be meeting Mom. In addition, since this new book is a *companion* book to its predecessor, not a *replacement*, it became clear that we needed a title that would differentiate it, while keeping close ties with the original. That's why CANADIAN NATIONAL'S WESTERN STATIONS was ultimately chosen as the new book's title.

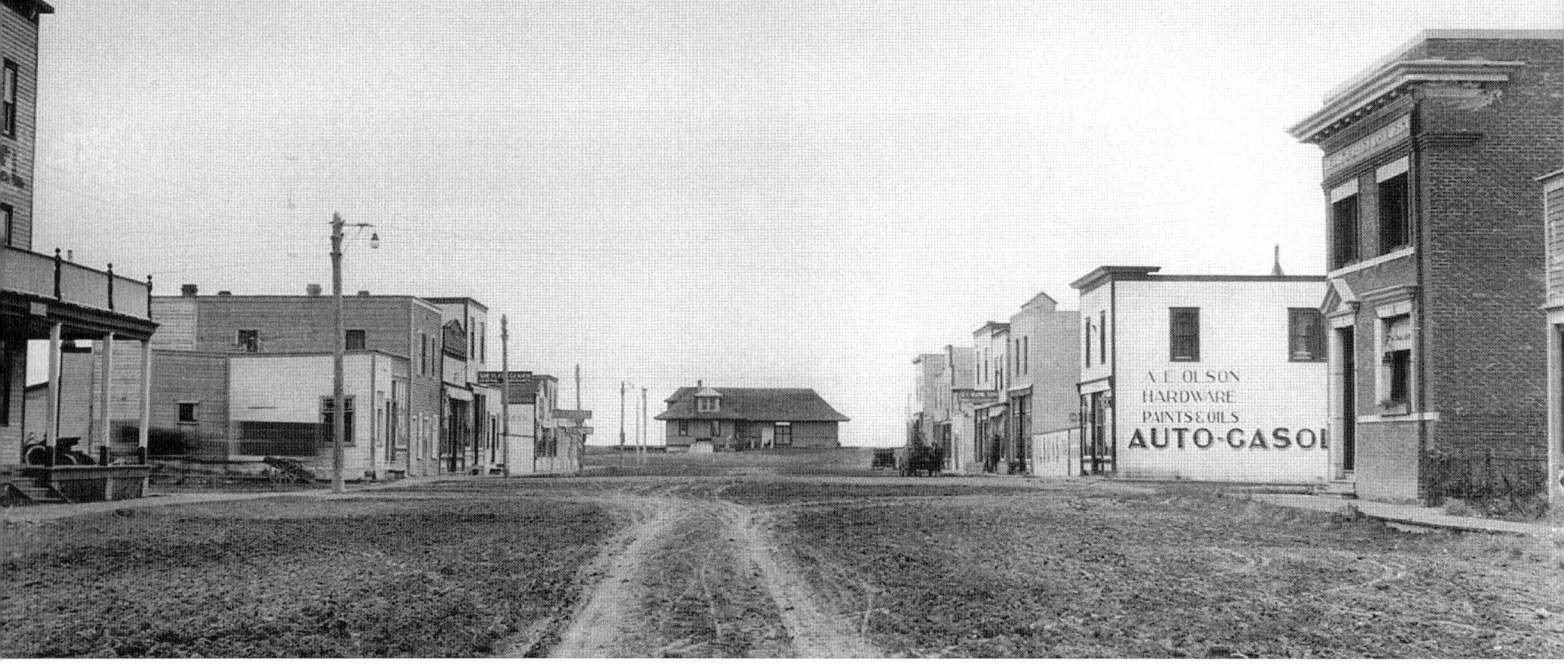

GTP Semans, Saskatchewan
(Leslie S. Kozma Collection), circa 1910s

Railways had a major impact on the urban morphology of rural towns in the Canadian west. Indeed, most of these communities, especially those on the Prairies, could trace their very existence to the railways. Many a fortune was won or lost on the location of new rail lines and the establishment of stations or town sites along them. For reasons of practicality and higher profit, western railways commonly employed the rectilinear grid for their town site plats. The GTP, in particular, had very rigid standards for its main line town sites. All but a handful were located north of the tracks. Railway Avenue was set back from and paralleled the track. Main Street commenced at the back door of the station, and ran perpendicular to the tracks. Queen and King Streets paralleled Main Street to the west and east, respectively. The GTP also enforced an early form of zoning, controlling the types and character of establishments that could be built facing onto Main Street or the station. Further, a discretionary Building Restriction Area in certain parts of the town site set a minimum specified value for the buildings constructed within that area and set a time limit for their completion. Sidings and business tracks were located across the tracks, away from the town site. Semans, Saskatchewan was just such a typical GTP town.

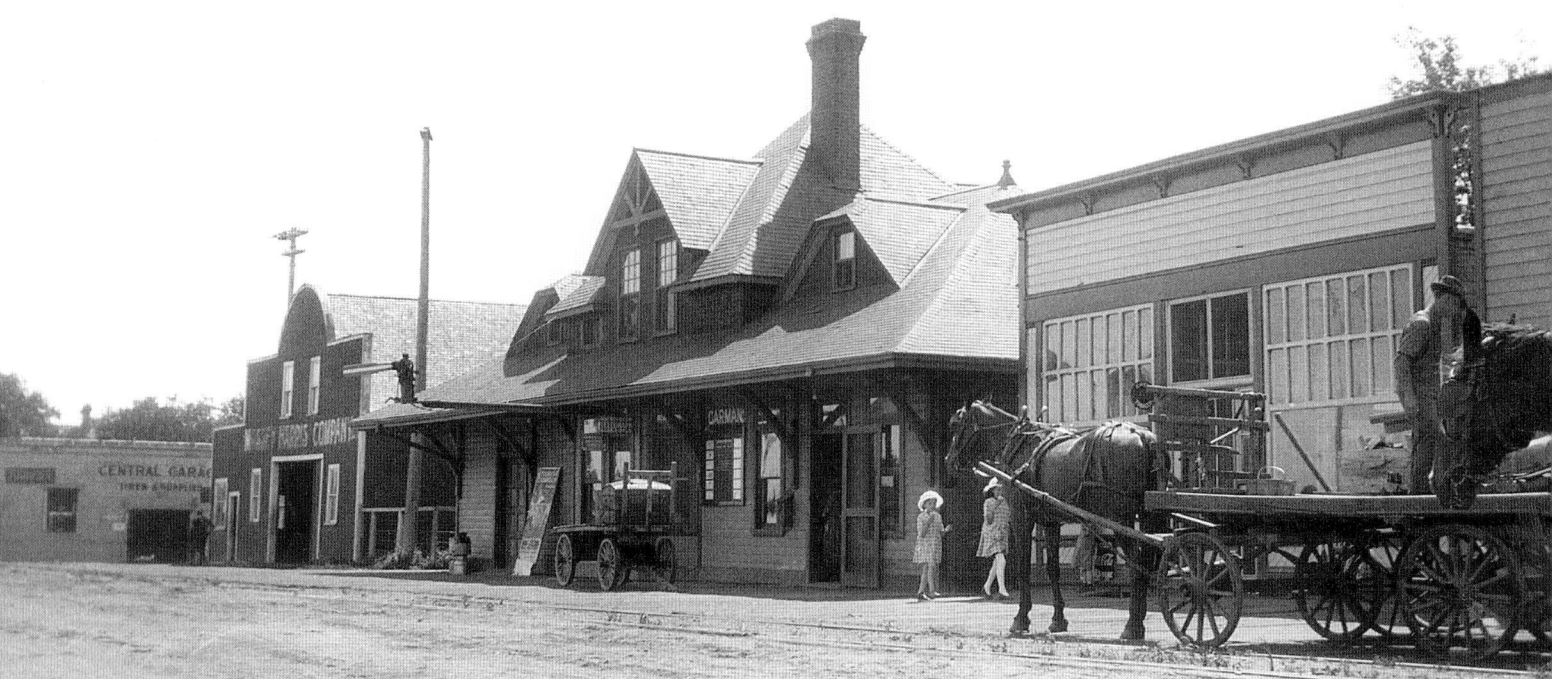

CNoR Carman, Manitoba
(Al Paterson Photo, Al Lill Collection), circa 1935

In the early 20th Century, railways were a key to prosperity in the Canadian west. During the railway boom it was believed that a town could never have too many railways: rival companies meant competition, hence lower fares and freight rates. Carman, Manitoba was one such town. It was a mere wayside station established on the Barnsley Branch of the Manitoba & Southwestern Western Colonization Railway (leased and operated by the CPR) which went through in 1889-90. Then, in 1901 the Canadian Northern acquired the Northern Pacific & Manitoba Railway (NP&M). With the CNoR intent on constructing a cut-off from Winnipeg to reach the old NP&M line to Brandon, Carman became a potential crossroads. But as in so many other western Canadian towns, the CPR owned virtually all the land on the approaches to Carman, and it was not about to let an upstart into town. By making the land prohibitively expensive it was hoped that the CNoR could be kept out, or at least suffer some costly delays. Recognizing that the Canadian Northern might bypass the community—with the very real possibility that it might create a rival town site—it appears that the Town of Carman acquired the necessary lands on behalf of the CNoR. The Canadian Northern constructed its line across South Railway Avenue, parallel to the Canadian Pacific. The CNoR's 2nd Class depot was plunked onto four lots facing onto the Avenue—virtually in the middle of downtown—just 1½ blocks east of the CPR station. The inconvenience of CNoR trains passing along and stopping upon one of the town's principal streets appears to have been of little consequence, although train speeds were severely limited as they negotiated the track on South Railway Avenue. The Carman agency was abolished in the 1960s and this depot sat vacant until 1972, when it was sold and refurbished as a seniors' drop-in centre.

SECTION I

Historical Perspective

NO NATION OWES ITS EXISTENCE MORE TO railways than Canada. A far-flung, sparsely populated land divided by formidable geographic barriers when it was formed at Confederation in 1867, as David P. Morgan observed in CANADIAN STEAM, *"…the 3,500 miles between its coasts were bonded by nothing more enduring than the tracks left by trappers' snowshoes and indians' [sic] moccasins."* [1] Since only railways could create the links that would make Canada a nation in fact, as well as name, it is not surprising that John A. Macdonald, Canada's first Prime Minister, made the completion of a transcontinental railway integral to his National Policy for unifying Canada.

Tying "Central Canada"—Quebec and Ontario—with its tariff-protected industries to an agriculture hinterland in the West, the Canadian Pacific Railway (CPR) secured that region for Canada. Not only was this railway a condition set by British Columbia for joining Canada, but also it was essential if the fertile agricultural land in the interior was to be kept from the United States. Emboldened by the successful end to its Civil War, believing in its "Manifest Destiny", many south of the border saw no reason not to add prairie Canada and British Columbia to its growing empire. Fear of its southern neighbor prompted the Canadian government to have the Canadian Pacific (CPR) build further south, burdening the Company with the difficult grades of Kicking Horse and Rogers passes, rather than the easier profiles offered by the Yellowhead Pass further to the north. The more arduous route aside, the Canadian Pacific did secure the West for Canada, politically. Morgan did not exaggerate when he said, *"It might be…argued that Canada's valid day of independence was November 7, 1885, for that was when the final spike on the Canadian Pacific between Montreal and Vancouver [actually Port Moody] was driven home."* [2]

If Canada needed railways, as historian W. A. Mackintosh noted, *"Railways and continually improving transportation were as essential as rain and sun to progressive settlement in the Canadian Prairie. Nearness to railways and to projected railways was of first importance to settlers."* [3] The story of the pioneering role played by the CPR in the West has been told often and needs no detailed recounting here. Suffice it to say that, between 1880 and 1893, with 3,000 miles built by the CPR and other lines, the transformation of the "great lone land" into a full-fledged agricultural region had begun. While the depression of 1893 slowed progress to a crawl, by 1901, with a population just over 400,000, the foundation for a massive economic expansion had been laid.[4] As the financial situation began to improve in 1896, with the best farmland in the United States already settled, and the development of farming methods more appropriate to the northern plains, western Canada became a desirable place to settle. All that was needed was more railways.

"Railroad iron is a magician's rod in its power to evoke the sleeping energies of land and water," proclaimed American lecturer Ralph Waldo Emerson.[5] In western Canada, especially after the turn of the century, the railways did exactly that. This burst of railway construction was accompanied by an economic boom of such magnitude that, as historian Alan Artibise noted, *"…[it was] sufficient to vitalize…the entire Canadian economy and to diffuse this economic vitality throughout the North Atlantic trading area."* [6] Between 1896 and 1914, the CPR, Canadian Northern Railway (CNoR) and the Grand Trunk Pacific (GTP) put down some 11,000 route miles of track. The population on the Canadian prairies had exploded, culminating in the creation of the provinces of Alberta and Saskatchewan in 1905. Acreage sown to wheat went from 2,495,000 in 1900 to 9,335,000 in 1914; wheat production that year was six times that of 1900-01.[7] World War I ended

---

NOTES:

1. David P. Morgan, editor, CANADIAN STEAM (Milwaukee, WI: Kalmbach Publishing Company, 1964), page 2.
2. Ibid.
3. W. A. Mackintosh, quoted by G. P. de T. Glazebrook, A HISTORY OF TRANSPORTATION IN CANADA (Toronto: The Ryerson Press, 1938) pages 315-16.
4. Glazebrook, op. cit., page 316.
5. Ralph Waldo Emerson, quoted by John R. Stilgoe, METROPOLITAN CORRIDOR: RAILROADS AND THE AMERICAN SCENE (New Haven, CT, Yale University Press, 1983), page ix.
6. Alan F. J. Artibise, "Prairie Urban Development: 1870-1930," HISTORICAL ASSOCIATION BOOKLET #34 (Ottawa, ON: Canadian Historical Association, 1981), page 22.
7. G. E. Britnell, THE WHEAT ECONOMY, (Toronto: University of Toronto Press, 1939), page 50.

GTP Agent

(SASKATCHEWAN ARCHIVES BOARD PHOTO R-A 25120), CIRCA 1910S

Looking very serious—and sporting a tie and a jacket, which may have been part of a formal uniform—the cap identifies him as a GTP station agent. He is standing in front of what appears to be a Type E depot. Since not all stations had agencies, the GTP, like its rivals, employed "train agents" who accompanied local freight or mixed trains. In this capacity, they practically took the place of a regular agent, in that their duties provided for taking orders for cars, supervising supply of same, issuing bills of lading for cars loaded, conveying information to the Operating Department as to cars ready to be lifted, waybilling freight. They dealt with all traffic at non-agency stations in the same manner as such traffic would be dealt with if a regular agent were there. Until the 1960s the local railway agent was perhaps the most important businessperson in most western Canadian rural communities, where the depot was the centre of life.

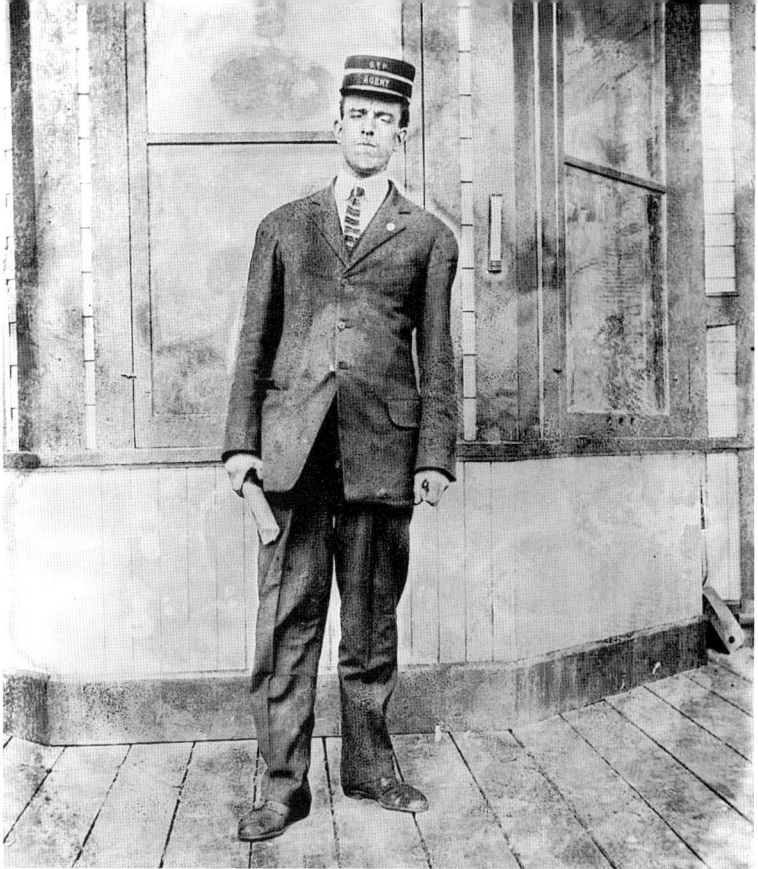

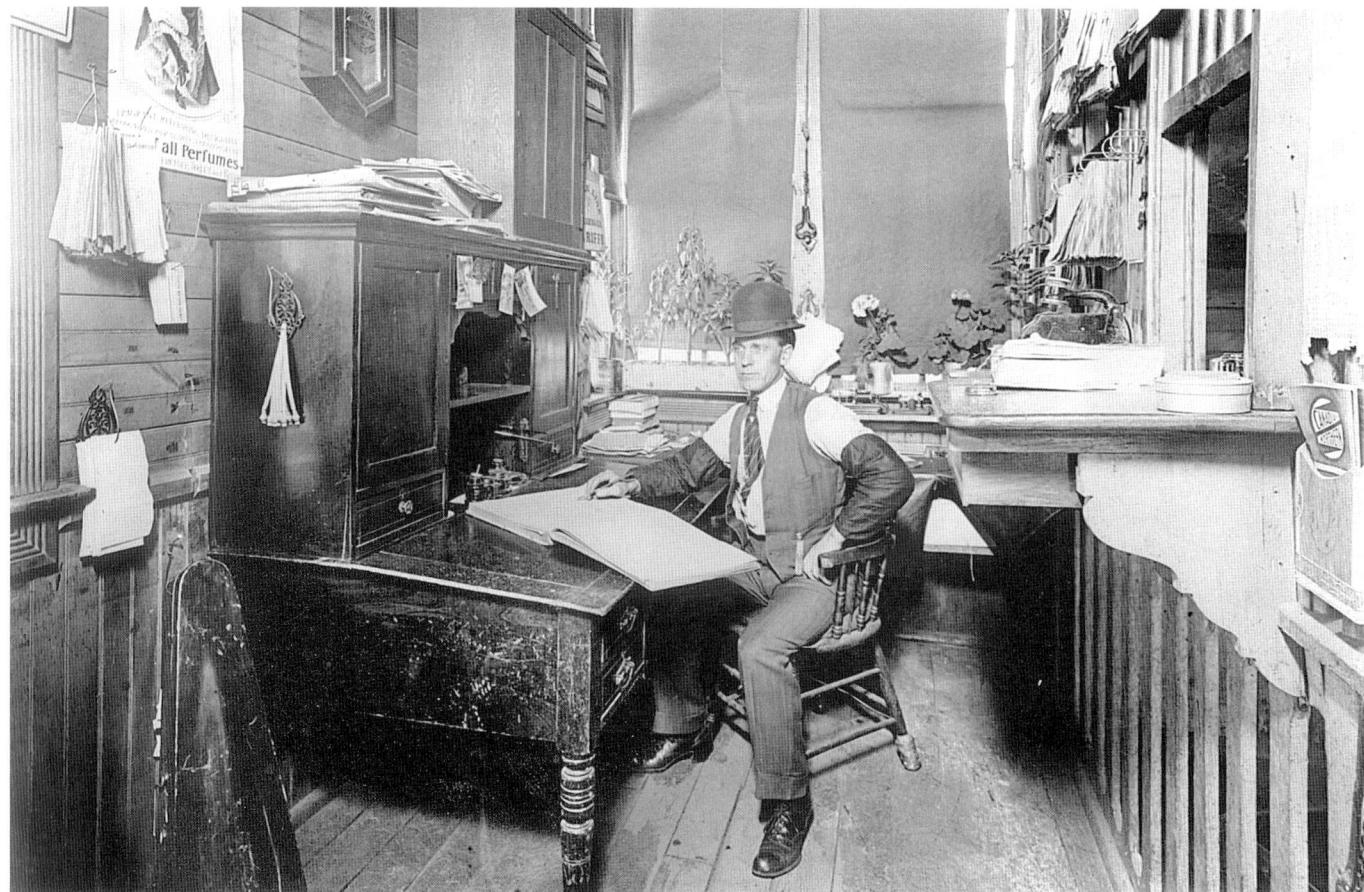

CNoR Underhill, Manitoba

(LEN STROH COLLECTION, VIA ERIC L. JOHNSON), CIRCA 1910S

CNoR Agent George Eckel nattily dressed in shirt and tie, vest, sleeve protectors and bowler hat, circa 1910s. There is a wealth of interior detail. The station ledger—in which all transactions and accounts were kept—was open on the desktop. The ledger had to be made available to the company auditor whenever he made his unannounced visits. The telegraph instruments were also on the desk. Further up, to his right, was another ticket case. To the left, the wall-mounted station timepiece and the poster advertising—of all things—perfume. The roller shades were pulled down in the bay window. What appear to be tomato plants and geraniums were on the operator's table. Above, on the post between the two windows, was the actuation device that operated the train-order signal by a wire. At the far right, beside the ticket wicket, the CNoR public timetable was in a wall mounted brochure rack still emblazoned with the Northern Pacific logo. Paperwork was everywhere, piled or bound on clipboards: waybills, car orders, tickets, and forms. Note the bundle of door seals on the near end of the desk. The interior details identify this as a standard Northern Pacific 4th Class depot: V-joint wall cladding and double V-joint wainscoting, the sawn decorative bracket for the ticket wicket and the "open grille" partition that separated the office from the waiting room. Missing from this view is the station safe. The location of this depot could not be confirmed, but it could have been at Underhill, Manitoba.

this growth and eventually led to the failure and nationalization of the CNoR and the GTP in 1918 and 1920, respectively. Out of this financial wreckage emerged the Canadian National Railways (CNR). Similarly, the Grand Trunk (GT), with its good system of lines in the United States and the St. Lawrence–Great Lakes basin, was undone by its commitments to the GTP and was swept into the CNR in 1923. Less well known is the branch line battle fought by the CPR and the CNR between 1919 and 1935 which added more than 4,000 miles to the western railway network. This proved to be the end of large-scale rural railway branch line construction in North America.[8]

By 1935 the prairie provinces—Manitoba, Saskatchewan and Alberta—had a railway system of some 19,000 miles. Of the prairie farms reported in the 1931 census, 74% were within 10 miles of a railway station. This was fortunate since 94% of these farms were served by dirt roads that were virtually impassable in poor weather.[9] The Saskatchewan road system actually deteriorated during the Depression and World War II.[10] With the significant geographical barriers on the prairies, most area residents would agree with historian H. Roger Grant's comment that, *"[When built,] every mile of railroad was needed."* [11] These numbers do not, however, convey the isolation felt by western Canadians during the railway era. In *BUTTER DOWN THE WELL*, Robert Collins recalled his boyhood in Shamrock, Saskatchewan, a hamlet southwest of Moose Jaw. During the 1939 Royal visit to Canada, the King and Queen were scheduled to stop in Moose Jaw, 60 miles away via the CP. *"If I had ever doubted the power of the king, not any more,"* Collins wrote. *"I was fourteen but I had never been in Moose Jaw nor ridden a train."* [12]

At the Shamrock depot a typical branch line train gathered its passengers. *"The whistle sent a great moaning wail echoing off the grain elevators and we were off to Moose Jaw to see the King."* Despite spending fifteen Depression-era dollars, *"…it was one of the moments in a lifetime…[that] gave us a glimpse not just of a king but of the world,"* a moment that began and ended at a rural railway station.[13]

For all the literary allusions and romantic views of the railway station at the head of Main Street, however, it was the depot's place in the economic life of the town that earned it its status as the centre of the community. For if railways were like rain to western farmers, it follows that every station was an oasis, a source of economic refreshment to farmers dependent on reaching markets thousands of miles away. The station was also the source of sustenance, with the railways bringing the necessities of life from the coalfields of Alberta and Saskatchewan, as well as the factories of Central Canada.

Typical of the blue-collar runs that called at most of the CNR's depots in prairie Canada was Mixed Train #M271-272, running between Prince Albert and Big River, Saskatchewan. In 1949, when railways were still at the heart of prairie life, the *WESTERN PRODUCER*, a farmer-oriented newspaper owned by the Saskatchewan Wheat Pool, sent Ken Cooper to ride this remote run. These so-called "Mixed Trains," hauling freight and passengers, represented a microcosm of rural railroading and prairie life.

The Big River Mixed, the link to the outside world for 14 communities, ran at a leisurely pace, scheduled to cover 85 miles in just over five hours. What with switching the ubiquitous grain elevators and livestock pens and the odd bulk fuel plant, adherence to the schedule was coincidental at best. Even so, this Mixed Train was literally the portal through which farmers and others gained access to their markets in far away Europe and Asia. Further, a thriving fishery at Big River loaded express refrigerator cars with fish for distant cities like Montreal and New York. Indeed, in 1948 alone, the remote community of Big River originated *"…more than 41,000 pounds of freight and express…and generated about a quarter million dollars [for the CNR]."* [14]

But there was still more. Inbound Less than Carload Lot (l.c.l.) merchandise brought the necessities of life to the isolated towns and hamlets along such routes. *"Groceries, hardware and automobile accessories were the most numerous, but there was furniture, chinaware…and a whole host of things for home, business and farm."* [15] Just as today's United Parcel Service truck can brighten the eyes of a child about to celebrate a birthday, so, too, must have children along #M271-272's route looked with anticipation as mysterious packages were unloaded from the train into the local depot's freight room. For virtually everything that came and went from a community passed through the station.

In many ways, the immediate postwar era represented the halcyon years of prairie Canada's passenger service. Along the mainlines ran the great name trains such as *"The Continental Limited,"* which paused only at divisional points and other major towns as they ran

---

NOTES:

8. Charles W. Bohi and Leslie S. Kozma, "The end of an era: The prairie province branch line boom: 1919-1935," TRAINS (November 1991), pages 48-52.
9. CANADA CENSUS, CENSUS OF CANADA: 1931, VOLUME 8, AGRICULTURE (Ottawa: King's Printer, 1932), pages 570, 630 and 698.
10. "Saskatchewan," ENCYCLOPEDIA CANADIANA (1966 edition), page 222.
11. H. H. Roger Grant, THE CORN BELT ROUTE, (Dekalb, IL: Northern University Press, 1984), page x.
12. Robert Collins, BUTTER DOWN THE WELL, (Vancouver: Douglas & McIntyre Ltd., 1997), page 129.
13. Ibid, page 132.
14. Ken W. F. Cooper, "Mixed Train," THE WESTERN PRODUCER MAGAZINE, April 14, 1949.
15. Ibid.

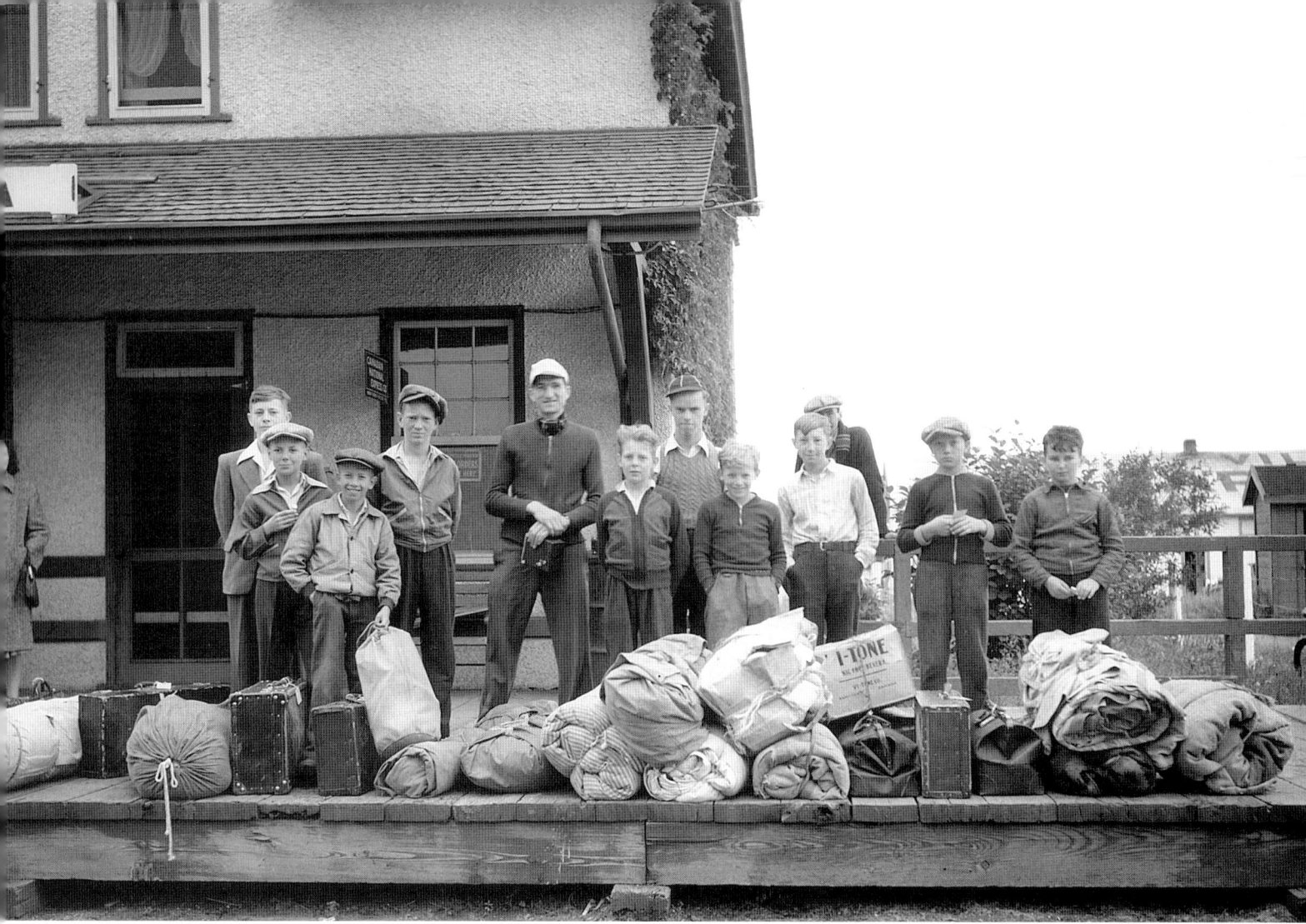

CNoR Vilna, Alberta (Provincial Archives of Alberta, Gavinchuk Collection, Photo G-1185), 1936

Anticipating the arrival of the train to take them away on an adventure, young campers pose on the station platform. With only a rudimentary road system until the early 1960s, the people of western Canada relied almost exclusively on railways for long-distance travel. The station was the town's portal to the world, whether it was buying tickets to the next station—for a dance or other social occasion—or making arrangements with the agent for a trip across the country or around the globe.

across western Canada. Though coaches carried most riders, affluent passengers who could afford sleeping cars relaxed in the lap of luxury, confident that their train would get them to the city in time for that important business appointment. No wonder those living along their routes would gather at wayside stations to watch these trains pass.

More important passenger routes also had Railway Post Office cars (RPOs) in their trains. Harried postal clerks, sorting the mail as they sped across the countryside, would dispatch mail at depots where the train did not stop by kicking sealed mail sacks out the door. Similarly, mail could also be picked up, "on the fly", by using a hook on the side of the RPO to snatch a mail sack from the track side "mail crane." Designated by their terminals, RPOs such as the *Rivers & Saskatoon*, and *Saskatoon Wainwright & Edmonton* handled the Royal Mail at the GTP depots along the mainline. On secondary routes RPOs such as the *Regina & North Battleford* brought the mail to city and hamlet alike. In the bush country along the Manitoba–Saskatchewan border the *Hudson Bay Junction & Flin Flon* helped break the isolation. Even branch lines like the routes northeast of Edmonton could have a RPO: for instance, the *Bonnyville & Edmonton*.[16]

But again, it was trains like the Big River Mixed that were much more typical. While today it is hard to imagine riding such slow trains, Saskatchewan, to cite one example, did not even maintain its rudimentary roads in the winter until the mid-1950s.[17] For that reason, even after World War II, these humble branch line Mixed Trains not only carried freight, but were a necessity for passengers as well. On the days he rode the Big River train, newspaper writer Cooper found the passengers going to Prince Albert to have a tooth pulled, to shop, to take a violin lesson and heading for the hospital. Coming out, the roll call on the Mixed included riders from Edmonton, a man headed to Canwood to take a new job with Imperial Oil, and a retired postal employee headed back after five months of visiting friends and relatives in Vancouver and the United States. The Big River Mixed also picked up and dropped off the Royal Mail.[18]

Often, a community's first depot consisted of a retired piece of rolling stock or a simple portable building. Where justified, however, larger more permanent buildings would be erected. Virtually every community in the prairie provinces that grew large enough to be incorporated as a village, and many which did not, got a permanent depot.[19] Since they were built late in the rural railway construction era, the CNR and its two predecessors could draw on almost a half-century of depot design experience from lines in the United States and Britain. Virtually all the permanent stations built by the CNR and its predecessors were "combination stations." That is, they included an attached freight shed for l.c.l., express and baggage and a waiting room for passengers. That way, one agent working in the office could handle both. Few communities in western Canada grew large enough to warrant a separate freight depot and passenger station. Moreover, most permanent stations built in the West included living quarters. This made it possible for an agent to be available in emergencies, or for delivering freight to patrons needing after-hours service. It also made burglaries less likely, an important matter given the large amount of cash that could be in the office.

While, by then, the role of a station "as an element of civic pride" was well accepted by most North American railway builders, the fact was that most small town depots were built to standardized plans that were easy and economical to replicate.[20] After all, railway building was expensive and costs had to be justified. That was especially true in western Canada where it often was not clear which towns would grow and which would not. That notwithstanding, both the Canadian Northern and the Grand Trunk Pacific evolved rural station plans that were attractive as well as functional.

As the first large CNR predecessor in the West, the CNoR, led by architect R. B. Pratt, developed a unique roofline that marked its depots as surely as architectural features identify fast food restaurants today. Starting as a draftsman for the CPR in 1895, three years later—at the age of 26—he became an architect for that company's Western Lines. In that role he designed two standard rural station plans with unique rooflines that were built in more than forty-five locations in western Canada. Joining the CNoR in 1901, Pratt developed yet another striking roof design that was to mark more than 320 small town "3rd Class" depots, 29 "2nd Class" stations at more important points, and urban buildings such as those in Port Arthur, Saskatoon, and Edmonton and the CNoR's operating hub at Dauphin, Manitoba. No other North American railway used a single architectural feature to mark so many of its stations.

The GTP also developed an attractive rural station design that we have classified as a *Type E* building.[21] In all at least 330 of these attractive stations were built west of the Lakehead. Deriving features from rural depots found along parent GT in eastern Canada and the United States, the wide use of the *Type E* made the GTP rural stations the most standardized of any railway in North America. This design was the most widely used plan in western Canada, accounting for more than 30% of the permanent CNR depots in the region. However, the standardization went far beyond the structure's design. Taking a carefully planned scientific approach, across the prairies, the GTP located almost all its stations and towns on the north side of the track. This gave the depots a southern exposure, making these uninsulated buildings easier to heat. To protect the agent in his office and the passengers in the waiting room, virtually every GTP station had its freight shed on the west end so that it could absorb the blasts of the prevailing northwest winds. By placing the elevators on the south side of the mainline about twice as far from the depot as its competitors did, the GTP protected its stations and towns from elevator fires. Moreover, snow on the leeward side of the granaries accumulated on the roads, not the tracks.

While rural branch line construction in the United States was virtually over by 1919, in Canada the CPR and the newly formed CNR built nearly 4,000 miles of line between the end of World War I and 1935. With this explosion of construction more depots were needed. In its early years the CNR used the depot designs of its predecessors, most commonly the CNoR Plan 100-72 3rd Class design. After 1923-24, the CNR most often employed a new "3rd Class Design." Though related to pre-World War I CNoR plans, this new CNR structure was much less flamboyant than their CNoR counterparts. Substantially built, these buildings usually included partial basements, concrete foundations and stucco surfaces.

NOTES:

16. Bryant Alden Long with William Jefferson Dennis, MAIL BY RAIL: THE STORY OF THE POSTAL TRANSPORTATION SERVICE, (New York: Simmons–Boardman Publishing Corporation, 1951), Appendix, Table 21.
17. Douglas N. W. Smith, ed., "The West's Own Great Express," CANADIAN RAIL PASSENGER YEARBOOK (Ottawa, ON: Trackside Canada, 1993), page 23.
18. Cooper, op. cit.
19. W. A. Mackintosh, ECONOMIC PROBLEMS OF THE PRAIRIE PROVINCES, (Vol. IV of CANADIAN FRONTIERS OF SETTLEMENT edited by W. A. Mackintosh and W. L. G. Joerg, Toronto: The Macmillan Company of Canada Ltd., at St. Martin's House, 1935), page 96. Typically, in 1935, to incorporate as a village required a minimum of 50 residents, a town, 500, and a city, 5,000.
20. John A. Dredge, PASSENGER TERMINALS AND TRAINS (1916; Milwaukee, WI: Klamath Publishing Co. 1969), page 260.
21. The Grand Trunk Pacific designated its depots by size. All of the small town station plans used were designated "Design A." To make it easier to discuss these plans in CANADIAN NATIONAL'S WESTERN DEPOTS: THE COUNTRY STATIONS OF WESTERN CANADA, the most commonly used plan—CNR Plan 100-152—was referred to as a *Type E* depot. Neither the GTP nor the CNR sanctioned these Type classifications.

In all, more than forty CNR 3rd Class depots were built to a variety of slightly different plans. Some were built along new lines, like those from Shellbrook to Turtleford, Saskatchewan, while others were replacements for stations lost to fire, or which had otherwise become inadequate. This was the last rural depot design used in large numbers by the CNR. After World War I, the CNR began to stucco the rural depots inherited from its predecessors. Not only did this "tighten up" the earlier buildings, but also it became an architectural symbol for the new "National Road."

Country railroad stations in western Canada remained at the heart of their communities until the mid-1960s, when better roads became much more common in the West. Why would people from Big River take a five-hour ride on the Mixed when they could hustle down to Prince Albert on their own schedule in two hours or less on the newly paved highways? Why would wholesalers send their goods in a boxcar when trucks could deliver so much more quickly? The same was true for the stock and oil traffic. All that was left to the railroads was coal and grain. But coal was quickly undercut by the increasing use of natural gas and heating oil. In the end, it was just as easy for elevator managers to call a centrally located office, called *Servocenters* on the CNR, to order their cars. Indeed, with the repeal of the so-called "Crow Rate" in 1995, the construction of "high-throughput" elevators made the older granaries economically obsolete. As a result, grain delivery points are further apart, and many branch lines became redundant. Since the late 1970s thousands of miles of branch line in western Canada have been removed, and more thousands sold to shortline "regional" railroads. In short, the era of the small town depot is over. On the CNR it lasted from about 1890 to 1980, a time so brief that some older residents who remembered seeing the building go up, also saw it removed. As one retiree put it, *"I'm going to outlive that depot."* [22]

Rural depots also lost their role in railway operations. Along high-traffic main lines *Centralized Traffic Control* (CTC) allowed train dispatchers to follow the progress of trains and to set switches and signals remotely, from offices hundreds of miles away. From these centralized *Rail Traffic Control* offices, the meeting and passing points for trains could be arranged without operators in line-side depots. *Manual Block Systems* using radio dispatching, cellular telephones and facsimile (fax) machines eventually allowed the same kind of centralized control on branch lines.[23] Their economic and operational functions gone, it is not surprising that after 1975, most rural depots were vacant. Within the following decade most of these depots were removed, closing another chapter in western Canadian railway history.[24]

Bibliography

Artibise, Alan F. J., *"Prairie Urban Development: 1870–1930,"* HISTORICAL ASSOCIATION BOOKLETS #34, Ottawa, ON: Canadian Historical Association, 1981.

Bohi, Charles W. and Leslie S. Kozma, *"The end of an era: The prairie province branch line boom: 1919–1935,"* TRAINS (November 1991).

Britnell, G. E., THE WHEAT ECONOMY, Toronto: University of Toronto Press, 1939.

Canada Census, CENSUS OF CANADA 1931 (VOLUME 8), Department of Agriculture, Ottawa, ON: King's Printer, 1932.

Collins, Robert, BUTTER DOWN THE WELL, Vancouver: Douglas & McIntyre Ltd., 1997.

Cooper, Ken W. F. *"Mixed Train,"* THE WESTERN PRODUCER MAGAZINE April 14, 1949.

Droege, John A., PASSENGER TERMINALS AND TRAINS, Milwaukee, WI: Kalmbach Publishing Company, reprinted 1969.

Glazebrook, G. P. de T., A HISTORY OF CANADA, Toronto: The Ryerson Press, 1938.

Grant, H. Roger, THE CORN BELT ROUTE, Dekalb, IL: Northern UP, 1984.

Kozma, Leslie S. and Charles W. Bohi, *"Canadian National's bee line over the prairie"*, TRAINS (June 1997).

Long, Bryant Alden with William Jefferson Dennis, MAIL BY RAIL: THE STORY OF THE POSTAL TRANSPORTATION SERVICE, New York: Simmons-Boardman Publishing Corporation, 1951.

Mackintosh, W. A., ECONOMIC PROBLEMS OF THE PRAIRIE PROVINCES, (VOLUME IV OF CANADIAN FRONTIERS OF SETTLEMENT), edited by W. A. Mackintosh and W. L. G. Joerg. Toronto: The Macmillan Company of Canada Ltd., at St. Martin's House, 1935.

Moss, Roger, CENTURY OF COLOR EXTERIOR DECORATION FOR AMERICAN BUILDINGS—1820/1920, New York: American Life Foundation, 1981.

NOTES:

22. Informal conversation with a resident of Czar, Alberta in August 1972.

23. Dispatchers' offices have been consolidated. Dispatchers are now known as Rail Traffic Controllers (RTCs). In 1958, CNR dispatching offices were located at Port Arthur, Ontario, Winnipeg, Dauphin and Flin Flon, Manitoba, Regina, Prince Albert and Saskatoon, Saskatchewan, Calgary and Edmonton, Alberta and Kamloops and Smithers, British Columbia. By 1999 all CNR dispatching in western Canada was handled from Edmonton.

24. The Canadian Northern Society has nearly a complete "set" of Canadian Northern depot designs. A refurbished 3rd Class depot—the most widely used of this design—is at Meeting Creek, Alberta. An enlarged version of this design is at Camrose, Alberta. Rowley represents the last 3rd Class design used in large numbers by the CNoR and CNR. The 2nd Class station at Big Valley, was the most commonly replicated plan of this size. At Donalda, Alberta, a 4th Class building was moved from Vandura, Saskatchewan.

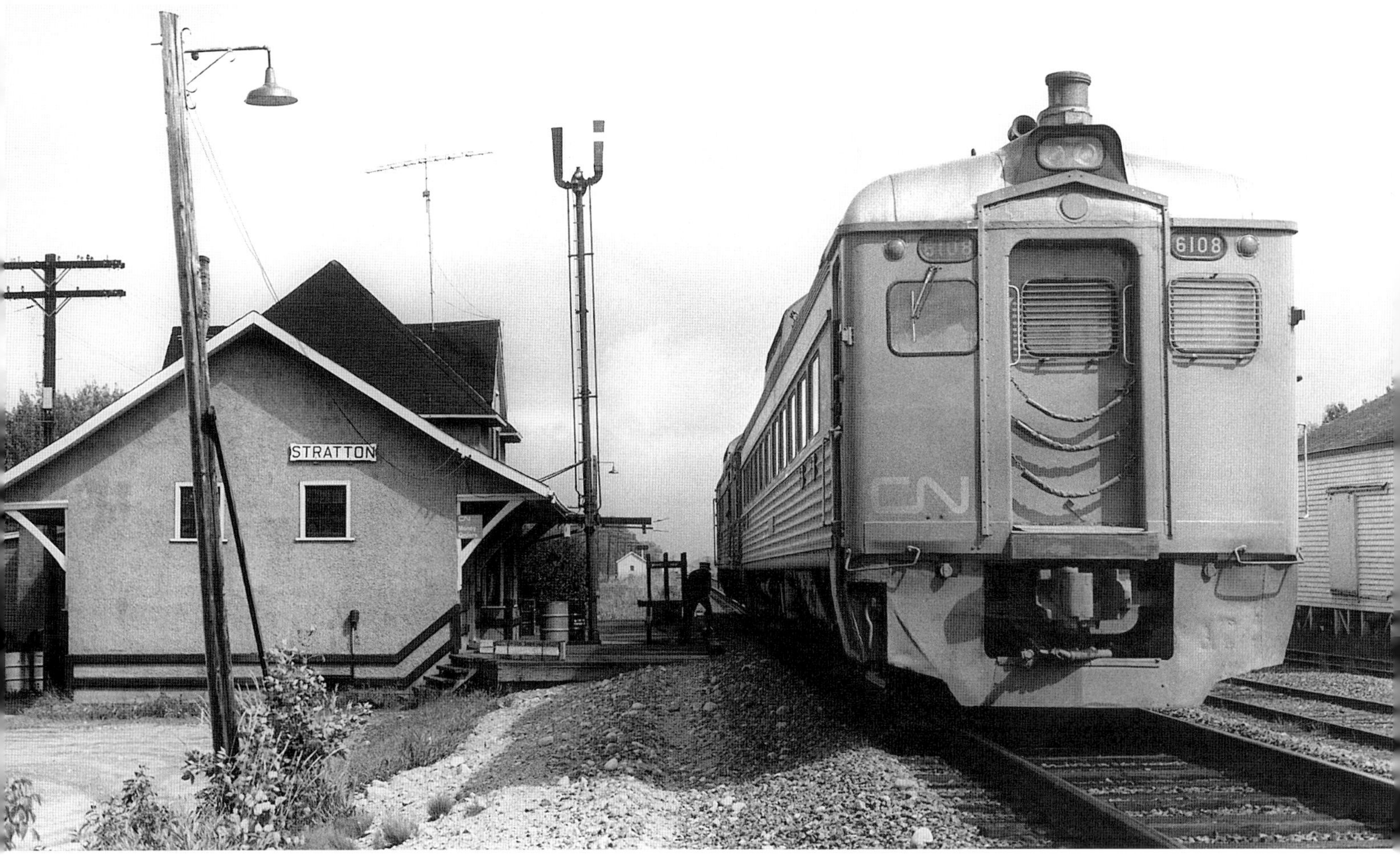

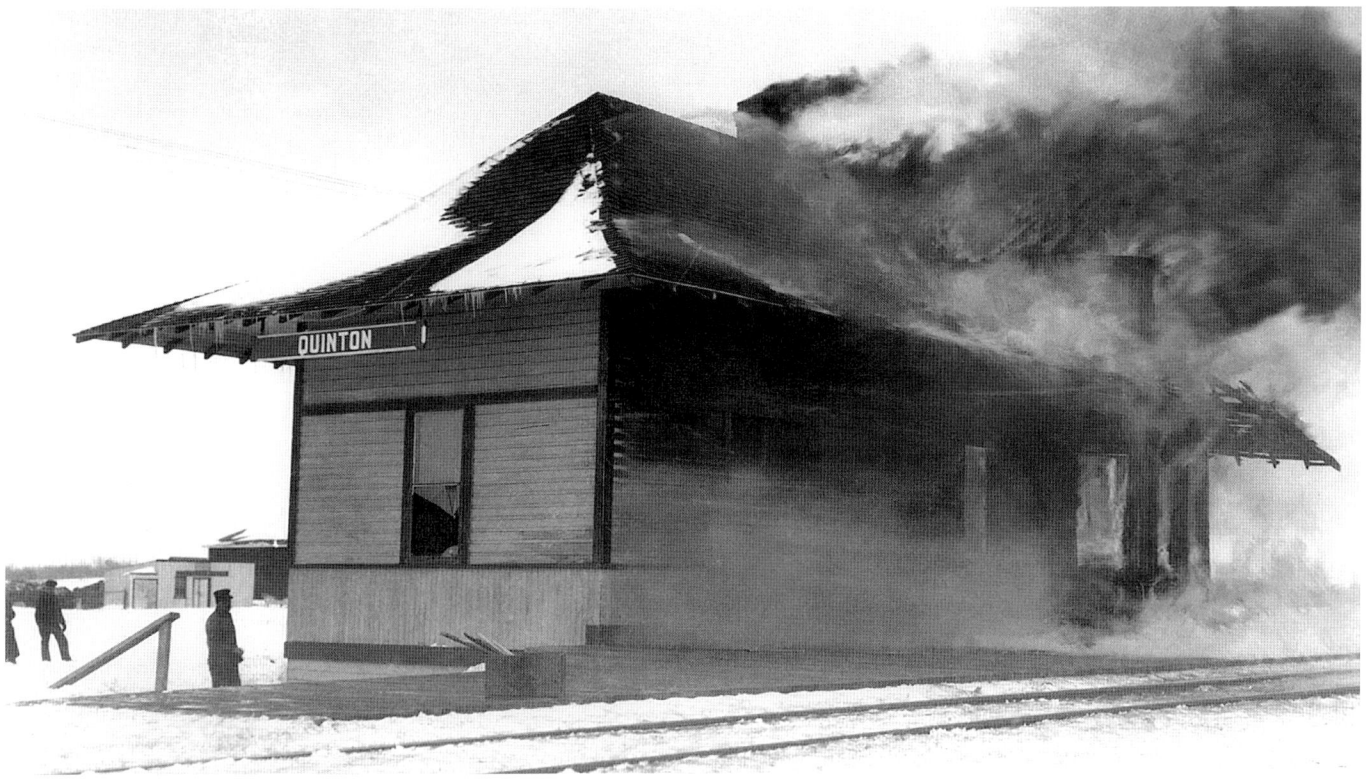

CNoR Stratton, Ontario (Charles Bohi Photo), 1971

Stopping at Stratton, Ontario is Train #696, *a Tuesday–Thursday–Saturday eastbound, running between Winnipeg and Thunder Bay. In the early 1970s, CN* Railiners *still protected a significant number of branch line passenger routes in the West. While the wooden platform had been reduced, the typical pole-mounted illumination remained. The television antenna on the roof indicates that this station was also still a home. The Stratton depot, erected in 1903, was sold in 1975.*

GTP Quinton, Saskatchewan #1 (Saskatchewan Archives Board, Photo R-A 8809-27), 1918

Since most early western Canadian combination depots were heated with one or more strategically placed coal-burning stoves, destruction by fire was a common fate. Here in 1918, Quinton, Saskatchewan's Type E depot meets its demise. Later CNR station designs employed a coal-burning furnace in a partial basement. Eventually, some of the company's earlier stations were retrofitted with such appliances. In the late 1940s, CNR experiments with oil-burning heaters for its Western Lines stations determined that these were more economical and cleaner burning than coal furnaces, so most of the important agencies were so equipped. Starting in the late 1950s the heating plants in some western stations were modified to burn natural gas.

Shelters, Portable Stations and Temporary Stations

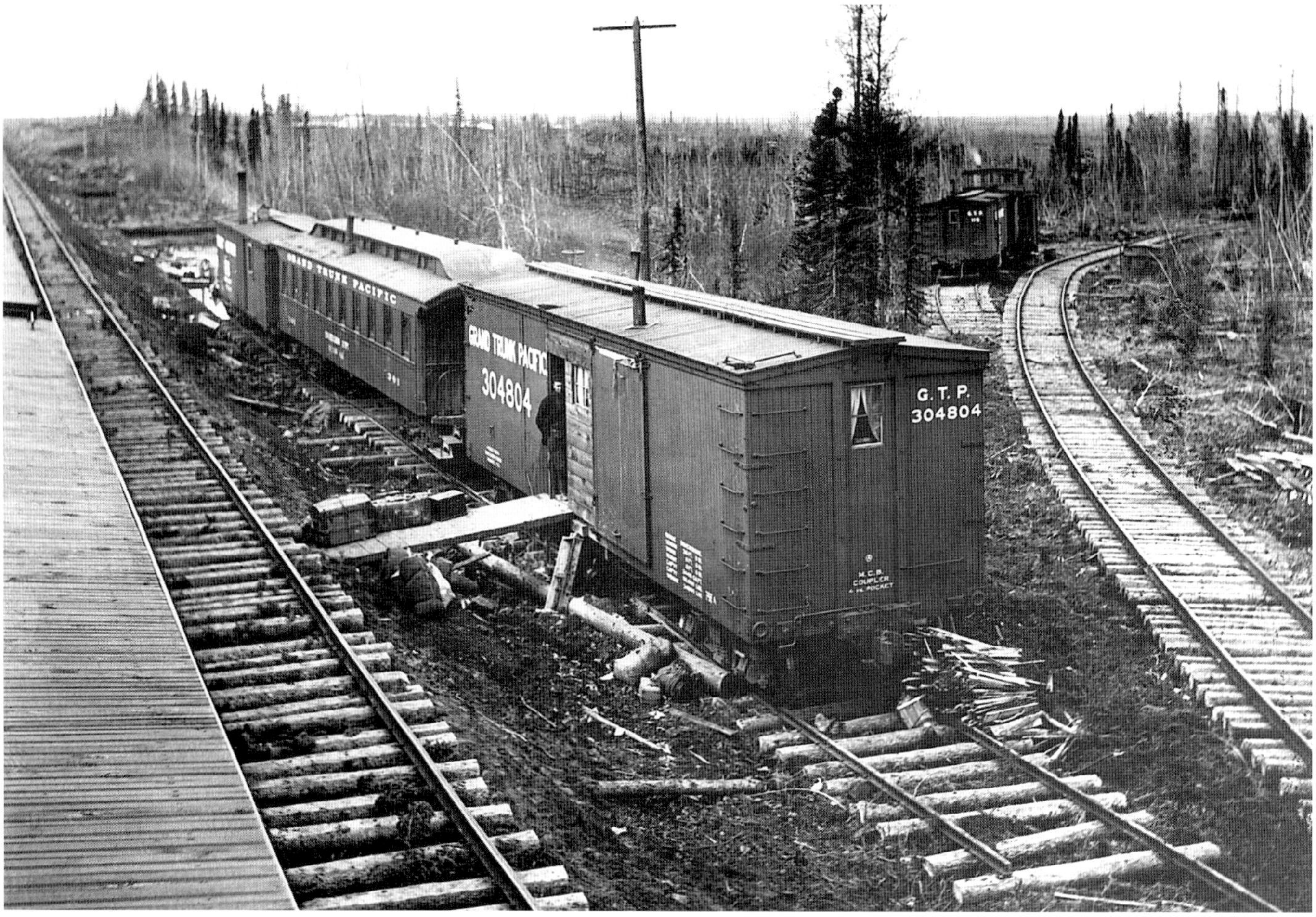

GTP Wolf Creek, Alberta #1 (Provincial Archives of Alberta, Photo A-15984), circa 1909

The GTP's temporary station—at either Bickerdike or Wolf Creek, Alberta—was comprised of Engineering Dept. Dining Car #301 (ex-GTR #1303, built 1894) and a box car set up as a freight shed, on a piece of disconnected track next to the main line. Such extemporaneous stations were common, especially during early line construction or in emergency situations, such as when a depot burned down. A truly portable design used by the GTP consisted of a 5'-0"x5'-0" hut, fitted with an operator's table inside and a pair of stretcher handles outside (Plan 100-174, 1912). These units were carried on company wrecking trains and deployed at derailment sites for a telegraph operator until rail service was restored.

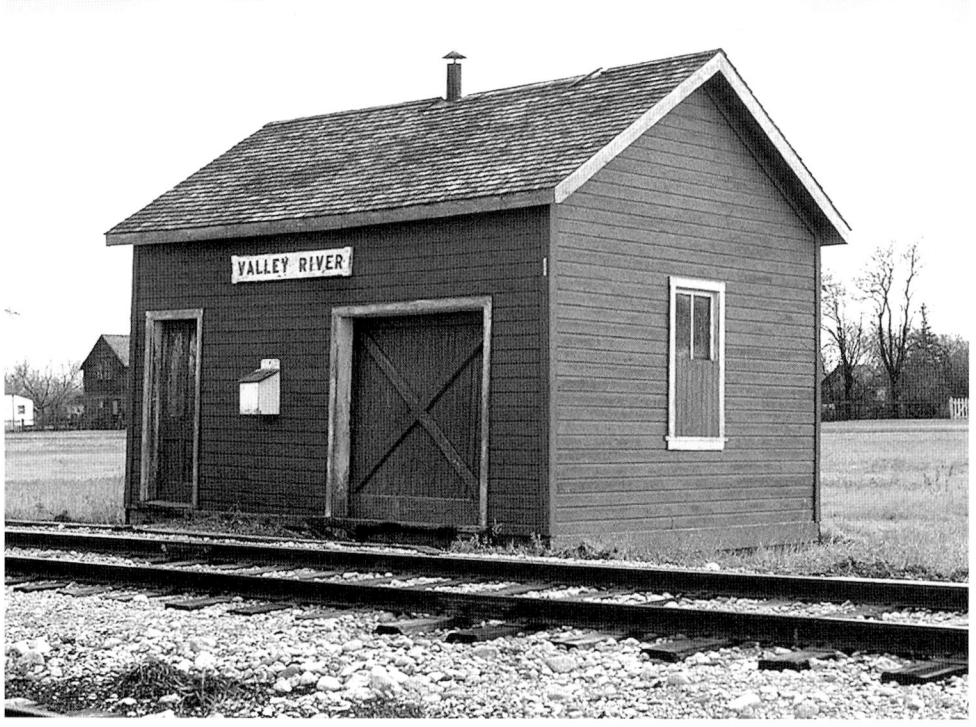

CNoR Valley River, Manitoba
(Hilt Friesen Photo), 1976

The 14'-0"x20'-0" freight and passenger shelter at Valley River, Manitoba—erected in 1897—is the earliest known CNoR building of this type. The lack of plans or other records suggests that this shelter was unique. The trackside platform, likely comprised of cinders within a timber curb, had long since been removed when Hilt Friesen took this photograph in 1976. The white box between the doors was for waybills.

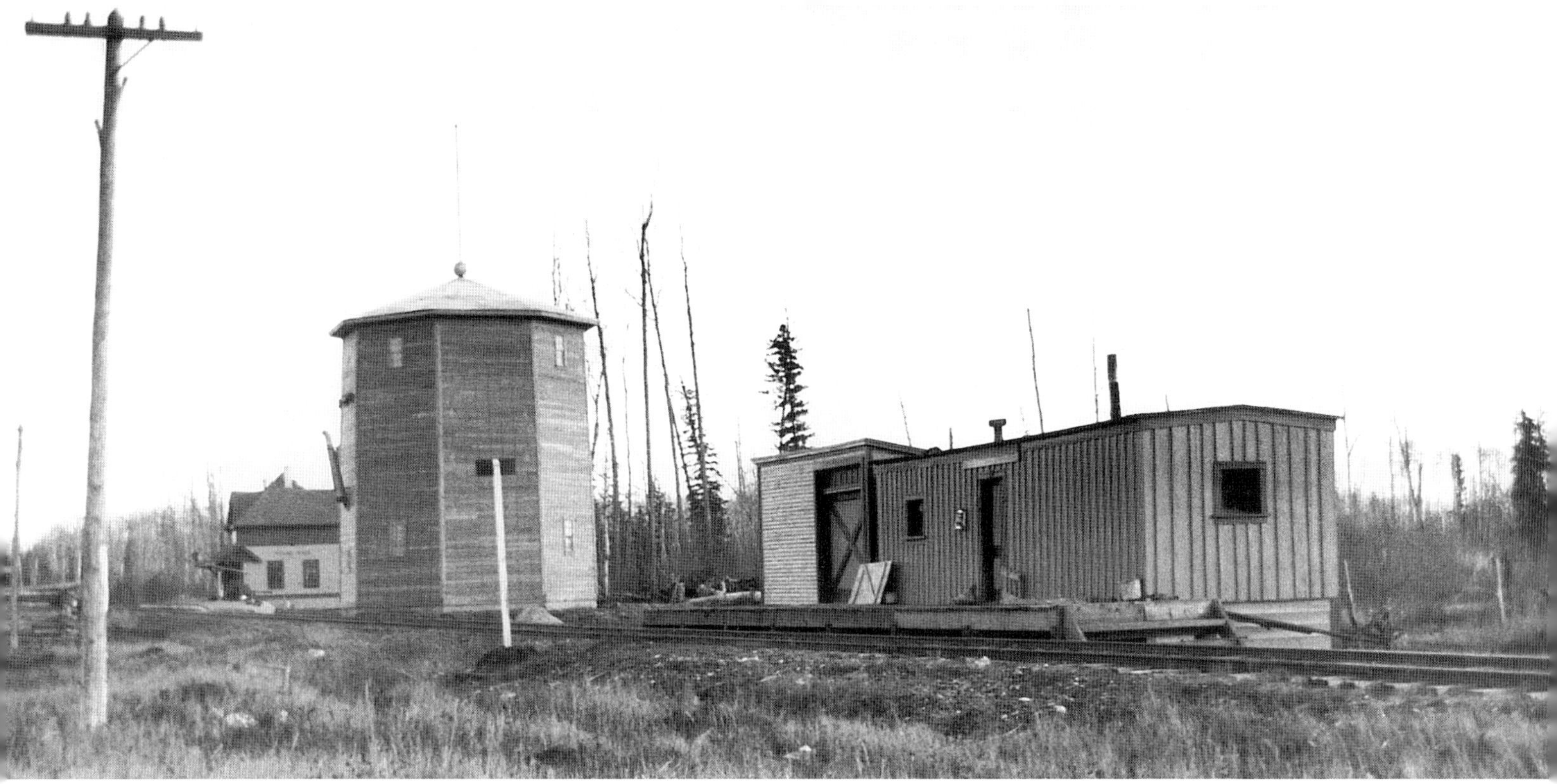

CNoR Prairie River, Saskatchewan #1 and #2 (NATIONAL ARCHIVES OF CANADA, PHOTO PA 18210), 1920

Three generations of station buildings at Prairie River, Saskatchewan are represented in this scene from 1920. CNoR Standard Portable Freight Shed (Plan 170-5), a simple 12'-0"x18'-0" wood-frame structure with a shed roof, was primarily used in conjunction with that company's early Standard Freight and Passenger Shelter (Plan 100-96). In at least one instance (Minburn, Alberta), such a freight shed served as a shelter. Although it is merely conjecture, it is likely that Prairie River's first depot was an FPS, which may have met an untimely end. It was replaced in 1919 by this Standard Portable Station moved from Durban, Manitoba. The Canadian Northern equivalent (Plan 100-24) to the CPR Portable Station (Plan H-14-38) was issued about 1907. These structures—finished with board-and-batten on the exterior—could easily be mistaken for a carbody shelter. Its interior was subdivided into a waiting room, an office and the operator's bedroom. Only 16 were recorded in western Canada. Once Prairie River's 3rd Class depot was opened in 1920, the former station buildings were moved away from the track and converted into section bunkhouses.

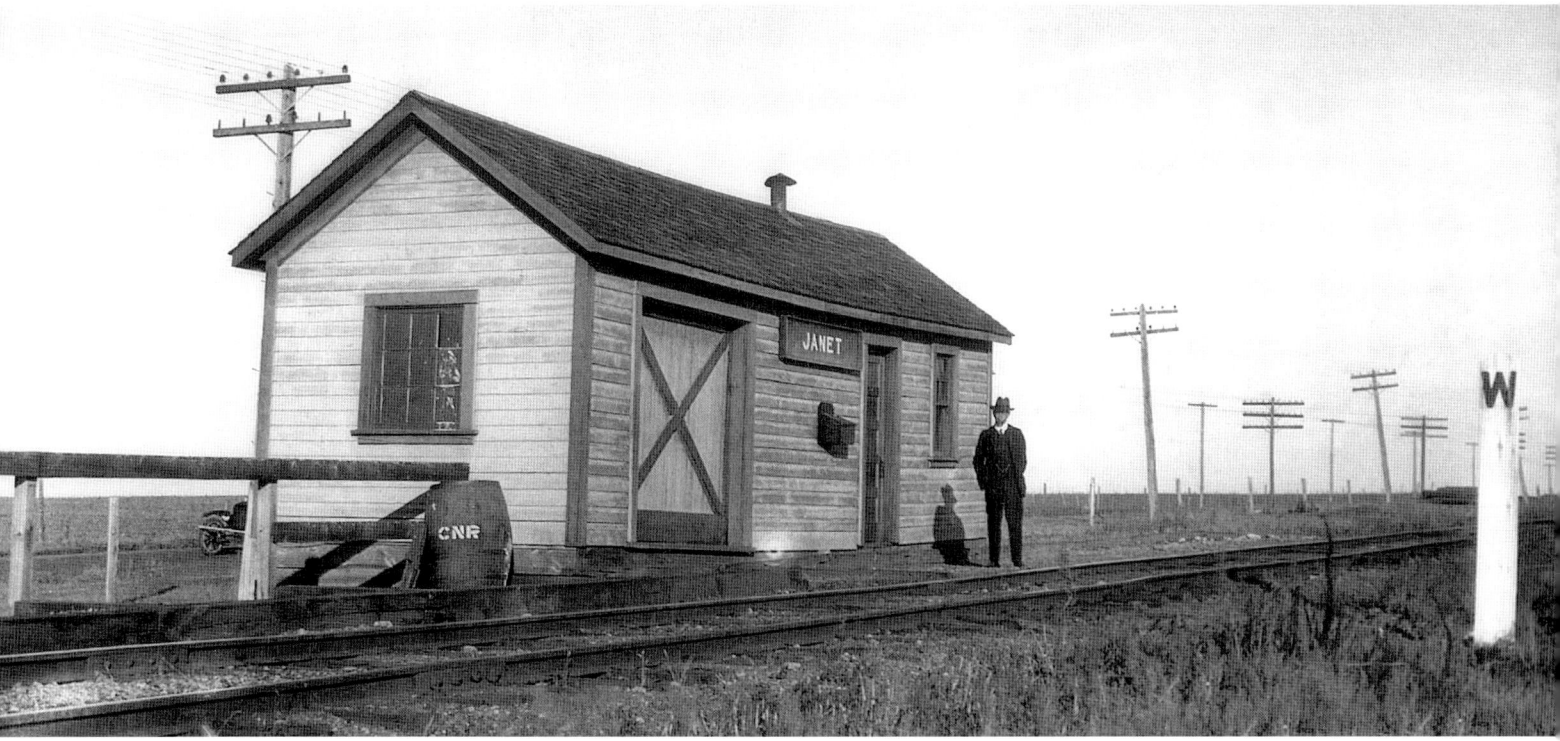

CNoR Janet, Alberta (B.C. ARCHIVES & RECORD SERVICE, BORDERTOWN COLLECTION, PHOTO F-08292), 1910s

The Canadian Northern issued plans for a passenger shelter in 1905 (Plan 100-95), but few were built. A mere 12'-0"x14'-0", they had a steeply pitched gable roof. The CNoR "Standard Waiting Room and Freight Shelter" (Plan 100-96), issued in 1908, was a 12'-0"x 30'-0" board-and-batten building with a shed roof. This design was modified in 1910, with a slight change in size—to 10'-0"x32'-0"—provided with a gable roof and clad with conventional drop siding. This "Standard Freight and Passenger Shelter" (Plan 100-41) was an economical design with an average construction cost of $481 per unit. It became a staple with at least 343 examples erected by the CNoR in the West between 1910 and 1923. The one at Janet, Alberta, just east of Calgary, was built in 1916. It was destroyed by fire in 1930. A handful of such shelters was purpose-built near larger station buildings and used as baggage and/or express sheds. By the mid- to late-1950s, with the demise of many branch line passenger services, freight and passenger shelters of this type became redundant. Many were converted into other uses, particularly as section bunkhouses or tool sheds.

SHELTERS, PORTABLE STATIONS AND TEMPORARY STATIONS

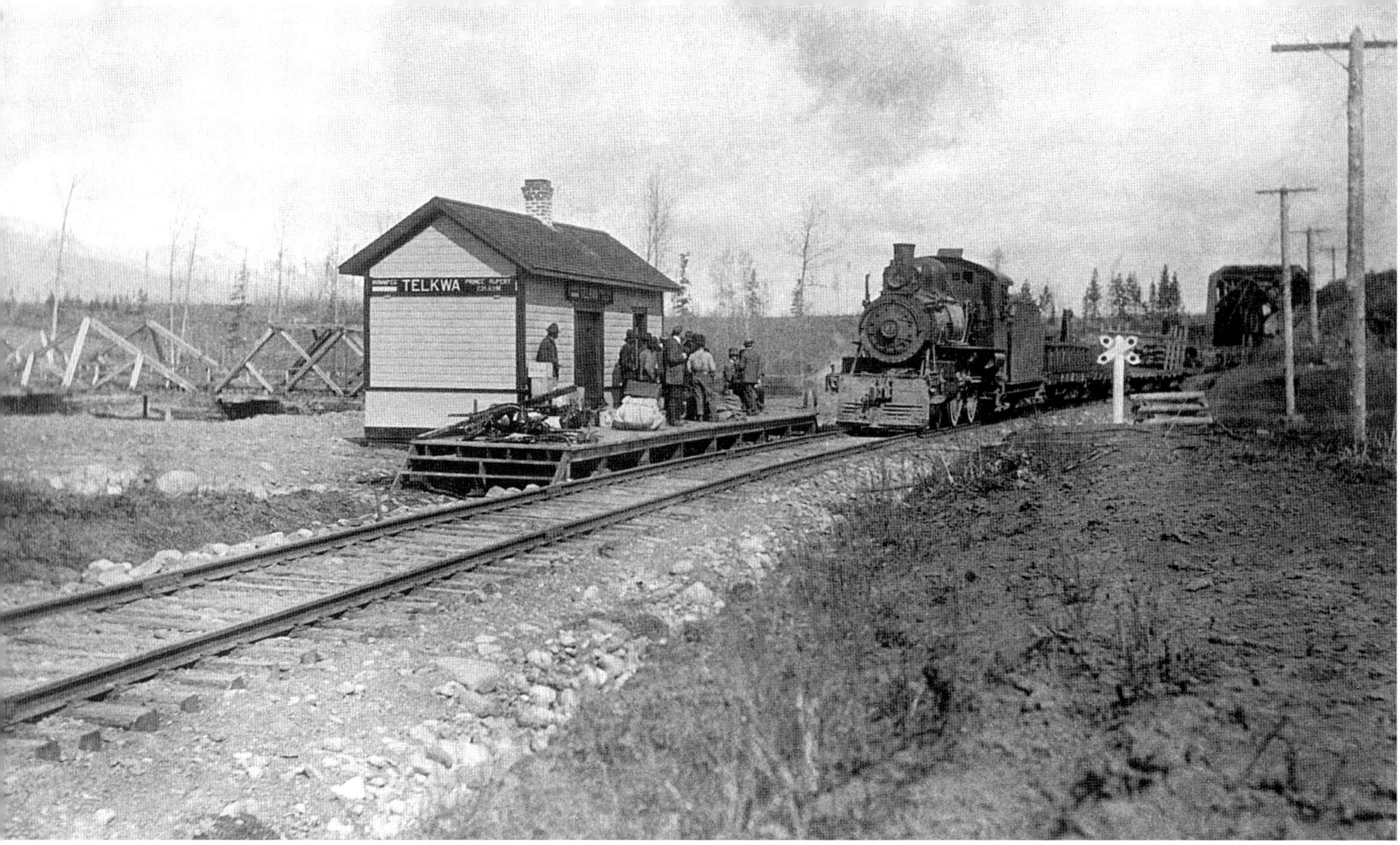

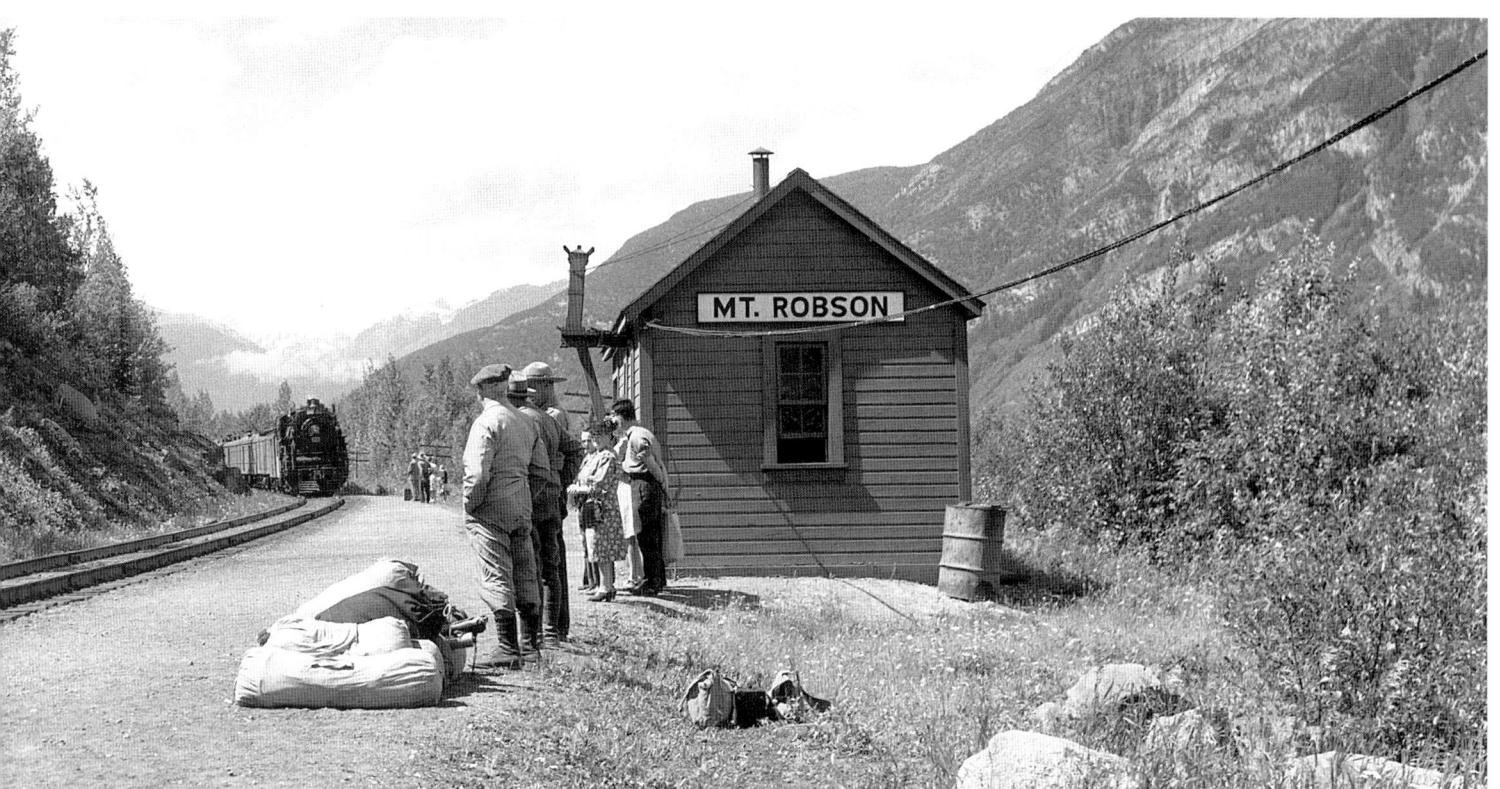

CNR Mount Robson, British Columbia

(CNR PHOTO X20165), 1930s

Even at an obscure station such as Mt. Robson, BC, train time could be a major event. A trio of adventurers awaits the arrival of the eastbound passenger train; Mt. Robson was a world-famous centre for packing and hiking and for mountaineers seeking to conquer the tallest mountain in the Canadian Rockies. The others, lacking baggage of any kind, could be the family members of a local section crew going into Redpass to shop, or they could be from the Robson Ranch—a resort just down the valley—waiting to exchange mail. Mt. Robson station was originally located about three miles east of here, where the CNoR erected a Type C depot in 1915. A disastrous snow slide on 26 February 1921 covered the tracks just beyond the train in this photograph, killing three people. As a result, in conjunction with the construction of a snow shed, in 1922 the CNR established a new station at this location, naming it Mt. Robson and re-naming the former point Foster. A Standard Portable Station and a Standard Freight and Passenger Shelter were installed at the new station in 1922. The local operator and a watchman who patrolled the tracks on either side of the new snow shed ensured that the tragic results of the 1921 snowslide would not recur. Still prominent on the Mt. Robson station here is the cantilever bracket for the train-order signal, which has been removed. The Portable Station was removed in the 1940s, leaving only the shelter. Until October 1963, employee operating timetables instructed passenger trains to stop for five minutes to let on-board patrons catch a glimpse of the station's namesake mountain, to the right and behind the photographer.

◀ **GTP Telkwa, British Columbia #1** (Bulkley Valley Historical and Museum Society, Photo P-0619), circa 1910s

The Grand Trunk Pacific was not a big believer in shelters, constructing few such buildings. Its freight and passenger shelters were of typical size (10'-0"x32'-0") and layout, and were covered by a simple gable roof. Two variants were built, differing only in the location of the door to the freight shed: either on the trackside (CNR Plan 100-162) or in the end wall (CNR Plan 100-173). One of the GTP's diminutive Moguls hauls an eastbound Mixed train, past Telkwa, BC's Standard Freight and Passenger Shelter erected in 1913. Its short wooden platform is crammed with people, baggage, l.c.l. freight and mail. While the Company showed a clear preference for locating its stations north of the tracks on the Prairies, this was not the case on its Mountain Division. The Telkwa station was south of the main line. The station name board, incorporating the route mileages from the company's Winnipeg and Prince Rupert terminals, was a standard feature on GTP main line depots, harkening back to a similar practice on parent Grand Trunk in the East. While this was the "ideal" standard for GTP main line stations, photographic evidence indicates that most name boards lacked the route mileages. With the consolidation of parallel CNoR trackage west of Edmonton in 1917, the mileages from Winnipeg were later painted out, pending re-laying of the lifted portions of the GTP track (dating this photo as post-1917). Subsequently, the terminal mileages on the name boards at each station were revised to reflect the trackage changes. The CNR continued the practice of indicating the terminal mileages from Vancouver and Montreal on the name boards at many of its main line stations in BC. At Telkwa, a detached freight shed was added next to the shelter in 1919. A Type G depot, built directly across the track from the shelter in 1922, was one of the last GTP-designed stations to be built. In 1923 this shelter was relocated to Quick, 22 miles to the east.

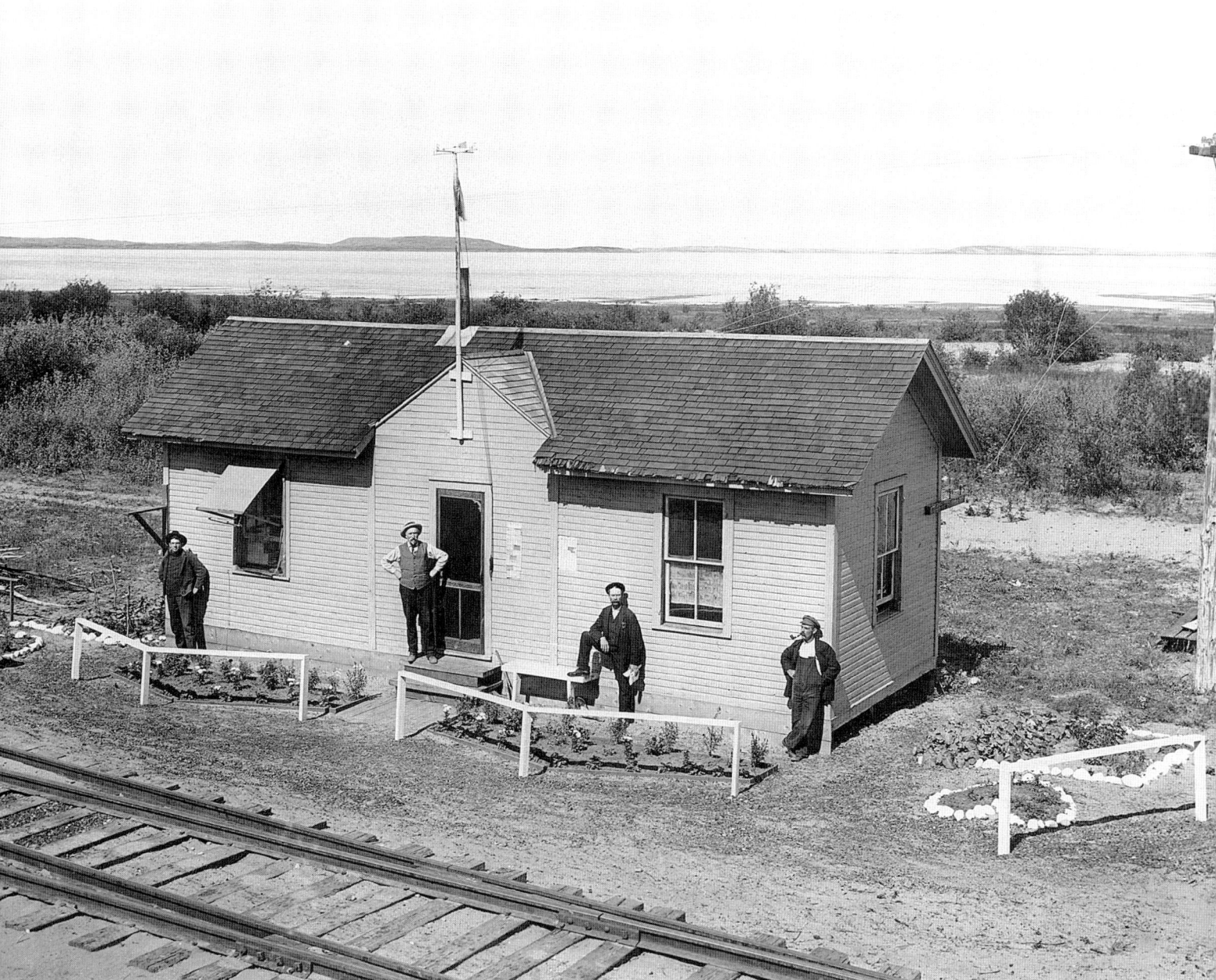

GTP Yonker, Saskatchewan #1 (Saskatchewan Archives Board, Photo R-B 9808), circa 1910

The Grand Trunk Pacific devised plans in 1907 for a "Standard Portable Station" (Plan 100-172)—based on a CPR design (Plan H-14-38)—but none was apparently constructed. Instead, at numerous locations, standard bunkhouses (CNR Plan 110-101) were fitted out as portable stations. The front porch, typical to the bunkhouse, was omitted when these buildings were used as stations, leaving the prominent gable over the door. Note the lack of a station name board, and the improvised awning over the operator's window at left. But even in the middle of nowhere—Yonker, Saskatchewan— the agent planted an extensive garden, complete with painted barricades and whitewashed rocks. Railway companies encouraged such gardens as they conveyed the fertility of the region to potential settlers riding their trains. This portable was replaced by a Type E depot in 1911.

SHELTERS, PORTABLE STATIONS AND TEMPORARY STATIONS

CNR Barlow Jct., Alberta

(B.C. ARCHIVES & RECORD SERVICE, BORDERTOWN COLLECTION, PHOTO F-08283), 1920S

Portable stations on western Canadian transcontinental lines can trace their heritage to a CPR standard (Plan H-14-38) issued in 1902. The GTP adopted the design (Plan 100-172) in 1907, although none was built. The first version appeared on the CNoR in 1908 (Plan 100-24). The CNoR's Eastern Lines (EL) Portable Station of 1912 was a copy of the CPR's. The Canadian National Railways' new EL Portable Station (Plan 100-132) issued in 1919 changed to 9'-0"x35'-0", with the same basic interior layout, and was covered by a hip roof. In the West, beginning in 1921, the CNR also erected a small number of portable stations (Plan 110-73A) based on a standard bunkhouse design of 1920 (Plan 110-73). It was 10'-0"x32'-0" and retained the usual office, waiting room and agent's bedroom and had a gable roof. From the exterior its most distinctive identifying feature was the two doors facing trackside. The Portable Station erected at Barlow Jct., just east of Calgary, in 1921 was the reverse of the standard plan. On the CNR many section bunkhouse and other buildings were later converted into portable-type stations.

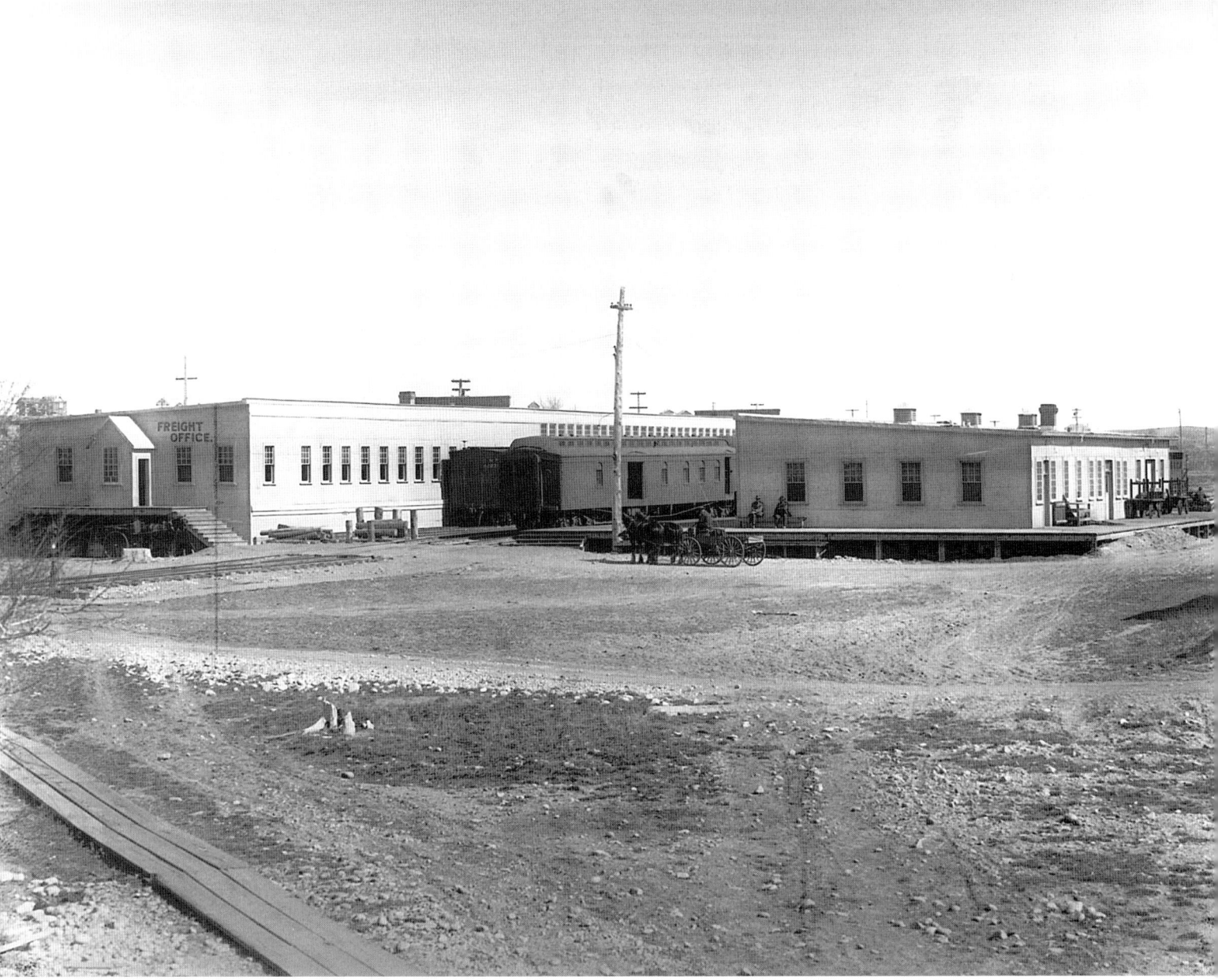

CNoR Calgary, Alberta #1

(PROVINCIAL ARCHIVES OF ALBERTA, H. POLLARD COLLECTION PHOTO P4131), CIRCA 1915

In 1910 the CNoR filed its right-of-way plans for entry into the City of Calgary. However, its proposed station, facing onto 1st Street West and 11th Avenue, encountered serious resistance by nearby landowners and the City since it entailed the closing of numerous cross streets. Subsequently, due to the high cost of the subways that would have been required, it was suggested that the CNoR line should extend only as far north as 17th Avenue. In 1911, CNoR acquired the St. Mary's Parish Hall property and a large tract of land on the westerly bend of the Elbow River, the latter for its freight terminals. It immediately set up offices in the former Hall. Preliminary plans prepared by R. B. Pratt, showing a monumental three-storey station in Neo-classical Style facing onto on 17th Avenue, were submitted to the City in August 1912 and were approved. Legal wrangling with the CPR delayed the CNoR's entry into Calgary until February 1914, however. The previous November the company constructed a temporary station on the east side of the Elbow River. This very plain 40'-0"x96'-0" wood-frame building was clad with corrugated metal and had a shed roof. Inside was a ticket office, large ladies' and general waiting rooms complete with washrooms, and a baggage and express room. A large freight shed and office (30'-0"x400'-0") was built across the platform from the station. The economic downturn of 1913 and the outbreak of war the following summer, forced the CNoR into an austerity programme. Construction of the proposed 17th Avenue station was shelved indefinitely. Instead, minor alterations were made to the former Parish Hall and a small addition was built onto it. The rail line was extended across the Elbow River and Calgary's new station opened in 1916. The temporary station was then converted into a freight shed, which was demolished in 1923. Here the temporary station and the freight shed are shown in their prime, about 1915.

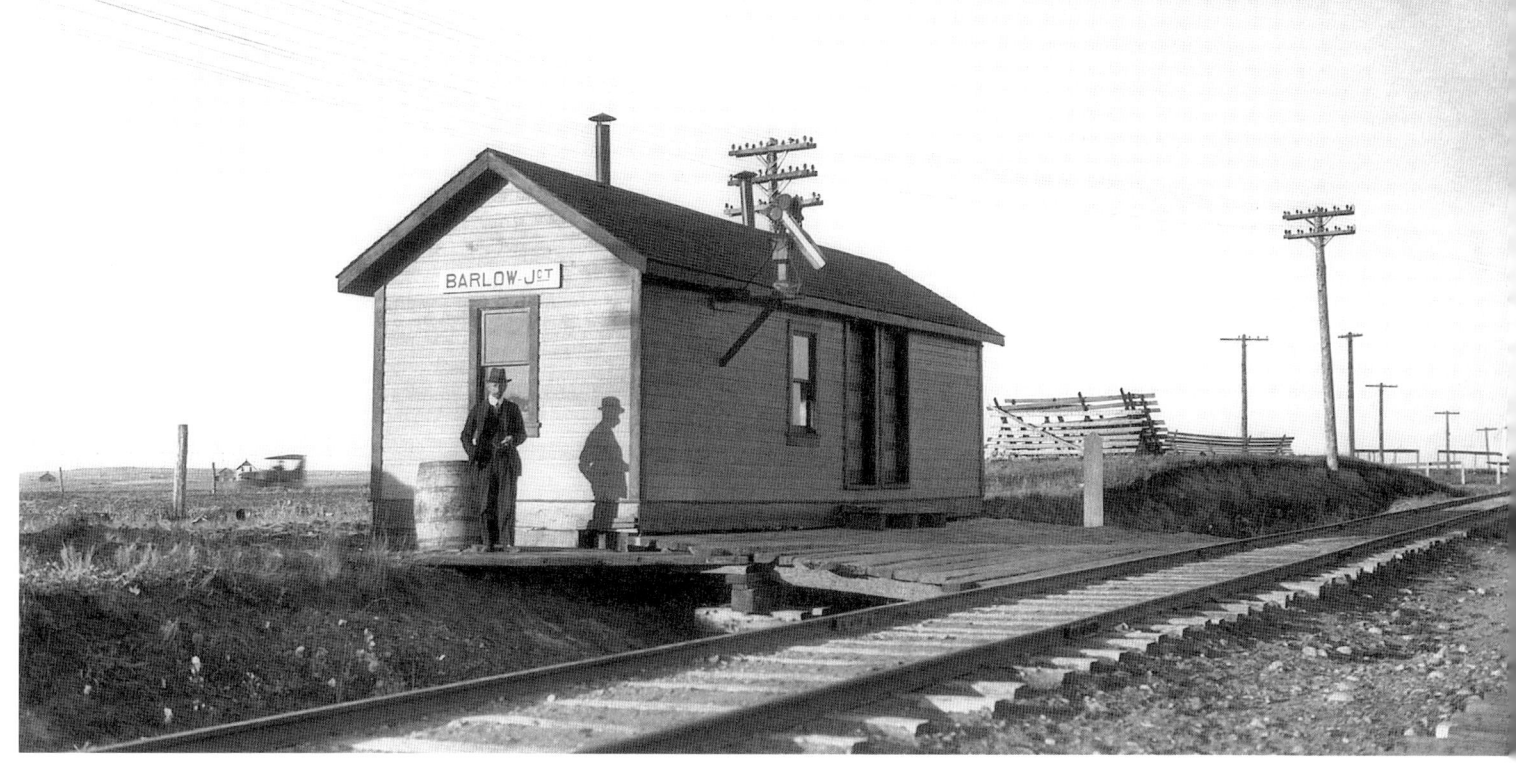

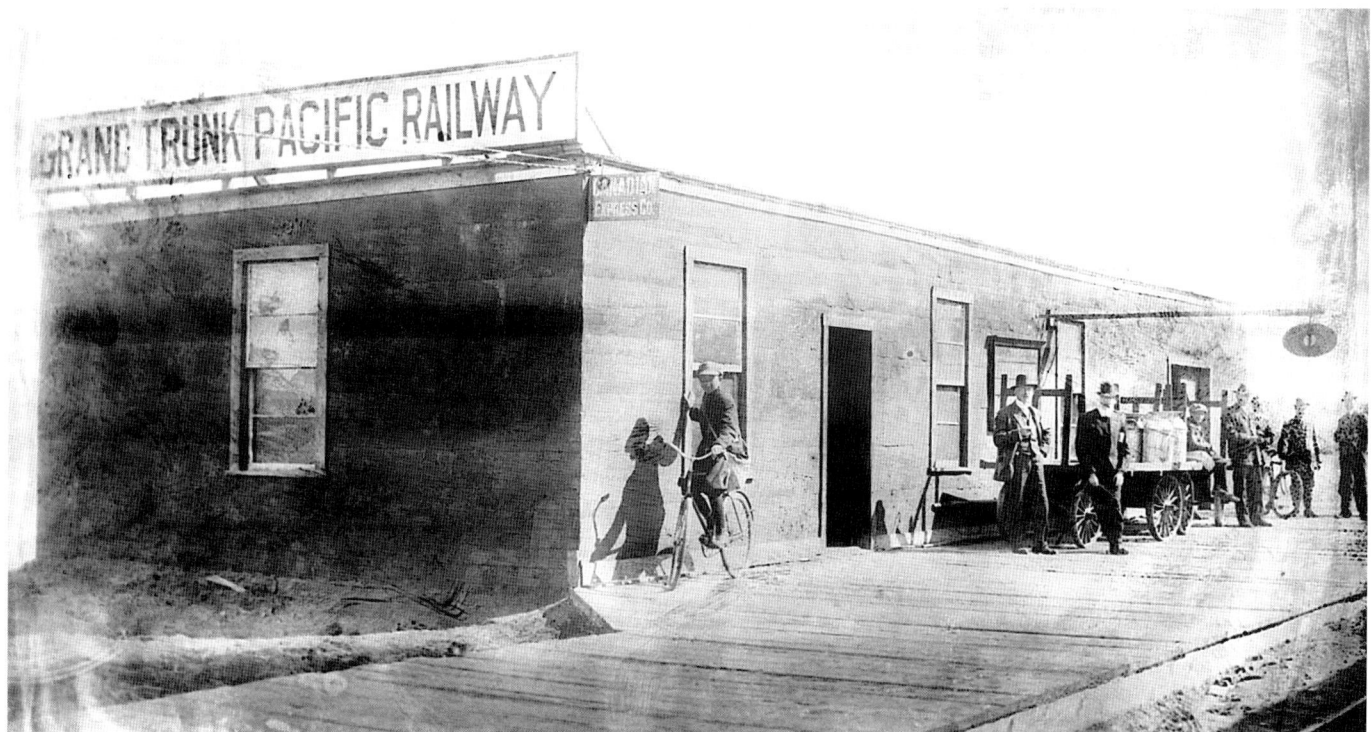

GTP Calgary, Alberta #1 (Provincial Archives of Alberta, H. Pollard Collection, Photo P4037), circa 1914

Although the Grand Trunk Pacific's direct route between Winnipeg and Prince Rupert on the Pacific coast resulted in significant savings in travel time over that of rival CNoR, it was symptomatic of the GTP's poor execution: it avoided every major city along the length of its main line. To gain access to these large population centres the GTP was forced to negotiate running-rights and union station agreements with its competitors. The Grand Trunk Pacific shared station accommodation with the CNoR at Winnipeg and Edmonton, and later with the CPR at Saskatoon. At its western terminus, the Prince Rupert Inn was relocated next to the track and refurbished to serve as a station. Its branch lines were a different proposition however. At Regina the GTP purchased a private residence near the western periphery of that city, and converted it into a depot. In 1914, the GTP acquired the North West Mounted Police barracks site in central Calgary, where it developed a station and freight yard. The GTP intended to construct its own elaborate stations at every major urban point, but World War I intervened, so none of these plans came to fruition. This very unassuming building was the GTP's temporary station at Calgary, on the corner of 6th Avenue and 6th Street S.E. It was of wood-frame construction with a waiting room, office and freight shed. The exterior was finished with metal sheeting stamped to simulate brick. The GTP's main ticket sales were handled through Niblock and Tull's, in the downtown Grain Exchange Building. On August 20, 1914 this station was relocated to suit a more desirable yard layout. The building was raised, placed on rollers and shifted to its new site near the corner of 9th Avenue and 6th Street S.E., next to a pair of newly laid spurs. A rather peculiar feature of the move was that the station staff was busy working in the building while it was traveling to its new location. Telephonic communication was kept going and business was being transacted as if nothing out of the ordinary was going on! With the construction in 1921 of a track connection at Barlow Jct., southeast of Calgary, the Canadian Northern yard became the new terminus in the city and the GTP line was reclassified as an industrial spur. By 1923, the former GTP station was leased to Hy Grade Coal and used as a coal shed. It was removed in 1924 to make way for the CNR's new inbound freight shed.

CNR Bjorkdale, Saskatchewan #2

(Hilt Friesen Photo), 1977

The "Freight and Passenger Shelter with Office," erected at Bjorkdale, Saskatchewan in 1948 (Plan 100-323)—as a replacement for a shelter destroyed by fire—had a bay window. Essentially a portable station, it was the only one erected to this Plan. A number of standard Freight and Passenger Shelters, such as Amaranth, Manitoba, were however upgraded in similar fashion. A standard section bunkhouse was subsequently moved just west of the station. The two-direction, three-aspect, upper quadrant train-order with its cantilevered bracket seems totally out of proportion to the station. The blades of the signal were actuated—by the operator-agent—by means of rods, solid jaws and a crank connecting to the two-lever machine bolted to the inside wall of the bay window. The flex conduit up the bracket indicates that the former kerosene lamp for the signal has long since been replaced by an electric light.

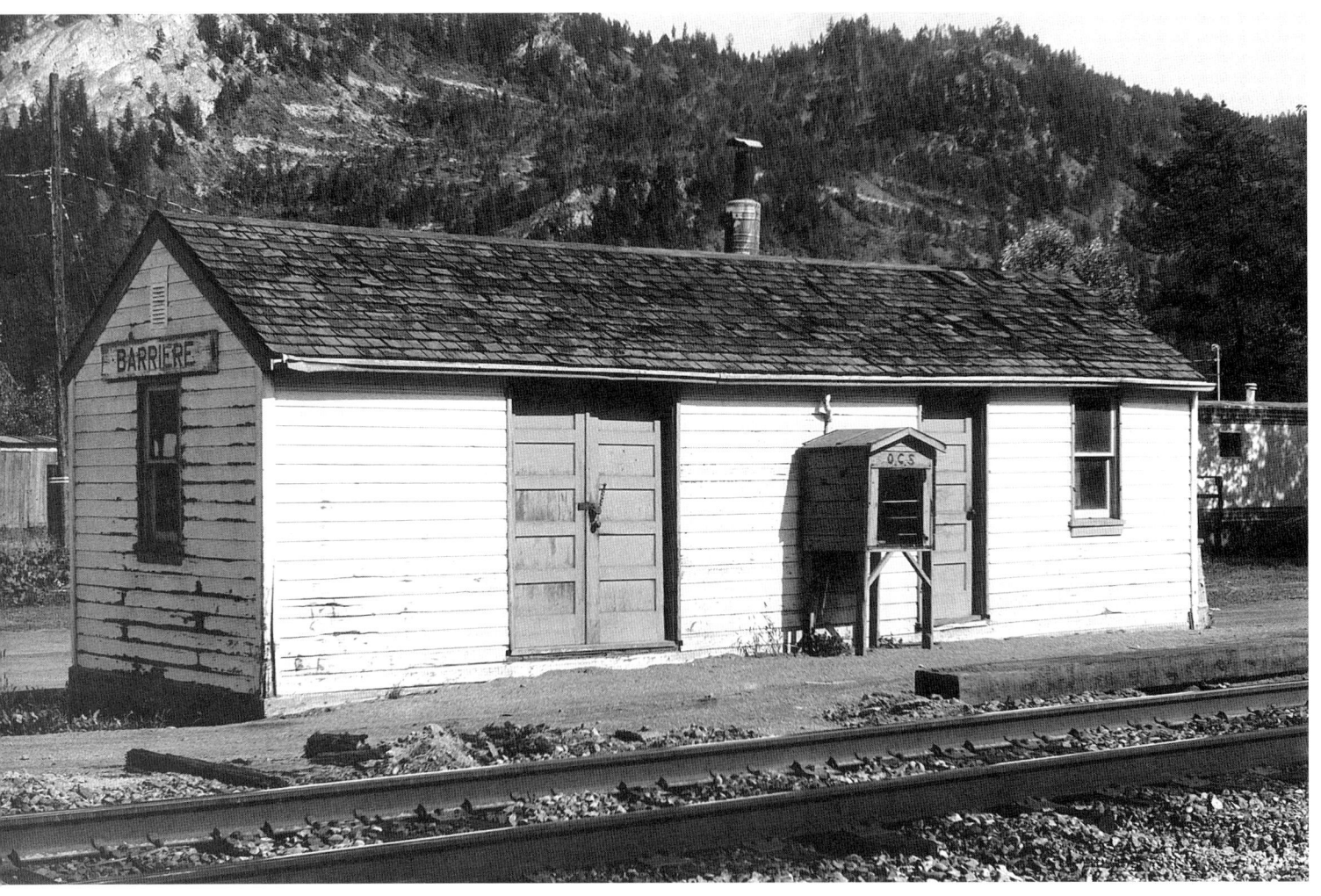

CNR Barriere, British Columbia #2

(Leslie S. Kozma Photo), 1975

The Freight and Passenger Shelter (Plan 100-334) erected at Barriere, BC in 1954—replacing a Type C depot razed by fire—was the culmination of nearly fifty years of evolution of CNR Freight and Passenger Shelters (FPS). In 1918 the Canadian National adopted the CNoR's Standard FPS (Plan 100-41). Some later versions had a window in the back wall of the waiting room, but were otherwise unchanged from the original 1910-design. The plans were modified slightly and re-issued as "Plan 100-41B" by the CNR in 1923. The sliding freight door of the former plan was replaced by a pair of cheaper swinging doors and a brick chimney was provided in lieu of the usual metal smoke jack. Inside, the small bench along the back wall had a hinged seat, the locker for the equipment used by patrons to flag down trains. Work on some of these freight-and-passenger shelters along new branch lines was halted during the early stages of the Depression; these "bare bones" versions of the building being classified as "Plan 100-41C." Minor improvements were made to "Plan 100-41B" and it was re-issued in 1947 (Plan 100-320) and 1951 (Plan 100-334), with only a few examples of each constructed.

CNoR Amaranth, Manitoba

(Hilt Friesen Photo), 1974

The station at Amaranth, Manitoba—well past its prime when this photograph was taken in 1974—was indicative of the extent to which changes to the standard building could render it virtually unrecognizable. With the need for an agent, the CNoR's "Old" Standard Freight and Passenger Shelter (Plan 100-96) was rebuilt into a permanent station. The freight room was relocated into an extension. The far door was likely for the new coal bin. An office was created in the former freight shed. A unique bay window was also added to the trackside of the office. No doubt, patrons were advised to "Watch that first step out of the waiting room onto the platform!"

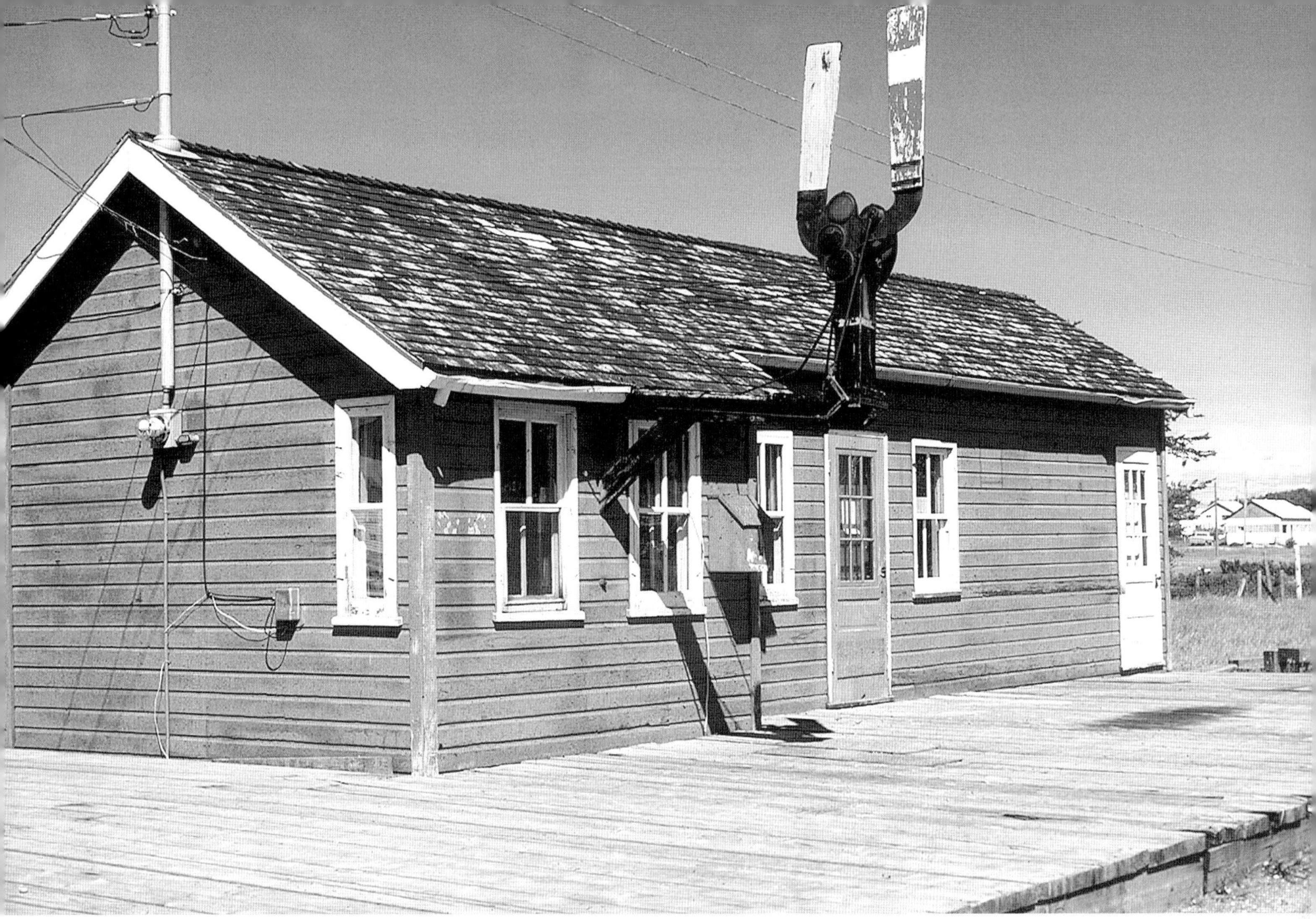

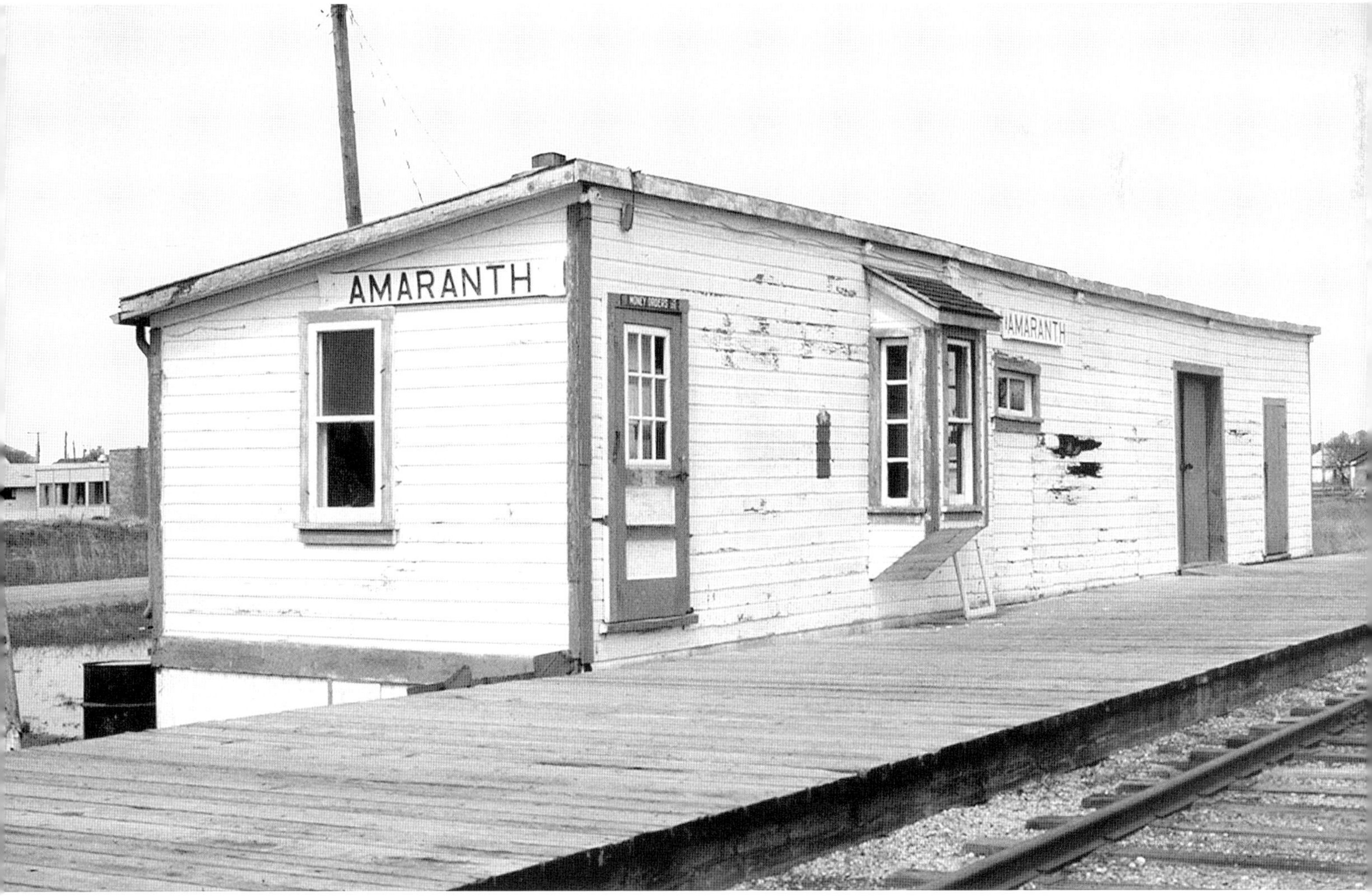

Shelters, Portable Stations and Temporary Stations

Combination Station-and-Section-Houses

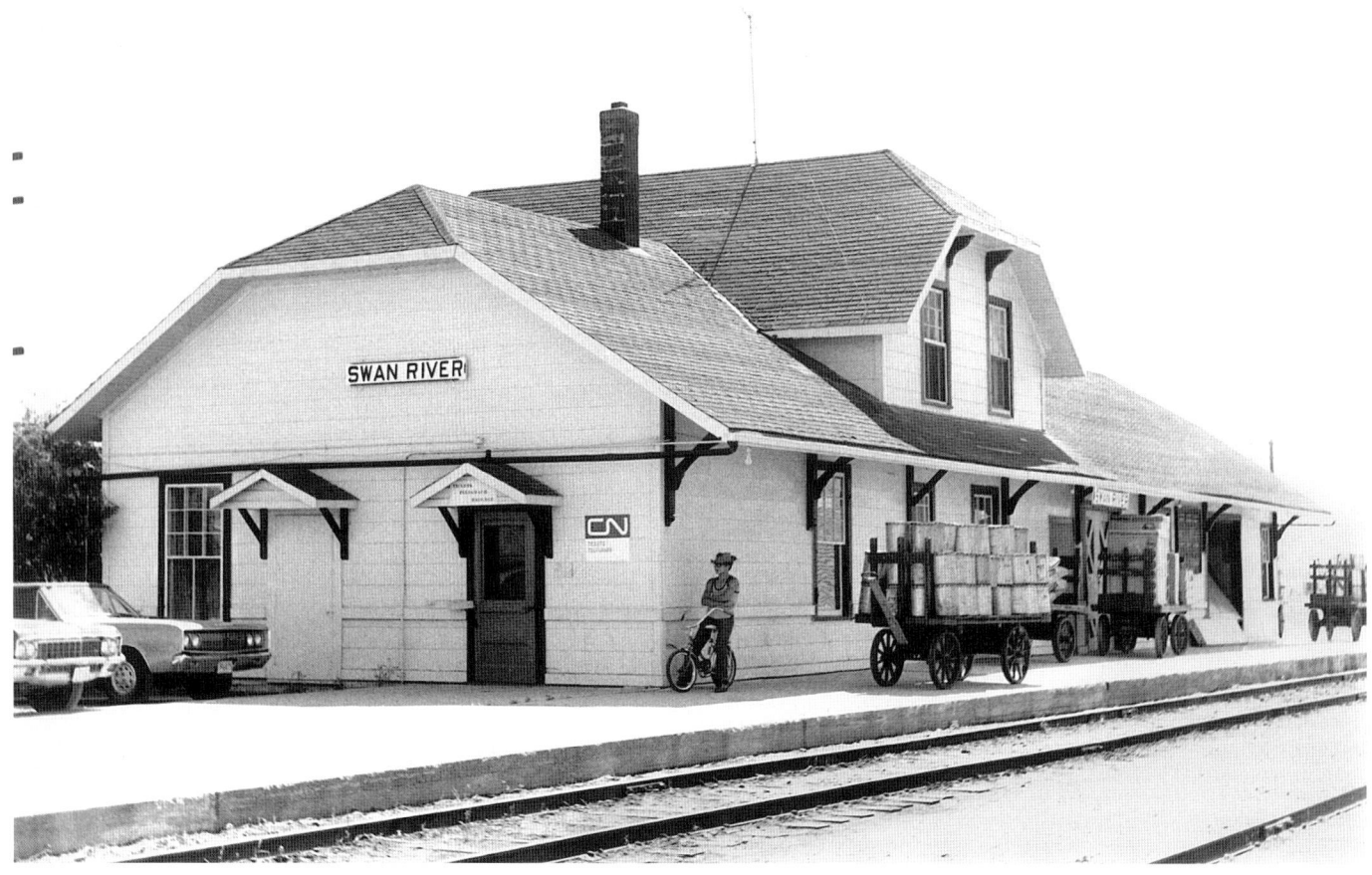

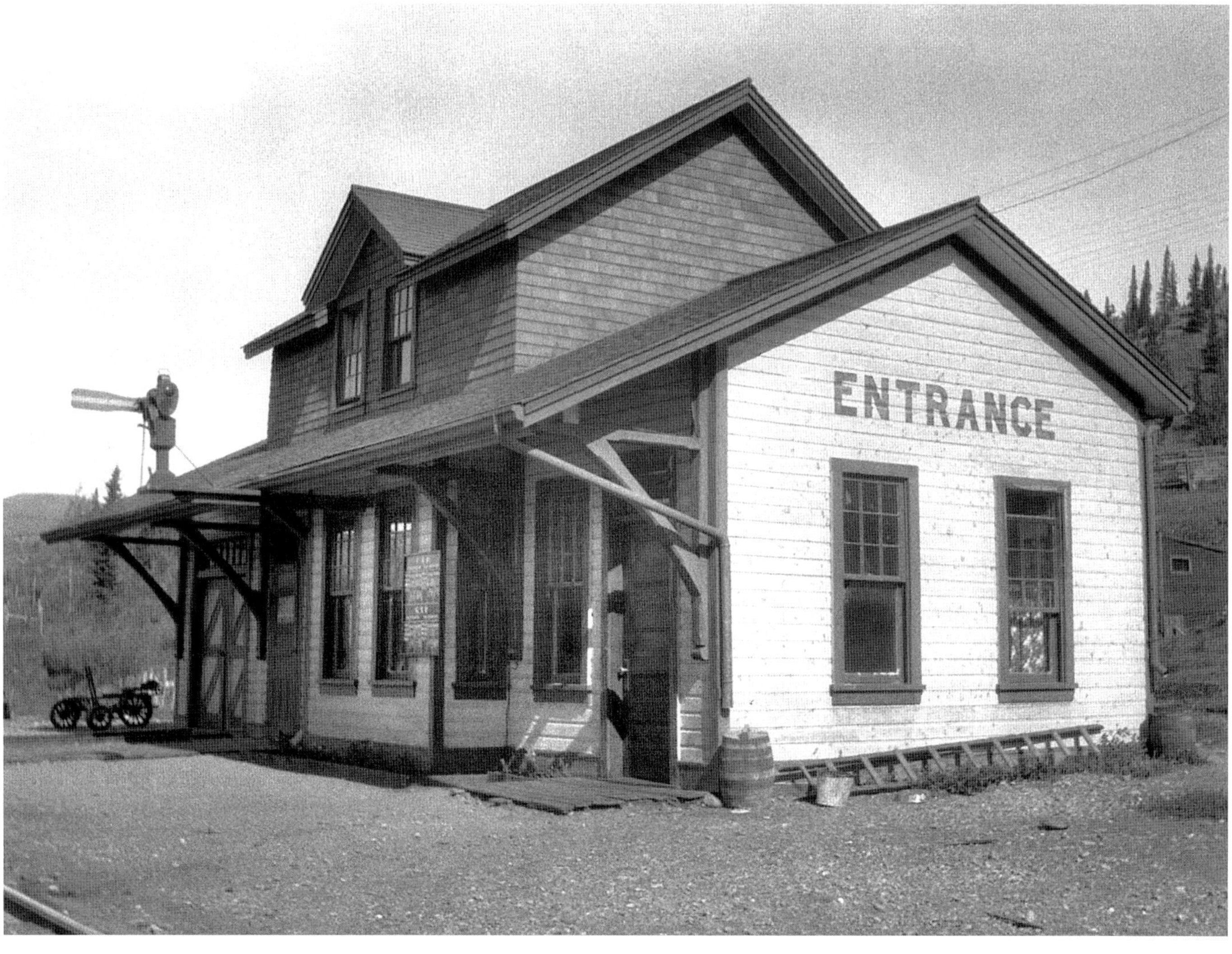

◀ **CNoR Swan River, Manitoba** (Charles W. Bohi Photo), 1971

Combination station-and-section-houses (CSS) took many forms on the CNoR. The first was a design used on the Gladstone and Winnipegosis Subdivisions before 1900 (Type A depot). The Canadian Northern Railway's earliest standard station (Plan 100-63) appears to have been based on a Canadian Pacific Railway (CPR) design. This was no mere coincidence, since William Mackenzie and his brothers were contracted to build the stations and water tanks along the CPR main line and the later Qu'Appelle Long Lake & Saskatchewan and Calgary & Edmonton branches. These slightly larger CNoR structures borrowed many architectural features from the CPR's combined station-and-section-houses of 1890 (CPR Type 2). All eleven of these CNoR CSS were erected in Manitoba. Judging by the wagons piled high with merchandise, l.c.l. and express were still important sources of traffic on the line as late as 1971. Another CSS, developed by the CNoR in 1904, was simply a standard section house provided with a trackside awning and wooden platform. One of the main floor bedrooms served as a waiting room (Plan 110-10).

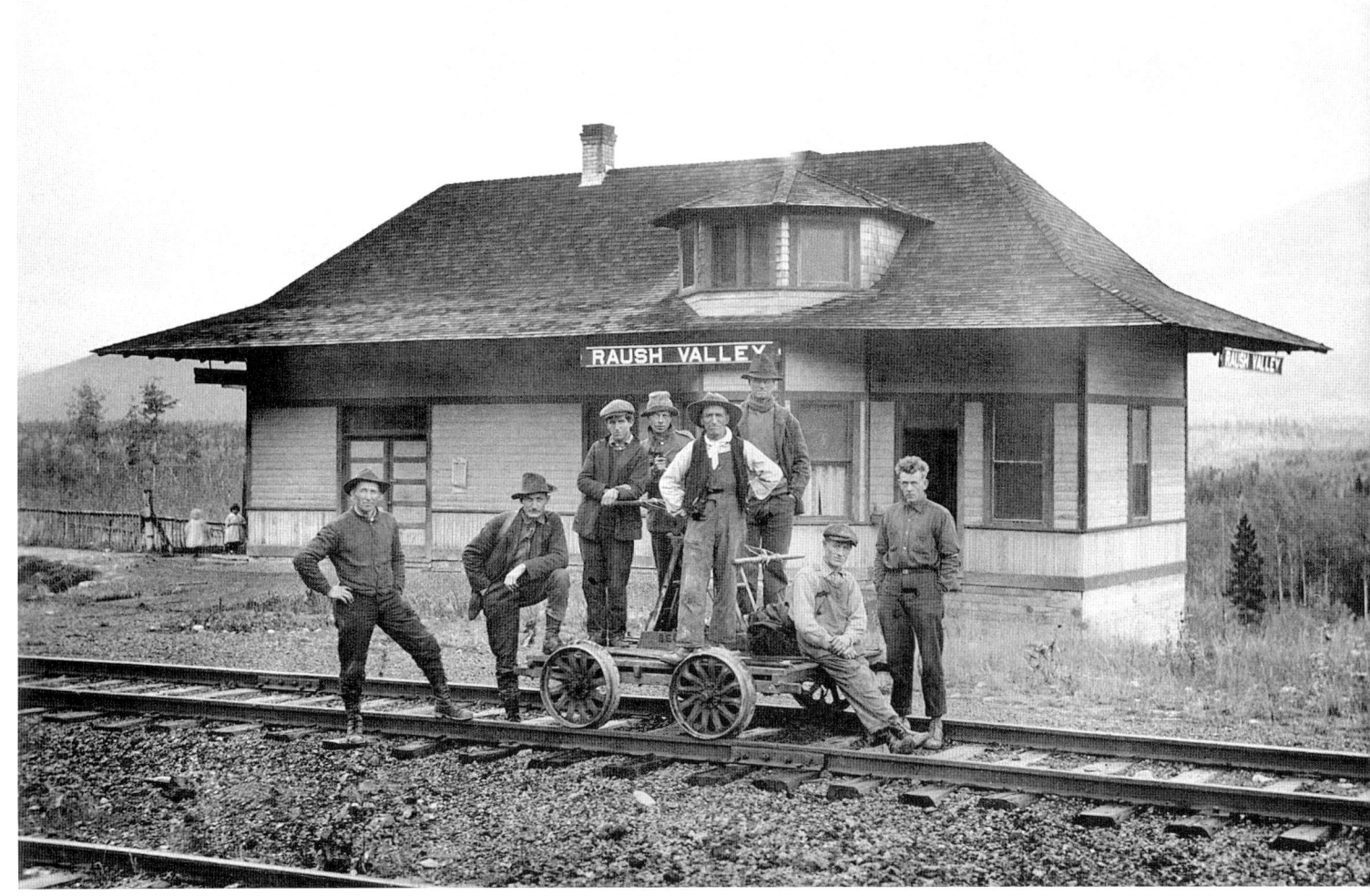

GTP Raush Valley, British Columbia (Adams Collection, Valley Museum & Archives, McBride #1999.16), 1921

Many GTP depots along the sparsely settled line through northern BC were built primarily to house section crews with the understanding that once traffic warranted, these buildings would be converted into operational stations. The men posing on the classic handcar were likely the local section gang that resided in the depot. The lack of a train bulletin, an order board or a trackside platform is a good indication that this building was used as a section house rather than a depot. In such cases, the freight shed of Type E *stations was often used as a bunkroom by the section laborers, while the balance of the building was occupied by the section foreman and his family (note the two children in the background, left). The name board lacked the main line route mileages, but was otherwise standard: an 11¾" high by 1¾" board, length to suit the name, with chamfered edges;* White *painted letters 8" high on a* Black *field; the chamfers were painted* White. *In the early 1950s many underused combination stations were converted into freight and passenger shelters: all but the freight shed being demolished or removed, while the remaining portion was re-configured (Plan 100-318). At least twenty-five* Type E *stations, mostly along the BC North Line, were transformed into such FPS. The Raush Valley depot, built in 1913, had an exterior treatment of roughcast stucco and wooden walers added in 1927. The walls and ceiling were insulated in 1941. This depot was sold and removed in 1963.*

◀ **CNoR Entrance, Alberta** (National Archives of Canada, Photo PA 100222), circa 1919

The most common CNoR CSS was the Type C *depot (Plan 110-26, later Plans 100-47, and 100-98 in BC), first drawn in 1912. It was also adopted for the CNoR Eastern Lines as Standard Station Number 7. Entrance, Alberta was an isolated community with little local passenger traffic, as evidenced by the lack of a trackside platform. Most of these types of buildings had at least a cinder platform. The bulletin board, to the right of the bay window, notes both GTP and CNoR trains, dating this photograph between 1917 and 1920. This station closed in 1927 with completion of the new 2.9-mile Dyke–Solomon connection and rehabilitation of the GTP between Obed and Dyke, which had lain abandoned since 1917. The ex-GTP station of Dyke was subsequently renamed Entrance, while the old CNoR site became "Old Entrance." The CNoR line east of Solomon was retained as a spur to the gravel pit at Bliss. When this spur was abandoned in 1932, the Entrance depot was sold* in situ *to the Alberta Forestry Department. It was subsequently re-sold and used as a cabin, remaining on its original site until about 1990, when it was relocated up the hill.*

Combination Station-and-Section-Houses

Combination Stations

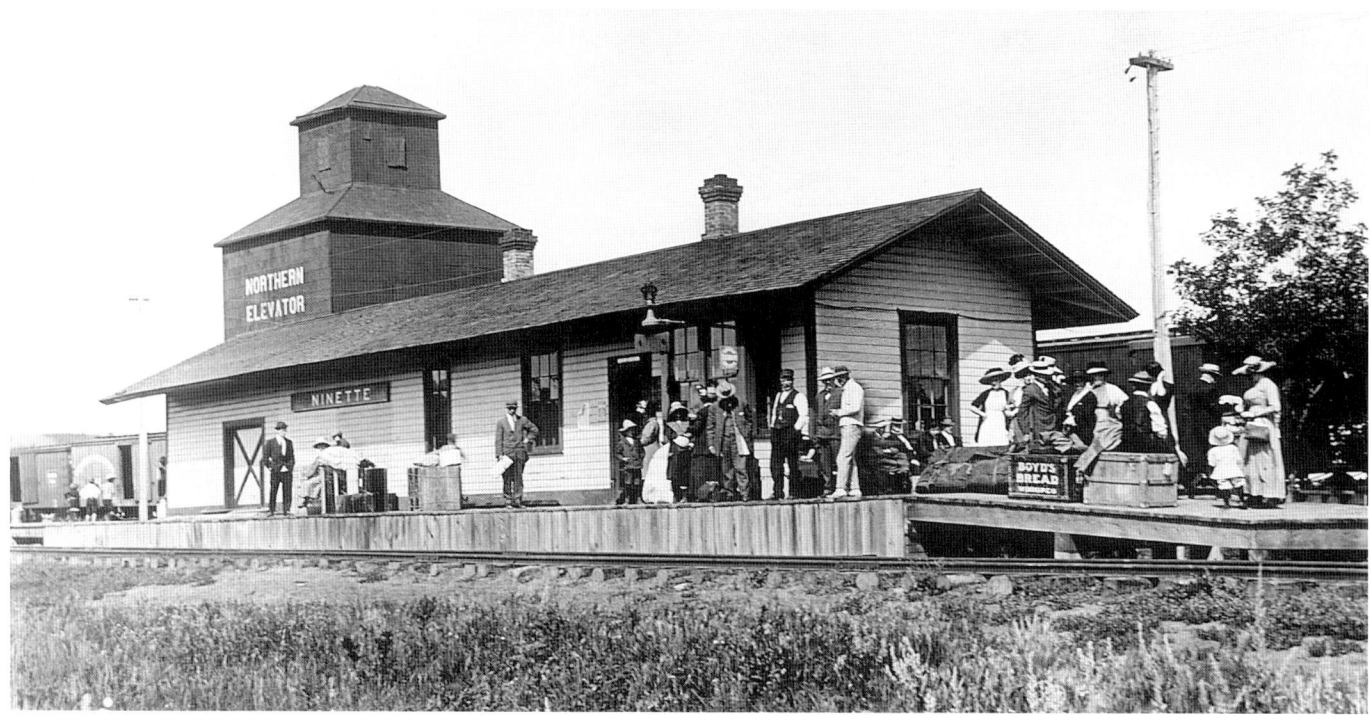

NP Ninette, Manitoba (Provincial Archives of Manitoba, Photo Ninette 4), 1910

Generally speaking, Northern Pacific Railway (NPR) stations erected in Canada reflected that company's early American standards. Ninette, Manitoba embodied the NPR's typical 4th Class Combination Depot (Plan S-26-31). They were narrow and long (16'-0"x48'-0") with a trackside bay window near one end, and had a simple gable roof. The interior was partitioned into an office, waiting room and freight shed. The length of the freight shed varied according to the expected volume of business. These NPR stations were the basis for later CNoR 4th and 5th Class stations. The Ninette depot, erected in 1898, was one of the later versions of the NPR design. It was sold in 1976, virtually unchanged from the day it opened.

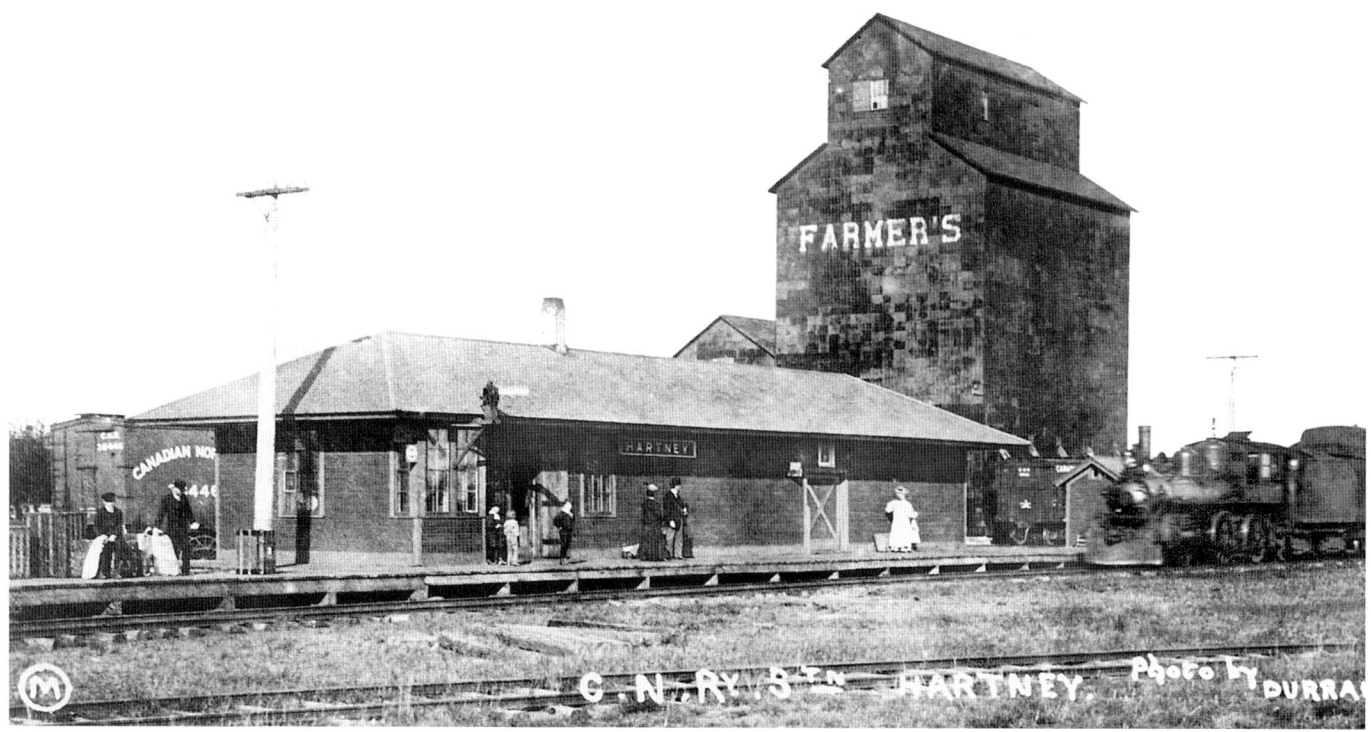

NP Hartney, Manitoba (Provincial Archives of Manitoba, Durant Collection, Photo Hartney–Buildings–CNR 1), circa 1901

Built in 1900, the Hartney, Manitoba depot was a mirror image of the Ninette plan and had a hip roof. The basic floor plan, in conjunction with variations in exterior finish—board-and-batten or drop siding—and/or roof line—hip, gable and clipped gable—dramatically altered the appearance of the standard NPR 4th Class depot. Some might argue that it did not make much difference, as these depots were still very plain. The square bay forming the corner at the end wall was a feature used by the CNoR on some of its early combination depots. Hartney was the end of the steel until 1905 when the line was extended to Virden.

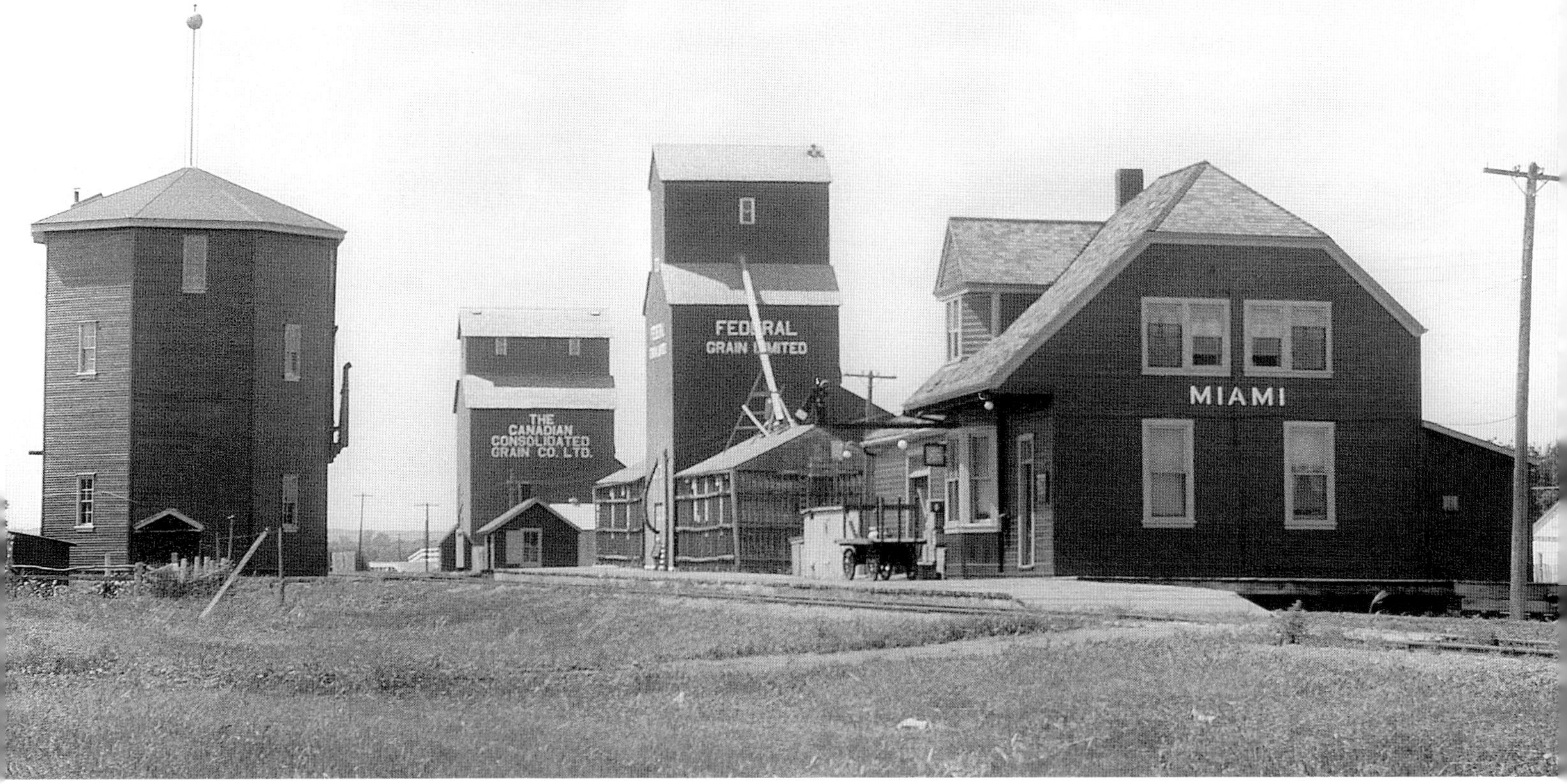

NP Miami, Manitoba (AL PATERSON PHOTO, STAFFORD SWAIN COLLECTION), 1945

Clearly, the station at Miami, Manitoba was a variant of the Northern Pacific's "3rd Class 2 Story Combination Depot" (Plan S-26-14, issued 1883). The two-storey design, incorporating an agent's apartment, was a departure from most other NPR depots, which were usually a single-storey without living accommodations. The NPR 3rd Class depot saw limited duty in the northwestern U.S. There is reason to believe that most of those erected in Manitoba were intended as combination station-and-section-houses. Miami was without a freight shed until the CNoR added one in 1903. The stuccoed version of this design at Wawanesa—the mirror image of the Miami depot—had an even longer freight shed added. With a few adjustments to the exterior, the basic elements for the massing of the CNoR 3rd Class depot are recognizable in this NPR building. Could this have been Pratt's inspiration for the CNoR's 3rd Class station?

NP Wawanesa, Manitoba (AL PATERSON PHOTO, STAFFORD SWAIN COLLECTION), NO DATE

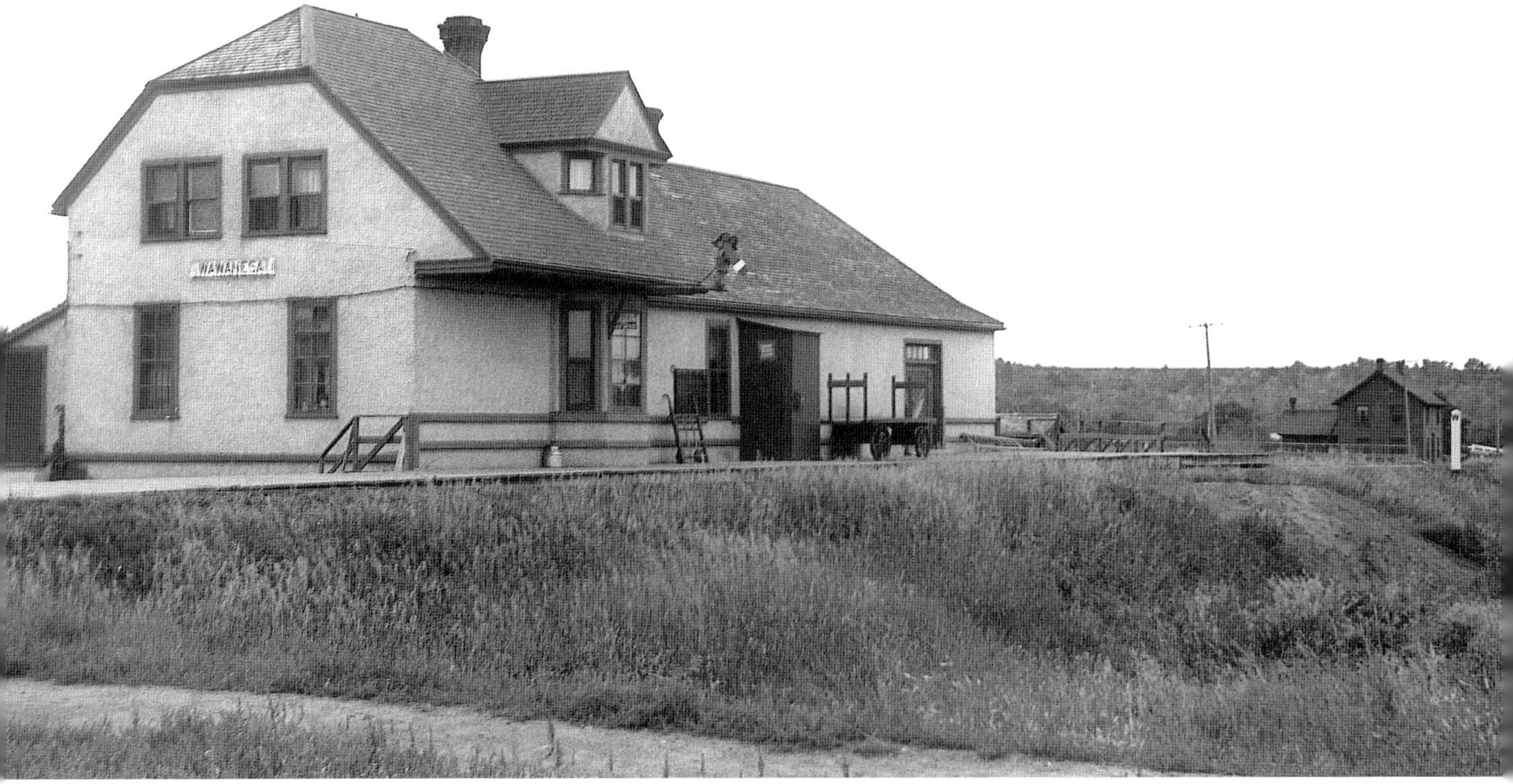

COMBINATION STATIONS

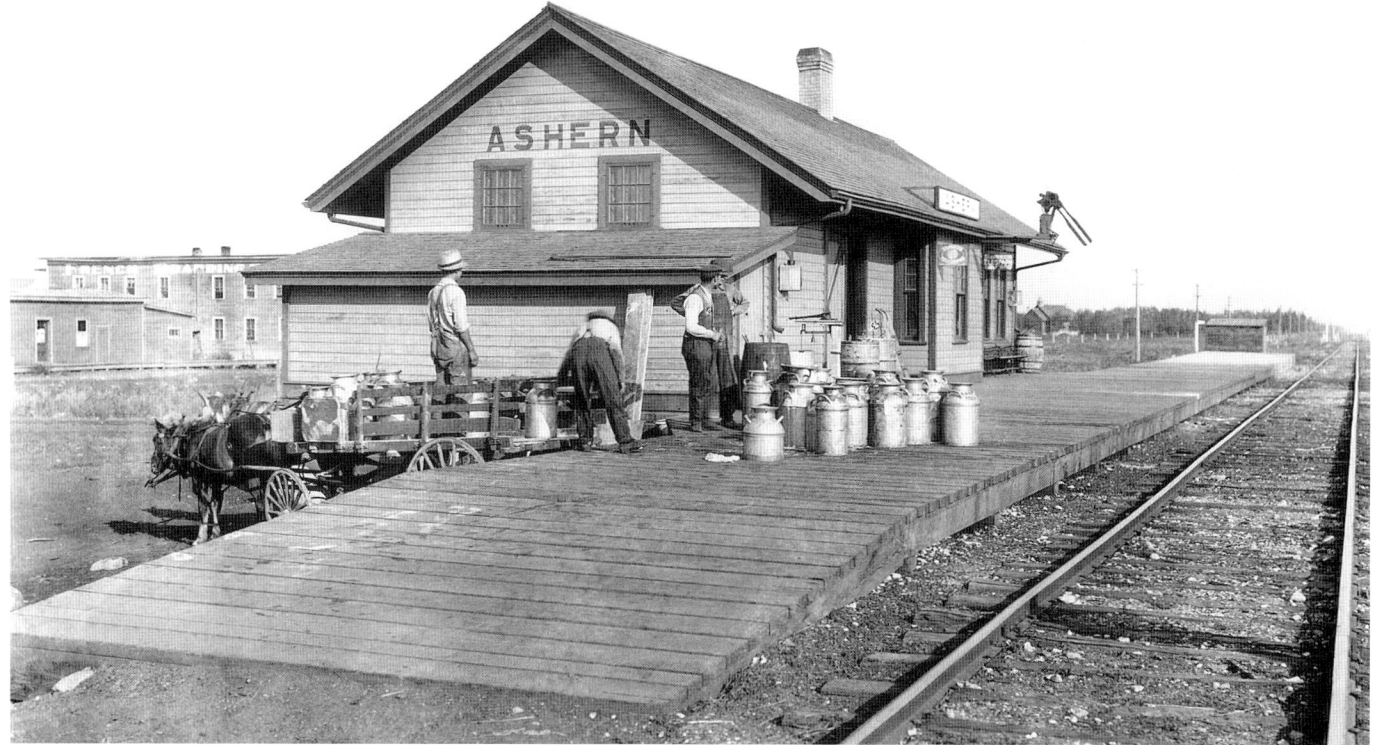

CNoR Ashern, Manitoba
(Provincial Archives of Manitoba, Photo Ashern 1), circa 1925

The CNoR 4th Class Station (Plan 100-68) at Ashern, Manitoba replaced a standard FPS (Plan 100-41) in 1918. The coal shed on this end of the building marks it as one of the later versions. "Milk run" was a railway term that entered the common lexicon, describing a train that stopped at every station to pick up milk or cream, and sometimes eggs. While such trains were the butt of many jokes, such local runs were an important source of revenue for the railways. Here, milk cans were being unloaded onto the platform for pick up by the next Winnipeg-bound train. In 1920, shipments of fresh fish also commenced moving over the Oak Point Subdivision, with Ashern being one of the primary shipping points. Passenger trains on this line would often have six or more express cars dedicated to fish traffic, bound for eastern Canada and the United States. The station name was painted onto the end walls in 12"-high Black letters. Note the one-direction, two-aspect, lower quadrant order board, the platform scale and the elaborate bench ends. The rainwater leaders emptied into water barrels on the platform. Such barrels were always kept full as a precaution against fire. This station—insulated in 1937 and stuccoed in 1941—was sold in 1977.

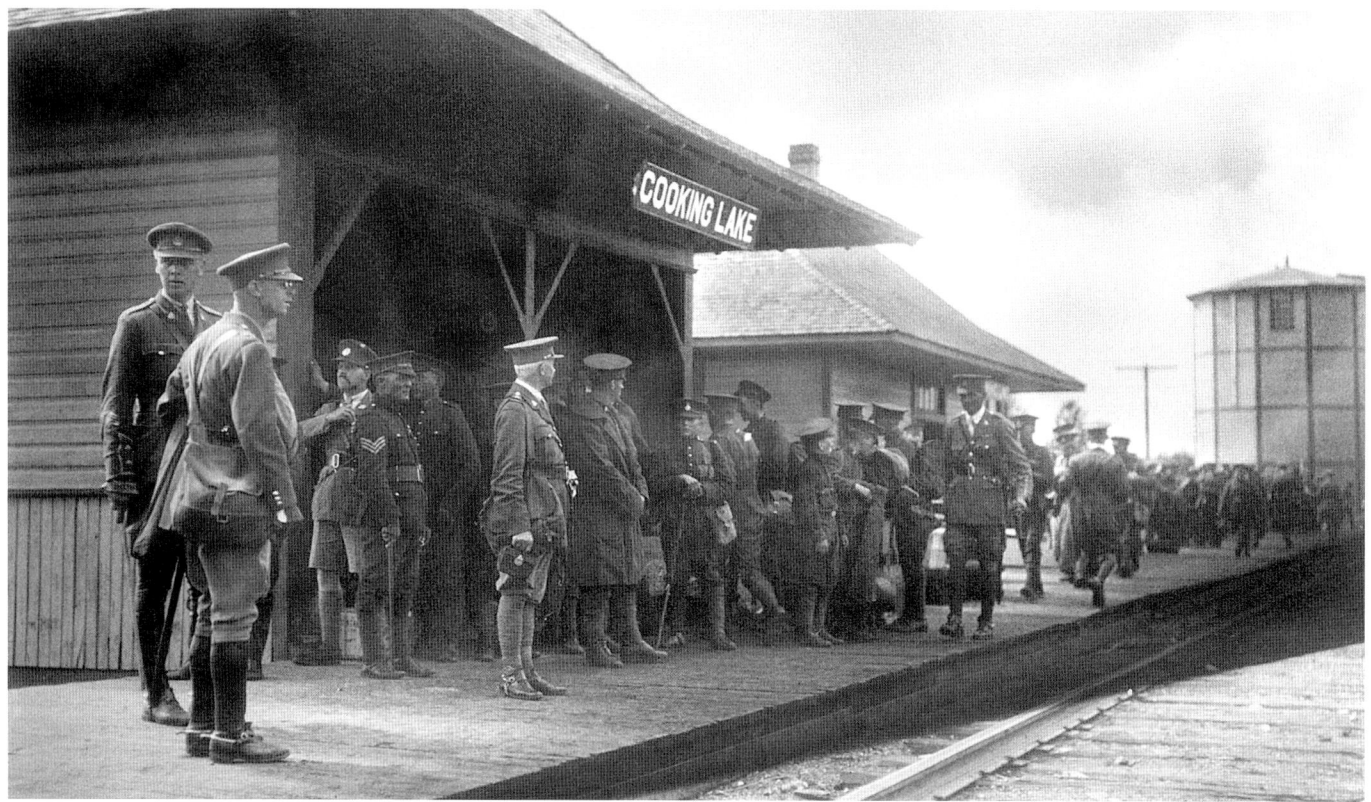

GTP Cooking Lake, Alberta
(City of Edmonton Archives, Photo EA-29-123), 1910s

A GTP 'Design B' Station (Plan 100-153) at Cooking Lake, Alberta, behind the semi-enclosed shelter and all those troops. Looming up beyond was the standard GTP water tank. Only three such stations were built on the GTP, including two at Uno, Manitoba (one destroyed by fire was rebuilt in kind). Measuring 18'-0"x35'-3", they had a small office and waiting room in one end, with the freight shed occupying most of the interior. Cooking Lake's transformation into a summer resort resulted in the addition of the detached shelter. At least two buildings similar to the GTP 'Design B' were built as express sheds erected next to their respective depots: at South Saskatoon and Unity, Saskatchewan. The latter building was relocated to the Saskatchewan Railroad Historical Association Museum, near Saskatoon, where it has been restored.

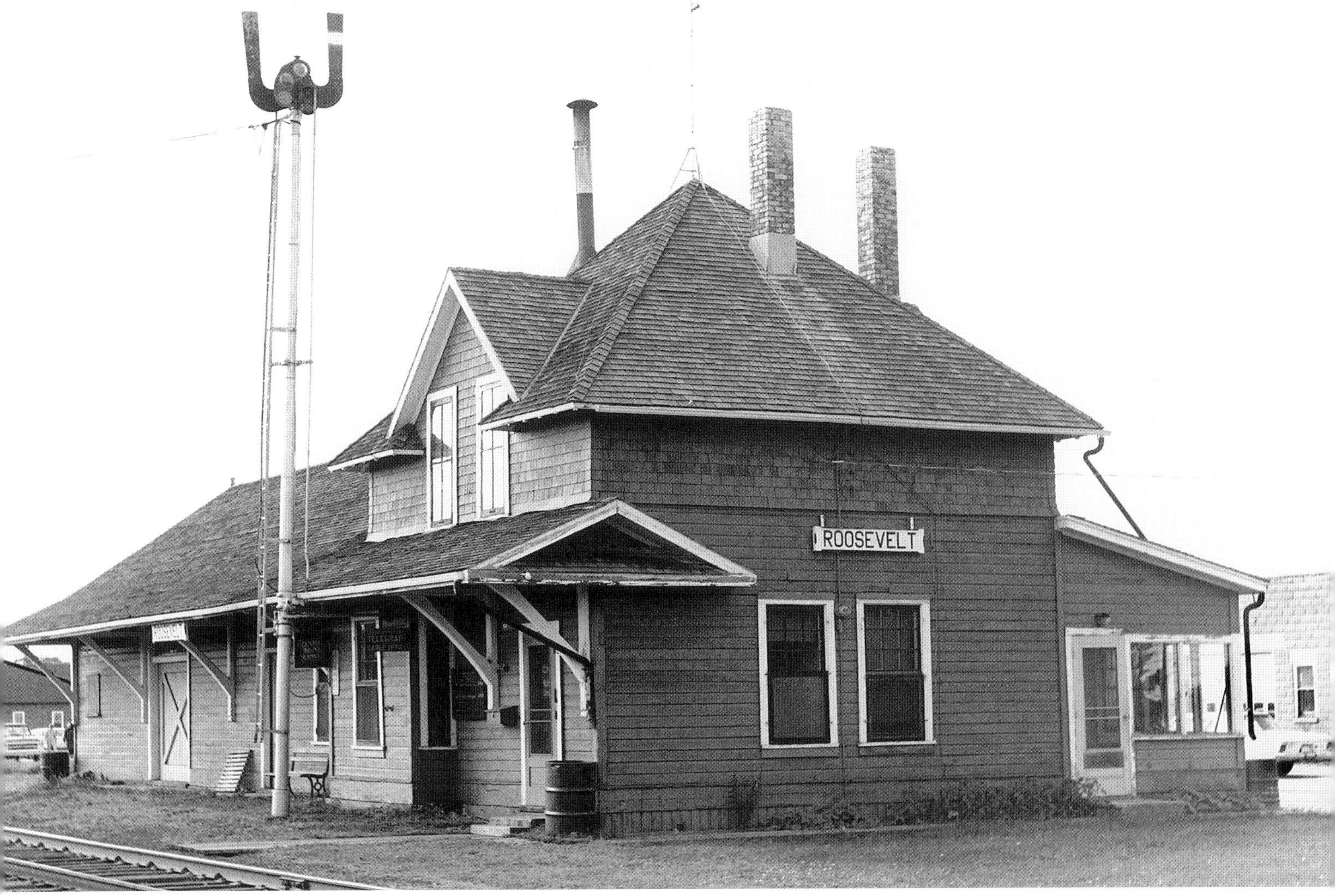

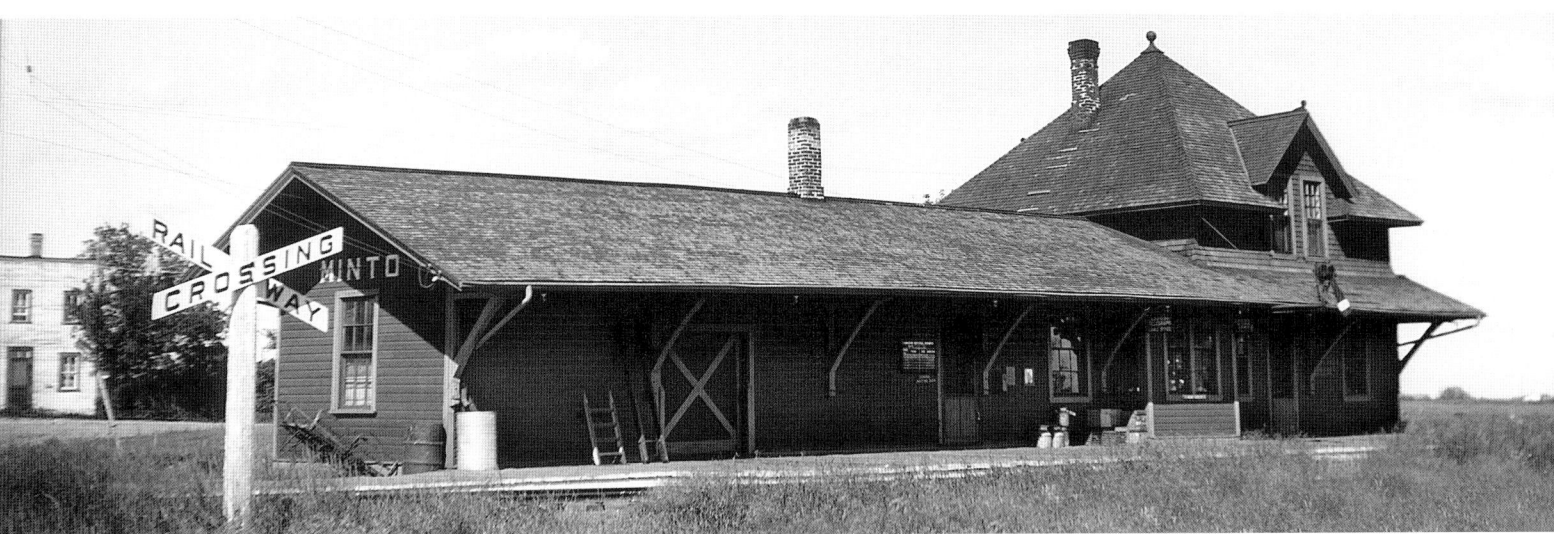

CNoR Roosevelt, Minnesota (Charles W. Bohi Photo), 1971

Architect Ralph Benjamin Pratt developed the CNoR's "Standard 3rd Class Station" in 1901 (Plan 100-3). It was 22'-0"x42'-0", with an office, waiting room and agent's living room on the main floor; with a 10'-0"x12'-0" kitchen annex to the rear; and four bedrooms upstairs. Examples were erected on all early CNoR lines, including those in Minnesota. Roosevelt, Minnesota, erected in 1904, was typical of these buildings. The freight shed was extended in 1914. This was one of only a few early CNoR stations to escape the application of stucco to its exterior. Here, the train-order signal was mounted on the standard 32'-0" high steel pipe mast located next to the building. The extra elevation was required when grades or curves on either approach to the station would have obscured the train engineers' views of the train-order signals at its usual height. In some cases, the mast was located across the track from the depot, the signals being actuated by means of rods and cranks running under the track. Steel masts like these—typically dating from the late 1920s—were painted Black, later Aluminum.

NP/CNoR Minto, Manitoba #1-B (B. Bergson Photo), 1942

In the early 1900s the CNoR upgraded at least three former Northern Pacific (NPR) depots in Manitoba by grafting the two-storey, waiting room/agent's apartment portion of a CNoR Standard 3rd Class station (Plan 100-3) onto the end of the original NPR structure. These hybrid stations were recognizable by their narrow freight sheds, large NPR-style fenestration and offset bay windows. Further, since these buildings remained unstuccoed, the parentage of each section remained obvious. By altering the former NPR depots in this manner, the CNoR had symbolically declared to its clientele that the line was "under new management." By contrast, at Elgin, Manitoba in 1904, the CNoR chose to erect a new 3rd Class station, then relocated the former NPR depot to Fairfax. Here the later standard blade was used on the lower quadrant train-order signal.

COMBINATION STATIONS

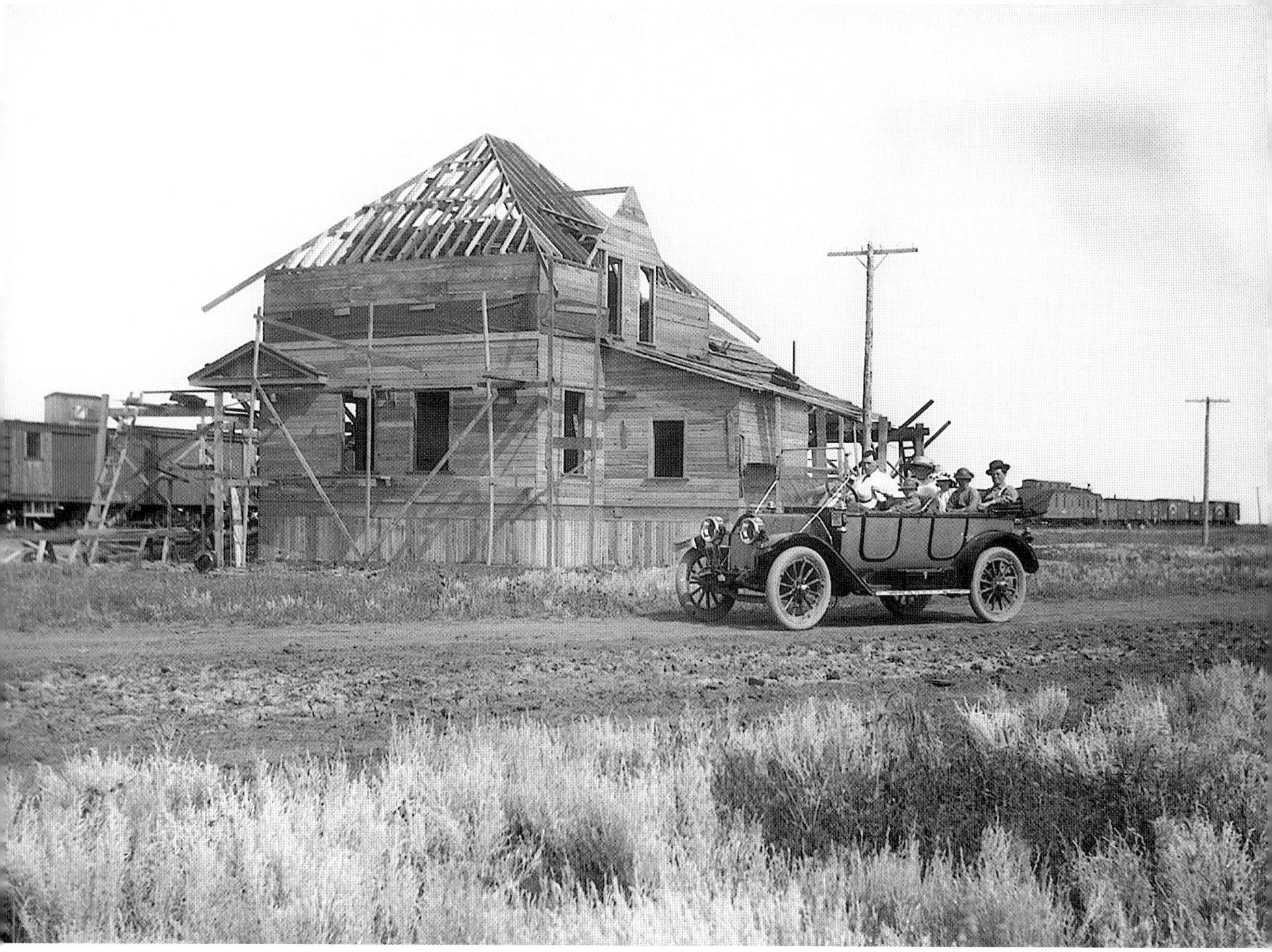

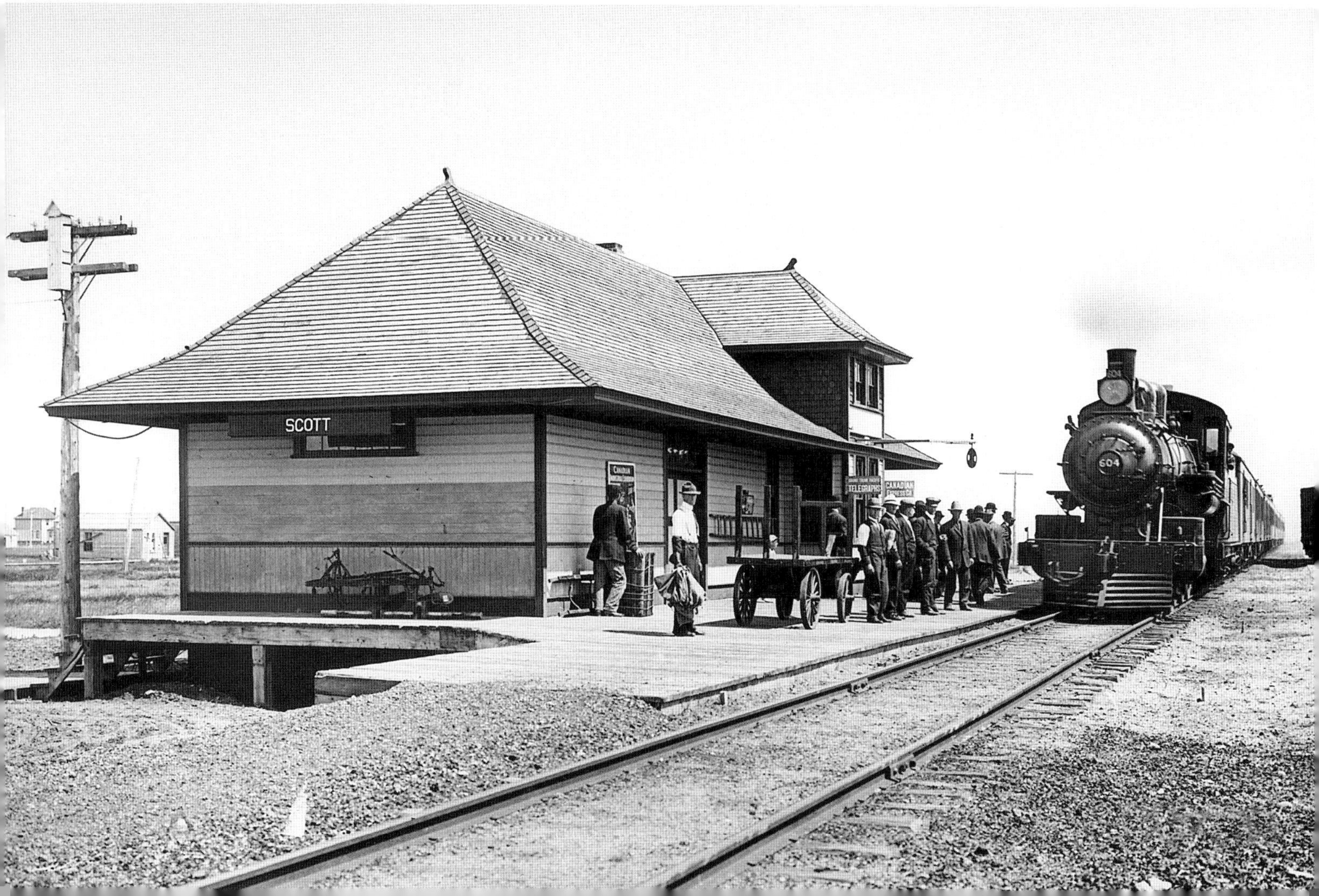

◀ CNoR Briercrest, Saskatchewan
(Moose Jaw Public Library, Photo 75-34), 1912

Most of the CNoR's early stations were very quickly outgrown, and required numerous additions to contend with the large volumes of traffic. Reacting to protests from the public, primarily regarding the small waiting room of the "Plan 100-3" stations, numerous minor changes were made to the 3rd Class design. It was modified in 1907 (Plan 100-29) by extending the waiting room and the office each by 2'-0" This lengthening necessitated changing the roof to a hip configuration, but the building retained its exterior character. A coal shed, adjoining the end of the freight shed, was added to this design and was subsequently retrofitted (Plan 110-56) to many of the earlier stations (necessitating the relocation of the pair of windows higher up in end wall of the freight shed). Third Class depots of this design were built in BC under Plan 100-64, which was identical to Plan 100-29. In 1914 the CNoR issued what could be termed as an "austerity" 3rd Class station (Plan 100-75). Apparently to save money, the rear kitchen annex was replaced by a small enclosed porch and the living room was reduced in size to accommodate the kitchen within the building-proper. In addition, the waiting room was extended an additional foot (overall building length increased to 47'-0"). A small number of 3rd Class Station variants, incorporating larger waiting rooms or extended freight sheds was also erected between 1904 and 1917. Third Class stations formed the backbone of the CNoR's agency accommodation in the West, with over 320 representatives built. Following numerous complaints by the residents of Briercrest, the CNoR appointed an agent and commenced construction of this 3rd Class station. The Board of Railway Commissioners had ordered its completion by December 1, 1912.

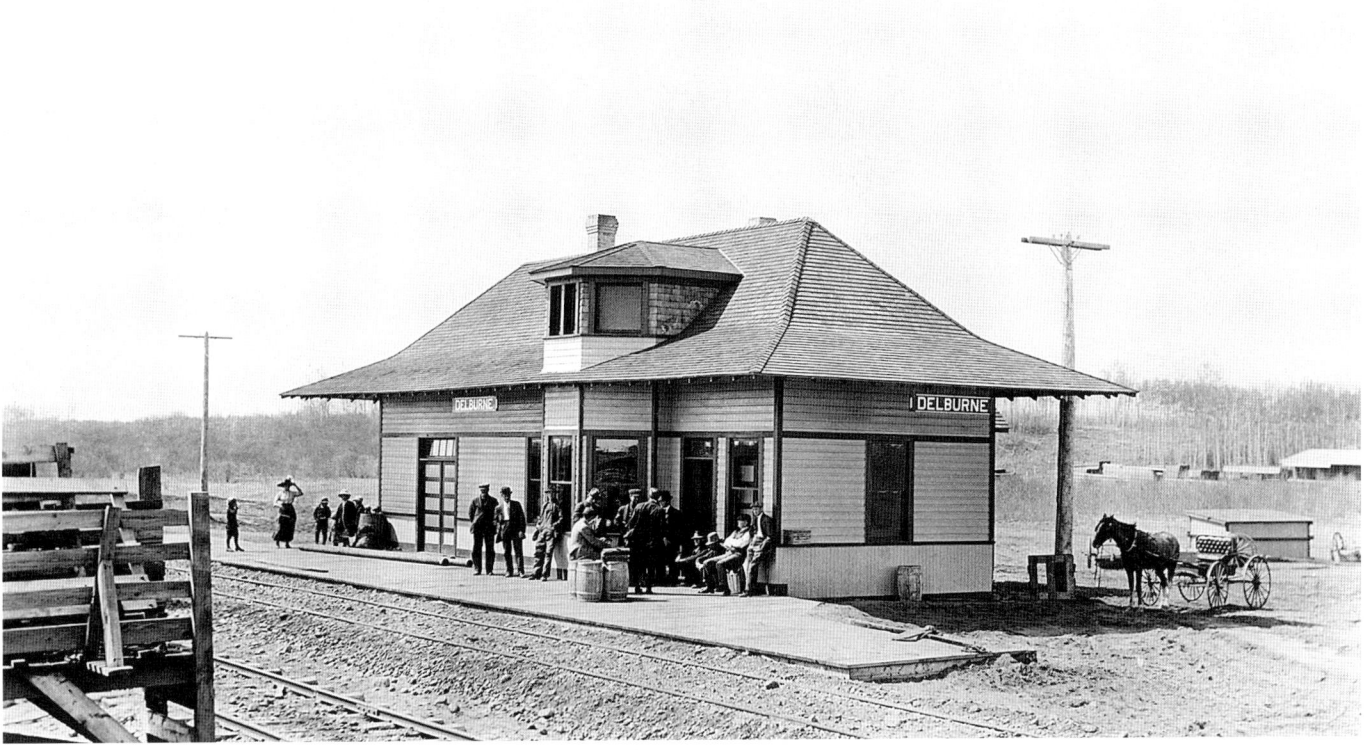

GTP Delburne, Alberta
(Glenbow Archives, Photo NA-4542-6), 1910s

The GTP was a firm believer in standardization. Nowhere was this more apparent than in its depots. The GTP's Design 'A' Station, classified as Type E, comprised nearly two-thirds of that company's depots in the West. A handful was also built on the NTR. The design borrowed many architectural features from earlier Grand Trunk designs found in the East, namely: a bellcast hip roof incorporating a wide overhang without support brackets, exposed, dressed rafter ends at the eaves, and a prominent polygonal bay which penetrated the roof overhang and terminated with a hip-roofed dormer on the second storey. Although most of the GTP's early depot plans were signed by Chief Engineer B. B. Kelliher, some contemporary railway journals credit French-born Joseph Gaston Legrand as being the designer of the GTP's permanent bridges, stations, roundhouses, coaling plants and fuel oil stations. Legrand had a long and illustrious railway career after arriving to Canada in 1891, including work with the Dominion Bridge Company and the Locomotive & Machine Company, Montreal (later Montreal Locomotive Works). He joined the GTP in 1906 but also found the time to be on the design board for the Quebec Bridge Co. and be Consulting Bridge Engineer for the Edmonton, Dunvegan & British Columbia and the Pacific Great Eastern railways. The Delburne station was built in 1912. It was stuccoed in 1922 and was subsequently fitted with electric lighting, plumbing and gas heating. It was sold to the town in 1976 and relocated to a museum site in town, next to the CNR water tank enclosure, which was also saved.

◀ GTP Scott, Saskatchewan #1
(National Archives of Canada, Photo PA-37778), 1910s

GTP #604 Ten Wheeler (Class A1, MLW 1910) pulls an 8-car passenger train up to the platform at Scott, Saskatchewan. Not a woman is in sight on the crowded platform. The mail courier, with a sealed mailbag in hand, is poised to make the swap as soon as postal clerk in the RPO opens the door. Similarly, the express truck has been carefully spotted on the platform, awaiting unloading of "head-end traffic." The GTP's Standard "24Ft.x53Ft." Station was that company's first combination station design (Plan 100-160). The lone example of this plan (later NTR No. 1) west of Winnipeg was erected at Nokomis, Saskatchewan. Instead of this design, the GTP began using the "26Ft.x60Ft." Station (Plan 100-154, authors' Type D), but these structures were likely too large and expensive for local way stations, so relatively few were built (22). Again, some were erected on the NTR. The GTR-style name board over the trackside bay window was a feature unique to this and GTP 'Design E' stations. Some other details worthy of note: the enameled signs for "Canadian Express Co." and "Grand Trunk Pacific Telegraphs," the scalloped shingles on the side of the second-storey bay and the wooden finials on the roof. The two-aspect disk train-order signal was about as simple as it got. This station exhibited the first GTP station livery, with the bottom 5' clearly being a different color than the wall above. This depot, which burned down in 1935, was replaced by a CNR 3rd Class Station, one of the last such structures built.

Combination Stations

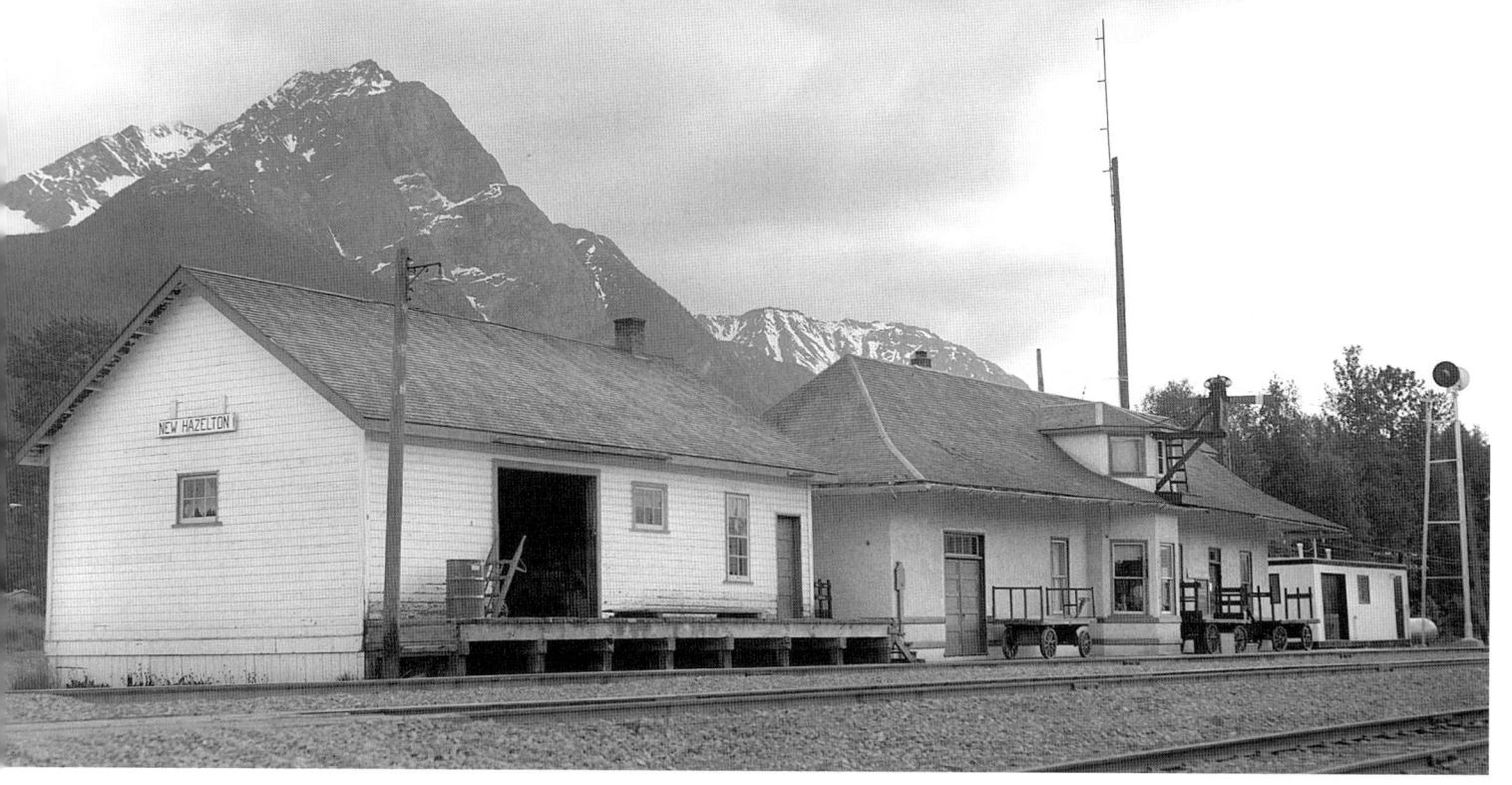

GTP New Hazelton, British Columbia (GTC Collectibles, Stan Styles Photo, CNR-NEWHAZ-1), 1975

Detached freight sheds were a common feature at the busier local stations. Occasionally, standard shelters were moved next to the depot as baggage or express sheds. At New Hazelton, BC, the 24'-0"x40'-0" freight shed, built in 1946, had an elevated platform facing directly onto the main line to expedite the transfer of l.c.l freight. The Type E depot's waiting room was also extended (16'-0"x20'-0") in 1946, with the former freight room being reserved for baggage. This arrangement was reminiscent of much earlier station layouts, which were more prevalent in the East.

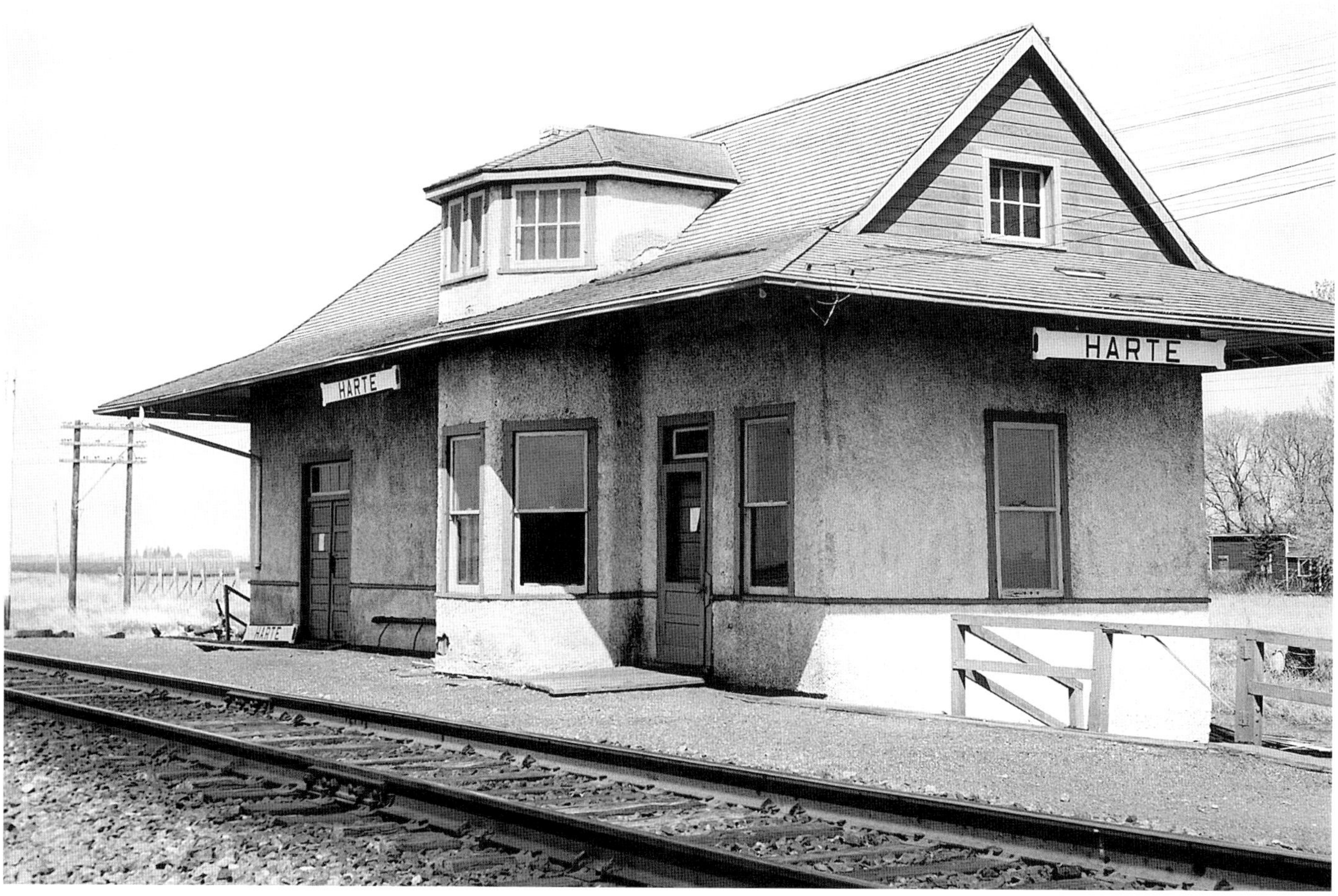

GTP Harte, Manitoba (Provincial Archives of Manitoba, Photo Architectural Survey—Harte-1), 1967

One of the biggest complaints from those living in the Type E depot was the lack of natural light and ventilation in the two upstairs bedrooms. Subsequently, in many cases, extra dormers were punched into the roof in an attempt to alleviate the problem. This was sometimes done in conjunction with extending the second floor over the freight shed. At Harte, Manitoba, yet another solution was employed. Modifying the hip roof into a gable end increased the headroom on the second floor. This modification was made after the stucco was applied as the new gable is finished with wood siding. The cleats on the roof, leading from the gable window to the eave, were likely intended as a means for a quick exit during an emergency. This photograph dates to 1967, just before this station was removed.

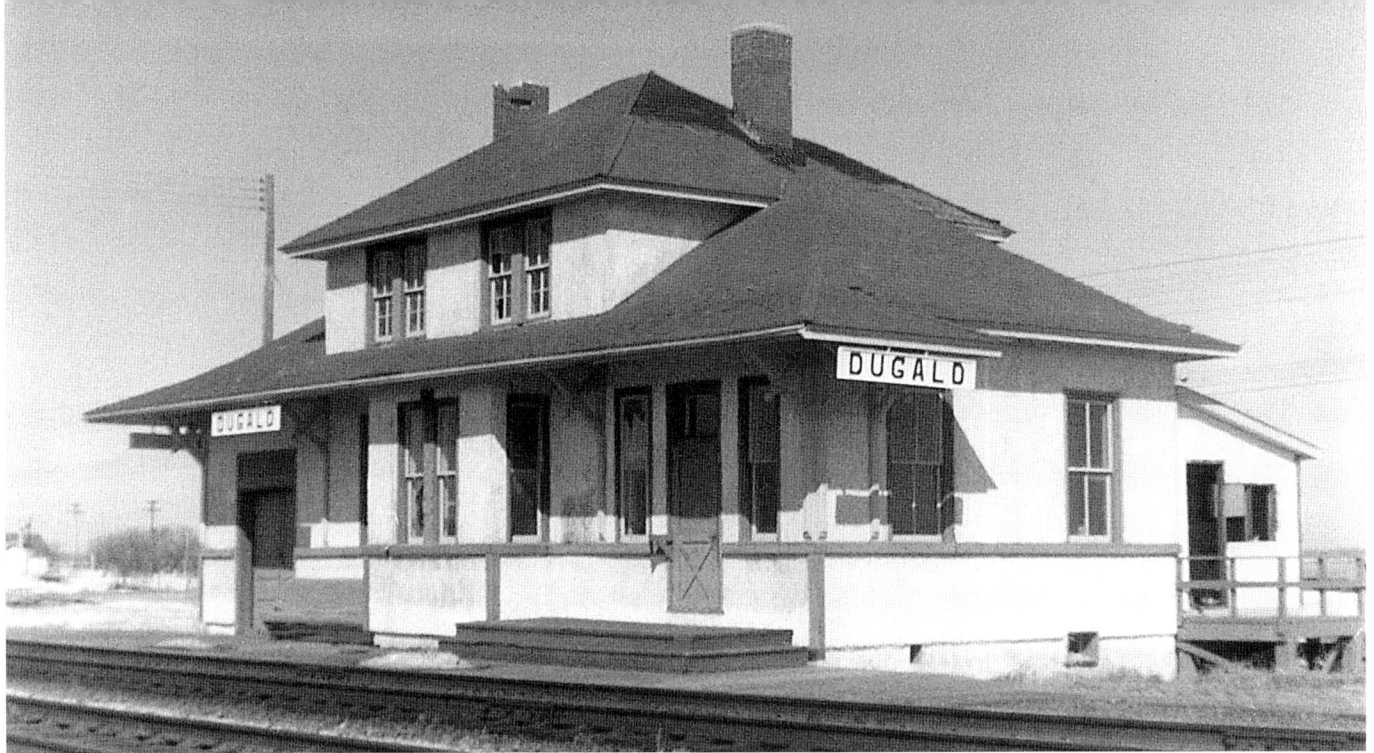

NTR Dugald, Manitoba
(PROVINCIAL ARCHIVES OF MANITOBA—DUGALD-1), 19??

Dugald, Manitoba was representative of a group of National Transcontinental Railway (NTR) stations erected in 1910, between Transcona, Manitoba and Sioux Lookout, Ontario. In 1907, the GTP was given access to the Canadian Pacific Railway's Engineering Department. The NTR's Standard No. 1 Station was that company's interpretation of the CPR's Standard No. 5 Station, originally developed in 1902. The NTR Standard No. 2 Station appears to be a smaller variant. The No. 3 plan was smaller still. Dugald was one of only eight NTR Standard No. 2 stations to be erected. None of these early NTR station designs was replicated east of Sioux Lookout. Just why this was so probably had a lot to do with the NTR Investigation Committee of 1914 which condemned the free-spending ways of the contractor, the GTP. At Redditt, Ontario, a turnaround point, a Standard No. 1 NTR depot erected in 1910, would have sufficed. Yet in 1912, the company erected a huge 'Design D' station.

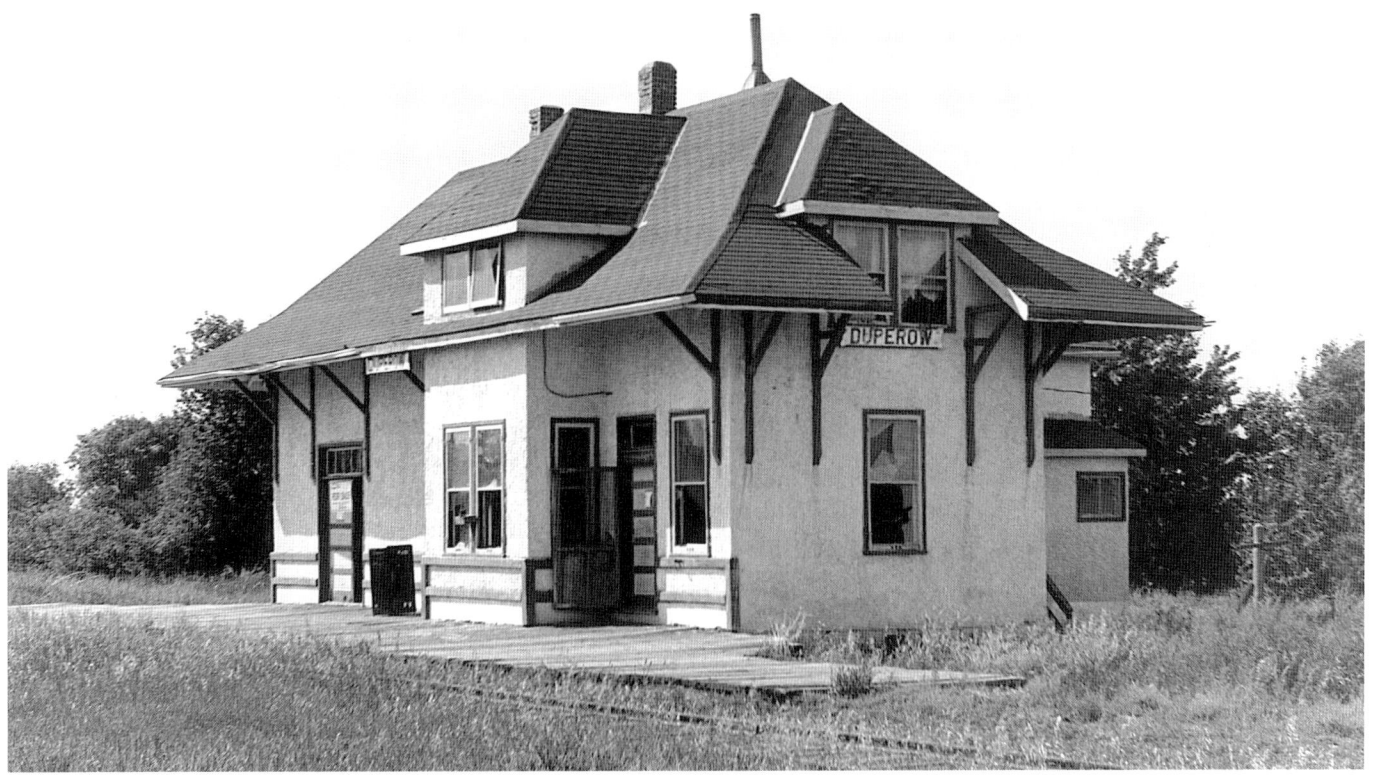

GTP Duperow, Saskatchewan #2
(CHARLES W. BOHI PHOTO), 1972

Prior to 1913, eastern counterpart National Transcontinental Railway (NTR) borrowed the GTP's Standard 'Design A' Station and simplified it (Plan 100-151). The main floor layout was virtually unchanged, except that the polygonal bay was squared off, and the upstairs apartment was extended over the freight shed, creating an additional bedroom. Hip dormers with large windows into each bedroom provided superior accommodations, with ample natural light and ventilation. The NTR 'Design A' station's exterior presented a very "boxy" appearance, amplified by the narrow overhangs of the hip roof—supported by simple "stick-built" brackets—and dormers reminiscent of the "CNR Plan 100-154"-design. This plan—classified by the authors as Type F—*was adopted by the GTP about 1917, primarily in a replacement role. The* Type F *depot at Duperow, Saskatchewan replaced an unidentified shelter in 1919. Like the other station buildings along the Dodsland Subdivision, it was stuccoed relatively late, in 1945.*

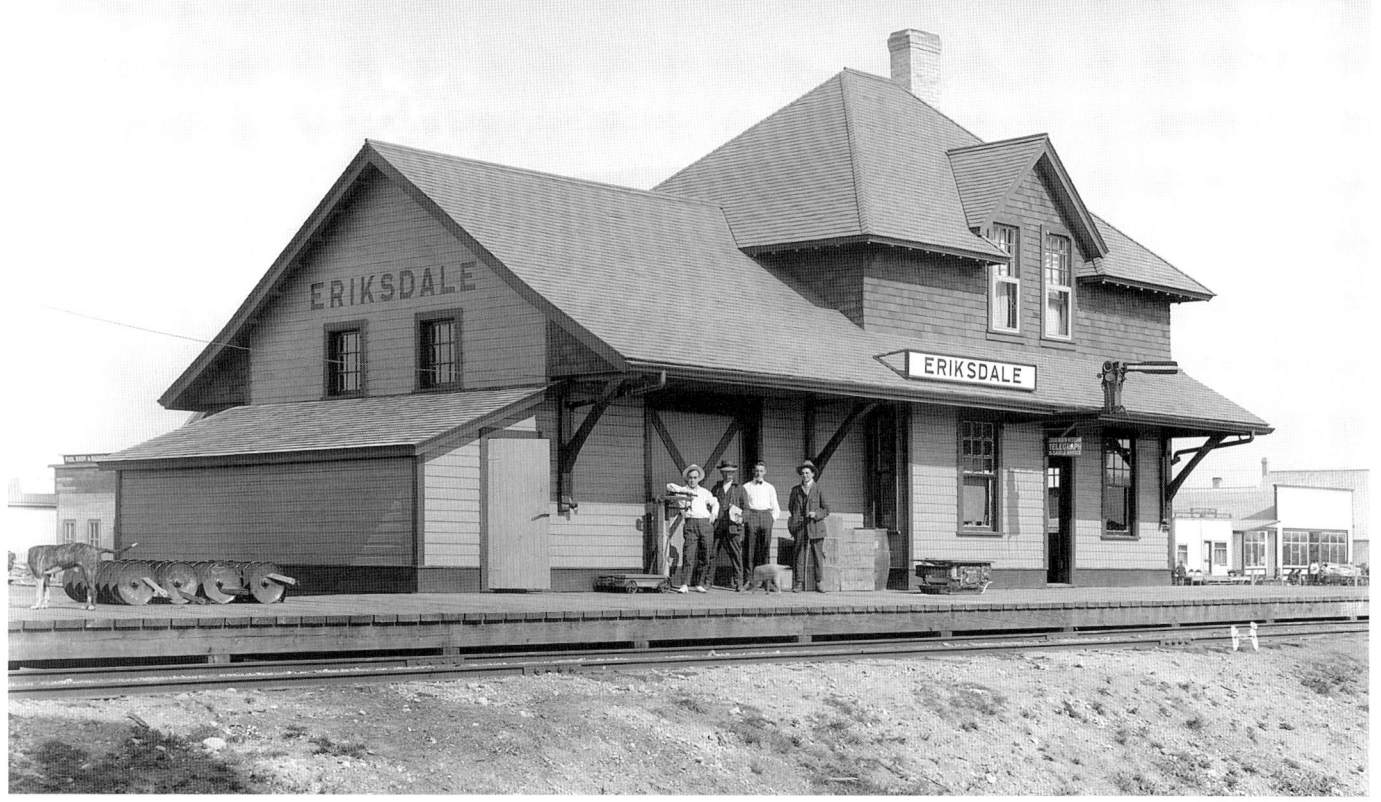

CNoR Eriksdale, Manitoba #2 (FOOTE COLLECTION, MANITOBA ARCHIVES, PHOTO N1856), CIRCA 1918

In its formative years the CNR was hard-pressed to develop its own set of building standards. Since many of its managers were formerly with the Canadian Northern, that company's designs were adopted for most of the structures erected by the CNR on its Western Lines between 1918 and 1924. Most of those built in the West were much-needed replacements for freight and passenger shelters. Some of these "CNoR-designed" 3rd, and 4th Class depots were also constructed on former GTP lines. The freshly minted 3rd Class depot erected at Eriksdale, Manitoba in 1918 replaced an earlier building. The coal bin attached to the end of the freight shed was a standard feature of these later designs (Plan 100-72). Compare Eriksdale with the newly stuccoed Smoky Lake, Alberta station in 1936. The wooden walers at the sill line and below protected the stucco from the heavy baggage and express trucks that rolled along the platform. On most of these stuccoed stations there was smooth-trowelled parging below the bottom waler. The application of stucco significantly reduced heating and painting costs. Stucco was not without its faults. Since most of these early buildings had wooden surface foundations, differential settlement due to frost heaving usually cracked the stucco. Further, the door and window openings in these depots were sometimes altered to suit changing operating requirements. Adding new openings into walls with a stucco finish was not usually a problem, but doors and windows that were filled in were usually stuccoed with little regard for matching the color or texture of the adjacent surface. Sometimes the entire wall area affected by the change would be repainted, making it less obvious, at least for a while.

CNoR Smoky Lake, Alberta (PROVINCIAL ARCHIVES OF ALBERTA, GAVINCHUK COLLECTION, PHOTO G297), APRIL 21, 1936

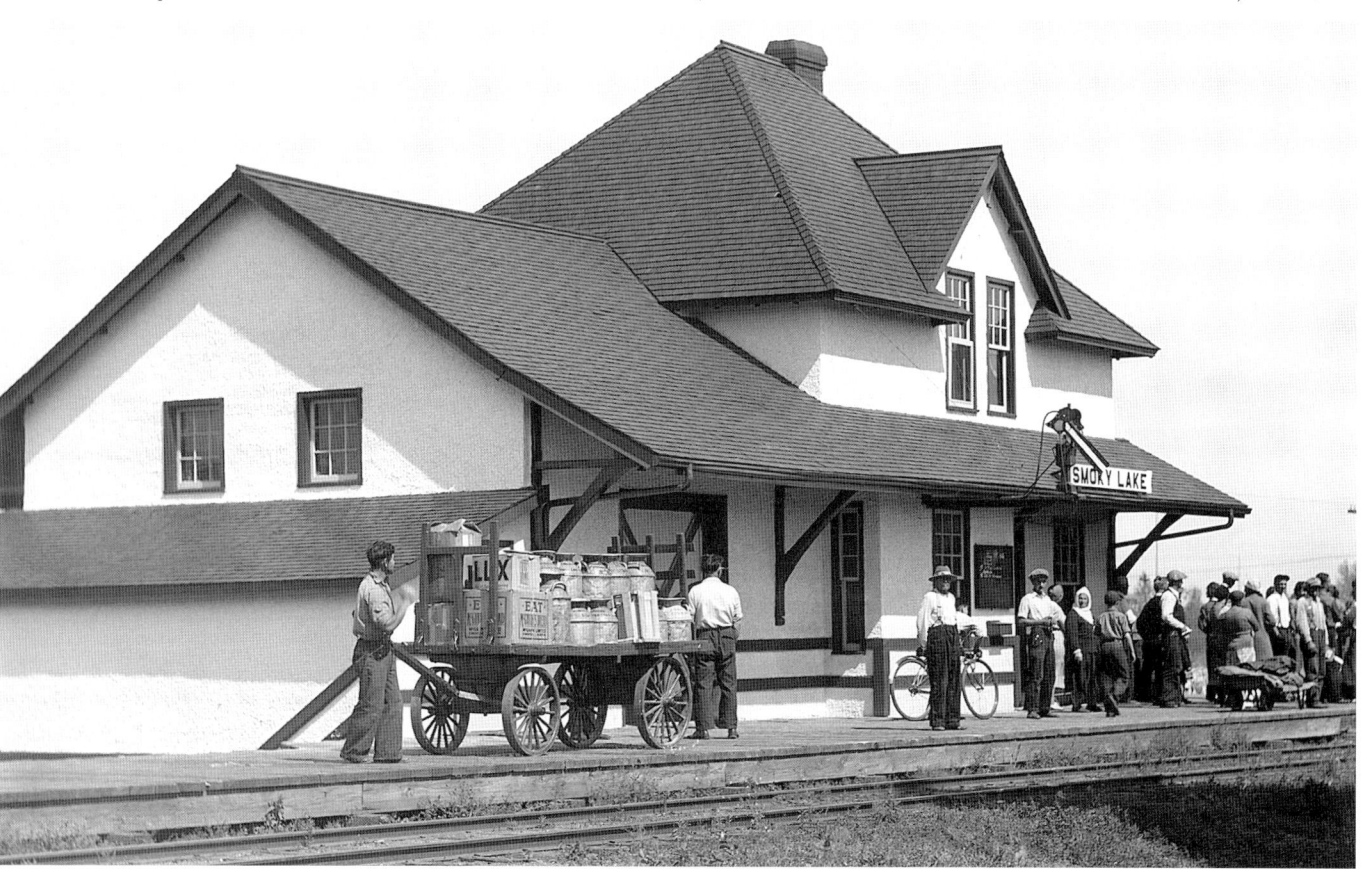

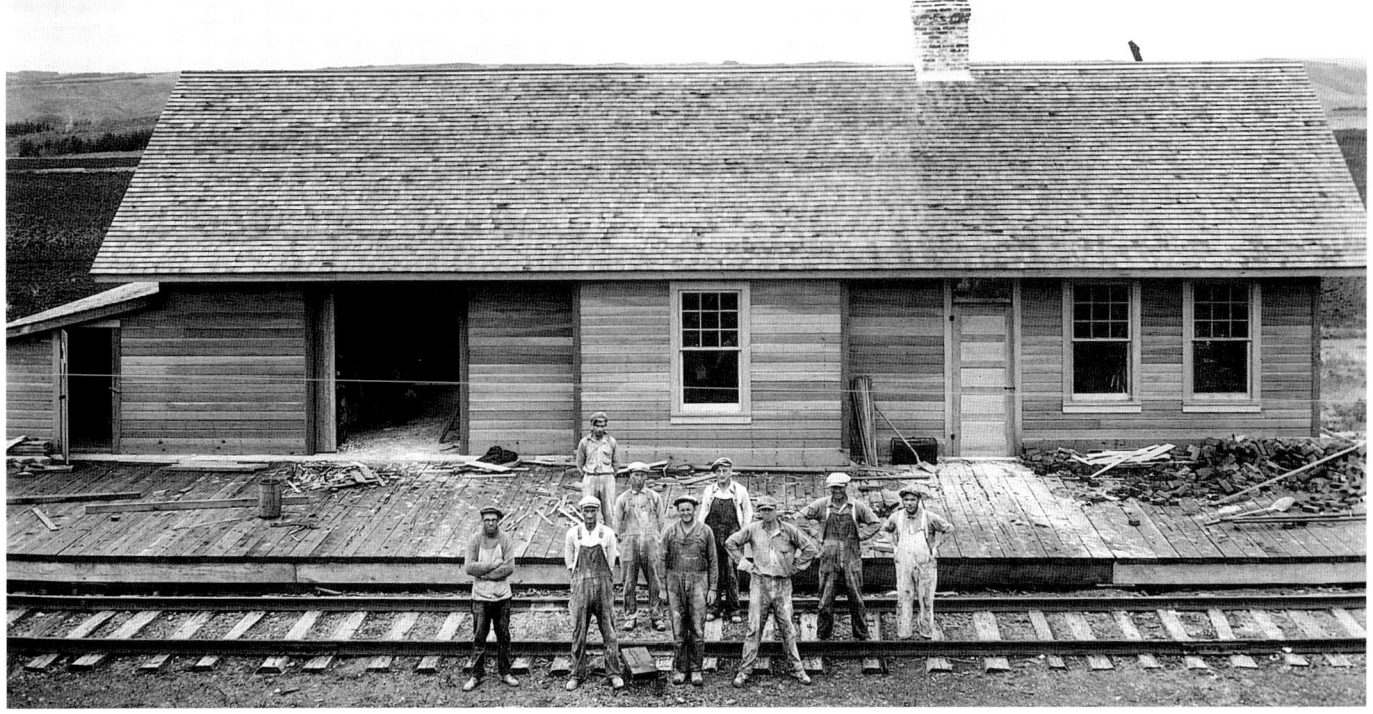

CNR Fabyan, Alberta #3 (Provincial Archives of Alberta, A17621), 1925

Using the floor layout of the latest CNoR "Plan 100-68" (1920) as the basis, the CNR developed plans for a new "Standard 4th Class Station" in 1925 (Plan 100-207). It measured 20'-0"x62'-2," with an 11'-10"x12'-0" kitchen lean-to at the rear. Foundations were concrete, but no provision was made for a basement. Later versions had a hip-gable roof over the main portion of the building. In the 1929-version of the station the kitchen annex was enlarged by 2'-0" (Plan 100-252). Per the CNR's newly-established exterior standards, the building had a concrete plinth with a rough-cast stucco finish above. Fabyan, Alberta had an early version of CNR 4th Class (Plan 100-207) replacing the Type E that burned down in 1924. This station was sold and removed in 1964.

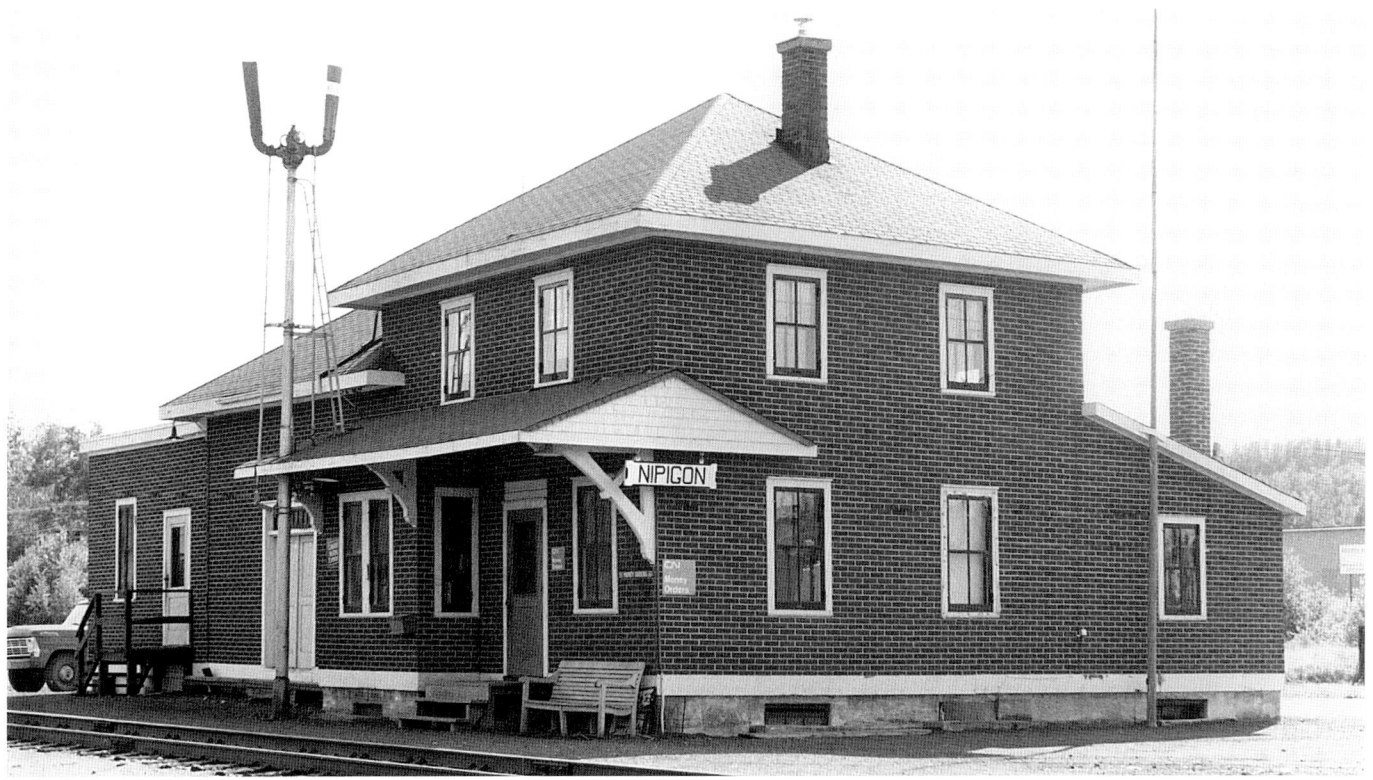

CNoR Nipigon, Ontario (Charles W. Bohi Photo), 1971

The CNoR Eastern Lines Standard No. 5 Station at Nipigon, Ontario represented a bridge of sorts between CNoR and CNR depot designs in western Canada. This can be attributed primarily to George Carruthers Briggs. He arrived to Canada in 1903 and was engaged in various architectural work in Toronto, until joining Mackenzie Mann & Co. (MM&Co.) in 1906, as a draftsman in the Engineering Department. In 1912 he was appointed Architect Building Department, then Inspector of Buildings (1914). Within two years Briggs became Supervisor of Bridges and Buildings, Eastern Lines CNoR, Toronto, responsible for the design and construction of new buildings. He was appointed Architect Eastern Lines CNR, Toronto in 1920, then Architect Western Lines CNR, Winnipeg on 21 June 1921, succeeding John Schofield. Many early CNoR Eastern Lines station plans bear Briggs' signature. The CNR's Western Lines standard stations after the mid-1920s appear to have been either designed by Briggs, or prepared under his supervision. While the basic floor layouts of the former CNoR western stations were retained, their exterior appearance was greatly influenced by their Eastern forebears. The Nipigon station as shown in this photograph has been clad with Insul Brick® *instead of the more common stucco. In the 1940s and 1950s, the exteriors of some other western lines stations were finished with asbestos shingles.*

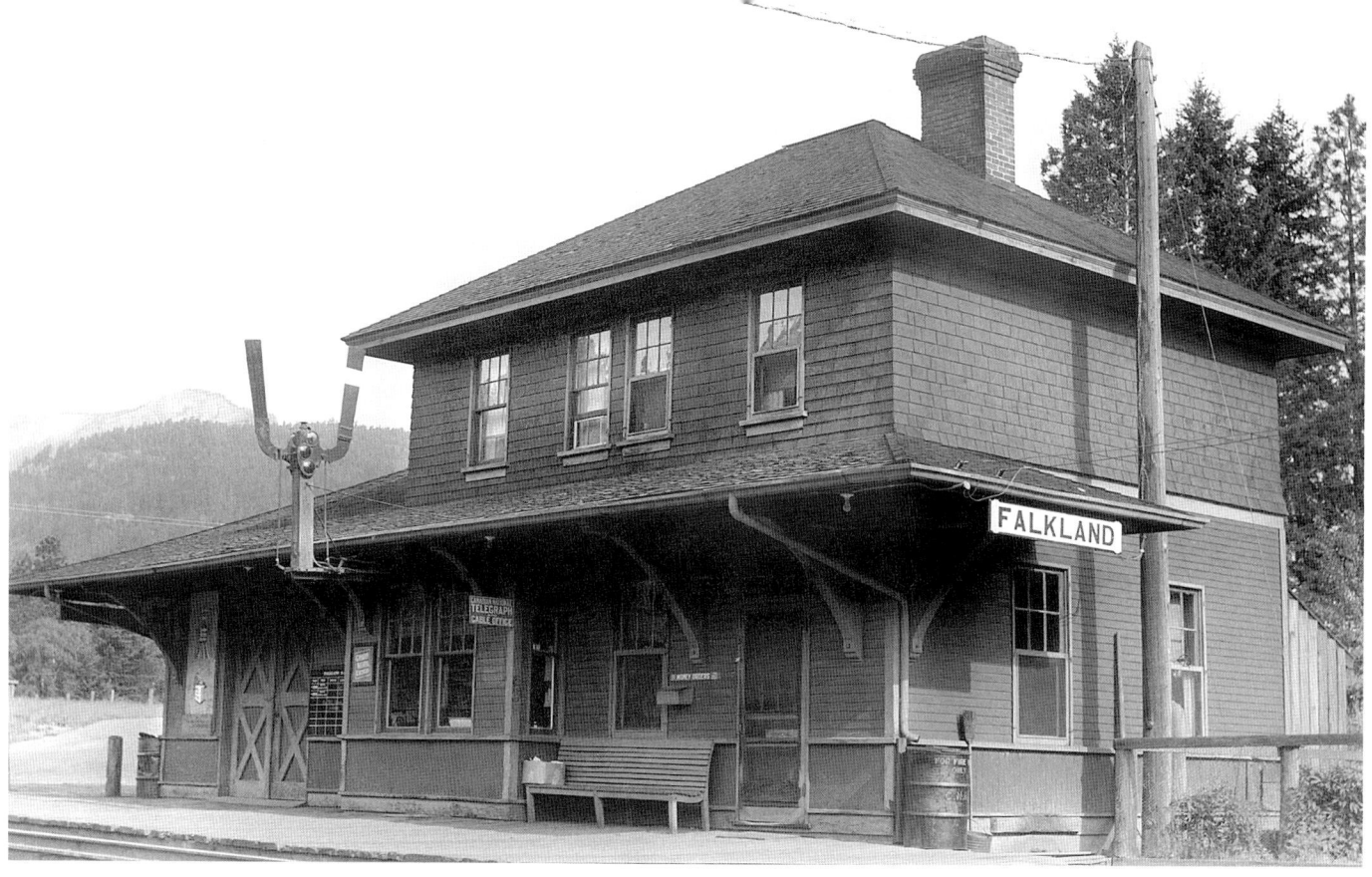

CNR Falkland, British Columbia

(AL PATERSON PHOTO), CIRCA 1960S

New depot designs for the Canadian National Railway's Western Lines emerged as early as 1922, but these were primarily for special situations (Red Deer, Alberta). Plans for standard stations did not appear for at least another three years. The architectural elements used on CNR's early 3rd Class Stations recalled the constituent companies west of the Lakehead: its floor plan and the bracket-supported shingled awning along the track side were borrowed from the Canadian Northern (Plan 100-72, et al) and the vertical V-joint wainscoting in combination with horizontal siding on the exterior recalled old Grand Trunk Pacific standards (Plans 100-154 and 100-152). The simple roofline came from the CNoR's Eastern Lines. Plans for the CNR's first original "Standard 3rd Class Station" were issued in 1925 (Plan 100-197). Its overall dimensions (22'-0"x46'-6") and interior layout were based on the 1920-version of "Plan 100-72." All subsequent CNR 3rd Class stations employed concrete foundations, built with or without (Plan 100-197A) a partial basement. Yet even within the same design, there were variations. Falkland, BC (1925) and Rorketon, Manitoba (1926) were built to the same plan, yet Rorketon's depot omitted the wainscoting.

CNR Rorketon, Manitoba

(CHARLES W. BOHI PHOTO), 1973

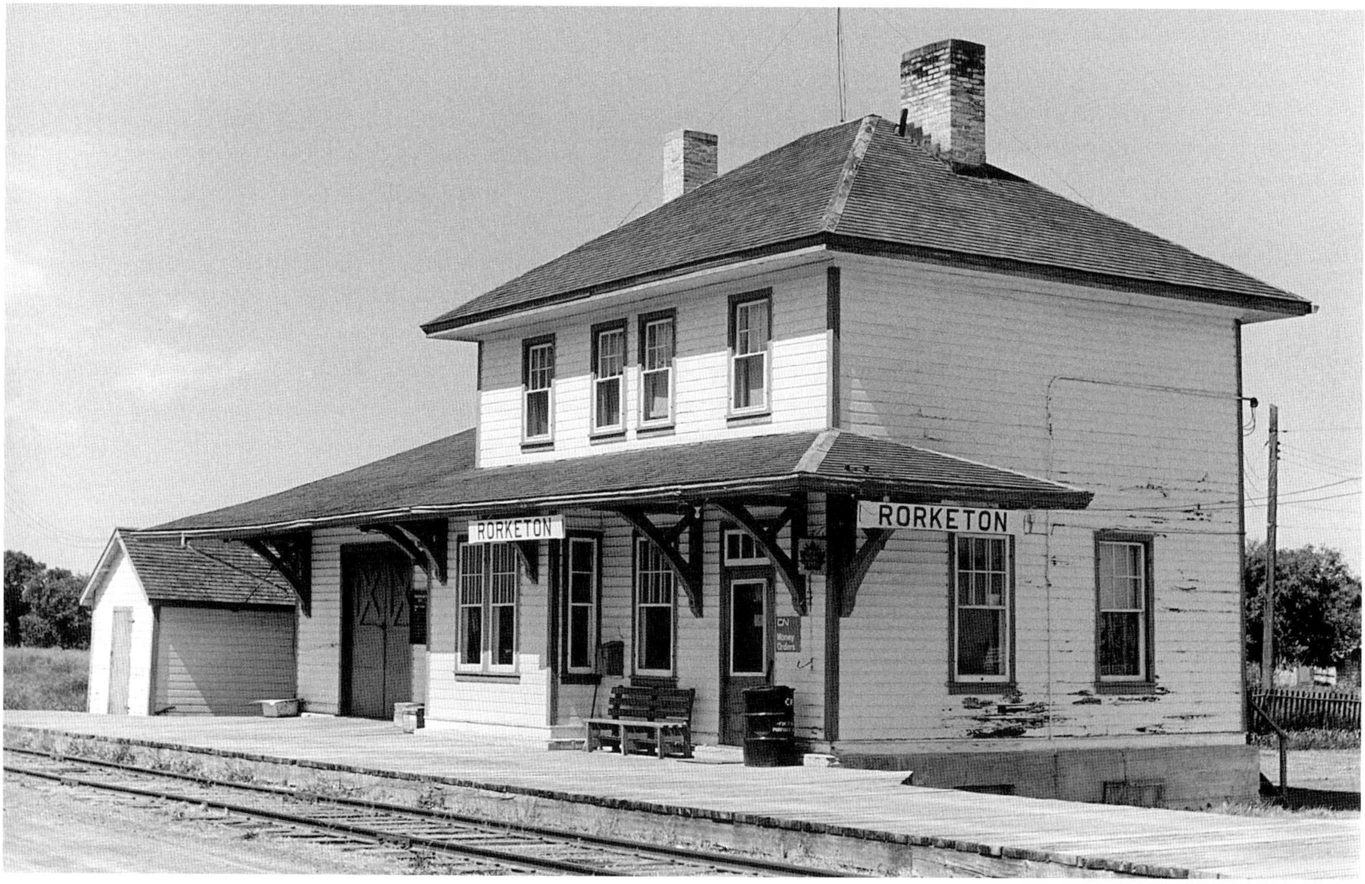

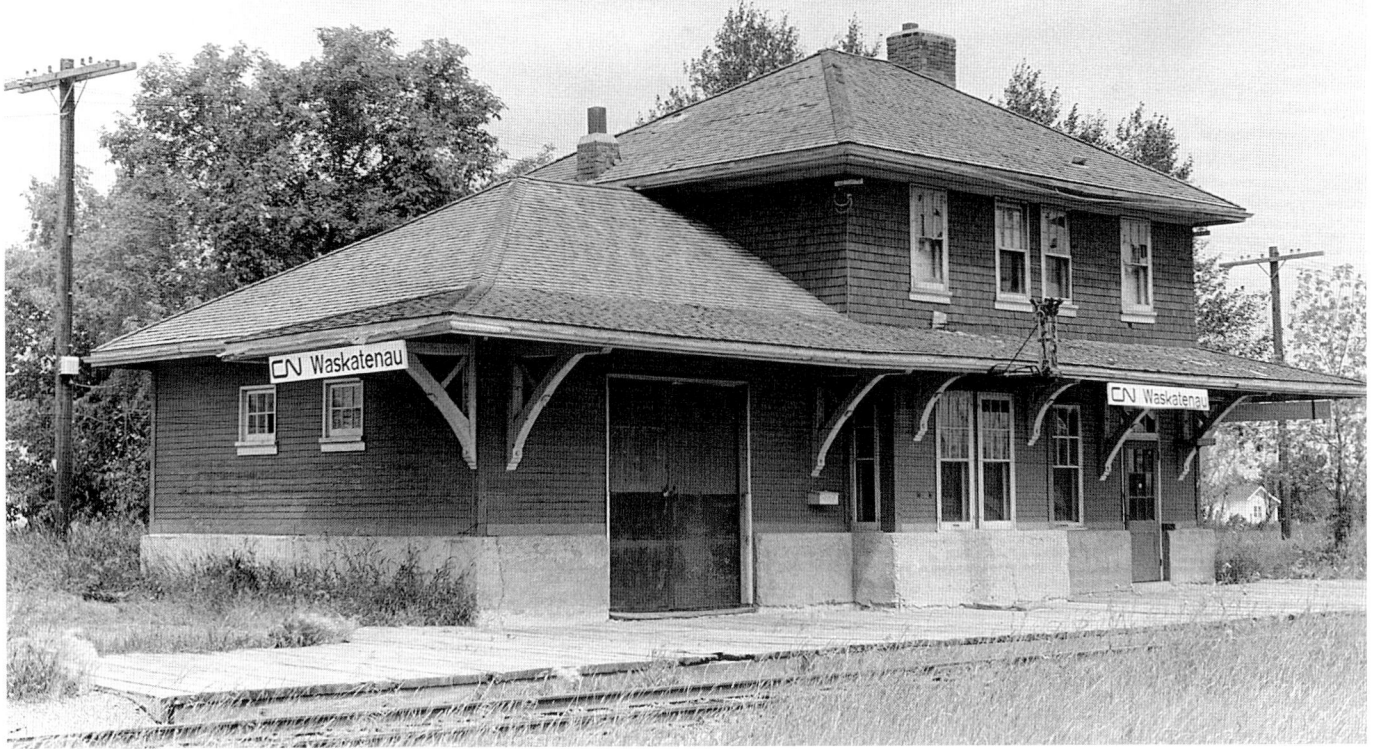

CNR Waskatenau, Alberta #2 (Charles W. Bohi Photo), 1973

CNR "Plan 100-197" was modified in early 1927, incorporating a partial basement and a concrete plinth (Plan 100-227). It proved short-lived, however, as an updated design was released in August that year (Plan 100-184). The footprint was changed by moving the kitchen into a rear 13'-0"x14'-6" annex, to make way for a dining room on the main floor. Beginning in 1927 all new Canadian National stations were built with a concrete plinth to the window sill-line, merely an above-grade extension of the foundations. It was an idea modeled on GTP precedents (Prince Albert, Saskatchewan 1916; McBride and Smithers, British Columbia, 1919), which provided protection for the lower part of the wall, and was cheaper than stone or brick. Starting in 1929, the concrete plinth was used in conjunction with a roughcast stucco finish above. Waskatenau, Alberta #2 was representative of "Plan 100-184" depots. Note the CN "wet noodle" logo on the station name boards.

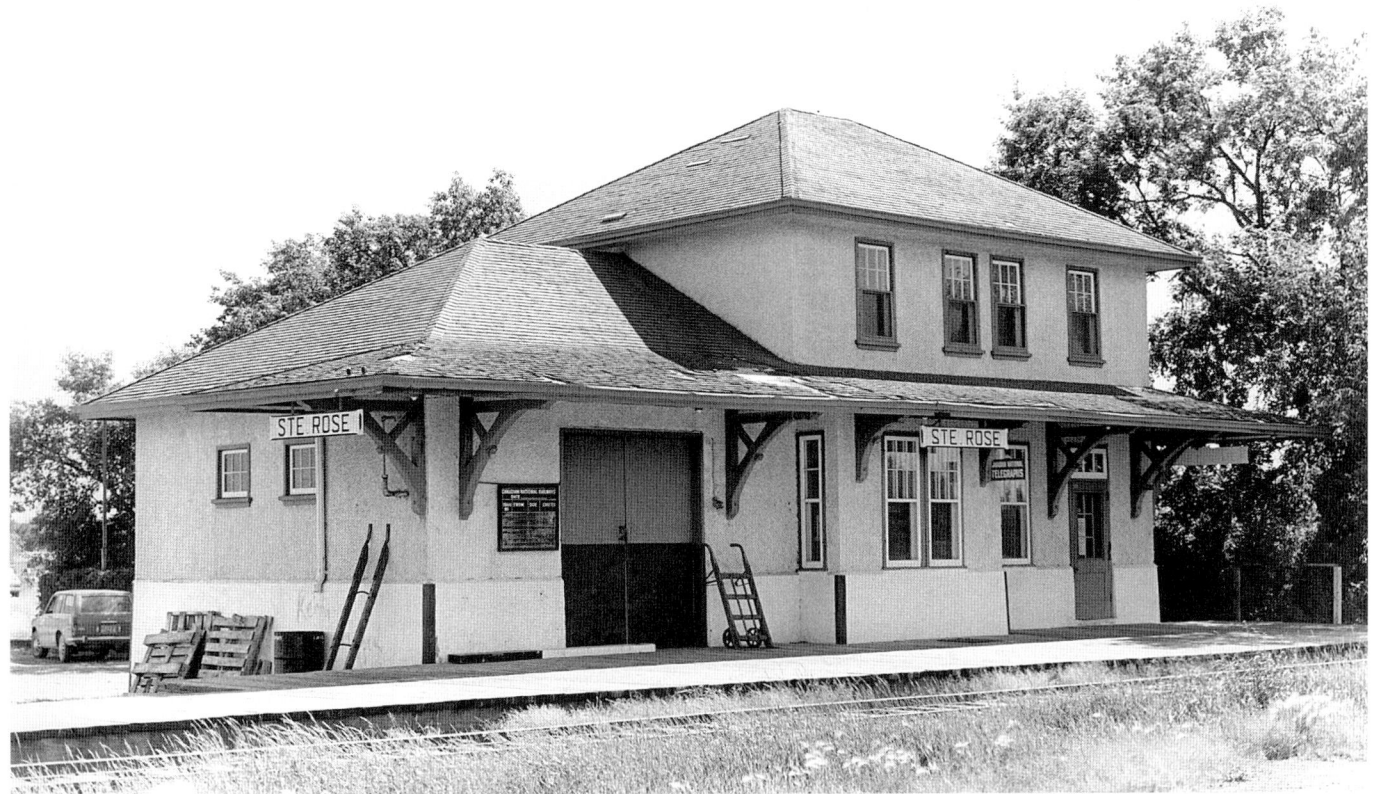

CNR Ste. Rose, Manitoba (Charles W. Bohi Photo), 1973

Through its clever use of rough-cast stucco, the Canadian National Railways achieved a subtle family resemblance. The Company borrowed this GTP practice of the late teens—used as a means to reduce maintenance—and it became an architectural characteristic on most standard CNR stations and section houses erected after the mid-1920s. As the decade continued, many former CNoR and GTP stations and section houses were stuccoed in similar fashion, further creating a "unified, company appearance." A stucco finish was added above the plinth of the "Plan 100-184" in 1929, creating "Plan 100-253." Another variant of this 1929 design had no basement and was slightly longer (22'-0"x54'-6") to provide a furnace room and attached coal bin on the main floor (Plan 100-250). The Ste. Rose, Manitoba station exhibits the clean lines of "Plan 100-253." Note the angle iron corner guards on the concrete plinth on either jamb of the freight shed door and the corners facing the platform.

Combination Stations

Passenger Stations

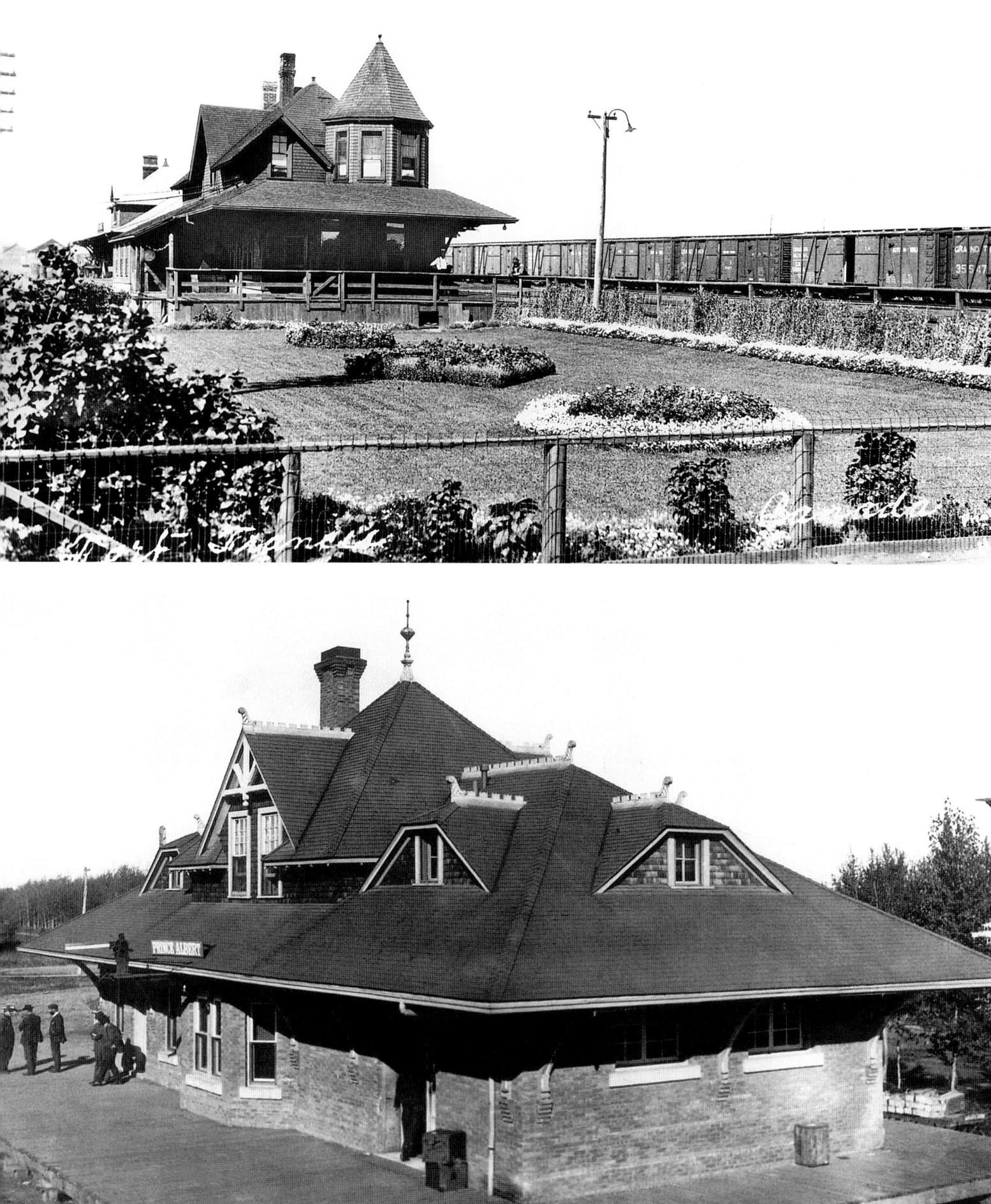

◀ **CNoR Fort Frances, Ontario #1 and #2** (PROVINCIAL ARCHIVES OF MANITOBA, HOWARD COLLECTION, PHOTO FORT FRANCES—BUILDINGS 1), 1920S

R. B. Pratt's arrival from the CPR had an immediate impact on the CNoR's station architecture. The so-called 2nd Class depots erected in 1901 at St. Boniface, Manitoba and Fort Frances, Ontario (Plan 100-4) were the first CNoR stations to incorporate, among other things, a high pyramidal roof with prominent gable dormers front and back, and a shingled, bracket-supported awning along the track side. These architectural devices were subsequently used on most CNoR stations erected in the West, and in doing so, became a Company trademark. The polygonal corner tower was a feature common to many eastern Canadian depots and was rarely repeated on the CNoR's Western Lines stations. In 1913, the Fort Frances depot was relocated to make room for a replacement station. With the opening of the new building (beyond), the former station was renovated into a restaurant–dining room–lunch counter. The old station was sold and removed in 1968.

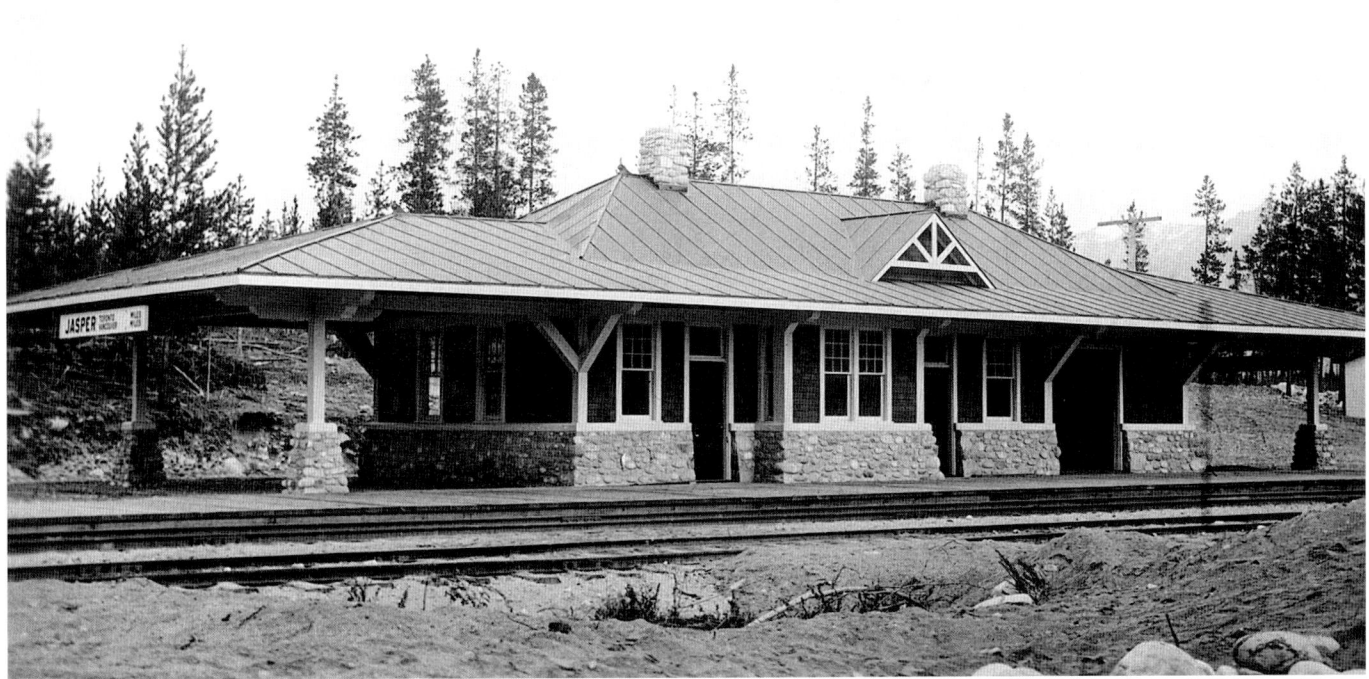

CNoR Jasper, Alberta (PROVINCIAL ARCHIVES OF ALBERTA, PHOTO A-1360), CIRCA 1916

The GTP and CNR serviced many resorts in the West. Not surprisingly, the GTP utilized standard structures at these locations, for example at Nakina, Ontario; Watrous, Saskatchewan; Cooking Lake, Wabamun and Jasper, Alberta. In contrast, many CNoR resorts had special depots. In 1910 R. B. Pratt designed a simple station for Westside, Manitoba, later renamed St. James. It was comprised of a single storey building (22'-0"x52'-10") with 24'-0" canopies on each end. Inside was a large waiting room, a small office with a bay window, and a freight and baggage room. This became the prototype for at least four other depots, including the one built at Jasper in 1915, shown above. The Jasper station virtually repeated Westside's floor plan, but was finished to a higher standard, with a stone plinth and metal roofing. A slightly larger variant (24'-0"x54'-0") constructed in 1913 at Chestermere Lake, east of Calgary, incorporated 32'-0" canopies on each end and had two small bedrooms upstairs for the agent. In 1917 two smaller variants were built at Delta, Manitoba and Alberta Beach. Additions and alterations to the St. James depot in 1921 dramatically changed its exterior appearance.

◀ **CNoR Prince Albert, Saskatchewan #2** (SASKATCHEWAN ARCHIVES BOARD, R-A 1313), 1910S

The first two Canadian Northern divisional points on the new main line west of Dauphin, Manitoba—Canora and Humboldt, Saskatchewan—were simply enlarged versions of 3rd Class buildings. Subsequent divisional points were equipped with larger "Standard 2nd Class Stations" (Plan 100-22), developed in 1905, which improved on the layout of the prototype buildings erected at Gladstone and Neepawa, Manitoba and Rainy River, Ontario #1. The 24'-0"x78'-2" main floor contained a baggage and express room, an office, a general waiting room, a ladies' waiting room with a polygonal bay and a lunch room with its associated kitchen and serving pantry. The station agent was provided with commodious living quarters upstairs. The chief architectural feature of these buildings was a central pyramidal roof flanked by hip gable dormers with similar dormers also located at each end. Here is the attractive brick variant erected in 1908 at Prince Albert, Saskatchewan (Plan 100-25).

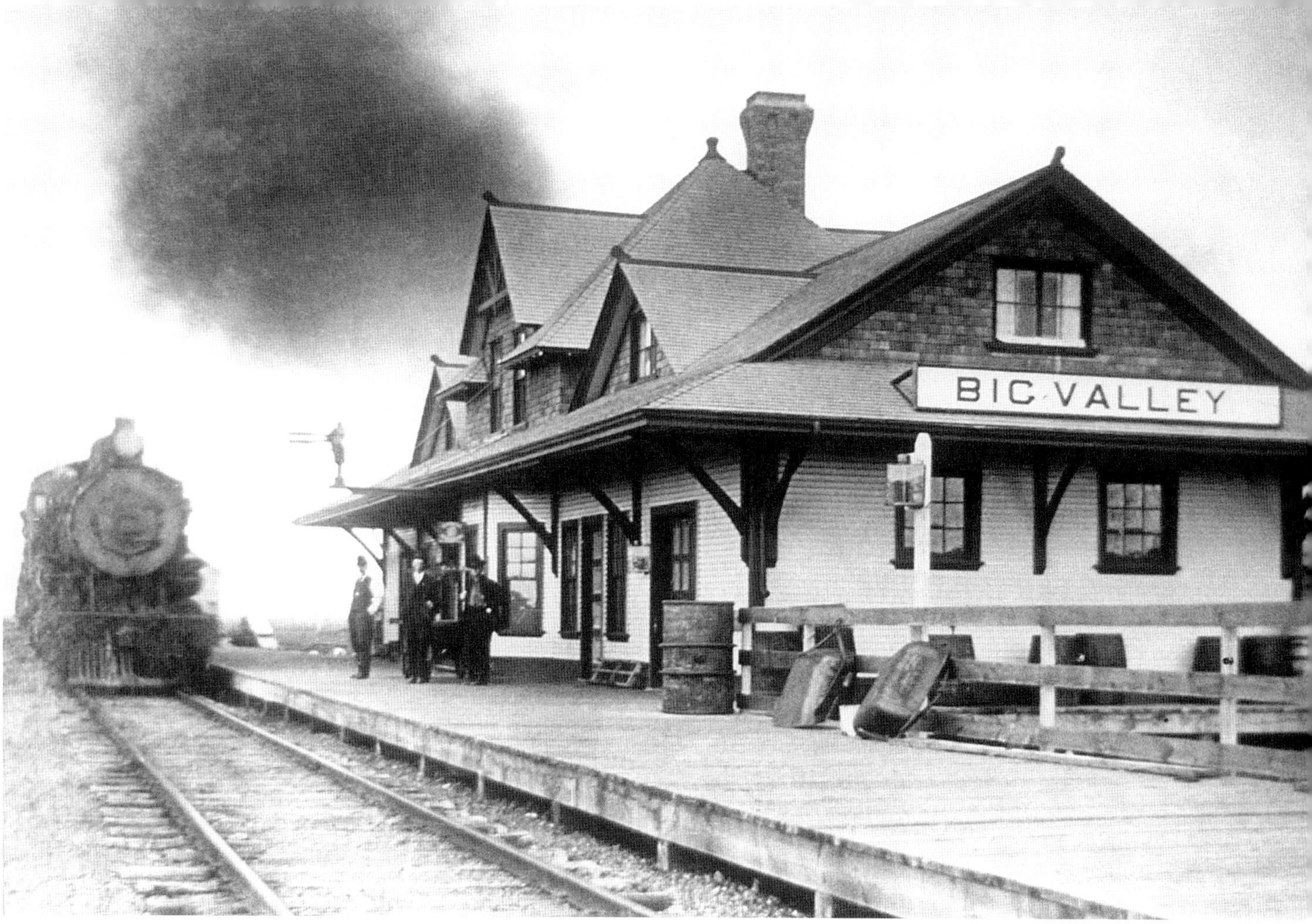

Canadian National's Western Stations

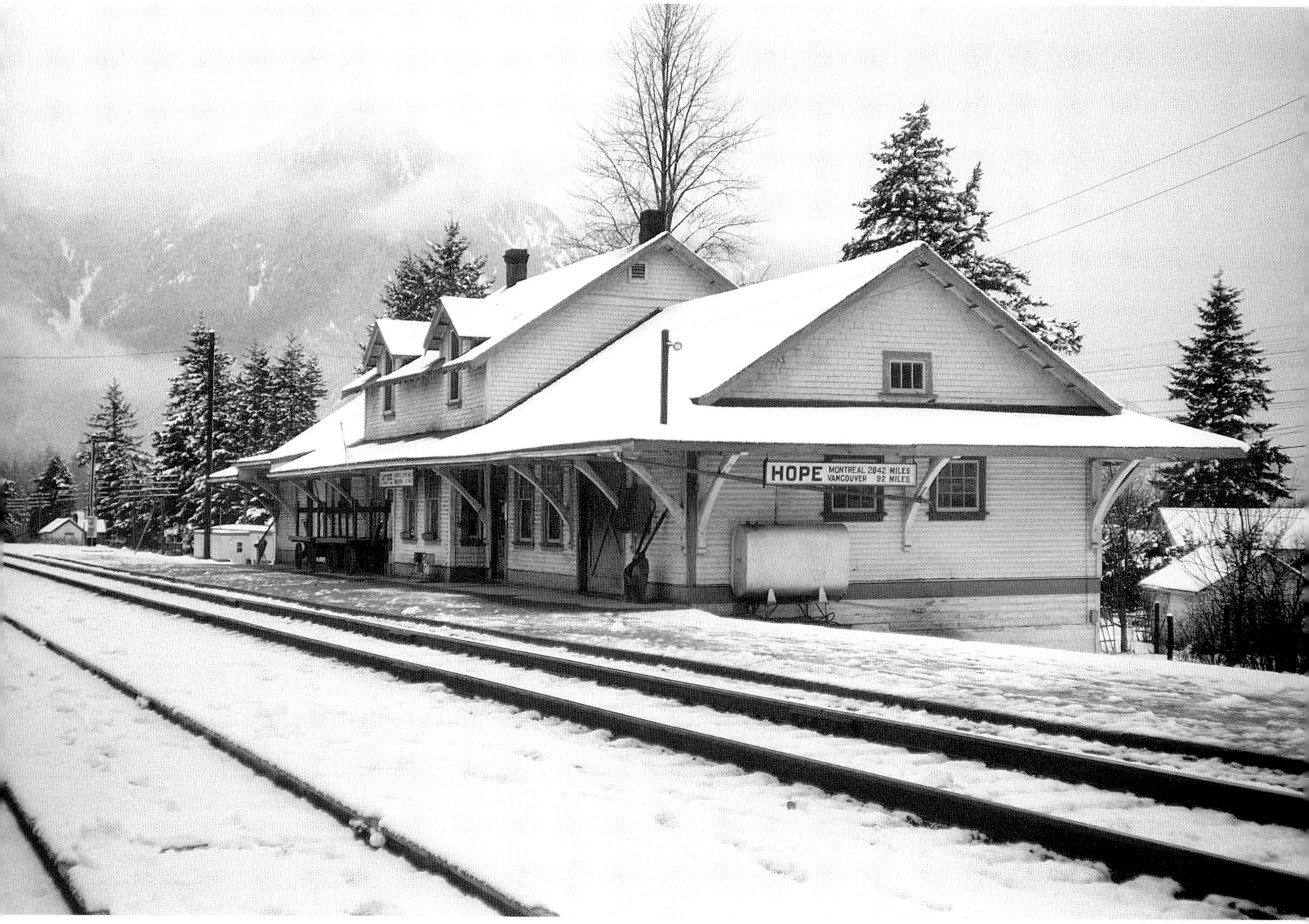

◀ CNoR Big Valley, Alberta　　　　　　　　　　　　　　　　　　　　　　　　　　　　　　　　　　　　(Canadian Northern Society Collection), 1910s

About 1910 a slightly larger (24'-0"x84'-4") frame variant of the "Plan 100-22" was developed for branch line terminals and other important points (Plan 100-39). In this design, the lunchroom and attendant facilities were dropped, the ladies' waiting room was relocated to trackside and separate rooms were provided for baggage and express. From the exterior, plain gable dormers in lieu of clipped gable dormers differentiated this plan from its predecessor. Big Valley was the headquarters for freight crews running north to Edmonton, west to Rocky Mountain House and south to Calgary. It remained an important terminal until 1923, when it was superseded by Mirror, a divisional point on the nearby GTP. The Big Valley depot was acquired by the Canadian Northern Society in 1989. It was refurbished to represent the 1940s-50s and is now a museum.

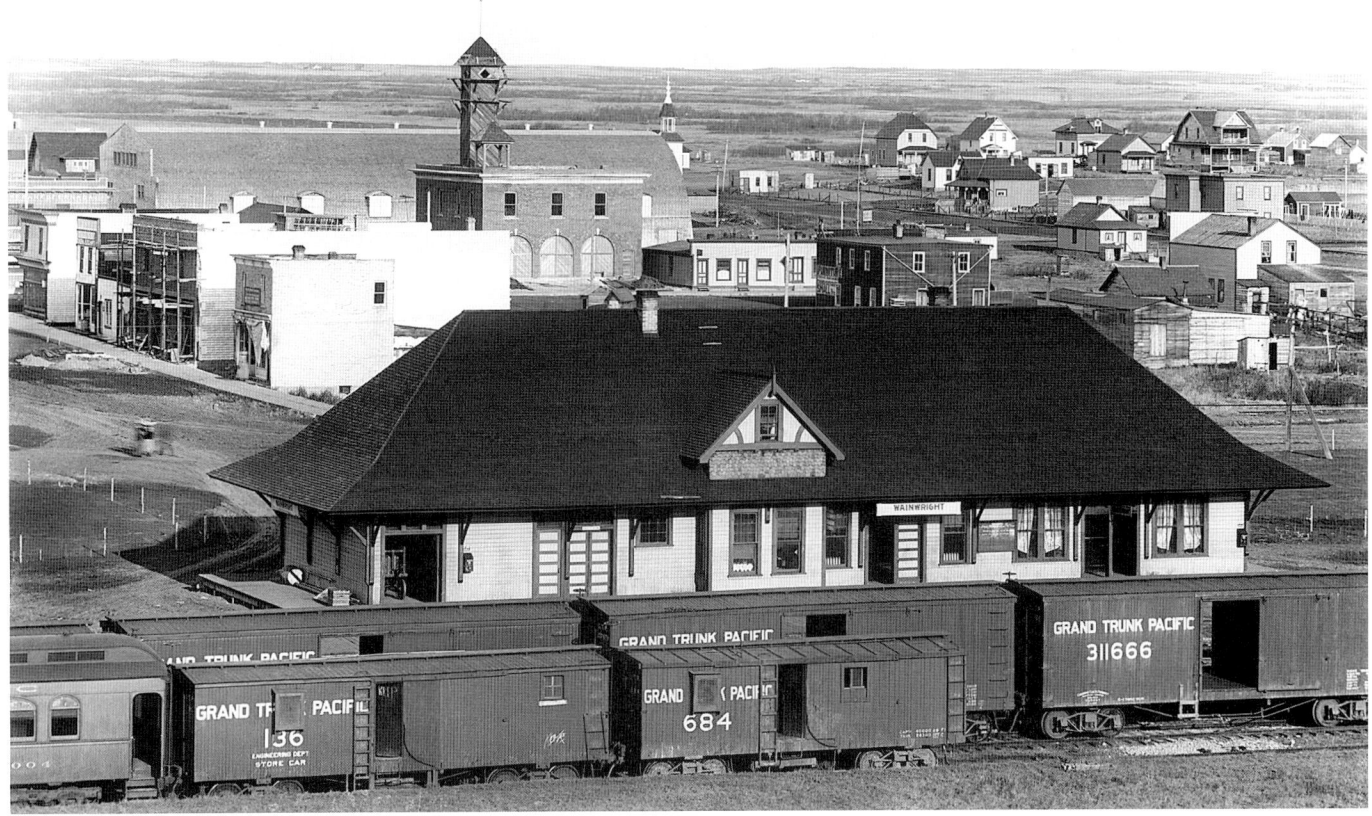

GTP Wainwright, Alberta #1　　　　　　　　　　　　　　　　　　　　　　　　　　　　　　　　　　　　(Glenbow Archives, Photo ND-18-7), circa 1910

A study in early GTP depot architecture, rolling stock and urban design. Wainwright, Alberta was a turnaround point for GTP, and later CNR, freight engine and train crews from Biggar, Saskatchewan and North Edmonton (Calder Yard). The GTP employed four standard passenger station designs at its main line divisional points. All were wood-frame construction and classified on the basis of size. The lone single-storey design—classified as "30 Ft.x102 Ft. 6 In. Station"—was also known as the "Standard No. 2 Terminal Station" (Plan 100-155). The furnace and coal store were in the partial basement. The main floor had a large waiting room that terminated into an open alcove, which served as a ladies waiting area. Washrooms were located at the rear. Other public spaces included a ticket office and a lunchroom, with a kitchen and a pantry. Separate baggage and express and freight rooms were provided. When the GTP finally did construct detached freight sheds at these locations, the baggage and express functions expanded into the vacated freight room. The building was covered by a bellcast hip roof that sloped down to all sides to form a bracket-supported overhang. The immensity of the high hip roof was broken by a small gable dormer over the trackside bay. This was the most common GTP passenger station, with three examples built. The variants at Jasper #1, Alberta and Pacific #1, BC had much larger dining rooms, but were otherwise the same. The Wainwright station burned down on 28 November 1928. The railway operator and a car inspector who were on duty at the time only managed to save the station clock. The replacement station (Plan 100-249) opened in early 1930. Note the boxes for the Royal Mail near each end wall, and the wagon peeking out from the express room door.

◀ CNoR Hope, British Columbia　　　　　　　　　　　　　　　　　　　　　　　　　　　　　　　　　　　　(Leslie S. Kozma Photo), 1974

The wood-frame stations at Hope and Port Mann, British Columbia (Plan 100-84), erected in 1916, were relatively inexpensive 2nd Class buildings designed by John Schofield in a style reminiscent of Pratt's 1912 Combination Station-and-Section-House (Plans 100-47/100-98). The main floor (24'-8"x107'-6") had an office, a general waiting room, a ladies' waiting room, a baggage and express room, a large freight room and an attached coal shed. An agent's apartment, with a kitchen, a pantry, a living room and two bedrooms, was upstairs. The previous year smaller variants (23'-10"x69'-8") were built at Estevan, Saskatchewan and Chilliwack, British Columbia. Schofield was born in Ireland. He emigrated to Canada in 1904, joining the CPR's Winnipeg Engineering office in 1904. Three years later, he went to the CNoR, and by 1909 had worked his way up to Assistant Architect. He assumed the title of Architect CNoR Western Lines in 1911. In 1920 he became Architect Western Lines for the Canadian National. He moved to the CNR's Toronto office in 1921, then to Montreal in 1923. From 1937, with the development of Trans-Canada Airlines (later Air Canada), Schofield expanded his design range and responsibilities, becoming Chief Architect of that airline, then a subsidiary of CNR. He was appointed Chief Architect CNR in 1942. His most notable stations in the West were: Jasper #3 (1925), Edmonton #2 (1927), and Saskatoon #3 (1938).

Passenger Stations

GTP Edson, Alberta

(Dave Shaw Collection Photo), 1967

Edson was the turnaround for GTP crews running west from Edmonton and east from Jasper. Its principal claim to fame was being the headquarters for trains running on the Alberta Coal Branch, a rich source of "black diamonds" for domestic and railway use. While Edson's 'Design D' depot was the only such example built west of Winnipeg, at least 12 were constructed on the NTR. There was ample room on the main floor: a trainmen's room, large general and ladies' waiting rooms, washrooms, baggage room and a huge lunch room, with attendant kitchen and pantry. Except for the large washroom, the second floor was occupied by offices. The size of this building suggests that it was erected in anticipation of the staff required to operate the Coal Branch. But when operations commenced in 1913, trains on the Branch were dispatched from Jasper. The dispatching office opened at Edson in 1918. The Edson station was stuccoed in 1938. Here in 1967, an express train lead by RS18s awaits its crew prior to proceeding westward. In 1977 this station was offered to the town, but it did not have the necessary resources for its preservation. The station was demolished.

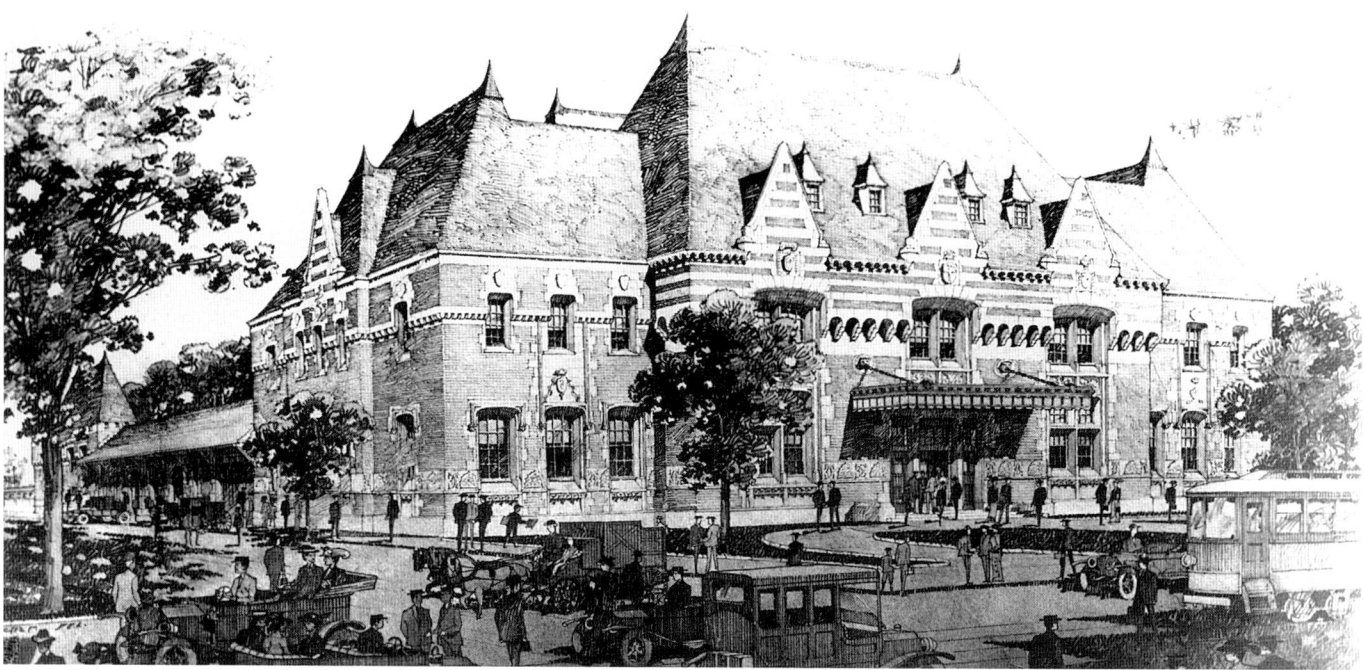

Proposed stations at GTP Moose Jaw, Saskatchewan

(Saskatchewan Archives Board, Photos R-B8763 and R-B8761), circa 1912

Ross & MacFarlane Architects, Montreal, formed in 1905, designed the GTR Union Station—Ottawa, the Chateau Laurier (Ottawa), Fort Garry (Winnipeg) and MacDonald (Edmonton) hotels and the stillborn GTP station at Edmonton. This firm also prepared proposals for the GTP station at Moose Jaw in the two styles in vogue prior to World War I: Chateauesque and Neo-Classical. The fenestration of both proposals indicates that the interior layout of the buildings was likely identical. Regrettably, the War intervened and neither building was constructed. Subsequently, the GTP was absorbed, with the CNoR, into the Canadian National Railways. The union station built at Moose Jaw in 1919, while dignified, reflected the CNR's limited means (Canadian National's Western Depots, page 75). Ross & MacFarlane may have had early involvement in the development of the GTP's standard stations, but nothing has come to light. Similarly, another important Canadian architect, Francis M. Rattenbury, also had ties to the GTP, but any influences he may have had on that company's standard station designs have yet to be established.

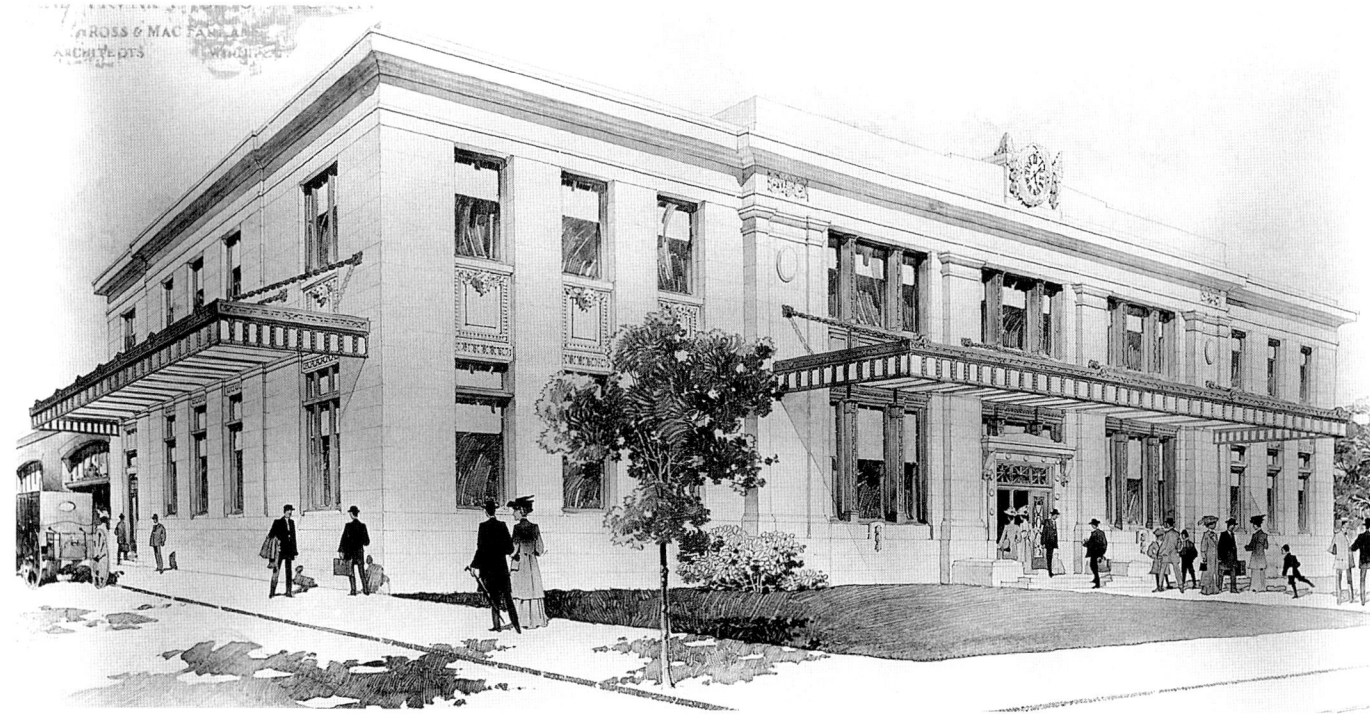

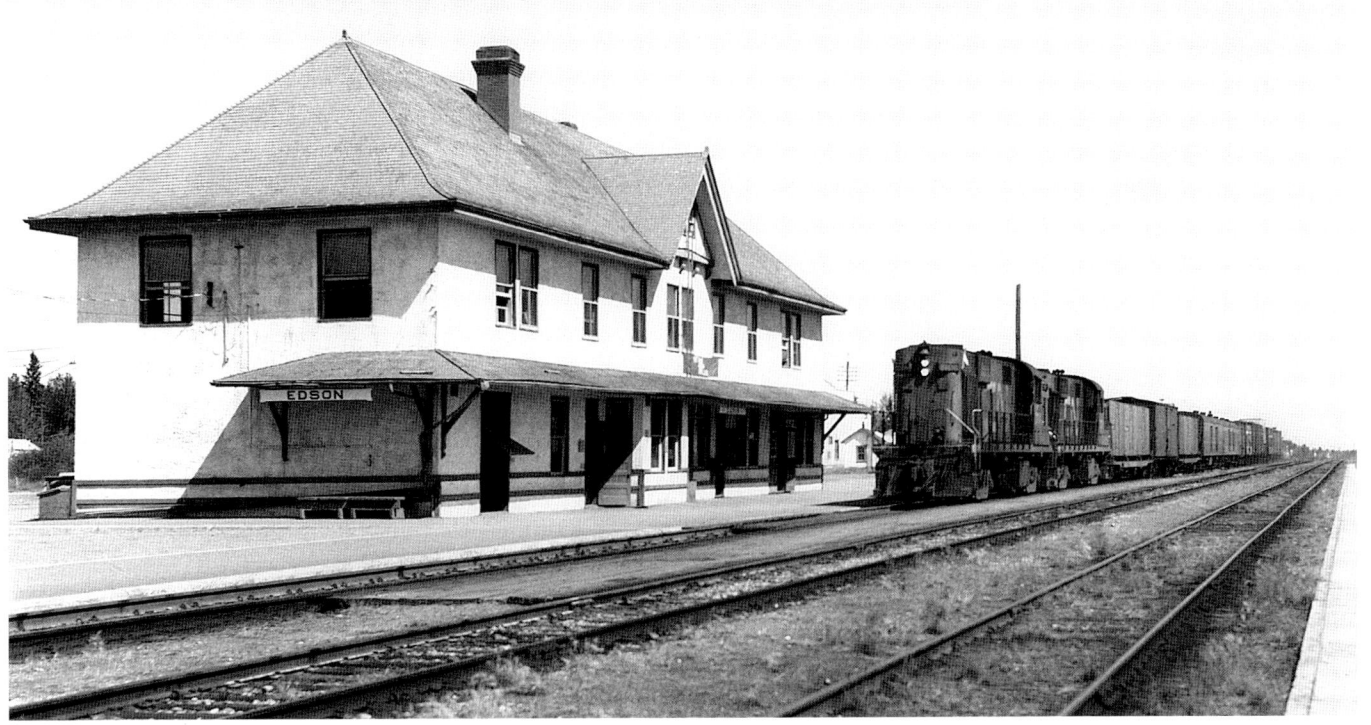

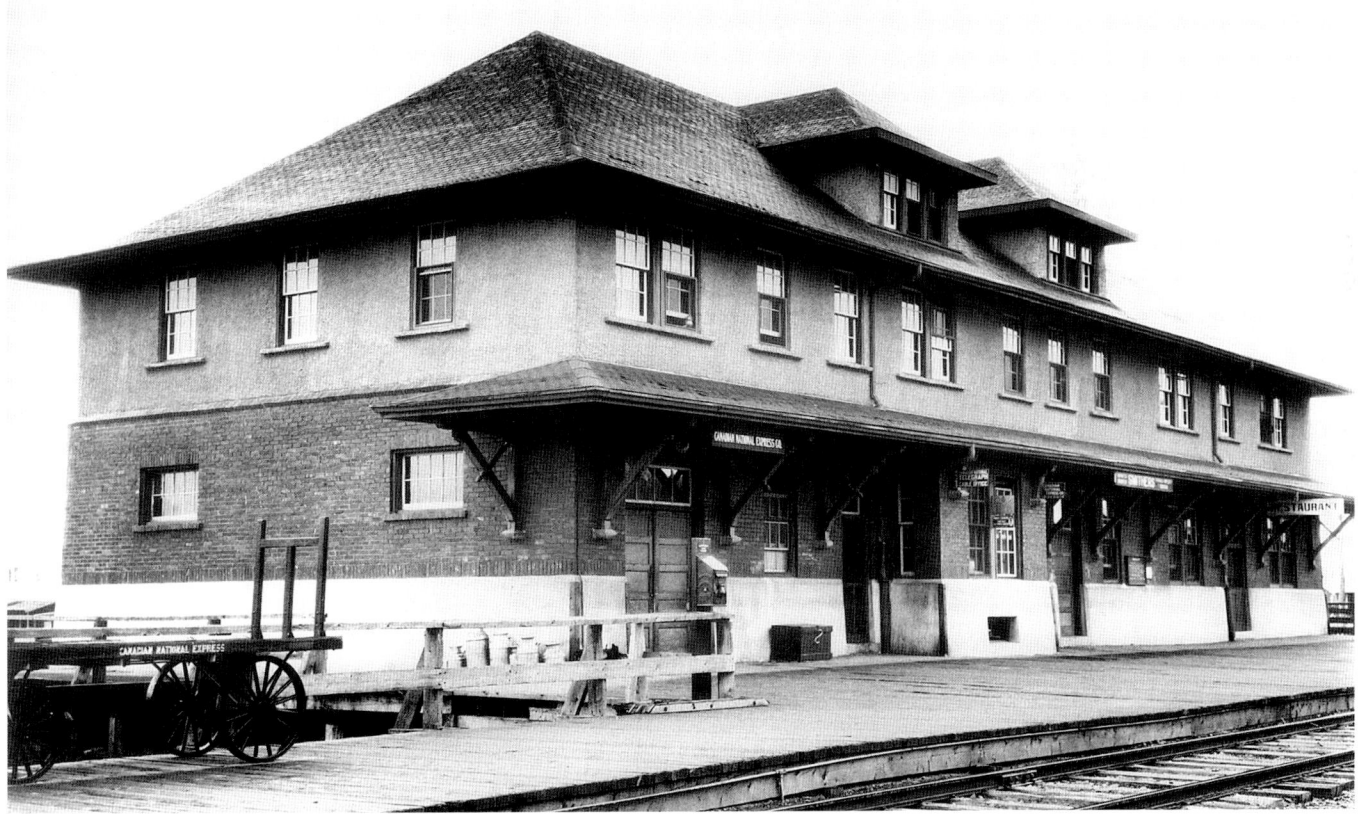

GTP Smithers, British Columbia
(Canadian National Photo 33916), circa 1950s

In 1914, the dispatchers responsible for operating GTP trains between Prince George and the coast were squeezed—along with the station staff—into a small, single floor frame building at Smithers. Due to the outbreak of War the earlier forecasts for the rapid growth of Smithers did not materialize, but in 1918 its outlook improved when the provincial government relocated its district offices and court registry from Old Hazelton. This may have been the primary motivation—despite the GTP's precarious financial situation—to erect this substantial 2½-storey structure (38'-10"x105'-10"), just east of the existing station. On the main floor, the large waiting room was flanked by the women's washroom, kitchen and lunch counter to the east, and the men's washroom, agent's office, trainmen's room and baggage room to the west. The second floor was subdivided into offices for the Smithers Divisional staff, including two sets of washrooms. In April 1919, the Master Mechanic and the Engineering Department relocated into the upstairs offices from Prince George and Prince Rupert, respectively. In the attic, three-bedrooms were provided for the restaurant employees. They shared a washroom on that level, a rare convenience at that time. This building was heated by steam, fed by underground pipes from the stationary plant at the nearby roundhouse. Although originally planned to be built entirely of wood, the destruction of the McBride station by fire earlier in 1918 prompted the GTP to alter the blueprints for the Smithers station. As such, the exterior walls were constructed entirely of load-bearing hollow clay tile. While the massing of this building owed much to the GTP 'Design D' station, its finishes were far superior. The concrete plinth and red face brick on the main floor, with rough-cast stucco above, gave the station a much different character than earlier company depots of this scale, and the quality of its exterior finishes harkened back to the GTP's 1917 Prince Albert, Saskatchewan station. The restaurant, opened in May 1919, served primarily passengers and railroaders, although locals were also welcome. The lunch counter was closed in 1955 and the area was converted into a CN–CP Telecommunications repeater station, with the former kitchen serving as its power room. The Smithers station is preserved.

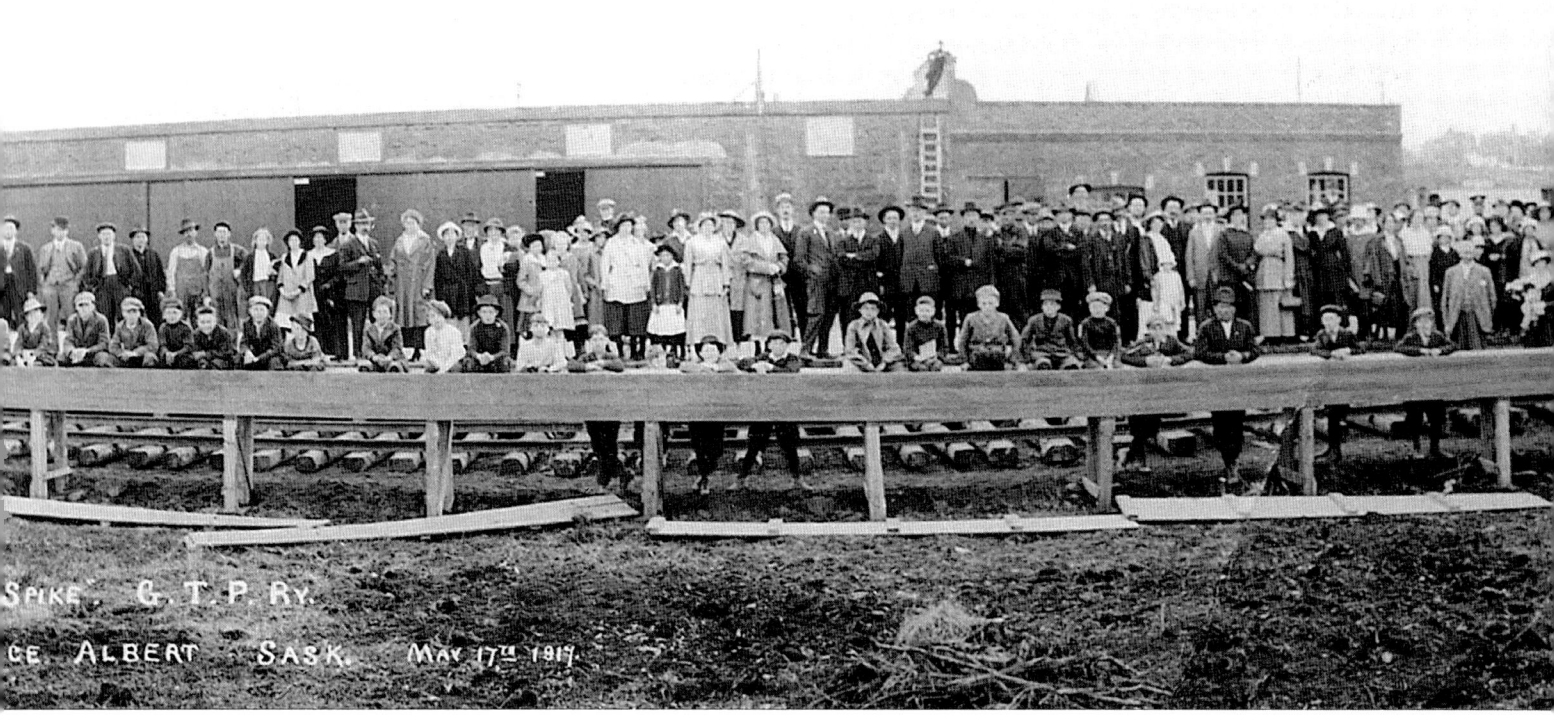

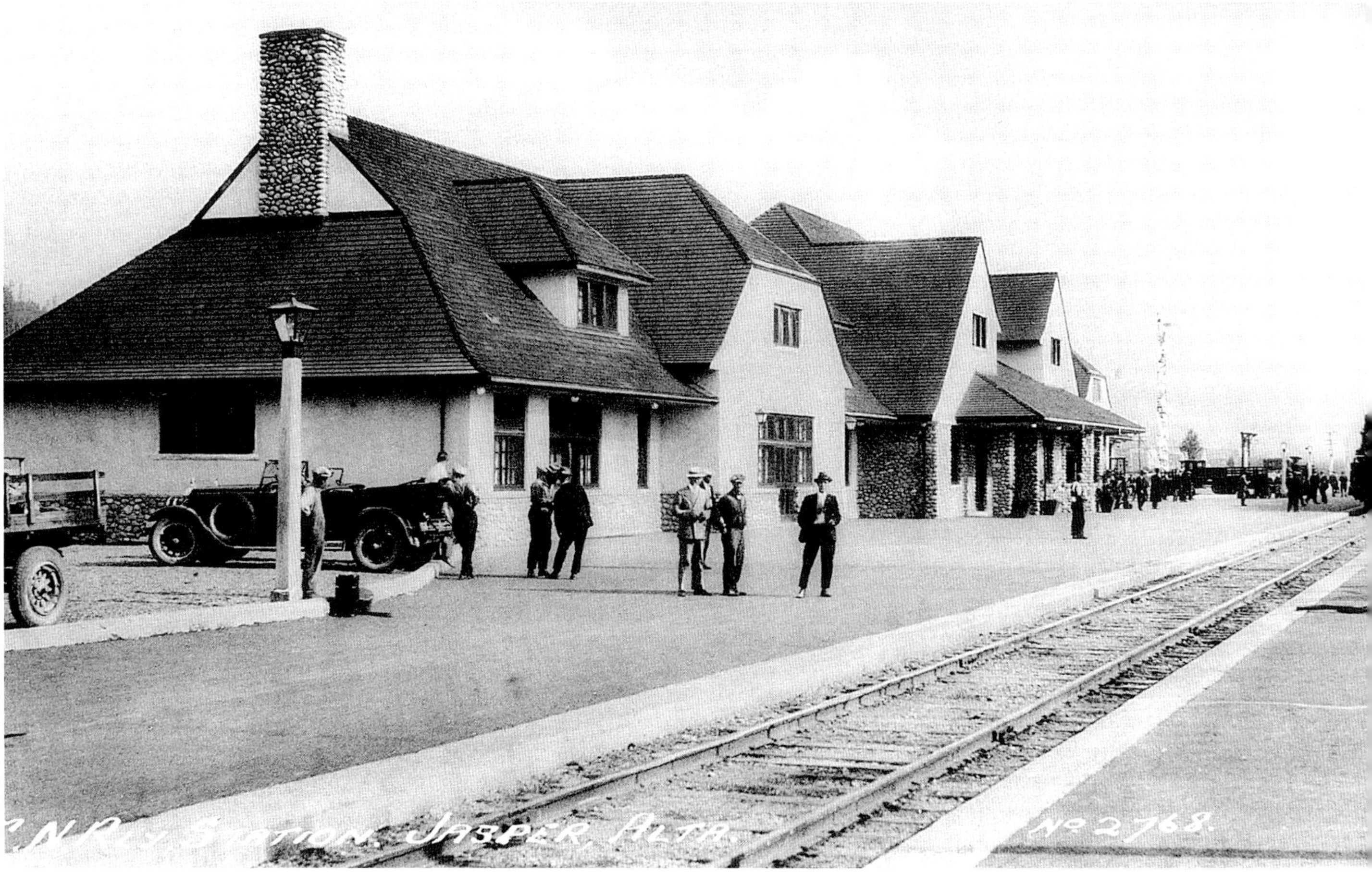

CNR Jasper, Alberta #3 (LESLIE S. KOZMA COLLECTION), CIRCA LATE 1920S

The former GTP station at Jasper, Alberta burned down late 1924. In keeping with its reputation as a world-class tourist destination, CNR Architect Schofield designed a replacement station that was a masterpiece. Its massing borrowed freely from English rural residential architecture and featured a plinth of local cobblestones capped with a course of Tyndall stone. The walls above were of brick, finished on the exterior with rough-cast stucco. The plaster and oak-beamed, vaulted ceiling in the general waiting room was naturally lighted by clerestory glazing. Other services included a restaurant and a dining room, with a feature fireplace and massive cobble chimney. Living accommodation for station staff was provided on the second level. In 1938, the central block of the Jasper #3, was used as the basis for a new station proposed for Prince Albert, Saskatchewan. The wings on either end however, were quite different from the Jasper prototype. It was not built. The Jasper station was restored under the auspices of Parks Canada in 2001.

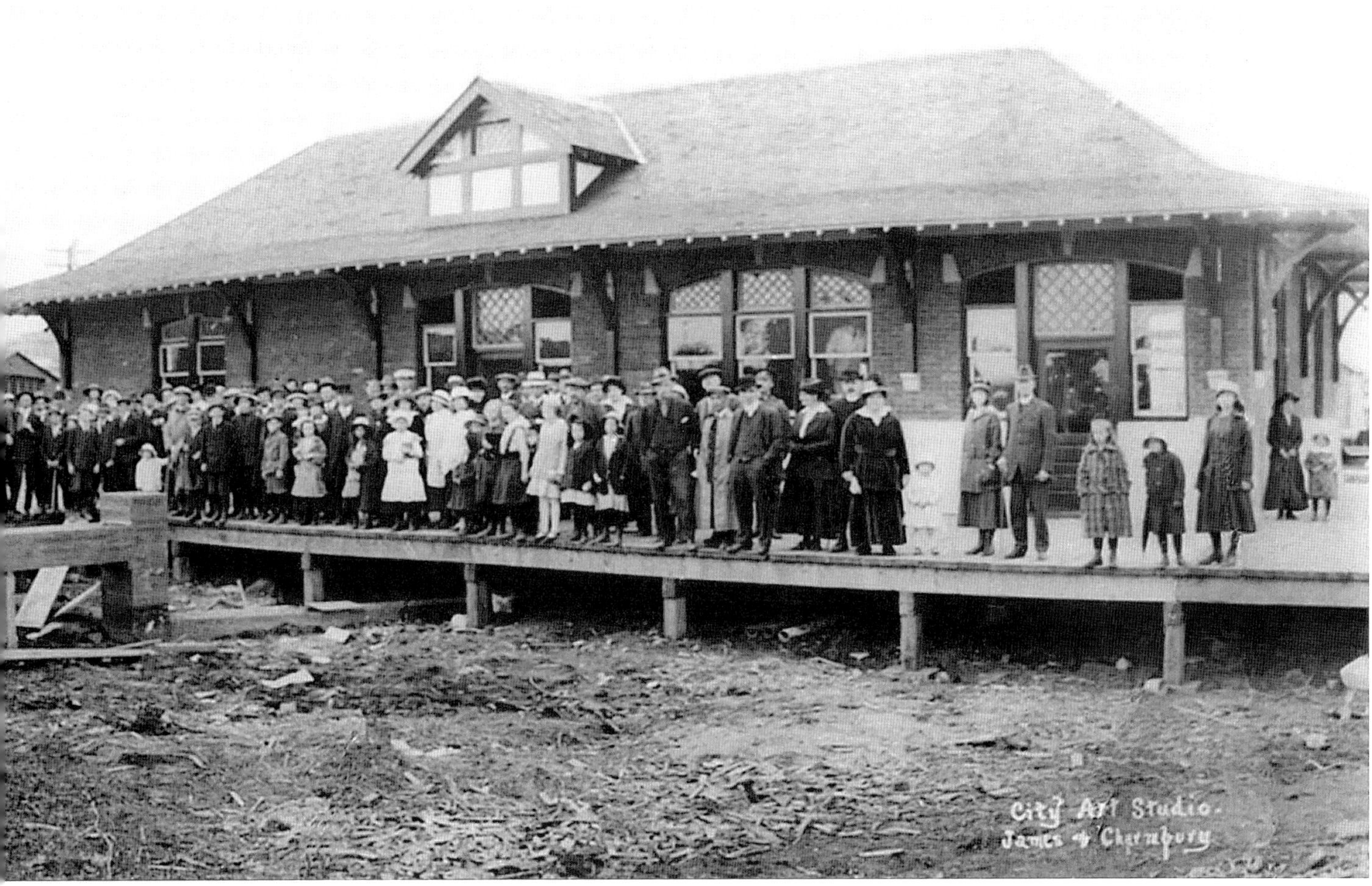

GTP Prince Albert, Saskatchewan (Saskatchewan Archives Board, Photo R-A 4364), 1917

The last spike, completing the GTP's Prince Albert Branch, was driven home on 17 May 1917. Behind the crowd was the GTP freight shed. To the right, the newly completed passenger station (Plan 100-171), a 25'-0"x70'-0" single-storey building, at the end of a stub-track yard, directly north of the CNoR terminals. A general waiting room, ladies' waiting room, office, washrooms, and separate express and baggage rooms were provided. The GTP's Prince Albert depot was easily the Company's finest passenger station in Saskatchewan and proved to be influential in the development of later GTP and CNR station designs. Many of the architectural elements that appeared for the first time on this building lived on in many non-standard Canadian National stations built in the West after 1925: concrete plinths, bellcast roofs with wide bracket-supported overhangs, rough-cast stucco and half-timbering in the dormers (Wainwright and Vegreville, Alberta). Other architectural devices from early GTP passenger stations—such as swept dormers and bellcast hip dormers—also found their way onto the CNR's large, rural passenger stations of the 1920s. Compare this to Jasper #3 and Kelowna, built in 1925 and 1926, respectively. While the station facilities at Prince Albert were consolidated at the former CNoR station in 1921, the GTP depot survived as an office building until 1957 when it was demolished.

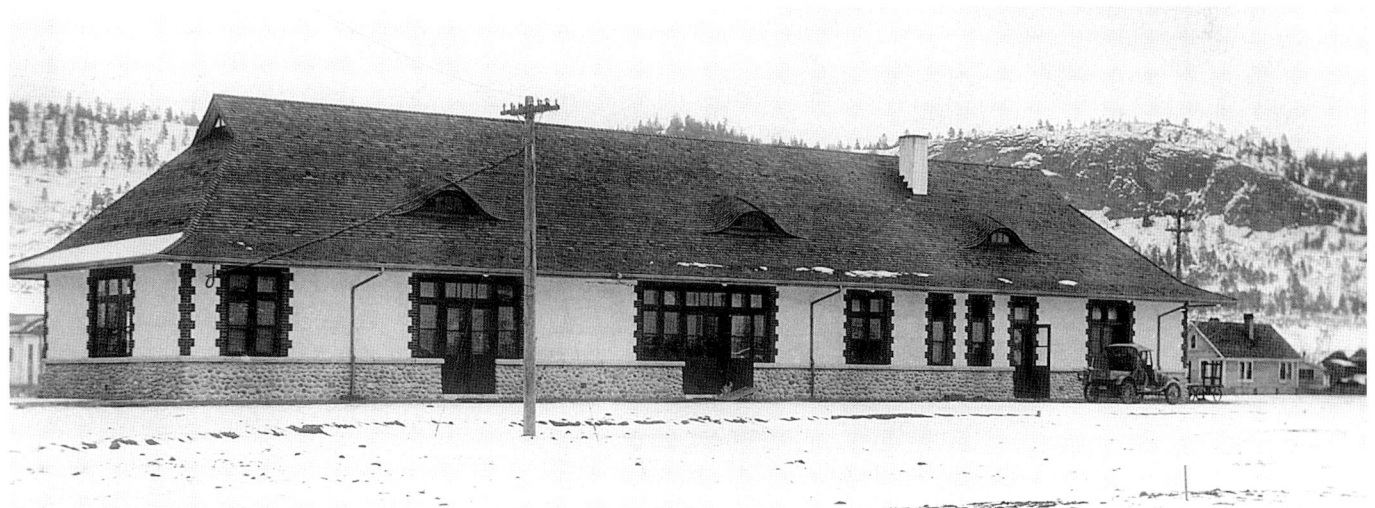

CNR Kelowna, British Columbia (Leslie S. Kozma Collection), 1929

The CNR finished many former Canadian Northern projects abandoned during World War One. Among these was the Okanagan Branch, connecting the CNR main line at Kamloops with the rich ranching and farming country of British Columbia's famous Okanagan valley. In exchange for running rights over the southern stretch of the new branch, the CNR received running rights over portions of the Canadian Pacific main line, between Kamloops to Campbell Creek, and the CPR Okanagan Subdivision, between Armstrong and Vernon. The CNR Okanagan Branch opened for service on 14 September 1925. In addition to being a major fruit-packing centre for the local growers, Kelowna's salubrious climate ensured that it would become a popular destination with tourists. The passenger station erected at Kelowna in 1926 reflected the fledgling CNR's confidence in the community's future. The station incorporated a cobble plinth capped with dressed stone, used with such success at Jasper #3, built the previous year. The exterior walls were finished with rough-cast stucco, with red brick accents on the corners and on the door and window jambs. The large expanse of the hip-gable roof was broken up by three eyebrow dormers and detail, previously employed on GTP Prince Albert (1917), and later repeated on Wainwright #3 (1929).

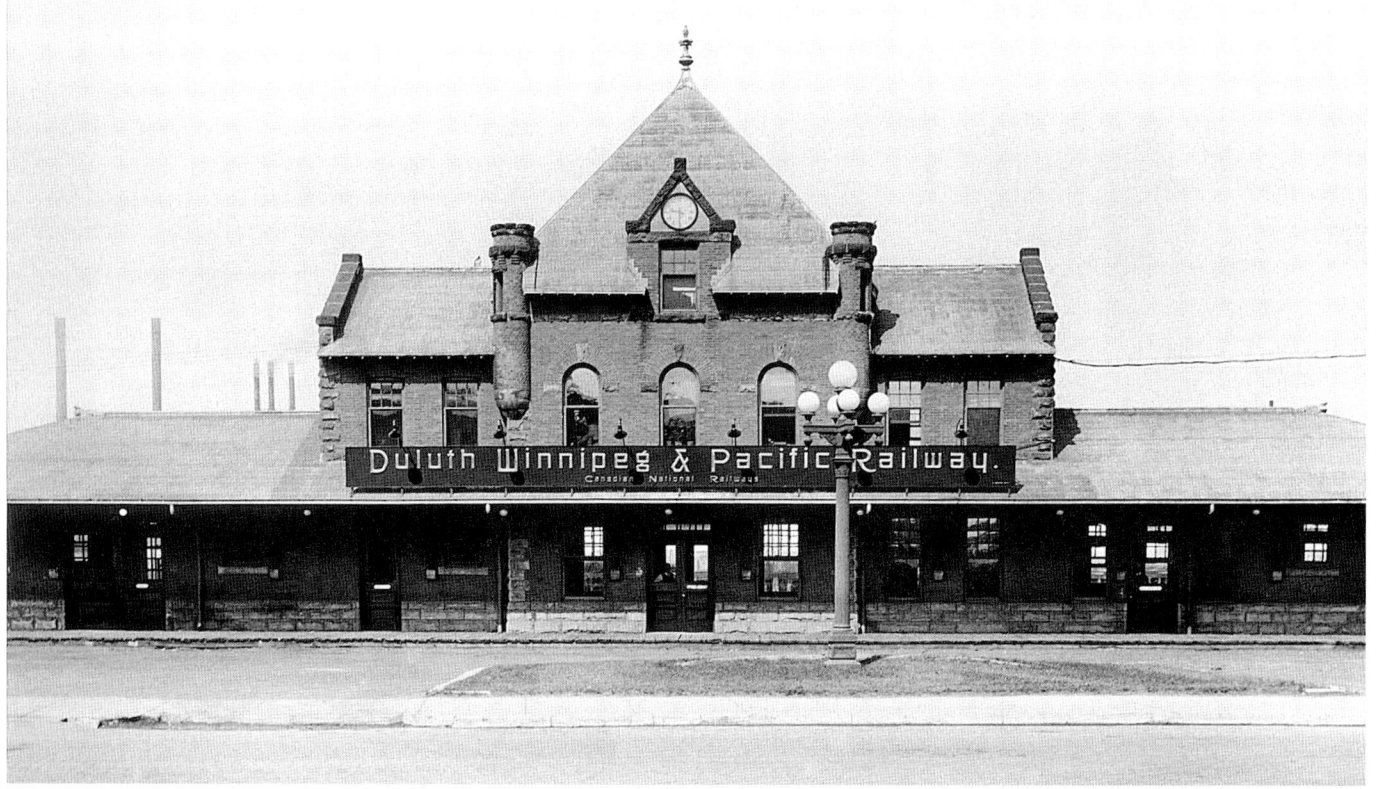

DW&P Virginia, Minnesota (Western Canada Pictorial Index Inc., Photo A1483-44911), 19??

The Duluth Winnipeg & Pacific adopted CNoR building standards, including station buildings, in 1910 and 1911. Pratt's high pyramid roof with its gable dormers and the clasping turrets on the corners, seemed right at home, even in Virginia, Minnesota. The most noticeable variation from the other stations of this class was the large clock in the dormer pediment, in lieu of the usual shock of wheat chiseled out of stone.

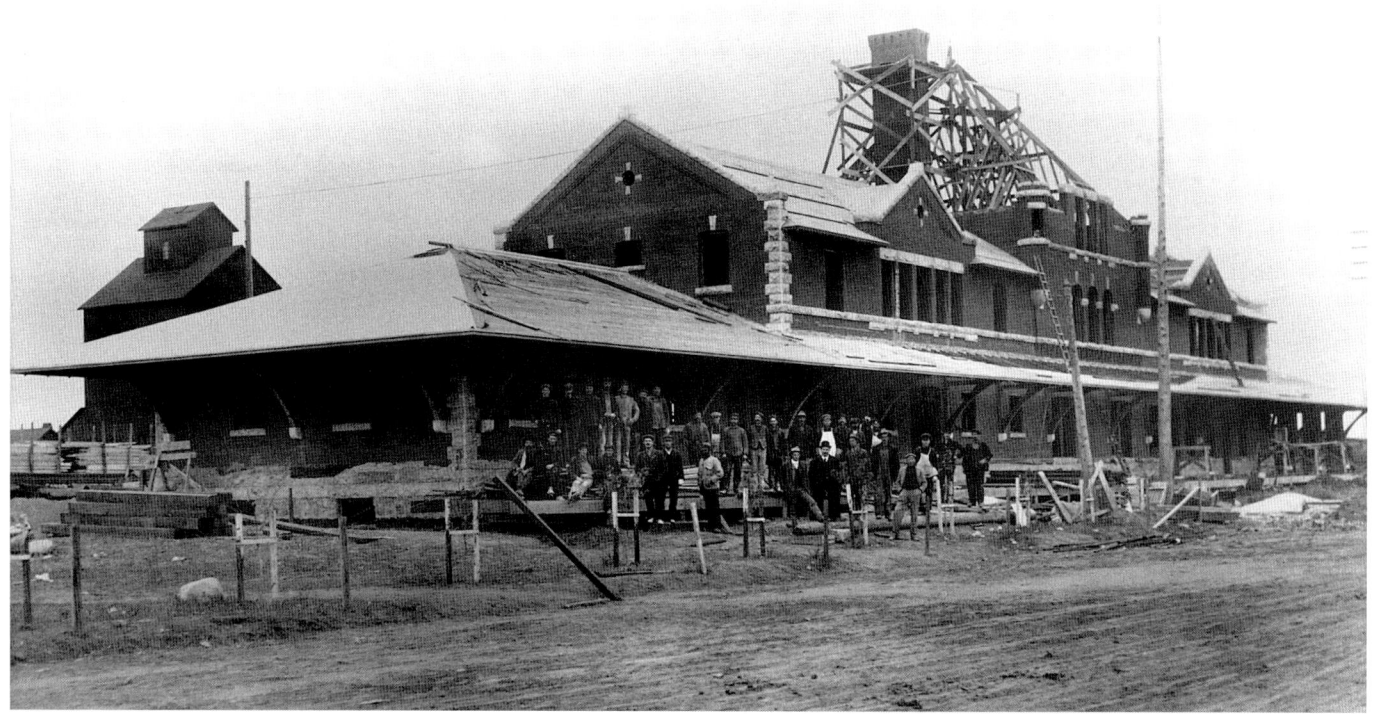

CNoR Saskatoon, Saskatchewan #2 (Saskatoon Public Library, Local History Room, Photo PH 90-63-3), 1910

Here, the proud tradesmen assembled in front of their handiwork. The brickwork is completed and the carpenters are putting the finishing touches onto the CNoR's classic roofline. The CNoR passenger station that loomed over First Avenue and 23rd Street in Saskatoon (Plan 100-33), was the third of a quintet of CNoR brick-and-stone passenger stations that showcased Pratt's roof line. The others were erected at Port Arthur (1905) and Edmonton (1906), Dauphin (1913), and Virginia, Minnesota (1913). Originally proposed in 1907, the Saskatoon building was completed in 1910. At the time, the 62'x218' structure was surely the finest CNoR station in Saskatchewan. It had a full-basement for the steam heating plant, fuel bin, storage and sleeping and dining car stores. The main floor included a ticket lobby, a ticket office, general and ladies' waiting rooms, toilets, parcel and baggage room, and express room and office. The second floor contained offices for the Divisional officers and other railway staff. Provision was made for a future second floor over the single-storey wings. Its central hip roof, punctuated with gable dormers and corbelled corner turrets, reached a height of 58'. The ground floor was extended and extensively remodeled in 1916, providing additional space for the Sleeping & Dining Car Department and more office staff. This station was demolished in 1940. Interestingly however, in 1990 a modern adaptation of the facade of this station was reconstructed on this site, in conjunction with the renovation and expansion of Midtown Shopping Centre.

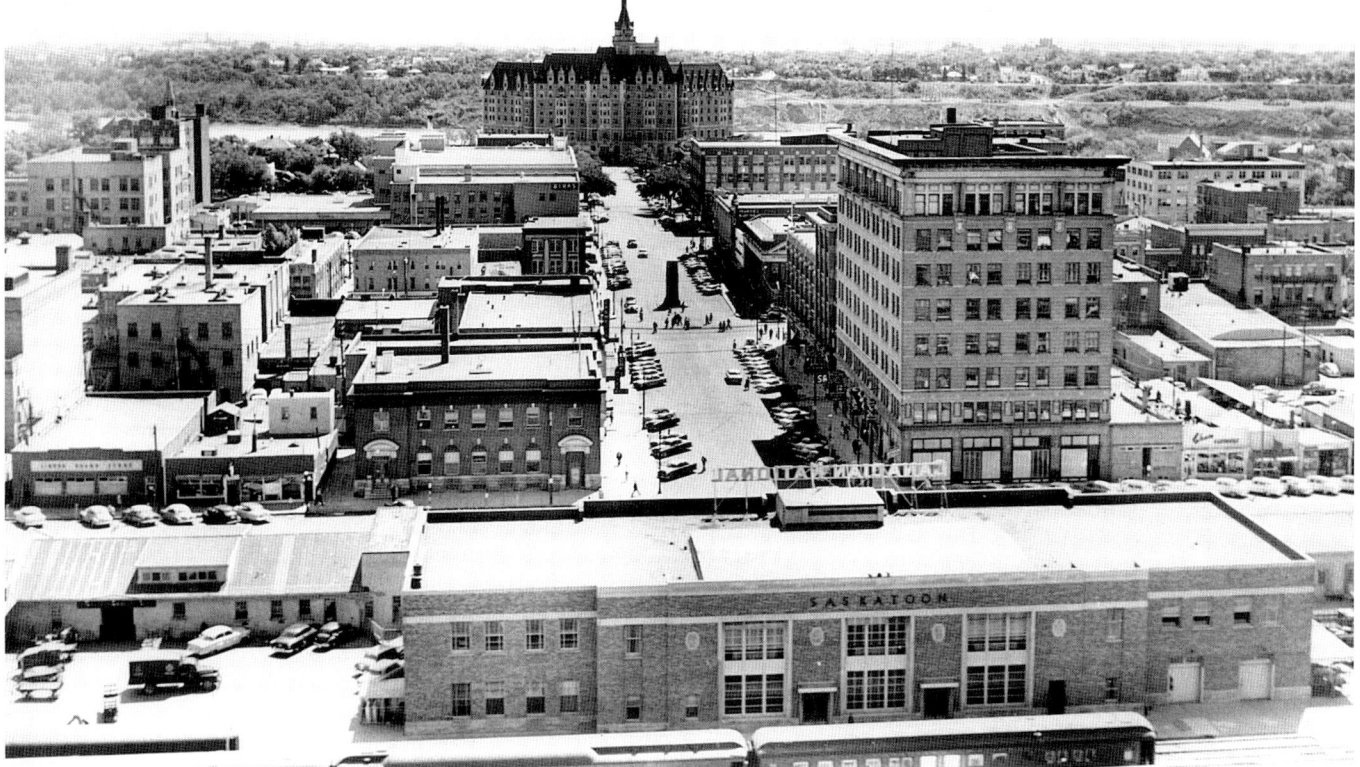

CNR Saskatoon, Saskatchewan #3   (Saskatoon Public Library, Local History Room, Photo LH 9835), mid-1950s

Saskatoon's third CNR station, built just south of the CNoR's 1910-depot, was opened in December 1939. It was built in a modernized Classic Style that contrasted sharply with the Chateau Style of the recently completed Bessborough Hotel, a few blocks down 21st Street. Yet, by using identical finish materials—buff brick and Tyndal stone—the structures complemented one another. Both structures were designed by CNR Architect John Schofield. The siting of the company's Bessborough Hotel in relation to the depot was critical. Indeed, in the case of railway hotels, if they could not be situated immediately across the street from the depot—such as at the Chateau Laurier in Ottawa or the Royal York Hotel in Toronto—it was essential that the hotel be at least a reasonable distance down the street from the rear of the station. This kindred relationship was repeated at Edmonton and Winnipeg. Major redevelopment of the Saskatoon's downtown CNR rail yards saw the new terminals established on the east end of the city in 1964. The inner city station was used by CNR as an office building until 1969 when it was demolished to make way for an office tower.

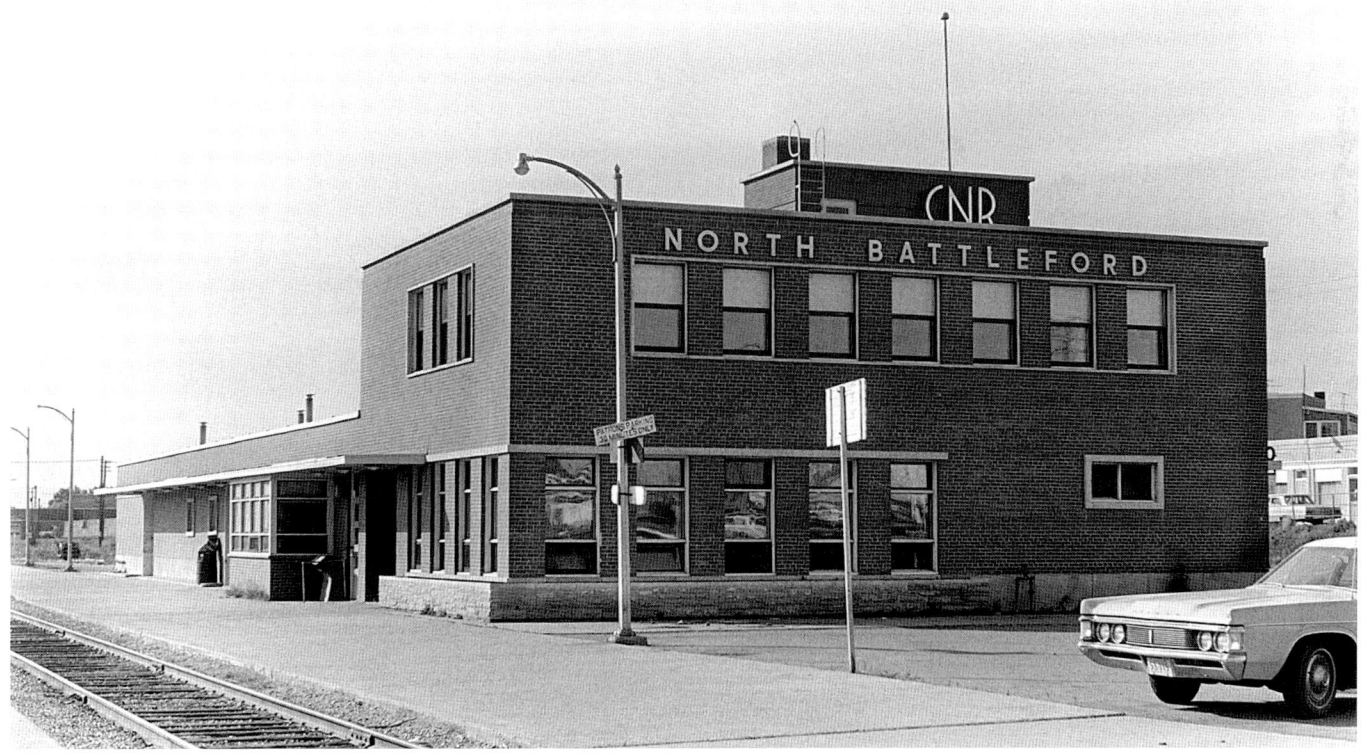

CNR North Battleford, Saskatchewan #3   (Charles W. Bohi Photo), 1973

At about 10 o'clock on the evening of January 22, 1908, fire was discovered in North Battleford's 2nd Class depot. While most of the building's contents were saved, one occupant was injured and another died of smoke inhalation. The gutted building was rebuilt, in kind, and was soon back in operation. By the 1950s the station required replacement. The passenger stations erected at North Battleford #3 and Prince Albert #3 in 1954 and 1958, respectively, incorporated architectural devices characteristic of the "Moderne Style," such as slab canopies, pylons and corner fenestration. CNR stations of this generation lacked the flair of earlier Canadian Pacific Railway attempts in this vein. On these larger CNR passenger stations, in lieu of conventional "two-dimensional" painted signboards, individual stainless steel letters spelled out the station name on the end of the building. Stylized stainless steel "CNR" letters on the penthouse—the forerunner of the company's "wet noodle" logo—were retained and remain to this day.

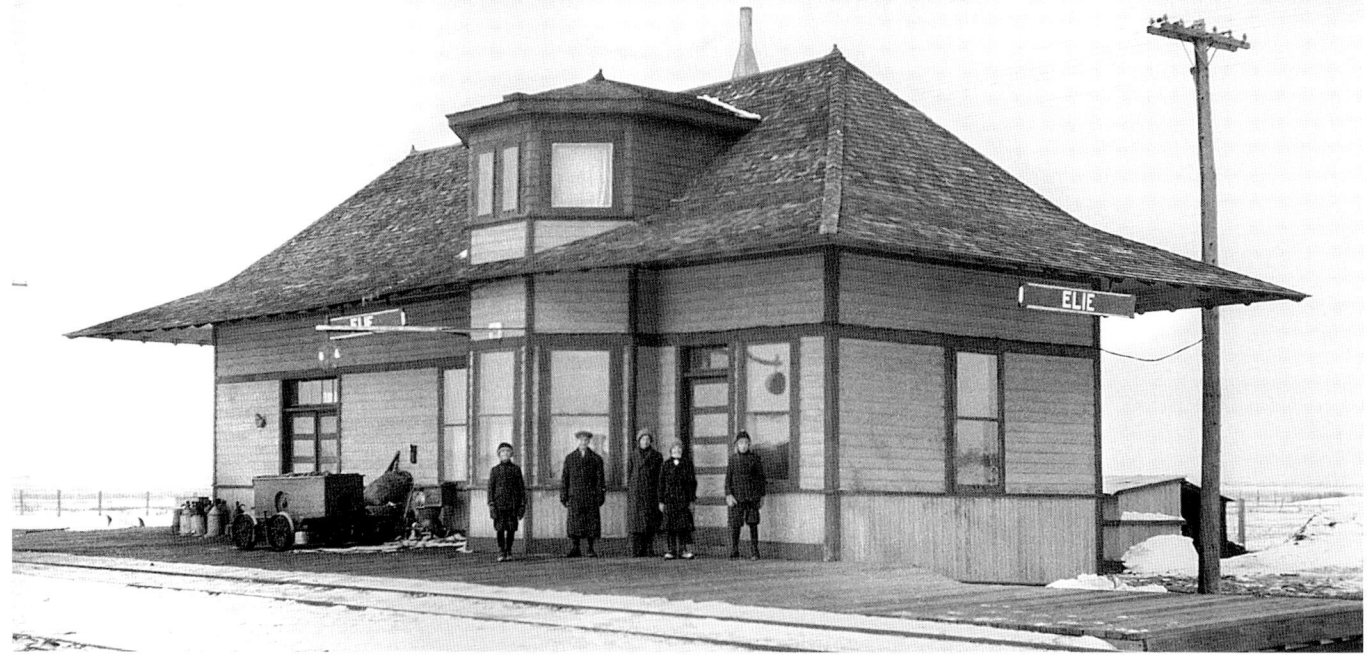

Exterior Paint Schedule—*GTP Phases A and B*: GTP Elie, Manitoba (AL PATERSON PHOTO, STAFFORD SWAIN COLLECTION), NO DATE

During the pre-World War I railway boom, the Grand Trunk Railway used an elaborate colour scheme for its wood-frame depots. The wainscoting— usually vertical V-joint siding—was painted Olive Green; *the belt line trim was a* Dark Green. *The rest of the body above this was* Grey. *Window and doorframes were* Dark Grey *while the doors and window sashes were* Cranberry. *The fascia around the main roof was a brownish colour. The overhang support brackets, shingling on the roof and the walls of the dormers and turrets matched the belt line trim. Upper storey fascias, window frames, finials and ridge boards were* White. *The window sashes were* Cranberry. *Early (pre-1909) Grand Trunk Pacific station colour schemes shared a similar complexity with its GTR parent. Unfortunately, the exact colours could not be established for the* GTP Phase A. *At Rivers, Manitoba and Nokomis, Saskatchewan, the body was likely* Yellow *with* Cranberry *trim while the wainscot and the wall shingling was painted a dark colour, possibly* Brown. *At Melville, Kelliher and Scott #1, Saskatchewan, the walls and wainscoting—five to six feet above top of platform—were painted darker shade (*Sand?*) than the body colour. This GTP paint scheme was simplified about 1909; the* GTP Phase-B: *the main body and soffit of the depot were* Yellow, *while the doors and window sashes were* Cream. *The fascia and casings were painted* Cranberry. *The shingles were stained* Gold. *The ends of the exposed rafters were the same colour as trim. As an interesting sidelight, the station of Fallis, about 50 miles west of Edmonton, was named after W. S. Fallis, President of the Sherwin-Williams Company, no doubt a good friend of GTP President Hays. Sherwin-Williams paints and stains were of the highest standard since the 1870s and the company was one of the primary suppliers to North American railways.*

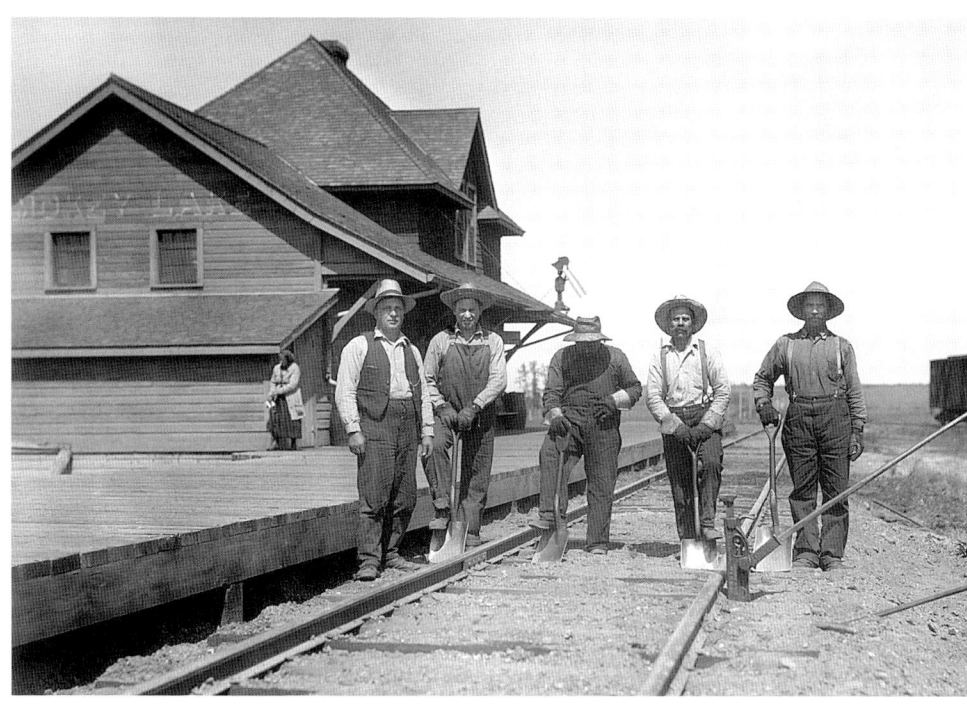

Exterior Paint Schedule— CNR Phase I— "Utilitarian" 1919: CNoR Smoky Lake, Alberta
(PROVINCIAL ARCHIVES OF ALBERTA PHOTO, GAVINCHUK COLLECTION G163), 1927

At some point in their history, most North American railways used utilitarian colour schemes for their depots. Sometimes, it was as if the painters were given brushes, scaffolding and a barrel of Oxide Red *paint and ordered to "do the job". Everything but the roof shingles was painted this one colour. By 1915, with limited means and a lot of work left to finish on many of its lines, the Canadian Northern was forced to economize. One way was to simplify the painting of its new structures. The newly formed Canadian National Railways, also looking for ways to save money, continued using this very simple livery, which the authors have designated the* CNR Phase I *scheme. It appears to have been revived again during the Depression being used well into World War II, when deferred maintenance was the rule. Indeed, it appears that sometimes, the* Green *trim was omitted. The Smoky Lake, Alberta station built in 1919 and shown here about 1927 was likely originally painted in the* Phase I *scheme: a* Red Oxide *body with* Green *fascia, trim sashes and doors. The dormers and the second storey walls of these buildings were usually* Red Oxide. *This scheme has also been documented on many CNR Eastern Lines stations and section houses. The Northern Alberta Railways and its predecessors also painted some of its depots in this scheme. Note the misspelled "Smokey Lake" painted onto the end wall of the freight shed. This was an unusual rendition of the station name lettering, possibly* Green *outlined in* White *or* Cream.

SECTION II

Exterior Colour Schemes

THE AVAILABILITY OF RELATIVELY CHEAP timber throughout much of the West made it the building material of choice, particularly for railway stations and other structures. Rapidity of construction, by relatively unskilled tradesmen, was another advantage offered by wood-frame construction. But, unlike masonry, untreated wood left exposed to the elements becomes weathered and unattractive. Thus, paint or stain is applied to the surface of the woodwork for protection and to improve its appearance.

In the West of the early 1900s, the railway depot was usually one of only a handful of buildings in an entire pioneer town to be painted. This made these railway structures that much more conspicuous.

While the colour schemes chosen by railway architects for their stations were carefully conceived, they were—by any standard—quite conservative. Indeed, based on the evidence, the railways of western Canada could not claim to be trendsetters as far as paint schemes for structures were concerned.[1]

Unfortunately, the colour cards issued by the CNoR and GTP's respective Engineering Departments for the painting of their buildings and structures have eluded the authors. The films of the early 20th century have provided the researcher of today with images in only black, white and the greys in between. Hand-tinted postcards sometimes provide some interesting "broad brush" insights into the liveries of older buildings and pieces of equipment, but there was sometimes considerable artistic license used. Therefore, hand-tinted post cards cannot be considered accurate enough to establish the true colours. While colour films came into popular use after World War II, they were expensive. As such, photographs, specifically of railway stations taken prior to 1950 are scarce. Finally, there are tremendous inconsistencies in the information that is available. Thus, anyone researching the colouration of these structures faces a daunting task.

Nevertheless, the authors obtained one of at least four CNR colour cards known to have been issued[2] and, using other notes, the colours of a second card could be approximated. Based primarily on these and some accurately-dated photographs, notations on railway blueprints, field work and other miscellaneous sources[3], the authors have compiled a representative sampling of generic CNoR, GTP and CNR colour schemes found in the West. It is hoped that these colours will suffice as a guide, at least until more conclusive evidence is found.

The first coats of paint were usually applied by the station's builder, often a contractor but sometimes the railway itself. The subsequent re-painting of these buildings was usually handled by the company's Divisional B&B Gang. The frequency of re-painting railway structures was based on many factors including location (high or low profile), importance (main or branch line), and budgetary considerations. In any given period there could be considerable variations in colour schemes and station identification, on the same Division, or even on the same Subdivision. In most cases, there were simply too many buildings to bring them all up to the latest standard at the same time. There were also inexplicable deviations on specific divisions.

NOTES:

1. Certainly after 1900, the palette of most North American railways seem to have been confined to Reds/Browns and a few subdued Greys, Creams/Yellows and Greens, and White and Black.

   Roger Moss, CENTURY OF COLOR EXTERIOR DECORATION FOR AMERICAN BUILDINGS — 1820/1920, page 93. "Normally, in the 1880s, the first floor of a building would be painted a darker color than the second when a two-tone scheme was adopted for the body... [but on many later depots] the colors were reversed, probably to compensate for the shadow cast by the [roof overhang or awnings]."

2. There is also reference in CNR's Western plan files to a "COLOUR PANEL 1941 STANDARD," which could not be located.

   At first glance the two known CNR colour cards appear to apply system-wide as they make no distinction between Western and Eastern Lines. Yet, there were significant differences in some of the colour schemes employed in the respective areas. One of the major differences was the application of rough-cast stucco to the exterior of wood-frame stations and section houses, something commonplace in the West but quite rare in the East.

3. In 1983, the Alberta Historic Sites Service (AHSS) acquired and relocated the Bellis, Alberta station to the Ukrainian Cultural Heritage Village, west of Edmonton. As a "living" display representative of the 1920s, the stucco was to be removed, the exterior siding was to be repaired and the building was to be re-painted in period colours. Lacking the necessary data, the AHSS commissioned a chromochronology of the depot, painstakingly removing the stucco and analyzing samples from selected wooden components of the building, layer by layer. From this and the 1937 CNR colour card, certain generalizations could be made about CNR paint schemes after 1923.

   The authors used the colour images of over 260 stations in western Canada —taken between 1953 and 1980—to create this database of latter-day CNR colour schemes.

For the purposes of this work, the exterior colour schemes used by the CNR and its predecessors on their "Western Lines" depots are divided into seven basic eras, or "*Phases*:" the Northern Pacific, the Canadian Northern, the Grand Trunk Pacific (including the National Transcontinental) and five on the Canadian National Railways.

The Northern Pacific & Manitoba likely used its parent company's colours, which the authors have not researched. During its 18-year history, the CNoR probably had a few different colour schemes for its stations. By contrast, the GTP built most of its stations within a relatively brief period—about a decade—so its livery had little opportunity to change, although at least one variation is documented. Colours for stations on the National Transcontinental Railway could not be established; perhaps they were the same as that of the GTR or the GTP. Then, there were the five distinct colour schemes employed by the CNR.

Each *Phase* had adaptations for the painting of shelters and the various classes of combination and passenger stations: some were one storey, while others had multiple storeys.

There are other factors to consider. While the CNR and its predecessors had exacting specifications for the paints used on their buildings and structures,[4] it is unclear how stringently company officials enforced the exact colouration. For instance, did the B&B Master or Superintendent actually take his colour card and compare it with the painted finish on the structure?

While each railway had standards for painting stations and other buildings, these were sometimes not followed to the letter. This is confirmed by this notation on the Canadian Pacific Railway Standard Colours for Buildings, 1923, "*…the colour samples illustrating how buildings may be painted are given as an indication of what can be done with these colours to get the best effects…for each class of building, but it is not intended that these combinations of colour shall be absolutely adhered to, but rather that local officers should use their own discretion in using these combinations and are free to select other combinations from the standard colours, provided the effects produced are simple and harmonious.*" A similar policy appears to have prevailed on the Canadian National Railways.

In addition to the local and regional variations in paint colours "when applied," further differences were brought about by discolouration due to fading and air pollution. The frequency of traffic was also a consideration, especially where coal was used as locomotive fuel. Indeed, the same colours sometimes varied on different parts of the same building, those portions subjected to constant sun or rain fading more rapidly than those portions protected from the elements. Sometimes, colour differences on the same building were due to poor matching following repairs undertaken years after the building was last painted.

Other than the *Red–White–Blue* scheme of the 1960s, the authors were unable to find any direct relationship between the colour schemes of railway company passenger rolling stock and that of western Canadian railway stations.[5]

By the 1970s, CNR Western Lines stations still in service were in five of the post-War colour schemes. Of these, the *Phase III-B/III-C* was by far the most prevalent. While the *Phase IV* scheme appears to have been originally applied only to stations along lines with passenger service, its application was later expanded, to the extent that it became the new standard for all stations. It was the second most common livery by the 1970s. During the same period, many depots were still in the *Red Oxide–Cream–Green* colours (*Phase III-A*), primarily along branch lines. There was also the small scattering of those in the *HBR Scheme*.[6]

The reason for some of this colour variation in the region may be attributed to the waning importance of the railway station. After all, money is not usually spent repainting redundant buildings. But this diversity was very much at odds with a standard livery, something that was supposed to tie all these depots to a common owner.[7]

NOTES:

4. *CPR Specification for Station Paint, 1 March 1924.* "The colour and shade shall conform to the CPR standard sample for each paint, obtained from the General Purchasing Agent."

5. Al Lill, George Carpenter and Brian West, "*CN Passenger Car Paint Schemes,*" CN LINES (Volume 7, Number 2), pages 12-15. The CNR issued a new colour card for its buildings in 1937. Coincidentally, that same year the CNR revised its passenger car colour from Pullman Green to Green No. 11 (Olive Green).

   Al Lill with George Carpenter, Bud Harcus, Stafford Swain and Brian West, "*CN Passenger Car Paint Schemes (Part 3),*" CN LINES (Volume 8, Number 1), pages 38-42. The reintroduction of the *Phase III-C* scheme may have coincided with the 1954 introduction of the new Green–Yellow–Black livery for CNR passenger cars.

6. Based on the database derived from the colour images noted in Footnote 2: *Phase III-B/III-C* (50%), *Phase IV* (38%), *Phase III-A* (10%), *HBR* and other (2%). Conclusions drawn from these statistics may be misleading, primarily because many of the older colour schemes were noted on retired buildings (most of these having been off-site for many years). Nevertheless, earlier in the 1970s there were significantly more stations in *Phase III-B/III-C* than *Phase IV*, that was still in its infancy.

7. *CN Signs Manual,* January 1965. "A continuing Visual Design Program is directed towards ensuring that CN's exterior appearance…[as] seen by the public eye has a consistent and smartly-designed appearance that can be readily identified…"

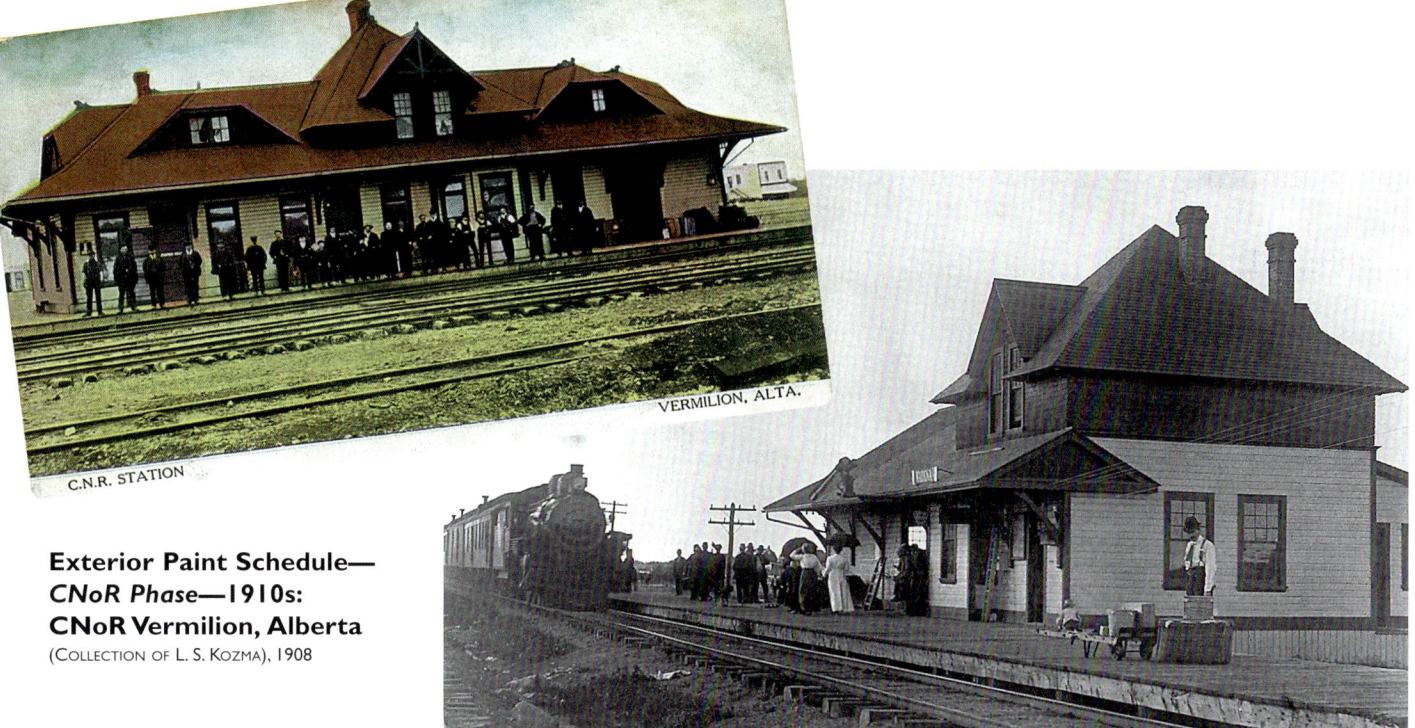

**Exterior Paint Schedule—
CNoR Phase—1910s:
CNoR Vermilion, Alberta**
(COLLECTION OF L. S. KOZMA), 1908

CNoR Wadena, Saskatchewan (SASKATCHEWAN ARCHIVES BOARD, PHOTO R-A2261), CIRCA 1910

When placed side by side, it is easy to visualize the colours on the hand-tinted post card of the Vermilion, Alberta depot on the black and white photograph of Wadena, Saskatchewan's 3rd Class station. A Dark Grey *stained shingle roof (contrary to what is shown, plus some early stations were stained* Red*),* Cream *body,* Light Brown *stain to the shingled walls of the second storey, and* Dark Brown *trim and overhang support brackets. The doors and the window sashes were painted a lighter* Brown*. The finials and ridge boards were sometimes painted* White*; other times they were finished to match the roof shingles. This* CNoR Phase *livery had much in common with contemporary residential and Canadian Pacific Railway depot colour schemes, particularly in the use of the* Cream *and the* Brown*. The enameled iron name board on the front awning of the Wadena depot became standard on the CNoR's local stations about 1900. They were especially evident along its main line between Grandview, Manitoba and Edmonton. It appears that the CNoR stopped purchasing this type of sign by 1906, although some of those installed remained in service into the 1970s. The signs—manufactured in England—were imported by The Acton Burrows Co. of Toronto. The Style no. 1 sign, used by the CPR and the CNoR, was 12" high with 9" high* White *lettering on a* Dark Blue *field; the length of the board varied according to the number of letters in the name. The Grand Trunk Railway used the Acton Company's Style no. 2 sign, 14" high, with* Black *lettering on a* White *background. As was custom on the GTR, the names and mileages to the terminals on either side of the station were also noted. This latter feature was later borrowed by the Grand Trunk Pacific, for some of its wooden name boards.*

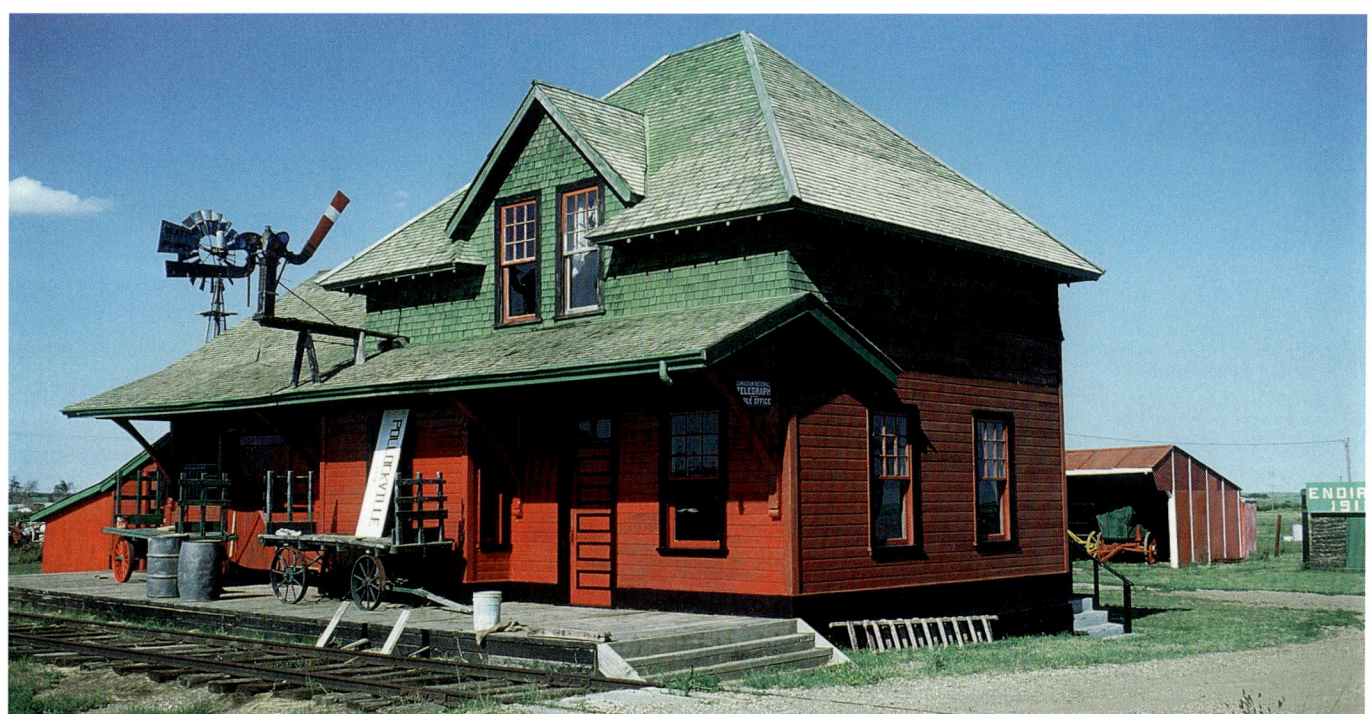

Exterior Paint Schedule—CNoR Pollockville, Alberta #2 (CHARLES W. BOHI PHOTO), 1970S

To further confound those researching depot colouration, many "pseudo-paint schemes"—incorporating elements of railway liveries—have been applied by well-intentioned museums. The station at Pollockville was sold in 1969 and relocated to the Town of Hanna in a museum exhibit. Was this the Phase I scheme? The Black *window trim should probably be* Green*. The actual shades of the colours used on this building are also debatable. As of this writing, Pollockville is the only recorded example in the West painted in the manner depicted here. Whether this scheme is unique, or, indeed, whether such a scheme ever saw service in this region is impossible to say without further documentation.*

EXTERIOR COLOUR SCHEMES

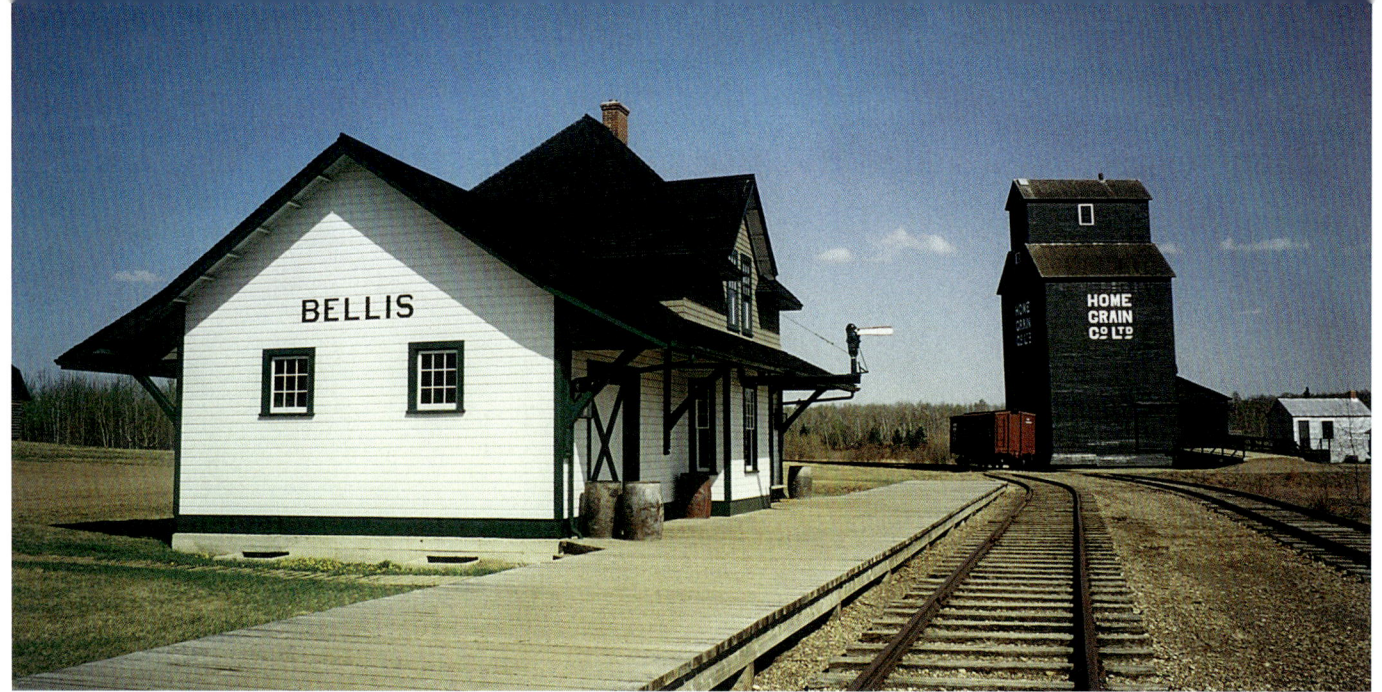

**Exterior Paint Schedule—*CNR Phase II*—"Marketing Scheme" 1920s:
CNoR Bellis, Alberta at the Ukranian Heritage Village** (DAVID KOSHMAN PHOTOS), 2001

There appears to be at least a tenuous link between the exterior finishing of English rural residences and some western Canadian railway stations. The fashionable English countryside houses of the early 1910s had red brick plinths, roughcast stucco walls—colour-washed either White *or a* Light Cream *above—wood trims and shutters painted a* Dark Green *and* Red *tile roofs. Some latter-day GTP depots, such as Smithers, BC clearly borrowed many of these elements. Articles in trade publications such as* CONSTRUCTION, *and the fact that many of the designers of western Canadian depots had an English connection likely had some influence. Indeed, R. E. Taylor, a draftsman in the GTP Building Department volunteered for overseas service, returning to CN railway service after the Great War. Further, the CNR's new President, Sir Henry Thornton, was fresh from England when he took over the corporation's reigns of power in 1922. By this time the integration of the former Canadian Northern and Grand Trunk Pacific lines was well underway. The Grand Trunk lines in the East were just being taken over. What better way to show that the CNR was now one unified company, under new management, than to have a common paint scheme for each of its locomotives, rolling stock and buildings? The authors have identified this depot livery as the* Phase II *"Marketing Scheme," issued about 1923 or 1924. The body and window sashes were painted* Grey. *The second storey wall shingling and the gable end of the awning were stained a "Moss Green," while the overhang support brackets and trim were painted a deeper* Green. *The roof shingles were stained* Red Oxide. *The Ukrainian Heritage Village (east of Edmonton) repainted its 3rd Class Bellis station in this scheme. While the GTR and CNR* Greys *appear to be the same, the GTR buildings continued to use the* Olive Green, *while those in the West were a deeper* Green. *The 1920s must have been a colourful era, with stations in former CNoR and GTP liveries, the latest CNR livery with* Grey *wood siding and those recently refinished with* White *stucco. Even the odd CPR-painted station may have survived into this era, a legacy of the CNoR takeover of the Qu'Appelle Long Lake-line between Regina and Prince Albert.*

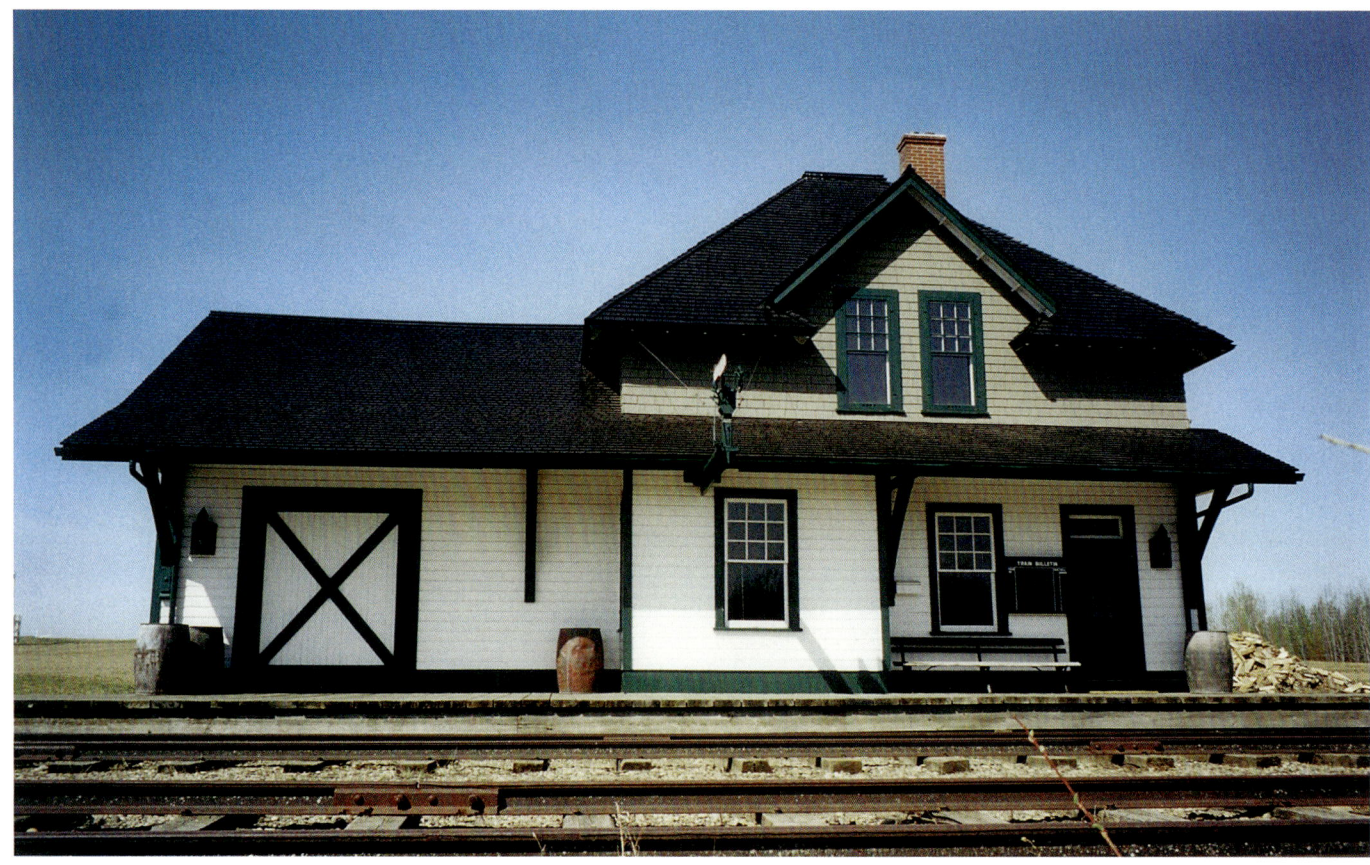

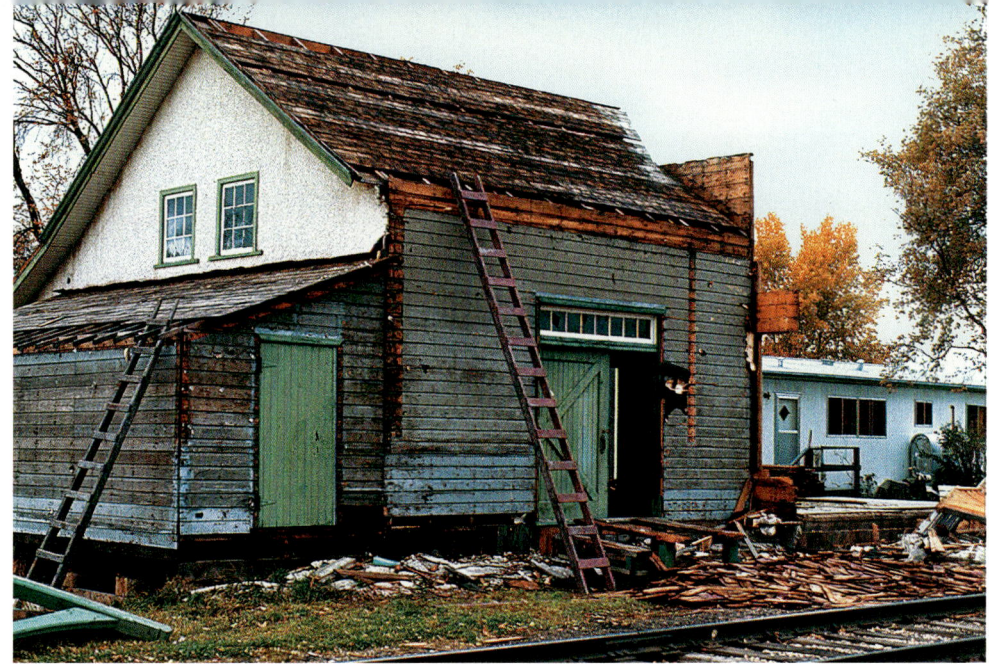

Exterior Paint Schedule—*CNR Phases II and III-B*: CNoR Grosse Isle, Manitoba
(Hilt Friesen Photo), 1974

The GTP began applying rough-cast stucco to the exterior of its wayside stations beginning in 1918. Its New 'Design A' Station (Type G) was the first western Canadian standard combination station to use the material as an "as-built" overall exterior finish. The CNR continued applying stucco to the exterior of existing wood-frame stations and section houses in western Canada and the practice became increasingly common after the 1920s, adding another element into the equation of colour schemes. The stucco finish helped keep company buildings warmer and more comfortable, significantly reduced heating costs and maintenance: on a stuccoed building—as on masonry ones—only the exposed wood and metal trim required painting. On some stations the stucco had a Cream/Yellow *wash instead of* White. *It is important to note that on stations where wooden walers were installed, the rough-cast stucco ended above the lowest waler. A float-finished (smooth) parging was applied below the bottom waler. The wall and dormer shingling above the main floor, when left unstuccoed, were usually painted the same colour as the body below. This photograph of the CNoR 3rd Class Station at Grosse Isle, Manitoba—under demolition in October 1974—reveals some interesting details. The siding on the main building and the coal shed lean-to did not line up, clearly indicating the latter was an addition. These standard coal sheds (Plan 110-56) were built onto many older CNoR stations. In most cases the windows on the end of the existing freight shed had to be raised to suit the roof of the addition. Here, the* Hyrib *lath and stucco applied to this building in 1941 was knocked off, exposing the original siding painted in the* Phase II Grey. *The bluish coloration may have been a wood preservative applied to these surfaces prior to the application of the lath and the stucco. In this case, the trim and doors were painted in the later* Phase III-B Green. *The sashes were* White, *an even later revision.*

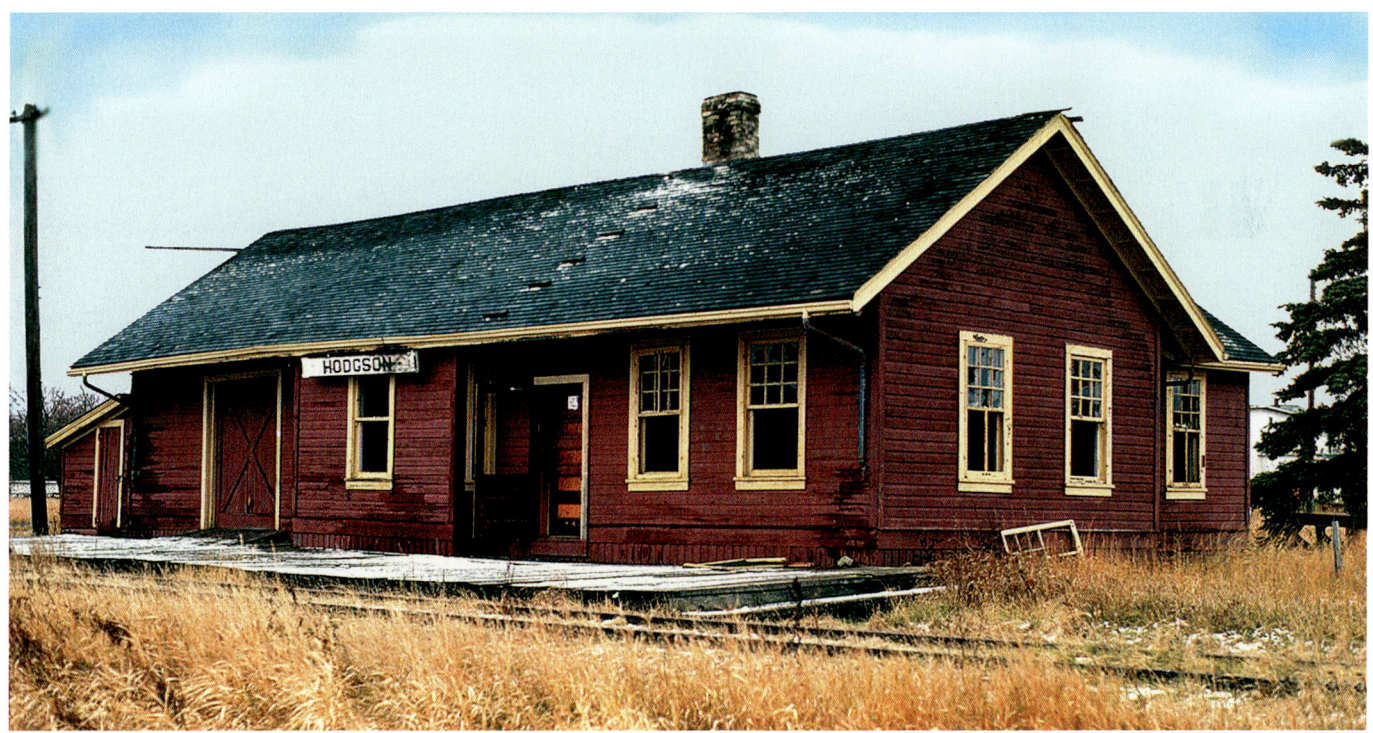

Exterior Paint Schedule—*CNR Phase III-A*: CNoR Hodgson, Manitoba (Hilt Friesen Photo), 1974

Red Oxide/Mineral Brown—*the colour most commonly associated with North American railways—was used extensively on rolling stock and buildings of all types. The CNR was no exception. The CNR's Standard Colours for 1949 revived a variant of the* Phase I *scheme for, "...[older] buildings with poor surfaces that have suffered from deferred maintenance or old buildings of size and type unsuited for present day traffic needs: body to be painted with an efficient* Red [Oxide] *paint, and sash painted* Cream." *On some buildings the sash was left* Oxide Red. *The classic CNR* Phase III-A Oxide Red-Cream *scheme, for unstuccoed stations such as Hodgson, Manitoba, was just a step above. The majority of the building was still one colour, but the* Cream *on the fascia, soffit, window trim and sash and brackets and beams added considerable "life." The roof was stained* Black. *A common variation on stations in the East was a browner shade of* Red Oxide *on the wainscoting, with lighter* Red Oxide *walls above, or the lighter* Red *on the entire body with the* Brownish-Red *on the shingling in the gables or dormers.*

Exterior Colour Schemes

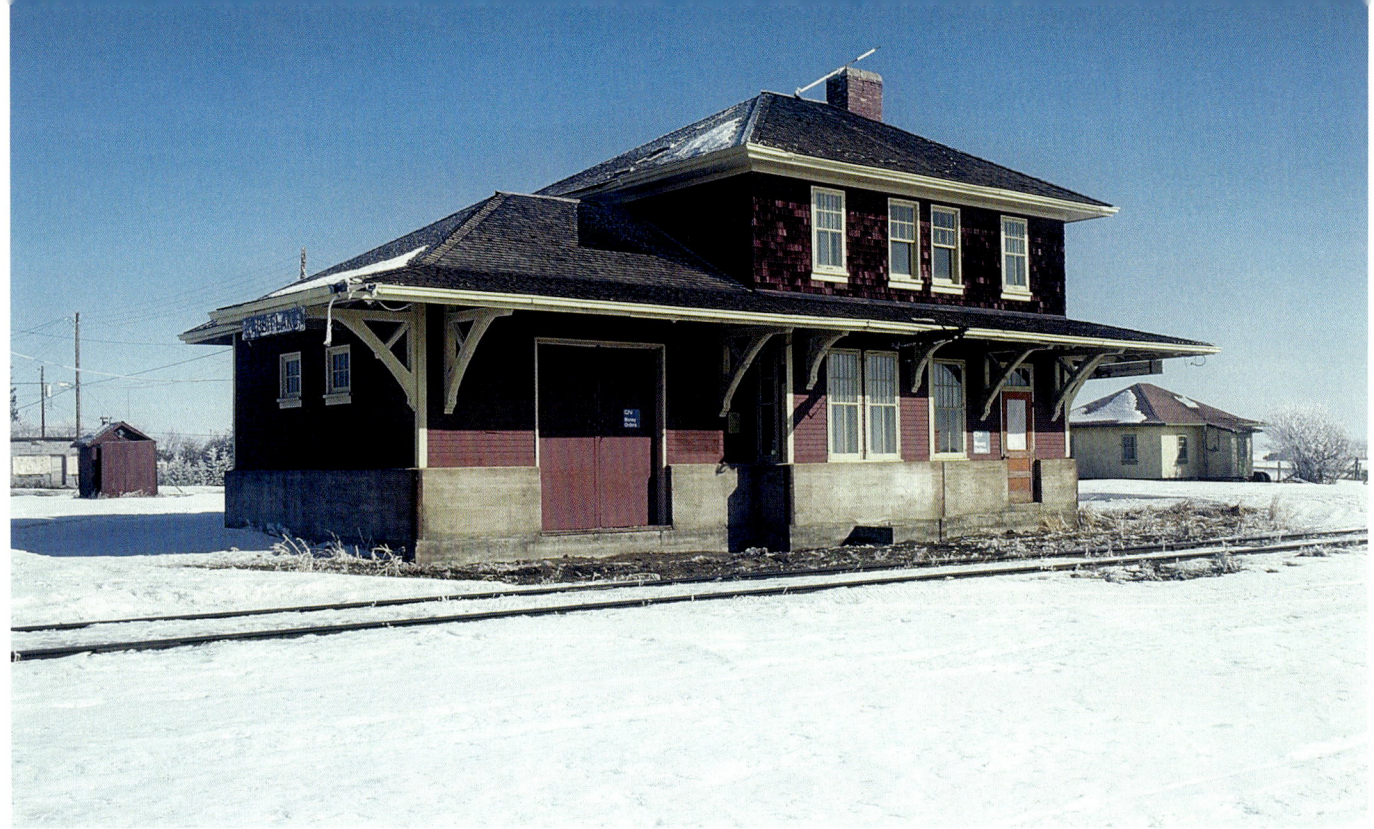

Exterior Paint Schedule—*CNR Phase III-A*: CNR Rabbit Lake, Saskatchewan (Charles W. Bohi Photo), 1981

Subsequently, the corner trims on some Phase III-A stations, such as this one at Rabbit Lake, Saskatchewan, were also painted Cream. *Like the brick on earlier stations, the concrete plinths were left unpainted. There was a great variation in the door treatments on the* Phase III-A *livery. Doors were usually* Red Oxide, *but some doors had* Red Oxide *stiles, rails and cross bracing with* Cream *panels. After about 1955, the window sashes were sometimes painted* Green, *and by the 1970s the sashes were sometimes* White. *The section house in the background was in the* Phase III-B *scheme.*

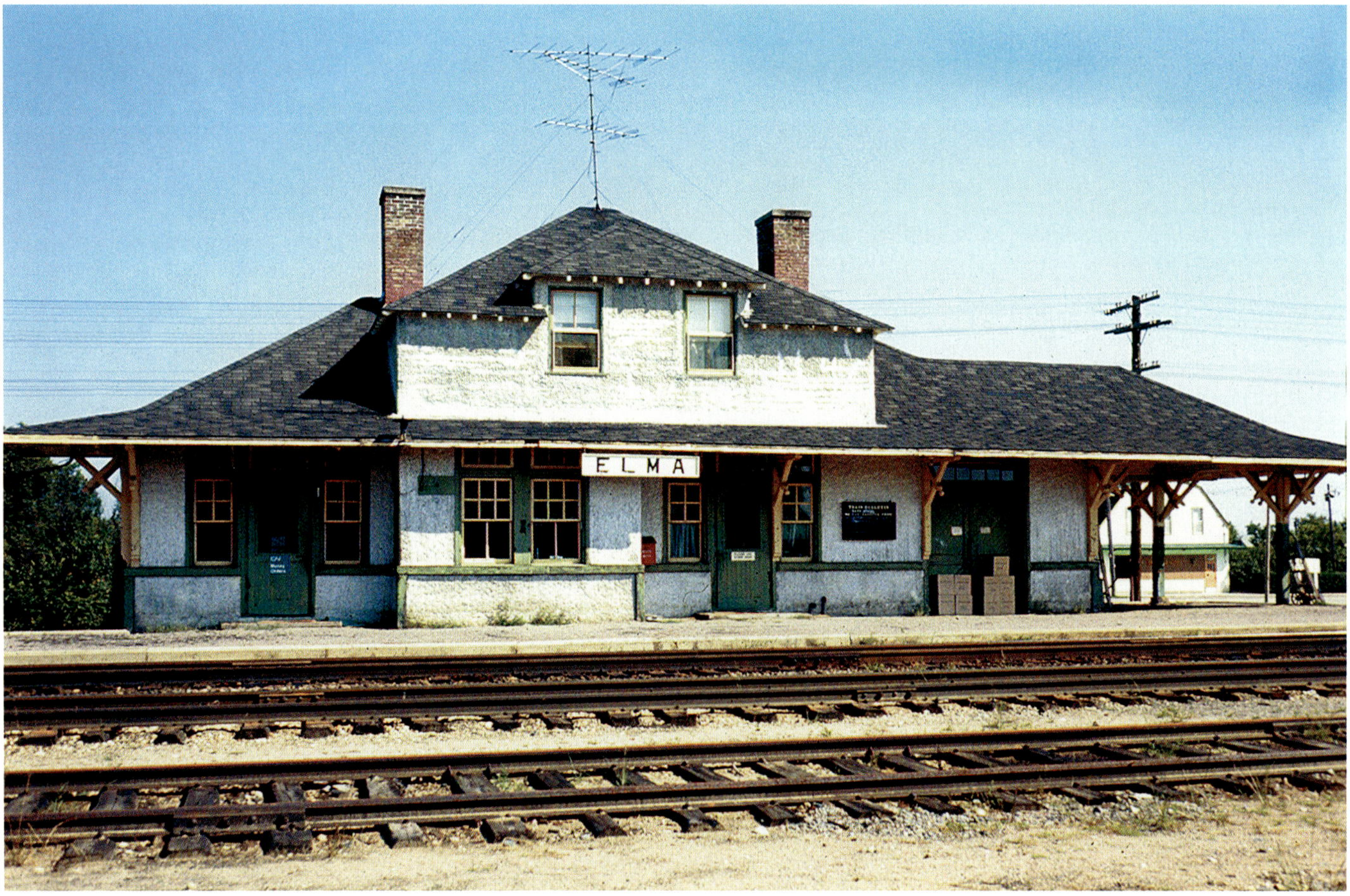

Exterior Paint Schedule—*CNR Early Phase III-B*; NTR Elma, Manitoba (Hilt Friesen Photo), 1975

Except for the recently applied Grey *asphalt roof shingles, the NTR No. 1 depot at Elma, Manitoba was a typical early* Phase III-B *scheme:* White *roughcast stucco,* Green *walers and trim,* Cream *fascia, soffit, window sashes, brackets and beams. Note the* Green *and* Cream *treatment of the roof overhang support posts (right). The roof in this 1949 scheme was stained* Red Oxide. *On some stations, the attached coal bin and the upper storey fascias were painted* Green. *Masonry stations were treated a bit differently; the window trims were painted* Cream *and the roofs were stained* Black. *Many stations painted in this early scheme were re-painted in kind, even after the standard was revised.*

**Exterior Paint Schedule—
CNR Later Phase III-B:
CNoR Kelwood, Manitoba**
(Hilt Friesen Photo), 1975

The muted colours, from years of weathering, are obvious on the 3rd Class depot at Kelwood, Manitoba. The later Phase III-B standard, issued about 1955, saw the fascia and brackets change colour from Cream to Green. The former Red Oxide roof shingles had evolved into a true Red. The White sashes on this station however, were a latter-day revision. Perhaps CNR no longer wanted to stock older colours such as the Cream, so the sashes were just painted the standard at that time, White. Other station details are also apparent in this excellent view: the scroll-sawn wood finial atop the dormer, the dressed rafter ends on the second storey eave and the typical enameled signs for the company's telegraph and express services. Note the surface-run wiring, indicating that electric power was added after the stucco was applied.

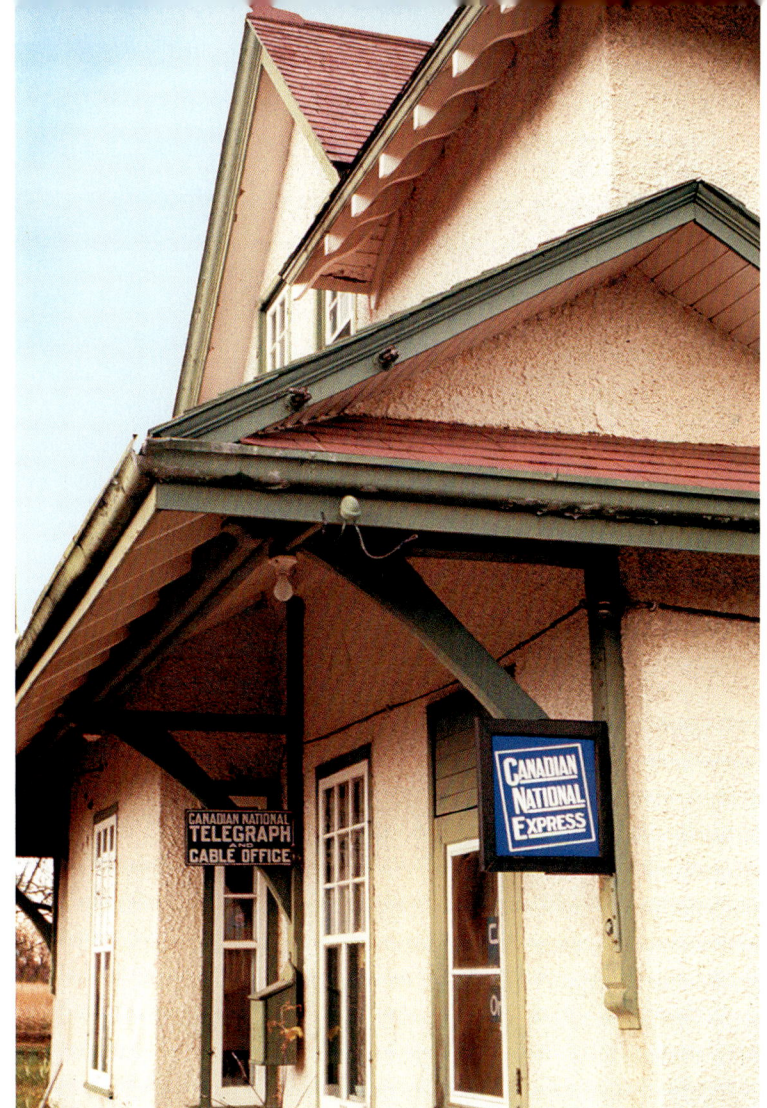

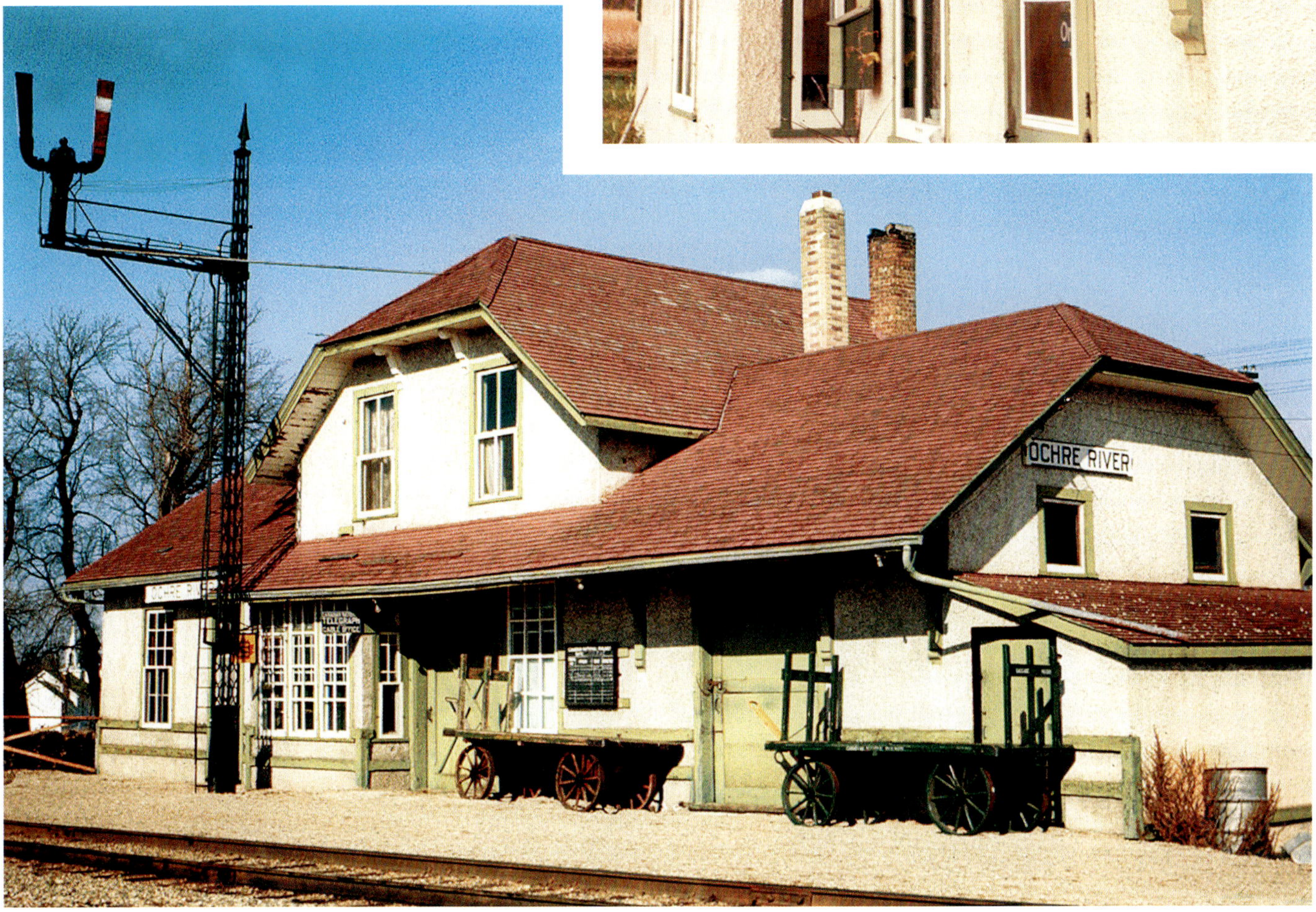

Exterior Paint Schedule—*CNR Later Phase III-B*: CNoR Ochre River, Manitoba (Hilt Friesen Photo), 1973

The combination station-and-section-house at Ochre River, Manitoba was erected in 1899. In 1973, the stucco, soffit, and the overhang brackets on the second floor were White and the walers and trim were Green, the later Phase III-B. Door colouration for buildings in the Phase III-B varied widely, with Green being the most common, with recorded instances of Green stiles, rails and cross bracing with Cream panels. Note the contrasting greens of the faded depot trim on the Ochre River building and the more recently painted express wagon on the platform. Both Greens were originally the same shade. This roof was stained Red, but on some stations the shingles were Black. The intricate cantilevered train-order signal mast—an interesting and unusual feature—was painted Black.

Exterior Colour Schemes

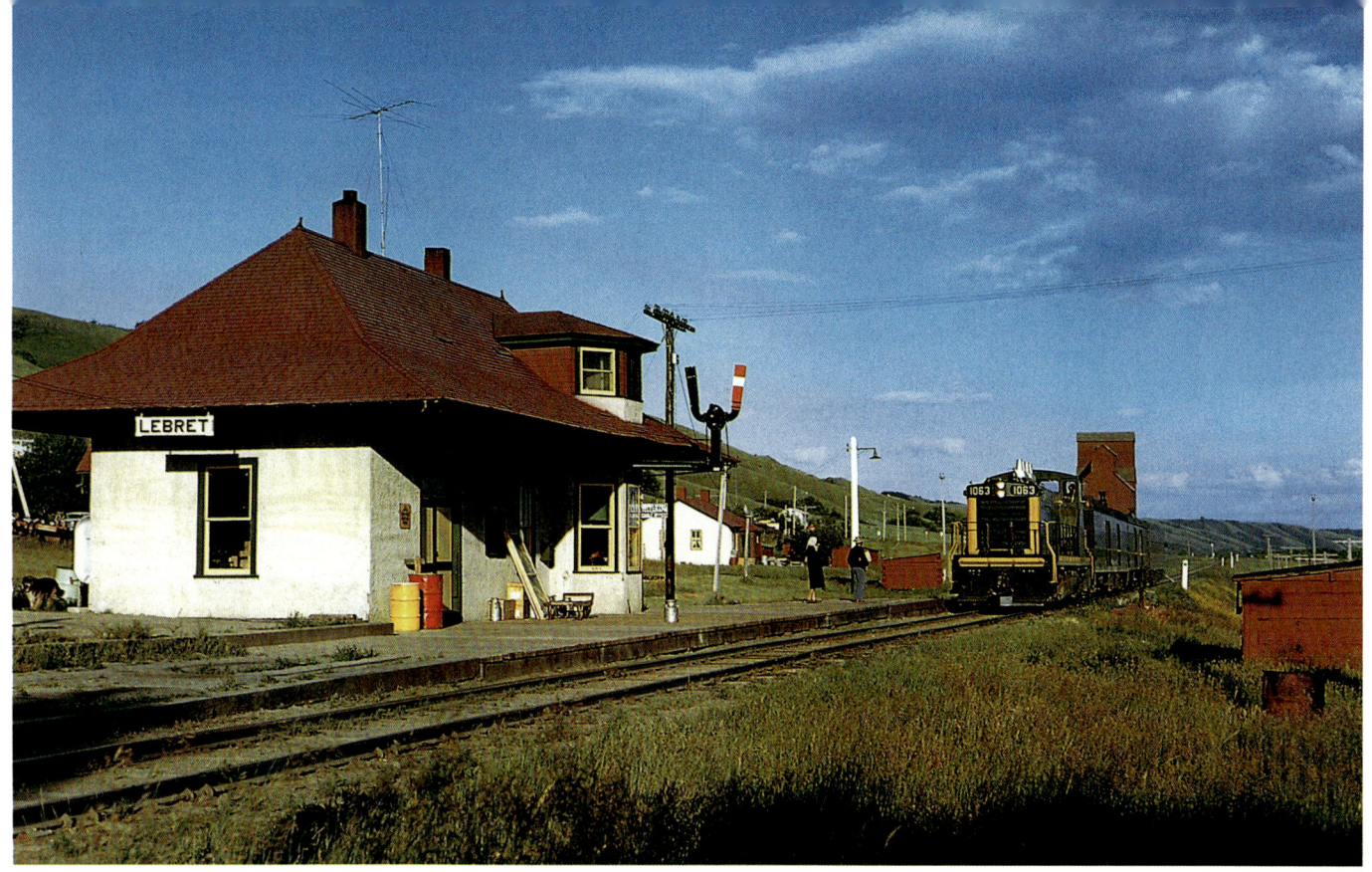

Exterior Paint Schedule—*CNR Later Phase III-B*: GTP Lebret, Saskatchewan (Robert J. Sandusky Photo), 1960

While this wonderful Robert Sandusky photo has appeared in numerous publications, it is worthy of inclusion here. The Lebret, Saskatchewan station exhibits some interesting colour variations. At first glance, it appears to be a standard later Phase III-B *scheme. The roof was* Red. *The body was* White *stucco; the unstuccoed dormer shingling was painted* Oxide Red. *Here the walers along the platform were omitted, an economy measure at about half the CNR stations that were stuccoed. The window sashes were* Cream *while the window and door trim were* Olive Green *rather than the usual* Green. *This is an odd coincidence, since parent Grand Trunk Railway's colours for its depots called for a* Grey *body with* Olive Green *wainscoting and* Cranberry *trim.*

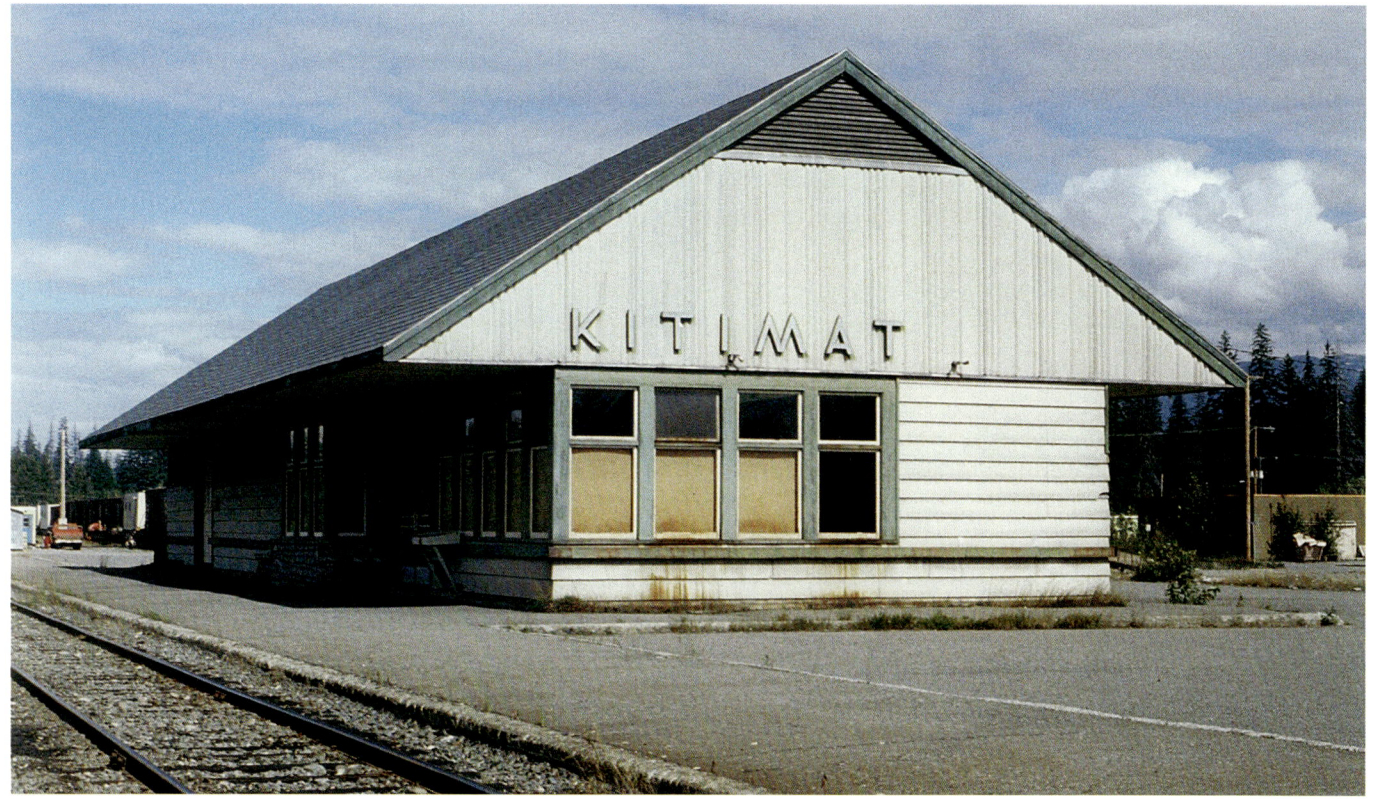

Exterior Paint Schedule—*CNR Phase III-C*: CNR Kitimat, British Columbia (Ken Haun Photo), 1978

The CNR continued upgrading the exterior of its stations and section houses with stucco well into the mid-1940s. By 1944 it also began using asbestos shingles and siding for its new buildings and for remedial work. These shingles were relatively easy to install and maintain, had fire resistive qualities, and had a certain aesthetic appeal. In contrast, the CPR seemed to favour Insul Brick®, *although both transcontinental lines used both products to some extent. The Kitimat, BC station, erected in 1955, was unique in layout and appearance, and used some of these new exterior finishes. The* Light Grey *asbestos shingle body and siding and* Green *trim recalled the earlier* Phase II *scheme.*

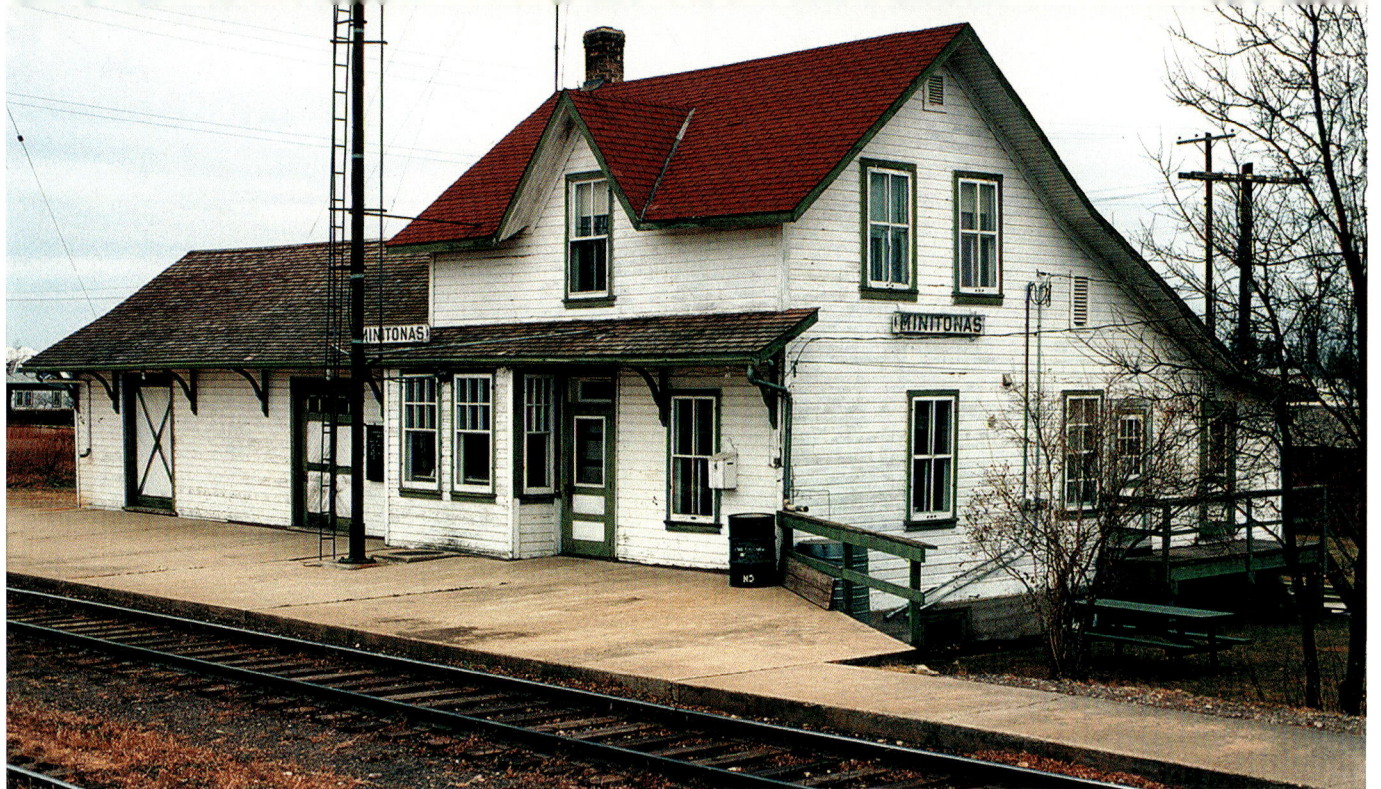

Exterior Paint Schedule—*CNR Phase III-C*: CNoR Minitonas, Manitoba   (Hilt Friesen Photo), 1976

When did the Phase III-C *colour scheme appear? It does not appear on the CNR's 1937 and 1948 colour cards. Yet, black and white photographs of the stations at Birch Hills, Saskatchewan (1948) and Minitonas, Manitoba (1953) show what was apparently the* White *and* Green *colour scheme. A possible explanation may lie with Colour Panel 1941 Standard, which has not been located. Perhaps the* Grey *of the 1937 scheme was changed to* White *to save lead during the War. Following the armistice the* White *and* Green *scheme may have fallen into disfavour, then re-surfaced again in the early 1950s. A surprisingly large number of the CNR's western combination and passenger stations were not "retro-finished" with stucco on the exterior. Indeed, on a few CNR Subdivisions only a handful or no stations at all were stuccoed: Albreda, Carman, Cowan, Cusson, Erwood, Hartney, Mantario, Miami, Oakland, Sheerness and Yale. The geographic randomness of this renders it inexplicable. The combination station-and-section house at Minitonas was erected in 1899 to Plan 100-99. Unlike the standard plan however, the "clipped gables" of the upper roof were built with conventional gables. This* Phase III-C *scheme is to the letter, except for the roof and the window sashes. The low roof was the standard* Black, *while the high roof was* Red. *In the latter years of service there appeared to have been little regard for the colour of the roof, particularly when asphalt shingles were installed. The sashes, which are supposed to be* Cream *in this livery, are the later* White. *Note the landing at the back door, and the picnic table. The* Phase III-C *scheme, apparently appearing in the early 1940s, recalled the* Phase II *scheme but with a* White *instead of* Grey *body and a different shade of* Green *for the trim.*

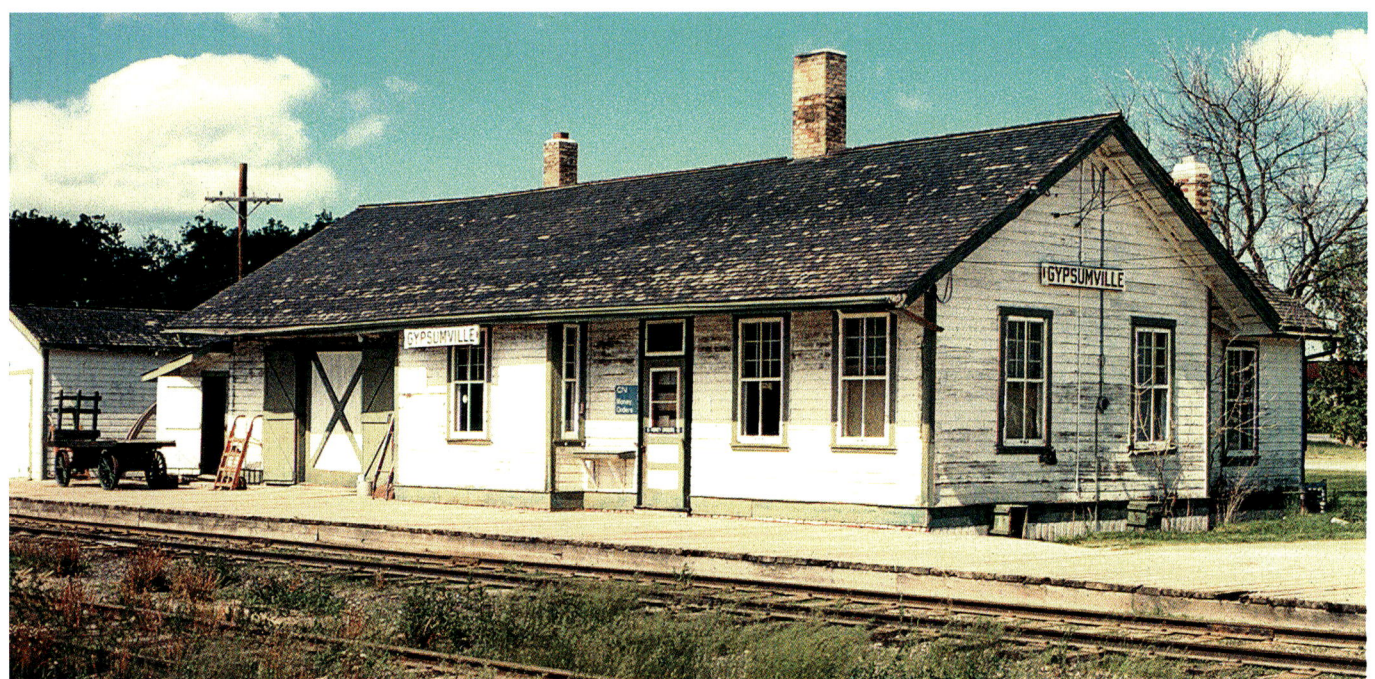

Exterior Paint Schedule—*CNR Phase III-C*: CNoR Gypsumville, Manitoba   (Hilt Friesen Photo), mid-1970s

The paint on the 4th Class Station at Gypsumville, Manitoba was considerably weathered when Hilt Friesen took this view in the mid-1970s. The Phase III-C *scheme was clearly intended to supersede the* Phase III-A *livery. Here, the former* Red Oxide *was showing through the* White *on the walls. Similarly, some patches of* Red *were evident on the* Black *shingle roof. Clearly, based on the poor paint coverage, the three-coat specification of old was not followed (blame it on the B&B Department?). The fascia, sill, and the door, window and corner trim were* Green. *The soffit and sashes were* White, *the later CNR standard. The stiles and rails of the doors and the cross bracing on the sliding door were* Green, *while the door panels were* White.

Exterior Colour Schemes

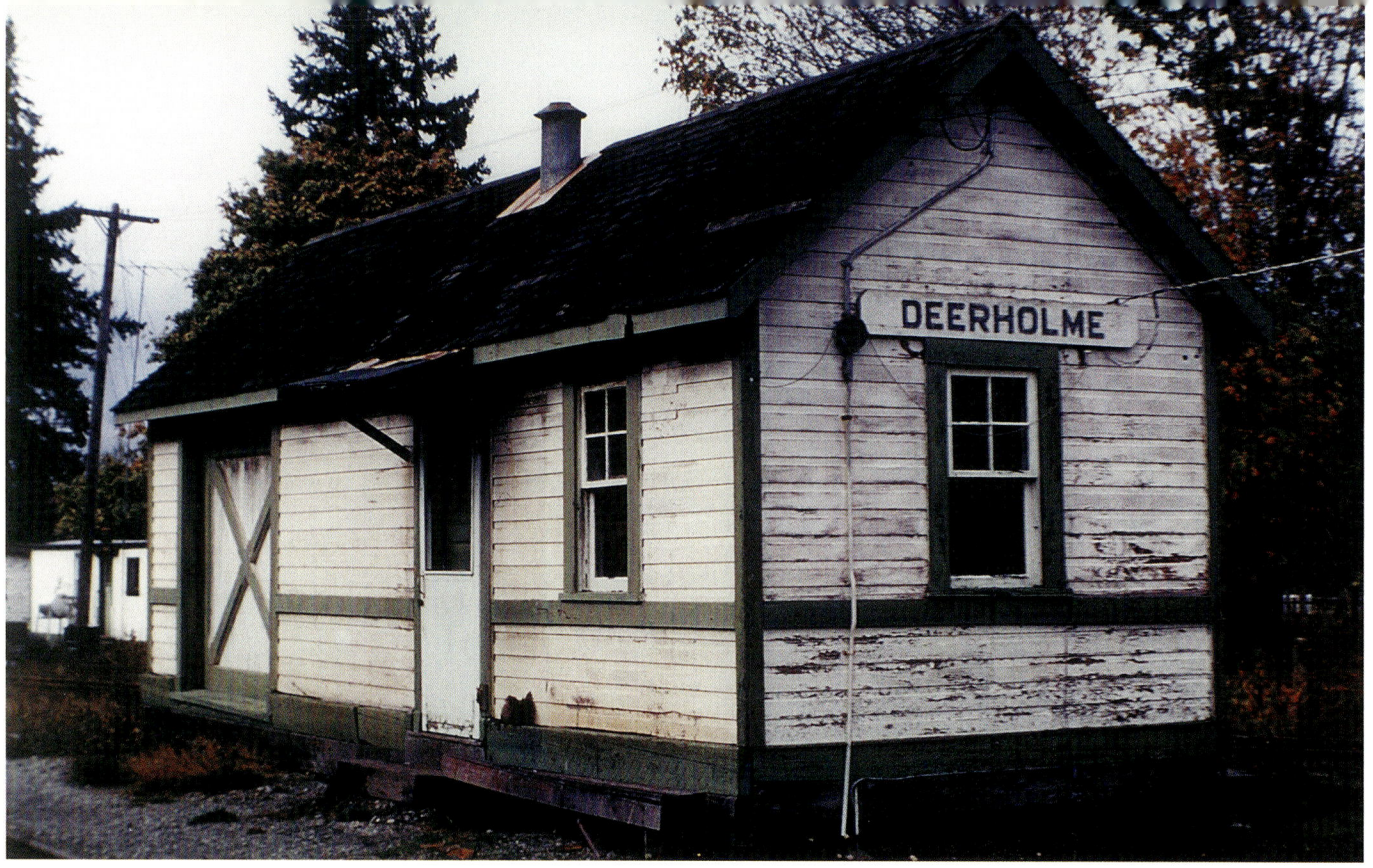

Exterior Paint Schedule—*CNR Phase III-C*: CNoR Deerholme, B.C. (AL LILL PHOTO), 19??

The Deerholme, BC freight and passenger shelter (Plan 100-41) in the Phase III-C *scheme. The belt-line trim—just below windowsill level around the building—and a similar trim above the windows on the end walls (not on this example), were traits of early versions of Plan 100-41. These simple "paste-on" details were later eliminated, likely to economize. Note the awning over the door, a local adaptation to shed rainwater and snow away from the entrance.*

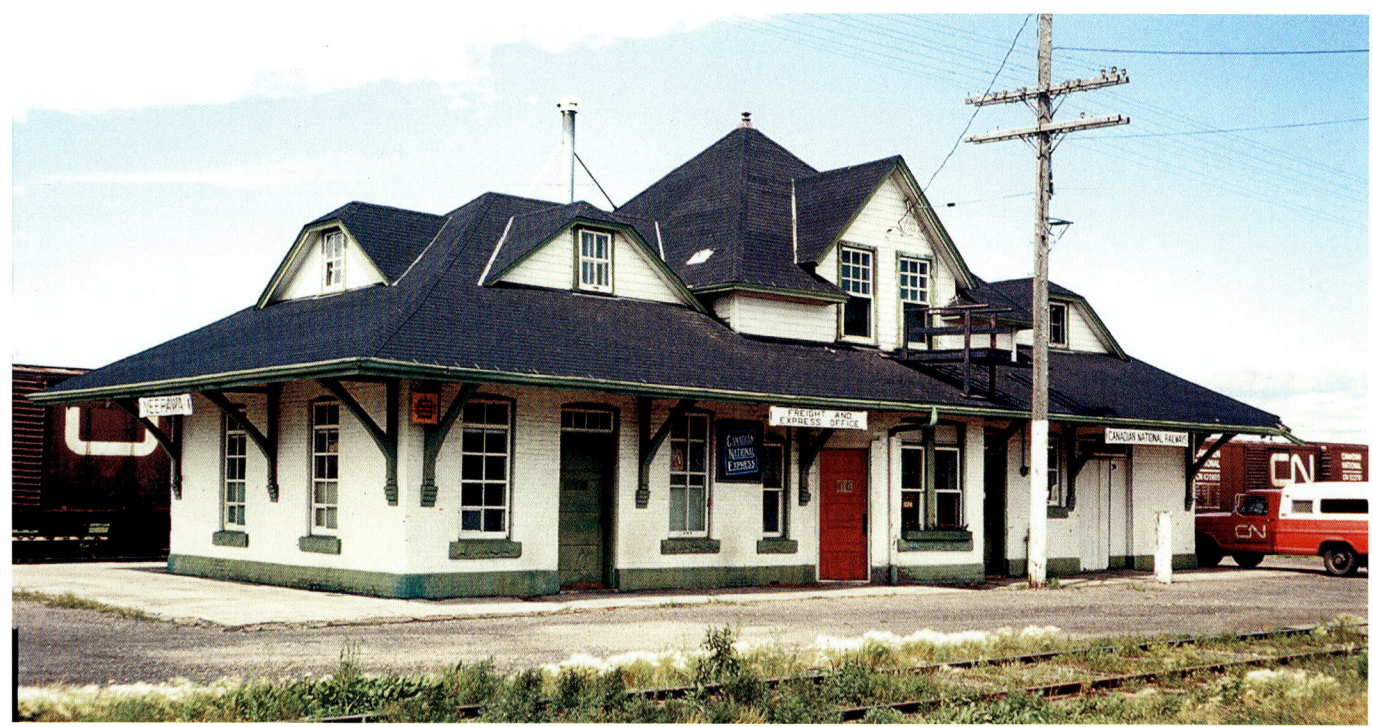

Exterior Paint Schedule—*CNR Phase III-C*: CNoR Neepawa, Manitoba (HILT FRIESEN PHOTO), 1973

Neepawa, Manitoba was one of only a few masonry versions of the CNoR's 2nd Class Station. The walls of the main floors were of brick while the second storey was of wood-frame. The front was virtually identical to the rear, shown here. As originally constructed, most early CNoR depots utilized red face brick and stone plinths, caps and sills, all of which usually appeared grey. The roof shingles were stained Grey. *St. Boniface, Manitoba #2 utilized local granite (grey) face brick with a reddish mortar. The brick and the stone sills on all CNoR masonry stations were unpainted and subsequent CNR specifications mandated they remain so. By the late 1950s, for whatever reason, the Neepawa station was painted in the* Phase III-C *scheme. The walls and upper storey were* White. *The overhang brackets, doors, trim, including the stone windowsills, were* Green. *The bottom five courses of brick around the base of the building were also painted* Green. *Window sashes were* White. *The roof was either* Grey *or a very faded* Black. *The door to the office was later painted* Orange, *corresponding with the 1960s image. Note the painting of the rainwater leader,* Green *top and bottom,* White *along the wall. The power pole was also painted* White *from the ground up to the eave line. This depot was acquired by the Beautiful Plains Museum and has since been modified and repainted.*

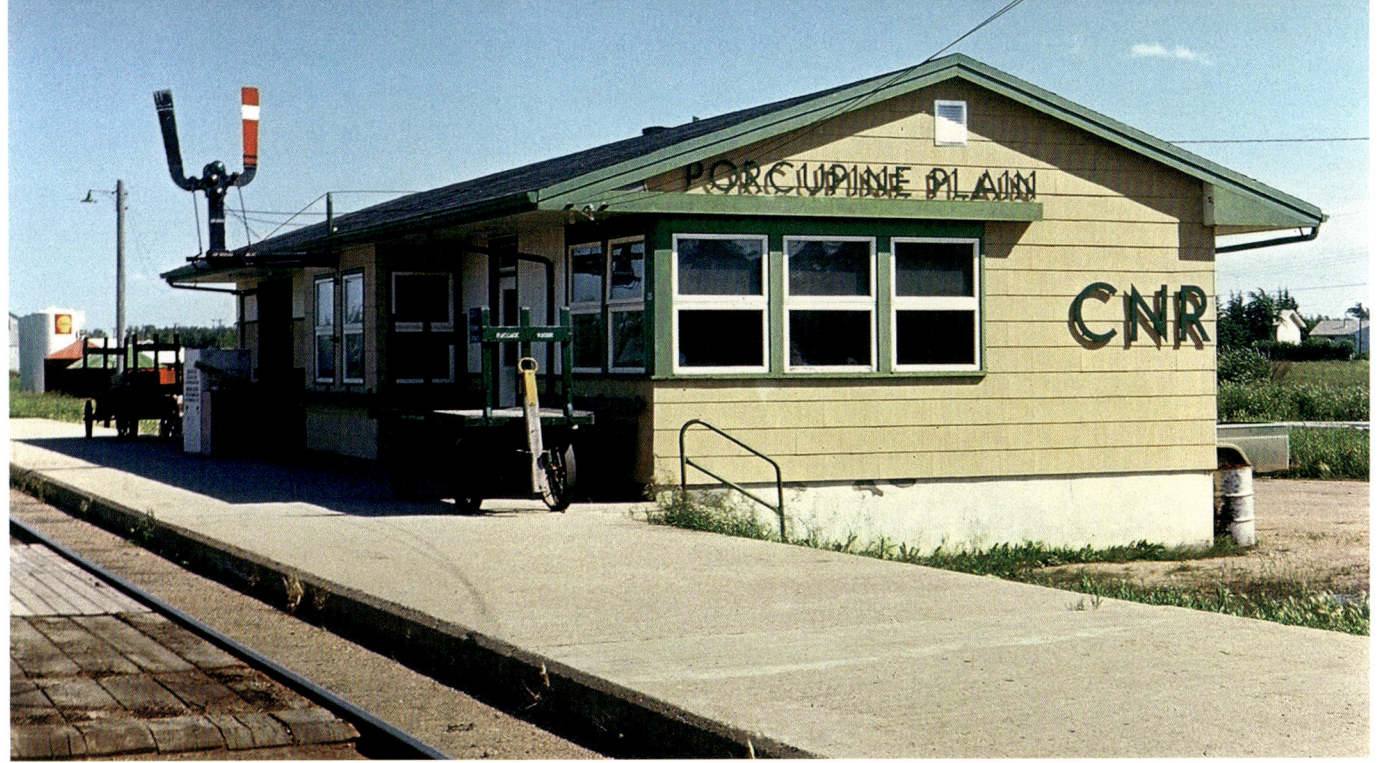

Exterior Paint Schedule—*CNR Phase HBR*:
CNR Porcupine Plain, Saskatchewan #3 (George Else Photo, David Else Collection), 1967

The depots on the line to Hudson Bay appear to have had a distinct livery that was later adopted, in modified form, on some adjoining CNR divisions. These HBR colours were from the standard CNR range, primarily Cream *and* Red Oxide. *In the mid-1950s, the body of the special station at Churchill, Manitoba was comprised of* Grey *asbestos shingles, the walers and trim were* Red Oxide *and the roof was* Red. *At Wabowden, Manitoba the body was mostly* Cream. *The Porcupine Plain, Saskatchewan #2 depot, built in 1959, was representative of the CNR's latest "bungalow style" depot, but clearly borrowed elements of the HBR livery: the* Cream *horizontal wall siding with* White *transite paneling above, paler than CNR standard* Green *trim,* White *sash and* Black *roof. An experimental colour scheme? The CNR 3rd Class station at Hyas, Saskatchewan had a* White *roughcast stucco body with an unpainted concrete plinth. The fascia, brackets and trim were* Red Oxide *while the window sash was* White. *The former* Green *showing through the* Red Oxide *paint on the fascia, clearly indicates that this HBR scheme was a later adaptation. The station at Stenen, Saskatchewan was treated similarly. All of these variations are loosely designated as the* HBR Scheme.

CNR Hyas, Saskatchewan #2 (Hilt Friesen Photo), 1977

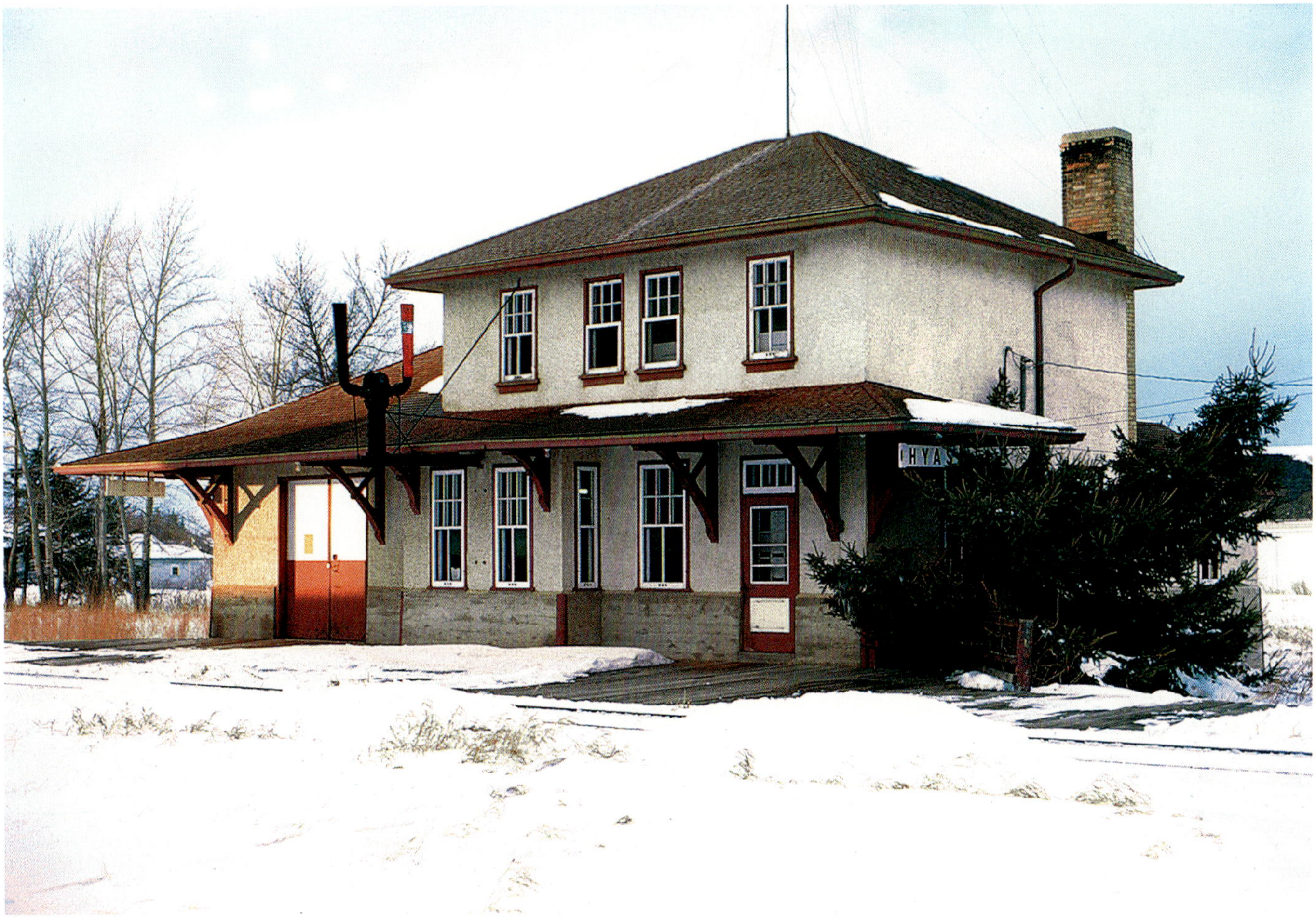

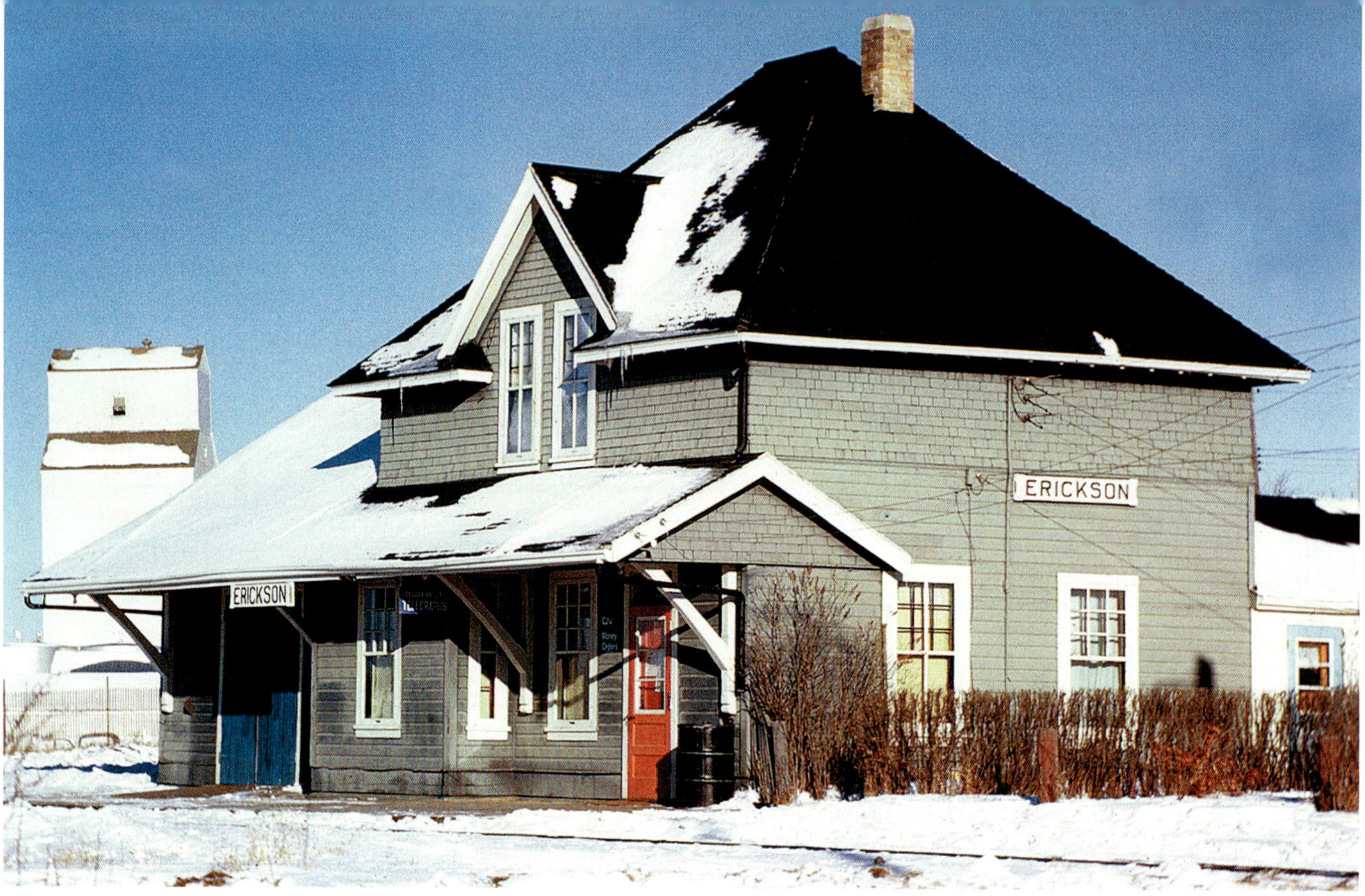

Exterior Paint Schedule—*CNR Phase IV*: CNoR Erickson, Manitoba #2 (Hilt Friesen Photo), 1973

In 1961 the new CNR corporate image emerged, which included a makeover of the company's diesel locomotives in an Orange–Grey–Black *colour scheme. The CNR's* Phase IV Red–White–Blue *colour scheme for stations appears to have coincided with the introduction of the CNR's new passenger service marketing promotion of the same name in April 1962. The siding/stucco body was* Grey, *evoking the earlier GTR and CNR's Western Lines body colours. The door and window frames, support brackets, walers and rainwater leaders were painted* Black, *while the window sashes, fascias, eavestroughing and soffit were painted* White. *All "public" doors were* Orange, *while all "service" and "freight" doors were* Blue. *Even so, there were considerable variations, some the polar opposite of the supposed standard. The unstuccoed station at Erickson, Manitoba received the "full treatment," except that the brackets and the door and window frames were* White *instead of* Black. *The unstuccoed lean-to at the rear was also painted* White.

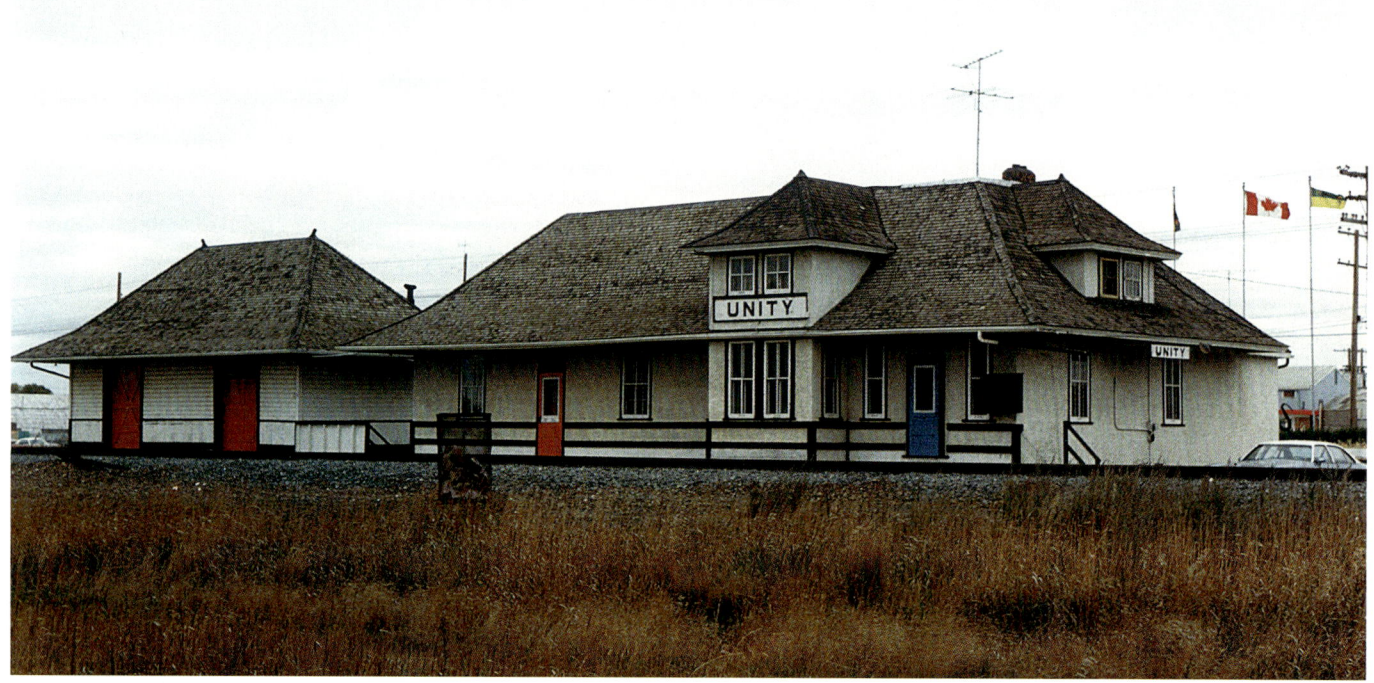

Exterior Paint Schedule—*CNR Phase IV*: GTP Unity, Saskatchewan (Keith Ewart Photo), 1985

Unity, Saskatchewan station and its attendant baggage-express shed looked right at home in the Phase IV *scheme. The stucco on the station and the siding on the shed were both* White. *Window and door trims and the walers were* Black, *with* White *window sashes. According to the standard, the* Blue *door leading to the waiting room should have been* Orange, *and the other three doors should have been* Blue. *It retained its original station name board over the bay window. This station was sold in 1993 and relocated to the east end of town, where it was converted into a restaurant. The baggage-express shed was moved to the Saskatchewan Railway Historical Association's museum near Saskatoon, where it is a feature exhibit painted in GTP Phase B colours.*

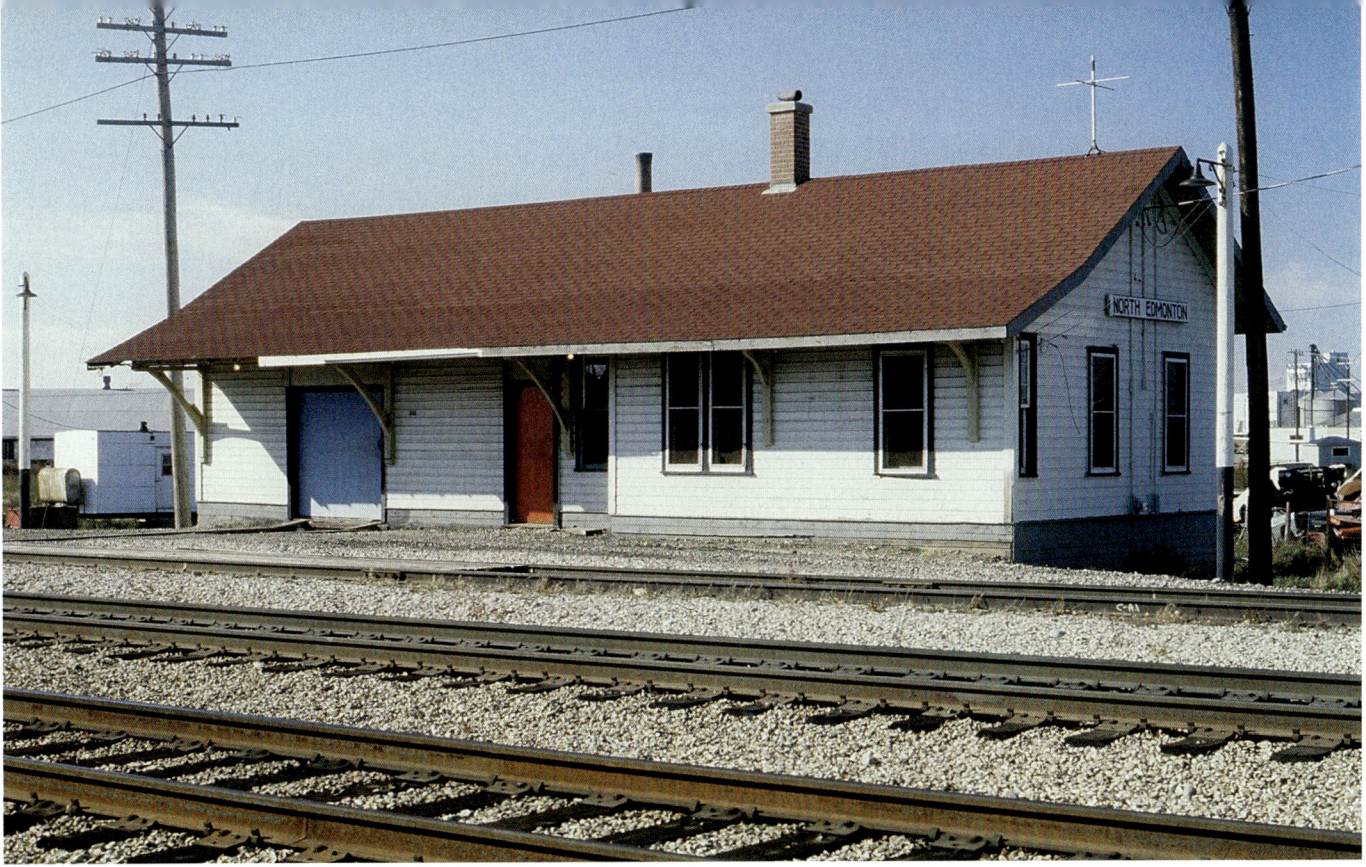

Exterior Paint Schedule—*CNR Phase IV*: CNoR North Edmonton, Alberta　　　(Leslie S. Kozma Photo), 1978

On the North Edmonton Jct. depot the wood siding and corner trims were White. *Window and doorframes were* Black *while the sashes were* White. *The fascia and the V-joint vertical siding on the skirt below the sill were* Grey. *In an unusual variation of the* Phase IV, *the overhang brackets were painted a* Pale Yellow. *By 1978 the roof had* Red *asphalt shingles.*

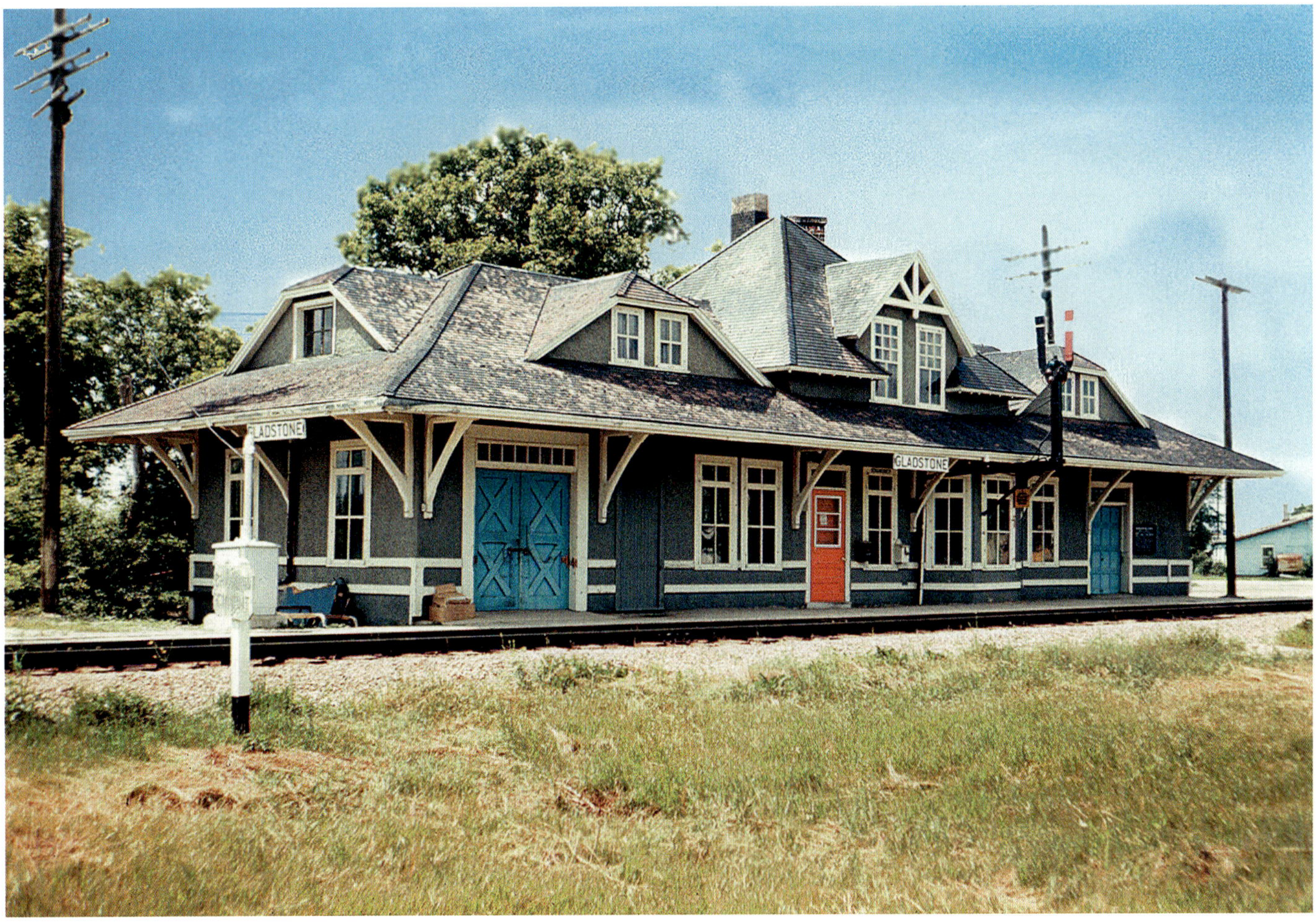

Exterior Paint Schedule—*CNR Phase IV*: CNoR Gladstone, Manitoba　　　(Hilt Friesen Photo), 1975

The 2nd Class station at Gladstone, Manitoba Phase IV *scheme featured a* Grey *stucco body. The fascia and gutters, walers, brackets and main floor door and window trim were* Pale Yellow. *The dormer fascias and second floor windows and sashes were painted* White. *Some of the former* Red *stain showed through the* Black *on the roof shingles.*

Exterior Colour Schemes

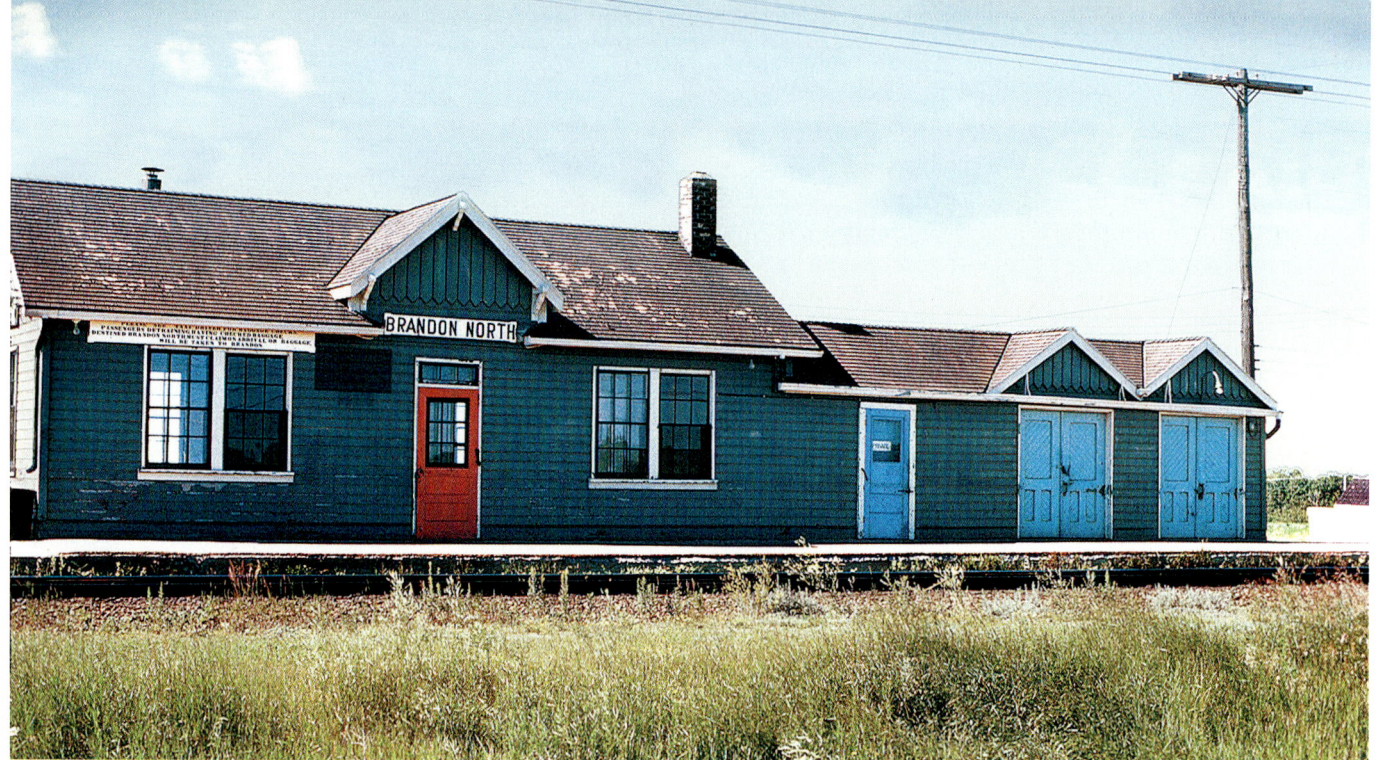

Exterior Paint Schedule—*CNR Phase IV*: CNR Brandon North, Manitoba (Hilt Friesen Photo), 1974

In 1909, the Brandon Board of Trade considered some of the new "upstart" towns on the GTP main line as threats to its hegemony over regional trade. Seeking a direct connection with the GTP, it lobbied political friends in Ottawa. Finally, after much agitation, in 1911 the GTP secured a subsidy to build a spur, from its main line at Harte, to connect with the existing Great Northern station in downtown Brandon. Grading was halted on October 1913 by a deepening economic recession. Although numerous large bridges had been built or were underway, no steel was ever laid on the line. Following consolidation of the CNoR and GTP, in 1920 the CNR negotiated a deal with the Canadian Pacific Railway and a transfer track was installed at the crossing just west of Knox. This indirect rail connection via the CPR apparently satisfied Brandon's business interests. Subsequently, for rail passengers, the new station of Brandon North was established between Knox and Levine, an "18-minute" taxi ride from downtown Brandon. In 1940 the CNR inaugurated a motor truck Express service between Brandon North and its namesake city. The following year the CNR built what was essentially a large passenger shelter (Plan 100-294), rather inconveniently located on the high, narrow embankment adjacent to the highway. The small annex to the east (right) was for stowing baggage and express wagons. The sign above the window read, "Please see that driver for baggage check passengers detraining having checked baggage destined Brandon North must claim on arrival or baggage will be taken to Brandon." The early Phase IV *scheme in July 1974:* Grey *body,* White *trim,* Black *roof and sashes, and* Blue *and* Orange *doors. In the later version, shown in December 1977, the body was painted* White *and the sill trim was* Black. *Perhaps because the* Grey *body made many stations look too dark and austere, the* Phase IV Red–White–Blue *scheme was revised. Commencing about early 1965, the siding or stucco on the body of some depots was painted* White. *The change to the* White *body certainly brightened the building's appearance. Examples of both* Phase IV *schemes were found system-wide. Little changed with the VIA Rail take-over of passenger services on the CNR in 1976 as most of the stations were leased to VIA but they continued to be maintained by Canadian National.*

CNR Brandon North, Manitoba (Hilt Friesen Photo), 1977

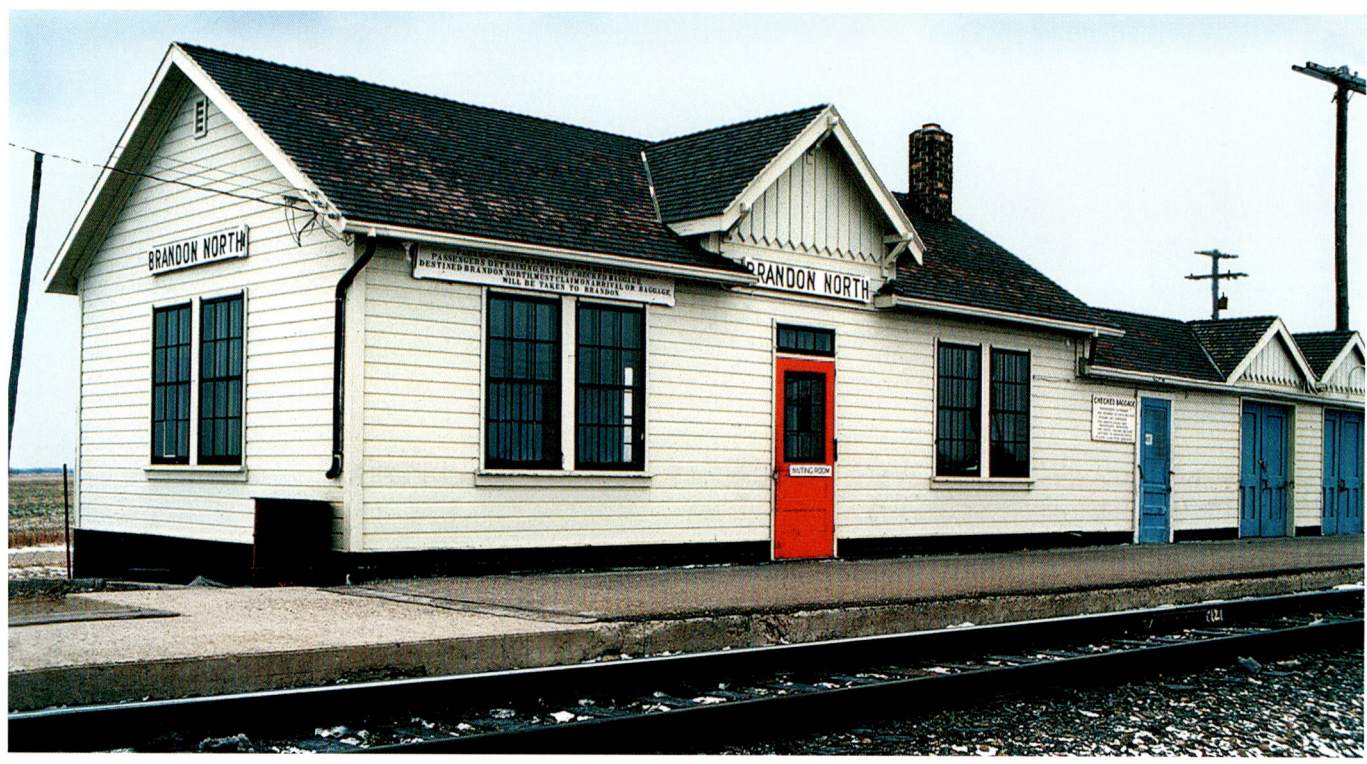

60   Canadian National's Western Stations

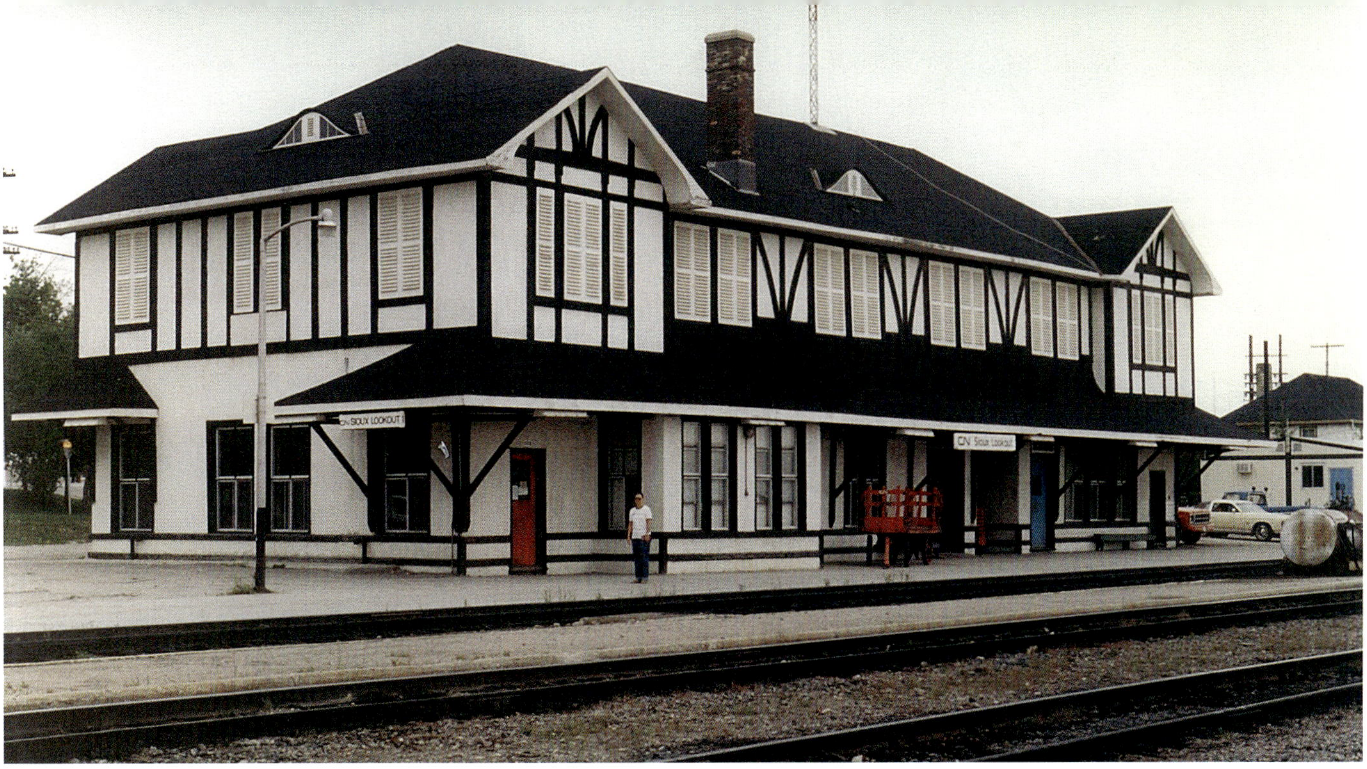

Exterior Paint Schedule—*CNR Phase IV*: NTR Sioux Lookout, Ontario (AL LILL PHOTO), 1982

The CNR Phase IV *scheme was used on all sizes of station buildings, including shelters. At Sioux Lookout, Ontario, the smattering of color on the doors was overwhelmed by the* White *body and the* Black *roof and trim. The symmetry, the half-timbering effect and the shuttered windows give this station a very European appearance. As of this writing, it was still being used by VIA Rail.*

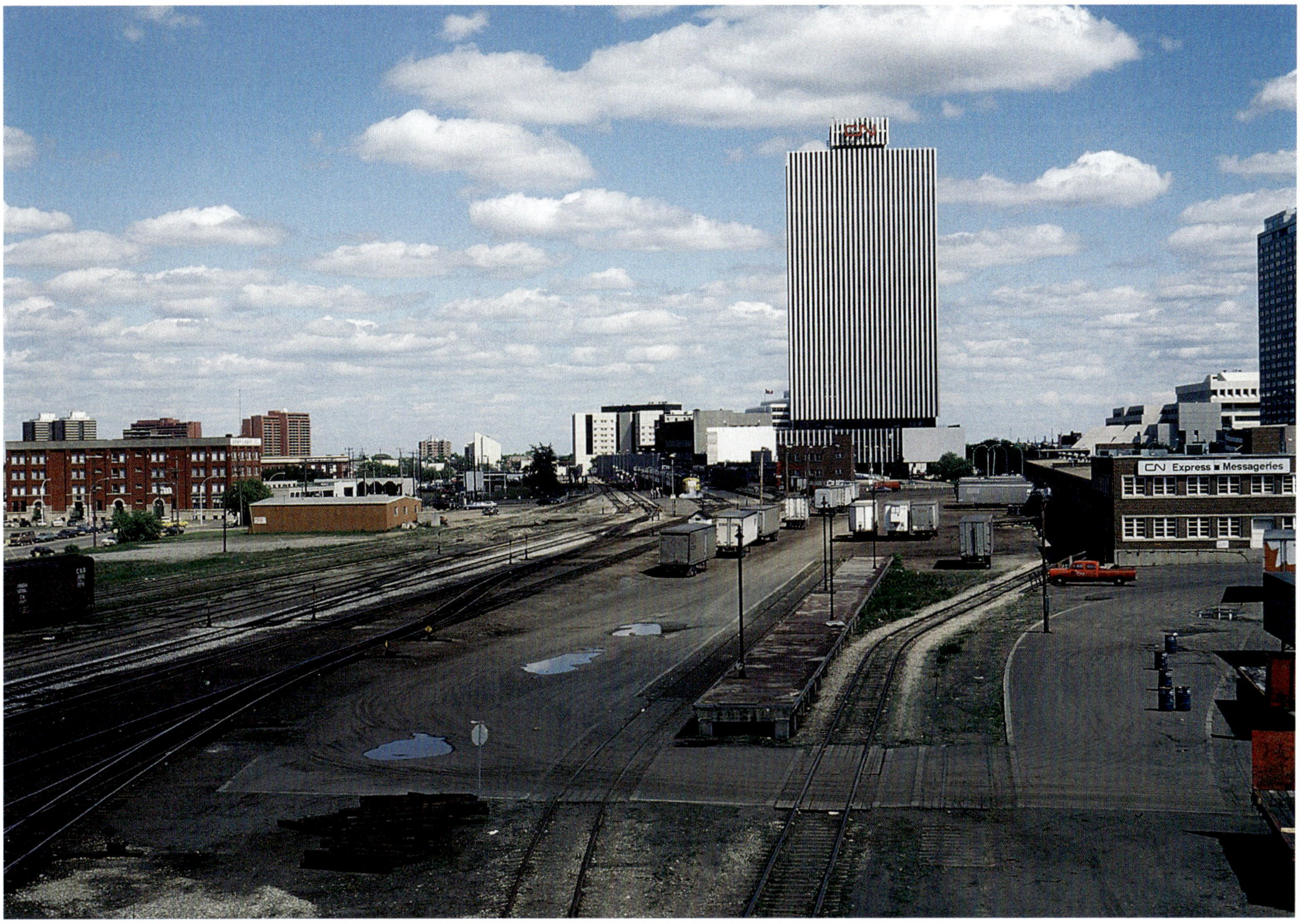

Exterior Paint Schedule—*CNR Phase IV*: CN Tower Edmonton, Alberta #4 (AL LILL PHOTO), 1985

The Phase IV *scheme reached its zenith with the construction of new office towers on CNR properties in Edmonton (1966) and Saskatoon (1969). Both buildings utilized the* Black *and* White, *topped by the CN's "wet noodle" logo in* Orange, *to create a bold corporate statement. In Saskatoon, the railway facilities were removed to the outskirts of the city. In Edmonton, the tracks were left at grade while a new station was incorporated into the basement of the 26-storey development. The flanking wings for baggage, express and mail—part of the former station—were retained. Precast concrete accent panels, painted* White—*were added to the fenestration along the south facades of both wings. The brick and stone facing street side were painted* Grey, *while the trackside remained unpainted. All of the doors received the standard treatment of* Blue *or* Orange.

EXTERIOR COLOUR SCHEMES

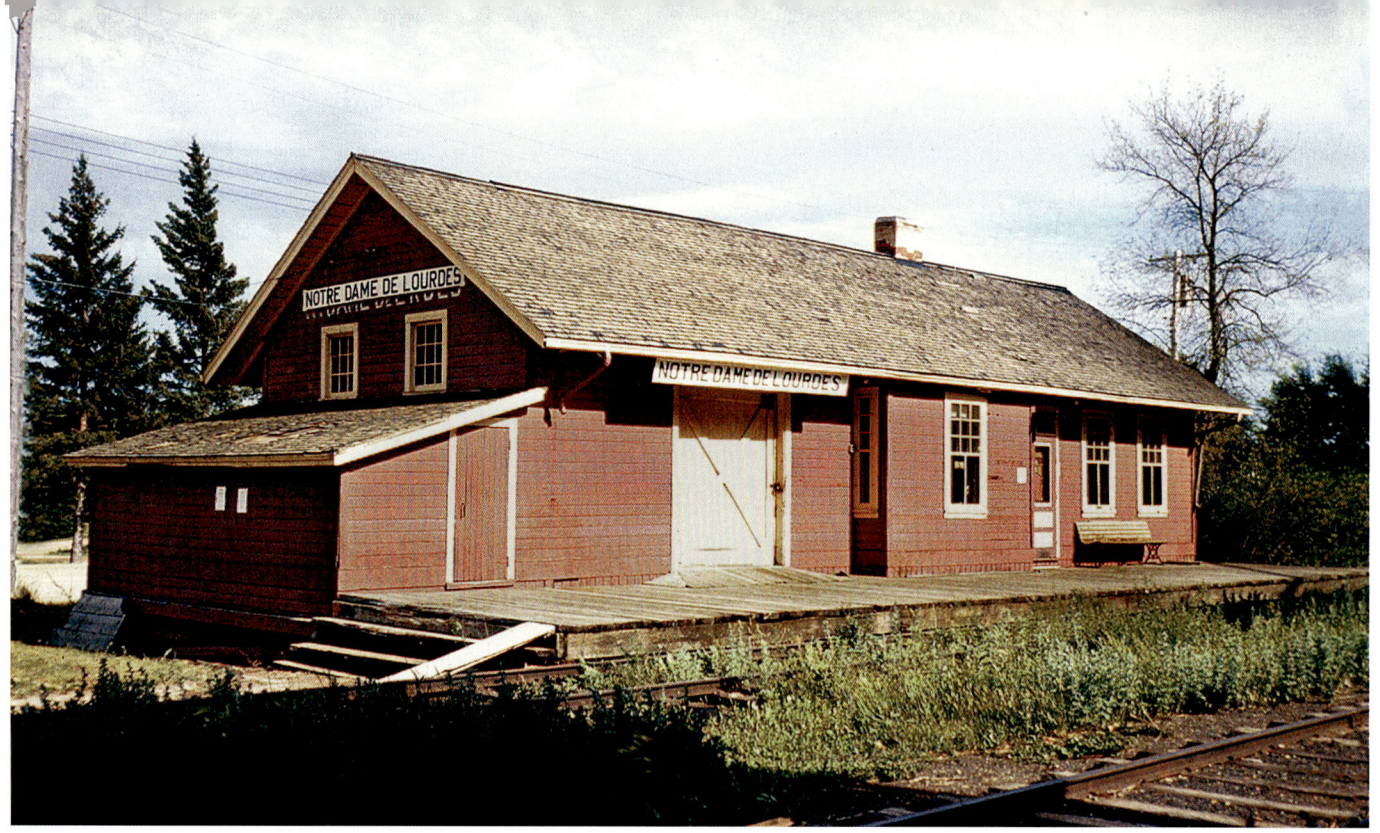

Exterior Paint Schedule—CNoR Notre Dame de Lourdes, Manitoba (Hilt Friesen Photo), 1973

Identification standards for stations were legion, and it would take a separate book to explain them all in detail. On the CNR, names were either painted directly onto the end walls (or sometimes onto the roof) or painted onto a flat wooden or sheet metal name board that was either secured to the end walls or roof, or hung from the eaves. All of these methods had also been employed by the Canadian Northern on its depots and shelters. When painting the name directly onto the building, for the Phase III-A *scheme, the* Cream-colored *letters were 12 inches (three boards) high; those on the stucco walls of* Phase III-B *stations were the same height, but were painted* Black. *In either case the station name was centred on the end walls, but its vertical positioning seemed to be at the discretion of the painter. On the waiting room end of the 3rd Class station, for instance, the location of the painted name was sometimes dictated by the prominent moulding between the wall shingling and the drop siding. On about half the CNoR 3rd Class depots, this moulding was removed prior to the application of the stucco. Here, at Wiseton, Saskatchewan, the name was painted about 4" above the moulding. In other cases, the name was higher above the moulding or centered between the top of the window trim and the bottom of the moulding. On the freight shed end of the Wroxton, Saskatchewan station, the name was painted at the same height as that on the waiting room end. This was not always the case; the respective locations of the lettering on either end of a depot were not always coordinated. At Shellmouth, Manitoba, the bottom of the letters was 12" above the moulding, while on the freight shed end the bottom of the letters was lower, practically at the top of the window header. By the early 1970s the stations on a handful of western Subdivisions still had their names painted onto their end walls: Albreda, Drumheller, Elrose, Mantario, Oyen, Sheerness, Tonkin and Yale. Some, such at Notre Dame de Lourdes, Manitoba had the newer name board installed partially obscuring the older painted station name. CNR station name boards of the "modern" era had 8" high* Gloss Black *lettering on an 11" high sign on a* Pale Yellow *field, later changed to* White. *The edges of station name boards were either chamfered or had a perimeter wood trim; both were usually painted a* Gloss Black. *Name boards were lag-bolted into the walls, suspended from metal strap brackets under the eaves or gables, or set on the awning over the bay window with a pair of metal supports bolted onto the roof (Wroxton). In some cases, the tops of these awning name boards were braced back to the roof with metal "tie straps" at either end.*

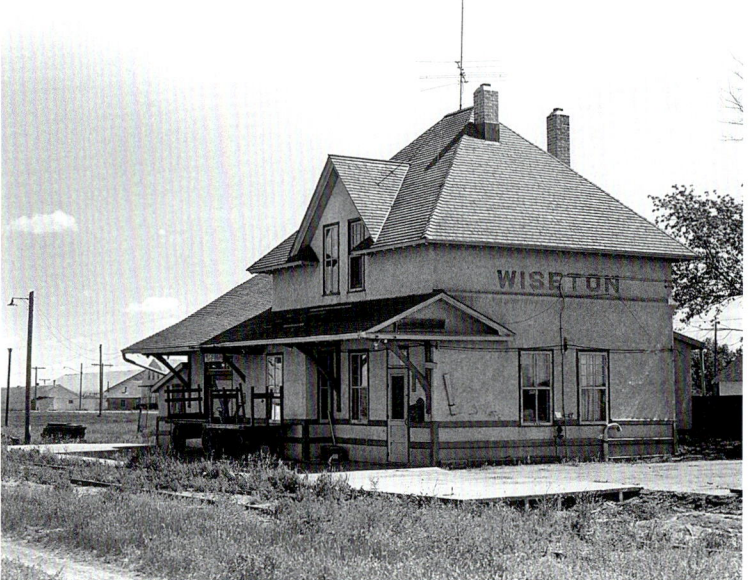

CNoR Wiseton, Saskatchewan (Charles W. Bohi Photo), 1971

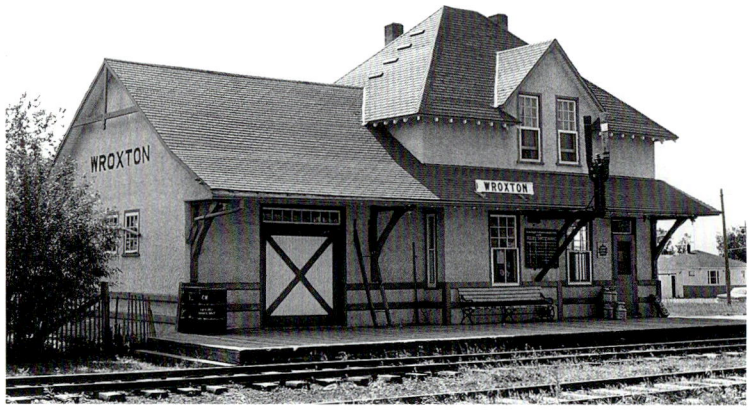

CNoR Wroxton, Saskatchewan (Charles W. Bohi Photo), 1971

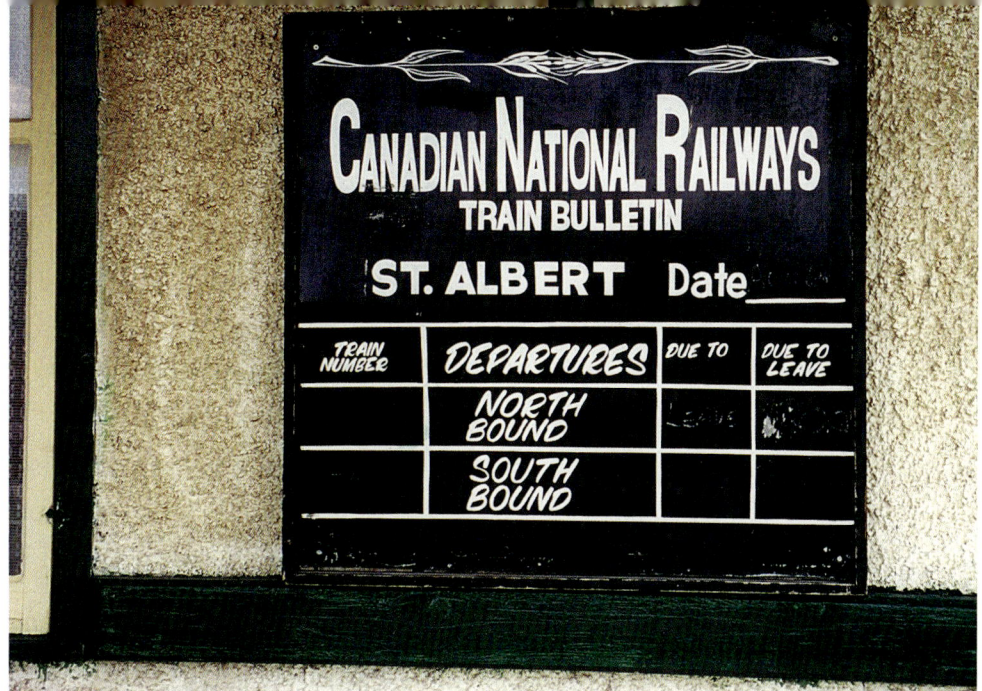

St. Albert, Alberta (L.S. Kozma Photo), 2001

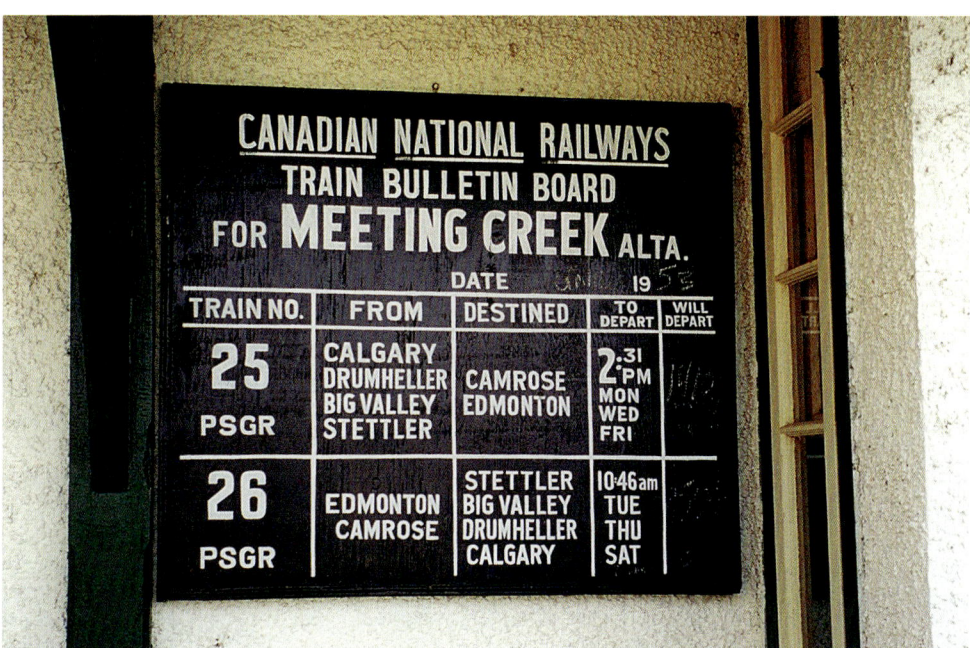

Meeting Creek, Alberta (L.S. Kozma Photo), 2001

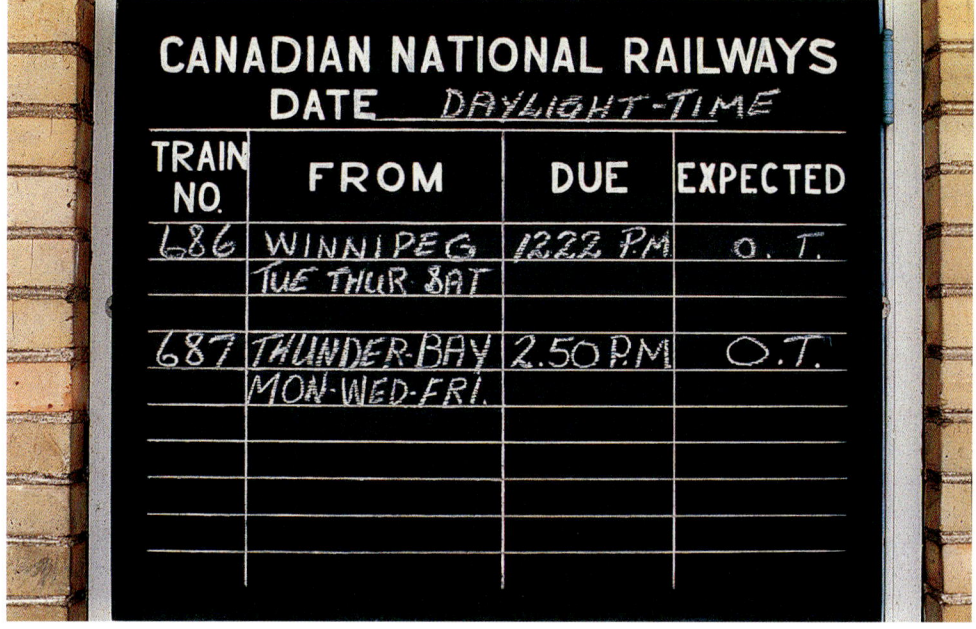

Baudette, Minnesota (Hilt Friesen Photo)

CN Train Bulletin Boards

All active agencies were required, under the Railway Act, to have a blackboard upon which the arrival times of late trains were to be noted in white chalk. It became standard practice to install formal Train Bulletins, a framed blackboard, usually mounted on an outside wall conspicuous to the waiting room door. Early bulletins were simply blackboards with the necessary information chalked thereon by the agent. By World War One, basic information—the company name (sometimes the corporate logo), station name, date, train number, point of origin (from), time due according to the timetable and time expected— was usually painted onto the Black *board in* White. *The painted lines for the columns and rows (the number of which varied) were also painted* White. *In many cases, the train number and schedules were also painted onto the board. The train due times were then "chalked up" by the local agent as required. The header "Canadian National Railways," with enlarged first letters and the "artistic flourishes," made the St. Albert, Alberta Bulletin (38"x38 1/2") unusual. By contrast, the Meeting Creek, Alberta Bulletin (38"x38"), to a later CNR standard (circa 1926), offered considerably more information. The painted "Train Numbers" and "Times Due" were changed to reflect revised schedules; in this case the spring 1955 change of timecard. The Baudette, Minnesota Bulletin was greatly simplified and was typical of those used on the CNR from the 1960s to the end of the station era. On these later bulletins the painted station name was usually omitted. When a local agency closed, the Train Bulletin, train-order signal, enameled metal express and telegraph signage, telegraph instruments/telephone, and office furnishings (including the all-important clock) were removed for possible reuse at other locations.*

EXTERIOR COLOUR SCHEMES

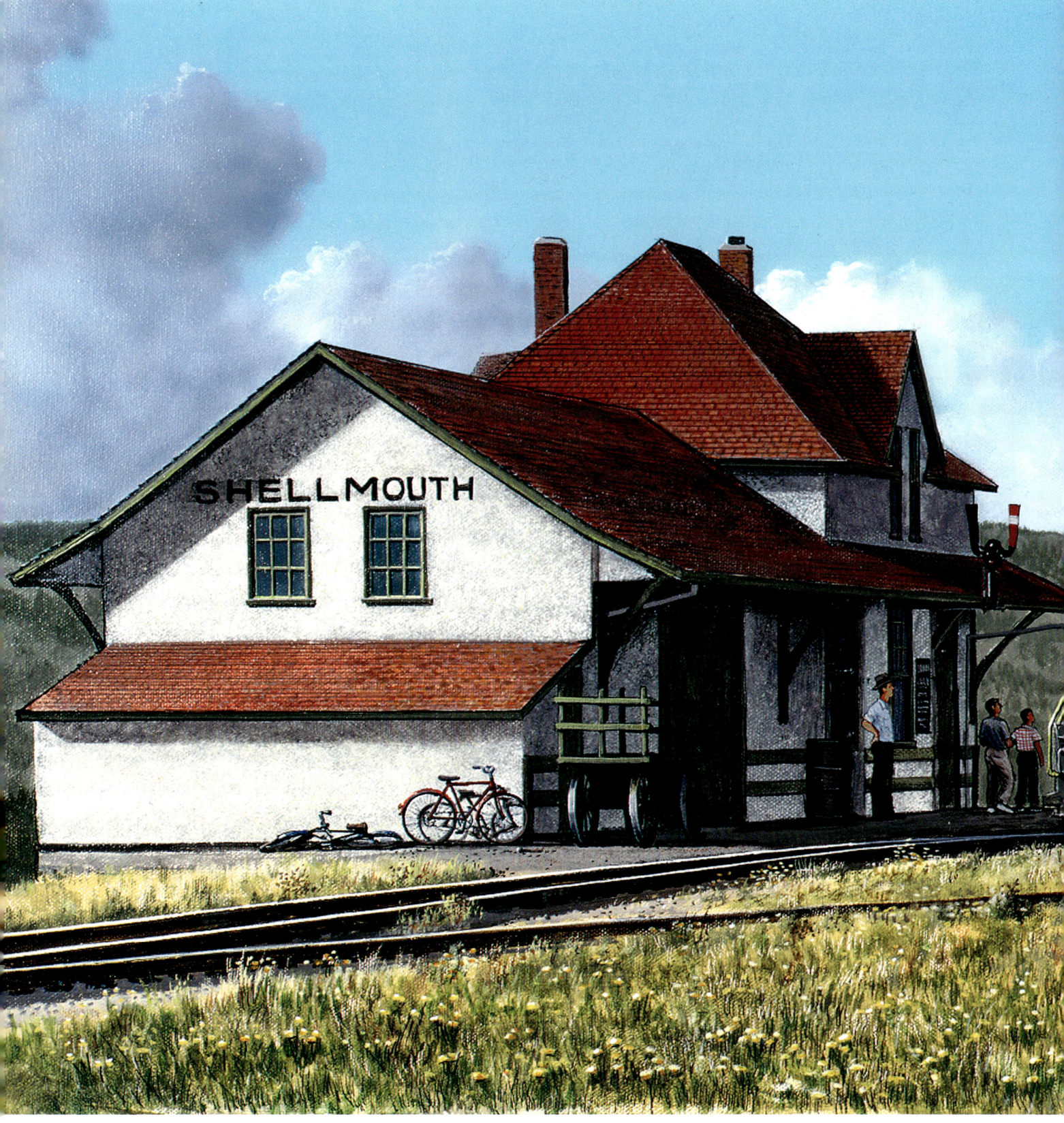

Shellmouth, Manitoba (Original Painting by Max Jacquiard)

In western Canada, all roads lead to the local depot… A brand new GMD1 1063 pulls an abbreviated mixed train up the grade out of the Assiniboine valley to the Shellmouth station. In a custom reminiscent of the glory days of the railway era, two local boys have traveled miles of dusty country roads on their bicycles just to catch a glimpse of the train at the depot. In time-honoured tradition, the engineer will call them up into the cab of the engine to show them around the new unit, and perhaps even let them try his coveted seat.

SECTION III

Rosters

CANADIAN NATIONAL'S WESTERN DEPOTS did an excellent job of discussing CNR's combination and passenger stations. However, it touched only very briefly on standard shelters, portable stations and temporary stations.

There is a friendly debate among railway *aficionados* as to what constitutes a depot. For the purposes of this work, a depot is defined as any building located at a station, which was used for train operation and/or passengers and freight service. Detached freight or express sheds, unless used as a station, are beyond the scope of this work.

Since nearly half of the communities in the West had only a shelter or a portable for a depot, the authors felt that these "lowly buildings"—in their many incarnations—have been neglected for far too long. It is hoped that adding these to rosters will fill this void in the railway station record.

The authors have identified over 2,000 depots in western Canada, which were built or acquired by Canadian National Railways. To present as much information as possible about each of these stations, three rosters are included in this work. The data were collected from a number of sources, primarily building and construction records found in company files. Other significant material was gleaned from numerous archives, photographic collections, local histories, newspapers, periodicals and fieldwork by the authors and their colleagues. These rosters represent at least ninety-five per cent of the depots erected by the CNR and its predecessors in western Canada.

Tracking down many of the depots built by the Canadian Northern prior to 1900 and also the former Northern Pacific depots, acquired by the CNoR in 1901, has proven to be difficult. Other than these exceptions, it is believed that the vast majority of those stations not noted in these rosters were likely portable buildings or shelters of little architectural significance, such as car bodies, recycled bunkhouses or tool sheds.

Some clarification is also required concerning some recent architectural studies which generalized that Grand Trunk Pacific (GTP) stations were built to the highest standard, relative to those erected by its chief rivals, the Canadian Northern (CNoR) and the Canadian Pacific (CPR).

While the GTP maintained exceedingly high engineering standards for its main line location and track work, the same cannot be said of most of its buildings, and certainly not about its combination stations. While its early depot designs, such as the *Type D* and the *Type E*, were aesthetically pleasing from the exterior, their interiors were finished with cheap V-Joint boards. In contrast, the standard depots of the CPR and CNoR were more substantially constructed and their interiors were much more highly finished, using plaster.

One had only to spend a typical prairie winter in a GTP depot to understand the difference. The V-Joint boards in the Grand Trunk Pacific structures tended to shrink shortly after construction, so that the wind literally howled through these buildings, making them very difficult to heat. Plaster walls and ceilings provided superior protection from the wind. By the 1930s, insulation (usually wood shavings) installed into the walls and ceilings and the application of stucco or *Insul-Brick*® siding to the exterior were all means of trying to keep these buildings livable through the seasons.

After about 1900 the Canadian Pacific generally employed concrete or stone foundations under the office and apartment portions of its western depots, while the attached freight sheds continued to rest on wooden surface foundations or posts. The GTP had a similar philosophy, while most CNoR depots used wooden surface foundations throughout.

Generally speaking, in terms of overall quality, the CPR engineered and built the best combination stations in western Canada, with the Canadian Northern coming in a close second. The GTP was a distant third. By 1925 the Canadian National's new standards for its Western Lines combination depots had achieved parity with those erected by the CPR.

> Station buildings converted to museums
> In the following roster pages, look for these entries under the "Notes" column:
> Museum 1: Converted to museum; remaining on site.
> Museum 2: Converted to museum; removed from original site.
> Museum *: Dispositions shown with an asterisk are cross-referenced to the Canadian Railway Station Guide (Bruce Ballantyne—Editor, The Bytown Railway Society Inc., 1998), which provides directions to off-site stations.

ROSTER I

CNR Stations in Western Canada, Listed Alphabetically by Province

This listing is an overview of the various types of stations found in specific communities served by Canadian National Railways, and is a guide to further information presented in the other two rosters. Entries in Roster I are listed in the following format:

ALBERTA

Station Name	Proposed/Former Name	Division	Subdivision	Type of Depot	Plan	Year	Notes	see page
Alberta Beach	<<Britannia>>	Edson	Lac Ste. Anne	SPEC-CNoR	100-90	1917	Note 36	118/134
Alexo	x-Stolberg	Calgary	Brazeau	FPS-CNR	100-41B	1924		115/138
Alix–CNoR		Calgary	Endiang	3rd	100-29	1912	Note 59	115/131

"Station Name" is the location in which a specific depot was built. In cases where a community's name differs from the one used by Canadian National, the latter is used. Where more than one station building was built at a location, a separate entry is made for each known depot (#1, #2, etc.)

"Proposed/Former Station Name." Names in double parentheses, thus "<<Name>>", indicate proposed station names for the location. Names indicated thus, "x-Name," provide the former name of the station.

"Division" refers to the operating area in which a locality/station is situated. Since the early 1960s brought tremendous changes to the CNR's Western Region, the authors arbitrarily chose the 1958 operating structure, as the Subdivisions are more workable for the Rosters.

Canadian National's Western Region—between Armstrong and Thunder Bay, Ontario and the Pacific coast—was divided into four Districts, from east to west: Manitoba, Saskatchewan, Alberta and British Columbia. These Districts were further subdivided into 15 Divisions:

MANITOBA DISTRICT:
Dauphin, Hudson Bay, Port Arthur (also incorporating the Lakehead Division) and Portage-Brandon Divisions;

SASKATCHEWAN DISTRICT:
Prince Albert, Regina and Saskatoon Divisions;

ALBERTA DISTRICT:
Calgary, Edmonton and Edson Divisions;

BRITISH COLUMBIA DISTRICT:
Kamloops (incorporating the Vancouver Terminals and Vancouver Island Divisions) and Smithers Divisions.

Lines abandoned prior to 1958 are listed under the Division under which they would probably have been listed had they remained in service.

"Subdivision" refers to the specific section of track within a given Division, on which a station is located. This reference also directs the reader to Roster II, where further information may be found.

"Type of Depot" refers to the *authors' classification* of the depot design built at the listed location. *Sometimes* the authors' classifications coincide with the railway designations. Over three quarters of the stations built by the CNR in western Canada fit into the "standard" classifications noted in CANADIAN NATIONAL'S WESTERN DEPOTS. The authors felt that revising the designations used in the original would cause too much confusion. *The authors' classifications are noted in italics.*

Sometimes, to further clarify the type of depot, the railway responsible for the design is noted. In some cases, Canadian Northern depot designs were constructed by the Canadian National on former Grand Trunk Pacific lines. The following abbreviations are used:

C&E	Calgary and Edmonton Railway
CNR	Canadian National Railways
CNoR	Canadian Northern Railway
CPR	Canadian Pacific Railway
DW&P	Duluth Winnipeg and Pacific Railway
GTP	Grand Trunk Pacific Railway
MRM	Midland Railway of Manitoba
NPR	Northern Pacific Railway
NTR	National Transcontinental Railway
QLL&S	Qu'Appelle Long Lake and Saskatchewan Railway

"Plan Number." The CNR adopted the Canadian Northern plan numbering scheme. Since the Grand Trunk Pacific (GTP) lacked a consistent designation policy for its station designs, in 1910 the Board of Railway Commissioners (BRC) recommended a simple identification system to expedite the approval of station location plans. These BRC number designations were used in reference to all GTP stations until 1923. Subsequently, the classification of GTP stations in CANADIAN NATIONAL'S WESTERN DEPOTS led to even more confusion regarding the designation of these buildings. The following table is presented to finally resolve the issue of GTP station design classifications:

Designation:			Plan Number:		
BRC	GTP	Bohi	GTP	CNR	Example
1	Design 'A'	Type E	3666	100-152	Hinton
2	Design 'B'	N/A	3693	100-153	Uno
3	26Ft.x60 Ft.	Type D	2786, 4416	100-154	Unity
	(also referred to in some GTP records as "early" Design 'A')				
4	30Ft.x102Ft.6In.	Special	2236	100-155	Wainwright #1
	(GTP Standard Terminal Depot No. 2)				
4	Spec. Design 'F'	Special	5955	100-159	Jasper #1
5	41Ft.x137Ft.6In.	Special	1618	100-156	Melville
6	Design 'E'	Special	4378	100-157	Mirror
7	Design 'D'	Special	4168	100-163	Edson
8	NTR Design 'A'	Type F		100-151	Duperow
9	New Design 'A-1'	Type G		100-168	Domremy
–	24Ft.x53Ft./NTR #1	NTR No. 1	1216, 2159	100-160	Nokomis
–	Design 'G'	N/A	8340	100-165	McBride #1
1A	BRC Shelter 1A	N/A	3702	100-162	Lorlie #1
1B	BRC Shelter 1B	N/A	3702	100-162/173	Telkwa #1
2	BRC Plan 2	N/A	3702	100-162	Fraser

Small groups of similar stations, or individually designed "custom" buildings, are referred to as "**Special Stations**."

The most notable change in the rosters from the original book is the inclusion of shelters, portable stations and temporary stations, described as follows:

- **FPS** Freight and Passenger Shelter
- **PORT** Portable Station
- **SHLT** Passenger Shelter
- **TOS** Train Order Station

These are further described in terms of their character, since some of these structures were not purpose-built as stations. Where known, the following designations are used to describe them:

- **CB** Carbody (superannuated rolling stock, usually without trucks.)
- **CO** Converted from coal shed.
- **FT** Converted from freight shed.
- **PH** Converted from a pump house.
- **SMBH** A variant of a sectionmen's bunkhouse or a bunkhouse converted for this purpose.
- **ST** Converted from a section tool house.

"**Year**" indicates the year the subject station building was constructed. Refer to Roster III for further information.

The "**Notes**" column is used to present further information that may be pertinent. The most common entries in this column are "**Probable**", "**Temporary**" and "**Note**." "**Probable**" indicates that while conclusive evidence about the design of the subject depot was not available to the authors, the data are sufficient to make a *reasonable hypothesis* about the type of depot at that location. "**Temporary**" is a relative term, and is used to indicate a building intended to serve for only a brief period. The remark "**Note**," followed by a numeral, indicates there are further relevant facts relating to the particular depot. The Notes for the rosters are found in the box at the bottom right of each page spread.

The "**see page**" column provides a page number reference to the corresponding entries for a particular station in Rosters II and III. The number preceding the slash "/" refers to Roster II, the number following to Roster III. "—" means that there is no corresponding entry.

ALBERTA

Station Name	Proposed/Former Name	Division	Subdivision	Type of Depot	Plan	Year	Notes	see page
Abilene	x-Gabriel Jct.	Edmonton	Coronado	SHLT-CNR		1928		117/143
Acadia Valley		Calgary	Acadia Valley	CN3rd	100-227	1927		114/142
Acheson #1		Edson	Wabamun	Type E	100-152	1911		119/135
Acheson #2		Edson	Wabamun	FPS-CNR	GTP-FT	1951		119/140
Alberta Beach	<<Britannia>>	Edson	Lac Ste. Anne	SPEC-CNoR	100-90	1917	Note 36	118/134
Alexo	x-Stolberg	Calgary	Brazeau	FPS-CNR	100-41B	1924		115/138
Alix–CNoR		Calgary	Endiang	3rd	100-29	1912	Note 59	115/131
Alix–GTP #1		Calgary	Three Hills	Type E	100-152	1911	Note 60	116/135
Alix–GTP #2		Calgary	Three Hills	3rd	100-29	—	Note 59	116/131
Alliance		Edmonton	Alliance	3rd	100-72	1916		116/132
Alness		Calgary	Oyen	FPS	100-41			115/125
Anatole		Saskatoon	Dodsland	FPS-CNR	100-41B	1927		113/138
Ancona	x-Pollock	Calgary	Brazeau	FPS	100-41			115/125
Ankerton		Edmonton	Alliance	FPS	100-41	—		116/125
Ansell		Edson	Brule	Type E	100-152	1911		118/135
Anshaw		Edmonton	Bonnyville	FPS-CNR	100-41B	1929		116/138
Ardenode #1		Calgary	Drumheller	3rd	100-29	1913		115/131
Ardenode #2		Calgary	Drumheller	FPS-CNR				115/143
Ardley		Calgary	Three Hills	Type E	100-152	1911		116/135
Ardmore	x-Cote	Edmonton	Bonnyville	FPS-CNR		1939		116/144
Ardrossan		Edmonton	Viking	Type E	100-152	1910		118/135
Armena		Edmonton	Camrose	FPS	100-41	1915		117/125
Armistice		Edmonton	Coronado	FPS-CNR	100-41B	1927		117/138
Arneson		Calgary	Acadia Valley	FPS-CNR	100-41B	1927		114/139
Ashmont #1		Edmonton	Coronado	FPS	100-41	1921		117/125
Ashmont #2		Edmonton	Coronado	CN3rd	100-250	1929		117/141
Athabasca	x-Athabaska	Edmonton	Athabasca	2nd	100-39	1912		116/134
Baintree		Calgary	Drumheller	FPS	100-41	1915		115/125

ROSTER NOTES:

36 The former CNoR line between Peace River Jct. and Darson Jct. (near Magnolia) was abandoned in June 1936.

59 Following trackage changes on the Brazeau Subdivision, this station was abandoned on site in 1922. The west end of the Endiang Subdivision was subsequently extended to include a portion of the Brazeau Subdivision. This depot was relocated to the GTP station grounds in 1927.

60 In 1927, after the former CNoR depot was moved to the Alix–GTP station grounds, the former GTP depot was converted into a section house.

ALBERTA

Station Name	Proposed/Former Name	Division	Subdivision	Type of Depot	Plan	Year	Notes	see page
Ballenden		Calgary	Spondin	FPS-CNR	100-41B	1932	Note 79	116/139
Bardo #1		Edmonton	Kingman	Type E	100-152	1913		117/135
Bardo #2		Edmonton	Kingman	FPS				117/144
Barlow		Calgary	Drumheller	FPS	100-41	1915		115/125
Barlow Jct.		Calgary	Drumheller	PORT-CNoR	110-73A	1921	SMBH, Reverse	115/128
Bashaw		Edmonton	Camrose	Type E	100-152	1911		117/135
Battle		Edmonton	Camrose	SHLT-CNoR		1918		117/144
Beaver River		Edmonton	Bonnyville	FPS	CB			117/143
Beiseker	x-Bartle	Calgary	Three Hills	Type E	100-152	1913		116/135
Bellis #1		Edmonton	Coronado	FPS	100-41	1919		117/125
Bellis #2		Edmonton	Coronado	3rd	100-72	1923		117/132
Benton #1		Calgary	Oyen	FPS	100-41	1913		115/125
Benton #2		Calgary	Oyen	3rd	100-72	1918		115/132
Berks		Edson	Lucerne	FPS	CB	1914	Note 40	118/143
Beynon		Calgary	Drumheller	FPS	100-41	1915		115/125
Bickerdike		Edson	Brule	Type E	100-152	1911		118/135
Big Valley		Calgary	Stettler	2nd	100-39	1912	Museum-1	116/134
Bilby #1		Edson	Sangudo	CSS-C	100-47	1913		119/128
Bilby #2		Edson	Sangudo	SHLT-CNR		1959		119/144
Bircham		Calgary	Three Hills	Type E	100-152	1912		116/135
Bissell #1		Edson	Wabamun	Type E	100-152	1910		119/130
Bissell #2		Edson	Wabamun	4th	100-68	1922		119/130
Blackfoot #1-A		Edmonton	Blackfoot	SHLT-CNoR	100-95	1908		116/124
Blackfoot #1-B		Edmonton	Blackfoot	FPS	100-41	1911		116/125
Blackfoot #2		Edmonton	Blackfoot	3rd	100-72	1922		116/132
Bliss		Edson	Lucerne	CSS-C	100-47	1914		118/128
Blue Ridge	x-Lonira	Edson	Sangudo	FPS	100-41	1922		119/125
Bodo	x-Rosenheim	Edmonton	Bodo	FPS-CNR	100-41C	1932		116/140
Bonar		Calgary	Oyen	FPS	100-41	1913		115/125
Bonnyville		Edmonton	Bonnyville	CN3rd	100-253	1929		116/142
Borradaile		Edmonton	Blackfoot	FPS	100-41	1911		116/125
Boscombe		Edmonton	Bonnyville	FPS-CNR	100-41B	1929		116/139
Brazeau #1-A	x-Nordegg	Calgary	Brazeau	3rd	100-29	1914		115/132
Brazeau #1-B		Calgary	Brazeau	FPS	100-41	——	Express Shed	115/125
Bremner		Edmonton	Viking	FPS-GTP	100-162	1913		118/134
Bretona		Edmonton	Camrose	3rd	100-29	1913		117/131
Bretville Jct.		Edmonton	Camrose					116/——
Bretville Jct.		Edmonton	Viking	PORT-CNR			Note 13	118/144
Briggs	x-Tannis	Calgary	Brazeau	FPS	100-41	1919		114/125
Bruce		Edmonton	Viking	Type E	100-152	1910		118/135
Brule #1		Edson	Brule	CSS-C	100-47	1914		118/128
Brule #2		Edson	Brule	FPS-CNR	100-320	1953		118/140
Burbank		Calgary	Brazeau	FPS	100-41	1915		114/125
Butze		Edmonton	Unity	PORT-GTP	110-101	——	SMBH	117/134
Byemoor		Calgary	Endiang	CN3rd	100-197	1927		115/141
Cadomin #1-A		Edson	Mountain Park	FPS	CB	1923		118/143
Cadomin #1-B		Edson	Mountain Park	FPS-CNR	100-41B	1923		118/139
Calahoo #1		Edson	Sangudo	CSS-C	100-47	1913		119/128
Calahoo #2		Edson	Sangudo	FPS	100-41	——		119/125
Calgary-CNoR #1		Calgary	Drumheller	STA	100-56	1914	Temporary	115/134
Calgary-CNoR #2		Calgary	Drumheller	SPEC-CNoR	100-91	1916	Note 27	115/134
Calgary-GTP		Calgary	Three Hills	SPEC-GTP		1914	Temporary	116/138
Calthorpe	x-Holt	Saskatoon	Dodsland	FPS-CNR	100-41B	1926		113/139
Camrose-CNoR		Edmonton	Camrose	3rd	100-29	1911		117/131
Camrose-GTP	On Aban. GTP	Edmonton	Kingman	SPEC-GTP	100-157	1910	Note 12	117/138
Cannel		Edson	Sangudo	FPS	100-41			119/125
Carolside		Calgary	Sheerness	FPS	100-41	1920		115/125
Carrot Creek-CNoR		Edson	Tollerton	CSS-C	100-47	1915	Note 62	119/128
Carrot Creek-GTP #1	x-Otley	Edson	Wabamun	Type E	100-152	1911		119/135
Carrot Creek-GTP #2		Edson	Wabamun	FPS-CNR	GTP-FT	1951		119/140
Carvel		Edson	Wabamun	Type E	100-152	1910		119/135
Cereal		Calgary	Oyen	3rd	100-29	1913		115/131
Cessford		Calgary	Sheerness	4th	100-68	1920		116/130
Cherhill		Edson	Sangudo	FPS	100-41	1916		119/125
Chestermere Lake		Calgary	Drumheller	SPEC-CNoR	100-51	1913		115/134
Chauvin		Edmonton	Unity	Type D	100-154	1909		117/135
Chinook		Calgary	Oyen	3rd	100-29	1913		115/131
Chip Lake #1		Edson	Wabamun	CSS-C	100-47	1913		119/128
Chip Lake #2		Edson	Wabamun	FPS-CNR	CNoR-FT	1951		119/140
Chipman		Edmonton	Vegreville	3rd	100-3	1907		118/130
Claysmore		Edmonton	Vegreville	FPS	100-41	1911		118/125
Clover Bar #1		Edmonton	Viking	Type E	100-152	1911		118/135
Clover Bar #2		Edmonton	Viking	FPS	100-41	——		118/125
Clyde		Edmonton	Athabasca	3rd	100-29	1912		116/131
Coalspur #1-A		Edson	Foothills	Type E	100-152	1913		118/135
Coalspur #1-B		Edson	Foothills	PORT-CNoR	110-73A	1923	SMBH	118/128
Codner		Calgary	Brazeau	FPS	100-41	1920		115/125
Coghill		Calgary	Brazeau					114/——
Colinton		Edmonton	Athabasca	CSS-C	100-47	1913		116/128
Conrich		Calgary	Three Hills	SHLT				116/144
Cooking Lake #1-A		Edmonton	Viking	SPEC-GTP	100-153	1910		118/138
Cooking Lake #1-B		Edmonton	Viking	SHLT-GTP		By15		118/134

ALBERTA

Station Name	Proposed/Former Name	Division	Subdivision	Type of Depot	Plan	Year	Notes	see page
Coronado #1		Edmonton	Coronado	4th	100-68	1921	Note 14	117/130
Coronado #2		Edmonton	Coronado	FPS-CNR	CNoR-FT	1939	Note 14	117/140
Craigmyle #2		Calgary	Drumheller	3rd	100-72	1916		115/132
Dalehurst–CNoR		Edson	Lucerne	CSS-C	100-47	1915	Note 73	118/128
Dalehurst–GTP	x-Roundcroft	Edson	Brule	Type E	100-152	1911		118/135
Dandurand–CNoR		Edson	Lucerne				Note 42	118/—
Darwell		Edson	Lac Ste. Anne	CSS-C	100-47	1913	Note 36	118/128
Dayson		Edson	Tollerton	CSS-C	100-47	1913	Note 62	119/128
Decoigne	x-Mt. Cavell/xx-Mt. Geikie	Kamloops	Albreda	CSS-C	100-47	1914		119/128
Delacour		Calgary	Three Hills	Type E	100-152	1913		116/135
Delburne		Calgary	Three Hills	Type E	100-152	1912	Museum-2	116/135
Delia		Calgary	Drumheller	3rd	100-29	1913		115/131
Demay		Edmonton	Demay	FPS	100-41	—		117/125
Deville #1-A		Edmonton	Viking	Type E	100-152	1910		118/135
Deville #1-B		Edmonton	Viking	FPS-CNR	100-41B	—		118/139
Dinant		Edmonton	Kingman	Type E	100-152	1912		117/135
Dinosaur	x-Munson Jct.	Calgary	Drumheller	FPS	100-41	1921	Note 25	115/125
Dobson #1		Calgary	Oyen	FPS	100-41	1913		115/125
Dobson #2		Calgary	Oyen	FPS-CNR	100-41B	1924		115/139
Dodds		Edmonton	Demay	3rd	100-29	1910		117/131
Donalda #1	<<Wallace>>	Calgary	Stettler	3rd	100-29	1911		116/131
Donalda #2		Calgary	Stettler	4th	100-31	—	Museum-2, Note 23	116/130
Dorenlee		Edmonton	Camrose	Type E	100-152	1912		117/135
Dowling		Calgary	Endiang	FPS-CNR	100-41B	1926		115/139
Drinnan		Edson	Brule	FPS				118/144
Drumheller #1		Calgary	Drumheller	3rd	100-29	1912		115/131
Drumheller #2		Calgary	Drumheller		170-2	1915	Note 26	115/141
Duagh		Edmonton	Coronado	FPS	100-41	1921		117/125
Duffield		Edson	Wabamun	Type E	100-152	1911		119/135
Duhamel		Edmonton	Camrose	Type E	100-152	1911		117/135
Dunshalt		Calgary	Drumheller	FPS	100-41	1922		115/125
East Edmonton	x-Valesso	Edmonton	Camrose	PORT	110-159	—	x-SMBH	117/141
Eckville		Calgary	Brazeau	3rd	100-29	1912		115/131
Edberg		Calgary	Stettler	3rd	100-29	1910		116/131
Edgerton		Edmonton	Unity	Type E	100-152	1911		117/135
Edmonton #1-A	Joint with GTP	Edmonton	Vegreville	SPEC-CNoR	100-34	1906	Note 13	118/134
Edmonton #1-B	Joint with GTP	Edmonton	Vegreville	FPS	100-41	1914	Notes 13, 64	118/125
Edmonton #2	Joint with NAR	Edmonton	Vegreville	SPEC-CNR	100-219	1927	Note 13	118/142
Edmonton #3		Edmonton	Vegreville	SPEC-CNR		1965	Notes 13, 65	118/142
Edmonton #4		Edmonton	Vegreville	SPEC-CNR		1966	Notes 13, 66	118/142
Edmonton–Calder Yard	x-North Yard	Edmonton	Viking	FPS	100-41	—	TOS, Note 13	118/125
Edmonton–EY&P–Ross Grade		Edmonton	Camrose	4th	100-6	1903	Notes 10, 13	116/130
Edson		Edson	Wabamun	SPEC-GTP	100-163	1910		119/138
Eduoardville	x-Heenan	Edmonton	Coronado	FPS-CNR	100-41B	1927		117/139
Edwand		Edmonton	Coronado	FPS	100-41	1919		117/125
Elk Point		Edmonton	Coronado	CN3rd	100-227	1927		117/142
Elnora	x-Perbeck	Calgary	Three Hills	Type E	100-152	1911		116/135
Elspeth		Calgary	Brazeau	3rd	100-29	1913		114/131
Embarras		Edson	Foothills	Type E	100-152	1912		118/135
Endiang		Calgary	Endiang	CN3rd	100-227	1927		115/142
Entrance–CNoR	<<Heda>>	Edson	Lucerne	CSS-C	100-47	1914		118/128
Entrance–GTP	x-Dyke	Edson	Brule	Type E	100-152	1911		118/135

ROSTER NOTES:

10 This 4th Class station, erected at the foot of Ross grade, was relocated in 1906 to the CNoR yard in Edmonton. It was used as Petty Stores until replaced in 1916. Final disposition is unknown, but it was likely demolished in 1916.

12 The GTP line though Camrose was abandoned in 1923. The disposition of this station is unknown, but it is believed to have been sold shortly after abandonment.

13 This station was technically on the Edmonton Terminals Subdivision.

14 Portion converted into section house; the freight shed was converted into FPS #2 in 1939.

23 Following inauguration of tourist passenger service on portions of the former CNR Stettler Subdivision in 1990, the Village of Donalda approached the Canadian Northern Society to acquire a station. The Society obtained an early design Canadian Northern 4th Class Station (Plan 100-31) from Vandura, Saskatchewan. It was moved onto the site of the original depot, extensively refurbished and opened in 1992 as an interpretive display in conjunction with the excursion trains that stopped here. The rail line serving Donalda was abandoned in 1997.

25 A train-order station was set up at this junction by late 1921. The former scale house from Drumheller was joined to a Standard FPS north of the junction switch. The shelter building was converted into living quarters and the scale house into a telegraph office, complete with order-board. This arrangement lasted until May 1927, after which all operating was handled out of the nearby Munson depot. The train-order station was removed, replaced by a register booth.

26 Following the demolition of the station at Drumheller, the nearby freight shed office was occupied by the agent and used as the *ad hoc* station.

27 The St. Mary's Hall was constructed in 1894. The CNoR obtained an option on the property in 1911, but did not take over the building until 1914. Conversion into a railway depot was completed in 1916.

36 The former CNoR line between Peace River Jct. and Darson Jct. (near Magnolia) was abandoned in June 1936.

40 Abandoned on grade in 1917. Final dispositions unknown; likely sold and demolished.

42 Abandoned on grade in 1917. Relocated to CNR Mile 15.3 Brule Subdivision in 1923, used as residence by the CNR pumpman for the new water tank erected here. Relocated to Galloway (#3) in 1940. Sold to the Town of Edson in 1976 and relocated to Centennial Park on the western outskirts of the community. Converted into museum. The station's signboards read "Edson."

62 Dayson, Carrot Creek–CNoR, Fulstow, Horner, Scriven and Tollerton, Ab. These stations were abandoned on grade in 1917. The following year, the CNoR apparently stripped all re-usable millwork (windows, doors, interior fittings, etc.) from these buildings. A local history makes reference to Carrot Creek–CNoR and Fulstow as being sold about 1923. It is likely that all of these stations were sold and removed at the same time.

64 This FPS was set up as a stores building for the Sleeping & Dining Car Department.

65 This was a temporary station set up during construction of the CN Tower (#4), on the site of the former station (#2).

66 The station facilities were located in the basement of this 26-floor office tower. VIA Rail Canada took over passenger operations in the building in 1978. In 1998, these premises were vacated in favour of a new VIA station built in northwestern Edmonton.

73 CNR building records are somewhat unclear regarding this station. One record clearly shows that Pedley had a 'Design A' (*Type E*) station, but another also notes it as Plan 100-47, with stucco and rehabilitation in 1927. It is likely that the original GTP station burned down and that this building was relocated from Dalehurst–CNoR, then abandoned in 1928.

79 The line between Hemaruka and Spondin never passed from the Construction to the Operating Department. This section was rarely operated.

ALBERTA

Station Name	Proposed/Former Name	Division	Subdivision	Type of Depot	Plan	Year	Notes	see page
Entwistle–CNoR #1		Edson	Tollerton	FPS	100-41	1914		119/125
Entwistle–CNoR #2		Edson	Tollerton	4th	100-68	1915		119/130
Entwistle–GTP		Edson	Wabamun	Type E	100-152	1910		119/135
Equity	x-Ghost Pine	Calgary	Three Hills					116/135
Erith		Edson	Foothills	Type E	100-152	1912		118/135
Errington		Edson	Brule	PORT	CB			118/143
Esther		Saskatoon	Dodsland	FPS-CNR	100-41B	1926		113/139
Evansburg–CNoR #1		Edson	Tollerton	FPS	100-41	1916		119/125
Evansburg–CNoR #2		Edson	Tollerton	3rd	100-72	1920		119/132
Evansburg–GTP #1-A		Edson	Wabamun	FPS-GTP	100-162	1914	Note 41	119/134
Evansburg–GTP #1-B		Edson	Wabamun	PORT-GTP	110-101	1918	SMBH	119/134
Evansburg–GTP #2		Edson	Wabamun	3rd	100-72			119/132
Everest		Edson	Lucerne					118/—
Excel #1		Calgary	Oyen	FPS	100-41	1913		115/125
Excel #2		Calgary	Oyen	3rd	100-72	1917		115/133
Fabyan #1		Edmonton	Viking	Type E	100-152	1910		118/135
Fabyan #2		Edmonton	Viking	Temp	xSMBH			118/—
Fabyan #3		Edmonton	Viking	CN4th	100-207	1925		118/142
Fallis		Edson	Wabamun	Type E	100-152	1910		119/135
Fenn		Calgary	Stettler	FPS	100-41	1916		116/125
Ferintosh		Edmonton	Camrose	Type E	100-152	1911		117/135
Ferrier		Calgary	Brazeau	FPS	100-41			115/125
Fidler		Edson	Mountain Park					118/—
Foothills	x-Mudge	Edson	Foothills	Type E	100-152	—		118/135
Forestburg		Edmonton	Alliance	CSS-C	100-47	1916		116/128
Fort Kent		Edmonton	Bonnyville	SHLT-CNR		1934		116/144
Ft. Saskatchewan		Edmonton	Vegreville	3rd	100-19	1905	Variant	118/131
Franchere		Edmonton	Bonnyville	FPS-CNR	100-41B	1929		116/139
Fulstow		Edson	Tollerton	CSS-C	100-47	1914	Note 62	119/128
Gainford		Edson	Wabamun	Type E	100-152	1911		119/135
Galahad		Edmonton	Alliance	CSS-C	100-47	1916		116/128
Galloway #1		Edson	Brule	Type E	100-152	1911		118/135
Galloway #2		Edson	Brule	FPS	100-41	—		118/125
Galloway #3		Edson	Brule	CSS-C	100-47			118/128
Garden Plain		Calgary	Spondin	FPS-CNR	100-41B	1930		116/139
Gartly		Calgary	Drumheller	FPS	100-41	1913		115/125
Geikie		Kamloops	Albreda	Type E	100-152	1912		119/135
Gibbons #1		Edmonton	Coronado	FPS	100-41	1919		117/125
Gibbons #2		Edmonton	Coronado	CN4th	100-186	1927		117/142
Glendon #1	x-Alcock	Edmonton	Bonnyville	FPS-CNR	100-41B	1929		116/139
Glendon #2		Edmonton	Bonnyville	FPS		—	x-SMBH	116/141
Glenevis		Edson	Sangudo	FPS	100-41	1916		119/125
Grainger #1		Calgary	Three Hills	SHLT-GTP				116/144
Grainger #2		Calgary	Three Hills	Type F	100-151	1919		116/137
Grainger #3		Calgary	Three Hills	STA-CNR		1928	Temporary	116/144
Granada		Edson	Wabamun	FPS		—	x-SMBH	119/141
Grand Centre		Edmonton	Bonnyville	SPEC-CNR	100-373	1958		116/142
Green Court	x-Greencourt	Edson	Sangudo	FPS	100-41	—		119/125
Greenshields		Edmonton	Unity	Type E	100-152	1911		117/135
Gunn		Edson	Sangudo	FPS	100-41	—		119/125
Hackett		Calgary	Endiang	FPS-CNR	100-41B	1927		115/139
Haight		Edmonton	Haight	3rd	100-29	1910		117/131
Halliday		Calgary	Sheerness	FPS	100-41	—		115/125
Hanna		Calgary	Oyen	2nd	100-39	1913		115/134
Hargwen #1		Edson	Brule	Type E	100-152	1911		118/135
Hargwen #2		Edson	Brule	Type G	100-168	1920	Note 9	118/138
Harlech		Calgary	Brazeau					115/—
Hawes	x-Jasper House	Edson	Pocahontas Branch	Type E	100-152	1913	Note 52	118/135
Hawkins #1		Edmonton	Viking	Type E	100-152	1911		118/135
Hawkins #2		Edmonton	Viking	FPS-CNR	100-41B	1950	x-? or new?	118/139
Hay Lakes #1	x-Hay Lake	Edmonton	Camrose	3rd	100-29	1913		117/131
Hay Lakes #2	x-Hay Lake	Edmonton	Camrose	FPS	100-41	—	Temporary	117/139
Hay Lakes #3	x-Hay Lake	Edmonton	Camrose	CN3rd	100-197A	1925		117/141
Haynes #1		Calgary	Brazeau	3rd	100-29	1913		114/131
Haynes #2		Calgary	Brazeau	FPS	110-73	—	x-SMBH	114/141
Heatburg	x-Bullocksville	Calgary	Three Hills	FPS-CNR	CB	1927		116/143
Heath		Edmonton	Unity	FPS-GTP	100-162	1913		117/134
Heinsburg #1		Edmonton	Coronado	FPS-CNR	100-41B	1930		117/139
Heinsburg #2		Edmonton	Coronado	CN4A	100-310	1950		117/142
Heisler		Edmonton	Alliance	CSS-C	100-47	1916		116/128
Hemaruka		Saskatoon	Dodsland	CN3rd	100-227	1927		113/142
Henry House–CNoR		Edson	Lucerne	CSS-C	100-47	1914	Note 44	118/128
Henry House–GTP		Edson	Brule	Type E	100-152	1911		118/135
Hilliard		Edmonton	Vegreville	FPS	100-41	1917		118/125
Hinton		Edson	Brule	Type E	100-152	1912	Note 8	118/135
Holden		Edmonton	Viking	Type E	100-152	1910		118/135
Horburg		Calgary	Brazeau	FPS	100-41	1918		115/125
Horner		Edson	Tollerton	CSS-C	100-47	1914	Note 62	119/128
Hubalta		Calgary	Three Hills	Type F	100-151	1913		116/137
Huxley		Calgary	Three Hills	Type E	100-152	1913		116/135
Innisfree #1	x-Delnorte	Edmonton	Vegreville	3rd	100-3	1906		118/130
Innisfree #2		Edmonton	Vegreville	PORT		—	x-SMBH	118/141

ALBERTA

Station Name	Proposed/Former Name	Division	Subdivision	Type of Depot	Plan	Year	Notes	see page
Inland		Edmonton	Haight	FPS	100-41	1922		117/125
Interlaken		Edson	Pocahontas Branch	Type E	100-152	1913	Note 53	118/135
Irma		Edmonton	Viking	Type E	100-152	1910		118/135
Irricana		Calgary	Three Hills	Type E	100-152	1911		116/135
Islay #1		Edmonton	Blackfoot	3rd	100-3	1906		116/130
Islay #2		Edmonton	Blackfoot	PORT-CNR	CB	1945		116/143
Islay #3		Edmonton	Blackfoot	CN4B	100-328	1952		116/142
Janet		Calgary	Drumheller	FPS	100-41	1916		115/125
Jarrow	<<Junkins>>	Edmonton	Viking	Type E	100-152	1910		118/135
Jasper #1	x-Fitzhugh	Edson	Brule	SPEC-GTP	100-155	1912	Variant	118/138
Jasper #2		Edson	Brule	SPEC-CNR	100-206	1925	Temporary	118/142
Jasper #3		Edson	Brule	SPEC-CNR	100-205	1925		118/142
Jasper Park	later Sleepy Hollow	Edson	Lucerne	SPEC-CNoR	100-80	1915	Note 45	118/134
Joffre		Calgary	Brazeau	FPS	100-41	1916		114/125
Junkins–GTP		Edson	Wabamun	Type E	100-152	1911	Note 67	119/135
Kapasiwin	x-Kapasiwin Beach	Edson	Wabamun	FPS-GTP	100-162	1918		119/134
Kathyrn #1		Calgary	Three Hills	SHLT-GTP				116/144
Kathyrn #2		Calgary	Three Hills	CN3rd	100-184	1928		116/141
Kelsey #1		Edmonton	Alliance	CSS-C	100-47	1916		116/128
Kelsey #2		Edmonton	Alliance	FPS		——		116/144
Kerensky		Edmonton	Coronado	FPS	100-41	1919		117/125
Keston		Edson	Wabamun	Type E	100-152	1913	Note 68	119/135
Kingman		Edmonton	Kingman	Type E	100-152	1910		117/135
Kinsella #1		Edmonton	Viking	Type E	100-152	1911		118/135
Kinsella #2		Edmonton	Viking	FPS		——	x-SMBH	118/141
Kiron		Edmonton	Alliance	FPS	100-41	——		116/125
Kitscoty		Edmonton	Blackfoot	3rd	100-29	1911		116/131
Lac Ste. Anne		Edson	Lac Ste. Anne	3rd	100-29	1912	Note 36	118/131
Lake Isle #1	<<Clearwater>>	Edson	Lac Ste. Anne	FPS-CNoR	100-41	1916		118/125
Lake Isle #2		Edson	Lac Ste. Anne	FPS-CNR	CB	1923	Note 36	118/143
Lamont		Edmonton	Vegreville	3rd	100-3	1907		118/130
Lamoral		Calgary	Brazeau					115/——
Lanfine #1		Calgary	Oyen	FPS	100-41			115/125
Lanfine #2		Calgary	Oyen	3rd	100-72	1918		115/133
Lavoy		Edmonton	Vegreville	3rd	100-3	1906		118/130
Leahurst		Calgary	Stettler	FPS	100-41	1918		116/125
Leaman		Edson	Wabamun	Type E	100-152	1911		119/135
Legal #1		Edmonton	Athabasca	SHLT-CNoR	100-95	1912		116/124
Legal #2		Edmonton	Athabasca	FPS	100-41	1917		116/125
Legal #3		Edmonton	Athabasca	4th	100-68	1917		116/130
Le Goff		Edmonton	Bonnyville	FPS-CNR	100-41B	1930		116/139
Leo		Calgary	Endiang	FPS-CNR	100-41B	1927		115/139
Leslieville		Calgary	Brazeau	3rd	100-29	1913		115/131
Leyland #1		Edson	Mountain Park	SPEC-GTP		1921	Note 48	118/144
Leyland #2		Edson	Mountain Park	CN4A	100-310	1951		118/142
Lindbergh		Edmonton	Coronado	FPS-CNR	100-41B	1930		117/139
Lindbrook		Edmonton	Viking	FPS-GTP	100-162	1914		118/134
Lisburn		Edson	Sangudo	FPS	100-41	1917		119/125
Little Gem		Saskatoon	Dodsland	FPS-CNR	100-41B	1927		113/139
Lloydminster #1-A		Edmonton	Blackfoot	3rd	100-19	1906		116/131
Lloydminster #1-B		Edmonton	Blackfoot	FPS	100-41	1917		116/125
Lobstick		Edson	Wabamun	CSS-C	100-47	1913		119/128
Lochearn	Joint with CPR	Calgary	Brazeau					115/——
Lodge	Joint with CPR	Calgary	Brazeau					115/——
Lombell		Edson	Sangudo					119/——
Looma		Edmonton	Camrose	FPS	100-41	1915		117/125
Lousana #1		Calgary	Three Hills	Type E	100-152	1912		116/135
Lousana #2		Calgary	Three Hills	FPS				116/144
Lovett		Edson	Foothills	Type E	100-152	1913		118/136
Luscar		Edson	Mountain Park	FPS	CB	——	Note 74	118/143
Lyalta		Calgary	Drumheller	3rd	100-29	1913		115/131
MacKay		Edson	Wabamun	Type E	100-152	1911		119/136
Macleod Jct.		Calgary	Drumheller	FPS	100-41	——		115/125
Magnolia	<<Borian>>	Edson	Lac Ste. Anne	CSS-C	100-47	1913	Note 36	118/128

ROSTER NOTES:

8 Left vacant on the abandoned GTP grade in 1917. This station was rehabilitated in 1927, when the Obed-Entrance (x-Dyke) section of the line was re-opened.

9 Demolished in derailment 1967.

36 The former CNoR line between Peace River Jct. and Darson Jct. (near Magnolia) was abandoned in June 1936.

41 There is a discrepancy in CNR records; one stating that a carbody (#6997) was placed here in 1914, while the GTP cost record indicates that a formal shelter costing $652 was erected here. A photograph in a local history clearly shows an FPS. Perhaps the carbody was a temporary station and there was a mix-up in record keeping.

44 Abandoned on grade in 1917. Turned over to Department of the Interior (Parks) circa 1923.

45 Abandoned on site in 1917. Converted into section house.

48 Constructed by the Mountain Park Collieries.

52 Abandoned on site in 1921; final disposition unknown.

53 Abandoned on site in 1921; turned over to Parks Department in 1923, for use as a base for Park fire rangers.

62 Dayson, Carrot Creek–CNoR, Fulstow, Horner, Scriven and Tollerton, Ab. These stations were abandoned on grade in 1917. The following year, the CNoR apparently stripped all re-usable millwork (windows, doors, interior fittings, etc.) from these buildings. A local history makes reference to Carrot Creek–CNoR and Fulstow as being sold about 1923. It is likely that all of these stations were sold and removed at the same time.

67 The GTP depot was relocated from the abandoned grade to the CNoR station grounds by 1918.

68 Abandoned on site in 1917, sold in 1930.

74 Luscar is actually on the Luscar Spur 5.2 miles from its junction with the Mountain Park Subdivision at Leyland.

ALBERTA

Station Name	Proposed/Former Name	Division	Subdivision	Type of Depot	Plan	Year	Notes	see page
Magnolia Bridge #1		Edson	Wabamun	FPS	110-117	—	x-ST	119/141
Magnolia Bridge #2		Edson	Wabamun	FPS-CNR	100-41B	1926		119/139
Mallaig		Edmonton	Bonnyville	FPS-CNR	100-41B	1929		116/139
Mannville #1	x-Manville	Edmonton	Vegreville	3rd	100-3	1906		118/130
Mannville #2		Edmonton	Vegreville	FPS		—	x-SMBH	118/141
Marlboro–CNoR		Edson	Lucerne	CSS-C	100-47	1914	Note 41	118/128
Marlboro–GTP #1	x-Dandurand-GTP	Edson	Brule	Type E	100-152	1911		118/136
Marlboro–GTP #2		Edson	Brule	FPS	100-41			118/125
Mayerthorpe #1		Edson	Sangudo	FPS	100-41	1922		119/125
Mayerthorpe #2		Edson	Sangudo	CN4th	100-220	1928		119/142
McLeod River		Edson	Foothills	Type E	100-152	1912	Museum-2	118/136
Meanook		Edmonton	Athabasca	FPS	100-41	1915		116/125
Medicine Lodge #1		Edson	Brule	Type E	100-152	1911		118/136
Medicine Lodge #2		Edson	Brule	FPS-CNR	GTP-FT	1951		118/140
Meeting Creek	<<Edenville>>	Calgary	Stettler	3rd	100-29	1912	Museum-1	116/131
Mercoal		Edson	Mountain Park	FPS	100-41	—		118/125
Michichi #1	x-Mecheche	Calgary	Drumheller	FPS	100-41	1913		115/125
Michichi #2		Calgary	Drumheller	3rd	100-72	1924		115/133
Middle Creek		Edmonton	Coronado	FPS-CNR	100-41B	1930		117/139
Midland		Calgary	Drumheller					115/—
Miette	x-Bedson	Edson	Brule	CSS-C	100-47	1914		118/128
Mileage 2.2		Edmonton	Camrose	PORT	110-258	1952	x-SMBH	116/141
Mileage 48.5		Edson	Foothills	FPS	100-41	—		118/125
Minburn #1		Edmonton	Vegreville	SHLT-CNoR		1908		118/124
Minburn #2		Edmonton	Vegreville	4th	100-68	1914		118/130
Mirror		Edmonton	Camrose	SPEC-GTP	100-157	1911		117/138
Morinville		Edmonton	Athabasca	3rd	100-3	1906		116/130
Morrin		Calgary	Stettler	3rd	100-29	1912		116/131
Mountain Park #2		Edson	Mountain Park	SPEC-CNR		1920	Note 48	118/138
Mundare		Edmonton	Vegreville	3rd	100-3	1906		118/130
Munson		Calgary	Drumheller	3rd	100-29	1912		115/131
Naco		Saskatoon	Dodsland	FPS-CNR	100-41B	1927		113/139
Nestow		Edmonton	Athabasca	FPS	100-41	1914		116/125
Nevis		Calgary	Endiang	3rd	100-29	1912		115/131
New Brigden #1		Saskatoon	Dodsland	FPS-CNR	100-41B	1926		113/139
New Brigden #2		Saskatoon	Dodsland	CN3rd	100-197	1927		113/141
New Norway		Edmonton	Camrose	Type E	100-152	1911		117/136
New Sarepta		Edmonton	Camrose	FPS	100-41	1915		117/125
Nightingale		Calgary	Drumheller	PORT-CNoR	110-73A	1922	SMBH	115/128
Niton		Edson	Wabamun	Type E	100-152	1911		119/136
Norfolk		Calgary	Drumheller	FPS	100-41	1915		115/125
North Edmonton		Edmonton	Vegreville	4th	100-31	1910	Note 13	118/130
North Jct.		Calgary	Red Deer	PORT-GTP	110-101	—	x-SMBH	115/141
Obed–CNoR		Edson	Lucerne	CSS-C	100-47	1914	Note 43	118/128
Obed–GTP		Edson	Brule	Type E	100-152	1911		118/136
Oberlin		Calgary	Endiang	FPS	100-41	—		115/125
Olin	x-Rosenroll	Edmonton	Kingman				Note 12	117/—
Oliver		Edmonton	Vegreville	SHLT-CNoR	100-95	1912		118/124
Onoway		Edson	Sangudo	3rd	100-29	1913		119/131
Otway	Joint with CPR	Calgary	Brazeau					115/—
Owlseye	x-Baffin	Edmonton	Coronado	FPS	100-41	1921		117/125
Oyen		Calgary	Oyen	3rd	100-29	1913		115/131
Parkgate		Edson	Pocahontas Branch	Type E	100-152	1913	Note 51	118/136
Peace River Jct.		Edson	Sangudo	PORT-CNoR		1916	Note 36	119/144
Peavey		Edmonton	Athabasca	SHLT-CNR		1945		116/144
Pedley #1		Edson	Brule	Type E	100-152	1913		118/136
Pedley #2		Edson	Brule	CSS-C	100-47	—		118/128
Peers		Edson	Wabamun	Type E	100-152	1911		119/136
Perryvale	x-Lewiston	Edmonton	Athabasca	CSS-C	100-47	1913		116/128
Philips		Edmonton	Viking	Type E	100-152	1910		118/136
Phoenix		Calgary	Brazeau	FPS	CB			115/143
Pocahontas		Edson	Pocahontas Branch	Type E	100-152	1913	Note 52	118/136
Poe		Edmonton	Viking	Type E	100-152	1911		118/136
Pollockville #1		Calgary	Sheerness	FPS	100-41	1920		115/125
Pollockville #2		Calgary	Sheerness	3rd	100-72	1920	Museum-2	115/133
Prentiss		Calgary	Brazeau	3rd	100-29	1912		114/131
Prevo		Calgary	Brazeau	FPS	100-41			114/125
Radway	x-Radway Centre	Edmonton	Coronado	3rd	100-72	1919		117/133
Ranfurly #1-A	x-Blair Siding	Edmonton	Vegreville	PORT-CNoR	100-24	1907		118/128
Ranfurly #1-B		Edmonton	Vegreville	SHLT-CNoR	100-95	1909		118/124
Ranfurly #2		Edmonton	Vegreville	3rd	100-72	1922		118/133
Red Deer #1		Calgary	Red Deer	CN3rd	100-148	1923	Variant	115/142
Red Deer #2		Calgary	Red Deer	STA-CNR	170-154	1961	FT	115/141
Redland #1		Calgary	Drumheller	FPS	100-41	1915		115/125
Redland #2		Calgary	Drumheller	3rd	100-72	1921		115/133
Redwater #1		Edmonton	Coronado	FPS	100-41	1920		117/125
Redwater #2		Edmonton	Coronado	STA-CNR	110-259	1952	x-SMBH, Note 15	117/141
Red Willow		Calgary	Stettler	3rd	100-29	1910		116/131
Ribstone #1		Edmonton	Unity	FPS-GTP	100-162	1914		117/134
Ribstone #2		Edmonton	Unity	Type G	100-154	1920		117/138
Richdale		Calgary	Oyen	3rd	100-29	1913		115/131
Riverbend		Edmonton	Vegreville	FPS	100-41	1912		118/125

ALBERTA

Station Name	Proposed/Former Name	Division	Subdivision	Type of Depot	Plan	Year	Notes	see page
Robb	x-Minehead	Edson	Foothills	Type E	100-152	1912		118/136
Robinsons #1		Edson	Sangudo	FPS-CNR	CB	1921		119/143
Robinsons #2		Edson	Sangudo	FPS-CNR	CB	1940		119/143
Rochester		Edmonton	Athabasca	CSS-C	100-47	1913		116/128
Rochfort Bridge #1		Edson	Sangudo	FPS	100-41	1922		119/125
Rochfort Bridge #2		Edson	Sangudo	CN4th	100-252	1930		119/142
Rockyford		Calgary	Drumheller	3rd	100-29	1913		115/131
Rocky Mountain House	Joint with CPR	Calgary	Brazeau					115/—
Rosalind		Edmonton	Alliance	FPS	100-41	—		116/125
Rosebud #1		Calgary	Drumheller	FPS	100-41	1913		115/125
Rosebud #2		Calgary	Drumheller	3rd	100-72	1919		115/133
Rosedale #1		Calgary	Drumheller	FPS	100-41	1913		115/125
Rosedale #2		Calgary	Drumheller	4th	100-68	1919		115/130
Rosedale #3		Calgary	Drumheller	PORT-CNoR	100-73A	—	SMBH	115/128
Rose Lynn		Calgary	Sheerness	FPS	100-41	1922		115/125
Rosevear		Edson	Wabamun	Type E	100-152	1911		119/136
Round Hill		Edmonton	Demay	3rd	100-29	1910		117/132
Rowley #1		Calgary	Stettler	FPS	100-41	1915		116/125
Rowley #2		Calgary	Stettler	3rd	100-72	1922	Museum-1	116/133
Royal Park	x-Raith	Edmonton	Vegreville	FPS	100-96	1909		118/124
Rumsey		Calgary	Stettler	3rd	100-29	1912		116/132
Ryley #1		Edmonton	Viking	FPS-GTP	100-162	1910		118/134
Ryley #2		Edmonton	Viking	Type E	100-152	1913		118/136
Sabine		Calgary	Endiang	FPS-CNR	100-41B	1927		115/139
St. Albert #2		Edson	Sangudo	4th	100-6	1909	Museum-2	119/130
St. Paul	x-St. Paul des Metis	Edmonton	Coronado	3rd	100-138	1921	Variant	117/133
Sangudo #2		Edson	Sangudo	4th	100-68	1918		119/130
Saunders		Calgary	Brazeau	FPS	100-41	1918		115/125
Scapa		Calgary	Endiang	FPS-CNR	100-41B	1926		115/139
Scollard		Calgary	Stettler	3rd	100-29	1911		116/132
Scotfield		Calgary	Oyen	FPS	100-41	1913		115/125
Scotford		Edmonton	Vegreville	FPS	100-41	1911		118/125
Scriven		Edson	Tollerton	CSS-C	100-47	1915	Note 62	119/129
Seba Beach		Edson	Wabamun	FPS-GTP	100-162	1917		119/134
Sedalia #1		Saskatoon	Dodsland	FPS-CNR	100-41B	1926		113/139
Sedalia #2		Saskatoon	Dodsland	CN4th	100-252	1930		113/142
Shaw		Edson	Mountain Park					118/—
Sheerness		Calgary	Sheerness	3rd	100-72	1920		115/133
Shonts		Edmonton	Viking	Type E	100-152	1911		118/136
Sibbald #1		Calgary	Oyen	PORT-CNoR	110-73A	1913		115/128
Sibbald #2		Calgary	Oyen	3rd	100-72	1917		115/133
Smoky Lake		Edmonton	Coronado	3rd	100-72	1919		117/133
Snaring		Edson	Brule	CSS-C	100-47	1915		118/129
Solomon		Edson	Brule	PORT-CNoR	CB			118/143
South Edmonton	x-Strathcona	Edmonton	Camrose	SPEC-CNoR	100-50	1912	Notes 11, 13	116/134
Spedden		Edmonton	Coronado	FPS	100-41	1919		117/125
Spondin		Calgary	Spondin	FPS-CNR	100-41B	1930		116/139
Spruce Grove–CNoR #1		Edmonton	Stony Plains Branch	FPS	100-96	1907		117/124
Spruce Grove–CNoR #2		Edmonton	Stony Plains Branch	5th	100-17	1914	Probable	117/129
Spruce Grove–GTP		Edson	Wabamun	Type E	100-152	1910		119/136
Stanmore #1		Calgary	Oyen	FPS	100-41	1913		115/125
Stanmore #2		Calgary	Oyen	4th	100-68	1917		115/130
Steeper		Edson	Mountain Park					118/—
Stegund	x-Gunderson	Edmonton	Camrose					117/—
Sterco	x-Basing	Edson	Foothills	FPS	100-41	1922		118/125
Stettler		Calgary	Stettler	2nd	100-39	1911	Museum-2	116/134
Steveville		Calgary	Sheerness	4th	100-68	1921	Note 55	116/130
Stony Plain–GTP		Edson	Wabamun	Type E	100-152	1911		119/136
Stony Plains–CNoR		Edmonton	Stony Plains Branch	3rd	100-3	1907	Reverse, Note 57	117/130
Styal	x-Imrie, <<Isfield>>	Edson	Wabamun	Type E	100-152	1911		119/136
Sundance		Edson	Lucerne	CSS-C	100-47	1914	Note 40	118/129
Sunnynook	x-Konowall	Calgary	Sheerness	4th	100-68	1920		115/130

ROSTER NOTES:

11 This station was little used after operations commenced on the Bretona to Bretville Jct. cut-off in 1929. The building was sold in 1954 and demolished the following year. It was rumoured that the boilers from this building were salvaged and re-used in the shopping complex erected on this site.

12 The GTP line though Camrose was abandoned in 1923. The disposition of this station is unknown, but it is believed to have been sold shortly after abandonment.

13 This station was technically on the Edmonton Terminals Subdivision.

15 Constructed from two second-hand section bunkhouses.

36 The former CNoR line between Peace River Jct. and Darson Jct. (near Magnolia) was abandoned in June 1936.

40 Abandoned on grade in 1917. Final dispositions unknown; likely sold and demolished.

41 There is a discrepancy in CNR records; one stating that a carbody (#6997) was placed here in 1914, while the GTP cost record indicates that a formal shelter costing $652 was erected here. A photograph in a local history clearly shows an FPS. Perhaps the carbody was a temporary station and there was a mix-up in record keeping.

43 Abandoned on grade 1928, relocated to nearby GTP station grounds by 1934. Used by CNR for storage.

48 Constructed by the Mountain Park Collieries.

51 This station was left vacant on the abandoned on grade in 1917. It was turned over to the Parks Department in 1924. The station is extant, but is gradually being pushed over by the constantly shifting sand dunes.

52 Abandoned on site in 1921; final disposition unknown.

55 The track laid to this point in 1921 was abandoned in 1927. It could not be established whether this depot was ever built.

57 This depot was left on site in 1923. It was occupied by the local CNR operator as a dwelling until it was demolished in 1934.

62 Dayson, Carrot Creek–CNoR, Fulstow, Horner, Scriven and Tollerton, Ab. These stations were abandoned on grade in 1917. The following year, the CNoR apparently stripped all re-usable millwork (windows, doors, interior fittings, etc.) from these buildings. A local history makes reference to Carrot Creek–CNoR and Fulstow as being sold about 1923. It is likely that all of these stations were sold and removed at the same time.

ALBERTA

Station Name	Proposed/Former Name	Division	Subdivision	Type of Depot	Plan	Year	Notes	see page
Swalwell		Calgary	Three Hills	Type E	100-152	1912		116/136
Sylvan Lake		Calgary	Brazeau	3rd	100-29	1913		114/132
Taplow		Calgary	Sheerness	FPS	100-41	1920		115/125
Tawatinaw		Edmonton	Athabasca	CSS-C	100-47	1913		116/129
Therien	x-Gabriel	Edmonton	Bonnyville	FPS-CNR	100-41B	1929	Note 78	116/139
Three Hills #1		Calgary	Three Hills	Type E	100-152	1912		116/136
Three Hills #2		Calgary	Three Hills	Type F	100-151	1919	Museum-2	116/137
Tofield		Edmonton	Viking	SPEC-GTP	100-157	1911		118/138
Tollerton		Edson	Tollerton	2nd	100-39	1913	Note 62	119/134
Torlea	x-Nestor	Edmonton	Viking	Type E	100-152	1911		118/136
Trochu #1		Calgary	Three Hills	Type E	100-152	1912		116/136
Trochu #2		Calgary	Three Hills	SPEC-CNR	100-365	1959		116/142
Troon		Calgary	Endiang	FPS	100-41		Probable	115/125
Twining		Calgary	Three Hills	SHLT				116/144
Ullin	Joint with CPR	Calgary	Brazeau					115/—
Uncas		Edmonton	Viking	Type E	100-152	1911		118/136
Vegreville #1-A		Edmonton	Vegreville	3rd	100-3	1905		118/130
Vegreville #1-B		Edmonton	Vegreville	FPS	100-41	1920	Express Shed	118/144
Vegreville #2		Edmonton	Vegreville	SPEC-CNR	100-255	1930		118/142
Vermilion		Edmonton	Blackfoot	2nd	100-22	1906		116/134
Viewpoint	x-White's Siding	Calgary	Stettler	3rd	100-29	1910		116/132
Viking	x-Meighen	Edmonton	Viking	Type D	100-154	1909		118/135
Villeneuve		Edson	Sangudo	CSS-C	100-47	1913		119/129
Vilna #1		Edmonton	Coronado	FPS	100-41	1919		117/125
Vilna #2		Edmonton	Coronado	3rd	100-72	1922		117/133
Vimy #1	x-Dunrobin	Edmonton	Athabasca	FPS	100-41	1914		116/125
Vimy #2		Edmonton	Athabasca	FPS-CNR	100-334	1952		116/140
Volmer		Edmonton	Athabasca	FPS	100-41	1913	Note 5	116/125
Wabamun		Edson	Wabamun	Type E	100-152	1911		119/136
Wainwright #1		Edmonton	Unity	SPEC-GTP	100-155	1909		117/138
Wainwright #2		Edmonton	Unity	FPS-CNR	CB	1929	Temporary	117/143
Wainwright #3		Edmonton	Unity	SPEC-CNR	100-249	1929	Museum-1	117/142
Warden #1		Calgary	Stettler	4th	100-68	1915		116/130
Warden #2		Calgary	Stettler	3rd	100-72	1919		116/133
Wardlow		Calgary	Sheerness	FPS	100-41	1921		116/125
Warspite #1		Edmonton	Coronado	FPS	100-41	1919		117/125
Warspite #2		Edmonton	Coronado	FPS			Temporary	117/144
Warspite #3		Edmonton	Coronado	CN4A	100-310	1950		117/142
Waskatenau #1	x-Waskateneau	Edmonton	Coronado	FPS	100-41	1920		117/125
Waskatenau #2		Edmonton	Coronado	CN3rd	100-184	1928		117/141
Watts		Calgary	Drumheller	FPS	100-41	1913		115/125
Wayne #1	x-Rosedeer	Calgary	Drumheller	FPS	100-41	1913		115/125
Wayne #2-A		Calgary	Drumheller	4th	100-68	1918		115/130
Wayne #2-B		Calgary	Drumheller	PORT-CNoR	110-73A	1919	SMBH	115/128
Weald		Edson	Foothills	Type E	100-152	1912		118/136
West Jct.		Edson	Wabamun	FPS-GTP	100-162	1913	Note 13	119/134
West Saunders		Calgary	Brazeau					115/—
Whatcher		Calgary	Spondin	FPS-CNR	100-41B	1930		116/139
Whitecourt #1-A		Edson	Sangudo	FPS	100-41	1922		119/125
Whitecourt #1-B		Edson	Sangudo	FPS	100-41	1922		119/125
Whitecourt #2		Edson	Sangudo	3rd	100-72	1922		119/133
Whitecourt #3		Edson	Sangudo	SPEC-CNR		1973		119/142
Wildwood	x-Junkins-CNoR	Edson	Wabamun	Type E	100-152	—	Note 67	119/136
Withrow		Calgary	Brazeau	FPS	100-41			115/125
Wolf Creek	x-Thornton	Edson	Wabamun	Type E	100-152	1911		119/136
Yates #1		Edson	Wabamun	Type E	100-152	1913		119/136
Yates #2		Edson	Wabamun	FPS-GTP	100-162	—		119/134
Yelger	x-Ryley-CNoR	Edmonton	Demay	3rd	100-29	1910		117/132
Youngstown		Calgary	Oyen	3rd	100-29	1913		115/132

BRITISH COLUMBIA

Station Name	Proposed/Former Name	Division	Subdivision	Type of Depot	Plan	Year	Notes	see page
Albreda–CNoR		Kamloops	Albreda	CSS-C	100-98	1915		120/129
Aleza Lake #1		Smithers	Fraser	Type E	100-152	1914		121/136
Aleza Lake #2		Smithers	Fraser	STA				121/144
Alpland #1	x-Mt. Robson-GTP	Smithers	Tete Jaune	Type E	100-152	1913		122/136
Alpland #2		Smithers	Tete Jaune	FPS-CNR		1922		122/144
Amsbury		Smithers	Skeena	Type E	100-152	1911		121/136
Andimaul #1		Smithers	Bulkley	Type E	100-152	1912		121/136
Andimaul #2		Smithers	Bulkley	FPS-CNR	GTP-FT	1951		121/140
Anglesey		Kamloops	Ashcroft	FPS	100-41	1917		120/125
Armstrong Jct.	Joint with CPR	Kamloops	Okanagan					120/—
Arnold		Kamloops	Yale	FPS	100-41	1915		120/125
Ashcroft		Kamloops	Ashcroft	3rd	100-64	1915		120/132
Avola #1		Kamloops	Clearwater	CSS-C	100-98	1915		120/129
Avola #2		Kamloops	Clearwater	FPS				120/144
Barrett #1		Smithers	Telkwa	Type E	100-152	1914		122/136
Barrett #2		Smithers	Telkwa	FPS-CNR	GTP-FT	1951		122/140
Barriere #1		Kamloops	Clearwater	CSS-C	100-98	1916		120/129
Barriere #2		Kamloops	Clearwater	FPS-CNR	100-334	1954		120/140
Basque		Kamloops	Ashcroft	CSS-C	100-98	1915		120/129
Bazan		Vancouver Terminals	Patricia Bay					122/—

BRITISH COLUMBIA

Station Name	Proposed/Former Name	Division	Subdivision	Type of Depot	Plan	Year	Notes	see page
Beament #1		Smithers	Bulkley	Type E	100-152	1913		121/136
Beamont #2		Smithers	Bulkley	FPS-CNR	GTP-FT	1949		121/140
Bednesti		Smithers	Nechako	Type E	100-152	1914		121/136
Bend #1		Smithers	Fraser	Type E	100-152	1914		121/136
Bend #2		Smithers	Fraser	FPS				121/—
Birch Island		Kamloops	Clearwater	CSS-C	100-98	1915		120/129
Blackpool		Kamloops	Clearwater	CSS-C	100-98	1915		120/129
Blue River		Kamloops	Albreda	2nd	100-82	1915		120/133
Boothroyd		Kamloops	Ashcroft	CSS-SH	110-12	1915		—/—
Boston Bar		Kamloops	Ashcroft	2nd	100-82	1915		120/133
Boulder		Kamloops	Clearwater	CSS-C	100-98	1915		120/129
Brynmoor		Vancouver Terminals	Patricia Bay					122/—
Bulkley Canyon #1	x-Giles	Smithers	Bulkley	Type E	100-152	1913		121/136
Bulkley Canyon #2		Smithers	Bulkley	FPS-CNR	GTP-FT			121/140
Burns Lake #1		Smithers	Telkwa	Type E	100-152	1914		122/136
Burns Lake #2		Smithers	Telkwa	SPEC-CNR	100-332	1952		122/142
Campbell Creek Jct.	x-Bostock Jct.	Kamloops	Okanagan	STA-CNR	110-189	1940	SH	120/141
Camscot		Vancouver Terminals	Cowichan					122/—
Cannor		Kamloops	Yale	SHLT-CNR		1927		120/144
Canoe River		Kamloops	Albreda	CSS-C	100-98	1915		120/129
Carnaby		Smithers	Bulkley	Type E	100-152	1913		121/136
Cedarvale #1		Smithers	Bulkley	Type E	100-152	1912		121/136
Cedarvale #2		Smithers	Bulkley	FPS-CNR	100-41B	1931		121/139
Chanlog		Vancouver Terminals	Cowichan					122/—
Chapmans		Kamloops	Yale	CSS-C	100-98	1916		120/129
Cheam View		Kamloops	Yale	CSS-C	100-98	1915		120/129
Chilako #1		Smithers	Nechako	Type E	100-152	1914		121/136
Chilako #2		Smithers	Nechako	FPS-CNR	GTP-FT	1952		121/140
Chilliwack		Kamloops	Yale	2nd	100-83	1915		120/134
Chinook Cove		Kamloops	Clearwater	CSS-C	100-98	1915		120/129
Chu Chua		Kamloops	Clearwater	3rd	100-64	1915		120/132
Cisco		Kamloops	Ashcroft	FPS	100-41	1917		120/125
Clearwater #1		Kamloops	Clearwater	FPS	100-41	1918		120/125
Clearwater #2		Kamloops	Clearwater	SPEC-CNR	1920-1	1961		120/142
Clemina		Kamloops	Albreda	CSS-C	100-98	1915		120/129
Coldstream		Kamloops	Lumby	FPS-CNR	100-41B	1926		120/139
Coldstream Ranch		Kamloops	Lumby	FPS				120/144
Colwood		Vancouver Terminals	Cowichan	FPS	100-41	By24		122/139
Copper Creek		Kamloops	Ashcroft	CSS-C	100-98	1916		120/129
Cordova	x-Cordova Bay	Vancouver Terminals	Patricia Bay					122/—
Cottonwood Flats		Kamloops	Clearwater	FPS	100-41			120/125
Cox	x-Sumas	Kamloops	Yale	FPS	100-41	1915		120/125
CPR Jct.	Joint with CPR	Kamloops	Okanagan					120/—
Craibenn		Smithers	Fraser	FPS				121/144
Crescent Spur #1	x-Leboe	Smithers	Fraser	FPS				121/144
Crescent Spur #2		Smithers	Fraser	FPS				121/144
Crescent Spur #3		Smithers	Fraser	FPS				121/144
Croydon #1		Smithers	Tete Jaune	Type E	100-152	1913		122/136
Croydon #2		Smithers	Tete Jaune	FPS-CNR	GTP-FT	1954		122/140
Culchillum		Vancouver Terminals	Cowichan	FPS-CNR	100-41B			122/139
Decker Lake		Smithers	Telkwa	Type E	100-152	1915		122/136
Deerholme		Vancouver Terminals	Cowichan	FPS	100-41	1921		122/125
Dewey		Smithers	Fraser	Type E	100-152	1914		121/136
Dooley		Vancouver Terminals	Patricia Bay	FPS	100-41	1917		122/125
Doreen	later Grand Trunk	Smithers	Bulkley	Type E	100-152	1913		121/136
Doughty #1		Smithers	Bulkley	Type E	100-152	1913		121/136
Doughty #2		Smithers	Bulkley	FPS-CNR	GTP-FT	1950		121/140
Duck Meadow	x-Ducks Meadow	Kamloops	Okanagan	FPS-CNR	100-41B	1927		120/139
Dunster		Smithers	Tete Jaune	Type E	100-152	1913	Museum-2	122/136
Eddy #1		Smithers	Tete Jaune	Type E	100-152	1913		122/136
Eddy #2		Smithers	Tete Jaune	FPS-GTP	110-101		x-SMBH	122/141
Elk Lake		Vancouver Terminals	Patricia Bay					122/—
Emperor		Smithers	Tete Jaune	SHLT-CNR		1926		122/144
Encombe #1	x-Midlake	Smithers	Nechako	Type E	100-152	1914		121/136
Encombe #2		Smithers	Nechako	FPS-CNR	GTP-FT	1950		121/140
Endako #1		Smithers	Nechako	STA-GTP		1914	Temporary	121/138
Endako #2		Smithers	Nechako	SPEC-CNR	100-143	1922	Similar to 100-142	121/142
Endako #3		Smithers	Nechako	TOS-CNR	Trailer	1970		121/144
Endako #4		Smithers	Nechako	SPEC-CNR	(see note)	1985	Comb. Sta/EMBH	121/142
Engen		Smithers	Nechako	Type E	100-152	1915		121/136

ROSTER NOTES:

5   The line between St. Albert and Morinville, Ab was abandoned effective 1 September 1947.

13   This station was technically on the Edmonton Terminals Subdivision.

62   Dayson, Carrot Creek–CNoR, Fulstow, Horner, Scriven and Tollerton, Ab. These stations were abandoned on grade in 1917. The following year, the CNoR apparently stripped all re-usable millwork (windows, doors, interior fittings, etc.) from these buildings. A local history makes reference to Carrot Creek–CNoR and Fulstow as being sold about 1923. It is likely that all of these stations were sold and removed at the same time.

67   The GTP depot was relocated from the abandoned grade to the CNoR station grounds by 1918.

78   The extension made in 1947 was comprised of the CPR Portable Station (CPR Plan H-14-38) purchased by the CNR and relocated from Sancroft, Alberta (built 1930). It was added onto the east end of the existing shelter. A door was cut into the end walls of the adjoining buildings. A bay window was installed on the trackside of the former CPR portion, which was the Agent's office and apartment. A carbody was moved next to the depot as a freight shed. The original section was removed (burned?) in 1976.

BRITISH COLUMBIA

Station Name	Proposed/Former Name	Division	Subdivision	Type of Depot	Plan	Year	Notes	see page
Evelyn		Smithers	Bulkley	Type E	100-152	1913		121/136
Exstew		Smithers	Skeena	Type E	100-152	1911		121/136
Falkland		Kamloops	Okanagan	CN3rd	100-197	1926		120/141
Falls Creek		Kamloops	Ashcroft	CSS-C	100-98	1915		120/129
Finmoore #1	x-Stuart	Smithers	Nechako	Type E	100-152	1914		121/136
Finmoore #2		Smithers	Nechako	FPS-CNR	CB			121/143
Fitzwilliam	x-Alpland	Kamloops	Albreda	Type E	100-152	1913	Note 1	120/136
Floods		Kamloops	Yale	FPS				120/144
Foreman #1		Smithers	Fraser	Type E	100-152	1914		121/136
Foreman #2		Smithers	Fraser	FPS-CNR	GTP-FT	1948		121/140
Forestdale #1		Smithers	Telkwa	Type E	100-152	1915		122/136
Forestdale #2		Smithers	Telkwa	FPS-CNR	GTP-FT	1948		122/140
Fort Fraser #1		Smithers	Nechako	FPS-GTP	100-162	1916		121/134
Fort Fraser #2		Smithers	Nechako	3rd	100-72	1923		121/133
Fort Fraser #3		Smithers	Nechako	FPS-CNR	100-41B	—		121/139
Fraser Lake		Smithers	Nechako	Type E	100-152	1914		121/136
Frederick		Kamloops	Ashcroft					120/—
Giscome		Smithers	Fraser	Type E	100-152	1914		121/136
Glen Lake		Vancouver Terminals	Cowichan	SHLT		By24		122/144
Glen Valley		Kamloops	Yale	FPS	100-41	1915		120/125
Goat River #1	x-Rooney, xx-Brundell	Smithers	Fraser	Type E	100-152	1914		121/136
Goat River #2		Smithers	Fraser	FPS	110-254	—	x-SMBH	121/141
Gorge	x-Hellsgate	Kamloops	Yale	CSS-SH	110-12	1916	Note 2	120/129
Grant Brook–CNoR		Kamloops	Albreda	CSS-C	100-98	1915		120/129
Grant Brook–GTP		Kamloops	Albreda	Type E	100-152	1913	Note 1	120/136
Guilford #1		Smithers	Fraser	Type E	100-152	1914		121/136
Guilford #2		Smithers	Fraser	FPS-CNR	GTP-FT	1950		121/140
Gyproc	x-Brownsville, xx-Liverpool; Joint with GN	Kamloops	Yale				Note 70	120/—
Halston	x-Mytton	Kamloops	Ashcroft	SPEC-CNoR	100-87	1916		120/130
Hansard		Smithers	Fraser	Type E	100-152	1914		121/136
Hawes		Vancouver Terminals	Cowichan					122/—
Haysport		Smithers	Skeena	PORT-GTP	110-101		SMBH	121/134
Hazelton		Smithers	Bulkley	Type E	100-152	1913		121/136
Heffley	Heffley 2nd site	Kamloops	Clearwater	FPS	100-41	—		120/125
Hope		Kamloops	Yale	2nd	100-84	1916		120/134
Houston #1		Smithers	Telkwa	Type E	100-152	1914		122/136
Houston #2		Smithers	Telkwa	Type G	100-168	1920		122/138
Houston #3		Smithers	Telkwa	STA				122/144
Hubert #1		Smithers	Telkwa	Type E	100-152	1914		122/136
Hubert #2		Smithers	Telkwa	FPS-CNR	GTP-FT	1949		122/140
Hulatt		Smithers	Nechako	Type E	100-152	1915		121/136
Hutchison		Smithers	Nechako	Type E	100-152	1914		121/136
Hutton		Smithers	Fraser	Type E	100-152	1914		121/136
Inkitsaph #1		Kamloops	Ashcroft	SHLT-CNoR		1917		120/144
Inkitsaph #2		Kamloops	Ashcroft	FPS-CNR	100-41B	1929		120/139
Inverness Cannery		Smithers	Skeena	FPS		—	x-ST	122/141
Irvine #1		Kamloops	Clearwater	CSS-C	100-98	1915		120/129
Irvine #2		Kamloops	Clearwater	FPS-CNR	100-290	1926		120/140
Isle Pierre #1		Smithers	Nechako	Type E	100-152	1914		121/136
Isle Pierre #2		Smithers	Nechako	FPS	100-41	—		121/125
Jackman		Kamloops	Albreda	CSS-C	100-98	1915		120/129
Kaien		Smithers	Skeena	FPS-CNR		—	x-ST	122/141
Kamloops #1	North of river	Kamloops	Okanagan	STA-CNoR		1913	Temporary, Note 49	120/134
Kamloops #2	South of river	Kamloops	Okanagan	STA-CNR		1921	Temporary	120/134
Kamloops #3-A	South of river	Kamloops	Okanagan	SPEC-CNR	100-210	1927		120/142
Kamloops #3-B	South of river	Kamloops	Okanagan	FPS-CNR	100-41B	1927	Note 50	120/139
Kamloops Jct.		Kamloops	Clearwater	2nd	100-81	1915		120/133
Kapoor		Vancouver Terminals	Cowichan					122/—
Kelowna	Joint with CPR	Kamloops	Okanagan	SPEC-CNR	100-214	1926		120/142
Kidd #1		Smithers	Fraser	Type E	100-152	1914		121/136
Kidd #2		Smithers	Fraser	FPS-CNR	GTP-FT	1953		121/140
Kinsol		Vancouver Terminals	Cowichan					122/—
Kissinger		Vancouver Terminals	Cowichan	SHLT-CNR		1929		122/144
Kitimat		Smithers	Kitimat	SPEC-CNR	100-356	1955		121/142
Kitselas	x-Vanarsdol	Smithers	Skeena	Type E	100-152	1911		121/136
Kitwanga		Smithers	Bulkley	Type E	100-152	1912		121/136
Knockholt #1		Smithers	Telkwa	Type E	100-152	1914		122/136
Knockholt #2		Smithers	Telkwa	FPS-CNR	GTP-FT	1951		122/140
Kwinitsa		Smithers	Skeena	Type E	100-152	1911	Museum-2	121/136
Laidlaw		Kamloops	Yale	CSS-C	100-98	1916		120/129
Lake Cowichan	x-Cowichan Lake	Vancouver Terminals	Cowichan	FPS-CNR	100-41B	—		122/139
Lake Kathlyn		Smithers	Bulkley	Type F	100-151	1917		121/138
Lakend		Vancouver Terminals	Cowichan					122/—
Lamming Mills		Smithers	Fraser	FPS-CNR		—		121/144
Langley	x-Fort Langley	Kamloops	Yale	3rd	100-64	1915	Museum-2	120/132
Lavington		Kamloops	Lumby					120/—
Leechtown		Vancouver Terminals	Cowichan	FPS		By24		122/144
Legrand	x-Fleet	Smithers	Fraser	Type E	100-152	1914		121/136
Lejac #1	x-Revsa	Smithers	Nechako	SHLT-CNR		—	x-PH	121/141
Lejac #2		Smithers	Nechako	FPS-CNR	100-41B	1945		121/139
Lempriere		Kamloops	Albreda	CSS-C	100-98	1915		120/129

BRITISH COLUMBIA

Station Name	Proposed/Former Name	Division	Subdivision	Type of Depot	Plan	Year	Notes	see page
Lindup #1		Smithers	Fraser	Type E	100-152	1914		121/136
Lindup #2		Smithers	Fraser	FPS-GTP	110-101	—	x-SMBH	121/141
Little Fort	x-Mt. Olie	Kamloops	Clearwater	3rd	100-64	1916		120/132
Longworth		Smithers	Fraser	Type E	100-152	1914		121/136
Loos #1	x-Crescent Island	Smithers	Fraser	Type E	100-152	1914		121/136
Loos #2		Smithers	Fraser	FPS	100-41			121/125
Louis Creek		Kamloops	Clearwater	CSS-C	100-98	1915		120/129
Lucerne–CNoR, BC		Edson	Lucerne	2nd	100-79	1915	Note 46	118/134
Lucerne–GTP		Kamloops	Albreda	Type E	100-152	1912	Note 1	120/136
Lumby #1		Kamloops	Lumby	FPS-CNR	100-41B	1926		120/139
Lumby #2		Kamloops	Lumby	FPS-CNR	100-333	1951		120/140
Lytton		Kamloops	Ashcroft	3rd	100-64	1915		120/132
Martel		Kamloops	Ashcroft	FPS	100-41	1917		120/125
Marten Lake #1		Smithers	Nechako	Type E	100-152	1915		121/136
Marten Lake #2		Smithers	Nechako	FPS-CNR	GTP-FT	1950		121/140
Matsqui		Kamloops	Yale	3rd	100-64	1915		120/132
McAbee		Kamloops	Ashcroft	CSS-C	100-98	1915		120/129
McBride #1		Smithers	Tete Jaune	SPEC-GTP	100-156	1913		122/138
McBride #2		Smithers	Tete Jaune	SPEC-GTP		1918	Temporary	122/138
McBride #3		Smithers	Tete Jaune	SPEC-GTP	100-167	1919		122/138
McCall		Smithers	Nechako	Type E	100-152	1915		121/136
McLure		Kamloops	Clearwater	CSS-C	100-98	1915		120/129
McMurphy		Kamloops	Clearwater	CSS-C	100-98	1915		120/129
Messiter		Kamloops	Clearwater	CSS-C	100-98	1915		120/129
Metchosin		Vancouver Terminals	Cowichan	FPS	100-41	By24		122/139
Mileage 98.5		Kamloops	Ashcroft	FPS	100-41	1916		120/125
Mileage 129.3		Kamloops	Clearwater	FPS	100-41	1916		120/125
Milnes Landing		Vancouver Terminals	Cowichan	FPS		By24		122/139
Minnibariet		Kamloops	Ashcroft					120/—
Miworth #1		Smithers	Nechako	Type E	100-152	1915		121/136
Miworth #2		Smithers	Nechako	FPS-CNR	GTP-FT	1948		121/140
Monte Lake		Kamloops	Okanagan	FPS-CNR	100-41B	1927		120/139
Moricetown		Smithers	Bulkley	Type E	100-152	1913		121/136
Mt. Douglas		Vancouver Terminals	Patricia Bay					122/—
Mt. Lehman		Kamloops	Yale	FPS	100-41	1916		120/125
Mt. Robson–CNoR	1st location	Kamloops	Albreda	CSS-C	100-98	1915	Renamed Foster	120/129
Mt. Robson–CNoR #1-A	2nd location	Kamloops	Albreda	FPS	100-41	1922		120/125
Mt. Robson–CNoR #1-B	2nd location	Kamloops	Albreda	PORT-CNR		1922		120/144
Nash		Smithers	Bulkley	Type E	100-152	1912		121/136
New Hazelton #1		Smithers	Bulkley	Type E	100-152	1913		121/136
New Hazelton #2		Smithers	Bulkley	PORT-CNR		1980		121/144
Newlands #1		Smithers	Fraser	Type E	100-152	1914		121/136
Newlands #2		Smithers	Fraser	FPS-CNR	GTP-FT	1949		121/140
Nichol #1		Smithers	Nechako	Type E	100-152	1914		121/136
Nichol #2		Smithers	Nechako	FPS-GTP	100-162	1918		121/134
North Westminster	x-Sapperton, Joint with GN	Kamloops	Yale				Note 70	120/—
O'Keefe		Kamloops	Okanagan	FPS-CNR	100-41B	1926		120/139
Otway		Smithers	Nechako	Type E	100-152	1915		121/136
Oyama		Kamloops	Okanagan	FPS-CNR	100-41B	1926		120/139
Pacific #1		Smithers	Bulkley	SPEC-GTP	100-155	1913		121/138
Pacific #2		Smithers	Bulkley	SPEC-CNR	100-277	1935		121/142
Palling #1		Smithers	Telkwa	Type E	100-152	1914		122/136
Palling #2		Smithers	Telkwa	FPS-CNR	GTP-FT	1950		122/140
Patricia Bay #1-A		Vancouver Terminals	Patricia Bay	FPS	100-41	1916		122/125
Patricia Bay #1-B		Vancouver Terminals	Patricia Bay	FPS	100-41	1916		122/125
Patricia Bay #1-C		Vancouver Terminals	Patricia Bay	FPS	100-41	1916		122/125
Penny #1-A		Smithers	Fraser	FPS		—	x-ST	121/141
Penny #1-B		Smithers	Fraser	FPS-GTP	110-101	—	x-SMBH	121/141
Penny #2		Smithers	Fraser	Type E	100-152			121/136
Perow		Smithers	Telkwa	Type E	100-152	1914		122/136
Phelan		Smithers	Skeena	Type E	100-152	1911		122/136
Pitman #1		Smithers	Skeena	Type E	100-152	1912		121/136
Pitman #2		Smithers	Skeena	FPS-CNR	GTP-FT	1947		121/140
Pitquah	x-Gosset	Kamloops	Ashcroft	CSS-SH	110-12	1915	Note 2	—/129
Popkum		Kamloops	Yale	FPS	100-41	1917		120/125
Port Mann		Kamloops	Yale	2nd	100-83	1915	Note 70	120/134
Postill	x-Hood	Kamloops	Okanagan	FPS-CNR	100-41B	1926		120/139
Priestly		Smithers	Telkwa	Type E	100-152	1915		122/136
Prince George #1		Smithers	Fraser	SPEC-GTP		1913		121/138
Prince George #2		Smithers	Fraser	SPEC-GTP	100-136	1922		121/142
Prince George #3		Smithers	Fraser	SPEC-CNR		1971		121/142

ROSTER NOTES:

1 These depots were left vacant on the abandoned GTP grade in 1917. Rainbow–GTP was relocated to Redpass in 1917 and Yellowhead burned down about 1918. The stations at Fitzwilliam, Grant Brook and Lucerne–GTP, BC were rehabilitated in 1924, when that section of the line was re-opened.

2 This was a conventional section house apparently used as station. It does not appear as if these buildings had bracket-supported awnings or formal waiting rooms as did earlier combination station-and-section-house designs such as Plan 110-10.

46 Abandoned when the rehabilitated GTP line reopened 1 November 1924. It remained vacant until World War II when Lucerne was used as a Japanese internment camp, and the station was used as a bunkhouse for internees. The depot was finally razed by the Parks Department in the mid-1950s.

49 The temporary station for the Canadian Northern and the Northern Construction Company (involved in building the railway line) was situated north of the South Thompson River.

50 For trainmen's equipment.

70 This station was technically on the Vancouver Terminals Subdivision.

BRITISH COLUMBIA

Station Name	Proposed/Former Name	Division	Subdivision	Type of Depot	Plan	Year	Notes	see page
Prince Rupert #1		Smithers	Skeena	SPEC-GTP	140-210	1907	Temporary, Note 56	122/138
Prince Rupert #2		Smithers	Skeena	SPEC-CNR	100-135	1922		122/142
Pyramid		Kamloops	Albreda	CSS-C	100-98	1915		120/129
Quick		Smithers	Telkwa	FPS-GTP	100-162	———		122/134
Rainbow–GTP		Kamloops	Albreda	Type E	100-152	1913	Note 1	120/136
Rainbow–CNoR		Kamloops	Albreda	CSS-C	100-98	1915		120/129
Ramage		Kamloops	Clearwater	FPS-CNR	100-41B	1927		120/139
Raush Valley #1		Smithers	Tete Jaune	Type E	100-152	1913		122/136
Raush Valley #2		Smithers	Tete Jaune	FPS-CNR		———		122/141
Rayleigh	x-St. Paul	Kamloops	Clearwater	CSS-C	100-98	1916		120/129
Rearguard #1	x-Albreda–GTP	Smithers	Tete Jaune	Type E	100-152	1913		122/136
Rearguard #2		Smithers	Tete Jaune	SHLT-CNR		1949		122/144
Redpass Jct. #1		Kamloops	Albreda	Type E	100-152		Note 1	120/136
Redpass Jct. #2		Kamloops	Albreda	STA-CNR	Trailer	1977		120/144
Resplendent–CNoR		Kamloops	Albreda	CSS-C	100-98	1915		120/129
Rider	x-Knole	Smithers	Fraser	Type E	100-152	1914		121/136
Rocky Point Siding		Vancouver Terminals	Cowichan	FPS		By24		122/144
Rosedale		Kamloops	Yale	3rd	100-64	1915		120/132
Rose Lake		Smithers	Telkwa	Type E	100-152	1915		122/136
Rutland #1-A		Kamloops	Okanagan	FPS-CNR	100-41B	1926		120/139
Rutland #1-B		Kamloops	Okanagan	FPS-CNR	100-41B	———		120/139
Saanichton		Vancouver Terminals	Patricia Bay					122/—
St. Elmo		Kamloops	Yale	FPS	100-41	1915		120/125
Salvus #1		Smithers	Skeena	Type E	100-152	1912		121/136
Salvus #2		Smithers	Skeena	CN3rd	100-256	1928	Variant	121/142
Sassenos	x-McNeil	Vancouver Terminals	Cowichan	FPS		By24		122/144
Savona		Kamloops	Ashcroft	CSS-C	100-98	1915		120/129
Savory		Smithers	Telkwa	Type E	100-152	1915		122/136
Scott		Vancouver Terminals	Patricia Bay					122/—
Seaton		Smithers	Bulkley	Type E	100-152	1913		121/136
Seddell		Kamloops	Ashcroft	CSS-C	100-98	1915		120/129
Selwyn	x-Resplendent–GTP	Smithers	Tete Jaune	Type E	100-152	1912		122/136
Shames		Smithers	Skeena	Type E	100-152	1912		121/136
Shawnigan Lake		Vancouver Terminals	Cowichan					122/—
Shelley #1		Smithers	Fraser	Type E	100-152	1914		121/136
Shelley #2		Smithers	Fraser	FPS-CNR	GTP-FT	———		121/140
Shelley #3		Smithers	Fraser	STA-CNR				121/144
Sheraton #1		Smithers	Telkwa	Type E	100-152	1915		122/136
Sheraton #2		Smithers	Telkwa	FPS-CNR	GTP-FT	1948		122/140
Shere		Smithers	Tete Jaune	Type E	100-152	1913		122/136
Shushten	x-Shusten	Kamloops	Ashcroft					120/—
Sidney		Vancouver Terminals	Patricia Bay					122/—
Sinclair Mills		Smithers	Fraser	FPS	110-217	———	x-SMBH	121/141
Sinkut #1	x-Tsinkut	Smithers	Nechako	Type E	100-152	1914		121/136
Sinkut #2		Smithers	Nechako	FPS-CNR	GTP-FT	1948		121/140
Skeena	x-Skeena City	Smithers	Skeena	Type E	100-152	1912		121/136
Skeena Crossing #1		Smithers	Bulkley	FPS-GTP	CB	1917		121/143
Skeena Crossing #2		Smithers	Bulkley	FPS-CNR		1943		121/144
Skoonka		Kamloops	Ashcroft					120/—
Smithers #1		Smithers	Telkwa	SPEC-GTP		1915	Temporary, Note 58	122/138
Smithers #2		Smithers	Telkwa	SPEC-GTP	100-166	1919	Museum-1	122/138
Smithvale		Kamloops	Yale	FPS	100-41	1922		120/125
Sockeye #1		Smithers	Skeena	Type E	100-152	1911		122/136
Sockeye #2		Smithers	Skeena	FPS		———	x-ST	122/141
Sooke Lake		Vancouver Terminals	Cowichan	SHLT		1920		122/144
Spences Bridge #1		Kamloops	Ashcroft	3rd	100-64	1915		120/132
Spences Bridge #2		Kamloops	Ashcroft	FPS	100-41	1922		120/125
Spences Bridge #3		Kamloops	Ashcroft	3rd	100-72	1923		120/133
Squeah		Kamloops	Yale	CSS-SH	110-12	1916	Note 2	120/129
Stout		Kamloops	Yale					120/—
Sweetsbridge		Kamloops	Okanagan	FPS-CNR	100-41B	1926		120/139
Swift Creek		Kamloops	Albreda	CSS-C	100-98	1915		120/129
Swiftwater		Smithers	Tete Jaune	Type E	100-152	1913		122/136
Sydney		Vancouver Terminals	Patricia Bay					122/—
Tatlow		Smithers	Telkwa	Type E	100-152	1914		122/136
Telkwa #1		Smithers	Telkwa	FPS-GTP	100-162	1914		122/134
Telkwa #2		Smithers	Telkwa	Type G	100-168	1922		122/138
Telkwa #3		Smithers	Telkwa	STA-CNR				122/144
Terrace #1		Smithers	Skeena	Type E	100-152	1911		121/136
Terrace #2		Smithers	Skeena	SPEC-CNR	100-391	1960		121/—
Tete Jaune		Smithers	Tete Jaune	Type E	100-152	1912		122/136
Thunder River		Kamloops	Albreda	CSS-C	100-98	1915		120/129
Tintagel		Smithers	Telkwa	Type E	100-152	1915		122/136
Topley		Smithers	Telkwa	Type E	100-152	1914		122/136
Trafalgar		Kamloops	Yale					120/—
Tranquille		Kamloops	Ashcroft	CSS-C	100-98	1916		120/129
Trout Creek		Kamloops	Clearwater					120/—
Tyee		Smithers	Skeena	Type E	100-152	1911		121/136
Tynehead		Kamloops	Yale	FPS-CNR	CB	1925		120/143
Urling #1		Smithers	Fraser	Type E	100-152	1914		121/136
Urling #2		Smithers	Fraser	FPS-CNR		———		121/—

BRITISH COLUMBIA

Station Name	Proposed/Former Name	Division	Subdivision	Type of Depot	Plan	Year	Notes	see page
Usk #1		Smithers	Skeena	Type E	100-152	1912		121/136
Usk #2		Smithers	Skeena	FPS-CNR				121/141
Valemount	x-Cranberry	Kamloops	Albreda	CSS-C	100-98			120/129
Vancouver #1	Joint with GN	Kamloops	Yale	SPEC-CNoR		1916	Temporary, Note 69	120/134
Vancouver #2		Kamloops	Yale	SPEC-CNoR	100-224	1917	Note 70	120/134
Vanderhoof #1		Smithers	Nechako	Type E	100-152	1914		121/136
Vanderhoof #2		Smithers	Nechako	3rd	100-72	1924		121/133
Vanderhoof #3		Smithers	Nechako	SPEC-CNR	100-345	1960		121/142
Vavenby		Kamloops	Clearwater	CSS-C	100-98	1915		120/129
Victoria–Point Ellice		Vancouver Terminals	Cowichan	SPEC-CNoR				122/142
Victoria–Alpha Street		Vancouver Terminals	Cowichan	SPEC-CNoR				122/134
Vinsulla	x-Hefferley/xx-Heffley 1st	Kamloops	Clearwater	CSS-C	100-98	1915		120/129
Walcott #1		Smithers	Telkwa	Type E	100-152	1913		122/136
Walcott #2		Smithers	Telkwa	FPS				122/144
Walhachin		Kamloops	Ashcroft	CSS-C	100-98	1915		120/129
Wedgwood #1		Smithers	Nechako	Type E	100-152	1915		121/136
Wedgwood #2		Smithers	Nechako	FPS-CNR	GTP-FT	1949		121/140
Westlang	x-Latimer Road, xx-Port Kells	Kamloops	Yale	FPS		1921		120/144
Westwold	x-West Wold	Kamloops	Okanagan	FPS-CNR	100-41B	1927		120/139
Willow River #1		Smithers	Fraser	Type E	100-152	1914		121/136
Willow River #2		Smithers	Fraser	FPS-CNR				121/144
Winfield		Kamloops	Okanagan	FPS-CNR	100-41B	1926		120/139
Wire Cache		Kamloops	Clearwater	FPS	100-41			120/125
Wolfenden		Kamloops	Clearwater	CSS-C	100-98	1915		120/129
Woodcock		Smithers	Bulkley	Type E	100-152	1912		121/136
Yale		Kamloops	Yale	CSS-C	100-98	1916		120/129
Yellowhead #1	x-Yelsum/xx-Summit	Kamloops	Albreda	Type E	100-152	1912	Note 1	119/136
Yellowhead #2		Kamloops	Albreda	CSS-C	100-47			120/129
Youbou		Vancouver Terminals	Cowichan	FPS-CNR	100-41B			122/139

MANITOBA

Station Name	Proposed/Former Name	Division	Subdivision	Type of Depot	Plan	Year	Notes	see page
Adelpha		Portage-Brandon	Wakopa	FPS	100-41	1916		107/125
Agar		Portage-Brandon	Cromer	FPS	100-41	1911		104/126
Agnew #1		Portage-Brandon	Hartney	PORT-CNoR	100-24		Probable	105/128
Agnew #2		Portage-Brandon	Hartney	FPS-CNR	100-41B	1923		105/139
Albert		Portage-Brandon	Victoria Beach	FPS	100-41	1918		106/126
Alcock		Port Arthur	Minaki					108/—
Alfretta		Portage-Brandon	Rapid City					106/—
Alonsa		Portage-Brandon	Oakland	4th	100-68	1922		106/130
Alpha		Portage-Brandon	Oakland					106/—
Altamont #1		Portage-Brandon	Miami	CSS-NPR	100-16	1899		105/128
Altamont #2		Portage-Brandon	Miami	SHLT-CNR			x-CO	105/141
Amanda		Portage-Brandon	Victoria Beach					106/—
Amaranth		Portage-Brandon	Oakland	FPS	100-96	1909		106/124
Angusville		Portage-Brandon	Rossburn	3rd	100-29	1909		106/132
Anola		Port Arthur	Minaki	NTR3	100-181	1910		108/138
Argue		Portage-Brandon	Hartney	FPS	100-41	1910	Probable	105/126
Argyle		Portage-Brandon	Inwood	FPS	100-41	1912		105/126
Arizona #1		Portage-Brandon	Pleasant Point	3rd	100-3	1905		106/130
Arizona #2		Portage-Brandon	Pleasant Point	FPS	100-41			106/126
Armstrongs		Portage-Brandon	Victoria Beach					107/—
Arona		Portage-Brandon	Harte					104/—
Ashdown		Portage-Brandon	Wawanesa	FPS	100-41	1912		107/126
Ashern #1		Portage-Brandon	Oak Point	FPS	100-41	1914		106/126
Ashern #2		Portage-Brandon	Oak Point	4th	100-68	1920		106/130
Ashville		Dauphin	Togo	FPS	100-41	1912		103/126
Athapap		Hudson Bay	Flin Flon	FPS-CNR	CB	1939		103/143
Atik		Hudson Bay	Flin Flon	FPS				103/—
Atikameg Lake		Hudson Bay	Wekusko	FPS-CNR	100-290	1928		104/140
Aulds		Portage-Brandon	Ridgeville					106/—
Babcock	Comm'l Cement	Portage-Brandon	Carman	SHLT-CNoR	100-95	1909	Probable	104/124
Baden		Dauphin	Erwood	CSS-B	100-99	1901		102/128
Badger		Port Arthur	Sprague	4th	100-31	1909		108/130
Baldur		Portage-Brandon	Carman	NPR-4th	100-26	1890	Museum-2	104/129
Balsam Bay		Portage-Brandon	Victoria Beach	FPS	100-41	1915		106/126
Barrows #1	x-Elksgate Jct.	Dauphin	Erwood	CSS-B	100-99	1908		102/128
Barrows #2		Dauphin	Erwood	FPS	100-41	1923		102/126
Barrows #3		Dauphin	Erwood	4th	100-68	1923		102/130
Baynham		Port Arthur	Sprague					108/—

ROSTER NOTES:

1 These depots were left vacant on the abandoned GTP grade in 1917. Rainbow–GTP was relocated to Redpass in 1917 and Yellowhead burned down about 1918. The stations at Fitzwilliam, Grant Brook and Lucerne–GTP, BC were rehabilitated in 1924, when that section of the line was re-opened.

2 This was a conventional section house apparently used as station. It does not appear as if these buildings had bracket-supported awnings or formal waiting rooms as did earlier combination station-and-section-house designs such as Plan 110-10.

56 The Prince Rupert Inn was the first of what was supposed to be a string of cross-country hostelries designed by Francis Mawson Rattenbury for the GTP. As it turned out, it was the only Rattenbury-designed hotel built by the company. The Inn was opened in 1907 and it was subsequently acquired by the Operating Department and converted into an ad hoc station. Associated costs: purchase $9,419, annex $21,303, remodeling $1,540 and temporary baggage room $346.

58 Replaced in 1919, converted into B&B shop in 1921.

69 The Great Northern Railway station on Pender Street was used by the CNoR commencing October 1915, until temporary passenger accommodations were built. These were apparently abandoned once the new depot on Main Street opened in 1917.

70 This station was technically on the Vancouver Terminals Subdivision.

MANITOBA

Station Name	Proposed/Former Name	Division	Subdivision	Type of Depot	Plan	Year	Notes	see page
Beaconia #2		Portage-Brandon	Victoria Beach	FPS-CNR	100-41B	1927		106/139
Beaudry		Portage-Brandon	Harte	Type E	100-152	1911		104/136
Beaver	x-Beaver River	Portage-Brandon	Gladstone	NPR-4th	100-26	1900		104/129
Bedford #1		Port Arthur	Sprague	FPS	100-41	1915		108/126
Bedford #2		Port Arthur	Sprague	FPS-CNR	100-290	1952		108/140
Belair		Portage-Brandon	Victoria Beach	FPS	100-41			106/126
Belleview		Portage-Brandon	Hartney	3rd	100-29	1915		105/132
Bellsite		Dauphin	Erwood	FPS-CNR	100-41B	1929		102/139
Belmont #1-A		Portage-Brandon	Carman	CSS-NPR	100-16	1889		104/128
Belmont #1-B		Portage-Brandon	Carman	3rd	100-3	1907	Add to Sta #1-A	104/130
Benard	x-Eustache	Portage-Brandon	Gladstone	FPS	100-41	1912		104/126
Benito		Dauphin	Preeceville	3rd	100-29	1909		102/132
Bethany #1		Portage-Brandon	Rossburn	FPS	100-96			106/124
Bethany #2		Portage-Brandon	Rossburn	CN4th	100-220	1927		106/142
Beulah		Portage-Brandon	Rapid City	3rd	100-29	1911		106/132
Bield		Dauphin	Togo	FPS	100-41	1912		103/126
Birch Bay		Portage-Brandon	Oak Point	FPS	100-41	1918		106/126
Birch River #1		Dauphin	Erwood	FPS	100-41	1911		102/126
Birch River #2		Dauphin	Erwood	CN4A	100-310	1948		102/142
Bird #1		Hudson Bay	Herchmer	PORT	110-148	1927	SMBH	103/141
Bird #2		Hudson Bay	Herchmer	FPS-CNR		1961		103/144
Bird's Hill		Portage-Brandon	Victoria Beach					106/—
Birdtail		Portage-Brandon	Rossburn	FPS	100-41	1915		106/126
Birnie		Portage-Brandon	Neepawa	5th	100-17	1904		105/129
Bloom		Portage-Brandon	Harte	FPS	100-41			104/128
Bowsman		Dauphin	Erwood	CSS-B	100-99	1900	Museum-2	102/128
Brainerd		Portage-Brandon	Victoria Beach	FPS-CNR	100-41B	1935		106/139
Brandon #1		Portage-Brandon	Pleasant Point	SPEC-NPR		1890		106/134
Brandon #2	On Spur	Portage-Brandon	Pleasant Point	SPEC-CNoR	140-144	1911		106/134
Brandon Jct.		Portage-Brandon	Pleasant Point	FPS-CNR	100-41B	1929		106/139
Brandon North	x-Knox Bridge	Portage-Brandon	Harte	SPEC-CNR	100-294	1941		104/142
Brandon–Sixth Street		Portage-Brandon	Cromer	TOS				104/—
Brereton Lake		Port Arthur	Minaki	FPS				108/144
Broad Valley		Portage-Brandon	Inwood	FPS	100-41	1915		105/126
Brumlie		Portage-Brandon	Rapid City	FPS	100-41	1914		106/126
Brunkild		Portage-Brandon	Carman	3rd	100-29	1909		104/132
Butler		Portage-Brandon	Cromer	FPS	100-41	1910		104/126
Cabot		Portage-Brandon	Harte	Type E	100-152	1911		104/136
Caliento		Portage-Brandon	Ridgeville	FPS	100-41	1913		106/126
Calrin		Portage-Brandon	Gladstone	FPS	100-41	1912		104/126
Camper		Portage-Brandon	Oak Point	FPS	100-41	1913		106/126
Carberry		Portage-Brandon	Carberry	2nd	100-21	1904		104/133
Carberry Jct.		Portage-Brandon	Neepawa					105/—
Cardale #2		Portage-Brandon	Rapid City	3rd	100-75	1914		106/133
Cardinal		Portage-Brandon	Carman	4th	100-31	1911		104/130
Carman		Portage-Brandon	Carman	2nd	100-2	1902		104/133
Carrick #2	x-Spurgrave	Port Arthur	Sprague	FPS-CNR	100-41B	1934		108/139
Cartier		Portage-Brandon	Letellier	FPS	100-41	1919		105/126
Cawdor		Portage-Brandon	Oakland	FPS	100-41			106/126
Caye		Portage-Brandon	Harte	Type E	100-152	1911		104/136
Channing		Hudson Bay	Flin Flon	FPS-CNR	CB	1929		103/143
Chatfield		Portage-Brandon	Inwood	FPS	100-41	1915		105/126
Chisel Lake #1-A		Hudson Bay	Chisel Lake	FPS-CNR	100-41B			103/139
Chisel Lake #1-B		Hudson Bay	Chisel Lake	FPS-CNR	100-41B			103/139
Christie	x-Christies	Portage-Brandon	Letellier	PORT-CNR	100-290	1939		105/140
Churchill		Hudson Bay	Herchmer	SPEC-CNR	100-271	1930		103/142
Clanwilliam #2		Portage-Brandon	Rossburn	3rd	100-29	1914		106/132
Clarkleigh		Portage-Brandon	Oak Point	PORT-CNoR	100-24	1911		105/128
Coatstone		Portage-Brandon	Wakopa	FPS-CNR	CB	1928		107/143
Colby		Portage-Brandon	Gladstone	FPS	100-41	1916		104/126
Cordova		Portage-Brandon	Rapid City	FPS	100-41	1912		106/126
Cormorant		Hudson Bay	Wekusko	FPS	100-41			104/126
Cowan #1		Dauphin	Cowan	CSS-A	100-99	1899		102/128
Cowan #2		Dauphin	Cowan	FPS	100-41			102/126
Craig Siding		Port Arthur	Minaki	FPS-CNR	100-290	1936		108/140
Cranberry Portage		Hudson Bay	Flin Flon	CN3rd	100-251	1929	Variant	103/142
Crocus		Portage-Brandon	Rossburn	FPS	100-41	1922		106/126
Cromer		Portage-Brandon	Cromer	3rd	100-29	1911		104/132
Curtis		Portage-Brandon	Gladstone	FPS	100-41	1911		104/126
Dacotah		Portage-Brandon	Gladstone	FPS	100-41	1917		104/126
Dauphin #1		Portage-Brandon	Gladstone	CSS-A	100-63	1897		104/128
Dauphin #2		Portage-Brandon	Gladstone	SPEC-CNoR	100-44	1913		104/134
Decimal	x-Dott	Port Arthur	Minaki	NTR3	100-181	1910		108/138
Decker		Portage-Brandon	Rapid City	3rd	100-29	1913		106/132
Deepdale #1		Dauphin	Togo	FPS	100-41	1915		103/126
Deepdale #2		Dauphin	Togo	3rd	100-72	1922		103/133
Deer		Portage-Brandon	Harte	FPS-CNR	100-41B			104/139
Deerhorn		Portage-Brandon	Oak Point	FPS	100-41	1915		105/126
Deerwood		Portage-Brandon	Miami	FPS	100-96	1908		105/124
Deloraine #2		Portage-Brandon	Wakopa	3rd	100-72	1915		107/133
Delta	x-Delta Beach	Portage-Brandon	Delta	SPEC-CNoR	100-90	1917	Note 24	104/134
Diamond	x-Headingly	Portage-Brandon	Gladstone	SHLT-CNoR		1904		104/144

MANITOBA

Station Name	Proposed/Former Name	Division	Subdivision	Type of Depot	Plan	Year	Notes	see page
Dipples		Portage-Brandon	Carman	FPS-CNoR	CB	1919		104/143
Dock		Portage-Brandon	Harte					104/—
Dropmore #1		Dauphin	Tonkin	FPS	100-41			103/126
Dropmore #2		Dauphin	Tonkin	4th	100-68	1921		103/130
Dufresne		Port Arthur	Sprague	FPS	100-41	1913		108/126
Dugald		Port Arthur	Minaki	NTR2	100-180	1910		108/138
Dugas		Portage-Brandon	Harte	FPS-CNR	CB	1925		104/143
Dunrea		Portage-Brandon	Hartney	NPR-4th		1898		105/129
Durban #1		Dauphin	Preeceville	PORT-CNoR	100-24			102/128
Durban #2		Dauphin	Preeceville	3rd	100-75	1919		102/133
Dutton		Dauphin	Togo					103/—
Eastments Siding		Dauphin	Togo					—/—
East Selkirk		Portage-Brandon	Victoria Beach	FPS	100-41	1915		106/126
East Tower		Portage-Brandon	Harte					104/—
Eden		Portage-Brandon	Neepawa	3rd	100-3	1903		105/130
Edwin		Portage-Brandon	Pleasant Point	FPS	100-96	1909		106/124
Ekhart	x-Drake	Portage-Brandon	Inwood	FPS	CB	1916		105/143
Elgin #1-A		Portage-Brandon	Hartney	NPR-4th		1898		105/129
Elgin #1-B		Portage-Brandon	Hartney	3rd	100-3	1904	Add to Sta #1-A	105/130
Elie–CNoR #2		Portage-Brandon	Gladstone	3rd	100-72	1919		104/133
Elliotts		Portage-Brandon	Wawanesa	FPS	100-41	1912		107/126
Elma		Port Arthur	Minaki	NTR1	100-179	1910		108/138
Elphinstone		Portage-Brandon	Rossburn	3rd	100-3	1904		106/130
Embury		Portage-Brandon	Oakland	FPS	CB			106/143
Emerson #1		Portage-Brandon	Ridgeville	SPEC-NPR	100-7	1904?		106/134
Emerson #2		Portage-Brandon	Ridgeville	SPEC-CNR	100-191	1923		106/142
Emerson Jct.		Portage-Brandon	Letellier	SPEC-NPR	100-52	1888		105/134
Emerson Jct.		Portage-Brandon	Ridgeville					106/—
Endcliffe		Dauphin	Tonkin	PORT-CNoR	100-24	1910		105/128
Enterprise		Portage-Brandon	Wakopa	SHLT-CNoR	100-95	1909		107/124
Erickson #1		Portage-Brandon	Rossburn	FPS	100-41	1911		106/126
Erickson #2		Portage-Brandon	Rossburn	3rd	100-72	1923		106/133
Eriksdale #2		Portage-Brandon	Oak Point	3rd	100-72	1918		105/133
Erinview		Portage-Brandon	Inwood	FPS	100-41	1912		105/126
Ethelbert		Dauphin	Cowan	CSS-A	100-63	1898		102/128
Exira		Portage-Brandon	Harte	Type E	100-152	1911		104/136
Fairfax		Portage-Brandon	Hartney	NPR-4th		—		105/129
Fairford #2		Portage-Brandon	Oak Point	FPS-CNR	100-41B	1943		106/139
Fairview		Portage-Brandon	Carberry	FPS	100-41	1912		104/126
Faulkner		Portage-Brandon	Steep Rock	FPS	100-41	1916		106/126
Findlay		Portage-Brandon	Hartney					105/—
Findlay Crossing		Portage-Brandon	Hartney	SHLT-CNoR	100-95	1905		105/124
Firdale		Portage-Brandon	Harte	FPS-GTP	100-162	1909		104/134
Fisher Branch		Portage-Brandon	Inwood	3rd	100-72	1915		105/133
Fishing River		Dauphin	Winnipegosis	STA-NPR		1898		103/—
Flin Flon		Hudson Bay	Flin Flon	SPEC-CNR	100-275	1934	Museum-1	103/142
Fork River #1		Dauphin	Winnipegosis	CSS-A	100-63	1899		103/128
Fork River #2		Dauphin	Winnipegosis	3rd	100-75	1920		103/133
Fork River #3		Dauphin	Winnipegosis	FPS	100-41	—		103/126
Fortier #1		Portage-Brandon	Harte	Type E	100-152	1911		104/136
Fortier #2		Portage-Brandon	Harte	FPS	100-41	1923		104/126
Fredenstahl		Portage-Brandon	Ridgeville	FPS	100-41	1910		106/126
Freshford		Hudson Bay	Turnberry					103/—
Fulton		Portage-Brandon	Oakland	FPS	100-41	1911		106/126
Gardenton	x-Stuartburn	Portage-Brandon	Ridgeville	3rd	100-3	1905		106/130
Garland		Dauphin	Cowan	FPS	100-41	1911		102/126
Gateside		Portage-Brandon	Pleasant Point	FPS	100-41	1912		106/126
Gervais #1		Portage-Brandon	Harte	Type E	100-152	1911		104/136
Gervais #2		Portage-Brandon	Harte	PORT-GTP	110-101	—	SMBH	104/141
Gilbert Plains		Dauphin	Togo	CSS-B	100-99	1900		103/128
Gilbert Plains Jct.		Dauphin	Togo					103/—
Gillam		Hudson Bay	Thicket	SPEC-CNR	100-244	1930		103/142
Giroux #2		Port Arthur	Sprague	SPEC-CNR	100-190	1923		108/142
Giroux #3		Port Arthur	Sprague	FPS-CNR	100-41B	1944	Temporary	108/139
Giroux #4		Port Arthur	Sprague	CN4A	100-305	1946		108/142
Gladstone #2		Portage-Brandon	Gladstone	2nd	100-5	1901	Museum-2	104/133
Glass		Port Arthur	Minaki	FPS-CNR		1922		108/—
Glencairn		Portage-Brandon	Gladstone	CSS-A	100-63		Probable	104/128
Glenella #1		Portage-Brandon	Gladstone	CSS-A	100-63	1897		104/128
Glenella #2		Portage-Brandon	Gladstone	3rd	100-29	1913		104/132
Glenforsa		Portage-Brandon	Rossburn	FPS	100-41	1910		106/126
Glenlea		Portage-Brandon	Letellier	FPS	100-41	1916		105/126
Glenora	x-Greenway	Portage-Brandon	Wakopa	PORT-CNoR	100-24	1908		107/128
Golden Stream		Portage-Brandon	Gladstone	SHLT-CNoR	100-95	1906		104/124
Gonor		Portage-Brandon	Victoria Beach	FPS	100-41	1915		106/126
Gordon		Portage-Brandon	Oak Point	FPS	100-41	1910		105/126
Grahamdale	x-Deerfield	Portage-Brandon	Oak Point	PORT-CNoR	100-24	1913		106/128
Grand Beach		Portage-Brandon	Victoria Beach	2nd	100-89	1916	Variant	106/133

ROSTER NOTES:

24 The Delta Subdivision was abandoned 1 March 1941. The Delta station was apparently sold *in situ* in 1941, being used as a fish warehouse until it burned down in the mid-1940s.

MANITOBA

Station Name	Proposed/Former Name	Division	Subdivision	Type of Depot	Plan	Year	Notes	see page
Grande Clariere #1		Portage-Brandon	Hartney	FPS	100-96	1908	Probable	105/124
Grande Clariere #2		Portage-Brandon	Hartney	FPS	100-41	1919	Probable	105/126
Grande Clariere #3		Portage-Brandon	Hartney	FPS	100-41	—		105/126
Grand Marais		Portage-Brandon	Victoria Beach	PORT-CNoR	110-73A	1921	SMBH	106/128
Grandview		Dauphin	Togo	CSS-A	100-63	1900		103/128
Grant's Cut		Portage-Brandon	Harte					104/—
Graysville #2	x-Gray's	Portage-Brandon	Carman	4th	100-68	1920		104/130
Gregg		Portage-Brandon	Harte	Type D	100-154	1909		104/135
Greenway		Portage-Brandon	Carman	4th	100-31	1910		104/130
Grosse Isle		Portage-Brandon	Oak Point	3rd	100-3	1904		105/130
Gruber		Dauphin	Winnipegosis					103/—
Guilbault		Portage-Brandon	Ridgeville					106/—
Gypsumville #2		Portage-Brandon	Oak Point	4th	100-68	1916		106/130
Hallboro #2		Portage-Brandon	Neepawa	3rd	100-29	1912		105/132
Hallboro #3		Portage-Brandon	Neepawa	FPS	100-41	—	Temporary	105/126
Hallboro #4		Portage-Brandon	Neepawa	4th	100-68	—		105/130
Harcus		Portage-Brandon	Oakland	FPS	100-41	1922		106/126
Hargrave		Portage-Brandon	Victoria Beach					106/—
Harte		Portage-Brandon	Harte	Type E	100-152	1911		104/136
Hartney		Portage-Brandon	Hartney	NPR-4th		1898		105/129
Hartney Crossing		Portage-Brandon	Hartney	SHLT-CNoR	100-95	1905		105/124
Hazeldean		Portage-Brandon	Wakopa	SHLT-CNoR	100-95	1914		107/124
Hazell		Port Arthur	Minaki	NTR3	100-181	1910		108/138
Helston	x-Berton	Portage-Brandon	Neepawa	3rd	100-3	1901		105/130
Hickey		Port Arthur	Sprague					108/—
Hilbre		Portage-Brandon	Oak Point	FPS	100-41	1916		106/126
Hillside Beach		Portage-Brandon	Victoria Beach	FPS	100-41	—		106/126
Hilton		Portage-Brandon	Wawanesa	NPR-4th			Probable	107/129
Hobson	x-Walldon	Portage-Brandon	Gladstone	FPS	100-96	1909	Probable	104/124
Hoctor		Port Arthur	Minaki	NTR3	100-181	1910		108/138
Hodgson #1		Portage-Brandon	Inwood	FPS	100-41			105/126
Hodgson #2		Portage-Brandon	Inwood	4th	100-68	1920		105/130
Holmfield #2-A		Portage-Brandon	Wakopa	4th	100-31	1909		107/130
Holmfield #2-B		Portage-Brandon	Wakopa	FPS	100-41			107/126
Homewood		Portage-Brandon	Carman	3rd	100-3	1901		104/130
Horton		Portage-Brandon	Wakopa	FPS-CNR	CB	1920		107/143
Howden		Portage-Brandon	Neepawa	FPS	100-41	1910		105/126
Huddlestone		Portage-Brandon	Delta	FPS	CB?		Note 24	104/143
Hummerston		Portage-Brandon	Neepawa	FPS	100-41	1913		105/126
Ilford		Hudson Bay	Thicket	FPS-CNR	100-41B	1927		103/139
Indian Springs		Portage-Brandon	Carman	FPS	100-41	1911		104/126
Indigo	x-Brereton	Port Arthur	Minaki					108/—
Ingelow		Portage-Brandon	Harte	Type D	100-154	1909		104/135
Inwood		Portage-Brandon	Inwood	3rd	100-29	1912		105/132
Isabella		Portage-Brandon	Rapid City	3rd	100-29	1910		106/132
Jordan		Portage-Brandon	Miami	FPS	100-41	1917		105/126
Justice		Portage-Brandon	Harte	Type D	100-154	1909		104/135
Kane #1		Portage-Brandon	Miami	FPS	100-41	1916		105/126
Kane #2		Portage-Brandon	Miami	FPS	100-41	—		105/126
Katrime		Portage-Brandon	Gladstone	FPS	100-41	1919		104/126
Kelwood #1		Portage-Brandon	Neepawa	3rd	100-29	1912		105/132
Kenville		Dauphin	Preeceville	3rd	100-29	1908		102/132
Kilty		Dauphin	Togo					103/—
Knox		Portage-Brandon	Harte	Type E	100-152	1911		104/136
La Brouquerie		Port Arthur	Sprague	3rd	100-3	1905		108/130
Ladysmith		Portage-Brandon	Pleasant Point	FPS	100-96	1905		106/—
Lavenham		Portage-Brandon	Pleasant Point	3rd	100-3	1905		—/—
Lake Francis #1	x-Lake Frances	Portage-Brandon	Oak Point	3rd	100-3	1904		105/130
Lake Francis #2		Portage-Brandon	Oak Point	FPS-CNR	100-41B	—		105/139
Lakeland		Portage-Brandon	Oakland	FPS	100-41	1915		106/126
Langruth		Portage-Brandon	Oakland	4th	100-68	1916		106/130
Laurier		Portage-Brandon	Gladstone	CSS-A	100-63	1899		104/128
Ladysmith		Portage-Brandon	Pleasant Point	FPS	100-96	1905		106/124
Lavenham		Portage-Brandon	Pleasant Point	3rd	100-3	1905		106/130
Lavina		Portage-Brandon	Rapid City	FPS	100-41	1913		106/126
Leary's		Portage-Brandon	Carman	FPS	100-96	1908		104/124
Lelant		Portage-Brandon	Pleasant Point	FPS	100-41	1916		106/—
Lena		Portage-Brandon	Wakopa	3rd	100-3	1904		107/130
Lelant		Portage-Brandon	Pleasant Point	FPS	100-41	1916		106/126
Leon		Portage-Brandon	Pleasant Point					106/—
Letellier #1		Portage-Brandon	Letellier	STA-NPR	100-116	1894		105/133
Letellier #2		Portage-Brandon	Letellier	FPS		—		105/144
Levine		Portage-Brandon	Harte					104/—
Lewis		Port Arthur	Minaki	NTR3	100-181	1910		108/138
Libau		Portage-Brandon	Victoria Beach	FPS	100-41	1915		106/126
Liege		Portage-Brandon	Wakopa					107/—
Lobbville	x-Wood Siding	Portage-Brandon	Neepawa	FPS-CNR	CB	1929		105/143
Longburn		Portage-Brandon	Oakland	FPS	100-96	1906		106/124
Lorette		Port Arthur	Sprague	4th	100-31	1909		108/130
Louise		Portage-Brandon	Wakopa	SHLT-CNoR	100-95	1904		107/124
Lowe Farm		Portage-Brandon	Miami	3rd	100-3	1905		105/131
Lundar		Portage-Brandon	Oak Point	3rd	100-29	1913		105/132

MANITOBA

Station Name	Proposed/Former Name	Division	Subdivision	Type of Depot	Plan	Year	Notes	see page
Lynn Lake		Hudson Bay	Sherridon	SPEC-CNR	100-393	1966		103/142
M&B Jct.		Portage-Brandon	Pleasant Point					106/—
Mafeking		Dauphin	Erwood	4th	100-31	1909		102/130
Magnet		Portage-Brandon	Ste. Rose	FPS-CNR	100-41B	1926		106/139
Makaroff #1-A		Dauphin	Togo	FPS	100-41	1912		103/126
Makaroff #1-B		Dauphin	Togo	FPS-CNR	100-41B	1923		103/139
Makinak #2		Portage-Brandon	Gladstone	3rd	100-3	1903		104/131
Manlius		Portage-Brandon	Victoria Beach	FPS-CNR	100-41B	1929?		106/139
Maon #1		Portage-Brandon	Cromer	SHLT-CNoR		1910		104/144
Maon #2		Portage-Brandon	Cromer	FPS-CNR	100-41B	—		104/139
Maples		Portage-Brandon	Hartney	FPS	100-41	1910		105/139
Marchand #2		Port Arthur	Sprague	4th	100-68	1920		108/130
Margaret		Portage-Brandon	Hartney	3rd	100-3			105/131
Marieapolis		Portage-Brandon	Carman	3rd	100-3	1903		104/131
Marius		Portage-Brandon	Oakland	FPS-CNR	CB	1949		106/143
Martin's	x-Hope Farm	Portage-Brandon	Letellier					105/—
Martinville	x-Martin	Portage-Brandon	Wawanesa	FPS	100-41	1912		107/126
Mayfeld		Portage-Brandon	Neepawa	FPS	100-96	1909		105/124
McArthur		Portage-Brandon	Pleasant Point					106/—
McConnell		Portage-Brandon	Rapid City	3rd	100-29	1909	Museum-2	106/132
McCreary Jct.		Portage-Brandon	Gladstone					104/—
McCreary #2		Portage-Brandon	Gladstone	3rd	100-29	1912		104/132
McLean		Dauphin	Togo					103/—
Meharry #1		Dauphin	Togo	FPS	100-41	1911		103/126
Meharry #2		Dauphin	Togo	FPS-CNR	100-41B	1924		103/139
Menisino		Portage-Brandon	Ridgeville	FPS	100-41	1910		106/126
Mentmore		Portage-Brandon	Rapid City	FPS-CNR	100-41B	1943		106/139
Menzie		Portage-Brandon	Rossburn	FPS	100-96	1909		106/124
Merle		Portage-Brandon	Cromer	FPS	100-41	1910		104/126
Methley		Portage-Brandon	Ste. Rose	FPS-CNR	100-41B	1926		106/139
Methven Jct.		Portage-Brandon	Wawanesa	FPS	100-96	1909		107/124
Miami		Portage-Brandon	Miami	CSS-NPR	100-16	1889	Museum-1	105/128
Middlebro #2		Port Arthur	Sprague	FPS-CNR	100-290	1939		108/140
Mileage 4.2		Portage-Brandon	Oak Point	SHLT-CNR	100-434	1977	Note 34	105/144
Mileage 57.4		Port Arthur	Minaki	FPS-CNR		1926		108/144
Mileage 144.1		Portage-Brandon	Oak Point	FPS-CNR	CB	1949		106/143
Mileage 498.5		Hudson Bay	Herchmer	FPS	100-41	—		103/126
Millwater		Hudson Bay	Flin Flon	FPS-CNR	100-41B	—		103/126
Miniota		Saskatoon	Miniota	Type E	100-152	1912		114/136
Minitonas		Dauphin	Cowan	CSS-B	100-99	1899		102/128
Minmar		Portage-Brandon	Hartney					105/—
Minto #1-A		Portage-Brandon	Hartney	NPR-4th	100-13	1898		105/129
Minto #1-B		Portage-Brandon	Hartney	3rd	100-3	1906	Add to Sta #1-A	105/131
Minto #2		Portage-Brandon	Hartney	SHLT-CNR				105/141
Moline		Portage-Brandon	Rapid City	PORT-CNoR	100-24	1912		106/128
Mollard		Portage-Brandon	Carman					104/—
Moodie		Port Arthur	Sprague					108/—
Moore		Portage-Brandon	Oak Point	FPS	100-41	1910		105/126
Moosehorn #1		Portage-Brandon	Oak Point	FPS	100-41			106/126
Moosehorn #2		Portage-Brandon	Oak Point	4th	100-68	1918	Museum-2	106/130
Morris		Portage-Brandon	Letellier	STA-NPR		1894		105/133
Mountain Side		Portage-Brandon	Wakopa	FPS	100-41	1916		107/126
Moyer		Portage-Brandon	Miami					105/—
Muir	x-Neepawa Jct.	Portage-Brandon	Gladstone	FPS	100-41	1911		104/126
Mulvihill #2		Portage-Brandon	Oak Point	4th	100-68	1920		106/130
Mulvihill #3		Portage-Brandon	Oak Point	FPS	100-41	—		106/126
Munroe		Portage-Brandon	Carberry	SHLT-CNoR	100-95	1909		104/124
Myra #1		Saskatoon	Miniota	Type E	100-152	1911		114/136
Myra #2		Saskatoon	Miniota	FPS-CNR	100-41B	1931		114/139
Myrtle #2		Portage-Brandon	Miami	4th	100-31	1911		105/130
Myrtle #3		Portage-Brandon	Miami	FPS	CB	—		105/143
Narcisse		Portage-Brandon	Inwood	FPS	100-41	1915		105/126
National Mills #1		Dauphin	Erwood	FPS-CNR	CB	1943		102/143
National Mills #2		Dauphin	Erwood	FPS-CNR	100-41B	—		102/139
Navin		Port Arthur	Sprague	FPS	100-41	1910		108/126
Neelin		Portage-Brandon	Wakopa	3rd	100-3	1904		107/131
Neepawa #1		Portage-Brandon	Neepawa	2nd	100-8	1902	Museum-1	105/133
Neepawa #2		Portage-Brandon	Neepawa	PORT		1980		105/144
Newton		Portage-Brandon	Gladstone	FPS	100-41	1911		104/126
Ninette #1-A		Portage-Brandon	Hartney	NPR-4th		1898		105/129
Ninette #1-B		Portage-Brandon	Hartney	FPS	100-96	1917	Probable, Express Shed	105/124
Norman		Saskatoon	Miniota	Type E	100-152	1911		114/136
North Elie	x-Elie–GTP	Portage-Brandon	Harte	Type E	100-152	1911		104/136
Norwood	x-Norgate	Portage-Brandon	Neepawa	FPS-CNR	CB	1927		105/143
Notre Dame de Lourdes		Portage-Brandon	Carman	4th	100-68	1921		104/130
Nourse		Port Arthur	Minaki					108/—

ROSTER NOTES:

24 The Delta Subdivision was abandoned 1 March 1941. The Delta station was apparently sold in situ in 1941, being used as a fish warehouse until it burned down in the mid-1940s.

34 This station was technically on the Winnipeg Terminals Subdivision.

MANITOBA

Station Name	Proposed/Former Name	Division	Subdivision	Type of Depot	Plan	Year	Notes	see page
Novra		Dauphin	Erwood	CSS-B	100-99	1901		102/128
Oak Bluff		Portage-Brandon	Carman	PORT-CNoR	100-24	1910		104/128
Oakburn		Portage-Brandon	Rossburn	3rd	100-29	1907		106/132
Oakland		Portage-Brandon	Oakland	STA-NPR		1898		106/133
Oakner		Saskatoon	Miniota	Type E	100-152	1911		114/136
Oak Point		Portage-Brandon	Oak Point	3rd	100-29	1908		105/132
Oakville		Portage-Brandon	Gladstone	3rd	100-3			104/131
Ochre River #1-A		Portage-Brandon	Gladstone	CSS-A	100-63	1899		104/128
Ochre River #1-B		Portage-Brandon	Gladstone	FPS	100-41		Exp Shed	104/126
Ogilvie #2		Portage-Brandon	Gladstone	FPS	100-41	——	Probable	104/126
Onah		Portage-Brandon	Pleasant Point					106/——
Ontop		Portage-Brandon	Hartney					105/——
Ophir		Port Arthur	Minaki	SHLT-CNR	110-116	——	x-ST	108/141
Orrville		Portage-Brandon	Rossburn	FPS	100-96	1910		106/124
Osprey	x-Glendale	Portage-Brandon	Neepawa	FPS	100-41	1911		105/126
Overstone		Portage-Brandon	Ridgeville	SHLT-CNR	100-95			106/124
Pacific Jct. #1		Portage-Brandon	Harte	Type E	100-152	1911		104/136
Pacific Jct. #2		Portage-Brandon	Harte	PORT-CNR	CB	1927		104/143
Paddington		Port Arthur	Sprague	TOS		1911	Note 34	108/144
Parkmount		Portage-Brandon	Victoria Beach	FPS	100-41	1917		106/126
Paulson #2		Portage-Brandon	Gladstone	FPS-CNR	CB	1926		104/143
Pawstik		Hudson Bay	Sherridon	FPS	100-41	——		103/126
Petrel		Portage-Brandon	Carberry	FPS	100-41	1912		104/126
Petrel Jct.		Portage-Brandon	Carberry					104/——
Petrel Jct.		Portage-Brandon	Harte					104/——
Pine Falls		Portage-Brandon	Pine Falls	PORT-CNR	100-221	1926		106/141
Pine River #1		Dauphin	Cowan	CSS-B	100-99			102/128
Pine River #2		Dauphin	Cowan	FPS	110-296	——	x-SMBH	102/141
Piney		Portage-Brandon	Ridgeville	3rd	100-3	1905		106/131
Pit Siding #1-A		Hudson Bay	Thicket	FPS		——	x-SMBH	103/141
Pit Siding #1-B		Hudson Bay	Thicket	FPS-CNR	CB	1959		103/143
Pleasant Point		Portage-Brandon	Pleasant Point	PORT-CNoR	100-24	1910		106/128
Plumas		Portage-Brandon	Gladstone	CSS-A	100-63	1896		104/128
Pope #1		Saskatoon	Miniota	Type D	100-154	1909		114/135
Pope #2		Saskatoon	Miniota	FPS-CNR	110-117	——	x-ST	114/141
Poplarfield		Portage-Brandon	Inwood	FPS	100-41	1915		105/126
Portage Jct. #1		Portage-Brandon	Letellier	NPR-SH		1891	Notes 34, 38	105/129
Portage Jct. #2		Portage-Brandon	Letellier	SHLT-CNR	100-290	1949	Note 34	105/140
Portage la Prairie–CNoR #2		Portage-Brandon	Gladstone	2nd	100-45	1904	Note 31	104/133
Portage la Prairie–GTP	Joint with MRM	Portage-Brandon	Harte	SPEC-GTP	100-175	1908		104/138
Powell		Dauphin	Erwood	FPS	100-41	1919		102/126
Pratt		Portage-Brandon	Pleasant Point	FPS	100-96	1906		106/124
Prospector		Hudson Bay	Flin Flon	FPS				103/——
Prosser		Portage-Brandon	Pleasant Point					106/——
Quadra	x-Arrow River	Saskatoon	Miniota	Type E	100-152	1911		114/136
Rackham		Portage-Brandon	Rossburn	FPS	100-41	——		106/126
Ralston		Portage-Brandon	Cromer	FPS				104/——
Rapid City		Portage-Brandon	Rapid City	3rd	100-29	1909		106/132
Rea		Saskatoon	Miniota	FPS	CB			114/143
Reeve #1		Portage-Brandon	Gladstone	FPS-CNR	CB	1928		104/143
Reeve #2		Portage-Brandon	Gladstone	FPS-CNR	CB	1947		104/143
Reids		Portage-Brandon	Wawanesa	FPS	100-41	1911		107/126
Renwer	x-Fishers	Dauphin	Cowan	FPS	100-41	1912		102/126
Ridgeville		Portage-Brandon	Ridgeville	3rd	100-3	1906		106/131
Riding Mountain		Portage-Brandon	Neepawa	FPS	100-41	1910		105/126
Rignold		Portage-Brandon	Gladstone	NPR-4th		1901	Probable	104/129
Risteen		Portage-Brandon	Carman					104/——
Rivers #1		Portage-Brandon	Harte	SPEC-GTP		1909		104/138
Rivers #2		Portage-Brandon	Harte	SPEC-GTP	100-169	1917		104/138
Roblin		Dauphin	Togo	3rd	100-3	1906		103/131
Roland #1		Portage-Brandon	Miami	STA-NPR	100-116	1900		105/133
Roland #2		Portage-Brandon	Miami	FPS	CB			105/143
Rorketon	x-Edillen	Portage-Brandon	Ste. Rose	CN3rd	100-197	1926	Variant	106/141
Rosebank		Portage-Brandon	Miami	NPR-4th		1897		105/129
Roseisle		Portage-Brandon	Carman	3rd	100-3	1903		104/131
Rossburn		Portage-Brandon	Rossburn	3rd	100-3	1907		106/131
Rossburn Jct.		Portage-Brandon	Neepawa	FPS	100-41	——		105/126
Rossendale		Portage-Brandon	Pleasant Point	4th	100-31	1910		106/130
Rounthwaite	x-Naughton	Portage-Brandon	Wawanesa	NPR-4th			Probable	107/129
Rufford		Portage-Brandon	Rapid City	FPS	100-41	1912		106/126
Russell		Portage-Brandon	Rossburn	3rd	100-29	1908		106/132
St. Agathe #1		Portage-Brandon	Letellier	STA-NPR	100-116	1894		105/133
St. Agathe #2		Portage-Brandon	Letellier	FPS	CB	——		105/143
Ste. Anne #2		Port Arthur	Sprague	SPEC-CNR	100-133	1920		108/142
St. Boniface #1		Port Arthur	Sprague	2nd	100-4	1901	Variant, Notes 29, 34	108/134
St. Boniface #2		Port Arthur	Sprague	SPEC-CNoR	100-54	1914	Note 34	108/134
St. Charles		Portage-Brandon	Gladstone	FPS	100-41	1917	Note 34	104/126
St. James	x-West Side	Portage-Brandon	Oak Point	SPEC-CNoR	100-40	1910	Note 34	105/134
St. Jean Baptiste		Portage-Brandon	Letellier	3rd	100-3	1902	Reverse	105/131
St. Laurent		Portage-Brandon	Oak Point	3rd	100-3	1904		105/131
St. Lazare	x-Lazare	Saskatoon	Miniota	Type D	100-154	1909		114/135
St. Martin		Portage-Brandon	Oak Point	FPS	100-41	1914		106/126

MANITOBA

Station Name	Proposed/Former Name	Division	Subdivision	Type of Depot	Plan	Year	Notes	see page
St. Norbert		Portage-Brandon	Letellier	STA-NPR	100-116	1894		105/133
Ste. Rose #1		Portage-Brandon	Ste. Rose	4th	100-68	1916		106/130
Ste. Rose #2		Portage-Brandon	Ste. Rose	CN3rd	100-253	1930		106/142
St. Vital		Portage-Brandon	Letellier					105/—
Sanatorium	x-Sanatarium	Portage-Brandon	Hartney					105/—
Sandilands		Port Arthur	Sprague	FPS	100-41	1916		108/126
Sandridge		Portage-Brandon	Inwood	FPS	100-41	1916		105/126
Sandy Lake #1		Portage-Brandon	Rossburn	FPS	100-41			106/126
Sandy Lake #2		Portage-Brandon	Rossburn	3rd	100-72	1921		106/133
Sanford		Portage-Brandon	Carman	3rd	100-3	1901		104/131
Scanterbury		Portage-Brandon	Victoria Beach	FPS	100-41	1915		106/126
Scarth		Portage-Brandon	Cromer	3rd	100-29	1907		104/132
Sclater		Dauphin	Cowan	FPS	100-41	1911		102/126
Searle	x-Alcrest	Portage-Brandon	Harte	Type E	100-152	1911		104/136
Semple		Portage-Brandon	Victoria Beach	FPS	100-41	1918		106/126
Sevick		Dauphin	Cowan	FPS	100-41	1923		102/126
Shellmouth		Dauphin	Tonkin	3rd	100-29	1909		103/132
Sherridon #1A		Hudson Bay	Sherridon	STA-CNR		1928	Temporary	103/144
Sherridon #1-B		Hudson Bay	Sherridon	STA	110-148	1928	SMBH	103/141
Sherridon #2		Hudson Bay	Sherridon	STA-CNR	140-234	1953		103/142
Shevlin		Dauphin	Togo	FPS	100-41	1911		103/126
Shiloh–2nd site	x-Shiloh Camp	Portage-Brandon	Pleasant Point	SPEC-CNR	100-299	1942		106/142
Shortdale		Dauphin	Togo	FPS	100-41	1911		103/126
Sifton		Dauphin	Cowan	CSS-A	100-63	1897		102/128
Silver Plains #2		Portage-Brandon	Letellier	FPS-CNR	100-41B	1943		105/139
Silverton #1		Portage-Brandon	Rossburn	FPS	100-96			106/124
Silverton #2		Portage-Brandon	Rossburn	3rd	100-72	1922		106/133
Simonhouse		Hudson Bay	Flin Flon	FPS-CNR	CB	—		103/143
Smart		Portage-Brandon	Harte					104/—
Smiths		Portage-Brandon	Miami					105/—
Snyders Siding		Dauphin	Togo					103/—
Somerset #1-A		Portage-Brandon	Carman	NPR-4th	100-13	1889		104/129
Somerset #1-B		Portage-Brandon	Carman	3rd	100-3	1903	Add to Sta #1-A	104/131
South Jct. #1		Port Arthur	Sprague	FPS-CNR	100-290	1937		108/140
South Jct. #2		Port Arthur	Sprague	FPS	100-41			108/126
Sperling		Portage-Brandon	Carman	3rd	100-3	1901		104/131
Sprague #2		Port Arthur	Sprague	SPEC-CNoR	100-37	1910		108/134
Springhill		Portage-Brandon	Rossburn	FPS	100-96	1910		106/124
Stead		Portage-Brandon	Pine Falls	FPS-CNR	100-41B	1927		106/139
Steep Rock		Portage-Brandon	Steep Rock	4th	100-68	1916		106/130
Steep Rock Jct.		Portage-Brandon	Oak Point	FPS	100-41	1920		106/126
Stephanson		Portage-Brandon	Ridgeville					106/—
Stephenfield		Portage-Brandon	Carman	FPS	100-41	1911		104/126
Stockport		Portage-Brandon	Ridgeville					106/—
Sundown		Portage-Brandon	Ridgeville	FPS	100-41	1910		106/126
Swains		Portage-Brandon	Letellier					105/—
Swan Lake		Portage-Brandon	Carman	3rd	100-29	1913		104/132
Swan River		Dauphin	Cowan	CSS	100-63	1899		102/128
Tenby #1		Portage-Brandon	Gladstone	FPS-CNoR	CB	1911		104/143
Tenby #2		Portage-Brandon	Gladstone	SHLT		—		104/144
Terence		Portage-Brandon	Cromer	3rd	100-29	1910		104/132
The Pas #1		Hudson Bay	Turnberry	3rd	100-29	1908	Variant	103/132
The Pas #2		Hudson Bay	Turnberry	CN3rd	100-189	1928	Variant	103/142
Thicket Portage #1-A		Hudson Bay	Thicket	PORT		—	x-SMBH	103/141
Thicket Portage #1-B		Hudson Bay	Thicket	PORT		—	x-SMBH	103/141
Thompson		Hudson Bay	Thompson	SPEC-CNR	100-382	1960		103/142
Tiger Hills		Portage-Brandon	Hartney					105/—
Timberton #1	x-Strevel	Dauphin	Togo	PORT-CNoR	100-24	1909		103/128
Timberton #2		Dauphin	Togo	FPS	100-41	1918		103/126
Todds		Portage-Brandon	Oak Point					106/—
Tolstoi		Portage-Brandon	Ridgeville	FPS	100-41	1910		106/126
Totogan		Portage-Brandon	Oakland					106/—
Townline		Portage-Brandon	Oakland	FPS-CNoR	CB	1915		106/143
Transcona #1	<<Springfield>>	Port Arthur	Minaki	NTR1	100-179	1912	Note 34	108/138
Transcona #2-A		Port Arthur	Minaki	SHLT-CNR	100-258	1929	Note 34	108/144
Transcona #2-B		Port Arthur	Minaki	FPS	100-41	—	Note 34	108/126
Treat		Saskatoon	Miniota	FPS-CNR	CB	1936		114/143
Tremaine		Portage-Brandon	Rapid City	FPS	100-41	1915		106/126
Turnberry		Hudson Bay	Turnberry	PORT-CNR		1938	SMBH	103/141
Tuxedo		Portage-Brandon	Oak Point					105/—
Ukraina		Dauphin	Cowan	FPS	100-41	1913		102/126
Underhill		Portage-Brandon	Hartney	NPR-4th			Probable	105/129
Union Point		Portage-Brandon	Letellier	FPS	100-41	1915		105/126

ROSTER NOTES:

29 The CNoR classified this as a 2nd Class Station.

31 The CNoR and the joint GTP–Midland Railway of Manitoba (Great Northern) lines through Portage la Prairie were coordinated in 1923. Track connections between the two lines were made at either end of town. The GTP–MRM line was retained. The CNoR line was abandoned and pulled up. The CNoR's Portage station was retained on site and used by the railway for offices. The station gutted by fire in 1960, and subsequently demolished by the CNR.

34 This station was technically on the Winnipeg Terminals Subdivision.

38 Standard NP section house with a bay window on the trackside,

MANITOBA

Station Name	Proposed/Former Name	Division	Subdivision	Type of Depot	Plan	Year	Notes	see page
Uno #1		Saskatoon	Miniota	STA-GTP	100-153	1907		114/138
Uno #2		Saskatoon	Miniota	STA-GTP	100-153	1910		114/138
Valde Spur		Portage-Brandon	Carman					104/—
Valley River		Dauphin	Cowan	FPS		1897		102/124
Valpoy		Portage-Brandon	Ste. Rose	FPS-CNR	100-41B	1926		106/139
Vassar		Port Arthur	Sprague	4th	100-31	1907		108/130
Victor		Saskatoon	Miniota	FPS				114/—
Victoria Beach		Portage-Brandon	Victoria Beach	2nd	100-89	1916	Variant	107/134
Villette		Portage-Brandon	Cromer	FPS	100-41	1911		104/126
Virden		Portage-Brandon	Hartney	3rd	100-19	1907	Variant	105/131
Vista		Portage-Brandon	Rossburn	FPS	100-96	1909		106/124
Vita #2		Portage-Brandon	Ridgeville	4th	100-68	1923		106/130
Vivian		Port Arthur	Minaki	NTR2	100-180	1910		108/138
Wabowden		Hudson Bay	Wekusko	CN3rd	100-251	1930	Variant	104/142
Wakopa		Portage-Brandon	Wakopa	3rd	100-3	1904		107/131
Wampum		Portage-Brandon	Ridgeville	FPS	100-41	1913		106/126
Wanless		Hudson Bay	Flin Flon	FPS	100-41			103/126
Warren #2		Portage-Brandon	Oak Point	3rd	100-72	1922		105/133
Wassewa		Portage-Brandon	Wakopa	FPS-CNR	CB	1920		107/143
Wattsview		Saskatoon	Miniota					114/—
Wawanesa		Portage-Brandon	Wawanesa	CSS-NPR	100-16	1889		107/128
Wekusko		Hudson Bay	Wekusko	PORT			x-SMBH	104/141
Westgate		Dauphin	Erwood	CSS-B	100-99	1901		102/128
Westray		Hudson Bay	Turnberry					103/—
West Tower	x-Arizona Jct.	Portage-Brandon	Gladstone					104/—
West Transcona	x-Transcona–CNoR	Portage-Brandon	Victoria Beach	FPS	100-41	1913		106/126
West Winnipeg		Portage-Brandon	Harte	SPEC-GTP	100-177	1908		104/138
White Plains		Portage-Brandon	Gladstone	CSS-NPR	100-16	1891	Probable	104/128
Whithorn		Hudson Bay	Turnberry					103/—
Williams Spur		Port Arthur	Minaki					108/—
Willow Range		Portage-Brandon	Gladstone	FPS	100-41	1912		104/126
Winnitoba		Port Arthur	Minaki	FPS	CGR1			108/144
Winnipeg #1		Portage-Brandon	Letellier	SPEC-NPR	100-10	1889	Notes 34, 37	105/134
Winnipeg #2	Joint with GTP	Portage-Brandon	Letellier	SPEC-CNR	UD15	1911	Note 34	105/134
Winnipeg–Pembina Subway		Portage-Brandon	Letellier	FPS			Note 34	105/144
Winnipegosis		Dauphin	Winnipegosis	CSS-A	100-63	1897	Museum-1	103/128
Woodlands		Portage-Brandon	Oak Point	3rd	100-3	1904		105/131
Woodnorth #2		Portage-Brandon	Cromer	3rd	100-29	1916		104/133
Woodridge		Port Arthur	Sprague	CSS-B	100-99	1902		108/128
Woodroyd		Portage-Brandon	Inwood	FPS	100-41			105/126
Worby		Portage-Brandon	Pleasant Point	FPS	100-41			106/126
Wyntonville	x-Shiloh-1st site	Portage-Brandon	Pleasant Point	FPS	100-41	1914		106/126
Youill		Portage-Brandon	Gladstone	FPS	100-96	1907	Probable	104/124

ONTARIO

Station Name	Proposed/Former Name	Division	Subdivision	Type of Depot	Plan	Year	Notes	see page
Abiwin		Port Arthur	Kashabowie					108/—
Alcona		Port Arthur	Graham	Type E	100-152	1911		107/136
Allanwater		Port Arthur	Allanwater	Type F	100-151	1911		107/138
Amesdale	x-Freda	Port Arthur	Quibell	Type F	100-151	1911		108/138
Anita		Port Arthur	Kashabowie					108/—
Annex		Port Arthur	Kashabowie					108/—
Armstrong #1		Port Arthur	Allanwater	SPEC-GTP	100-158	1912		107/138
Armstrong #2		Port Arthur	Allanwater	SPEC-CNR		1927		107/142
Atikokan #2		Port Arthur	Kashabowie	SPEC-CNR	100-193	1923	Note 35	108/142
Baird		Port Arthur	Graham	Type E	100-152	1912	Note 32	107/136
Banning #1		Port Arthur	Fort Frances	STA-CNoR	100-12	1901		107/129
Banning #2		Port Arthur	Fort Frances	FPS	100-41			107/126
Barwick #1		Port Arthur	Fort Frances	3rd	100-3	1904		107/131
Barwick #2		Port Arthur	Fort Frances	FPS				107/144
Bear Pass #2	x-Bears Pass	Port Arthur	Fort Frances	4th	100-68	1920		107/130
Blalock		Port Arthur	Kashabowie					108/—
Brinka		Port Arthur	Quibell					108/—
Calm Lake	x-Progress	Port Arthur	Fort Frances					107/—
Cameo		Port Arthur	Allanwater	Type F	100-151	1911		107/138
Canyon		Port Arthur	Quibell					108/—
Clarkdon		Port Arthur	Graham	FPS-CNR	CB	1946		107/143
Collins #1		Port Arthur	Allanwater	Type F	100-151	1911		107/138
Collins #2		Port Arthur	Allanwater	FPS	100-41			107/126
Conmee		Port Arthur	Kashabowie	FPS	100-41	1923		108/126
Crest		Port Arthur	Graham	Type E	100-152	1912	Note 32	107/136
Crilly		Port Arthur	Fort Frances	SHLT-CNR		1926		107/144
Crozier		Port Arthur	Fort Frances	4th	100-31	1910		107/130
Devlin	x-Devlin Road	Port Arthur	Fort Frances	4th	100-31	1910		107/130
Dona		Port Arthur	Graham	Type E	100-152	1912	Note 32	107/136
Duluth Jct.		Port Arthur	Fort Frances					107/—
Elizabeth	x-Steep Rock	Port Arthur	Fort Frances	FPS-CNR	100-41B	1924		107/139
Ellis		Port Arthur	Graham	Type E	100-152	1912		107/136
Emo		Port Arthur	Fort Frances	3rd	100-3	1901		107/131
Ena		Port Arthur	Minaki					108/—
Farlane		Port Arthur	Quibell	NTR3	100-181	1910		108/138
Farrington #1		Port Arthur	Fort Frances	FPS	100-41	1911		107/127
Farrington #2		Port Arthur	Fort Frances	FPS-CNR	CB	1955		107/143

ONTARIO

Station Name	Proposed/Former Name	Division	Subdivision	Type of Depot	Plan	Year	Notes	see page
Favel		Port Arthur	Quibell					108/—
Flanders	x-Maflower	Port Arthur	Fort Frances	4th	100-68	1916		107/130
Flett		Port Arthur	Graham	Type E	100-152	1911		107/137
Fort Frances #1		Port Arthur	Fort Frances	2nd	100-4	1901	Note 29	107/134
Fort Frances #2		Port Arthur	Fort Frances	SPEC-CNoR	100-42	1913		107/134
Fort William		Port Arthur	Kashabowie	SPEC-CNoR	100-109	1918		107/134
Fowler		Port Arthur	Allanwater	Type F	100-151	1912		107/138
Garda		Port Arthur	Kashabowie					108/—
Ghost River	x-Smith	Port Arthur	Allanwater	Type F	100-151	1912		107/138
Glenorchy #2		Port Arthur	Fort Frances	FPS-CNR	100-290	1943		107/140
Glenwater	x-Mattawin	Port Arthur	Kashabowie	STA-CNoR	100-12	1901		108/129
Graham		Port Arthur	Graham	Type E	100-152	1910		107/137
Griff		Port Arthur	Graham	Type E	100-152	1911		107/137
Harvey		Port Arthur	Allanwater	Type F	100-151	1911		107/138
Hematite		Port Arthur	Kashabowie	FPS-CNoR	CB	1906		108/143
Horne		Port Arthur	Graham	Type E	100-152	1911		107/137
Hudson		Port Arthur	Quibell	NTR2	100-180	1911		108/138
Hume		Port Arthur	Kashabowie	FPS	100-41	1914		108/127
Huronian #1		Port Arthur	Kashabowie	4th	100-68	1918		108/130
Jacobs		Port Arthur	Allanwater	Type F	100-151	1911		107/138
James		Port Arthur	Graham	Type E	100-152	1910		107/137
Jelly		Port Arthur	Kashabowie					108/—
Jones #1		Port Arthur	Quibell	Type E	100-152	1911		108/137
Jones #2		Port Arthur	Quibell	FPS	100-41	—		108/127
Kabaigon		Port Arthur	Kashabowie					108/—
Kakabeka Falls #2		Port Arthur	Kashabowie	3rd	100-72	1915		108/133
Kashabowie		Port Arthur	Kashabowie	STA-CNoR	100-12	1901		108/129
Kawa		Port Arthur	Allanwater	Type F	100-151	1911		107/138
Kawene		Port Arthur	Kashabowie	STA-CNoR	100-12	1901		108/129
Keego		Port Arthur	Kashabowie					108/—
Kelly		Port Arthur	Graham	Type E	100-152	1911		107/137
Larson		Port Arthur	Graham	Type E	100-152	1911		107/137
Laseine		Port Arthur	Fort Frances	STA-CNoR	100-12	1901		107/129
Lash		Port Arthur	Quibell					108/—
La Vallee		Port Arthur	Fort Frances	3rd	100-29	1907		107/132
Linko		Port Arthur	Graham	Type E	100-152	1910		107/137
Mabella		Port Arthur	Kashabowie	STA-CNoR	100-12	1901		108/129
Mack		Port Arthur	Graham	Type E	100-152	1911		107/137
Malachi		Port Arthur	Minaki	NTR3	100-181			108/138
Mathieu		Port Arthur	Fort Frances					107/—
McIntosh #1		Port Arthur	Quibell	NTR2	100-180	1910		108/138
McIntosh #2		Port Arthur	Quibell	FPS	100-41	—		108/127
Mileage 53.9		Port Arthur	Allanwater	FPS-CNR	CB	1925		107/143
Mileage 68.1		Port Arthur	Fort Frances	FPS-CNR		1945		107/144
Millidge		Port Arthur	Quibell	NTR2	100-180	1910		108/138
Minaki		Port Arthur	Minaki	NTR2	100-180	1910		108/138
Mine Centre #1		Port Arthur	Fort Frances	STA-CNoR	100-12	1901	Note 30	107/129
Mine Centre #2		Port Arthur	Fort Frances	FPS-CNR	CB	1941		107/143
Mine Centre #3-A		Port Arthur	Fort Frances	FPS	CB	—		107/143
Mine Centre #3-B		Port Arthur	Fort Frances	PORT	110-159	—	x-SMBH	107/141
Mine Centre #4		Port Arthur	Fort Frances	PORT	110-237	—	x-SMBH	107/141
Mokomon		Port Arthur	Kashabowie	STA-CNoR	100-12	1901		108/129
Morgan		Port Arthur	Quibell					108/—
Mount		Port Arthur	Kashabowie					107/—
Neebing #1		Port Arthur	Kashabowie	SHLT-CNR		1923		107/144
Neebing #2		Port Arthur	Kashabowie	SHLT-CNR	100-433	1977		107/144
Nickel Lake	x-Nickle Lake	Port Arthur	Fort Frances	FPS-CNR	CB	1939		107/143
Niddrie	x-Hunter	Port Arthur	Quibell	NTR2	100-180	1910		108/138
North Pines		Port Arthur	Quibell	SHLT	CGR1			108/144
Ogaki		Port Arthur	Allanwater	Type F	100-151	1911		107/138
Olcott		Port Arthur	Kashabowie	PORT-CNR	CB	1950		108/143
Olive		Port Arthur	Fort Frances	FPS-CNR	CB	1942		107/143
Onaping		Port Arthur	Allanwater	Type F	100-151	1911		107/138
Oscar #1		Port Arthur	Graham	Type E	100-152	1910		107/137
Oscar #2		Port Arthur	Graham	FPS-CNR	100-290	1949		107/140
Ottermere		Port Arthur	Minaki	FPS-CNR	100-290	1937		108/140
Overflow		Port Arthur	Fort Frances					107/—
Owakonze	x-Baril Lake	Port Arthur	Kashabowie	FPS-CNR		1924		108/—
Pascopee		Port Arthur	Allanwater	Type F	100-151	1911		107/138
Pelican		Port Arthur	Quibell	NTR3	100-181	1910		108/138

ROSTER NOTES:

29 The CNoR classified this as a 2nd Class Station.

30 The disposition of the first depot could not be established. It may have burned down and been replaced by a 4th Class structure.

32 The 26-mile section between Conmee and Fort William was abandoned in 1925. The final disposition of this station could not be established.

34 This station was technically on the Winnipeg Terminals Subdivision.

35 The second storey was removed in 1947.

37 In 1889, the Northern Pacific & Manitoba Railway constructed this three-storey brick station-hotel on Water Avenue. The hotel portion of the complex was destroyed in a spectacular fire in February 1899. After the opening of the new Union depot in 1911, the old station was integrated into the Winnipeg Industrial Bureau and used as a convention hall. In 1926 it was converted into an immigration shed. During the Depression it was used as a hostel by the unemployed and homeless. The military took over the building during World War II, after which it again served as a shelter for the homeless. The third floor of the station was removed in 1954.

ONTARIO

Station Name	Proposed/Former Name	Division	Subdivision	Type of Depot	Plan	Year	Notes	see page
Petry #1		Port Arthur	Graham	Type E	100-152	1910		107/137
Petry #2		Port Arthur	Graham	FPS-CNR	100-290	1943		107/140
Pinewood		Port Arthur	Fort Frances	3rd	100-3	1901		107/131
Planet	x-Tebo	Port Arthur	Kashabowie					108/——
Port Arthur #2	later Thunder Bay	Port Arthur	Kashabowie	SPEC-CNoR	100-49	1905		107/134
Postans		Port Arthur	Kashabowie					108/——
Quetico	x-Windigo	Port Arthur	Kashabowie	STA-CNoR	100-12	1901		108/129
Quibell		Port Arthur	Quibell	NTR3	100-181	1910		108/138
Quorn #1		Port Arthur	Graham	Type E	100-152	1910		107/137
Quorn #2		Port Arthur	Graham	FPS-CNR	100-132	1947		107/141
Rainy River #1	x-Beaver Mills	Port Arthur	Fort Frances	2nd	100-1	1901	Variant	107/133
Rainy River #2		Port Arthur	Fort Frances	SPEC-CNoR	100-120	1918	Add to Sta #1	107/134
Raith		Port Arthur	Graham	Type E	100-152	1910		107/137
Reba		Port Arthur	Graham	Type E	100-152	1911		107/137
Redditt #1		Port Arthur	Quibell	NTR1	100-179	1910		108/138
Redditt #2		Port Arthur	Quibell	SPEC-GTP	100-158	1912		108/138
Red Lake Road #1		Port Arthur	Quibell	FPS-CNR	CB	1946		108/143
Red Lake Road #2		Port Arthur	Quibell	CN4A	100-317	1947		108/142
Rice Lake		Port Arthur	Minaki					108/——
Ritchan #1		Port Arthur	Quibell	Type E	100-152	1912		108/137
Ritchan #2		Port Arthur	Quibell	FPS-CNR	100-290	1937		108/140
Robinson		Port Arthur	Allanwater	Type F	100-151	1912		107/138
Rocky Inlet		Port Arthur	Fort Frances	FPS	100-41	1911	Probable	107/127
Rosnel		Port Arthur	Allanwater	Type F	100-151	1912		107/138
Rossmere		Port Arthur	Kashabowie					108/——
Rowan	x-Fonger	Port Arthur	Kashabowie					108/——
Sapawe	x-Iron Spur	Port Arthur	Kashabowie	FPS-CNR	100-41B	1950		108/139
Savant Lake	x-Bucke	Port Arthur	Allanwater	Type F	100-151	1912		107/138
Seibert		Port Arthur	Fort Frances					107/——
Shabaqua		Port Arthur	Kashabowie	FPS-CNR		1921		108/——
Shebandowan		Port Arthur	Kashabowie	FPS-CNR		1923		108/——
Sims		Port Arthur	Fort Frances					107/——
Sioux Lookout		Port Arthur	Allanwater	SPEC-GTP	100-195	1911		107/138
Slate River		Port Arthur	Kashabowie					108/——
Snowden		Port Arthur	Graham	Type E	100-152	1911		107/137
Stanley		Port Arthur	Kashabowie	SPEC-CNoR		1900	Note 75	108/130
Staunton		Port Arthur	Allanwater	Type F	100-151	1912		107/138
Stratton		Port Arthur	Fort Frances	3rd	100-3	1903		107/131
Sunstrum		Port Arthur	Quibell	Type E	100-152	1912		108/137
Superior Jct. #1		Port Arthur	Allanwater	NTR2	100-180	1910		107/138
Superior Jct. #2		Port Arthur	Allanwater	FPS-CNR	100-290	——		107/140
Taggart		Port Arthur	Quibell					108/——
Tannin		Port Arthur	Graham	Type E	100-152	1910		107/137
Tebo		Port Arthur	Minaki					108/——
Turtle		Port Arthur	Fort Frances					107/——
Twin City		Port Arthur	Kashabowie	FPS	100-41	1912		107/127
Umfreville #1	x-Hunt	Port Arthur	Graham	Type E	100-152	1910		107/137
Umfreville #2		Port Arthur	Graham	SPEC-CNR	100-218	1927		107/142
Umfreville #3		Port Arthur	Graham	FPS	100-41	——		107/127
Unaka		Port Arthur	Graham	Type E	100-152	1911		107/137
Valora #1		Port Arthur	Graham	Type E	100-152	1911		107/137
Valora #2		Port Arthur	Graham	SPEC-CNR	100-218	1926		107/142
Wade #1-A		Port Arthur	Minaki	SHLT-CNR		1920		108/144
Wade #1-B		Port Arthur	Minaki	SHLT-CNR	100-201	1926		108/144
Watcomb	x-Wako	Port Arthur	Graham	Type E	100-152	1910		107/137
Webster #1		Port Arthur	Quibell	NTR2	100-180	1910		108/138
Webster #2		Port Arthur	Quibell	PORT	110-42	——	x-SMBH	108/141
Webster #3		Port Arthur	Quibell	FPS	110-159	——	x-SMBH	108/141
Wells Camp		Port Arthur	Kashabowie	FPS-CNR	CB	1950		108/143
Westfort		Port Arthur	Graham	Type E	100-152	1912		107/137
West Fort William	x-Westfort	Port Arthur	Kashabowie	STA				107/134
White		Port Arthur	Minaki	Type E	100-152	1912		108/137
Ycliff #1		Port Arthur	Allanwater	Type F	100-151	1912		107/138
Ycliff #2		Port Arthur	Allanwater	PORT		——	x-SMBH	107/141
Yonde		Port Arthur	Graham	Type E	100-152	1911		107/137
Zarn		Port Arthur	Graham	Type E	100-152	1910		107/137

SASKATCHEWAN

Station Name	Proposed/Former Name	Division	Subdivision	Type of Depot	Plan	Year	Notes	see page
Abbott		Regina	Avonlea	FPS	100-41	1923		111/127
Aberdeen		Prince Albert	Aberdeen	3rd	100-3	1905		108/131
Aberfeldy		Edmonton	Blackfoot	FPS	100-96	1909		116/124
Adams		Regina	Central Butte	FPS	100-41	——		111/127
Akosane	x-Etomami	Dauphin	Assiniboine	FPS-CNR	100-41B	1930		102/139
Allan		Saskatoon	Asquith	Type D	100-154	1909		113/135
Alsask		Calgary	Oyen	3rd	100-29	1911		115/132
Alticane		Prince Albert	Robinhood	FPS-CNR	100-41B	1929		110/139
Alvena		Prince Albert	Meskanaw	CN3rd	100-253	1931		110/142
Amiens		Prince Albert	Amiens	FPS-CNR	100-41B	1930		109/139
Amsterdam		Dauphin	Assiniboine	FPS	100-41	1915		102/127
Ancrum #1		Prince Albert	Cudworth	Type E	100-152	1912		109/137
Ancrum #2		Prince Albert	Cudworth	SHLT-CNR	150-52	——	x-PH	109/141

SASKATCHEWAN

Station Name	Proposed/Former Name	Division	Subdivision	Type of Depot	Plan	Year	Notes	see page
Anerley #1		Saskatoon	Elrose	FPS	100-41	1913		114/127
Anerley #2		Saskatoon	Elrose	CN4th	100-252	1930		114/142
Antar	x-South Moose Jaw	Regina	Avonlea	FPS	100-41	1913		111/127
Aquadell		Regina	Main Centre	FPS-CNR	CB	1930		112/143
Arborfield		Prince Albert	Arborfield	CN3rd	100-250	1930		109/141
Archydal		Regina	Central Butte	Type E	100-152	1913		111/137
Ardath		Saskatoon	Conquest	3rd	100-29	1912		113/132
Ardill #1		Regina	Gravelbourg	FPS	100-41	1913		112/127
Ardill #2		Regina	Gravelbourg	4th	100-68	1923		112/130
Argo		Saskatoon	Dodsland	Type E	100-152	1913		113/137
Arma		Prince Albert	Duck Lake	FPS	100-41	——		110/127
Armit #1	x-Meaks	Dauphin	Erwood	FPS-CNR		1943		102/144
Armit #2		Dauphin	Erwood	FPS-CNR	100-41B	——		102/139
Arran #1		Dauphin	Preeceville	FPS	100-41	1911		102/127
Arran #2		Dauphin	Preeceville	3rd	100-72	1919	Museum-2	102/133
Artland		Edmonton	Unity	Type E	100-152	1911		117/137
Asquith #1	x-Iwana	Saskatoon	Asquith	Type E	100-152	By15		113/137
Asquith #2		Saskatoon	Asquith	Type F	100-151	1918		113/138
Atwater #1		Saskatoon	Miniota	Type D	100-154	1909		114/135
Atwater #2		Saskatoon	Miniota	FPS-CNR		——		114/144
Ava	x-Fort	Saskatoon	Dodsland	Type E	100-152	1913		113/137
Avonhurst #1		Regina	Qu'Appelle	FPS-GTP	CB	1914		112/143
Avonhurst #2		Regina	Qu'Appelle	Type G	100-168	1920		112/138
Avonlea		Regina	Avonlea	3rd	100-29	1912		111/132
Aylsebury		Regina	Craik	4th	100-31	1910		111/130
Aylsham #1		Prince Albert	Brooksby	FPS-CNR	100-41C	1932		109/140
Aylsham #2		Prince Albert	Brooksby	CN4A	100-313	1949		109/142
Baildon		Regina	Avonlea	3rd	100-29	1913		111/132
Balcarres #1		Regina	Qu'Appelle	SPEC-GTP	100-157	1910		112/138
Balcarres #2		Regina	Qu'Appelle	CN3rd	100-253	1932		112/142
Bangor		Saskatoon	Miniota	Type E	100-152	1913		114/137
Bannock #1		Prince Albert	Tisdale	CSS-SH	110-10	1909		110/129
Bannock #2		Prince Albert	Tisdale	FPS	100-41	——		110/127
Bannock #3		Prince Albert	Tisdale	FPS-CNR		1954		110/144
Bapaume		Prince Albert	Amiens	FPS-CNR	100-41B	1930		109/139
Barbour	x-Dunleath	Dauphin	Tonkin	FPS	100-41	1916	Not moved?	103/127
Barvas		Dauphin	Tonkin	FPS	100-41	1915		103/127
Bateman		Regina	Gravelbourg	4th	100-68	1923		112/130
Battleford–CNoR		Prince Albert	Battleford	3rd	100-19	1907	Variant	109/131
Battleford–GTP		Saskatoon	Porter	SPEC-GTP	100-157	1912		114/138
Bayard		Regina	Gravelbourg	3rd	100-29	1913		112/132
Bazentin		Prince Albert	Amiens	FPS-CNR	100-41B	1930		109/139
Beadle #1		Saskatoon	Rosetown	FPS	100-41	By12		114/127
Beadle #2		Saskatoon	Rosetown	4th	100-68	1916		114/130
Beatty #1		Prince Albert	Tisdale	FPS				110/144
Beatty #2		Prince Albert	Tisdale	3rd	100-72	1918		110/133
Beaufield #1		Saskatoon	Dodsland	Type E	100-152	1913		113/137
Beaufield #2		Saskatoon	Dodsland	SHLT-CNR		——	x-PH	113/141
Beaverdale		Dauphin	Tonkin	FPS-CNR	100-41B	1929		103/139
Bechard #1	x-Lindley	Regina	Lewvan	FPS-GTP	CB	1917		112/143
Bechard #2		Regina	Lewvan	3rd	100-72	1921		112/133
Beechy #1		Saskatoon	Beechy	FPS	100-41	1921		113/127
Beechy #2		Saskatoon	Beechy	4th	100-68	1923		113/130
Belbutte		Prince Albert	Amiens	FPS-CNR	100-41B	1930		109/139
Bemersyde		Regina	Corning	FPS-CNR	100-41B	1925		111/139
Bengough		Regina	Bengough	3rd	100-29	1912		111/132
Benson	x-Hill Hall	Regina	Lewvan	Type E	100-152	1913		112/137
Bertwell	x-Kakwa	Dauphin	Assiniboine	FPS-CNR	100-41B	1930		102/139
Bethune		Regina	Craik	CSS-CP	100-100	1890	Note 71	111/128
Bienfait #1		Regina	Bienfait	FPS	100-41	1913		111/127
Bienfait #2		Regina	Bienfait	3rd	100-72	1915	Note 77	111/133
Big River		Prince Albert	Big River	3rd	100-29	1910		109/132
Biggar		Saskatoon	Asquith	SPEC-GTP	100-155	1909		113/138
Birch Hills		Prince Albert	Tisdale	3rd	100-3	1905		110/131
Birling		Edmonton	Blackfoot	FPS	100-41	1911		116/127
Birmingham		Saskatoon	Touchwood	Type E	100-152	1911		114/137
Birsay		Saskatoon	Beechy	4th	100-68	1920		113/130
Bjorkdale #1		Prince Albert	Chelan	FPS-CNR	100-41B	1930		109/139
Bjorkdale #2		Prince Albert	Chelan	PORT-CNR	CB	1948	Temporary	109/143
Bjorkdale #3		Prince Albert	Chelan	PORT-CNR	100-323	1948	Add to Sta #2	109/141
Bladworth		Regina	Craik	3rd	100-29	1908		111/132

ROSTER NOTES:

71 This station was built by the Canadian Pacific Railway that operated the Qu'Appelle Long Lake and Saskatchewan Railway until 1906, when the line was acquired by the Canadian Northern Railway.

75 This station was constructed at the junction of the Ontario and Rainy River section and the "old" Port Arthur, Duluth & Western Railway. A photograph in THUNDER BAY TO GUNFLINT by Elinor Barr (Thunder Bay Historical Society, 1999), page 107, shows a 1½-storey wood-frame structure unlike anything else constructed by the CNoR.

77 For clarity, the Lampman Subdivision is shown in its pre-1952 configuration: Maryfield to Radville. Flooding in the spring of 1948 knocked out three bridges in the Souris valley, closing the line between Blewett and Goodwater. The resulting stub lines were dubbed the Blewett (Lampman to Blewett) and Goodwater (Radville to Goodwater) Subdivisions and train services were operated to the respective ends of track. CNR studies in 1951 determined it was uneconomic to rebuild the bridges and rebuild the closed stretch of rail line, so it was abandoned. Subsequently, the former Bienfait Subdivision (Lampman to Estevan) was incorporated into the south end of the Lampman Subdivision.

SASKATCHEWAN

Station Name	Proposed/Former Name	Division	Subdivision	Type of Depot	Plan	Year	Notes	see page
Blaine Lake		Prince Albert	Blaine Lake	3rd	100-29	1912		109/132
Blewett		Regina	Lampman	3rd	100-29	1911	Note 77	112/132
Bodmin		Prince Albert	Big River	FPS	100-41	—		109/127
Bolney		Prince Albert	Bolney	FPS-CNR	100-41B	1929		109/139
Borden		Prince Albert	Langham	3rd	100-3	1907		110/131
Bournemouth		Prince Albert	Robinhood	FPS-CNR	100-41B	1928		110/139
Brada		Prince Albert	Langham	FPS	100-96	1909		110/124
Bradwell #1		Saskatoon	Asquith	Type D	100-154	1909	Probable	113/135
Bradwell #2		Saskatoon	Asquith	Type E	100-152	1910		113/137
Brancepeth #1		Prince Albert	Tisdale	FPS	100-41			110/127
Brancepeth #2		Prince Albert	Tisdale	SPEC-CNR	100-280	1935		110/142
Brancepeth #3		Prince Albert	Tisdale	FPS-CNR	100-41B	—		110/139
Bratton		Saskatoon	Conquest	FPS	100-41	1912		113/127
Bredin		Regina	Craik	FPS	100-41	1922		111/127
Breeze		Regina	Northgate					112/—
Bremen		Prince Albert	Cudworth	Type E	100-152	1911		109/137
Bresaylor #1		Edmonton	Blackfoot	PORT-CNoR	100-24	1908		116/128
Bresaylor #2		Edmonton	Blackfoot	FPS	100-41	1923		116/127
Brett	later Irvington	Prince Albert	Brooksby	SHLT-CNR	110-153	—	x-ST	109/141
Brewer		Dauphin	Yorkton	Type E	100-152	1910		103/137
Briercrest		Regina	Avonlea	3rd	100-29	1912		111/132
Brisbin		Saskatoon	Rosetown	FPS	100-41	—	Museum-2	114/127
Brock		Saskatoon	Rosetown	3rd	100-29	1909		114/132
Brooking		Regina	Bengough	3rd	100-29	1913		111/132
Brooksby		Prince Albert	Brooksby	4th	100-68	1923		109/130
Browning #1		Regina	Lampman	FPS	100-41	1912		112/127
Browning #2		Regina	Lampman	SHLT-CNoR		1917		112/144
Browning #3		Regina	Lampman	4th	100-68	1923		112/130
Bruno		Prince Albert	Aberdeen	3rd	100-3	1904		108/131
Bryant		Regina	Lampman	FPS	100-41	1912		112/127
Buchanan		Dauphin	Margo	3rd	100-3	1904		102/131
Buckland		Prince Albert	Blaine Lake	FPS	100-41	1914		109/127
Burdick		Regina	Central Butte	Type E	100-152	1913		111/137
Burgis #1		Dauphin	Yorkton	Type E	100-152	1911		103/137
Burgis #2		Dauphin	Yorkton	FPS-CNR	CB	1950		103/143
Burnham		Regina	Gravelbourg				Note 33	112/—
Burt		Regina	Central Butte	PORT-GTP	110-101		SMBH, Probable	111/134
Cactus Lake	x-Grosswerder	Edmonton	Bodo	FPS-CNR	100-41C	1932		116/140
Calder #1		Dauphin	Tonkin	FPS	100-41	1912		103/127
Calder #2		Dauphin	Tonkin	3rd	100-75	1914		103/133
Calderbank		Regina	Main Centre	FPS-CNR	100-41C	1932		112/140
Calley		Dauphin	Tonkin	FPS	100-41	1916		103/127
Cameo		Prince Albert	Amiens	FPS-CNR	100-41B	1929		109/139
Cana #1		Saskatoon	Miniota	Type E	100-152	1911		114/137
Cana #2		Saskatoon	Miniota	FPS-CNR		1965		114/—
Candiac		Regina	Glenavon	4th	100-31	1913		112/130
Cando		Saskatoon	Porter	Type E	100-152	1913		114/137
Canora		Dauphin	Margo	3rd	100-3	1904	Museum-1	102/131
Cantyre		Hudson Bay	Turnberry					103/—
Canwood #1	x-McOwan	Prince Albert	Big River	FPS	100-41			109/127
Canwood #2	Joint with CPR	Prince Albert	Big River	4th	100-68	1916		109/130
Carlea		Prince Albert	Brooksby	FPS-CNR	100-41C	1932		109/140
Carlsberg		Regina	Glenavon	3rd	100-29			112/132
Carlyle		Regina	Lampman	3rd	100-29	1909	Museum-2	112/132
Carlton		Prince Albert	Carlton	FPS	100-41	—		109/127
Carmel #1		Prince Albert	Aberdeen	FPS	100-96	1908		108/124
Carmel #2		Prince Albert	Aberdeen	CSS-SH	110-10	1911		108/129
Carmel #3		Prince Albert	Aberdeen	4th	100-68	1917		108/130
Carpenter		Prince Albert	Meskanaw	FPS-CNR	100-41B	1931		110/139
Carragana		Prince Albert	Chelan	FPS-CNR	100-41B	1930		109/139
Carrot River #1		Prince Albert	Brooksby	FPS-CNR	100-41C	1932	Note 7	109/140
Carrot River #2		Prince Albert	Brooksby	CN4A	100-309	1947		109/142
Carruthers		Prince Albert	Cutknife	Type G	100-168	1920		110/138
Cavalier		Prince Albert	Turtleford	FPS-CNR	CB	1927		111/143
Cavell	x-Coblenz	Edmonton	Unity	Type D	100-154	1910		117/135
Cazalet		Saskatoon	Asquith	SHLT-CNR	150-53	—	x-PH	113/141
Ceba		Hudson Bay	Turnberry					103/—
Cedoux		Regina	Lewvan	Type E	100-152	1912		112/137
Ceepee	<<Elbow>>	Prince Albert	Langham	FPS	100-41	1911		110/127
Central Butte #1		Regina	Central Butte	FPS	CB			111/143
Central Butte #2		Regina	Central Butte	Type F	100-151	1919		111/138
Ceylon		Regina	Bengough	3rd	100-29	1912		111/132
Chamberlain		Regina	Craik	CSS-CP	100-100	1890	Note 71	111/128
Chambers		Saskatoon	Conquest	FPS	100-41	1912		113/127
Chandler		Regina	Lampman	3rd	100-29	1912	Note 77	112/132
Chappell		Saskatoon	Asquith	TOS				113/144
Chelan		Prince Albert	Chelan	FPS-CNR	100-41B	1930		109/139
Chemong		Hudson Bay	Turnberry	SHLT		By20		103/144
Claggett		Prince Albert	Meskanaw	FPS-CNR	100-41B	1931		110/139
Clair	<<Englefeldt>>	Dauphin	Margo	FPS	100-41	1912		102/127
Clarkboro		Prince Albert	Aberdeen	FPS	100-96	1909		108/124

SASKATCHEWAN

Station Name	Proposed/Former Name	Division	Subdivision	Type of Depot	Plan	Year	Notes	see page
Clark's Crossing #1		Prince Albert	Duck Lake	FPS	100-96	1910		110/124
Clark's Crossing #2		Prince Albert	Duck Lake	FPS	CB	—		110/143
Clashmoor		Prince Albert	Arborfield	FPS-CNR	100-41B	1930		109/139
Clavet		Saskatoon	Asquith	Type E	100-152	1911		113/137
Claybank		Regina	Gravelbourg	FPS	100-41	1913		112/127
Cleardale		Regina	Weyburn	FPS-CNR	100-41B	1928		113/139
Cleeves		Prince Albert	Turtleford	FPS	100-41	1922		111/127
Clemenceau		Dauphin	Assiniboine	FPS-CNR	100-41B	1930		102/139
Clouston		Prince Albert	Duck Lake	FPS	100-41	1914		110/127
Coleville		Saskatoon	Dodsland	Type E	100-152	1913		113/137
Colfax #1		Regina	Lewvan	Type E	100-152	1913		112/137
Colfax #2		Regina	Lewvan	CN3rd	100-250	1930		112/142
Colgate		Regina	Lampman	3rd	100-29	1912	Upgr. to 100-72, Note 77	112/132
Colmer		Regin	Qu'Appelle	Type E	100-152	1911		112/137
Condie		Regina	Craik	3rd	100-29	1911		111/132
Conquest		Saskatoon	Conquest	3rd	100-29	1912		113/132
Coppen		Regina	Gravelbourg	FPS	100-41	1923		112/127
Corning	x-St. Kilda	Regina	Corning	CN3rd	100-197	1925		111/141
Cosine		Edmonton	Bodo	FPS-CNR	100-41C	1932		116/140
Cote		Dauphin	Togo	FPS	100-41	1912		103/127
Cowper		Regina	Lampman	FPS	100-41	1912		112/127
Craik		Regina	Craik	CSS-CP	100-100	1890	Note 71	111/128
Crooked River #1-A		Prince Albert	Tisdale	PORT-CNoR	100-24	1907		110/128
Crooked River #1-B		Prince Albert	Tisdale	FPS	110-159	—		110/141
Crutwell #1		Prince Albert	Blaine Lake	FPS	100-41	1912		109/127
Crutwell #2		Prince Albert	Blaine Lake	FPS-CNR	100-41B	1947		109/139
Crystal Beach		Saskatoon	Rosetown	SHLT-CNR		1927		114/144
Cudworth #1		Prince Albert	Cudworth	Type E	100-152	1911		109/137
Cudworth #2		Prince Albert	Cudworth	CN3rd	100-197	1925		109/141
Cudworth Jct.		Prince Albert	Cudworth					109/—
Cullen		Regina	Lampman	FPS	100-41	1916		112/127
Cuthbert	x-Magiddo	Calgary	Acadia Valley	FPS-CNR	100-41B	1927		114/139
Cutknife	x-Rossman	Prince Albert	Cutknife	Type E	100-152	1913		110/137
Dacer #1		Saskatoon	Porter	Type E	100-152	1913		114/137
Dacer #2		Saskatoon	Porter	FPS-CNR	CB	1941		114/143
Dana #1		Prince Albert	Aberdeen	CSS-SH	110-10	1905		108/129
Dana #2		Prince Albert	Aberdeen	SHLT-CNR	CB	1934		108/143
Dalmeny		Prince Albert	Langham	3rd	100-3	1907		110/131
Dalzell		Regina	Glenavon	PORT-CNoR	100-24	1911		112/128
Dankin		Calgary	Mantario	FPS-CNR	100-41B	1923		115/139
D'Arcy #1		Saskatoon	Rosetown	FPS	100-41	1915		114/127
D'Arcy #2		Saskatoon	Rosetown	4th	100-68	1916		114/130
Darmody		Regina	Central Butte	Type E	100-152	1914	Reverse	111/137
Davidson #2		Regina	Craik	CP#5	100-110	1905	Notes 18, 71	111/133
Davin		Regina	Glenavon	3rd	100-29	1912		112/132
Davis	Joint with CPR	Prince Albert	Tisdale	FPS	100-96	1910		110/124
Daylesford		Prince Albert	St. Brieux	FPS	100-41	1921		110/127
Debden #1		Prince Albert	Big River	FPS	100-41	1914		109/127
Debden #2	Joint with CPR	Prince Albert	Big River	4th	100-68	1918		109/130
Deer Creek	x-Tangleflags	Prince Albert	Bolney	FPS-CNR	100-41B	1929		109/139
Delisle		Saskatoon	Rosetown	3rd	100-29	1908		114/131
Delmas		Edmonton	Blackfoot	3rd	100-3	1905		116/131
Demaine	x-Scapa	Saskatoon	Beechy	4th	100-68	1922		113/130
Denholm #1		Prince Albert	Langham	3rd	100-29	1912		110/132
Denholm #2		Prince Albert	Langham	CN4th	100-279	1936		110/142
Denny	x-Druse	Saskatoon	Conquest	FPS-CNR	CB	1939		113/143
Dewar Lake #1		Saskatoon	Dodsland	FPS		By15		113/144
Dewar Lake #2		Saskatoon	Dodsland	Type F	100-151	1920		113/138
Dillabough		Prince Albert	Chelan	FPS-CNR	100-41B	1930		109/139
Dinsmore		Saskatoon	Elrose	3rd	100-29	1913		114/132
Disley		Regina	Craik	4th	100-31	1914		111/130
Dixon		Prince Albert	Aberdeen	FPS	100-96	1908		108/124
Dodsland #1		Saskatoon	Dodsland	Type E	100-152	1913		113/137
Dodsland #2		Saskatoon	Dodsland	CN4A	100-315	1948	Variant	113/142
Domremy #1		Prince Albert	Cudworth	Type E	100-152	1915		109/137
Domremy #2		Prince Albert	Cudworth	Type G	100-168	1919		109/138
Donegal		Edmonton	Bodo	FPS-CNR	100-41C	1931		116/140

ROSTER NOTES:

7 Converted into section tool house in 1947. Converted into enginemen's bunkhouse in 1967.

18 The first depot was actually built by the Qu'Appelle Long Lake and Saskatchewan Railway at a station named Finsbury, located two miles south of present day Davidson, was abandoned in 1905. As this CSS-CPR (#1) was removed prior to the acquisition of the QLL&S by the CNoR in 1906, it is not listed here.

33 The stretch between Neidpath and Swift Current was operated on a sporadic basis until abandoned in September 1958. Standard freight and passenger shelters (CNR Plan 100-41B) are noted on the respective station grounds plans as "Shelter Site", therefore it appears that these shelters may not have been constructed and are thus excluded from this listing. The CNR had a Union Station agreement with the CPR to use that company's Swift Current depot.

71 This station was built by the Canadian Pacific Railway that operated the Qu'Appelle Long Lake and Saskatchewan Railway until 1906, when the line was acquired by the Canadian Northern Railway.

77 For clarity, the Lampman Subdivision is shown in its pre-1952 configuration: Maryfield to Radville. Flooding in the spring of 1948 knocked out three bridges in the Souris valley, closing the line between Blewett and Goodwater. The resulting stub lines were dubbed the Blewett (Lampman to Blewett) and Goodwater (Radville to Goodwater) Subdivisions and train services were operated to the respective ends of track. CNR studies in 1951 determined it was uneconomic to rebuild the bridges and rebuild the closed stretch of rail line, so it was abandoned. Subsequently, the former Bienfait Subdivision (Lampman to Estevan) was incorporated into the south end of the Lampman Subdivision.

SASKATCHEWAN

Station Name	Proposed/Former Name	Division	Subdivision	Type of Depot	Plan	Year	Notes	see page
Donovan #1	x-Birdview	Saskatoon	Conquest	FPS	100-41	1913		113/127
Donovan #2		Saskatoon	Conquest	3rd	100-72	1917		113/133
Donwell		Dauphin	Rhein	FPS	100-41	1913		103/127
Doonside		Portage-Brandon	Cromer	FPS	100-41	1911		104/127
Dracup		Dauphin	Tonkin					103/—
Dreghorn		Regina	Glenavon	FPS	100-41	1912		112/127
Driver		Saskatoon	Dodsland	FPS-GTP	100-162	1920		113/134
Duck Lake		Prince Albert	Duck Lake	CSS-CP	100-100	1891	Note 71, Museum-2*	110/128
Dudley		Saskatoon	Beechy	FPS	100-41	1922		113/127
Duff		Regina	Qu'Appelle	Type E	100-152	1913	Museum-2	112/137
Dulwich	x-Longstaff	Prince Albert	Turtleford	FPS-CNR	CB	1929		111/143
Dumble		Prince Albert	Big River	FPS	110-42	—	x-SMBH	109/141
Dummer #1		Regina	Avonlea	PORT-CNoR	100-24	1913		111/128
Dummer #2		Regina	Avonlea	4th	100-68	1916		111/130
Dunblane #1		Regina	Central Butte	FPS	100-41			111/127
Dunblane #2		Regina	Central Butte	3rd	100-72	1917		111/133
Dundurn		Regina	Craik	CSS-CP	100-100	1892	Note 71	112/128
Dunning	x-Webster	Regina	Lampman	3rd	100-29	1912	Note 77	112/132
Duperow #1	x-Lydden	Saskatoon	Dodsland	FPS		1915	Temporary	113/144
Duperow #2		Saskatoon	Dodsland	Type F	100-151	1919		113/138
Duro		Saskatoon	Asquith	Type E	100-152	1911		113/137
East Prince Albert		Prince Albert	Duck Lake	BK-7		1898	Note 71	110/133
Eastview #1		Regina	Central Butte	FPS		1915		111/144
Eastview #2		Regina	Central Butte	FPS		—		111/141
Eatonia #1	x-Eaton–2nd	Calgary	Mantario	PORT-CNoR	110-73A	1922	SMBH	115/128
Eatonia #2		Calgary	Mantario	3rd	100-199	1924	Variant, Museum-1	115/142
Ebenezer		Dauphin	Yorkton	Type E	100-152	1911		103/137
Edam		Prince Albert	Turtleford	3rd	100-29	1913	Museum-1	111/132
Edenwold		Regina	Qu'Appelle	Type E	100-152	1911		112/137
Edgeley		Regina	Qu'Appelle	Type E	100-152	1911		112/137
Elcott		Regina	Northgate	Type E	100-152	1912		112/137
Eldersley #1	x-Osgood	Prince Albert	Tisdale	SHLT-CNoR	100-95			110/124
Eldersley #2		Prince Albert	Tisdale	4th	100-68	1922		110/130
Eldred		Prince Albert	Big River	FPS	100-41	1911		109/127
Elrose		Saskatoon	Elrose	3rd	100-29	1913		114/132
Elswick	x-Lowell	Regina	Lampman	FPS-CNR	CB	1937	Note 77	112/143
Endeavour #1-A		Dauphin	Assiniboine	FPS-CNR	100-41B	1930		102/139
Endeavour #1-B		Dauphin	Assiniboine	PORT	110-159	—	SMBH	102/141
Endeavour #2		Dauphin	Assiniboine	CN4A	100-310	1948		102/142
End Lake		Edmonton	Bodo	FPS-CNR	100-41C	1931		116/140
Englefeld	<<Clairvaux>>	Dauphin	Margo	4th	100-31	1912		102/130
Ens		Prince Albert	Cudworth	SHLT	110-153	—	x-ST	109/141
Erinferry	x-Wrixon	Prince Albert	Big River	FPS	CB			109/143
Erwood #1		Dauphin	Erwood	CSS-B	100-99	1901		102/128
Erwood #2		Dauphin	Erwood	FPS	100-41	1918		102/127
Eskbank #1		Regina	Central Butte	FPS	CB			111/143
Eskbank #2		Regina	Central Butte	FPS-CNR	100-41B	1928	Probable	111/140
Estevan		Regina	Bienfait	2nd	100-83	1915	Note 77	111/134
Estlin		Regina	Lewvan	Type E	100-152	1912		112/137
Eston #1		Saskatoon	Elrose	3rd	100-72	1915		114/133
Eston #2		Saskatoon	Elrose	FPS	110-159	—	x-SMBH	114/141
Ethelton		Prince Albert	Meskanaw	FPS-CNR	100-41B	1931		110/140
Ettington #1		Regina	Gravelbourg	FPS	100-41	1913		112/127
Ettington #2		Regina	Gravelbourg	3rd	100-29	1914		112/132
Euclid	x-Thresher	Regina	Central Butte	FPS-CNR	100-41B	1927		111/140
Eyre		Calgary	Mantario	4th	100-68	1920		115/130
Fairholme		Prince Albert	Robinhood	FPS-CNR	100-41B	1928		110/140
Fairlight		Portage-Brandon	Cromer	3rd	100-29	1907		104/132
Fairmount #1		Calgary	Oyen	FPS	100-41	By14		—/127
Fairmount #2		Calgary	Oyen	4th	100-68	1917		115/130
Fairmount #3		Calgary	Oyen	FPS-CNR	100-41B	—		115/140
Farley		Saskatoon	Asquith	Type E	100-152	1911		113/137
Fenton #1		Prince Albert	Tisdale	PORT-CNoR	100-24	1907		110/128
Fenton #2	Joint with CPR	Prince Albert	Tisdale	FPS	100-41	1914		110/127
Fenwood		Saskatoon	Touchwood	Type E	100-152	1911		114/137
Fielding		Prince Albert	Langham	3rd	100-3	1907		110/131
Findlater #1		Regina	Craik	FPS	100-96	1909		111/124
Findlater #2		Regina	Craik	4th	100-31	1911		111/130
Finnie		Regina	Qu'Appelle	Type E	100-152	1910		112/137
Fiske		Saskatoon	Rosetown	3rd	100-29	1910		114/132
Fitzmaurice		Dauphin	Tonkin	FPS-CNR	100-41B	1929		103/140
Flaxcombe	x-Harwell	Calgary	Oyen	3rd	100-29	1912		115/132
Fonehill		Dauphin	Tonkin	3rd	100-72	1915		103/133
Forgan		Saskatoon	Elrose	3rd	100-29	1913		114/132
Fort Qu'Appelle		Regina	Qu'Appelle	Type E	100-152	1911	Museum-1	112/137
Forward		Regina	Avonlea	3rd	100-29	1912		111/132
Frankslake #1	x-Frank's Lake	Regina	Qu'Appelle	FPS-GTP	CB	1916		112/143
Frankslake #2		Regina	Qu'Appelle	FPS		—	SMBH	113/141
Frederick		Prince Albert	Aberdeen	FPS		1922		108/144
Frenchman Butte		Prince Albert	Bolney	CN3rd	100-253	1929		109/142
Friend		Regina	Gravelbourg				Note 33	112/—
Frobisher		Regina	Northgate	Type E	100-152	1913		112/137

SASKATCHEWAN

Station Name	Proposed/Former Name	Division	Subdivision	Type of Depot	Plan	Year	Notes	see page
Galilee		Regina	Gravelbourg	FPS	100-41	1916		112/127
Gallivan		Prince Albert	Cutknife	Type E	100-152	1913		110/137
Gerald		Saskatoon	Miniota	Type E	100-152	1911		114/137
Gillespie		Regina	Qu'Appelle	Type E	100-152	1910		112/137
Gilroy #1		Regina	Riverhurst	FPS-GTP		By15	Temporary	113/144
Gilroy #2		Regina	Riverhurst	Type G	100-168	1919		113/138
Girvin #2		Regina	Craik	3rd	100-29	1910		111/132
Glaslyn		Prince Albert	Robinhood	CN3rd	100-184	1928	Museum-1	110/141
Glenavon		Regina	Glenavon	3rd	100-29	1911		112/132
Glenbush		Prince Albert	Robinhood	FPS-CNR	100-41B	1928		110/140
Glen Kerr		Regina	Main Centre	FPS-CNR	100-41C	1930		112/140
Glidden		Saskatoon	Elrose	3rd	100-72	1918		114/133
Goodeve		Saskatoon	Touchwood	Type D	100-154	1909		114/135
Goodwater		Regina	Lampman	3rd	100-29	1911	Note 77	112/132
Gorlitz		Dauphin	Yorkton	Type E	100-152	1913		103/137
Gouldtown		Regina	Main Centre	FPS-CNR	100-41C	1930		112/140
Grainland		Regina	Central Butte	FPS-CNR	100-41B	1927		111/140
Grandora		Saskatoon	Asquith	Type E	100-152	1911		113/137
Grassdale		Regina	Weyburn	FPS-CNR	100-41B	1928		113/140
Grasswood	x-Grindlay	Regina	Craik	FPS	100-41	——	Note 21	112/127
Gravelbourg		Regina	Gravelbourg	3rd	100-53	1913	Variant	112/132
Gray		Regina	Lewvan	Type E	100-152	1914		112/137
Grayburn	x-Forgray	Regina	Central Butte	Type E	100-152	1914		111/137
Greenan		Saskatoon	Elrose	FPS	100-41	1915		114/127
Greenbush #1		Prince Albert	Tisdale	CSS-SH	110-10	1902		110/129
Greenbush #2		Prince Albert	Tisdale	FPS			x-SMBH	110/143
Greene		Saskatoon	Dodsland	FPS-GTP	CB	1914		113/143
Griffin #1		Regina	Lewvan	Type E	100-152	1913		112/137
Griffin #2		Regina	Lewvan	FPS		1921	Temporary	112/144
Griffin #3		Regina	Lewvan	3rd	100-72	1921		112/133
Gye		Regina	Bengough	FPS-CNR	100-41B	1926		111/140
Hafford		Prince Albert	Blaine Lake	3rd	100-29	1913		109/132
Hague		Prince Albert	Duck Lake	CPR#5	100-110	1905	Note 71	110/133
Halvorgate		Regina	Main Centre	FPS-CNR	100-41C	1932		112/140
Hamlin		Prince Albert	Turtleford	FPS	100-41	1914		110/127
Hamton #1		Dauphin	Rhein	FPS	100-41	1913		103/127
Hamton #2		Dauphin	Rhein	4th	100-68	1924		103/130
Handsworth		Regina	Corning	FPS-CNR	100-41B	1925		111/140
Hanley #2		Regina	Craik	CP#5	100-110	1905	Notes 20, 71	112/133
Hardene		Calgary	Mantario	FPS	100-41	1920		115/127
Hardy #1		Regina	Bengough	FPS	100-41	1913		111/127
Hardy #2		Regina	Bengough	4th	100-68	1918		111/130
Harptree		Regina	Bengough	FPS-CNR	100-41B	1926		111/140
Harris		Saskatoon	Rosetown	3rd	100-29	1909		114/132
Hartwell		Prince Albert	Robinhood	FPS-CNR	100-41B	1928		110/140
Hassan		Dauphin	Assiniboine	FPS	100-41	1915		102/127
Hatherleigh		Prince Albert	Hatherleigh	CN3rd	100-253	1931		110/142
Haultain		Regina	Craik	SHLT-CNoR	100-95	1908		112/124
Hawker	x-Eaton—1st	Saskatoon	Rosetown	PORT-CNoR	110-73A	1914	SMBH	114/128
Hawkeye	x-Lynwood	Prince Albert	Amiens	FPS-CNR	100-41B	1930		109/140
Hawoods #1		Saskatoon	Asquith	Type E	100-152	1911		113/137
Hawoods #2		Saskatoon	Asquith	FPS-GTP		1920		113/144
Hazel Dell		Dauphin	Preeceville	FPS	100-41	1921		102/127
Hearne #1		Regina	Avonlea	FPS	100-41	1913		111/127
Hearne #2		Regina	Avonlea	4th	100-68	1917		111/130
Hearts Hill		Edmonton	Bodo	FPS-CNR	100-41C	1933		116/140
Henribourg	Joint with CPR	Prince Albert	Paddockwood	CN3rd	100-197	1925		110/141
Hepburn #1		Prince Albert	Carlton	FPS	100-41			109/127
Hepburn #2		Prince Albert	Carlton	CN4th	100-252	1930		109/142
Highgate		Edmonton	Blackfoot	FPS	100-41	1919		116/127
Hinchcliffe		Dauphin	Assiniboine	FPS-CNR	100-41B	1930		102/140
Hodgeville		Regina	Gravelbourg	3rd	100-72	1922		112/133
Hoey #1		Prince Albert	Cudworth	FPS-GTP	100-162	1914		109/134
Hoey #2		Prince Albert	Cudworth	Type G	100-168	1920		109/138
Holbein		Prince Albert	Blaine Lake	FPS	100-41	1915		109/127
Holmes		Prince Albert	Cudworth					109/——
Hoosier	x-Fee	Saskatoon	Dodsland	Type E	100-152	1913		113/137
Hubbard		Saskatoon	Touchwood	Type E	100-152	1911		114/137

ROSTER NOTES:

20 The original site of Hanley station grounds was about three miles north of its present location.

21 The sources regarding the disposition of this station are contradictory. One record indicates that both buildings were moved to Redpass Jct., BC while another source states that they were both relocated to McBride, BC.

33 The stretch between Neidpath and Swift Current was operated on a sporadic basis until abandoned in September 1958. Standard freight and passenger shelters (CNR Plan 100-41B) are noted on the respective station grounds plans as "Shelter Site," therefore it appears that these shelters may not have been constructed and are thus excluded from this listing. The CNR had a Union Station agreement with the CPR to use that company's Swift Current depot.

71 This station was built by the Canadian Pacific Railway that operated the Qu'Appelle Long Lake and Saskatchewan Railway until 1906, when the line was acquired by the Canadian Northern Railway.

77 For clarity, the Lampman Subdivision is shown in its pre-1952 configuration: Maryfield to Radville. Flooding in the spring of 1948 knocked out three bridges in the Souris valley, closing the line between Blewett and Goodwater. The resulting stub lines were dubbed the Blewett (Lampman to Blewett) and Goodwater (Radville to Goodwater) Subdivisions and train services were operated to the respective ends of track. CNR studies in 1951 determined it was uneconomic to rebuild the bridges and rebuild the closed stretch of rail line, so it was abandoned. Subsequently, the former Bienfait Subdivision (Lampman to Estevan) was incorporated into the south end of the Lampman Subdivision.

SASKATCHEWAN

Station Name	Proposed/Former Name	Division	Subdivision	Type of Depot	Plan	Year	Notes	see page
Hudson Bay	x-Hudson Bay Jct.	Dauphin	Erwood	3rd	100-29	1911	Variant	102/132
Hughton		Saskatoon	Elrose	3rd	100-75	1914		114/133
Humboldt	x-Humbolt	Dauphin	Margo	3rd	100-18	1905	Variant	102/131
Huntoon #1		Regina	Lewvan	Type E	100-152	1913		112/137
Huntoon #2		Regina	Lewvan	SHLT-CNR	110-117	—	x-ST	112/141
Hyas #1		Dauphin	Preeceville	FPS	100-41	1912		102/127
Hyas #2		Dauphin	Preeceville	CN3rd	100-253	1937		102/142
Ibstone	x-Charlton	Saskatoon	Porter	Type E	100-152	1913		114/137
Iffley		Prince Albert	Hatherleigh	FPS-CNR	100-41B	1931		110/140
Inchkeith	x-Hawthorne	Portage-Brandon	Cromer	FPS	100-41	1911		104/127
Indi		Regina	Craik	FPS	100-41	1915		112/127
Inglenook		Saskatoon	Elrose	FPS-CNR	100-41B	1929		114/140
Innes		Regina	Lewvan	PORT-GTP	110-101		SMBH	112/134
Invermay		Dauphin	Margo	3rd	100-3	1904		102/131
Isham		Saskatoon	White Bear	FPS-CNR	100-41B	1927		114/140
Ituna		Saskatoon	Touchwood	Type E	100-152	1911		114/137
Jameson		Regina	Glenavon	3rd	100-29	1914		112/132
Jasmin		Saskatoon	Touchwood	Type E	100-152	1911		114/137
Jedburgh		Dauphin	Tonkin	CN3rd	100-250	1929		103/142
Juniata		Saskatoon	Asquith	Type E	100-152	1911		113/137
Juniper		Saskatoon	Elrose	FPS	100-41	1913		114/127
Kamsack #1		Dauphin	Togo	3rd	100-18	1904	Variant	103/131
Kamsack #2		Dauphin	Togo	SPEC-CNR	100-399	1968		103/142
Keatley	x-Peacedale	Prince Albert	Robinhood	FPS-CNR	100-41B	1929		110/140
Kegworth #1	x-Lovat	Regina	Glenavon	FPS	100-41	1911	Probable	112/127
Kegworth #2		Regina	Glenavon	FPS-CNR	100-41B	1926		112/140
Kelliher		Saskatoon	Touchwood	Type D	100-154	1909		114/135
Kelso		Portage-Brandon	Cromer	3rd	100-29	1907		104/132
Kelvington #1		Dauphin	Preeceville	PORT-CNoR	110-73A	1922	SMBH	103/128
Kelvington #2		Dauphin	Preeceville	3rd	100-75	1922	Museum-2	103/133
Kenaston		Regina	Craik	CSS-CP	100-100	1890	Note 71	112/128
Kendal #1		Regina	Glenavon	FPS	100-41			112/127
Kendal #2		Regina	Glenavon	4th	100-31	1913		112/130
Kessock		Dauphin	Tonkin	FPS	100-41	1916		103/127
Ketchen		Dauphin	Preeceville	FPS	100-41	1920		102/127
Kettlehut		Regina	Main Centre	FPS-CNR	CB	1931		112/143
Keystown		Regina	Central Butte	Type E	100-152	1913		111/137
Kilwinning		Prince Albert	Blaine Lake	FPS	100-41	1913		109/127
Kindersley #1		Saskatoon	Rosetown	PORT-CNoR	CB	1910	Temporary	114/143
Kindersley #2		Saskatoon	Rosetown	FPS	100-96	1910	Variant, Temporary	114/124
Kindersley #3		Saskatoon	Rosetown	2nd	100-39	1910		114/134
Kingsford		Regina	Bienfait	FPS	100-41	1917	Note 77	111/127
Kinhop		Saskatoon	Rosetown	FPS	100-41	—		114/127
Kinistino		Prince Albert	Tisdale	3rd	100-3	1905		110/131
Kinley		Saskatoon	Asquith	Type D	100-154	1909		113/135
Kipling		Portage-Brandon	Cromer	2nd	100-22	1908		104/133
Krydor #1	<<Ballock>>	Prince Albert	Blaine Lake	FPS	100-41	1913		109/127
Krydor #2		Prince Albert	Blaine Lake	4th	100-68	1917		109/130
Kuroki #1		Dauphin	Margo	CSS-SH	110-10	1905		102/129
Kuroki #2		Dauphin	Margo	FPS	100-41	1917		102/127
Kylemore #1		Dauphin	Margo	FPS	100-96	1909		102/124
Kylemore #2		Dauphin	Margo	FPS	100-41	—		102/127
Lacadena		Saskatoon	White Bear	CN3rd	100-227	1927		114/142
Lady Lake		Dauphin	Assiniboine	FPS-CNR	100-41B	1930		102/140
Laird		Prince Albert	Carlton	3rd	100-29	1909		109/132
Lake Lenore		Prince Albert	St. Brieux	3rd	100-72	1921		110/133
Lake Valley #1	x-Linstrom	Regina	Central Butte	Type E	100-152	1914		111/137
Lake Valley #2		Regina	Central Butte	FPS-CNR	100-41B	—	Probable	111/140
Lampman		Regina	Lampman	3rd	100-29	1910	Note 76	112/132
Landis		Edmonton	Unity	Type E	100-152	1911		117/137
Langbank		Portage-Brandon	Cromer	3rd	100-29	1911		104/132
Langham		Prince Albert	Langham	3rd	100-3	1905		110/131
Laporte		Calgary	Mantario	4th	100-68	1920		115/130
Lashburn		Edmonton	Blackfoot	3rd	100-3	1907		116/131
Laura #1		Saskatoon	Rosetown	SHLT-CNoR	100-95	1908		114/124
Laura #2		Saskatoon	Rosetown	4th	100-31	1911		114/130
Lawson #1		Regina	Riverhurst	FPS-GTP	CB	1914		113/143
Lawson #2		Regina	Riverhurst	Type F	100-151	1919		113/138
Leask		Prince Albert	Blaine Lake	3rd	100-29	1912		109/132
Lebret		Regina	Qu'Appelle	Type E	100-152	1911		112/137
Leckford	x-Bonne Plaine	Prince Albert	Duck Lake	FPS	100-41	1911		110/127
Leney		Saskatoon	Asquith	Type D	100-154	1910		113/135
Lepine		Prince Albert	Meskanaw	FPS-CNR	100-41B	1931		110/140
Leross		Saskatoon	Touchwood	Type E	100-152	1911		114/137
Lestock	x-Mostyn	Saskatoon	Touchwood	Type E	100-152	1911		114/137
Lett		Saskatoon	Porter	Type E	100-152	1913		114/137
Levuka		Regina	Avonlea					111/—
Lewvan		Regina	Lewvan	Type E	100-152	1912		112/137
Lilac	2nd location (1916)	Prince Albert	Blaine Lake	FPS	100-41	1917		109/127
Lintlaw #1		Dauphin	Preeceville	FPS	100-41			102/127
Lintlaw #2		Dauphin	Preeceville	4th	100-68	1920		102/130
Lipsett	x-Pleasant Valley	Prince Albert	St. Brieux	FPS	100-41	1915		110/127

SASKATCHEWAN

Station Name	Proposed/Former Name	Division	Subdivision	Type of Depot	Plan	Year	Notes	see page
Livelong		Prince Albert	Robinhood	FPS-CNR	100-41B	1928		110/140
Longacre		Regina	Central Butte	FPS-CNR	100-41B	1927		111/140
Lorlie #1		Regina	Qu'Appelle	FPS-GTP	CB	1915		112/143
Lorlie #2		Regina	Qu'Appelle	Type G	100-168	1920		112/138
Loverna		Saskatoon	Dodsland	Type E	100-152	1913		113/137
Lucky Lake		Saskatoon	Beechy	3rd	100-72	1923		113/133
Lumsden #1		Regina	Craik	CSS-CP	100-100	1890	Note 71	111/128
Lumsden #2		Regina	Craik	3rd	100-3	1908		111/131
MacDowall		Prince Albert	Duck Lake	CSS-CP	100-100	1891	Note 71	110/128
MacNutt		Dauphin	Tonkin	3rd	100-29	1910		103/132
Macrorie		Saskatoon	Conquest	3rd	100-29	1912		113/132
Madison		Saskatoon	Elrose	3rd	100-72	1917		114/133
Maidstone		Edmonton	Blackfoot	3rd	100-3	1905		116/131
Main Centre		Regina	Main Centre	FPS-CNR	100-41C	1932		112/140
Mair		Regina	Lampman	FPS	100-41	1910	Probable	112/127
Mansur #1		Regina	Weyburn	FPS	CB			113/143
Mansur #2		Regina	Weyburn	SHLT-CNR		—	x-PH	113/141
Mantario		Calgary	Mantario	3rd	100-72	1920		115/133
Marcelin		Prince Albert	Blaine Lake	3rd	100-29	1911		109/132
Marengo		Calgary	Oyen	3rd	100-29	1911		115/132
Margo #1		Dauphin	Margo	4th	100-31	1911		102/130
Margo #2		Dauphin	Margo	FPS	CBx2	—	Temporary	102/143
Margo #3		Dauphin	Margo	CN4B	100-328	1953		102/142
Marshall		Edmonton	Blackfoot	3rd	100-3	1905		116/131
Maryfield #1	Joint with CPR	Portage-Brandon	Cromer	CP A-2	100-86	—		104/133
Maryfield #2	Joint with CPR	Portage-Brandon	Cromer	4th	100-68	—		104/130
Mattes	Joint with CPR	Prince Albert	Big River	FPS-CNR		1920		109/144
Mawer #1		Regina	Central Butte	Type E	100-152	1913		111/137
Mawer #2		Regina	Central Butte	CN3rd	100-197	1924		111/141
Mayfair		Prince Albert	Robinhood	CN3rd	100-250	1929		110/142
Maymont		Prince Albert	Langham	3rd	100-29	1908		110/132
Mazenod		Regina	Gravelbourg	3rd	100-29	1913		112/132
McCallum–CN Jct.	1st site	Regina	Glenavon	FPS-CNR	100-41B	1926		112/140
McGee #1		Saskatoon	Rosetown	FPS				114/144
McGee #2		Saskatoon	Rosetown	3rd	100-29	1913		114/132
McKim	x-Peoples	Dauphin	Yorkton	FPS-CNR	CB	1927		103/143
McMichael		Prince Albert	Meskanaw	FPS-CNR	100-41B	1931		110/140
Meacham		Prince Albert	Cudworth	Type E	100-152	1911		109/137
Mead #1		Saskatoon	Asquith	FPS-GTP	100-162	1908		113/134
Mead #2		Saskatoon	Asquith	Type F	100-151	1917		113/138
Medstead		Prince Albert	Robinhood	CN3rd	100-184	1928		110/141
Mehan #1		Dauphin	Yorkton	Type E	100-152	1911		103/137
Mehan #2		Dauphin	Yorkton	PORT-CNR		1959		103/144
Melfort	Joint with CPR	Prince Albert	Tisdale	3rd	100-19	1904	Variant	110/131
Melville		Saskatoon	Miniota	SPEC-GTP	100-156	1908		114/138
Mennon		Prince Albert	Carlton	FPS	100-41	1913		109/127
Meota		Prince Albert	Turtleford	3rd	100-29	1910	Reverse	111/132
Merid #1		Calgary	Oyen	FPS	100-41	1910		115/127
Merid #2		Calgary	Oyen	3rd	100-72	1918		115/133
Mervin		Prince Albert	Turtleford	3rd	100-29	1914	Note 63	111/132
Meskanaw		Prince Albert	Meskanaw	PORT-CNR	100-132	1931		110/141
Mikado #1		Dauphin	Margo	FPS	100-41			102/127
Mikado #2		Dauphin	Margo	3rd	100-72	1917		102/133
Mildred	x-Arleux	Prince Albert	Amiens	FPS-CNR	100-41B	1930		109/140
Mileage 81.5		Dauphin	Togo	FPS	100-41	—		103/127
Mileage 34.4		Hudson Bay	Turnberry	SHLT		By20		103/144
Millerdale		Saskatoon	Dodsland	Type E	100-152	1913		113/137
Minard		Regina	Lewvan	Type E	100-152	1913		112/137
Mistatim #1-A		Prince Albert	Tisdale	FPS	100-41	—		110/127
Mistatim #1-B		Prince Albert	Tisdale	FPS		—	x-SMBH	110/141
Mitchellton		Regina	Gravelbourg	3rd	100-29	1913		112/132
Montmartre		Regina	Glenavon	3rd	100-29			112/132
Mont Nebo		Prince Albert	Amiens	FPS-CNR	100-41B	1930		109/140
Moose Jaw–CNoR #1	On Home Street South	Regina	Avonlea	SPEC-CNoR	100-57	1913	Temporary	111/134
Moose Jaw–CNoR #2		Regina	Avonlea	SPEC-CNR	100-123	1918		111/134
Moose Jaw–CNoR #3	Union Sta. w/GTP	Regina	Avonlea	SPEC-CNR	100-124	1919		111/134
Moose Jaw–GTP		Regina	Central Butte	PORT-GTP	110-101	1914	SMBH	111/134
Moose Range #1-A		Prince Albert	Brooksby	FPS-CNR	100-41C	1931		109/140
Moose Range #1-B		Prince Albert	Brooksby	FPS				109/144
Moreland		Regina	Avonlea	FPS	100-41	1913		111/127
Moseley		Prince Albert	St. Brieux	PORT-CNoR	110-73A	—	SMBH	110/128

ROSTER NOTES:

63 CNR records classify this as Plan 100-29, but it incorporates all the features of Plan 100-72.

71 This station was built by the Canadian Pacific Railway that operated the Qu'Appelle Long Lake and Saskatchewan Railway until 1906, when the line was acquired by the Canadian Northern Railway.

76 The second storey was removed, circa 1941, rendering it unrecognizable as a 3rd Class station.

77 For clarity, the Lampman Subdivision is shown in its pre-1952 configuration: Maryfield to Radville. Flooding in the spring of 1948 knocked out three bridges in the Souris valley, closing the line between Blewett and Goodwater. The resulting stub lines were dubbed the Blewett (Lampman to Blewett) and Goodwater (Radville to Goodwater) Subdivisions and train services were operated to the respective ends of track. CNR studies in 1951 determined it was uneconomic to rebuild the bridges and rebuild the closed stretch of rail line, so it was abandoned. Subsequently, the former Bienfait Subdivision (Lampman to Estevan) was incorporated into the south end of the Lampman Subdivision.

SASKATCHEWAN

Station Name	Proposed/Former Name	Division	Subdivision	Type of Depot	Plan	Year	Notes	see page
Mossbank		Regina	Gravelbourg	3rd	100-29	1913		112/132
Muenster		Dauphin	Margo	4th	100-31	1908		102/130
Mullingar		Prince Albert	Robinhood	FPS-CNR	100-41B	1929		110/140
Murphy's #1	<<Crooked River>>	Prince Albert	Tisdale	SHLT-CNoR	100-95	By14		110/124
Murphy's #2		Prince Albert	Tisdale	CN3rd	100-250	1929		110/142
Muscow		Regina	Qu'Appelle	Type E	100-152	1911		112/137
Naisberry	x-Wentworth	Prince Albert	Tisdale	FPS	100-96	1906		110/124
Neely		Prince Albert	Cudworth	Type E	100-152	1911		109/137
Neidpath		Regina	Gravelbourg	CN3rd	100-197	1925		112/141
Neola #1		Saskatoon	Asquith	SHLT-CNR	150-53	—	x-PH	113/141
Neola #2		Saskatoon	Asquith	FPS-CNR		1930		113/144
Netherhill		Saskatoon	Rosetown	3rd	100-29	1910	Museum-2	114/132
Newcross		Saskatoon	Asquith	TOS-CNR		1929		113/144
New Osgoode		Prince Albert	Arborfield	FPS-CNR	100-41B	1930		109/140
Nicklen #1	x-Armley	Prince Albert	Brooksby	FPS-CNR	100-41C	1930		109/140
Nicklen #2		Prince Albert	Brooksby	FPS-CNR	CB	1938		109/143
Nokomis		Saskatoon	Touchwood	NTR1	100-160	1908	Museum-2	114/138
North Battleford #1		Prince Albert	Langham	2nd	100-22	1905		110/134
North Battleford #2		Prince Albert	Langham	2nd	100-22	1908		110/134
North Battleford #3		Prince Albert	Langham	SPEC-CNR	100-330	1955		110/142
Northgate		Regina	Northgate	SPEC-GTP	100-164	1914		112/138
North Regina–CNoR		Regina	Craik	FPS-CNoR		1911	Note 17	111/144
North Regina–GTP	x-West Yard	Regina	Qu'Appelle	TOS			Note 22	113/144
North Saskatoon #1		Prince Albert	Duck Lake	FPS-CNoR		By14	Note 4	110/144
North Saskatoon #2		Prince Albert	Duck Lake	FPS-CNR	CB	1933	Note 4	110/143
North Saskatoon #3		Prince Albert	Duck Lake	FPS-CNR		1960s	Note 4, x-SMBH	110/141
Norquay		Dauphin	Preeceville	3rd	100-29	1911		102/132
Nutana		Saskatoon	Asquith	TOS-CNoR		1905	Note 4	113/144
Nut Mountain #1	x-Spall	Dauphin	Preeceville	FPS	100-41	1922		102/127
Nut Mountain #2		Dauphin	Preeceville	CN4A	100-305	1945		102/142
Oban #1		Edmonton	Unity	Type E	100-152	1911		117/137
Oban #2		Edmonton	Unity	FPS				117/144
Odessa		Regina	Glenavon	3rd	100-29	1913		112/132
Okla		Dauphin	Preeceville	FPS	100-41	1920		102/127
Openshaw		Regina	Northgate	Type E	100-152	1913		112/137
Ordale		Prince Albert	Amiens	FPS-CNR	100-41B	1930		109/140
Osler		Prince Albert	Duck Lake	CSS-CP	100-100	1892	Note 71	110/128
Otosquen #1-A		Hudson Bay	Turnberry	FPS-CNR	CB	1944		103/143
Otosquen #1-B		Hudson Bay	Turnberry	PORT-CNR	CB	1953		103/143
Otthon		Dauphin	Yorkton	Type E	100-152	1911		103/137
Paddockwood		Prince Albert	Paddockwood	FPS-CNR	100-41B	1925		110/140
Palmer #1		Regina	Gravelbourg	FPS	100-41	1913		112/127
Palmer #2		Regina	Gravelbourg	3rd	100-72	1917		112/133
Palo		Edmonton	Unity	FPS-GTP	100-162	1917		117/134
Paradise Hill	x-Digges	Prince Albert	Bolney	CN3rd	100-253	1929		109/142
Parkerview	x-Crowtherview	Dauphin	Tonkin	CN3rd	100-253	1929		103/142
Parkman		Regina	Lampman	3rd	100-29	1910		112/132
Parkside #1		Prince Albert	Blaine Lake	FPS	100-41	1912		109/127
Parkside #2		Prince Albert	Blaine Lake	3rd	100-72	1916		109/133
Parry #1		Regina	Avonlea	FPS	100-41	1913		111/127
Parry #2		Regina	Avonlea	3rd	100-29	1916		111/132
Paswegin #1		Dauphin	Margo	FPS	100-96	1908		102/124
Paswegin #2		Dauphin	Margo	FPS	100-41	1918		102/127
Pathlow #1		Prince Albert	St. Brieux	FPS	100-41	1915		110/127
Pathlow #2		Prince Albert	St. Brieux	3rd	100-72	1922		110/133
Pattee		Regina	Central Butte	FPS-CNR	100-41B	1923		111/140
Paynton		Edmonton	Blackfoot	3rd	100-3	1905		116/131
Peebles	x-Kaiser	Regina	Glenavon	FPS-CNR	100-41B	1927		112/140
Peesane #1	x-Midway?	Prince Albert	Tisdale	CSS-SH	110-10	1903	Note 61	110/129
Peesane #2		Prince Albert	Tisdale	FPS	100-41	1911		110/127
Pelly		Dauphin	Preeceville	3rd	100-29	1909		102/132
Peterson #1		Prince Albert	Cudworth	FPS-GTP	CB	1916		109/143
Peterson #2		Prince Albert	Cudworth	FPS	100-41	—		109/127
Pinkham #1		Calgary	Oyen	FPS	100-41	By14		115/127
Pinkham #2		Calgary	Oyen	4th	100-68	1915		115/130
Plato		Saskatoon	Elrose	3rd	100-72	1915		114/133
Polwarth	Joint with CPR	Prince Albert	Big River	FPS	100-41	1915		109/127
Porcupine Plain #1		Prince Albert	Chelan	FPS-CNR	100-41B	1930		109/140
Porcupine Plain #2		Prince Albert	Chelan	CN4A	100-310	1953		109/142
Porcupine Plain #3		Prince Albert	Chelan	SPEC-CNR	100-366	1959		109/142
Prairie River #1		Prince Albert	Tisdale	FPS	100-96	1908	Probable	110/124
Prairie River #2		Prince Albert	Tisdale	PORT-CNoR	100-24	—		110/128
Prairie River #3		Prince Albert	Tisdale	3rd	100-72	1920	Museum-1	110/133
Preeceville		Dauphin	Preeceville	3rd	100-71	1912	Variant	102/133
Prince #1		Prince Albert	Turtleford	FPS	100-41	1914		110/127
Prince #2		Prince Albert	Turtleford	CN4th	100-220	1928	Museum-2	110/142
Prince Albert–CNoR #1	x-W. Prince Albert	Prince Albert	Duck Lake	CSS-CP	100-100	1890	Notes 28, 71	110/128
Prince Albert–CNoR #2		Prince Albert	Duck Lake	FPS		1905	Temporary	110/144
Prince Albert–CNoR #3	Joint w/CPR	Prince Albert	Duck Lake	2nd	100-25	1906	Variant	110/133
Prince Albert–CNoR #4	Joint w/CPR	Prince Albert	Duck Lake	SPEC-CNR	100-385	1960		110/142
Prince Albert–GTP		Prince Albert	Cudworth	SPEC-GTP	100-171	1917		109/138
Prinham		Prince Albert	Turtleford	FPS-CNR	CB	1939		110/143

SASKATCHEWAN

Station Name	Proposed/Former Name	Division	Subdivision	Type of Depot	Plan	Year	Notes	see page
Prongua		Prince Albert	Cutknife	Type E	100-152	1913		110/137
Prudhomme #1	x-Howell	Prince Albert	Aberdeen	FPS	100-96			108/124
Prudhomme #2		Prince Albert	Aberdeen	4th	100-31	1910		108/130
Punnichy		Saskatoon	Touchwood	Type D	100-154	1909		114/135
Pym		Saskatoon	Rosetown	FPS	100-41	1915		114/127
Quill Lake	<<Rally>>	Dauphin	Margo	3rd	100-3	1904		102/131
Quinton #1		Saskatoon	Touchwood	Type E	100-152	1911		114/137
Quinton #2		Saskatoon	Touchwood	Type F	100-151	1918		114/138
Rabbit Lake	x-Roundstone	Prince Albert	Robinhood	CN3rd	100-184	1928	Museum-1	110/141
Radisson		Prince Albert	Langham	3rd	100-3	1905		110/131
Radville		Regina	Lampman	2nd	100-39	1912	Museum-1	112/134
Rak		Prince Albert	Meskanaw	FPS-CNR	100-41B	1931		110/140
Rama #1-A		Dauphin	Margo	FPS	100-96	1909		102/124
Rama #1-B		Dauphin	Margo	FPS	100-41	—		102/127
Rama #2		Dauphin	Margo	4th	100-68	—		102/130
Raymore #1		Saskatoon	Touchwood	Type D	100-154	1907		114/135
Raymore #2		Saskatoon	Touchwood	FPS-GTP	CB	1919	Temporary	114/143
Raymore #3		Saskatoon	Touchwood	Type G	100-168	1921		114/138
Redberry		Prince Albert	Blaine Lake	FPS	100-41	1913		109/127
Red Deer Hill		Prince Albert	Cudworth	Type F	100-151	1918		109/138
Red Pheasant #1		Saskatoon	Porter	FPS-GTP	CB?			114/143
Red Pheasant #2		Saskatoon	Porter	FPS-CNR	CB	1950		114/143
Reford		Edmonton	Unity	Type E	100-152	1911		117/137
Regina	Union Station	Regina	Craik	SPEC-CNoR	100-58	1912	Notes 16, 22	111/134
Regina–GTP	On Spur	Regina	Lewvan	SPEC-GTP	110-131	1914	Notes 22, 39	112/138
Reserve		Dauphin	Assiniboine	CN3rd	100-253	1930		102/142
Reward		Edmonton	Bodo	FPS-CNR	100-41C	1932		116/140
Reynaud		Prince Albert	Meskanaw	CN3rd	100-253	1931		110/142
Rhein		Dauphin	Rhein	3rd	100-29	1911		103/132
Riceton		Regina	Lewvan	Type E	100-152	1912		112/137
Richard #1		Prince Albert	Blaine Lake	FPS	100-41	1913		109/127
Richard #2		Prince Albert	Blaine Lake	3rd	100-29	1916		109/132
Richlea		Saskatoon	Elrose	3rd	100-72	1915		114/133
Richmond		Prince Albert	Duck Lake	STA				110/144
Ridgedale #1	x-Ealing	Prince Albert	Brooksby	FPS	100-41	1922	Note 6	109/127
Ridgedale #2		Prince Albert	Brooksby	3rd	100-72	1922		109/133
Ridpath #1		Saskatoon	Rosetown	3rd	100-29	1910		114/132
Ridpath #2		Saskatoon	Rosetown	FPS-CNR	100-41B	1925		114/140
Ritchie		Regina	Bengough	FPS	100-41	1916		111/127
Riverhurst		Regina	Riverhurst	Type F	100-151	1917		113/138
Robinhood		Prince Albert	Robinhood	FPS-CNR	100-41B	1928		110/140
Roddick		Prince Albert	Duck Lake	FPS	100-41	1916		110/127
Roderickville		Regina	Gravelbourg				Note 33	112/—
Roncott	x-Harvester	Regina	Bengough	FPS-CNR	100-41B	1926		111/140
Roscoe #1		Dauphin	Erwood	FPS	CB			102/143
Roscoe #2		Dauphin	Erwood	FPS	100-41	1918		102/127
Rosetown		Saskatoon	Rosetown	3rd	100-29	1909		114/132
Rosthern		Prince Albert	Duck Lake	CPR Type BK 8		1902	Note 71, Museum-2*	110/133
Rowatt		Regina	Lewvan	Type E	100-152	1912		112/137
Rowletta #1		Regina	Central Butte	FPS		1916	Temporary	111/144
Rowletta #2		Regina	Central Butte	FPS-CNR	CB	1940		111/143
Ruddell	<<Lucerne>>	Prince Albert	Langham	3rd	100-3	1905		110/131
Runnymede #1		Dauphin	Togo	FPS	100-41			103/127
Runnymede #2		Dauphin	Togo	4th	100-68	1923		103/130
Rutan		Prince Albert	Cudworth	SHLT-CNR	110-117	—	x-ST	109/141
Ruthilda		Saskatoon	Dodsland	Type E	100-152	1913		113/137
Ryerson		Regina	Lampman	FPS	100-41	1912		112/127
St. Boswells #1	x-Bellot	Regina	Gravelbourg	FPS	100-41	1923		112/127
St. Boswells #2		Regina	Gravelbourg	4th	100-68	1923		112/130

ROSTER NOTES:

4 This station was technically on the Saskatoon Terminals Subdivision.

6 The sources regarding the disposition of this station are contradictory. One says that the structure was cut in half, one portion being shipped to Birch Hills and the other to Star City, for use as section bunkhouses. Another source indicates that, in 1933, this building was relocated to Peterson as a section bunkhouse.

16 With the Canadian Northern take-over of the Qu'Appelle Long Lake and Saskatchewan Railway in December 1906, it retained the joint station agreement between the CPR and QLL&S for use of the Regina depot and freight sheds. This station—the CPR's second depot at Regina—was replaced in 1912 by a "Union Station" built by the CPR for joint use and occupancy by the CNoR, then later the GTP, and subsequently the CNR. Only the 1912 station is included in the rosters. It is located on the CPR main line in downtown Regina on that company's Indian Head Subdivision. The station was subsequently acquired by VIA Rail Canada. It has since been sold, "restored" and redeveloped into a casino.

17 The CNoR constructed a temporary station adjacent to its Regina divisional yards in 1911. No description of this structure has been found. It was likely removed after the downtown CPR-CNoR Union station opened in 1912.

22 This station was technically on the Regina Terminals Subdivision.

28 It appears that the apartment-office-waiting room portion of this building was converted into a section house, while the freight shed was relocated next to the new station (#2) and used as a baggage-express shed.

33 The stretch between Neidpath and Swift Current was operated on a sporadic basis until abandoned in September 1958. Standard freight and passenger shelters (CNR Plan 100-41B) are noted on the respective station grounds plans as "Shelter Site," therefore it appears that these shelters may not have been constructed and are thus excluded from this listing. The CNR had a Union Station agreement with the CPR to use that company's Swift Current depot.

39 This temporary station—opened at 16th and Albert streets in 1912—was a re-cycled residence, renovated to provide a waiting room and ticket and administrative offices. The station facilities were consolidated in 1920 with those of the CNoR and CPR, at the Union Depot. The GTP's Regina station was subsequently closed. In 1924 it was converted into a residence for the CNR Divisional Superintendent. The building was later sold and used as a boys' home. It survived until at least 1961.

61 Reference to the station name Midway was found on Plan 110-10. Other stations listed on this drawing suggest that Midway was situated on the east end of the Tisdale Subdivision. Since Peesane is the approximate mid-point between Hudson Bay Jct. and Melfort, it may have formerly been known as Midway.

71 This station was built by the Canadian Pacific Railway that operated the Qu'Appelle Long Lake and Saskatchewan Railway until 1906, when the line was acquired by the Canadian Northern Railway.

SASKATCHEWAN

Station Name	Proposed/Former Name	Division	Subdivision	Type of Depot	Plan	Year	Notes	see page
St. Brieux #1		Prince Albert	St. Brieux	FPS	100-41	1915		110/127
St. Brieux #2		Prince Albert	St. Brieux	3rd	100-72	1920		110/133
St. Gregor #1		Dauphin	Margo	FPS				102/144
St. Gregor #2		Dauphin	Margo	3rd	100-75	1914		102/133
St. Louis		Prince Albert	Cudworth	FPS-GTP	100-162	1914	Probable	109/134
St. Walburg #1		Prince Albert	Turtleford	PORT-CNoR	110-73A	1921	SMBH	111/128
St. Walburg #2		Prince Albert	Turtleford	4th	100-68	1922		111/130
Salter		Saskatoon	Porter	FPS-GTP	CB	1914		114/143
Salvador		Edmonton	Bodo	FPS-CNR	100-41C	1931		116/140
Sandwith		Prince Albert	Hatherleigh	FPS-CNR	100-41B	1931		110/140
Sandgren		Saskatoon	Elrose	FPS-CNR	100-41B	1929		114/140
Saskatoon–CNR		Saskatoon	Asquith	SPEC-CNR	100-419	1964		113/142
Saskatoon–CNoR #1		Regina	Craik	CSS-CP	100-100	1891	Notes 4, 71	112/128
Saskatoon–CNoR #2		Regina	Craik	SPEC-CNoR	100-33	1910	Note 4	112/134
Saskatoon–CNoR #3		Regina	Craik	SPEC-CNR	100-288	1939	Notes 4, 54	112/142
Saskatoon–Loop Jct.		Prince Albert	Duck Lake	TOS-CNR	110-73	—	Note 4, x-SMBH	110/141
Saskatoon–Lorne Avenue		Regina	Craik	TOS-CNR	110-250	1951	Note 4	112/144
Scentgrass		Prince Albert	Hatherleigh	FPS-CNR	100-41B	1931		110/140
Scott #1		Edmonton	Unity	Type D	100-154	1909		117/135
Scott #2		Edmonton	Unity	CN3rd	100-253	1935		117/142
Scottsburgh		Regina	Gravelbourg	FPS-CNR	100-41B	1925		112/140
Semans		Saskatoon	Touchwood	Type D	100-154	1909		114/135
Senator	Joint with CPR	Prince Albert	Tisdale	FPS		—	x-ST	110/141
Service		Regina	Lampman	FPS-CNR	100-41B	1924		112/140
Shellbrook		Prince Albert	Blaine Lake	3rd	100-29	1910		109/132
Shell Lake	x-Rastel	Prince Albert	Amiens	CN3rd	100-253	1930		109/142
Sidmar		Regina	Central Butte	Type E	100-152	1913		111/137
Smales	x-Holder	Regina	Craik	FPS-CNR	100-41B	1923		112/140
Smiley		Saskatoon	Dodsland	Type E	100-152	1913		113/137
Smoking Tent		Dauphin	Erwood	FPS-CNR	CB	1950		102/143
Smuts		Prince Albert	Meskanaw	FPS-CNR	100-41B	1931		110/140
Snipe Lake		Saskatoon	Elrose	3rd	100-72	1917		114/133
Somme		Prince Albert	Chelan	PORT-CNR	100-132	1930		109/141
Souris River		Regina	Northgate	FPS	CB			112/143
Souris Valley		Regina	Lampman	FPS	100-41	1913		112/127
South Canora	x-Canora–GTP	Dauphin	Yorkton	SPEC-GTP	100-157	1911		103/138
South Elbow	x-Ireton	Regina	Central Butte	CN3rd	100-197	1927		111/141
South Saskatoon #1	x-Earl	Saskatoon	Asquith	Type D	100-154	1909	Notes 3, 4	113/135
South Saskatoon #2		Saskatoon	Asquith	TOS		—		113/144
Speddington		Prince Albert	Chelan	FPS		1946		109/144
Speers		Prince Albert	Blaine Lake	3rd	100-29	1913		109/132
Spiritwood		Prince Albert	Amiens	CN3rd	100-250	1930		109/142
Spring Valley #1		Regina	Gravelbourg	FPS	100-41	1913		112/127
Spring Valley #2		Regina	Gravelbourg	4th	100-68	1916		112/130
Springwater		Saskatoon	Dodsland	Type E	100-152	1913		113/137
Spruce Lake	<<Alamac>>	Prince Albert	Turtleford	FPS	100-41	1922		111/127
Spy Hill #1		Saskatoon	Miniota	Type E	100-152	1910		114/137
Spy Hill #2		Saskatoon	Miniota	SPEC-CNR	100-187	—	Note 47	114/143
Star City		Prince Albert	Tisdale	3rd	100-3	1904		110/131
Steelman		Regina	Northgate	Type E	100-152	1913		112/137
Steen		Prince Albert	Chelan	FPS-CNR	100-41B	1930		109/140
Stenen		Dauphin	Preeceville	3rd	100-29	1912		102/132
Stony Beach		Regina	Central Butte	Type E	100-152	1913		111/137
Stornoway		Dauphin	Rhein	3rd	100-29	1913		103/132
Strehlow		Regina	Craik	FPS	100-41	1914		112/127
Strong		Regina	Craik	FPS	100-41	—	Note 19	112/127
Sturdee		Dauphin	Tonkin	FPS	100-41	1915		103/127
Sturgis #1		Dauphin	Preeceville	FPS	100-41	By14		102/127
Sturgis #2		Dauphin	Preeceville	3rd	100-72	1918	Museum-2	102/133
Sunny Glen		Edmonton	Bodo	FPS-CNR	100-41C	1931		116/140
Surbiton		Saskatoon	Elrose	FPS	100-41	1913		114/132
Swanson		Saskatoon	Conquest	3rd	100-29	1912		113/132
Swift Current	Joint with CPR	Regina	Gravelbourg				Note 33	112/—
Tadmore		Dauphin	Assiniboine	FPS	100-41	1915		102/127
Tako		Edmonton	Unity	Type E	100-152	1911		117/137
Tallman		Prince Albert	Blaine Lake	FPS-CNR	100-41B	1929		109/140
Tall Pines		Dauphin	Assiniboine	FPS-CNR	100-41B	1930		102/140
Talmage		Regina	Lewvan	Type E	100-152	1913		112/137
Tarnapol		Prince Albert	Meskanaw	FPS-CNR	100-41B	1931		110/140
Tate		Saskatoon	Touchwood	Type E	100-152	1911		114/137
Tatsfield		Prince Albert	Cutknife	FPS	CB?			110/143
Teakle		Regina	Main Centre	FPS-CNR	100-41C	1930		112/140
Tessier		Saskatoon	Rosetown	3rd	100-29	1908		114/132
Thunder Creek		Regina	Main Centre	FPS-CNR	CB	1931		112/143
Tichfield #1	x-Lyons	Saskatoon	Elrose	FPS	100-41	1918		114/127
Tichfield #2		Saskatoon	Elrose	FPS-CNR	100-320	1949		114/143
Tilney #1		Regina	Avonlea	FPS	100-41	1913		111/127
Tilney #2		Regina	Avonlea	4th	100-68	1922		111/130
Tiny		Dauphin	Margo	FPS	100-96	1909		102/124
Tisdale #1		Prince Albert	Tisdale	3rd	100-3	1904		110/131
Tisdale #2		Prince Albert	Tisdale	SPEC-CNR	100-412	1964		110/142
Togo		Dauphin	Togo	3rd	100-3	1907		103/131

SASKATCHEWAN

Station Name	Proposed/Former Name	Division	Subdivision	Type of Depot	Plan	Year	Notes	see page
Tonkin		Dauphin	Tonkin	FPS	100-41	1916		103/127
Toppingham		Regina	Gravelbourg				Note 33	112/—
Totzke #1		Prince Albert	Cudworth	Type E	100-152	1911		109/137
Totzke #2		Prince Albert	Cudworth	CN4th	—			109/142
Touchwood		Saskatoon	Touchwood	SPEC-CNR	100-298	1943		114/143
Truax		Regina	Avonlea	3rd	100-29	1912		111/132
Tullis		Saskatoon	Beechy	FPS	100-41	1921		113/128
Turtleford		Prince Albert	Turtleford	3rd	100-29	1914	Museum-2	111/132
Tyner		Saskatoon	White Bear	FPS-CNR	100-41B	1927		114/140
Undora		Saskatoon	Touchwood	Type E	100-152	1911		114/137
Unity		Edmonton	Unity	Type D	100-154	1909	Museum-2	117/135
Usherville		Dauphin	Assiniboine	FPS-CNR	100-41B	1930		102/140
Valparaiso #1		Prince Albert	Tisdale	FPS	100-41	1916		110/128
Valparaiso #2		Prince Albert	Tisdale	4th	100-68	1920		110/130
Vandura		Portage-Brandon	Cromer	4th	100-31	1909	Note 23	104/130
Vanscoy #1		Saskatoon	Rosetown	FPS	100-41	By11		114/128
Vanscoy #2		Saskatoon	Rosetown	3rd	100-29	1912		114/132
Vawn	<<St. Hippolyte>>	Prince Albert	Turtleford	3rd	100-29	1913		111/132
Veillardville		Prince Albert	Tisdale	FPS-CNR	100-41B	1929		110/140
Venn #1		Saskatoon	Touchwood	Type D	100-154	1907		114/135
Venn #2		Saskatoon	Touchwood	Type G	100-168	1924		114/138
Vera		Edmonton	Unity	FPS-GTP	100-162	1914		117/134
Veregin #1	x-Verigin	Dauphin	Margo	PORT-CNoR	100-24	1908		102/128
Veregin #2		Dauphin	Margo	3rd	100-29	1911		102/132
Verendrye		Saskatoon	Elrose	FPS-CNR	100-41B	1929		114/140
Vibank		Regina	Glenavon	3rd	100-29	1913		112/132
Victoria Plains	x-Mulcahey	Regina	Qu'Appelle	Type E	100-152	1911		113/137
Vonda		Prince Albert	Aberdeen	3rd	100-3	1905		108/131
Wachee		Hudson Bay	Turnberry					103/—
Wadena		Dauphin	Margo	3rd	100-3	1904		102/131
Wakaw #1		Prince Albert	Cudworth	Type E	100-152	1911		109/137
Wakaw #2		Prince Albert	Cudworth	Type G	100-168	1919		109/138
Wakaw Jct.		Prince Albert	Meskanaw					110/—
Waldheim #1		Prince Albert	Carlton	FPS	100-96	1909	Probable	109/124
Waldheim #2		Prince Albert	Carlton	3rd	100-29	1912		109/132
Waldron		Saskatoon	Miniota	Type E	100-152	1910		114/137
Wallisville		Saskatoon	Dodsland	FPS		1913		113/144
Warman #1		Prince Albert	Duck Lake	3rd	100-3	1905	x-Langham Sb	110/131
Warman #2		Prince Albert	Duck Lake	SPEC-CNR		1970s		110/144
Wartime		Saskatoon	Elrose	3rd	100-72	1915		114/133
Waseca #1		Edmonton	Blackfoot	SHLT-CNoR	100-95	1905		116/124
Waseca #2		Edmonton	Blackfoot	4th	100-31	1911		116/130
Watrous		Saskatoon	Touchwood	SPEC-GTP	100-155	1909		114/138
Watson		Dauphin	Margo	3rd	100-3	1905		102/131
Weekes		Prince Albert	Chelan	PORT-CNR	100-132	1930	Reverse	109/141
Welby #1		Saskatoon	Miniota	FPS-GTP	100-173	1910		114/134
Welby #2		Saskatoon	Miniota	STA-CNR	100-307	1946		114/143
Weldon #1		Prince Albert	Tisdale	FPS	100-41	By12		110/128
Weldon #2		Prince Albert	Tisdale	3rd	100-72	1916		110/133
Weyburn #1-A	On spur	Regina	Weyburn	PORT-GTP	110-101	1914	SMBH	113/135
Weyburn #1-B	On spur	Regina	Weyburn	FPS	CB			113/143
Weyburn #2	On spur	Regina	Weyburn	SPEC-CNR	100-238	1928		113/142
White Bear		Saskatoon	White Bear	CN3rd	100-227	1927		114/142
White Star	Joint with CPR	Prince Albert	Paddockwood	FPS-CNR	100-41B	1925		110/140
Whittome		Prince Albert	Brooksby	FPS	100-41	1923		109/128
Willmar		Regina	Lampman	3rd	100-29	1910		112/132
Willowbrook		Dauphin	Tonkin	3rd	100-72	1916		103/133
Willow Bunch #1-A		Regina	Bengough	PORT-CNoR	100-73A	1926		111/128
Willow Bunch #1-B		Regina	Bengough	FPS-CNR	100-41B	1926		111/140
Willow Bunch #2		Regina	Bengough	CN3rd	100-216	1927		111/142
Wimmer		Dauphin	Margo	FPS	100-41	1910		102/128
Winter #1		Edmonton	Unity	PORT-GTP	110-101	1914	SMBH	117/135
Winter #2		Edmonton	Unity	3rd	100-72	1922	Note 72	117/133
Wiseton		Saskatoon	Elrose	3rd	100-29	1913		114/132

ROSTER NOTES:

3 In 1927 the freight shed was converted into a dwelling for the coalman, while the balance of the depot was relocated to Nutana and converted into a section house.

4 This station was technically on the Saskatoon Terminals Subdivision.

19 The sources regarding the disposition of this station are contradictory. One states that it was relocated to McBride, BC, the other says it was moved to Redpass Jct., BC.

23 Following inauguration of tourist passenger service on portions of the former CNR Stettler Subdivision in 1990, the Village of Donalda approached the Canadian Northern Society to acquire a station. The Society obtained an early design Canadian Northern 4th Class Station (Plan 100-31) from Vandura, Saskatchewan. It was moved onto the site of the original depot, extensively refurbished and opened in 1992 as an interpretive display in conjunction with the excursion trains that stopped here. The rail line serving Donalda was abandoned in 1997.

33 The stretch between Neidpath and Swift Current was operated on a sporadic basis until abandoned in September 1958. Standard freight and passenger shelters (CNR Plan 100-41B) are noted on the respective station grounds plans as "Shelter Site", therefore it appears that these shelters may not have been constructed and are thus excluded from this listing. The CNR had a Union Station agreement with the CPR to use that company's Swift Current depot.

47 This was originally constructed as a telegraph repeater station in 1928. It was converted into a section house in 1951, and then into a station after the original depot was razed by fire in 1960.

54 In 1964, a new passenger station was established near the northwestern outskirts of the city in Chappell Yards. The former downtown station building was used by CNR as an office building until 1969. Once it was vacated, the building was razed and the site was re-developed.

71 This station was built by the Canadian Pacific Railway that operated the Qu'Appelle Long Lake and Saskatchewan Railway until 1906, when the line was acquired by the Canadian Northern Railway.

72 CNR records classify this as Plan 100-197, but it incorporates all the features of Plan 100-72.

SASKATCHEWAN

Station Name	Proposed/Former Name	Division	Subdivision	Type of Depot	Plan	Year	Notes	see page
Witley		Saskatoon	White Bear	FPS-CNR	100-41B	1927		114/140
Woodley #1	x-Sander	Regina	Lewvan	FPS-GTP	CB			112/143
Woodley #2		Regina	Lewvan	FPS	100-41	—		112/128
Worcester #1	x-Rainton	Regina	Lewvan	FPS-GTP	100-162	1917		112/134
Worcester #2		Regina	Lewvan	FPS-CNR	CB	1939		112/143
Wordsworth #1		Regina	Lampman	FPS	100-41	1912		112/128
Wordsworth #2		Regina	Lampman	CN3rd	100-250	1929		112/142
Wroxton		Dauphin	Tonkin	3rd	100-29	1913		103/132
Xena		Saskatoon	Asquith	Type E	100-152	1911		113/137
Yarbo #1		Saskatoon	Miniota	Type E	100-152	1911		114/137
Yarbo #2		Saskatoon	Miniota	SHLT-CNR		1934		114/144
Yarbo #3		Saskatoon	Miniota	SPEC-CNR	100-392	1960		114/142
Yellow Creek		Prince Albert	Meskanaw	PORT-CNR	100-132	1931		110/141
Yonker #1		Edmonton	Unity	PORT-GTP	110-101	1911	SMBH	117/135
Yonker #2		Edmonton	Unity	Type E	100-152	1911		117/137
York Lake		Dauphin	Yorkton	FPS-GTP	100-162	1912		103/134
Yorkton–CNoR #1		Dauphin	Tonkin	FPS				103/144
Yorkton–CNoR #2		Dauphin	Tonkin	2nd	100-85	1915		103/134
Yorkton–GTP #1		Dauphin	Yorkton	SPEC-GTP	100-157	1910		103/138
Yorkton–GTP #2		Dauphin	Yorkton	SPEC-CNR	100-210	1964		103/143
Young		Saskatoon	Asquith	Type E	100-152	1911		113/137
Zealandia		Saskatoon	Rosetown	3rd	100-29	1908		114/132
Zehner #1		Regina	Qu'Appelle	Type E	100-152	1911		113/137
Zehner #2		Regina	Qu'Appelle	SPEC-CNR	100-142	1921	Sim to 100-143	113/142
Zelma		Saskatoon	Asquith	Type E	100-152	1911		113/137
Zeneta #1		Saskatoon	Miniota	Type E	100-152	1911		114/137
Zeneta #2		Saskatoon	Miniota	CN3rd	100-184	1928		114/141
Zenon Park #1		Prince Albert	Arborfield	FPS-CNR	100-41B	1930		109/140
Zenon Park #2		Prince Albert	Arborfield	SPEC-CNR	100-280	—		109/142

MINNESOTA

Station Name	Proposed/Former Name	Division	Subdivision	Type of Depot	Plan	Year	Notes	see page
Angora #2		DW&P	Cusson	4th	100-144	1921		102/130
Arbutus #2		DW&P	Cusson	FPS		—		102/144
Ash Lake #2		DW&P	Cusson	FPS	100-96	—	Probable	102/124
Bailey		DW&P	Taft					102/—
Bartlett		DW&P	Taft					102/—
Baudette #1		Port Arthur	Sprague	2nd	100-28	1907	Variant	108/133
Baudette #2		Port Arthur	Sprague	SPEC-CNR	100-192	1923		108/142
Britt #2		DW&P	Cusson	3rd	100-72	1918		102/133
Cedar		Port Arthur	Sprague					108/—
Central Lakes		DW&P	Taft	STA		1909		102/144
Cook #2		DW&P	Cusson	3rd	100-55	1914		102/132
Cusson #2		DW&P	Cusson	FPS	100-41	—		102/126
De Forest		DW&P	Taft					102/—
Elsdon		DW&P	Cusson					102/—
Ericsburg #1		DW&P	Cusson	FPS	100-96	1910	Probable	102/124
Ericsburg #2		DW&P	Cusson	STA	100-111	1917		102/144
Ericsburg #3		DW&P	Cusson	3rd	100-72	1923		102/133
Falls Jct. #2		DW&P	Cusson	FPS	100-41	—		102/126
Gheen #2	x-Alvina	DW&P	Cusson	4th	100-145	1921		102/130
Glendale		DW&P	Cusson					102/—
Graceton #1		Port Arthur	Sprague	5th	100-17	1907		108/129
Graceton #2		Port Arthur	Sprague	4th	100-68	1919		108/130
Haley		DW&P	Cusson	FPS	100-41	1911		102/126
Harney #2		DW&P	Taft	3rd	100-72	1918		102/133
Idington		DW&P	Cusson					102/—
Kinmount		DW&P	Cusson					102/—
Leander		DW&P	Cusson					102/—
Longworth		Port Arthur	Sprague					108/—
Melrude	x-Ellsmere	DW&P	Taft	3rd	100-29	1913		102/132
Nopeming		DW&P	Taft	FPS	100-41	1913		102/126
Orr #1		DW&P	Cusson	5th	100-17			102/129
Orr #2		DW&P	Cusson	3rd	100-72	1921		102/133
Peary		DW&P	Taft	SHLT-CNoR	100-95	1917	Probable	102/124
Pitt		Port Arthur	Sprague	4th	100-31	1909		108/130
Rainier #1		DW&P	Cusson	4th	100-31	1908		102/130
Rainier #2		DW&P	Cusson	SPEC-CNoR	100-92	1916		102/134
Ray #1		DW&P	Cusson	4th	100-31	1911		102/130
Ray #2		DW&P	Cusson	3rd	100-72	1921		102/133
Roosevelt		Port Arthur	Sprague	3rd	100-3	1904		108/131
Shaw		DW&P	Taft					102/—
Simar		DW&P	Taft	FPS	100-41	1918		102/126
Swift		Port Arthur	Sprague	4th	100-31	1909		108/130
Taber		DW&P	Cusson					102/—
Taft #2		DW&P	Taft	CN3rd	100-250	1929		102/142
Trunk Road		DW&P	Taft					102/—
Twig		DW&P	Taft	FPS	100-41	1918		102/126
Virginia #2		DW&P	Taft	SPEC-CNoR	100-46	1913		102/134
Warroad #2		Port Arthur	Sprague	SPEC-CNoR	100-77	1914		108/134
West Duluth		DW&P	Taft	SPEC-CNoR	100-48	1912		102/134
Whiteface		DW&P	Taft	FPS	100-41	1921		102/126
Williams		Port Arthur	Sprague	4th	100-31	1909		108/130

ROSTER II

CNR Stations in Western Canada, Listed by Subdivision

In 1958, for operating purposes, CNR divided its Western Region into four Districts, comprised of fifteen Divisions. For expediency, as noted in Roster I, three of the smaller Divisions have been folded into larger Divisions. Roster II is arranged by District and Division as follows:

MANITOBA DISTRICT
Dauphin Division	Page 102
Hudson Bay Division	Page 103
Portage-Brandon Division	Page 104
Port Arthur Division	Page 107

SASKATCHEWAN DISTRICT
Prince Albert Division	Page 108
Regina Division	Page 111
Saskatoon Division	Page 113

ALBERTA DISTRICT
Calgary Division	Page 114
Edmonton Division	Page 116
Edson Division	Page 118

BRITISH COLUMBIA DISTRICT
Kamloops Division	Page 119
Smithers Division	Page 121
Vancouver Terminals Division	Page 122

These Divisions are further divided into "Subdivisions." The Subdivisions are listed alphabetically under the Division of which they are a part. To find the Division and Subdivision of a particular locality, refer to Roster I. Stations are listed by timetable mileage in each Subdivision.

The information in Roster II is presented as follows:

ALBERTA DISTRICT
Edson Division

WABAMUN SUBDIVISION
Edmonton, Ab to Edson, Ab—129.5 miles

Milepost	Locality	Proposed/Former Name	Type	Plan	Built	Notes
4.2	West Jct.		FPS-1B	100-162	1913	Note 13
7.1	Bissell #1		Type E	100-152	1910	
7.1	Bissell #2		4th	100-68	1922	
14.1	Acheson #1		Type E	100-152	1911	
14.1	Acheson #2		FPS	GTP-FT	1951	

At the beginning of the entry for each Subdivision, the respective terminals and total mileage is shown. Where terminals are merely junction points, the closest station is noted.

The following abbreviations are used to indicate the province or state in which a depot is located:

Ab	Alberta		Mn	Minnesota
BC	British Columbia		On	Ontario
Mb	Manitoba		Sk	Saskatchewan

"Milepost" is the distance, in miles, from the initial terminal or junction of the Subdivision as it appears in Employee Timetables. Mileages of stations abandoned due to line revisions are "reckoned" as if they were on the 1958 Subdivision.

"Station Name", as in Roster I, is the name of the community where a particular depot was erected. Spellings of station names are as they appear in railway employee operating timetables. The number following the station name indicates the chronology of the station buildings on the site (first, second, third, etc.).

"Proposed/Former Name". When applicable, the proposed station name is given in double parentheses following its present name, thus "<<Name>>", or its former name is noted thus, "x-Name".

"Type of Depot" refers to the authors' classification of the station building. As in Roster I, examples of small groups of similar depots or individually designed stations are referred to as "Special Stations."

"Plan Number" is the CNR plan number. For further information refer to Roster III.

"Built" refers to the nominal year in which a particular depot was constructed. The latest date of construction as noted in railway records is the one used. It is possible that depots may have been erected earlier than the date indicated. Three explanations may account for this discrepancy, all relating to company bookkeeping. While construction records may indicate that a depot was completed at a particular time, it may have been advantageous to the company to record that the building was opened later than it actually was (i.e. a line not deemed officially open for traffic was not subject to the current tariffs and thus the company could charge "construction rates" for shipments along that line); original records may have been lost and company personnel may have entered an estimated date of construction for valuation purposes. Alternately, since a "refurbished" building could sometimes be considered as "new", on paper, the date of major improvements or rebuilding in the records was substituted for the original date of construction. Dates not noted on company records or other source materials are left blank in the roster. Buildings relocated from another site are noted as "———" in this column to indicate a duplicate entry.

The "Notes" column provides data of further interest or more substantial detail. These Notes are found in the box at the bottom right of each page spread.

DULUTH, WINNIPEG & PACIFIC

CUSSON SUBDIVISION
Virginia, Mn to Rainier, Mn—91.2 miles

Milepost	Locality	Proposed/Former Name	Type	Plan	Built	Notes
82.5	Britt #2		3rd	100-72	1918	
88.6	Taber					
91.5	Idington					
93.9	Angora #2		4th	100-144	1921	Variant
96.1	Leander					
100.0	Cook #2			100-55	1914	
104.2	Haley		FPS	100-41	1911	
110.0	Gheen #2	x-Alvina	4th	100-145	1921	
114.5	Glendale					
116.0	Orr #1		5th	100-17		
116.0	Orr #2		3rd	100-72	1921	
119.4	Cusson #2		FPS	100-41	——	
121.0	Elsdon					
128.4	Ash Lake #2		FPS	100-96	——	Probable
133.3	Kinmount					
137.9	Arbutus #2		FPS		——	
148.7	Ray #1		4th	100-31	1911	
148.7	Ray #2		3rd	100-72	1921	
156.3	Ericsburg #1		FPS	100-96	1910	Probable
156.3	Ericsburg #2		STA	100-111	1917	
156.3	Ericsburg #3		3rd	100-72	1923	
164.4	Falls Jct. #2		FPS	100-41	——	
165.2	Rainier #1		4th	100-31	1908	
165.2	Rainier #2		SPEC.	100-92	1916	

TAFT SUBDIVISION
Duluth, Mn to Virginia, Mn—74.0 miles

Milepost	Locality	Proposed/Former Name	Type	Plan	Built	Notes
0.7	West Duluth		SPEC.	100-48	1912	
9.4	Nopeming		FPS	100-41	1913	
12.5	Harney #2		3rd	100-72	1918	
19.8	Simar		FPS	100-41	1918	
24.2	Twig		FPS	100-41	1918	
25.7	Bartlett					
33.0	Taft #2		CN3rd	100-250	1929	
41.9	Shaw					
46.6	Whiteface		FPS	100-41	1921	
51.7	Melrude	x-Ellsmere	3rd	100-29	1913	
56.1	Central Lakes		STA		1909	
57.8	Bailey					
59.7	Trunk Road					
62.5	Peary		SHLT	100-95	1917	Probable
69.5	De Forest					
74.0	Virginia #2		SPEC.	100-46	1913	

MANITOBA DISTRICT
Dauphin Division

ASSINIBOINE SUBDIVISION
Canora, Sk to Hudson Bay, Sk—93.7 miles

Milepost	Locality	Proposed/Former Name	Type	Plan	Built	Notes
7.8	Amsterdam		FPS	100-41	1915	
14.1	Tadmore		FPS	100-41	1915	
17.5	Hassan		FPS	100-41	1915	
29.5	Lady Lake		FPS	100-41B	1930	
32.2	Hinchcliffe		FPS	100-41B	1930	
39.7	Endeavour #1-A		FPS	100-41B	1930	
39.7	Endeavour #1-B		PORT	110-159	——	SMBH
39.7	Endeavour #2		CN4A	100-310	1948	
44.6	Usherville		FPS	100-41B	1930	
53.2	Tall Pines		FPS	100-41B	1930	
63.1	Reserve		CN3rd	100-253	1930	Museum-2
72.4	Bertwell	x-Kakwa	FPS	100-41B	1930	
77.5	Clemenceau		FPS	100-41B	1930	
82.9	Akosane	x-Etomami	FPS	100-41B	1930	

COWAN SUBDIVISION
Dauphin, Mb to Swan River, Mb—98.4 miles

Milepost	Locality	Proposed/Former Name	Type	Plan	Built	Notes
5.6	Valley River		FPS		1897	
13.2	Sifton		CSS-A	100-63	1897	
21.5	Ukraina		FPS	100-41	1913	
29.9	Ethelbert		CSS-A	100-63	1898	
38.7	Garland		FPS	100-41	1911	
48.9	Pine River #1		CSS-B	100-99		
48.9	Pine River #2		FPS	110-296	——	x-SMBH
59.3	Sclater		FPS	100-41	1911	
66.7	Cowan #1		CSS-A	100-99	1899	
66.7	Cowan #2		FPS	100-41	——	
77.5	Renwer	x-Fishers	FPS	100-41	1912	
87.3	Minitonas		CSS-B	100-99	1899	
93.2	Sevick		FPS	100-41	1923	
98.4	Swan River		CSS-A	100-63	1899	

MANITOBA DISTRICT
Dauphin Division

ERWOOD SUBDIVISION
Swan River, Mb to Hudson Bay, Sk—101.1 miles

Milepost	Locality	Proposed/Former Name	Type	Plan	Built	Notes
9.8	Bowsman		CSS-B	100-99	1900	Museum-2
21.5	Birch River #1		FPS	100-41	1911	
21.5	Birch River #2		CN4A	100-310	1948	
30.9	Novra		CSS-B	100-99	1901	
35.5	Bellsite		FPS	100-41B	1929	
42.1	Mafeking		4th	100-31	1909	
50.2	Baden		CSS-B	100-99	1901	
59.3	Powell		FPS	100-41	1919	
61.0	Barrows #1	x-Elksgate Jct.	CSS-B	100-99	1908	
61.0	Barrows #2		FPS	100-41	1923	
61.0	Barrows #3		4th	100-68	1923	
66.9	National Mills #1		FPS	CB	1943	
66.9	National Mills #2		FPS	100-41B	——	
70.0	Westgate, Mb		CSS-B	100-99	1901	
75.4	Armit, Sk #1	x-Meaks	FPS		1943	
75.4	Armit, Sk #2		FPS	100-41B		
80.0	Roscoe #1		FPS	CB		
80.0	Roscoe #2		FPS	100-41	1918	
86.4	Smoking Tent		FPS	CB	1950	
92.6	Erwood #1		CSS-B	100-99	1901	
92.6	Erwood #2		FPS	100-41	1918	
101.1	Hudson Bay	x-Hudson Bay Jct.	3rd	100-29	1911	Variant

MARGO SUBDIVISION
Kamsack, Sk to Humboldt, Sk—146.4 miles

Milepost	Locality	Proposed/Former Name	Type	Plan	Built	Notes
8.4	Veregin #1	x-Verigin	PORT	100-24	1908	
8.4	Veregin #2		3rd	100-29	1911	
16.6	Mikado #1		FPS	100-41		
16.6	Mikado #2		3rd	100-72	1917	
24.0	Canora		3rd	100-3	1904	Museum-1
31.4	Tiny		FPS	100-96	1909	
38.5	Buchanan		3rd	100-3	1904	
49.5	Rama #1-A		FPS	100-96	1909	
49.5	Rama #1-B		FPS	100-41	——	Add to #1-A
49.5	Rama #2		4th	100-68	——	
57.1	Invermay		3rd	100-3	1904	
64.9	Margo #1		4th	100-31	1911	
64.9	Margo #2		FPS	CBx2	——	Temporary
64.9	Margo #3		CN4B	100-328	1953	
72.3	Kuroki #1		CSS-SH	110-10	1905	
72.3	Kuroki #2		FPS	100-41	1917	
79.3	Kylemore #1		FPS	100-96	1909	
79.3	Kylemore #2		FPS	100-41	——	
86.7	Wadena		3rd	100-3	1904	
94.4	Paswegin #1		FPS	100-96	1908	
94.4	Paswegin #2		FPS	100-41	1918	
99.5	Clair	<<Englefeldt>>	FPS	100-41	1912	
108.0	Quill Lake	<<Rally>>	3rd	100-3	1904	
114.8	Wimmer		FPS	100-41	1910	
120.2	Watson		3rd	100-3	1905	
126.2	Englefeld	<<Clairvaux>>	4th	100-31	1912	
133.7	St. Gregor #1		FPS			
133.7	St. Gregor #2		3rd	100-75	1914	
141.0	Muenster		4th	100-31	1908	
146.4	Humboldt	x-Humbolt	3rd	100-18	1905	Variant

PREECEVILLE SUBDIVISION
Swan River, Mb to Kelvington, Sk—113.5 miles

Milepost	Locality	Proposed/Former Name	Type	Plan	Built	Notes
6.5	Kenville		3rd	100-29	1908	
14.1	Durban #1		PORT	100-24		
14.1	Durban #2		3rd	100-75	1919	
18.8	Benito, Mb		3rd	100-29	1909	
26.4	Arran #1, Sk		FPS	100-41	1911	
26.4	Arran #2, Sk		3rd	100-72	1919	Museum-2
35.7	Pelly		3rd	100-29	1909	
45.2	Norquay		3rd	100-29	1911	
52.6	Hyas #1		FPS	100-41	1912	
52.6	Hyas #2		CN3rd	100-253	1937	
57.9	Stenen		3rd	100-29	1912	
65.8	Sturgis #1		FPS	100-41	By14	
65.8	Sturgis #2		3rd	100-72	1918	Museum-2
72.1	Preeceville		3rd	100-71	1912	
79.3	Ketchen		FPS	100-41	1920	
86.7	Hazel Dell		FPS	100-41	1921	
92.9	Okla		FPS	100-41	1920	
99.8	Lintlaw #1		FPS	100-41		
99.8	Lintlaw #2		4th	100-68	1920	
106.9	Nut Mountain #1	x-Spall	FPS	100-41	1922	
106.9	Nut Mountain #2		CN4A	100-305	1945	

MANITOBA DISTRICT
Dauphin Division

PREECEVILLE SUBDIVISION
(continued)

Milepost	Locality	Proposed/Former Name	Type	Plan	Built	Notes
113.5	Kelvington #1		PORT	110-73A	1922	SMBH
113.5	Kelvington #2		3rd	100-75	1922	Museum-2

RHEIN SUBDIVISION
Ross Jct., Sk to Wroxton, Sk—37.8 miles

Milepost	Locality	Proposed/Former Name	Type	Plan	Built	Notes
5.9	Donwell		FPS	100-41	1913	
13.6	Hamton #1		FPS	100-41	1913	
13.6	Hamton #2		4th	100-68	1924	
21.9	Rhein		3rd	100-29	1911	
29.9	Stornoway		3rd	100-29	1913	

TOGO SUBDIVISION
Dauphin, Mb to Kamsack, Sk—100.9 miles

Milepost	Locality	Proposed/Former Name	Type	Plan	Built	Notes
3.0	Gilbert Plains Jct.					
6.3	Kilty					
11.4	Ashville		FPS	100-41	1912	
17.3	Snyders Siding					
20.0	Gilbert Plains		CSS-B	100-99	1900	
24.1	Dutton					
29.5	Grandview		CSS-A	100-63	1900	
37.0	Meharry #1		FPS	100-41	1911	
37.0	Meharry #2		FPS	100-41B	1924	
42.4	Timberton #1	x-Strevel	PORT	100-24	1909	
42.4	Timberton #2		FPS	100-41	1918	
45.3	Shortdale		FPS	100-41	1911	
50.7	Bield		FPS	100-41	1912	
54.7	Shevlin		FPS	100-41	1911	
62.6	Roblin		3rd	100-3	1906	
69.2	Deepdale #1		FPS	100-41	1915	
69.2	Deepdale #2		3rd	100-72	1922	
69.6	McLean					
74.5	Makaroff #1-A, Mb		FPS	100-41	1912	
74.5	Makaroff #1-B, Mb		FPS	100-41B	1923	
79.5	Togo, Sk		3rd	100-3	1907	
81.5	Mileage 81.5		FPS	100-41		
88.0	Runnymede #1		FPS	100-41		
88.0	Runnymede #2		4th	100-68	1923	
94.8	Cote		FPS	100-41	1912	
100.9	Kamsack #1		3rd	100-18	1904	Variant
100.9	Kamsack #2		SPEC.	100-399	1968	

TONKIN SUBDIVISION
Russell, Mb to Parkerview, Sk—112.3 miles

Milepost	Locality	Proposed/Former Name	Type	Plan	Built	Notes
7.5	Endcliffe		PORT	100-24	1910	
16.4	Shellmouth		3rd	100-29	1909	
24.3	Dropmore #1, Mb		FPS	100-41		
24.3	Dropmore #2, Mb		4th	100-68	1921	
32.7	MacNutt, Sk		3rd	100-29	1910	
40.9	Calder #1		FPS	100-41	1912	
40.9	Calder #2		3rd	100-75	1914	
48.4	Wroxton		3rd	100-29	1913	
53.6	Kessock		FPS	100-41	1916	
58.1	Barvas		FPS	100-41	1915	
63.0	Barbour	x-Dunleath	FPS	100-41	1916	Not moved?
65.0	Tonkin		FPS	100-41	1916	
68.8	Sturdee		FPS	100-41	1915	
70.9	Calley		FPS	100-41	1916	
73.5	Yorkton–CNoR #1		FPS			
73.5	Yorkton–CNoR #2		2nd	100-85	1915	
78.3	Dracup					
85.0	Fonehill		3rd	100-72	1915	
89.9	Willowbrook		3rd	100-72	1916	
95.9	Beaverdale		FPS	100-41B	1929	
101.2	Jedburgh		CN3rd	100-250	1929	
106.9	Fitzmaurice		FPS	100-41B	1929	
112.3	Parkerview	x-Crowtherview	CN3rd	100-253	1929	

WINNIPEGOSIS SUBDIVISION
Sifton, Mb to Winnipegosis—20.8 miles

Milepost	Locality	Proposed/Former Name	Type	Plan	Built	Notes
5.0	Fishing River		STA		1898	
10.4	Fork River #1		CSS-A	100-63	1899	
10.4	Fork River #2		3rd	100-75	1920	
10.4	Fork River #3		FPS	100-41		
[15]	Gruber					
20.8	Winnipegosis		CSS-A	100-63	1897	Museum-1

MANITOBA DISTRICT
Dauphin Division

YORKTON SUBDIVISION
Melville, Sk to Canora, Sk—54.0 miles

Milepost	Locality	Proposed/Former Name	Type	Plan	Built	Notes
6.1	Brewer		Type E	100-152	1910	
11.0	McKim	x-Peoples	FPS	CB	1927	
14.7	Otthon		Type E	100-152	1911	
21.4	York Lake		FPS-1B	100-162	1912	
25.0	Yorkton–GTP #1		SPEC.	100-157	1910	
25.0	Yorkton–GTP #2		SPEC.	100-210	1964	
30.8	Mehan #1		Type E	100-152	1911	
30.8	Mehan #2		PORT		1959	
35.9	Ebenezer		Type E	100-152	1911	
42.0	Gorlitz		Type E	100-152	1913	
48.6	Burgis #1		Type E	100-152	1911	
48.6	Burgis #2		FPS	CB	1950	
54.0	South Canora	x-Canora–GTP	SPEC.	100-157	1911	

Hudson Bay Division

CHISEL LAKE SUBDIVISION
Optic Lake, Mb to Osborne Lake, Mb—71.0 miles

Milepost	Locality	Proposed/Former Name	Type	Plan	Built	Notes
51.4	Chisel Lake #1-A		FPS	100-41B		
51.4	Chisel Lake #1-B		FPS	100-41B		

FLIN FLON SUBDIVISION
The Pas, Mb to Flin Flon, Mb—87.5 miles

Milepost	Locality	Proposed/Former Name	Type	Plan	Built	Notes
6.0	Prospector		FPS			
22.2	Wanless		FPS	100-41		
30.2	Atik		FPS			
41.0	Simonhouse		FPS	CB		
51.1	Cranberry Portage		CN3rd	100-251	1929	Variant
62.5	Millwater		FPS	100-41B		
66.0	Athapap		FPS	CB	1939	
81.7	Channing		FPS	CB	1929	
87.5	Flin Flon		SPEC.	100-275	1934	Museum-1

HERCHMER SUBDIVISION
Gillam, Mb to Churchill, Mb—183.7 miles

Milepost	Locality	Proposed/Former Name	Type	Plan	Built	Notes
347.1	Bird #1		PORT	110-148	1927	SMBH
347.1	Bird #2		FPS		1961	
498.5	Mileage 498.5		FPS	100-41		
509.9	Churchill		SPEC.	100-271	1930	

SHERRIDON SUBDIVISION
Cranberry Portage, Mb to Lynn Lake, Mb—184.8 miles

Milepost	Locality	Proposed/Former Name	Type	Plan	Built	Notes
40.4	Sherridon #1-A		STA		1928	Temporary
40.4	Sherridon #1-B		STA	110-148	1928	SMBH
40.4	Sherridon #2		STA	140-234	1953	
94.0	Pawstik		FPS	100-41		
184.8	Lynn Lake		SPEC.	100-393	1966	

THICKET SUBDIVISION
Wabowden, Mb to Gillam, Mb—189.7 miles

Milepost	Locality	Proposed/Former Name	Type	Plan	Built	Notes
184.3	Thicket Portage #1-A		PORT			x-SMBH
184.3	Thicket Portage #1-B		PORT			x-SMBH
256.2	Pit Siding #1-A		FPS			x-SMBH
256.2	Pit Siding #1-B		FPS	CB	1959	
285.7	Ilford		FPS	100-41B	1927	
326.1	Gillam		SPEC.	100-244	1930	

THOMPSON SUBDIVISION
Mileage 199.8 Hudson Bay Railway, Mb to Thompson, Mb—30.7 miles

Milepost	Locality	Proposed/Former Name	Type	Plan	Built	Notes
30.7	Thompson		SPEC.	100-382	1960	

TURNBERRY SUBDIVISION
Hudson Bay Jct., Sk to The Pas, Mb—87.5 miles

Milepost	Locality	Proposed/Former Name	Type	Plan	Built	Notes
9.0	Wachee					
18.0	Ceba					
27.1	Chemong		SHLT		By20	
34.4	Mileage 34.4		SHLT		By20	
43.0	Cantyre					
35.2	Otosquen #1-A, Sk		FPS	CB	1944	
35.2	Otosquen #1-B, Sk		PORT	CB	1953	
50.5	Turnberry, Mb		PORT		1938	SMBH
60.4	Whithorn					
68.2	Westray					
77.9	Freshford					
87.5	The Pas #1		3rd	100-29	1908	Variant
87.5	The Pas #2		CN3rd	100-189	1928	Variant

MANITOBA DISTRICT
Hudson Bay Division
WEKUSKO SUBDIVISION
The Pas, Mb to Wabowden, Mb—136.4 miles

Milepost	Locality	Proposed/Former Name	Type	Plan	Built	Notes
16.9	Atikameg Lake		FPS	100-290	1928	
41.4	Cormorant		FPS	100-41	—	
81.2	Wekusko		PORT		—	x-SMBH
136.4	Wabowden		CN3rd	100-251	1930	Variant

Portage-Brandon Division
CARBERRY SUBDIVISION
Brandon Jct., Mb to Carberry Jct., Mb—22.8 miles

Milepost	Locality	Proposed/Former Name	Type	Plan	Built	Notes
4.1	Carberry		SPEC.	100-21	1904	
8.5	Fairview		FPS	100-41	1912	
12.4	Petrel		FPS	100-41	1912	
12.9	Petrel Jct.					
17.7	Munroe		SHLT	100-95	1909	

CARMAN SUBDIVISION
near Winnipeg, Mb to Belmont, Mb—118.8 miles

Milepost	Locality	Proposed/Former Name	Type	Plan	Built	Notes
5.4	Oak Bluff		PORT	100-24	1910	
9.9	Dipples		FPS	CB	1919	
13.3	Sanford		3rd	100-3	1901	
21.8	Brunkild		3rd	100-29	1909	
26.0	Mollard					
30.1	Sperling		3rd	100-3	1901	
37.2	Homewood		3rd	100-3	1901	
43.6	Carman		2nd	100-2	1902	
50.5	Graysville #2	x-Gray's	4th	100-68	1920	
54.8	Stephenfield		FPS	100-41	1911	
59.0	Roseisle		3rd	100-3	1903	
63.2	Leary's		FPS	100-96	1908	
64.6	Babcock	Comm'l Cement	SHLT	100-95	1909	Probable
68.8	Valde Spur					
70.9	Cardinal		4th	100-31	1911	
73.1	Notre Dame de Lourdes		4th	100-68	1921	
73.5	Risteen					
78.9	Somerset #1-A		NPR-4th	100-13	1889	
78.9	Somerset #1-B		3rd	100-3	1903	Add to #1-A
85.2	Swan Lake		3rd	100-29	1913	
91.3	Indian Springs		FPS	100-41	1911	
96.0	Marieapolis		3rd	100-3	1903	
103.0	Greenway		4th	100-31	1910	
109.0	Baldur		NPR-4th	100-26	1890	Museum-2
118.8	Belmont #1-A		CSS-NPR	100-16	1889	
118.8	Belmont #1-B		3rd	100-3	1907	Add to #1-A

CROMER SUBDIVISION
Brandon, Mb to Kipling, Sk—128.3 miles

Milepost	Locality	Proposed/Former Name	Type	Plan	Built	Notes
[0.5]	Sixth Street		TOS			
7.5	Villette		FPS	100-41	1911	
14.9	Merle		FPS	100-41	1910	
19.8	Terence		3rd	100-29	1910	
25.3	Ralston		FPS			
32.4	Agar		FPS	100-41	1911	
39.3	Maon #1		SHLT		1910	
39.3	Maon #2		FPS	100-41B	—	
47.2	Scarth		3rd	100-29	1907	
53.0	Woodnorth #2		3rd	100-29	1916	
60.1	Cromer		3rd	100-29	1911	
67.4	Butler, Mb		FPS	100-41	1910	
75.2	Maryfield, Sk #1	Joint with CPR	CP A-2	100-86	—	
75.2	Maryfield, Sk #2	Joint with CPR	4th	100-68	—	
82.5	Fairlight		3rd	100-29	1907	
89.0	Doonside		FPS	100-41	1911	
96.6	Kelso		3rd	100-29	1907	
104.2	Vandura		4th	100-31	1909	Note 23
112.9	Langbank		3rd	100-29	1911	
120.8	Inchkeith	x-Hawthorne	FPS	100-41	1911	
128.3	Kipling		2nd	100-22	1908	

DELTA SUBDIVISION
Oakland, Mb to Delta, Mb—5.6 miles

Milepost	Locality	Proposed/Former Name	Type	Plan	Built	Notes
3.2	Huddlestone		FPS	CB?		
5.6	Delta	x-Delta Beach	SPEC.	100-90	1917	Note 24

GLADSTONE SUBDIVISION
Winnipeg, Mb to Dauphin, Mb—177.5 miles

Milepost	Locality	Proposed/Former Name	Type	Plan	Built	Notes
0.6	St. Charles		FPS	100-41	1917	Note 34
3.1	Diamond	x-Headingly	SHLT		1904	
7.2	Calrin		FPS	100-41	1912	
20.5	White Plains		CSS-NPR	100-16	1891	Probable
25.0	Dacotah		FPS	100-41	1917	

MANITOBA DISTRICT
Portage-Brandon Division
GLADSTONE SUBDIVISION
(continued)

Milepost	Locality	Proposed/Former Name	Type	Plan	Built	Notes
30.5	Elie–CNoR #2		3rd	100-72	1919	
34.8	Benard	x-Eustache	FPS	100-41	1912	
38.0	Willow Range		FPS	100-41	1912	
41.7	Oakville		3rd	100-3		
45.2	Newton		FPS	100-41	1911	
48.2	Curtis		FPS	100-41	1911	
54.1	East Tower					
54.3	Portage la Prairie–CNoR #2		2nd	100-45	1904	Note 31
56.1	West Tower	x-Arizona Jct.				
56.3	Portage Jct. #1		CSS		1891	Note 38
56.3	Portage Jct. #2		SHLT	100-318	1949	Probable
60.3	Hobson	x-Walldon	FPS	100-96	1909	Probable
65.7	Rignold		NPR-4th		1901	Probable
70.1	Youill		FPS	100-96	1907	Probable
74.3	Beaver	x-Beaver River	NPR-4th	100-26	1900	
79.0	Katrime		FPS	100-41	1919	
82.8	Muir	x-Neepawa Jct.	FPS	100-41	1911	
87.0	Golden Stream		SHLT	100-95	1906	
92.2	Gladstone #2		2nd	100-5	1901	Museum-2
99.9	Ogilvie #2		FPS	100-41	—	Probable
106.1	Plumas		CSS-A	100-63	1896	
110.4	Colby		FPS	100-41	1916	
114.4	Tenby #1		FPS	CB	1911	
114.4	Tenby #2		SHLT		—	
119.6	Glenella #1		CSS-A	100-63	1897	
119.6	Glenella #2		3rd	100-29	1913	
127.7	Glencairn		CSS-A	100-63		Probable
134.5	Reeve #1		FPS	CB	1928	
134.5	Reeve #2		FPS	CB	1947	
138.6	McCreary Jct.					
139.7	McCreary #2		3rd	100-29	1912	
148.2	Laurier		CSS-A	100-63	1899	
156.6	Makinak #2		3rd	100-3	1903	
163.9	Ochre River #1-A		CSS-A	100-63	1899	
163.9	Ochre River #1-B		FPS	100-41		Express Shed
171.8	Paulson #2		FPS	CB	1926	
177.5	Dauphin #1		CSS-A	100-63	1897	
177.5	Dauphin #2		SPEC.	100-44	1913	

HARTE SUBDIVISION
Winnipeg, Mb to Rivers, Mb—142.2 miles

Milepost	Locality	Proposed/Former Name	Type	Plan	Built	Notes
6.5	Pacific Jct. #1		Type E	100-152	1911	
6.5	Pacific Jct. #2		PORT	CB	1927	
7.1	Searle	x-Alcrest	Type E	100-152	1911	
14.4	West Winnipeg		SPEC.	100-177	1908	
17.7	Beaudry		Type E	100-152	1911	
22.2	Cabot		Type E	100-152	1911	
25.7	Dugas		FPS	CB	1925	
30.5	North Elie	x-Elie–GTP	Type E	100-152	1911	
37.1	Fortier #1		Type E	100-152	1911	
37.1	Fortier #2		FPS	100-41	1923	
44.3	Gervais #1		Type E	100-152	1911	
44.3	Gervais #2		PORT	110-101	—	SMBH
53.1	East Tower					
54.1	GN Jct.					
54.3	Portage la Prairie–GTP Joint with MRM		SPEC.	100-175	1908	Note 31
55.2	West Jct.					
59.7	Arona					
63.3	Bloom		FPS	100-41	—	
71.0	Caye		Type E	100-152	1911	
76.7	Deer		FPS	100-41B	—	
82.3	Dock					
84.3	Exira		Type E	100-152	1911	
91.2	Firdale		FPS-1B	100-162	1909	
99.7	Gregg		Type D	100-154	1909	
103.6	Petrel Jct.					
106.8	Harte		Type E	100-152	1911	
113.2	Ingelow		Type D	100-154	1909	
121.8	Justice		Type D	100-154	1909	
127.7	Brandon North	x-Knox Bridge	SPEC.	100-294	1941	
129.4	Knox		Type E	100-152	1911	
133.0	Smart					
136.6	Levine					
140.2	Grant's Cut					
142.2	Rivers #1		SPEC.	100-158	1909	
142.2	Rivers #2		SPEC.	100-169	1917	

MANITOBA DISTRICT
Portage-Brandon Division

HARTNEY SUBDIVISION
near Belmont, Mb to Virden, Mb—91.4 miles

Milepost	Locality	Proposed/Former Name	Type	Plan	Built	Notes
8.4	Tiger Hills					
12.0	Sanatorium	x-Sanatarium				
12.7	Ninette #1-A		NPR-4th		1898	
12.7	Ninette #1-B		FPS	100-96	1917	Probable, Expr. Shed
15.7	Ontop					
17.3	Dunrea		NPR-4th		1898	
22.9	Margaret		3rd	100-3		
27.0	Minmar					
30.4	Minto #1-A		NPR-4th	100-13	1898	
30.4	Minto #1-B		3rd	100-3	1906	Add to #1-A
30.4	Minto #2		SHLT			
35.6	Fairfax		NPR-4th		—	
42.0	Elgin #1-A		NPR-4th		1898	
42.0	Elgin #1-B		3rd	100-3	1904	Add to #1-A
47.2	Underhill		NPR-4th			Probable
49.8	Argue		FPS	100-41	1910	Probable
54.1	Hartney		NPR-4th		1898	
54.3	Hartney Crossing		SHLT	100-95	1905	
62.9	Grande Clariere #1		FPS	100-96	1908	Probable
62.9	Grande Clariere #2		FPS	100-41	1919	Probable
62.9	Grande Clariere #3		FPS	100-41	—	
68.1	Findlay Crossing		SHLT	100-95	1905	
69.2	Findlay					
72.3	Belleview		3rd	100-29	1915	
78.0	Agnew #1		PORT	100-24		Probable
78.0	Agnew #2		FPS	100-41B	1923	
[—]	Scarth	See Cromer Subdivision				
87.7	Maples		FPS	100-41	1910	
91.4	Virden		3rd	100-19	1907	

INWOOD SUBDIVISION
Grosse Isle, Mb to Hodgson, Mb—80.9 miles

Milepost	Locality	Proposed/Former Name	Type	Plan	Built	Notes
4.4	Ekhart	x-Drake	FPS	CB	1916	
7.8	Argyle		FPS	100-41	1912	
14.5	Woodroyd		FPS	100-41		
21.3	Erinview		FPS	100-41	1912	
30.7	Inwood		3rd	100-29	1912	
35.9	Sandridge		FPS	100-41	1916	
42.8	Narcisse		FPS	100-41	1915	
50.1	Chatfield		FPS	100-41	1915	
57.1	Poplarfield		FPS	100-41	1915	
64.5	Broad Valley		FPS	100-41	1915	
71.5	Fisher Branch		3rd	100-72	1915	
80.9	Hodgson #1		FPS	100-41		
80.9	Hodgson #2		4th	100-68	1920	

LETELLIER SUBDIVISION
Winnipeg, Mb to Emerson Jct., Mb—62.1 miles

Milepost	Locality	Proposed/Former Name	Type	Plan	Built	Notes
[0.0]	Winnipeg #1		SPEC-NPR	100-10	1889	Notes 34, 37
[0.0]	Winnipeg #2	Joint with GTP	SPEC.	UD15	1911	Note 34
[—]	Winnipeg–Pembina Subway		FPS			Note 34
2.6	Portage Jct. #1		NPR-SH		1891	Notes 34, 38
2.6	Portage Jct. #2		SHLT	100-290	1949	Note 34
4.1	St. Vital					
6.2	St. Norbert		STA-NPR	100-116	1894	
12.2	Cartier		FPS	100-41	1919	
15.6	Glenlea		FPS	100-41	1916	
20.5	St. Agathe #1		STA-NPR	100-116	1894	
20.5	St. Agathe #2		FPS	CB		
24.2	Union Point		FPS	100-41	1915	
29.4	Silver Plains #2		FPS	100-41B	1943	
34.1	Swains					
37.4	Morris		STA-NPR		1894	
43.7	St. Jean Baptiste		3rd	100-3	1902	Reverse Plan
46.9	Martin's	x-Hope Farm				
53.8	Letellier #1		STA-NPR	100-116	1894	
53.8	Letellier #2		FPS			
58.5	Christie	x-Christies	PORT	100-290	1939	
62.1	Emerson Jct.		SPEC-NPR	100-52	1888	

MIAMI SUBDIVISION
Morris, Mb to Somerset, Mb—62.1 miles

Milepost	Locality	Proposed/Former Name	Type	Plan	Built	Notes
3.7	Moyer					
6.0	Smiths					
9.9	Lowe Farm		3rd	100-3	1905	
16.2	Kane #1		FPS	100-41	1916	
16.2	Kane #2		FPS	100-41		
21.1	Myrtle #2		4th	100-31	1911	

MANITOBA DISTRICT
Portage-Brandon Division

MIAMI SUBDIVISION
(continued)

Milepost	Locality	Proposed/Former Name	Type	Plan	Built	Notes
21.1	Myrtle #3		FPS	CB	—	
25.6	Roland #1		STA-NPR	100-116	1900	
25.6	Roland #2		FPS	CB		
28.8	Jordan		FPS	100-41	1917	
33.7	Rosebank		NPR-4th		1897	
39.6	Miami		CSS-NPR	100-16	1889	Museum-1
49.1	Deerwood		FPS	100-96	1908	
54.4	Altamont #1		CSS-NPR	100-16	1899	
54.4	Altamont #2		SHLT		—	x-CO

NEEPAWA SUBDIVISION
near Gladstone, Mb to near McCreary, Mb—70.6 miles

Milepost	Locality	Proposed/Former Name	Type	Plan	Built	Notes
5.6	Mayfeld		FPS	100-96	1909	
10.9	Helston	x-Berton	3rd	100-3	1901	
14.4	Lobbville	x-Wood Siding	FPS	CB	1929	
20.1	Hummerston		FPS	100-41	1913	
23.4	Carberry Jct.					
26.9	Hallboro #2		3rd	100-29	1912	
26.9	Hallboro #3		FPS	100-41	—	Temporary
26.9	Hallboro #4		4th	100-68	—	
29.0	Osprey	x-Glendale	FPS	100-41	1911	
33.1	Neepawa #1		2nd	100-8	1902	Museum-1
33.1	Neepawa #2		PORT		1980	
37.8	Rossburn Jct.		FPS	100-41		
38.3	Howden		FPS	100-41	1910	
43.5	Eden		3rd	100-3	1903	
48.8	Birnie		5th	100-17	1904	
54.8	Riding Mountain		FPS	100-41	1910	
61.0	Kelwood #1		3rd	100-29	1912	
65.1	Norwood	x-Norgate	FPS	CB	1927	

OAK POINT SUBDIVISION
Winnipeg, Nb to Gypsumville, Mb—156.7 miles

Milepost	Locality	Proposed/Former Name	Type	Plan	Built	Notes
1.8	Tuxedo					
2.4	St. James	x-West Side	SPEC.	100-40	1910	Note 34
4.2	Mileage 4.2		SHLT	100-434	1977	Note 34
8.2	Moore		FPS	100-41	1910	
13.8	Gordon		FPS	100-41	1910	
20.2	Grosse Isle		3rd	100-3	1904	
26.6	Warren #2		3rd	100-72	1922	
33.8	Woodlands		3rd	100-3	1904	
43.3	Lake Francis #1	x-Lake Frances	3rd	100-3	1904	
43.3	Lake Francis #2		FPS	100-41B	—	
53.2	St. Laurent		3rd	100-3	1904	
60.7	Oak Point		3rd	100-29	1908	
67.1	Clarkleigh		PORT	100-24	1911	
73.9	Lundar		3rd	100-29	1913	
79.8	Deerhorn		FPS	100-41	1915	
86.2	Eriksdale #2		3rd	100-72	1918	

NOTES:

23 Following inauguration of tourist passenger service on portions of the former CNR Stettler Subdivision in 1990, the Village of Donalda approached the Canadian Northern Society to acquire a station. The Society obtained an early design Canadian Northern 4th Class Station (Plan 100-31) from Vandura, Saskatchewan. It was moved onto the site of the original depot, extensively refurbished and opened in 1992 as an interpretive display in conjunction with the excursion trains that stopped here. The rail line serving Donalda was abandoned in 1997.

24 The Delta Subdivision was abandoned 1 March 1941. The Delta station was apparently sold in situ in 1941, being used as a fish warehouse until it burned down in the mid-1940s.

31 The CNoR and the joint GTP-Midland Railway of Manitoba (Great Northern) lines through Portage la Prairie were coordinated in 1923. Track connections between the two lines were made at either end of town. The GTP-MRM line was retained. The CNoR line was abandoned and pulled up. The CNoR's Portage station was retained on site and used by the railway for offices. The station gutted by fire in 1960, and subsequently demolished by the CNR.

34 This station was technically on the Winnipeg Terminals Subdivision.

37 In 1889, the Northern Pacific & Manitoba Railway constructed this three-storey brick station-hotel on Water Avenue. The hotel portion of the complex was destroyed in a spectacular fire in February 1899. After the opening of the new Union depot in 1911, the old station was integrated into the Winnipeg Industrial Bureau and used as a convention hall. In 1926 it was converted into an immigration shed. During the Depression it was used as a hostel by the unemployed and homeless. The military took over the building during World War II, after which it again served as a shelter for the homeless. The third floor of the station was removed in 1954.

38 Standard NP section house with a bay window on the trackside.

MANITOBA DISTRICT
Portage-Brandon Division

OAK POINT SUBDIVISION
(continued)

Milepost	Locality	Proposed/Former Name	Type	Plan	Built	Notes
94.4	Mulvihill #2		4th	100-68	1920	
94.4	Mulvihill #3		FPS	100-41	—	
102.4	Camper		FPS	100-41	1913	
111.0	Ashern #1		FPS	100-41	1914	
111.0	Ashern #2		4th	100-68	1920	
119.3	Moosehorn #1		FPS	100-41		
119.3	Moosehorn #2		4th	100-68	1918	Museum-2
126.9	Grahamdale	x-Deerfield	PORT	100-24	1913	
129.7	Steep Rock Jct.		FPS	100-41	1920	
132.2	Birch Bay		FPS	100-41	1918	
135.7	Hilbre		FPS	100-41	1916	
143.4	Fairford #2		FPS	100-41B	1943	
144.1	Mileage 144.1		FPS	CB	1949	
149.1	Todds					
152.5	St. Martin		FPS	100-41	1914	
156.7	Gypsumville #2		4th	100-68	1916	

OAKLAND SUBDIVISION
Portage la Prairie, Mb to Alonsa, Mb—71.2 miles

Milepost	Locality	Proposed/Former Name	Type	Plan	Built	Notes
3.0	Alpha					
6.1	Townline		FPS	CB	1915	
9.1	Oakland		STA-NPR	100-116	1898	
11.0	Fulton		FPS	100-41	1911	
15.9	Longburn		FPS	100-96	1906	
21.0	Cawdor		FPS	100-41	—	
[26.4]	Totogan					
30.6	Lakeland		FPS	100-41	1915	
38.6	Langruth		4th	100-68	1916	
47.0	Embury		FPS	CB		
50.1	Marius		FPS	CB	1949	
53.4	Amaranth		FPS	100-96	1909	
63.5	Harcus		FPS	100-41	1922	
71.2	Alonsa		4th	100-68	1922	

PINE FALLS SUBDIVISION
Beaconia, Mb to Pine Falls, Mb—19.5 miles

Milepost	Locality	Proposed/Former Name	Type	Plan	Built	Notes
5.3	Stead		FPS	100-41B	1927	
19.5	Pine Falls		PORT	100-221	1926	

PLEASANT POINT SUBDIVISION
Portage la Prairie, Sk to Brandon, Mb—78.4 miles

Milepost	Locality	Proposed/Former Name	Type	Plan	Built	Notes
4.1	McArthur					
11.1	Edwin		FPS	100-96	1909	
14.3	Lelant		FPS	100-41	1916	
17.4	Rossendale		4th	100-31	1910	
22.6	Lavenham		3rd	100-3	1905	
27.7	Ladysmith		FPS	100-96	1905	
31.6	Pratt		FPS	100-96	1906	
35.6	Gateside		FPS	100-41	1912	
36.7	Worby		FPS	100-41	—	
39.0	Arizona #1		3rd	100-3	1905	
39.0	Arizona #2		FPS	100-41	—	
44.2	Pleasant Point		PORT	100-24	1910	
48.7	Prosser					
51.7	Brandon Jct.		FPS	100-41B	1929	
59.0	Onah					
64.7	Shiloh–2nd site	x-Shiloh Camp	SPEC.	100-299	1942	
66.5	Wyntonville	x-Shiloh–1st site	FPS	100-41	1914	
74.5	Leon					
77.0	M&B Jct.					
78.4	Brandon #1		SPEC-NPR		1890	
78.4	Brandon #2	On Spur	SPEC.	140-144	1911	

RAPID CITY SUBDIVISION
Hallboro, Mb to Beulah, Mb—74.4 miles

Milepost	Locality	Proposed/Former Name	Type	Plan	Built	Notes
5.7	Mentmore		FPS	100-41B	1943	
12.5	Cordova		FPS	100-41	1912	
20.5	Rufford		FPS	100-41	1912	
22.4	Tremaine		FPS	100-41	1915	
27.5	Rapid City		3rd	100-29	1909	
35.3	Moline		PORT	100-24	1912	
42.5	Cardale #2		3rd	100-75	1914	
45.9	Brumlie		FPS	100-41	1914	
51.9	McConnell		3rd	100-29	1909	Museum-2
55.1	Alfretta					
58.2	Lavina		FPS	100-41	1913	
63.2	Decker		3rd	100-29	1913	
67.3	Isabella		3rd	100-29	1910	
74.4	Beulah		3rd	100-29	1911	

MANITOBA DISTRICT
Portage-Brandon Division

RIDGEVILLE SUBDIVISION
near Sprague, Mb to Emerson Jct., Mb—72.6 miles

Milepost	Locality	Proposed/Former Name	Type	Plan	Built	Notes
3.3	Wampum		FPS	100-41	1913	
5.6	Guilbault					
10.8	Piney		3rd	100-3	1905	
15.0	Stephanson					
18.3	Menisino		FPS	100-41	1910	
24.7	Sundown		FPS	100-41	1910	
32.1	Caliento		FPS	100-41	1913	
38.7	Vita #2		4th	100-68	1923	
46.1	Gardenton	x-Stuartburn	3rd	100-3	1905	
51.8	Tolstoi		FPS	100-41	1910	
55.2	Overstone		SHLT	100-95		
60.0	Aulds					
61.1	Ridgeville		3rd	100-3	1906	
64.5	Fredenstahl		FPS	100-41	1910	
66.8	Stockport					
71.4	Emerson #1		SPEC-NPR	100-7	1904?	
71.4	Emerson #2		SPEC.	100-191	1923	
72.6	Emerson Jct.					

ROSSBURN SUBDIVISION
Rossburn Jct., Mb to Russell, Mb—104.2 miles

Milepost	Locality	Proposed/Former Name	Type	Plan	Built	Notes
5.0	Springhill		FPS	100-96	1910	
9.2	Orrville		FPS	100-96	1910	
15.3	Bethany #1		FPS	100-96		
15.3	Bethany #2		CN4th	100-220	1927	
20.1	Clanwilliam #2		3rd	100-29	1914	
24.7	Crocus		FPS	100-41	1922	
31.5	Erickson #1		FPS	100-41	1911	
31.5	Erickson #2		3rd	100-72	1923	
39.8	Rackham		FPS	100-41	—	
45.6	Sandy Lake #1		FPS	100-41		
45.6	Sandy Lake #2		3rd	100-72	1921	
52.9	Elphinstone		3rd	100-3	1904	
56.4	Glenforsa		FPS	100-41	1910	
61.0	Menzie		FPS	100-96	1909	
65.6	Oakburn		3rd	100-29	1907	
72.8	Vista		FPS	100-96	1909	
78.7	Rossburn		3rd	100-3	1907	
83.9	Birdtail		FPS	100-41	1915	
92.5	Angusville		3rd	100-29	1909	
98.9	Silverton #1		FPS	100-96		
98.9	Silverton #2		3rd	100-72	1922	
104.2	Russell		3rd	100-29	1908	

STE. ROSE SUBDIVISION
Ochre River, Mb to Rorketon, Mb—37.1 miles

Milepost	Locality	Proposed/Former Name	Type	Plan	Built	Notes
11.1	Ste. Rose #1		4th	100-68	1916	
11.1	Ste. Rose #2		CN3rd	100-253	1930	
16.2	Valpoy		FPS	100-41B	1926	
23.1	Methley		FPS	100-41B	1926	
30.6	Magnet		FPS	100-41B	1926	
37.1	Rorketon	x-Edillen	CN3rd	100-197	1926	Variant

STEEP ROCK SUBDIVISION
near Grahamdale, Mb to Steep Rock, Mb—12.1 miles

Milepost	Locality	Proposed/Former Name	Type	Plan	Built	Notes
5.9	Faulkner		FPS	100-41	1916	
12.1	Steep Rock		4th	100-68	1916	

VICTORIA BEACH SUBDIVISION
near Winnipeg, Mb to Victoria Beach, Mb—70.2 miles

Milepost	Locality	Proposed/Former Name	Type	Plan	Built	Notes
3.0	West Transcona	x-Transcona–CNoR	FPS	100-41	1913	
6.0	Parkmount		FPS	100-41	1917	
7.8	Bird's Hill					
10.2	Manlius		FPS	100-41B	1929?	
17.1	Gonor		FPS	100-41	1915	
22.3	Brainerd		FPS	100-41B	1935	
23.9	East Selkirk		FPS	100-41	1915	
29.7	Semple		FPS	100-41	1918	
34.2	Libau		FPS	100-41	1915	
42.2	Scanterbury		FPS	100-41	1915	
47.9	Beaconia #2		FPS	100-41B	1927	
52.4	Balsam Bay		FPS	100-41	1915	
56.2	Grand Marais		PORT	110-73A	1921	SMBH
57.1	Grand Beach		2nd	100-89	1916	Variant
61.0	Hargrave					
62.8	Belair		FPS	100-41	—	
65.4	Amanda					
66.8	Hillside Beach		FPS	100-41	—	
67.9	Albert		FPS	100-41	1918	

MANITOBA DISTRICT
Portage-Brandon Division

VICTORIA BEACH SUBDIVISION
(continued)

Milepost	Locality	Proposed/Former Name	Type	Plan	Built	Notes
68.3	Armstrongs					
70.2	Victoria Beach		2nd	100-89	1916	Variant

WAKOPA SUBDIVISION
Greenway, Mb to Deloraine, Mb—79.8 miles

Milepost	Locality	Proposed/Former Name	Type	Plan	Built	Notes
8.8	Glenora	x-Greenway	PORT	100-24	1908	
17.8	Neelin		3rd	100-3	1904	
22.9	Louise		SHLT	100-95	1904	
28.8	Holmfield #2-A		4th	100-31	1909	
28.8	Holmfield #2-B		FPS	100-41	—	
33.3	Enterprise		SHLT	100-95	1909	
38.8	Lena		3rd	100-3	1904	
47.1	Wakopa		3rd	100-3	1904	
51.8	Adelpha		FPS	100-41	1916	
57.8	Horton		FPS	CB	1920	
62.9	Wassewa		FPS	CB	1920	
67.9	Mountain Side		FPS	100-41	1916	
71.8	Hazeldean		SHLT	100-95	1914	
74.1	Coatstone		FPS	CB	1928	
77.2	Liege					
79.8	Deloraine #2		3rd	100-72	1915	

WAWANESA SUBDIVISION
Belmont, Mb to Martinville, Mb—32.3 miles

Milepost	Locality	Proposed/Former Name	Type	Plan	Built	Notes
4.5	Hilton		NPR-4th			Probable
9.1	Ashdown		FPS	100-41	1912	
14.7	Wawanesa		CSS-NPR	100-16	1889	
17.8	Elliotts		FPS	100-41	1912	
19.6	Methven Jct.		FPS	100-96	1909	
20.8	Reids		FPS	100-41	1911	
24.4	Rounthwaite	x-Naughton	NPR-4th			Probable
32.3	Martinville	x-Martin	FPS	100-41	1912	

Port Arthur Division

ALLANWATER SUBDIVISION
Armstrong, On to Sioux Lookout, On—138.9 miles

Milepost	Locality	Proposed/Former Name	Type	Plan	Built	Notes
0.0	Armstrong #1		SPEC.	100-158	1912	
0.0	Armstrong #2		SPEC.		1927	
7.4	Onaping		Type F	100-151	1911	
14.5	Pascopee		Type F	100-151	1911	
21.1	Collins #1		Type F	100-151	1911	
21.1	Collins #2		FPS	100-41	—	
28.6	Ogaki		Type F	100-151	1911	
38.9	Jacobs		Type F	100-151	1911	
46.1	Kawa		Type F	100-151	1911	
52.4	Cameo		Type F	100-151	1911	
53.9	Mileage 53.9		FPS	CB	1925	
55.9	Allanwater		Type F	100-151	1911	
65.5	Harvey		Type F	100-151	1911	
69.6	Staunton		Type F	100-151	1912	
78.6	Savant Lake	x-Bucke	Type F	100-151	1912	
90.7	Fowler		Type F	100-151	1912	
100.5	Ycliff #1		Type F	100-151	1912	
100.5	Ycliff #2		PORT		—	x-SMBH
108.8	Robinson		Type F	100-151	1912	
115.9	Ghost River	x-Smith	Type F	100-151	1912	
123.1	Rosnel		Type F	100-151	1912	
132.5	Superior Jct. #1		NTR2	100-180	1910	
132.5	Superior Jct. #2		FPS	100-290	—	
138.9	Sioux Lookout		SPEC.	100-195	1911	

FORT FRANCES SUBDIVISION
Atikokan, On to Rainy River, On—143.5 miles

Milepost	Locality	Proposed/Former Name	Type	Plan	Built	Notes
2.9	Overflow					
10.1	Elizabeth	x-Steep Rock	FPS	100-41B	1924	
17.4	Banning #1		STA	100-12	1901	
17.4	Banning #2		FPS	100-41	—	
22.6	Flanders	x-Maflower	4th	100-68	1916	
28.1	Calm Lake	x-Progress				
28.7	Laseine		STA	100-12	1901	
32.1	Crilly		SHLT		1926	
33.1	Mathieu					
38.5	Glenorchy #2		FPS	100-290	1943	
44.8	Turtle					
47.9	Mine Centre #1		STA	100-12	1901	Note 30
47.9	Mine Centre #2		FPS	CB	1941	
47.9	Mine Centre #3-A		FPS	CB	—	
47.9	Mine Centre #3-B		PORT	110-159	—	x-SMBH
47.9	Mine Centre #4		PORT	110-237	—	x-SMBH

MANITOBA DISTRICT
Port Arthur Division

FORT FRANCES SUBDIVISION
(continued)

Milepost	Locality	Proposed/Former Name	Type	Plan	Built	Notes
52.1	Olive		FPS	CB	1942	
57.3	Farrington #1		FPS	100-41	1911	
57.3	Farrington #2		FPS	CB	1955	
64.6	Bear Pass #2	x-Bears Pass	4th	100-68	1920	
68.1	Mileage 68.1		FPS		1945	
70.1	Nickel Lake	x-Nickle Lake	FPS	CB	1939	
[73.4]	Sims					
80.4	Rocky Inlet		FPS	100-41	1911	Probable
83.3	Seibert					
87.9	Duluth Jct.					
88.9	Fort Frances #1		2nd	100-4	1901	Note 29
88.9	Fort Frances #2		SPEC.	100-42	1913	
95.1	Crozier		4th	100-31	1910	
99.3	La Vallee		3rd	100-29	1907	
101.3	Devlin	x-Devlin Road	4th	100-31	1910	
109.2	Emo		3rd	100-3	1901	
116.0	Barwick #1		3rd	100-3	1904	
116.0	Barwick #2		FPS		—	
124.5	Stratton		3rd	100-3	1903	
131.1	Pinewood		3rd	100-3	1901	
143.5	Rainy River #1	x-Beaver Mills	2nd	100-1	1901	Variant
143.5	Rainy River #2		SPEC.	100-120	1918	Add to #1

GRAHAM SUBDIVISION
Westfort, On/Conmee, On to Superior Jct.—189.5/159.5 miles

Milepost	Locality	Proposed/Former Name	Type	Plan	Built	Notes
[0.0]	Westfort		Type E	100-152	1912	
[13.2]	Baird		Type E	100-152	1912	Note 32
[20.9]	Crest		Type E	100-152	1912	Note 32
[26.4]	Dona		Type E	100-152	1912	Note 32
3.2	Ellis		Type E	100-152	1912	
9.8	Flett		Type E	100-152	1911	
16.5	Griff		Type E	100-152	1911	
22.1	Horne		Type E	100-152	1911	
28.6	Raith		Type E	100-152	1910	
33.2	Linko		Type E	100-152	1910	
38.8	James		Type E	100-152	1910	
46.7	Kelly		Type E	100-152	1911	
53.1	Larson		Type E	100-152	1911	
59.2	Mack		Type E	100-152	1911	
70.8	Graham		Type E	100-152	1910	
78.3	Oscar #1		Type E	100-152	1910	
78.3	Oscar #2		FPS	100-290	1949	
85.5	Petry #1		Type E	100-152	1910	
85.5	Petry #2		FPS	100-290	1943	
92.7	Quorn #1		Type E	100-152	1910	
92.7	Quorn #2		FPS	100-132	1947	
98.0	Reba		Type E	100-152	1911	
105.5	Snowden		Type E	100-152	1911	
110.1	Tannin		Type E	100-152	1910	
116.2	Unaka		Type E	100-152	1911	
122.8	Valora #1		Type E	100-152	1911	
122.8	Valora #2		SPEC.	100-218	1926	
124.8	Clarkdon		FPS	CB	1946	
131.1	Watcomb	x-Wako	Type E	100-152	1910	
137.4	Umfreville #1	x-Hunt	Type E	100-152	1910	
137.4	Umfreville #2		SPEC.	100-218	1927	
137.4	Umfreville #3		FPS	100-41	—	
141.7	Yonde		Type E	100-152	1911	
149.1	Zarn		Type E	100-152	1910	
156.3	Alcona		Type E	100-152	1911	

KASHABOWIE SUBDIVISION
Port Arthur, On to Atikokan, On—141.4 miles

Milepost	Locality	Proposed/Former Name	Type	Plan	Built	Notes
0.0	Port Arthur #2	later Thunder Bay	SPEC.	100-49	1905	
3.8	Fort William		SPEC.	100-109	1918	
5.3	West Fort William	x-Westfort	STA			
[6.3]	Mount					
9.0	Neebing #1		SHLT		1923	
10.3	Neebing #2		SHLT	100-433	1977	
12.3	Twin City		FPS	100-41	1912	

NOTES:

29 The CNoR classified this as a 2nd Class Station.

30 The disposition of the first depot could not be established. It may have burned down and been replaced by a 4th Class structure.

32 The 26-mile section between Conmee and Fort William was abandoned in 1925. The final disposition of this station could not be established.

MANITOBA DISTRICT
Port Arthur Division
KASHABOWIE SUBDIVISION
(continued)

Milepost	Locality	Proposed/Former Name	Type	Plan	Built	Notes
13.0	Slate River					
16.2	Jelly					
[20]	Stanley		SPEC.		1900	Note 75
22.6	Kakabeka Falls #2		3rd	100-72	1915	
26.3	Hume		FPS	100-41	1914	
30.4	Mokomon		STA	100-12	1901	
34.8	Rowan	x-Fonger				
35.7	Conmee		FPS	100-41	1923	
38.9	Garda					
43.7	Glenwater	x-Mattawin	STA	100-12	1901	
46.6	Anita					
52.5	Shabaqua		FPS		1921	
57.6	Mabella		STA	100-12	1901	
60.3	Annex					
62.1	Shebandowan		FPS		1923	
65.8	Rossmere					
72.0	Kabaigon					
76.7	Postans					
80.9	Kashabowie		STA	100-12	1901	
86.2	Planet	x-Tebo				
89.8	Keego					
96.1	Huronian #1		4th	100-68	1918	
101.4	Owakonze	x-Baril Lake	FPS		1924	
103.9	Wells Camp		FPS	CB	1950	
105.0	Quetico	x-Windigo	STA	100-12	1901	
113.6	Abiwin					
120.5	Kawene		STA	100-12	1901	
125.6	Blalock					
127.4	Sapawe	x-Iron Spur	FPS	100-41B	1950	
130.5	Hematite		FPS	CB	1906	
135.9	Olcott		PORT	CB	1950	
141.4	Atikokan #2		SPEC.	100-193	1923	Note 35

MINAKI SUBDIVISION
Redditt, On to Transcona, Mb—121.8 miles

Milepost	Locality	Proposed/Former Name	Type	Plan	Built	Notes
6.6	Ena					
14.4	Minaki		NTR2	100-180	1910	
20.6	Wade #1-A		SHLT		1920	
20.6	Wade #1-B		SHLT	100-201	1926	
????	Tebo					
27.8	Ottermere		FPS	100-290	1937	
30.1	Malachi		NTR3	100-181		
36.1	White		Type E	100-152	1912	
37.5	Rice Lake, On					
41.1	Winnitoba, Mb		FPS	CGR1		
44.1	Ophir		SHLT	110-116		x-ST
51.6	Decimal	x-Dott	NTR3	100-181	1910	
56.6	Brereton Lake		FPS			
57.4	Mileage 57.4		FPS		1926	
58.7	Indigo	x-Brereton				
64.0	Hoctor		NTR3	100-181	1910	
68.8	Alcock					
73.7	Elma		NTR1	100-179	1910	
80.9	Lewis		NTR3	100-181	1910	
83.4	Williams Spur					
88.8	Hazell		NTR3	100-181	1910	
90.6	Craig Siding		FPS	100-290	1936	
94.3	Nourse					
98.3	Vivian		NTR2	100-180	1910	
106.4	Anola		NTR3	100-181	1910	
110.0	Glass		FPS		1922	
115.2	Dugald		NTR2	100-180	1910	
121.8	Transcona #1	<<Springfield>>	NTR1	100-179	1912	Note 34
121.8	Transcona #2-A		SHLT	100-258	1929	Note 34
121.8	Transcona #2-B		FPS	100-41		Note 34

QUIBELL SUBDIVISION
Sioux Lookout, On to Redditt, On—123.1 miles

Milepost	Locality	Proposed/Former Name	Type	Plan	Built	Notes
6.4	Pelican		NTR3	100-181	1910	
7.5	North Pines		SHLT	CGR1		
12.6	Hudson		NTR2	100-180	1911	
20.7	Webster #1		NTR2	100-180	1910	
20.7	Webster #2		PORT	110-42		x-SMBH
20.7	Webster #3		FPS	110-159		x-SMBH
27.5	Taggart					
32.1	Sunstrum		Type E	100-152	1912	
39.4	Millidge		NTR2	100-180	1910	
45.5	Ritchan #1		Type E	100-152	1912	
45.5	Ritchan #2		FPS	100-290	1937	

MANITOBA DISTRICT
Port Arthur Division
QUIBELL SUBDIVISION
(continued)

Milepost	Locality	Proposed/Former Name	Type	Plan	Built	Notes
50.9	Amesdale	x-Freda	Type F	100-151	1911	
57.8	Niddrie	x-Hunter	NTR2	100-180	1910	
65.5	Morgan					
69.5	Lash					
71.2	Red Lake Road #1		FPS	CB	1946	
71.2	Red Lake Road #2		CN4A	100-317	1947	
74.6	Quibell		NTR3	100-181	1910	
83.5	McIntosh #1		NTR2	100-180	1910	
83.5	McIntosh #2		FPS	100-41		
90.2	Canyon					
99.3	Favel					
106.0	Jones #1		Type E	100-152	1911	
106.0	Jones #2		FPS	100-41		
113.4	Farlane		NTR3	100-181	1910	
118.3	Brinka					
123.1	Redditt #1		NTR1	100-179	1910	
123.1	Redditt #2		SPEC.	100-158	1912	

SPRAGUE SUBDIVISION
Rainy River, On, to near Winnipeg, Mb—145.7 miles

Milepost	Locality	Proposed/Former Name	Type	Plan	Built	Notes
1.6	Baudette #1, Mn		2nd	100-28	1907	Variant
1.6	Baudette #2, Mn		SPEC.	100-192	1923	
7.9	Pitt		4th	100-31	1909	
12.8	Graceton #1		5th	100-17	1907	
12.8	Graceton #2		4th	100-68	1919	
15.3	Cedar					
18.5	Williams		4th	100-31	1909	
25.3	Roosevelt		3rd	100-3	1904	
32.0	Swift		4th	100-31	1909	
38.0	Warroad #2		SPEC.	100-77	1914	
43.8	Longworth, Mn					
49.3	Middlebro #2, Mb		FPS	100-290	1939	
51.5	Hickey					
57.6	Sprague #2		SPEC.	100-37	1910	
63.5	South Jct. #1		FPS	100-290	1937	
63.5	South Jct. #2		FPS	100-41		
68.6	Vassar		4th	100-31	1907	
73.4	Moodie					
77.5	Badger		4th	100-31	1909	
83.2	Carrick #2	x-Spurgrave	FPS	100-41B	1934	
88.6	Woodridge		CSS-B	100-99	1902	
94.4	Baynham					
96.0	Sandilands		FPS	100-41	1916	
99.8	Bedford #1		FPS	100-41	1915	
99.8	Bedford #2		FPS	100-290	1952	
105.9	Marchand #2		4th	100-68	1920	
113.2	La Brouquerie		3rd	100-3	1905	
118.3	Giroux #2		SPEC.	100-190	1923	
118.3	Giroux #3		FPS	100-41B	1944	Temporary
118.3	Giroux #4		CN4A	100-305	1946	
126.2	Ste. Anne #2		SPEC.	100-133	1920	
131.0	Dufresne		FPS	100-41	1913	
138.3	Lorette		4th	100-31	1909	
145.9	Navin		FPS	100-41	1910	
147.9	Paddington		TOS		1911	Note 34
[152.6]	St. Boniface #1		2nd	100-4	1901	Variant, Notes 29, 34
[152.6]	St. Boniface #2		SPEC.	100-54	1914	Note 34

SASKATCHEWAN DISTRICT
Prince Albert Division
ABERDEEN SUBDIVISION
Humboldt, Sk to Warman, Sk—65.5 miles

Milepost	Locality	Proposed/Former Name	Type	Plan	Built	Notes
4.4	Dixon		FPS	100-96	1908	
10.4	Carmel #1		FPS	100-96	1908	
10.4	Carmel #2		CSS-SH	110-10	1911	
10.4	Carmel #3		4th	100-68	1917	
18.3	Bruno		3rd	100-3	1904	
22.9	Frederick	x-Grain Spur	FPS		1922	
24.9	Totzke #2	See Cudworth Subdivision				
26.6	Dana #1		CSS-SH	110-10	1905	
26.6	Dana #2		SHLT	CB	1934	
35.5	Prudhomme #1	x-Howell	FPS	100-96		
35.5	Prudhomme #2		4th	100-31	1910	
44.3	Vonda		3rd	100-3	1905	
52.6	Aberdeen		3rd	100-3	1905	
59.7	Clarkboro		FPS	100-96	1909	

SASKATCHEWAN DISTRICT
Prince Albert Division

AMIENS SUBDIVISION
Shellbrook, Sk to Medstead, Sk—75.0 miles

Milepost	Locality	Proposed/Former Name	Type	Plan	Built	Notes
5.8	Cameo		FPS	100-41B	1929	
13.0	Ordale		FPS	100-41B	1930	
19.2	Mont Nebo		FPS	100-41B	1930	
24.1	Hawkeye	x-Lynwood	FPS	100-41B	1930	
29.0	Shell Lake	x-Rastel	CN3rd	100-253	1930	
37.2	Amiens		FPS	100-41B	1930	
41.6	Mildred	x-Arleux	FPS	100-41B	1930	
49.4	Spiritwood		CN3rd	100-250	1930	
56.0	Bapaume		FPS	100-41B	1930	
62.8	Belbutte		FPS	100-41B	1930	
67.7	Bazentin		FPS	100-41B	1930	

ARBORFIELD SUBDIVISION
Crooked River, Sk to Arborfield, Sk—19.4 miles

Milepost	Locality	Proposed/Former Name	Type	Plan	Built	Notes
3.9	Clashmoor		FPS	100-41B	1930	
8.4	New Osgoode		FPS	100-41B	1930	
14.3	Zenon Park #1		FPS	100-41B	1930	
14.3	Zenon Park #2		SPEC.	100-280	—	
19.4	Arborfield		CN3rd	100-250	1930	

BATTLEFORD SUBDIVISION
North Battleford, Sk to Battleford, Sk—6.0 miles

Milepost	Locality	Proposed/Former Name	Type	Plan	Built	Notes
6.0	Battleford		3rd	100-19	1907	Variant

BIG RIVER SUBDIVISION
Shellbrook, Sk to Big River, Sk—56.5 miles

Milepost	Locality	Proposed/Former Name	Type	Plan	Built	Notes
14.7	Canwood #1	x-McOwan	FPS	100-41		
14.7	Canwood #2	Joint with CPR	4th	100-68	1916	
22.1	Polwarth	Joint with CPR	FPS	100-41	1915	
26.9	Mattes	Joint with CPR	FPS		1920	
31.2	Debden #1		FPS	100-41	1914	
31.2	Debden #2	Joint with CPR	4th	100-68	1918	
37.0	Eldred		FPS	100-41	1911	
42.8	Erinferry	x-Wrixon	FPS	CB		
45.2	Dumble		FPS	110-42	—	x-SMBH
50.6	Bodmin		FPS	100-41	—	
56.5	Big River		3rd	100-29	1910	

BLAINE LAKE SUBDIVISION
Prince Albert, Sk to Denholm, Sk—116.5 miles

Milepost	Locality	Proposed/Former Name	Type	Plan	Built	Notes
8.0	Buckland		FPS	100-41	1914	
14.9	Crutwell #1		FPS	100-41	1912	
14.9	Crutwell #2		FPS	100-41B	1947	
20.5	Holbein		FPS	100-41	1915	
28.5	Shellbrook		3rd	100-29	1910	
35.7	Parkside #1		FPS	100-41	1912	
35.7	Parkside #2		3rd	100-72	1916	
43.3	Kilwinning		FPS	100-41	1913	
49.5	Leask		3rd	100-29	1912	
56.5	Marcelin		3rd	100-29	1911	
64.3	Blaine Lake		3rd	100-29	1912	
68.9	Tallman		FPS	100-41B	1929	
73.8	Krydor #1	<<Ballock>>	FPS	100-41	1913	
73.8	Krydor #2		4th	100-68	1917	
81.6	Redberry		FPS	100-41	1913	
86.7	Hafford		3rd	100-29	1913	
95.6	Speers		3rd	100-29	1913	
102.3	Richard #1		FPS	100-41	1913	
102.3	Richard #2		3rd	100-29	1916	
108.7	Lilac	2nd location (1916)	FPS	100-41	1917	

BOLNEY SUBDIVISION
Spruce Lake, Sk to Frenchman Butte, Sk—28.2 miles

Milepost	Locality	Proposed/Former Name	Type	Plan	Built	Notes
8.9	Bolney		FPS	100-41B	1929	
15.4	Paradise Hill	x-Digges	CN3rd	100-253	1929	
21.8	Deer Creek	x-Tangleflags	FPS	100-41B	1929	
28.2	Frenchman Butte		CN3rd	100-253	1929	

BROOKSBY SUBDIVISION
near Melfort, Sk to Carrot River, Sk—51.1 miles

Milepost	Locality	Proposed/Former Name	Type	Plan	Built	Notes
5.9	Whittome		FPS	100-41	1923	
10.0	Brett	later Irvington	SHLT	110-153	—	x-ST
14.8	Brooksby		4th	100-68	1923	
22.9	Ridgedale #1	x-Ealing	FPS	100-41	1922	Note 6
22.9	Ridgedale #2		3rd	100-72	1922	
29.2	Nicklen #1	x-Armley	FPS	100-41C	1930	
29.2	Nicklen #2		FPS	CB	1938	
35.1	Carlea		FPS	100-41C	1932	
40.2	Aylsham #1		FPS	100-41C	1932	

SASKATCHEWAN DISTRICT
Prince Albert Division

BROOKSBY SUBDIVISION
near Melfort, Sk to Carrot River, Sk—51.1 miles

Milepost	Locality	Proposed/Former Name	Type	Plan	Built	Notes
40.2	Aylsham #2		CN4A	100-313	1949	
45.0	Moose Range #1-A		FPS	100-41C	1931	
45.0	Moose Range #1-B		FPS			
51.1	Carrot River #1		FPS	100-41C	1932	Note 7
51.1	Carrot River #2		CN4A	100-309	1947	

CARLTON SUBDIVISION
Dalmeny, Sk To Carlton, Sk—35.9 miles

Milepost	Locality	Proposed/Former Name	Type	Plan	Built	Notes
6.5	Mennon		FPS	100-41	1913	
13.4	Hepburn #1		FPS	100-41		
13.4	Hepburn #2		CN4th	100-252	1930	
20.8	Waldheim #1		FPS	100-96	1909	Probable
20.8	Waldheim #2		3rd	100-29	1912	
27.8	Laird		3rd	100-29	1909	
35.9	Carlton		FPS	100-41	—	

CHELAN SUBDIVISION
Reserve, Sk to Crooked River, Sk—60.1 miles

Milepost	Locality	Proposed/Former Name	Type	Plan	Built	Notes
7.8	Dillabough		FPS	100-41B	1930	
13.0	Weekes		PORT	100-132	1930	Reverse
17.4	Somme		PORT	100-132	1930	
22.9	Carragana		FPS	100-41B	1930	
29.5	Porcupine Plain #1		FPS	100-41B	1930	
29.5	Porcupine Plain #2		CN4A	100-310	1953	
29.5	Porcupine Plain #3		SPEC.	100-366	1959	
35.6	Chelan		FPS	100-41B	1930	
43.3	Steen		FPS	100-41B	1930	
49.0	Bjorkdale #1		FPS	100-41B	1930	
49.0	Bjorkdale #2		PORT	CB	1948	Temporary
49.0	Bjorkdale #3		PORT	100-323	1948	Add to #2
54.6	Speddington		FPS		1946	

CUDWORTH SUBDIVISION
Young, Sk to Prince Albert, Sk—111.7 miles

Milepost	Locality	Proposed/Former Name	Type	Plan	Built	Notes
6.0	Ancrum #1		Type E	100-152	1912	
6.0	Ancrum #2		SHLT	150-52	—	x-PH
11.7	Neely		Type E	100-152	1911	
17.4	Rutan		SHLT	110-117	—	x-ST
24.1	Meacham		Type E	100-152	1911	
31.2	Peterson #1		FPS	CB	1916	
31.2	Peterson #2		FPS	100-41	—	
38.7	Totzke #1		Type E	100-152	1911	
38.7	Totzke #2		CN4th			
46.1	Bremen		Type E	100-152	1911	
54.9	Cudworth #1		Type E	100-152	1911	
54.9	Cudworth #2		CN3rd	100-197	1925	
66.4	Wakaw #1		Type E	100-152	1911	
66.4	Wakaw #2		Type G	100-168	1919	
70.0	Ens		SHLT	110-153	—	x-ST
76.4	Domremy #1		Type E	100-152	1915	
76.4	Domremy #2		Type G	100-168	1919	
82.5	Hoey #1		FPS-1B	100-162	1914	
82.5	Hoey #2		Type G	100-168	1920	
86.4	St. Louis		FPS	100-162	1914	Probable
93.9	Red Deer Hill		Type F	100-151	1918	
100.8	Holmes					
108.0	Cudworth Jct.					
111.7	Prince Albert–GTP		SPEC.	100-171	1917	

NOTES:

6 The sources regarding the disposition of this station are contradictory. One says that the structure was cut in half, one portion being shipped to Birch Hills and the other to Star City, for use as section bunkhouses. Another source indicates that, in 1933, this building was relocated to Peterson as a section bunkhouse.

7 Converted into section tool house in 1947. Converted into enginemen's bunkhouse in 1967.

29 The CNoR classified this as a 2nd Class Station.

34 This station was technically on the Winnipeg Terminals Subdivision.

35 The second storey was removed in 1947.

75 This station was constructed at the junction of the Ontario and Rainy River section and the "old" Port Arthur Duluth & Western Railway. A photograph in THUNDER BAY TO GUNFLINT by Elinor Barr (Thunder Bay Historical Society, 1999), page 107, shows a 1½-storey wood-frame structure unlike anything else constructed by the CNoR.

SASKATCHEWAN DISTRICT
Prince Albert Division

CUTKNIFE SUBDIVISION
Battleford, Sk to Carruthers, Sk—43.8 miles

Milepost	Locality	Proposed/Former Name	Type	Plan	Built	Notes
9.5	Prongua		Type E	100-152	1913	
23.0	Gallivan		Type E	100-152	1913	
30.9	Cutknife	x-Rossman	Type E	100-152	1913	
38.0	Tatsfield		FPS	CB?		
43.8	Carruthers		Type G	100-168	1920	

DUCK LAKE SUBDIVISION
Saskatoon, Sk to Prince Albert, Sk—87.8 miles

Milepost	Locality	Proposed/Former Name	Type	Plan	Built	Notes
[1.8]	Saskatoon–Loop Jct.		TOS	110-73	—	Note 4, x-SMBH
1.9	North Saskatoon #1		FPS		By14	Note 4
1.9	North Saskatoon #2		FPS	CB	1933	Note 4
1.9	North Saskatoon #3		FPS		1960s	Note 4, x-SMBH
6.0	Richmond		STA			
6.7	Clark's Crossing #1		FPS	100-96	1910	
6.7	Clark's Crossing #2		FPS	CB		
11.6	Warman #1		3rd	100-3	1905	x-Langham Sb
11.6	Warman #2		SPEC		1970s	
15.9	Osler		CSS-CPR	100-100	1892	Note 71
27.1	Hague		CPR#5	100-110	1905	Note 71
33.2	Arma		FPS	100-41	—	
38.2	Rosthern		CPR	100-18	1902	Note 71, Museum-2*
44.2	Leckford	x-Bonne Plaine	FPS	100-41	1911	
49.6	Duck Lake		CSS-CPR	100-100	1891	Note 71, Museum-2*
58.3	Roddick		FPS	100-41	1916	
66.9	MacDowall		CSS-CPR	100-100	1891	Note 71
76.1	Clouston		FPS	100-41	1914	
85.3	Prince Albert–CNoR #1	x-W. Prince Albert	CSS-CPR	100-100	1890	Notes 28, 71
85.3	Prince Albert–CNoR #2		FPS		1905	Temporary
85.3	Prince Albert–CNoR #3	Joint with CPR	2nd	100-25	1906	
85.3	Prince Albert–CNoR #4	Joint with CPR	SPEC.	100-385	1960	
[87.8]	East Prince Albert		BK-7		1898	Note 71

HATHERLEIGH SUBDIVISION
Prinham, Sk to Avery, Sk—31.6 miles

Milepost	Locality	Proposed/Former Name	Type	Plan	Built	Notes
3.3	Scentgrass		FPS	100-41B	1931	
7.7	Iffley		FPS	100-41B	1931	
14.3	Hatherleigh		CN3rd	100-253	1931	
23.2	Sandwith		FPS	100-41B	1931	

LANGHAM SUBDIVISION
Warman, Sk to North Battleford, Sk—82.4 miles

Milepost	Locality	Proposed/Former Name	Type	Plan	Built	Notes
8.9	Dalmeny		3rd	100-3	1907	
16.8	Langham		3rd	100-3	1905	
24.7	Ceepee	<<Elbow>>	FPS	100-41	1911	
30.7	Borden		3rd	100-3	1907	
38.6	Radisson		3rd	100-3	1905	
45.9	Fielding		3rd	100-3	1907	
53.5	Maymont		3rd	100-29	1908	
60.4	Ruddell	<<Lucerne>>	3rd	100-3	1905	
67.9	Denholm #1		3rd	100-29	1912	
67.9	Denholm #2		CN4th	100-279	1936	
76.4	Brada		FPS	100-96	1909	
82.4	North Battleford #1		2nd	100-22	1905	
82.4	North Battleford #2		2nd	100-22	1908	
82.4	North Battleford #3		SPEC.	100-330	1955	

MESKANAW SUBDIVISION
Melfort, Sk to Aberdeen, Sk—89.5 miles

Milepost	Locality	Proposed/Former Name	Type	Plan	Built	Notes
5.3	McMichael		FPS	100-41B	1931	
8.9	Claggett		FPS	100-41B	1931	
14.2	Ethelton		FPS	100-41B	1931	
20.4	Meskanaw		PORT	100-132	1931	
28.7	Yellow Creek		PORT	100-132	1931	
36.7	Tarnapol		FPS	100-41B	1931	
42.3	Reynaud		CN3rd	100-253	1931	
48.8	Lepine		FPS	100-41B	1931	
55.7	Wakaw Jct.					
64.6	Carpenter		FPS	100-41B	1931	
71.0	Alvena		CN3rd	100-253	1931	
78.8	Smuts		FPS	100-41B	1931	
83.6	Rak		FPS	100-41B	1931	

SASKATCHEWAN DISTRICT
Prince Albert Division

PADDOCKWOOD SUBDIVISION
near Prince Albert, Sk to Paddockwood, Sk—23.9 miles

Milepost	Locality	Proposed/Former Name	Type	Plan	Built	Notes
7.5	White Star	Joint with CPR	FPS	100-41B	1925	
15.6	Henribourg	Joint with CPR	CN3rd	100-197	1925	
23.9	Paddockwood		FPS	100-41B	1925	

ROBINHOOD SUBDIVISION
Speers, Sk to Turtleford, Sk—101.5 miles

Milepost	Locality	Proposed/Former Name	Type	Plan	Built	Notes
7.6	Keatley	x-Peacedale	FPS	100-41B	1929	
14.7	Alticane		FPS	100-41B	1929	
22.4	Mayfair		CN3rd	100-250	1929	
29.0	Mullingar		FPS	100-41B	1929	
36.4	Rabbit Lake	x-Roundstone	CN3rd	100-184	1928	Museum-1
42.2	Bournemouth		FPS	100-41B	1928	
50.5	Glenbush		FPS	100-41B	1928	
55.2	Medstead		CN3rd	100-184	1928	
61.0	Robinhood		FPS	100-41B	1928	
69.6	Glaslyn		CN3rd	100-184	1928	Museum-1
78.7	Fairholme		FPS	100-41B	1928	
86.6	Livelong		FPS	100-41B	1928	
96.2	Hartwell		FPS	100-41B	1928	

ST. BRIEUX SUBDIVISION
Thatch, Sk to Humboldt Jct., Sk—52.2 miles

Milepost	Locality	Proposed/Former Name	Type	Plan	Built	Notes
4.7	Lipsett	x-Pleasant Valley	FPS	100-41	1915	
12.4	Pathlow #1		FPS	100-41	1915	
12.4	Pathlow #2		3rd	100-72	1922	
19.5	St. Brieux #1		FPS	100-41	1915	
19.5	St. Brieux #2		3rd	100-72	1920	
28.8	Daylesford		FPS	100-41	1921	
37.6	Lake Lenore		3rd	100-72	1921	
44.7	Moseley		PORT	110-73A	—	SMBH

TISDALE SUBDIVISION
Hudson Bay Jct., Sk to near Prince Albert, Sk—157.7miles

Milepost	Locality	Proposed/Former Name	Type	Plan	Built	Notes
6.2	Veillardville		FPS	100-41B	1929	
13.6	Greenbush #1		CSS-SH	110-10	1902	
13.6	Greenbush #2		FPS		—	x-SMBH
25.6	Prairie River #1		FPS	100-96	1908	Probable
25.6	Prairie River #2		PORT	100-24	—	
25.6	Prairie River #3		3rd	100-72	1920	Museum-1
33.6	Bannock #1		CSS-SH	110-10	1909	
33.6	Bannock #2		FPS	100-41		
33.6	Bannock #3		FPS		1954	
41.5	Mistatim #1-A		FPS	100-41	—	
41.5	Mistatim #1-B		FPS		—	x-SMBH
51.4	Peesane #1	x-Midway?	CSS-SH	110-10	1903	Note 61
51.4	Peesane #2		FPS	100-41	1911	
59.2	Crooked River #1-A		PORT	100-24	1907	
59.2	Crooked River #1-B		FPS	110-159	—	x-SMBH
60.9	Murphy's #1	<<Crooked River>>	SHLT	100-95	By14	
60.9	Murphy's #2		CN3rd	100-250	1929	
63.1	Eldersley #1	x-Osgood	SHLT	100-95		
63.1	Eldersley #2		4th	100-68	1922	
72.8	Tisdale #1		3rd	100-3	1904	
72.8	Tisdale #2		SPEC.	100-412	1964	
78.3	Valparaiso #1		FPS	100-41	1916	
78.3	Valparaiso #2		4th	100-68	1920	
85.1	Star City		3rd	100-3	1904	
92.0	Naisberry	x-Wentworth	FPS	100-96	1906	
98.7	Melfort		3rd	100-19	1904	Variant
107.0	Beatty #1		FPS			
107.0	Beatty #2		3rd	100-72	1918	
117.4	Kinistino		3rd	100-3	1905	
123.5	Weldon #1		FPS	100-41	By12	
123.5	Weldon #2		3rd	100-72	1916	
128.5	Brancepeth #1		FPS	100-41		
128.5	Brancepeth #2		SPEC.	100-280	1935	
128.5	Brancepeth #3		FPS	100-41B	—	
135.7	Birch Hills		3rd	100-3	1905	
144.3	Fenton #1		PORT	100-24	1907	
144.3	Fenton #2	Joint with CPR	FPS	100-41	1914	
146.8	Senator	Joint with CPR	FPS		—	x-ST
151.8	Davis	Joint with CPR	FPS	100-96	1910	

TURTLEFORD SUBDIVISION
North Battleford, Sk to St. Walburg, Sk—77.0 miles

Milepost	Locality	Proposed/Former Name	Type	Plan	Built	Notes
7.5	Hamlin		FPS	100-41	1914	
10.9	Prinham		FPS	CB	1939	
14.4	Prince #1		FPS	100-41	1914	
14.4	Prince #2		CN4th	100-220	1928	Museum-2

SASKATCHEWAN DISTRICT
Prince Albert Division

TURTLEFORD SUBDIVISION
(continued)

Milepost	Locality	Proposed/Former Name	Type	Plan	Built	Notes
20.7	Meota		3rd	100-29	1910	Reverse
26.1	Cavalier		FPS	CB	1927	
31.0	Vawn	<<St. Hippolyte>>	3rd	100-29	1913	
38.4	Edam		3rd	100-29	1913	Museum-1
44.6	Dulwich	x-Longstaff	FPS	CB	1929	
49.7	Mervin		3rd	100-29	1914	Note 63
55.6	Turtleford		3rd	100-29	1914	Museum-2
62.7	Cleeves		FPS	100-41	1922	
68.5	Spruce Lake	<<Alamac>>	FPS	100-41	1922	
77.0	St. Walburg #1		PORT	110-73A	1921	SMBH
77.0	St. Walburg #2		4th	100-68	1922	

Regina Division

AVONLEA SUBDIVISION
near Radville, Sk to Moose Jaw, Sk—88.3 miles

Milepost	Locality	Proposed/Former Name	Type	Plan	Built	Notes
9.6	Abbott		FPS	100-41	1923	
14.4	Forward		3rd	100-29	1912	
23.0	Moreland		FPS	100-41	1913	
30.2	Parry #1		FPS	100-41	1913	
30.2	Parry #2		3rd	100-29	1916	
36.7	Dummer #1		PORT	100-24	1913	
36.7	Dummer #2		4th	100-68	1916	
43.1	Truax		3rd	100-29	1912	
52.2	Avonlea		3rd	100-29	1912	
59.2	Hearne #1		FPS	100-41	1913	
59.2	Hearne #2		4th	100-68	1917	
66.5	Briercrest		3rd	100-29	1912	
69.5	Levuka					
73.5	Tilney #1		FPS	100-41	1913	
73.5	Tilney #2		4th	100-68	1922	
78.1	Baildon		3rd	100-29	1913	
82.2	Antar	x-South Moose Jaw	FPS	100-41	1913	
87.7	Moose Jaw–CNoR #1	On Home St. South	SPEC.	100-57	1913	Temporary
87.7	Moose Jaw–CNoR #2		SPEC.	100-123	1918	
87.7	Moose Jaw–CNoR #3	Joint with GTP	SPEC	100-124	1919	

BENGOUGH SUBDIVISION
Radville, Sk to Willow Bunch, Sk—71.5 miles

Milepost	Locality	Proposed/Former Name	Type	Plan	Built	Notes
5.7	Brooking		3rd	100-29	1913	
15.7	Ceylon		3rd	100-29	1912	
21.7	Hardy #1		FPS	100-41	1913	
21.7	Hardy #2		4th	100-68	1918	
35.1	Ritchie		FPS	100-41	1916	
42.9	Bengough		3rd	100-29	1912	
48.9	Roncott	x-Harvester	FPS	100-41B	1926	
59.0	Harptree		FPS	100-41B	1926	
64.9	Gye		FPS	100-41B	1926	
71.5	Willow Bunch #1-A		PORT	100-73A	1926	
71.5	Willow Bunch #1-B		FPS	100-41B	1926	
71.5	Willow Bunch #2		CN3rd	100-216	1927	

BIENFAIT SUBDIVISION
Lampman, Sk to Estevan, Sk—25.1 miles

Milepost	Locality	Proposed/Former Name	Type	Plan	Built	Notes
7.6	Kingsford		FPS	100-41	1917	Note 77
16.3	Bienfait #1		FPS	100-41	1913	
16.3	Bienfait #2		3rd	100-72	1915	Note 77
25.1	Estevan		2nd	100-83	1915	Note 77

CENTRAL BUTTE SUBDIVISION
Regina, Sk to Dunblane, Sk—130.4 miles

Milepost	Locality	Proposed/Former Name	Type	Plan	Built	Notes
4.7	Sidmar		Type E	100-152	1913	
9.1	Adams		FPS	100-41	—	
12.2	Pattee		FPS	100-41B	1923	
16.9	Keystown		Type E	100-152	1913	
22.0	Stony Beach		Type E	100-152	1913	
28.1	Eastview #1		FPS		1915	
28.1	Eastview #2		FPS		—	
33.6	Burdick		Type E	100-152	1913	
39.8	Moose Jaw–GTP		PORT	110-101	1914	SMBH
45.9	Burt		PORT	110-101		Probable
52.0	Archydal		Type E	100-152	1913	
57.8	Grayburn	x-Forgray	Type E	100-152	1914	
63.4	Rowletta #1		FPS		1916	Temporary
63.4	Rowletta #2		FPS	CB	1940	
68.6	Lake Valley #1	x-Linstrom	Type E	100-152	1914	
68.6	Lake Valley #2		FPS	100-41B	—	Probable
74.2	Eskbank #1		FPS	CB		

SASKATCHEWAN DISTRICT
Regina Division

CENTRAL BUTTE SUBDIVISION
(continued)

Milepost	Locality	Proposed/Former Name	Type	Plan	Built	Notes
74.2	Eskbank #2		FPS	100-41B	1928	Probable
81.2	Darmody		Type E	100-152	1914	Reverse
86.1	Mawer #1		Type E	100-152	1913	
86.1	Mawer #2		CN3rd	100-197	1924	
92.3	Central Butte #1		FPS	CB		
92.3	Central Butte #2		Type F	100-151	1919	
99.5	Euclid	x-Thresher	FPS	100-41B	1927	
105.6	Grainland		FPS	100-41B	1927	
116.1	South Elbow	x-Ireton	CN3rd	100-197	1927	
124.7	Longacre		FPS	100-41B	1927	
130.4	Dunblane #1		FPS	100-41		
130.4	Dunblane #2		3rd	100-72	1917	

CORNING SUBDIVISION
near Kipling, Sk to Handsworth, Sk—22.3 miles

Milepost	Locality	Proposed/Former Name	Type	Plan	Built	Notes
8.2	Bemersyde		FPS	100-41B	1925	
14.4	Corning	x-St. Kilda	CN3rd	100-197	1925	
22.3	Handsworth		FPS	100-41B	1925	

CRAIK SUBDIVISION
Regina, Sk to Saskatoon, Sk—159.3 miles

Milepost	Locality	Proposed/Former Name	Type	Plan	Built	Notes
[0.0]	Regina	Union Station	SPEC.	100-58	1912	Notes 16, 22
[1.9]	North Regina-CNoR		FPS		1911	Notes 17, 22
7.4	Condie		3rd	100-29	1911	
12.2	Bredin		FPS	100-41	1922	
18.0	Lumsden #1		CSS-CPR	100-100	1890	Note 71
18.0	Lumsden #2		3rd	100-3	1908	
26.8	Disley		4th	100-31	1914	
35.1	Bethune		CSS-CPR	100-100	1890	Note 71
45.3	Findlater #1		FPS	100-96	1909	
45.3	Findlater #2		4th	100-31	1911	
54.0	Chamberlain		CSS-CPR	100-100	1890	Note 71
62.2	Aylsbury		4th	100-31	1910	
71.8	Craik		CSS-CPR	100-100	1890	Note 71
80.4	Girvin #2		3rd	100-29	1910	
88.6	Davidson #2		CP#5	100-110	1905	Notes 18, 71
98.4	Bladworth		3rd	100-29	1908	

NOTES:

4 This station was technically on the Saskatoon Terminals Subdivision.

16 With the Canadian Northern take-over of the Qu'Appelle Long Lake and Sakatchewan Railway in December 1906, it retained the joint station agreement between the CPR and QLL&S for use of the Regina depot and freight sheds. This station—the CPR's second depot at Regina—was replaced in 1912 by a "Union Station" built by the CPR for joint use and occupancy by the CNoR, and later the GTP, then subsequently the CNR. Only the 1912 station is included in the rosters. It is located on the CPR main line in downtown Regina on that company's Indian Head Subdivision. The station was subsequently acquired by VIA Rail Canada. It has since been sold, "restored" and redeveloped into a casino.

17 The CNoR constructed a temporary station adjacent to its Regina divisional yards in 1911. No description of this structure has been found. It was likely removed after the downtown CPR-CNoR Union station opened in 1912.

18 The first depot was actually built by the Qu'Appelle Long Lake and Sakatchewan Railway at a station named Finsbury, located two miles south of present day Davidson, was abandoned in 1905. As this CSS-CPR (#1) was removed prior to the acquisition of the QLL&S by the CNoR in 1906, it is not listed here.

22 This station was technically on the Regina Terminals Subdivision.

28 It appears that the apartment-office-waiting room portion of this building was converted into a section house, while the freight shed was relocated next to the new station (#2) and used as a baggage-express shed.

61 Reference to the station name Midway was found on Plan 110-10. Other stations listed on this drawing suggest that Midway was situated on the east end of the Tisdale Subdivision. Since Peesane is the approximate mid-point between Hudson Bay Jct. and Melfort, it may have formerly been known as Midway.

63 CNR records classify this as Plan 100-29, but it incorporates all the features of Plan 100-72.

71 This station was built by the Canadian Pacific Railway that operated the Qu'Appelle Long Lake and Saskatchewan Railway until 1906, when the line was acquired by the Canadian Northern Railway.

77 For clarity, the Lampman Subdivision is shown in its pre-1952 configuration: Maryfield to Radville. Flooding in the spring of 1948 knocked out three bridges in the Souris valley, closing the line between Blewett and Radville. The resulting stub lines were dubbed the Blewett (Lampman to Blewett) and Goodwater (Radville to Goodwater) subdivisions and train services were operated to the respective ends of track. CNR studies in 1951 determined it was uneconomic to rebuild the bridges and rebuild the closed stretch of rail line, so it was abandoned. Subsequently, the former Bienfait Subdivision (Lampman to Estevan) was incorporated into the south end of the Lampman Subdivision.

SASKATCHEWAN DISTRICT
Regina Division

CRAIK SUBDIVISION
(continued)

Milepost	Locality	Proposed/Former Name	Type	Plan	Built	Notes
104.6	Smales	x-Holder	FPS	100-41B	1923	
109.3	Kenaston		CSS-CPR	100-100	1890	Note 71
114.9	Strong		FPS	100-41	——	Note 19
120.7	Hanley #2		CP#5	100-110	1905	Notes 20, 71
129.6	Indi		FPS	100-41	1915	
134.8	Dundurn		CSS-CPR	100-100	1892	Note 71
141.1	Strehlow		FPS	100-41	1914	
145.7	Haultain		SHLT	100-95	1908	
150.6	Grasswood	x-Grindlay	FPS	100-41	——	Note 21
[157.2]	Saskatoon–Lorne Avenue		TOS	110-250	1951	Note 4
[159.3]	Saskatoon–CNoR #1		CSS-CP	100-100	1891	Notes 4, 71
[159.3]	Saskatoon–CNoR #2		SPEC.	100-33	1910	Note 4
[159.3]	Saskatoon–CNoR #3		SPEC.	100-288	1939	Notes 4, 54

GLENAVON SUBDIVISION
Kipling, Sk to McCallum Jct., Sk—91.8 miles

Milepost	Locality	Proposed/Former Name	Type	Plan	Built	Notes
6.0	Dalzell		PORT	100-24	1911	
12.3	Carlsberg		3rd	100-29		
14.4	Peebles	x-Kaiser	FPS	100-41B	1927	
17.5	Kegworth #1	x-Lovat	FPS	100-41	1911	Probable
17.5	Kegworth #2		FPS	100-41B	1926	
24.1	Glenavon		3rd	100-29	1911	
29.6	Candiac		4th	100-31	1913	
38.1	Montmartre		3rd	100-29		
46.0	Kendal #1		FPS	100-41		
46.0	Kendal #2		4th	100-31	1913	
54.0	Odessa		3rd	100-29	1913	
62.0	Vibank		3rd	100-29	1913	
69.9	Davin		3rd	100-29	1912	
78.1	Jameson		3rd	100-29	1914	
85.5	Dreghorn		FPS	100-41	1912	
	McCallum–CN Jct.–2nd site					
91.8	McCallum–CN Jct.–1st site		FPS	100-41B	1926	Note 22

GRAVELBOURG SUBDIVISION
near Avonlea, Sk to Swift Current, Sk—150.6 miles

Milepost	Locality	Proposed/Former Name	Type	Plan	Built	Notes
7.3	Claybank		FPS	100-41	1913	
10.4	Bayard		3rd	100-29	1913	
18.2	Spring Valley #1		FPS	100-41	1913	
18.2	Spring Valley #2		4th	100-68	1916	
27.2	Galilee		FPS	100-41	1916	
35.9	Mitchellton		3rd	100-29	1913	
42.6	Ardill #1		FPS	100-41	1913	
42.6	Ardill #2		4th	100-68	1923	
48.2	Mossbank		3rd	100-29	1913	
56.8	Ettington #1		FPS	100-41	1913	
56.8	Ettington #2		3rd	100-29	1914	
62.9	Mazenod		3rd	100-29	1913	
69.3	Palmer #1		FPS	100-41	1913	
69.3	Palmer #2		3rd	100-72	1917	
78.5	Gravelbourg		3rd	100-53	1913	Variant
85.7	Coppen		FPS	100-41	1923	
91.9	Bateman		4th	100-68	1923	
96.8	St. Boswells #1	x-Bellot	FPS	100-41	1923	
96.8	St. Boswells #2		4th	100-68	1923	
104.0	Hodgeville		3rd	100-72	1922	
112.2	Scottsburgh		FPS	100-41B	1925	
118.9	Neidpath		CN3rd	100-197	1925	
125	Roderickville					Note 33
132.6	Burnham					Note 33
138.1	Toppingham					Note 33
141.1	Friend					Note 33
150.6	Swift Current	Joint with CPR	CPR Station			Note 33

LAMPMAN SUBDIVISION
Maryfield, Sk to Radville, Sk—139.7 miles

Milepost	Locality	Proposed/Former Name	Type	Plan	Built	Notes
7.2	Ryerson		FPS	100-41	1912	
13.3	Mair		FPS	100-41	1910	Probable
19.9	Parkman		3rd	100-29	1910	
26.6	Service		FPS	100-41B	1924	
30.4	Cowper		FPS	100-41	1912	
37.3	Carlyle		3rd	100-29	1909	Museum-2
45.9	Wordsworth #1		FPS	100-41	1912	
45.9	Wordsworth #2		CN3rd	100-250	1929	
52.4	Willmar		3rd	100-29	1910	
60.3	Browning #1		FPS	100-41	1912	
60.3	Browning #2		SHLT		1917	
60.3	Browning #3		4th	100-68	1923	
67.4	Lampman		3rd	100-29	1910	Note 76

SASKATCHEWAN DISTRICT
Regina Division

LAMPMAN SUBDIVISION
(continued)

Milepost	Locality	Proposed/Former Name	Type	Plan	Built	Notes
76.2	Cullen		FPS	100-41	1916	
83.2	Bryant		FPS	100-41	1912	
[89.4]	Blewett		3rd	100-29	1911	Note 77
[97.4]	Chandler		3rd	100-29	1912	Note 77
[102.6]	Elswick	x-Lowell	FPS	CB	1937	Note 77
[111.7]	Goodwater		3rd	100-29	1911	Note 77
[120.3]	Colgate		3rd	100-29	1912	Upgrd to 100-72, Note 77
[127.0]	Dunning	x-Webster	3rd	100-29	1912	Note 77
[133.8]	Souris Valley		FPS	100-41	1913	Note 77
139.7	Radville		2nd	100-39	1912	Museum-1

LEWVAN SUBDIVISION
Lampman, Sk to North Regina, Sk—116.9 miles

Milepost	Locality	Proposed/Former Name	Type	Plan	Built	Notes
0.6	Minard		Type E	100-152	1913	
6.8	Woodley #1	x-Sander	FPS-1A	CB		
6.8	Woodley #2		FPS	100-41	——	
12.5	Benson	x-Hill Hall	Type E	100-152	1913	
24.7	Huntoon #1		Type E	100-152	1913	
24.7	Huntoon #2		SHLT	110-117	——	x-ST
30.5	Innes		PORT	110-101		SMBH
36.3	Griffin #1		Type E	100-152	1913	
36.3	Griffin #2		FPS		1921	Temporary
36.3	Griffin #3		3rd	100-72	1921	
49.4	Talmage		Type E	100-152	1913	
54.3	Worcester #1	x-Rainton	FPS-1B	100-162	1917	
54.3	Worcester #2		FPS	CB	1939	
61.0	Cedoux		Type E	100-152	1912	
68.1	Colfax #1		Type E	100-152	1913	
68.1	Colfax #2		CN3rd	100-250	1930	
74.2	Lewvan		Type E	100-152	1912	
80.6	Bechard #1	x-Lindley	FPS-1A	CB	1917	
80.6	Bechard #2		3rd	100-72	1921	
86.6	Riceton		Type E	100-152	1912	
93.6	Gray		Type E	100-152	1914	
100.4	Estlin		Type E	100-152	1912	
107.7	Rowatt		Type E	100-152	1912	
114.3	Regina–GTP	On Spur	SPEC.	110-131	1914	Notes 22, 39

MAIN CENTRE SUBDIVISION
Mawer, Sk to Main Centre, Sk—48.6 miles

Milepost	Locality	Proposed/Former Name	Type	Plan	Built	Notes
5.8	Kettlehut		FPS	CB	1931	
11.2	Thunder Creek		FPS	CB	1931	
16.8	Halvorgate		FPS	100-41C	1932	
22.2	Aquadell		FPS	CB	1930	
25.5	Calderbank		FPS	100-41C	1932	
32.4	Glen Kerr		FPS	100-41C	1930	
37.6	Teakle		FPS	100-41C	1930	
42.7	Gouldtown		FPS	100-41C	1930	
48.6	Main Centre		FPS	100-41C	1932	

NORTHGATE SUBDIVISION
Northgate, Sk to Lampman, Sk—39.4 miles

Milepost	Locality	Proposed/Former Name	Type	Plan	Built	Notes
0.2	Northgate		SPEC.	100-164	1914	
3.6	Elcott		Type E	100-152	1912	
7.2	Souris River		FPS	CB		
13.3	Openshaw		Type E	100-152	1913	
19.1	Frobisher		Type E	100-152	1913	
29.3	Steelman		Type E	100-152	1913	
34.4	Breeze					

QU'APPELLE SUBDIVISION
Meville, Sk to North Regina, Sk—95.4 miles

Milepost	Locality	Proposed/Former Name	Type	Plan	Built	Notes
6.7	Colmer		Type E	100-152	1911	
12.2	Duff		Type E	100-152	1913	Museum-2
17.6	Finnie		Type E	100-152	1910	
21.2	Lorlie #1		FPS-1A	CB	1915	
21.2	Lorlie #2		Type G	100-168	1920	
26.8	Gillespie		Type E	100-152	1910	
32.7	Balcarres #1		SPEC.	100-157	1910	
32.7	Balcarres #2		CN3rd	100-253	1932	
42.0	Lebret		Type E	100-152	1911	
46.4	Fort Qu'Appelle		Type E	100-152	1911	Museum-1
52.5	Muscow		Type E	100-152	1911	
61.2	Edgeley		Type E	100-152	1911	
66.9	Avonhurst #1		FPS-1A	CB	1914	
66.9	Avonhurst #2		Type G	100-168	1920	
72.4	Edenwold		Type E	100-152	1911	
78.1	Frankslake #1	x-Frank's Lake	FPS-1A	CB	1916	

SASKATCHEWAN DISTRICT
Regina Division

QU'APPELLE SUBDIVISION
(continued)

Milepost	Locality	Proposed/Former Name	Type	Plan	Built	Notes
78.1	Frankslake #2		FPS			SMBH
82.6	Zehner #1		Type E	100-152	1911	
82.6	Zehner #2		SPEC.	100-142	1921	Similar to 100-143
88.6	Victoria Plains	x-Mulcahey	Type E	100-152	1911	
95.4	North Regina–GTP	x-West Yard	TOS			Note 22

RIVERHURST SUBDIVISION
Central Butte, Sk to Riverhurst, Sk—18.0 miles

Milepost	Locality	Proposed/Former Name	Type	Plan	Built	Notes
7.0	Lawson #1		FPS-1A	CB	1914	
7.0	Lawson #2		Type F	100-151	1919	
12.1	Gilroy #1		FPS		By15	Temporary
12.1	Gilroy #2		Type G	100-168	1919	
18.0	Riverhurst		Type F	100-151	1917	

WEYBURN SUBDIVISION
Talmage, Sk to Radville, Sk—38.2 miles

Milepost	Locality	Proposed/Former Name	Type	Plan	Built	Notes
6.7	Mansur #1		FPS	CB		
6.7	Mansur #2		SHLT			x-PH
13.2	Weyburn #1-A	On spur	PORT	110-101	1914	SMBH
13.2	Weyburn #1-B	On spur	FPS	CB		
13.2	Weyburn #2	On spur	SPEC.	100-238	1928	
22.0	Grassdale		FPS	100-41B	1928	
28.5	Cleardale		FPS	100-41B	1928	

Saskatoon Division

ASQUITH SUBDIVISION
Watrous, Sk to Biggar, Sk—118.2 miles

Milepost	Locality	Proposed/Former Name	Type	Plan	Built	Notes
6.3	Xena		Type E	100-152	1911	
13.9	Young		Type E	100-152	1911	
22.5	Zelma		Type E	100-152	1911	
29.7	Allan		Type D	100-154	1909	
38.2	Bradwell #1		Type D	100-154	1909	Probable
38.2	Bradwell #2		Type E	100-152	1910	
45.3	Clavet		Type E	100-152	1911	
52.2	Duro		Type E	100-152	1911	
57.0	Newcross		TOS		1929	Note 4
58.2	South Saskatoon #1	x-Earl	Type D	100-154	1909	Notes 3, 4
58.2	South Saskatoon #2		TOS			Note 4
58.6	Nutana		TOS		1905	Note 4
61.9	Chappell		TOS			Note 4
62.8	Saskatoon–CNR		SPEC.	100-419	1964	Note 4
66.3	Farley		Type E	100-152	1911	
73.3	Grandora		Type E	100-152	1911	
78.0	Hawoods #1		Type E	100-152	1911	
78.0	Hawoods #2		FPS		1920	
83.4	Asquith #1	x-Iwana	Type E	100-152	By15	
83.4	Asquith #2		Type F	100-151	1918	
88.5	Juniata		Type E	100-152	1911	
93.0	Kinley		Type D	100-154	1909	
99.0	Leney		Type D	100-154	1910	
106.2	Mead #1		FPS-1B	100-162	1908	
106.2	Mead #2		Type F	100-151	1917	
109.5	Cazalet		SHLT	150-53		x-PH
111.2	Neola #1		SHLT	150-53		x-PH
111.2	Neola #2		FPS		1930	
118.2	Biggar		SPEC.	100-155	1909	

BEECHY SUBDIVISION
near Dunblane, Sk to Beechy, Sk—34.7 miles

Milepost	Locality	Proposed/Former Name	Type	Plan	Built	Notes
8.4	Birsay		4th	100-68	1920	
13.3	Tullis		FPS	100-41	1921	
19.5	Lucky Lake		3rd	100-72	1923	
24.3	Dudley		FPS	100-41	1922	
28.6	Demaine	x-Scapa	4th	100-68	1922	
34.7	Beechy #1		FPS	100-41	1921	
34.7	Beechy #2		4th	100-68	1923	

CONQUEST SUBDIVISION
near Deslisle, Sk to Dunblane, Sk—59.3 miles

Milepost	Locality	Proposed/Former Name	Type	Plan	Built	Notes
4.3	Chambers		FPS	100-41	1912	
8.0	Donovan #1	x-Birdview	FPS	100-41	1913	
8.0	Donovan #2		3rd	100-72	1917	
16.2	Swanson		3rd	100-29	1912	
22.8	Ardath		3rd	100-29	1912	
29.4	Conquest		3rd	100-29	1912	
33.4	Denny	x-Druse	FPS	CB	1939	
38.8	Bratton		FPS	100-41	1912	
45.7	Macrorie		3rd	100-29	1912	

SASKATCHEWAN DISTRICT
Saskatoon Division

DODSLAND SUBDIVISION
near Biggar, Sk to Hemaruka, Ab—154.0 miles

Milepost	Locality	Proposed/Former Name	Type	Plan	Built	Notes
6.0	Argo		Type E	100-152	1913	
12.2	Duperow #1	x-Lydden	FPS		1915	Temporary
12.2	Duperow #2		Type F	100-151	1919	
18.5	Springwater		Type E	100-152	1913	
25.6	Ruthilda		Type E	100-152	1913	
35.9	Ava	x-Fort	Type E	100-152	1913	
43.0	Wallisville		FPS		1913	
47.0	Dodsland #1		Type E	100-152	1913	
47.0	Dodsland #2		CN4A	100-315	1948	Variant
53.3	Millerdale		Type E	100-152	1913	
59.7	Beaufield #1		Type E	100-152	1913	
59.7	Beaufield #2		SHLT			x-PH
66.4	Coleville		Type E	100-152	1913	
72.6	Driver		FPS-1B	100-162	1920	
78.5	Smiley		Type E	100-152	1913	
85.9	Dewar Lake #1		FPS		By15	
85.9	Dewar Lake #2		Type F	100-151	1920	
90.4	Hoosier	x-Fee	Type E	100-152	1913	
96.5	Greene		FPS-1A	CB	1914	
103.5	Loverna, Sk		Type E	100-152	1913	
110.5	Calthorpe, Ab	x-Holt	FPS	100-41B	1926	
115.7	Esther		FPS	100-41B	1926	
120.8	Anatole		FPS	100-41B	1927	
126.3	New Brigden #1		FPS	100-41B	1926	
126.3	New Brigden #2		CN3rd	100-197	1927	
134.0	Sedalia #1		FPS	100-41B	1926	
134.0	Sedalia #2		CN4th	100-252	1930	
140.3	Naco		FPS	100-41B	1927	
148.3	Little Gem		FPS	100-41B	1927	
154.0	Hemaruka		CN3rd	100-227	1927	

NOTES:

3 In 1927 the freight shed was converted into a dwelling for the coalman, while the balance of the depot was relocated to Nutana and converted into a section house.

4 This station was technically on the Saskatoon Terminals Subdivision.

19 The sources regarding the disposition of this station are contradictory. One states that it was relocated to McBride, BC, the other says it was moved to Redpass Jct., BC.

20 The original site of Hanley station grounds was about three miles north of its present location.

21 The sources regarding the disposition of this station are contradictory. One record indicates that both buildings were moved to Redpass Jct., BC while another source states that they were both relocated to McBride, BC.

22 This station was technically on the Regina Terminals Subdivision.

33 The stretch between Neidpath and Swift Current was operated on a sporadic basis until abandoned in September 1958. Standard freight and passenger shelters (CNR Plan 100-41B) are noted on the respective station grounds plans as "Shelter Site", therefore it appears that these shelters may not have been constructed and are thus excluded from this listing. The CNR had a Union Station agreement with the CPR to use that company's Swift Current depot.

39 This temporary station—opened at 16th and Albert streets in 1912—was a recycled residence, renovated to provide a waiting room and ticket and administrative offices. The station facilities were consolidated in 1920 with those of the CNoR and CPR, at the Union Depot. The GTP's Regina station was subsequently closed. In 1924 it was converted into a residence for the CNR Divisional Superintendent. The building was later sold and used as a boys' home. It survived until at least 1961.

54 In 1964, a new passenger station was established near the northwestern outskirts of the city in Chappell Yards. The former downtown station building was used by CNR as an office building until 1969. Once it was vacated, the building was razed and the site was re-developed.

71 This station was built by the Canadian Pacific Railway that operated the Qu'Appelle Long Lake and Saskatchewan Railway until 1906, when the line was acquired by the Canadian Northern Railway.

76 The second storey was removed, circa 1941, rendering it unrecognizable as a 3rd Class station.

77 For clarity, the Lampman Subdivision is shown in its pre-1952 configuration: Maryfield to Radville. Flooding in the spring of 1948 knocked out three bridges in the Souris valley, closing the line between Blewett and Goodwater. The resulting stub lines were dubbed the Blewett (Lampman to Blewett) and Goodwater (Radville to Goodwater) subdivisions and train services were operated to the respective ends of track. CNR studies in 1951 determined it was uneconomic to rebuild the bridges and rebuild the closed stretch of rail line, so it was abandoned. Subsequently, the former Bienfait Subdivision (Lampman to Estevan) was incorporated into the south end of the Lampman Subdivision.

SASKATCHEWAN DISTRICT
Saskatoon Division

ELROSE SUBDIVISION
Dunblane, Sk to Kindersley, Sk—120.7 miles

Milepost	Locality	Proposed/Former Name	Type	Plan	Built	Notes
0.6	Tichfield #1	x-Lyons	FPS	100-41	1918	
0.6	Tichfield #2		FPS	100-320	1949	
4.7	Juniper		FPS	100-41	1913	
11.7	Surbiton		FPS	100-41	1913	
15.9	Anerley #1		FPS	100-41	1913	
15.9	Anerley #2		CN4th	100-252	1930	
22.3	Dinsmore		3rd	100-29	1913	
31.3	Wiseton		3rd	100-29	1913	
38.7	Forgan		3rd	100-29	1913	
44.2	Hughton		3rd	100-75	1914	
49.8	Elrose		3rd	100-29	1913	
57.2	Wartime		3rd	100-72	1915	
62.4	Greenan		FPS	100-41	1915	
70.0	Plato		3rd	100-72	1915	
76.9	Richlea		3rd	100-72	1915	
84.4	Eston #1		3rd	100-72	1915	
84.4	Eston #2		FPS	110-159	——	x-SMBH
91.0	Snipe Lake		3rd	100-72	1917	
97.7	Madison		3rd	100-72	1917	
104.2	Glidden		3rd	100-72	1918	
109.8	Sandgren		FPS	100-41B	1929	
112.4	Inglenook		FPS	100-41B	1929	
116.3	Verendrye		FPS	100-41B	1929	

MINIOTA SUBDIVISION
Rivers, Mb to Melville, Sk—137.1 miles

Milepost	Locality	Proposed/Former Name	Type	Plan	Built	Notes
5.8	Myra #1		Type E	100-152	1911	
5.8	Myra #2		FPS	100-41B	1931	
9.8	Norman		Type E	100-152	1911	
16.2	Oakner		Type E	100-152	1911	
22.5	Pope #1		Type D	100-154	1909	
22.5	Pope #2		FPS	110-117	——	x-ST
28.6	Quadra	x-Arrow River	Type E	100-152	1911	
34.2	Rea		FPS	CB		
36.7	Miniota #1		Type E	100-152	1912	
36.7	Miniota #2		FPS	CB	——	x-SMBH
43.7	Uno #1		FPS-2	100-153	1907	
43.7	Uno #2		FPS-2	100-153	1910	
51.2	Treat		FPS	CB	1936	
55.5	Wattsview					
61.3	St. Lazare	x-Lazare	Type D	100-154	1909	
66.8	Victor, Mb		FPS			
74.8	Welby, Sk #1		FPS-1B	100-173	1910	
74.8	Welby, Sk #2		STA	100-307	1946	
82.4	Spy Hill #1		Type E	100-152	1910	
82.4	Spy Hill #2		SPEC.	100-187	——	Note 47
88.9	Gerald		Type E	100-152	1911	
95.8	Yarbo #1		Type E	100-152	1911	
95.8	Yarbo #2		SHLT		1934	
95.8	Yarbo #3		SPEC.	100-392	1960	
101.9	Zeneta #1		Type E	100-152	1911	
101.9	Zeneta #2		CN3rd	100-184	1928	
109.6	Atwater #1		Type D	100-154	1909	
109.6	Atwater #2		FPS		——	
115.1	Bangor		Type E	100-152	1913	
123.2	Waldron		Type E	100-152	1910	
129.4	Cana #1		Type E	100-152	1911	
129.4	Cana #2		FPS		——	
137.1	Melville		SPEC.	100-156	1908	

PORTER SUBDIVISION
Oban, Sk to Battleford, Sk—48.2 miles

Milepost	Locality	Proposed/Former Name	Type	Plan	Built	Notes
5.8	Lett		Type E	100-152	1913	
11.4	Salter		FPS-1A	CB	1914	
17.5	Cando		Type E	100-152	1913	
23.6	Red Pheasant #1		FPS	CB?		
23.6	Red Pheasant #2		FPS	CB	1950	
31.9	Ibstone	x-Charlton	Type E	100-152	1913	
43.0	Dacer #1		Type E	100-152	1913	
43.0	Dacer #2		FPS	CB	1941	
48.2	Battleford-GTP		SPEC.	100-157	1912	

ROSETOWN SUBDIVISION
Saskatoon, Sk to Kindersley, Sk—123.2 miles

Milepost	Locality	Proposed/Former Name	Type	Plan	Built	Notes
4.5	Hawker	x-Eaton-1st	PORT	110-73A	1914	SMBH
14.2	Vanscoy #1		FPS	100-41	By11	
14.2	Vanscoy #2		3rd	100-29	1912	
23.0	Delisle		3rd	100-29	1908	
31.1	Laura #1		SHLT	100-95	1908	

SASKATCHEWAN DISTRICT
Saskatoon Division

ROSETOWN SUBDIVISION
(continued)

Milepost	Locality	Proposed/Former Name	Type	Plan	Built	Notes
31.1	Laura #2		4th	100-31	1911	
38.2	Tessier		3rd	100-29	1908	
41.8	Kinhop		FPS	100-41	——	
46.8	Harris		3rd	100-29	1909	
48.9	Crystal Beach		SHLT		1927	
52.4	Brisbin		FPS	100-41	——	Museum-2
57.5	Zealandia		3rd	100-29	1908	
63.6	Pym		FPS	100-41	1915	
69.0	Rosetown		3rd	100-29	1909	
75.7	Ridpath #1		3rd	100-29	1910	
75.7	Ridpath #2		FPS	100-41B	1925	
81.7	McGee #1		FPS			
81.7	McGee #2		3rd	100-29	1913	
89.0	Fiske		3rd	100-29	1910	
95.2	D'Arcy #1		FPS	100-41	1915	
95.2	D'Arcy #2		4th	100-68	1916	
103.6	Brock		3rd	100-29	1909	
110.1	Netherhill		3rd	100-29	1910	Museum-2
116.2	Beadle #1		FPS	100-41	By12	
116.2	Beadle #2		4th	100-68	1916	
123.2	Kindersley #1		PORT	CB	1910	Temporary
123.2	Kindersley #2		FPS	100-96	1910	Variant, Temporary
123.2	Kindersley #3		2nd	100-39	1910	

TOUCHWOOD SUBDIVISION
Melville, Sk to Watrous, Sk—129.0 miles

Milepost	Locality	Proposed/Former Name	Type	Plan	Built	Notes
6.6	Birmingham		Type E	100-152	1911	
12.1	Fenwood		Type E	100-152	1911	
18.8	Goodeve		Type D	100-154	1909	
28.4	Hubbard		Type E	100-152	1911	
34.5	Ituna		Type E	100-152	1911	
42.0	Jasmin		Type E	100-152	1911	
46.8	Kelliher		Type D	100-154	1909	
52.7	Leross		Type E	100-152	1911	
58.0	Lestock	x-Mostyn	Type E	100-152	1911	
65.7	Touchwood		SPEC.	100-298	1943	
72.5	Punnichy		Type D	100-154	1909	
77.6	Quinton #1		Type E	100-152	1911	
77.6	Quinton #2		Type F	100-151	1918	
82.9	Raymore #1		Type D	100-154	1907	
82.9	Raymore #2		FPS	CB	1919	Temporary
82.9	Raymore #3		Type G	100-168	1921	
92.2	Semans		Type D	100-154	1909	
97.2	Tate		Type E	100-152	1911	
106.2	Nokomis		NTR1	100-160	1908	Museum-2
114.1	Undora		Type E	100-152	1911	
120.7	Venn #1		Type D	100-154	1907	
120.7	Venn #2		Type G	100-168	1924	
129.0	Watrous		SPEC.	100-155	1909	

WHITE BEAR SUBDIVISION
Eston, Sk to White Bear, Sk—34.3 miles

Milepost	Locality	Proposed/Former Name	Type	Plan	Built	Notes
4.8	Witley		FPS	100-41B	1927	
10.2	Isham		FPS	100-41B	1927	
18.7	Tyner		FPS	100-41B	1927	
24.2	Lacadena		CN3rd	100-227	1927	
34.3	White Bear		CN3rd	100-227	1927	

ALBERTA DISTRICT
Calgary Division

ACADIA VALLEY SUBDIVISION
Eyre, Sk to Acadia Valley, Ab—23.5 miles

Milepost	Locality	Proposed/Former Name	Type	Plan	Built	Notes
7.7	Cuthbert, Sk	x-Magiddo	FPS	100-41B	1927	
16.1	Arneson, Ab		FPS	100-41B	1927	
23.5	Acadia Valley		CN3rd	100-227	1927	

BRAZEAU SUBDIVISION
Alix, Ab to Brazeau, Ab—149.9 miles

Milepost	Locality	Proposed/Former Name	Type	Plan	Built	Notes
4.1	Coghill					
10.0	Haynes #1		3rd	100-29	1913	
10.0	Haynes #2		FPS	110-73	——	x-SMBH
17.2	Joffre		FPS	100-41	1916	
22.3	Prentiss		3rd	100-29	1912	
35.1	Burbank		FPS	100-41	1915	
43.7	Briggs	x-Tannis	FPS	100-41	1919	
47.2	Prevo		FPS	100-41		
51.5	Sylvan Lake		3rd	100-29	1913	
57.7	Elspeth		3rd	100-29	1913	

ALBERTA DISTRICT
Calgary Division

BRAZEAU SUBDIVISION
(continued)

Milepost	Locality	Proposed/Former Name	Type	Plan	Built	Notes
65.7	Eckville		3rd	100-29	1912	
72.7	Withrow		FPS	100-41		
77.0	Leslieville		3rd	100-29	1913	
85.4	Codner		FPS	100-41	1920	
89.8	Lodge	Joint with CPR				
91.1	Otway	Joint with CPR				
91.2	Rocky Mountain House		Joint with CPR			
93.9	Lochearn	Joint with CPR				
95.4	Ullin	Joint with CPR				
98.5	Ferrier		FPS	100-41		
108.6	Horburg		FPS	100-41	1918	
115.6	Phoenix		FPS	CB		
119.2	Lamoral					
126.4	Ancona	x-Pollock	FPS	100-41		
131.8	Saunders		FPS	100-41	1918	
133.1	West Saunders					
134.9	Alexo	x-Stolberg	FPS	100-41B	1924	
142.5	Harlech					
149.6	Brazeau #1-A	x-Nordegg	3rd	100-29	1914	
149.6	Brazeau #1-B		FPS	100-41	—	

DRUMHELLER SUBDIVISION
Hanna, Ab to Calgary, Ab—136.8 miles

Milepost	Locality	Proposed/Former Name	Type	Plan	Built	Notes
7.7	Watts		FPS	100-41	1913	
14.5	Craigmyle #2		3rd	100-72	1916	
21.9	Delia		3rd	100-29	1913	
29.9	Michichi #1	x-Mecheche	FPS	100-41	1913	
29.9	Michichi #2		3rd	100-72	1924	
32.9	Gartly		FPS	100-41	1913	
40.3	Dinosaur	x-Munson Jct.	FPS	100-41	1921	Note 25
41.1	Munson		3rd	100-29	1912	
49.8	Midland					
52.4	Drumheller #1		3rd	100-29	1912	
52.4	Drumheller #2			170-2	1915	Note 26
56.8	Rosedale #1		FPS	100-41	1913	
56.8	Rosedale #2		4th	100-68	1919	
56.8	Rosedale #3		PORT	100-73A	—	SMBH
60.4	Wayne #1	x-Rosedeer	FPS	100-41	1913	
60.4	Wayne #2-A		4th	100-68	1918	
60.4	Wayne #2-B		PORT	110-73A	1919	SMBH
68.2	Beynon		FPS	100-41	1915	
76.4	Rosebud #1		FPS	100-41	1913	
76.4	Rosebud #2		3rd	100-72	1919	
79.0	Redland #1		FPS	100-41	1915	
79.0	Redland #2		3rd	100-72	1921	
87.1	Rockyford		3rd	100-29	1913	
93.5	Baintree		FPS	100-41	1915	
96.5	Dunshalt		FPS	100-41	1922	
96.6	Nightingale		PORT	110-73A	1922	SMBH
102.9	Ardenode #1		3rd	100-29	1913	
102.9	Ardenode #2		FPS			
111.1	Lyalta		3rd	100-29	1913	
118.3	Norfolk		FPS	100-41	1915	
[124.3]	Chestermere Lake		SPEC.	100-51	1913	
126.6	Janet		FPS	100-41	1916	
130.7	Barlow		FPS	100-41	1915	
132.2	Barlow Jct.		PORT	110-73A	1921	SMBH, Reverse
134.1	Macleod Jct.		FPS	100-41	—	
136.6	Calgary–CNoR #1			100-56	1914	Temporary
136.6	Calgary–CNoR #2		SPEC.	100-91	1916	Note 27

ENDIANG SUBDIVISION
Hanna, Ab to Alix, Ab—85.2 miles

Milepost	Locality	Proposed/Former Name	Type	Plan	Built	Notes
10.9	Dowling		FPS	100-41B	1926	
18.2	Scapa		FPS	100-41B	1926	
28.0	Endiang		CN3rd	100-227	1927	
34.3	Byemoor		CN3rd	100-197	1927	
40.2	Leo		FPS	100-41B	1927	
47.3	Hackett		FPS	100-41B	1927	
55.6	Sabine		FPS	100-41B	1927	
70.4	Oberlin		FPS	100-41	—	
75.4	Nevis		3rd	100-29	1912	
[83.1]	Troon		FPS	100-41		Probable
[85.2]	Alix–CNoR		3rd	100-29	1912	Note 59

ALBERTA DISTRICT
Calgary Division

MANTARIO SUBDIVISION
Glidden, Sk to Alsask, Sk—44.1 miles

Milepost	Locality	Proposed/Former Name	Type	Plan	Built	Notes
5.4	Dankin		FPS	100-41B	1923	
10.1	Eatonia #1	x-Eaton-2nd	PORT	110-73A	1922	SMBH
10.1	Eatonia #2		3rd	100-199	1924	Variant, Museum-1
16.4	Laporte		4th	100-68	1920	
25.6	Mantario		3rd	100-72	1920	
31.5	Eyre		4th	100-68	1920	
39.3	Hardene		FPS	100-41	1920	

OYEN SUBDIVISION
Kindersley, Sk to Hanna, Ab—136.4 miles

Milepost	Locality	Proposed/Former Name	Type	Plan	Built	Notes
8.3	Fairmount #2		4th	100-68	1917	
8.3	Fairmount #3		FPS	100-41B	—	
15.0	Pinkham #1		FPS	100-41	By14	
15.0	Pinkham #2		4th	100-68	1915	
22.6	Flaxcombe	x-Harwell	3rd	100-29	1912	
30.9	Marengo		3rd	100-29	1911	
36.8	Merid #1		FPS	100-41	1910	
36.8	Merid #2		3rd	100-72	1918	
44.0	Alsask, Sk		3rd	100-29	1911	
50.9	Sibbald, Ab #1		PORT	110-73A	1913	
50.9	Sibbald, Ab #2		3rd	100-72	1917	
60.7	Benton #1		FPS	100-41	1913	
60.7	Benton #2		3rd	100-72	1918	
66.7	Oyen		3rd	100-29	1913	
71.4	Excel #1		FPS	100-41	1913	
71.4	Excel #2		3rd	100-72	1917	
77.0	Lanfine #1		FPS	100-41		
77.0	Lanfine #2		3rd	100-72	1918	
83.0	Cereal		3rd	100-29	1913	
88.8	Chinook		3rd	100-29	1913	
97.2	Dobson #1		FPS	100-41	1913	
97.2	Dobson #2		FPS	100-41B	1924	
102.3	Youngstown		3rd	100-29	1913	
108.3	Scotfield		FPS	100-41	1913	
116.2	Stanmore #1		FPS	100-41	1913	
116.2	Stanmore #2		4th	100-68	1917	
120.7	Richdale		3rd	100-29	1913	
127.2	Alness		FPS	100-41		
131.1	Bonar		FPS	100-41	1913	
136.4	Hanna		2nd	100-39	1913	

RED DEER SPUR
North Jct., Ab to Red Deer, Ab—9.9 miles

Milepost	Locality	Proposed/Former Name	Type	Plan	Built	Notes
0.8	North Jct.		PORT	110-101	—	x-SMBH
9.9	Red Deer #1		CN3rd	100-148	1923	Variant
9.9	Red Deer #2		STA	170-154	1961	FT

SHEERNESS SUBDIVISION
near Bonar, Ab to Steveville, Ab—58.9 miles

Milepost	Locality	Proposed/Former Name	Type	Plan	Built	Notes
6.1	Taplow		FPS	100-41	1920	
11.4	Sheerness		3rd	100-72	1920	
16.9	Rose Lynn		FPS	100-41	1922	
20.0	Halliday		FPS	100-41	—	
25.6	Sunnynook	x-Konowall	4th	100-68	1920	
31.1	Carolside		FPS	100-41	1920	
39.2	Pollockville #1		FPS	100-41	1920	
39.2	Pollockville #2		3rd	100-72	1920	Museum-2

NOTES:

25 A train-order station was set up at this junction by late 1921. The former scale house from Drumheller was joined to a Standard FPS north of the junction switch. The shelter building was converted into living quarters and the scale house into a telegraph office, complete with order-board. This arrangement lasted until May 1927, after which all operating was handled out of the nearby Munson depot. The train-order station was removed, replaced by a register booth.

26 Following the demolition of the station at Drumheller, the nearby freight shed office was occupied by the agent and used as the ad hoc station.

27 The St. Mary's Hall was constructed in 1894. The CNoR obtained an option on the property in 1911, but did not take over the building until 1914. Conversion into a railway depot was completed in 1916.

47 This was originally constructed as a telegraph repeater station in 1928. It was converted into a section house in 1951, and then into a station after the original depot was razed by fire in 1960.

59 Following trackage changes on the Brazeau Subdivision, this station was abandoned on site in 1922. The west end of the Endiang Subdivision was subsequently extended to include a portion of the Brazeau Subdivision. This depot was relocated to the GTP station grounds in 1927.

ALBERTA DISTRICT
Calgary Division

SHEERNESS SUBDIVISION
(continued)

Milepost	Locality	Proposed/Former Name	Type	Plan	Built	Notes
46.3	Cessford		4th	100-68	1920	
53.6	Wardlow		FPS	100-41	1921	
[58.9]	Steveville		4th	100-68	1921	Note 55

SPONDIN SUBDIVISION
Scapa, Ab to Spondin, Ab—17.7 miles

Milepost	Locality	Proposed/Former Name	Type	Plan	Built	Notes
[160.9]	Ballenden		FPS	100-41B	1932	Note 79
178.3	Spondin		FPS	100-41B	1930	
187.1	Garden Plain		FPS	100-41B	1930	
170.6	Whatcher		FPS	100-41B	1930	

STETTLER SUBDIVISION
Ferlow Jct., Ab to Dinosaur Jct., Ab —108.0 miles

Milepost	Locality	Proposed/Former Name	Type	Plan	Built	Notes
5.3	Viewpoint	x-White's Siding	3rd	100-29	1910	
12.3	Edberg		3rd	100-29	1910	
21.2	Meeting Creek	<<Edenville>>	3rd	100-29	1912	Museum-1
30.9	Donalda #1	<<Wallace>>	3rd	100-29	1911	
30.9	Donalda #2		4th	100-31	—	Museum-2, Note 23
40.4	Red Willow		3rd	100-29	1910	
45.4	Leahurst		FPS	100-41	1918	
50.9	Stettler		2nd	100-39	1911	Museum-2
55.8	Warden #1		4th	100-68	1915	
55.8	Warden #2		3rd	100-72	1919	
64.3	Fenn		FPS	100-41	1916	
72.1	Big Valley		2nd	100-39	1912	Museum-1
79.9	Scollard		3rd	100-29	1911	
86.8	Rumsey		3rd	100-29	1912	
92.9	Rowley #1		FPS	100-41	1915	
92.9	Rowley #2		3rd	100-72	1922	Museum-1
100.4	Morrin		3rd	100-29	1912	

THREE HILLS SUBDIVISION
Mirror, Ab to Calgary-GTP, Ab—130.4 miles

Milepost	Locality	Proposed/Former Name	Type	Plan	Built	Notes
6.1	Alix–GTP #1		Type E	100-152	1911	Note 60
6.1	Alix–GTP #2		3rd	100-29	—	Note 59
11.3	Heatburg	x-Bullocksville	FPS	CB	1927	
16.3	Ardley		Type E	100-152	1911	
21.4	Delburne		Type E	100-152	1912	Museum-2
27.9	Lousana #1		Type E	100-152	1912	
27.9	Lousana #2		FPS			
37.8	Elnor	x-Perbeck	Type E	100-152	1911	
43.4	Huxley		Type E	100-152	1913	
50.4	Trochu #1		Type E	100-152	1912	
50.4	Trochu #2		SPEC.	100-365	1959	
53.8	Equity	x-Ghost Pine				
60.2	Three Hills #1		Type E	100-152	1912	
60.2	Three Hills #2		Type F	100-151	1919	Museum-2
66.9	Twining		SHLT			
73.2	Swalwell		Type E	100-152	1912	
79.4	Grainger #1		SHLT			
79.4	Grainger #2		Type F	100-151	1919	
79.4	Grainger #3		STA		1928	Temporary
85.0	Bircham		Type E	100-152	1912	
91.9	Beiseker	x-Bartle	Type E	100-152	1913	
97.5	Irricana		Type E	100-152	1911	
106.5	Kathyrn #1		SHLT			
106.5	Kathyrn #2		CN3rd	100-184	1928	
111.9	Delacour		Type E	100-152	1913	
117.7	Conrich		SHLT			
123.3	Hubalta		Type F	100-151	1913	
130.4	Calgary–GTP		STA		1914	Temporary

Edmonton Division

ALLIANCE SUBDIVISION
Camrose, Ab to Alliance, Ab—59.3 miles

Milepost	Locality	Proposed/Former Name	Type	Plan	Built	Notes
8.1	Kiron		FPS	100-41		
16.3	Kelsey #1		CSS-C	100-47	1916	
16.3	Kelsey #2		FPS		—	
22.4	Rosalind		FPS	100-41	—	
29.0	Ankerton		FPS	100-41	—	
34.7	Heisler		CSS-C	100-47	1916	
43.8	Forestburg		CSS-C	100-47	1916	
51.2	Galahad		CSS-C	100-47	1916	
59.3	Alliance		3rd	100-72	1916	

ALBERTA DISTRICT
Edmonton Division

ATHABASCA SUBDIVISION
St. Albert, Ab to Athabasca, Ab—84.8 miles

Milepost	Locality	Proposed/Former Name	Type	Plan	Built	Notes
[6.9]	Volmer		FPS	100-41	1913	Note 5
12.9	Morinville		3rd	100-3	1906	
18.4	Peavey		SHLT		1945	
23.3	Legal #1		SHLT	100-95	1912	
23.3	Legal #2		FPS	100-41	1917	
23.3	Legal #3		4th	100-68	1917	
31.2	Vimy #1	x-Dunrobin	FPS	100-41	1914	
31.2	Vimy #2		FPS	100-334	1952	
37.0	Clyde		3rd	100-29	1912	
43.9	Nestow		FPS	100-41	1914	
50.4	Tawatinaw		CSS-C	100-47	1913	
56.3	Rochester		CSS-C	100-47	1913	
64.1	Perryvale	x-Lewiston	CSS-C	100-47	1913	
72.6	Meanook		FPS	100-41	1915	
77.2	Colinton		CSS-C	100-47	1913	
84.8	Athabasca	x-Athabaska	2nd	100-39	1912	

BLACKFOOT SUBDIVISION
North Battleford, Sk to Vermilion, Ab—124.4 miles

Milepost	Locality	Proposed/Former Name	Type	Plan	Built	Notes
10.8	Highgate		FPS	100-41	1919	
18.9	Delmas		3rd	100-3	1905	
26.2	Bresaylor #1		PORT	100-24	1908	
26.2	Bresaylor #2		FPS	100-41	1923	
33.9	Paynton		3rd	100-3	1905	
43.4	Birling		FPS	100-41	1911	
49.9	Maidstone		3rd	100-3	1905	
57.6	Waseca #1		SHLT	100-95	1905	
57.6	Waseca #2		4th	100-31	1911	
64.3	Lashburn		3rd	100-3	1907	
72.6	Marshall		3rd	100-3	1905	
78.9	Aberfeldy, Sk		FPS	100-96	1909	
84.4	Lloydminster, Ab #1-A		3rd	100-19	1906	
84.4	Lloydminster, Ab #1-B		FPS	100-41	1917	
91.4	Blackfoot #1-A		SHLT	100-95	1908	
91.4	Blackfoot #1-B		FPS	100-41	1911	
91.4	Blackfoot #2		3rd	100-72	1922	
99.3	Kitscoty		3rd	100-29	1911	
109.6	Islay #1		3rd	100-3	1906	
109.6	Islay #2		PORT	CB	1945	
109.6	Islay #3		CN4B	100-328	1952	
117.3	Borradaile		FPS	100-41	1911	
124.4	Vermilion		2nd	100-22	1906	

BODO SUBDIVISION
Unity, Sk to Bodo, Ab—51.5 miles

Milepost	Locality	Proposed/Former Name	Type	Plan	Built	Notes
6.6	End Lake		FPS	100-41C	1931	
11.2	Sunny Glen		FPS	100-41C	1931	
14.6	Reward		FPS	100-41C	1932	
20.7	Donegal		FPS	100-41C	1931	
26.5	Salvador		FPS	100-41C	1931	
31.6	Hearts Hill		FPS	100-41C	1933	
39.5	Cactus Lake	x-Grosswerder	FPS	100-41C	1932	
44.8	Cosine, Sk		FPS	100-41C	1932	
51.5	Bodo, Ab	x-Rosenheim	FPS	100-41C	1932	

BONNYVILLE SUBDIVISION
Abilene, Ab to Grand Centre, Ab—61.0 miles

Milepost	Locality	Proposed/Former Name	Type	Plan	Built	Notes
3.8	Boscombe		FPS	100-41B	1929	
10.0	Mallaig		FPS	100-41B	1929	
14.8	Therien	x-Gabriel	FPS	100-41B	1929	Note 78
18.8	Glendon #1	x-Alcock	FPS	100-41B	1929	
18.8	Glendon #2		FPS		—	x-SMBH
24.1	Franchere		FPS	100-41B	1929	
31.2	Anshaw		FPS	100-41B	1929	
37.0	Bonnyville		CN3rd	100-253	1929	
42.9	Fort Kent		SHLT		1934	
48.2	Ardmore	x-Cote	FPS		1939	
54.4	Le Goff		FPS	100-41B	1930	
57.2	Beaver River		FPS	CB		
61.0	Grand Centre		SPEC.	100-373	1958	

CAMROSE SUBDIVISION
Edmonton, Ab to Mirror, Ab—95.1 miles

Milepost	Locality	Proposed/Former Name	Type	Plan	Built	Notes
0.0	Bretville Jct.	See Viking Subdivision				Note 13
[—]	Edmonton	EY&P-Ross Grade	4th	100-6	1903	Notes 10,13
[—]	South Edmonton	x-Strathcona	SPEC.	100-50	1912	Notes 11,13
2.2	Mileage 2.2		PORT	110-258	1952	x-SMBH, Note 13

ALBERTA DISTRICT
Edmonton Division

CAMROSE SUBDIVISION
(continued)

Milepost	Locality	Proposed/Former Name	Type	Plan	Built	Notes
4.5	East Edmonton	x-Valesso	PORT	110-159	—	x-SMBH, Note 13
9.9	Bretona		3rd	100-29	1913	
17.0	Looma		FPS	100-41	1915	
22.5	Stegund	x-Gunderson				
24.7	New Sarepta		FPS	100-41	1915	
31.3	Hay Lakes #1	x-Hay Lake	3rd	100-29	1913	
31.3	Hay Lakes #2	x-Hay Lake	FPS	100-41	—	Temporary
31.3	Hay Lakes #3	x-Hay Lake	CN3rd	100-197A	1925	
38.3	Armena		FPS	100-41	1915	
48.1	Camrose–CNoR		3rd	100-29	1911	
53.8	Battle		SHLT		1918	
59.8	Duhamel		Type E	100-152	1911	
63.1	New Norway		Type E	100-152	1911	
70.6	Ferintosh		Type E	100-152	1911	
75.8	Dorenlee		Type E	100-152	1912	
84.3	Bashaw		Type E	100-152	1911	
95.1	Mirror		SPEC.	100-157	1911	

CORONADO SUBDIVISION
St. Paul Jct., Ab to Heinsburg, Ab—160.0 miles

Milepost	Locality	Proposed/Former Name	Type	Plan	Built	Notes
7.2	Duagh		FPS	100-41	1921	
15.6	Gibbons #1		FPS	100-41	1919	
15.6	Gibbons #2		CN4th	100-186	1927	
20.6	Coronado #1		4th	100-68	1921	Note 14
20.6	Coronado #2		FPS	CNoR-FT	1939	Note 14
29.6	Redwater #1		FPS	100-41	1920	
29.6	Redwater #2		SPEC.	110-259	1952	x-SMBH, Note 15
34.9	Kerensky		FPS	100-41	1919	
43.1	Radway	x-Radway Centre	3rd	100-72	1919	
50.0	Waskatenau #1	x-Waskateneau	FPS	100-41	1920	
50.0	Waskatenau #2		CN3rd	100-184	1928	
57.0	Warspite #1		FPS	100-41	1919	
57.0	Warspite #2		FPS		—	Temporary
57.0	Warspite #3		CN4A	100-310	1950	
64.7	Smoky Lake		3rd	100-72	1919	
74.9	Edwand		FPS	100-41	1919	
80.1	Bellis #1		FPS	100-41	1919	
80.1	Bellis #2		3rd	100-72	1923	
90.0	Vilna #1		FPS	100-41	1919	
90.0	Vilna #2		3rd	100-72	1922	
98.5	Spedden		FPS	100-41	1919	
105.0	Ashmont #1		FPS	100-41	1921	
105.0	Ashmont #2		CN3rd	100-250	1929	
108.3	Abilene	x-Gabriel Jct.	SHLT		1928	
113.0	Owlseye	x-Baffin	FPS	100-41	1921	
120.5	St. Paul	x-St. Paul des Metis	3rd	100-138	1921	Variant
129.4	Eduoardville	x-Heenan	FPS	100-41B	1927	
134.2	Armistice		FPS	100-41B	1927	
139.6	Elk Point		CN3rd	100-227	1927	
149.5	Lindbergh		FPS	100-41B	1930	
154.5	Middle Creek		FPS	100-41B	1930	
160.0	Heinsburg #1		FPS	100-41B	1930	
160.0	Heinsburg #2		CN4A	100-310	1950	

DEMAY SUBDIVISION
near Ryley, Ab to Camrose Ab—24.2 miles

Milepost	Locality	Proposed/Former Name	Type	Plan	Built	Notes
7.4	Demay		FPS	100-41	—	
12.9	Round Hill		3rd	100-29	1910	
18.8	Dodds		3rd	100-29	1910	
24.2	Yelger	x-Ryley–CNoR	3rd	100-29	1910	

HAIGHT SUBDIVISION
near Ryley, Ab to near Vegreville, Ab—21.8 miles

Milepost	Locality	Proposed/Former Name	Type	Plan	Built	Notes
6.5	Haight		3rd	100-29	1910	
13.9	Inland		FPS	100-41	1922	

KINGMAN SUBDIVISION
Tofield, Ab to Camrose, Ab—23.7 miles

Milepost	Locality	Proposed/Former Name	Type	Plan	Built	Notes
5.7	Bardo #1		Type E	100-152	1913	
5.7	Bardo #2		FPS			
12.0	Kingman		Type E	100-152	1910	
18.4	Dinant		Type E	100-152	1912	
[25.8]	Camrose–GTP	On Aban. GTP	SPEC.	100-157	1910	Note 12
[29.9]	Olin	x-Rosenroll/On Abandoned GTP				

ALBERTA DISTRICT
Edmonton Division

STONY PLAINS BRANCH
near Edmonton, Ab to Stony Plains, Ab—19.5 miles

Milepost	Locality	Proposed/Former Name	Type	Plan	Built	Notes
[14.0]	Spruce Grove-CNoR		FPS	100-96	1907	
[14.0]	Spruce Grove-CNoR		5th	100-17	1914	Probable
[19.5]	Stony Plains–CNoR		3rd	100-3	1907	Reverse, Note 57

UNITY SUBDIVISION
Biggar, Sk to Wainwright, Ab—140.1 miles

Milepost	Locality	Proposed/Former Name	Type	Plan	Built	Notes
8.6	Oban #1		Type E	100-152	1911	
8.6	Oban #2		FPS			
16.3	Palo		FPS-1B	100-162	1917	
22.6	Landis		Type E	100-152	1911	
30.0	Cavell	x-Coblenz	Type D	100-154	1910	
36.6	Reford		Type E	100-152	1911	
42.7	Scott #1		Type D	100-154	1909	
42.7	Scott #2		CN3rd	100-253	1935	
51.2	Tako		Type E	100-152	1911	
57.9	Unity		Type D	100-154	1909	Museum-2
68.5	Vera		FPS	100-162	1914	
77.3	Winter #1		PORT	110-101	1914	SMBH
77.3	Winter #2		3rd	100-72	1922	Note 72
84.5	Yonker #1		PORT	110-101	1911	SMBH
84.5	Yonker #2		Type E	100-152	1911	
96.5	Artland, Sk		Type E	100-152	1911	
103.3	Butze, Ab		PORT	110-101	—	SMBH
106.9	Chauvin		Type D	100-154	1909	
112.0	Ribstone #1		FPS-1B	100-162	1914	
112.0	Ribstone #2		Type G	100-154	1920	
121.2	Edgerton		Type E	100-152	1911	
127.8	Heath		FPS-1B	100-162	1913	
135.3	Greenshields		Type E	100-152	1911	
140.1	Wainwright #1		SPEC.	100-155	1909	
140.1	Wainwright #2		FPS	CB	1929	Temporary
140.1	Wainwright #3		SPEC.	100-249	1929	Museum-1

NOTES:

5 The line between St. Albert and Morinville, Ab was abandoned effective 1 September 1947.

10 This 4th Class station, erected at the foot of Ross grade, was relocated in 1906 to the CNoR yard in Edmonton. It was used as Petty Stores until replaced in 1916. Final disposition is unknown, but it was likely demolished in 1916.

11 This station was little used after operations commenced on the Bretona to Bretville Jct. cut-off in 1929. The building was sold in 1954 and demolished the following year. It was rumoured that the boilers from this building were salvaged and re-used in the shopping complex erected on this site.

12 The GTP line though Camrose was abandoned in 1923. The disposition of this station is unknown, but it is believed to have been sold shortly after abandonment.

13 This station was technically on the Edmonton Terminals Subdivision.

14 Portion converted into section house; the freight shed was converted into FPS #2 in 1939.

15 Constructed from two second-hand section bunkhouses.

23 Following inauguration of tourist passenger service on portions of the former CNR Stettler Subdivision in 1990, the Village of Donalda approached the Canadian Northern Society to acquire a station. The Society obtained an early design Canadian Northern 4th Class Station (Plan 100-31) from Vandura, Saskatchewan. It was moved onto the site of the original depot, extensively refurbished and opened in 1992 as an interpretive display in conjunction with the excursion trains that stopped here. The rail line serving Donalda was abandoned in 1997.

55 The track laid to this point in 1921 was abandoned in 1927. It could not be established whether this depot was ever built.

57 This depot was left on site in 1923. It was occupied by the local CNR operator as a dwelling until it was demolished in 1934.

59 Following trackage changes on the Brazeau Subdivision, this station was abandoned on site in 1922. The west end of the Endiang Subdivision was subsequently extended to include a portion of the Brazeau Subdivision. This depot was relocated to the GTP station grounds in 1927.

60 In 1927, after the former CNoR depot was moved to the Alix–GTP station grounds, the former GTP depot was converted into a section house.

72 CNR records classify this as Plan 100-197, but it incorporates all the features of Plan 100-72.

78 The extension made in 1947 was comprised of the CPR Portable Station (CPR Plan H-14-38) purchased by the CNR and relocated from Sancroft, Alberta (built 1930). It was added onto the east end of the existing shelter. A door was cut into the end walls of the adjoining buildings. A bay window was installed on the trackside of the former CPR portion, which was the Agent's office and apartment. A carbody was moved next to the depot as a freight shed. The original section was removed (burned?) in 1976.

79 The line between Hemaruka and Spondin never passed from the Construction to the Operating Department. This section was rarely operated.

ALBERTA DISTRICT
Edmonton Division

VEGREVILLE SUBDIVISION
Vermilion, Ab to Edmonton, Ab—129.6 miles

Milepost	Locality	Proposed/Former Name	Type	Plan	Built	Notes
7.4	Claysmore		FPS	100-41	1911	
14.6	Mannville #1	x-Manville	3rd	100-3	1906	
14.5	Mannville #2		FPS			x-SMBH
22.6	Minburn #1		SHLT	100-60	1908	
22.6	Minburn #2		4th	100-68	1914	
31.6	Innisfree #1	x-Delnorte	3rd	100-3	1906	
31.6	Innisfree #2		PORT			x-SMBH
39.2	Ranfurly #1-A	x-Blair Siding	PORT	100-24	1907	
39.2	Ranfurly #1-B		SHLT	100-95	1909	
39.2	Ranfurly #2		3rd	100-72	1922	
48.2	Lavoy		3rd	100-3	1906	
57.1	Vegreville #1-A		3rd	100-3	1905	
57.1	Vegreville #1-B		FPS		1920	Express Shed
57.1	Vegreville #2		SPEC.	100-255	1930	
64.0	Royal Park	x-Raith	FPS	100-96	1909	
70.9	Mundare		3rd	100-3	1906	
77.6	Hilliard		FPS	100-41	1917	
85.1	Chipman		3rd	100-3	1907	
92.4	Lamont		3rd	100-3	1907	
106.2	Scotford		FPS	100-41	1911	
112.7	Ft. Saskatchewan		3rd	100-19	1905	Variant
118.0	Riverbend		FPS	100-41	1912	
121.7	Oliver		SHLT	100-95	1912	
[126.3]	North Edmonton		4th	100-31	1910	Note 13
[129.6]	Edmonton #1-A	Joint with GTP	SPEC.	100-34	1906	Note 13
[129.6]	Edmonton #1-B	Joint with GTP	FPS	100-41	1914	Notes 13, 64
[129.6]	Edmonton #2	Joint with NAR	SPEC.	100-219	1927	Note 13
[129.6]	Edmonton #3		SPEC.		1965	Notes 13, 65
[129.6]	Edmonton #4		SPEC.		1966	Notes 13, 66

VIKING SUBDIVISION
Wainwright, Ab to Bretville Jct., Ab—120.1 miles

Milepost	Locality	Proposed/Former Name	Type	Plan	Built	Notes
6.5	Fabyan #1		Type E	100-152	1910	
6.5	Fabyan #2		Temp	x-SMBH	……	
6.5	Fabyan #3		CN4th	100-207	1925	
11.5	Hawkins #1		Type E	100-152	1911	
11.5	Hawkins #2		FPS	100-41B	1950	x-? or new?
17.6	Irma		Type E	100-152	1910	
25.2	Jarrow	<<Junkins>>	Type E	100-152	1910	
32.0	Kinsella #1		Type E	100-152	1911	
32.0	Kinsella #2		FPS			x-SMBH
36.9	Philips		Type E	100-152	1910	
44.4	Viking	x-Meighen	Type D	100-154	1909	
51.2	Torlea	x-Nestor	Type E	100-152	1911	
56.6	Bruce		Type E	100-152	1910	
65.8	Holden		Type E	100-152	1910	
70.0	Poe		Type E	100-152	1911	
74.6	Ryley #1		FPS-1B	100-162	1910	
74.6	Ryley #2		Type E	100-152	1913	
81.1	Shonts		Type E	100-152	1911	
86.1	Tofield		SPEC.	100-157	1911	
92.3	Lindbrook		FPS-1B	100-162	1914	
98.0	Deville #1-A		Type E	100-152	1910	
98.0	Deville #1-B		FPS	100-41B		
99.9	Cooking Lake #1-A		SPEC.	100-153	1910	
99.9	Cooking Lake #1-B		SHLT		By15	
103.7	Uncas		Type E	100-152	1911	
109.9	Ardrossan		Type E	100-152	1910	
114.4	Bremner		FPS-1B	100-162	1913	
119.0	Clover Bar #1		Type E	100-152	1911	Note 13
119.0	Clover Bar #2		FPS	100-41		Note 13
120.1	Bretville Jct.		PORT			Note 13
[127.1]	Calder Yard	x-North Yard	TOS	100-41		Note 13

Edson Division

BRULE SUBDIVISION
Edson, Ab to Jasper, Ab—106.5 miles

Milepost	Locality	Proposed/Former Name	Type	Plan	Built	Notes
4.3	Ansell		Type E	100-152	1911	
9.4	Bickerdike		Type E	100-152	1911	
14.4	Marlboro–GTP #1	x-Dandurand–GTP	Type E	100-152	1911	
14.4	Marlboro–GTP #2		FPS	100-41		
19.6	Galloway #1		Type E	100-152	1911	
19.6	Galloway #2		FPS	100-41		
19.6	Galloway #3		CSS-C	100-47		
26.3	Medicine Lodge #1		Type E	100-152	1911	
26.3	Medicine Lodge #2		FPS	GTP-FT	1951	
30.9	Hargwen #1		Type E	100-152	1911	
30.9	Hargwen #2		Type G	100-168	1920	Note 9
35.7	Obed–GTP		Type E	100-152	1911	

ALBERTA DISTRICT
Edson Division

BRULE SUBDIVISION
(continued)

Milepost	Locality	Proposed/Former Name	Type	Plan	Built	Notes
41.2	Dalehurst–GTP	x-Roundcroft	Type E	100-152	1911	
47.5	Pedley #1		Type E	100-152	1913	
47.5	Pedley #2		CSS-C	100-47		Note 73
52.1	Drinnan		FPS			
55.1	Hinton		Type E	100-152	1912	Note 8
60.3	Entrance–GTP	x-Dyke	Type E	100-152	1911	
66.5	Solomon		PORT	CB		
70.3	Errington		PORT	CB		
71.6	Brule #1		CSS-C	100-47	1914	
71.6	Brule #2		FPS	100-320	1953	
78.6	Miette	x-Bedson	CSS-C	100-47	1914	
91.0	Snaring		CSS-C	100-47	1915	
98.1	Henry House–GTP		Type E	100-152	1911	
106.5	Jasper #1	x-Fitzhugh	SPEC.	100-155	1912	
106.5	Jasper #2		SPEC.	100-206	1925	Temporary
106.5	Jasper #3		SPEC.	100-205	1925	

FOOTHILLS SUBDIVISION
Bickerdike, Ab to Lovett, Ab—55.3 miles

Milepost	Locality	Proposed/Former Name	Type	Plan	Built	Notes
5.5	McLeod River		Type E	100-152	1912	Museum-2
10.7	Erith		Type E	100-152	1912	
16.3	Weald		Type E	100-152	1912	
24.8	Embarras		Type E	100-152	1912	
34.0	Robb	x-Minehead	Type E	100-152	1912	
36.6	Coalspur #1-A		Type E	100-152	1913	
36.6	Coalspur #1-B		PORT	110-73A	1923	SMBH
[47.3]	Sterco	x-Basing	FPS	100-41	1922	
[48.5]	Mileage 48.5		FPS	100-41		
[50.7]	Foothills	x-Mudge	Type E	100-152		
[55.3]	Lovett		Type E	100-152	1913	

LAC STE. ANNE SUBDIVISION
Peace River Jct., Ab to near Entwistle, Ab—43.0 miles

Milepost	Locality	Proposed/Former Name	Type	Plan	Built	Notes
[37.3]	Alberta Beach	<<Britannia>>	SPEC.	100-90	1917	Note 36
[41.9]	Lac Ste. Anne		3rd	100-29	1912	Note 36
[48.1]	Darwell		CSS-C	100-47	1913	Note 36
[53.7]	Lake Isle #1	<<Clearwater>>	FPS	100-41	1916	
[53.7]	Lake Isle #2		FPS	CB	1923	Note 36
[61.4]	Magnolia	<<Borian>>	CSS-C	100-47	1913	Note 36

LUCERNE SUBDIVISION
Tollerton, Ab to Lucerne, BC—128.9 miles

Milepost	Locality	Proposed/Former Name	Type	Plan	Built	Notes
[7.4]	Sundance		CSS-C	100-47	1914	Note 40
[14.3]	Dandurand–CNoR					Note 42
[15.7]	Marlboro		CSS-C	100-47	1914	Note 41
[21.0]	Berks		FPS	CB	1914	Note 40
[28.1]	Everest					
[35.1]	Obed–CNoR		CSS-C	100-47	1914	Note 43
[43.8]	Dalehurst–CNoR		CSS-C	100-47	1915	Note 73
[52.5]	Bliss		CSS-C	100-47	1914	
[61.4]	Entrance–CNoR	<<Heda>>	CSS-C	100-47	1914	
[98.0]	Henry House–CNoR		CSS-C	100-47	1914	Note 44
[107.3]	Jasper Park, Ab	later Sleepy Hollow	SPEC.	100-80	1915	Note 45
[128.9]	Lucerne–CNoR, BC		2nd	100-79	1915	Note 46

MOUNTAIN PARK SUBDIVISION
Coalspur, Ab to Mountain Park, Ab—31.0 miles

Milepost	Locality	Proposed/Former Name	Type	Plan	Built	Notes
6.9	Mercoal		FPS	100-41		
8.2	Steeper					
11.8	Shaw					
18.0	Fidler					
22.5	Leyland #1		SPEC.		1921	Note 48
22.5	Leyland #2		CN4A	100-310	1951	
[—]	Luscar		FPS	CB		Note 74
23.7	Cadomin #1-A		FPS	CB	1923	
23.7	Cadomin #1-B		FPS	100-41B	1923	
31.0	Mountain Park #2		SPEC.		1920	Note 48

POCAHONTAS BRANCH
Snaring Jct., Ab to Pocahontas, Ab—10.7 miles

Milepost	Locality	Proposed/Former Name	Type	Plan	Built	Notes
[—]	Parkgate		Type E	100-152	1913	Note 51
[0.0]	Pocahontas		Type E	100-152	1913	Note 52
[5.9]	Hawes	x-Jasper House	Type E	100-152	1913	Note 52
[10.7]	Interlaken		Type E	100-152	1913	Note 53

ALBERTA DISTRICT
Edson Division

SANGUDO SUBDIVISION
near Bissell, Ab to Whitecourt, Ab—103.1 miles

Milepost	Locality	Proposed/Former Name	Type	Plan	Built	Notes
1.7	Cannel		FPS	100-41		
5.0	St. Albert #2		4th	100-6	1909	Museum-2
13.0	Villeneuve		CSS-C	100-47	1913	
19.4	Calahoo #1		CSS-C	100-47	1913	
19.4	Calahoo #2		FPS	100-41	—	
25.3	Bilby #1		CSS-C	100-47	1913	
25.3	Bilby #2		SHLT		1959	
29.4	Onoway		3rd	100-29	1913	
31.0	Peace River Jct.		PORT		1916	
36.0	Gunn		FPS	100-41	—	
44.4	Glenevis		FPS	100-41	1916	
51.5	Cherhill		FPS	100-41	1916	
57.0	Lisburn		FPS	100-41	1917	
62.5	Sangudo #2		4th	100-68	1918	
64.8	Robinsons #1		FPS	CB	1921	
64.8	Robinsons #2		FPS	CB	1940	
68.9	Rochfort Bridge #1		FPS	100-41	1922	
68.9	Rochfort Bridge #2		CN4th	100-252	1930	
74.2	Mayerthorpe #1		FPS	100-41	1922	
74.2	Mayerthorpe #2		CN4th	100-220	1928	
79.8	Green Court	x-Greencourt	FPS	100-41	—	
85.3	Lombell					
89.7	Blue Ridge	x-Lonira	FPS	100-41	1922	
103.1	Whitecourt #1-A		FPS	100-41	1922	
103.1	Whitecourt #1-B		FPS	100-41	1922	
103.1	Whitecourt #2		3rd	100-72	1922	
103.1	Whitecourt #3		SPEC.		1973	

TOLLERTON SUBDIVISION
Edmonton, Ab/near Entwistle, Ab to Tollerton, At—136.9/ 67.7 miles
Refer to the Sangudo and Wabamun Subdivisions for the original eastern portion of the Tollerton Subdivision

Milepost	Locality	Proposed/Former Name	Type	Plan	Built	Notes
[71.9]	Entwistle–CNoR #1		FPS	100-41	1914	
[71.9]	Entwistle–CNoR #2		4th	100-68	1915	
[72.7]	Evansburg–CNoR #1		FPS	100-41	1916	
[72.7]	Evansburg–CNoR #2		3rd	100-72	1920	
[101.0]	Dayson		CSS-C	100-47	1913	Note 62
[108.9]	Carrot Creek–CNoR		CSS-C	100-47	1915	Note 62
[114.5]	Fulstow		CSS-C	100-47	1914	Note 62
[124.7]	Horner		CSS-C	100-47	1914	Note 62
[129.4]	Scriven		CSS-C	100-47	1915	Note 62
[136.9]	Tollerton		2nd	100-39	1913	Note 62

WABAMUN SUBDIVISION
Edmonton, Ab to Edson, Ab—129.5 miles

Milepost	Locality	Proposed/Former Name	Type	Plan	Built	Notes
4.2	West Jct.		FPS-1B	100-162	1913	Note 13
7.1	Bissell #1		Type E	100-152	1910	
7.1	Bissell #2		4th	100-68	1922	
14.1	Acheson #1		Type E	100-152	1911	
14.1	Acheson #2		FPS	GTP-FT	1951	
19.6	Spruce Grove–GTP		Type E	100-152	1910	
23.9	Stony Plain–GTP		Type E	100-152	1911	
32.4	Carvel		Type E	100-152	1910	
38.3	Duffield		Type E	100-152	1911	
42.7	Kapasiwin	x-Kapasiwin Beach	FPS-1B	100-162	1918	
44.2	Wabamun		Type E	100-152	1911	
51.7	Fallis		Type E	100-152	1910	
54.8	Seba Beach		FPS-1B	100-162	1917	
57.9	Gainford		Type E	100-152	1911	
61.1	Magnolia Bridge #1		FPS	110-117	—	x-ST
61.1	Magnolia Bridge #2		FPS	100-41B	1926	
66.3	Entwistle–GTP		Type E	100-152	1910	
67.9	Evansburg–GTP #1-A		FPS-1B	100-162	1914	Note 41
67.9	Evansburg–GTP #1-B		PORT	110-101	1918	SMBH
67.9	Evansburg–GTP #2		3rd	100-72	—	
72.1	Styal	x-Imrie	Type E	100-152	1911	
[—]	Junkins-GTP		Type E	100-152	1911	Note 67
[—]	Keston		Type E	100-152	1913	Note 68
73.6	Lobstick		CSS-C	100-47	1913	
77.4	Wildwood	x-Junkins-CNoR	Type E	100-152	—	Note 67
82.2	Granada		FPS		—	x-SMBH
86.2	Chip Lake #1		CSS-C	100-47	1913	
86.2	Chip Lake #2		FPS	CNoR-FT	1951	
87.9	Leaman		Type E	100-152	1911	
92.2	MacKay		Type E	100-152	1911	
99.5	Niton		Type E	100-152	1911	
102.9	Carrot Creek–GTP #1	x-Otley	Type E	100-152	1911	
102.9	Carrot Creek–GTP #2		FPS	GTP-FT	1951	
109.7	Peers		Type E	100-152	1911	

ALBERTA DISTRICT
Edson Division

WABAMUN SUBDIVISION
(continued)

Milepost	Locality	Proposed/Former Name	Type	Plan	Built	Notes
116.0	Rosevear		Type E	100-152	1911	
120.6	Wolf Creek	x-Thornton	Type E	100-152	1911	
124.1	Yates #1		Type E	100-152	1913	
124.1	Yates #2		FPS-1B	100-162	—	
129.5	Edson		SPEC.	100-163	1910	

BRITISH COLUMBIA DISTRICT
Kamloops Division

ALBREDA SUBDIVISION
Jasper, Ab to Blue River, BC—132.4 miles

Milepost	Locality	Proposed/Former Name	Type	Plan	Built	Notes
8.3	Geikie		Type E	100-152	1912	
12.9	Decoigne, Ab	x-Mt. Cavell/ xx-Mt. Geikie	CSS-C	100-47	1914	
17.6	Yellowhead #1, BC	x-Yelsum/ xx-Summit	Type E	100-152	1912	Note 1

NOTES:

1 These depots were left vacant on the abandoned GTP grade in 1917. Rainbow-GTP was relocated to Redpass in 1917 and Yellowhead burned down about 1918. The stations at Fitzwilliam, Grant Brook and Lucerne–GTP, BC were rehabilitated in 1924, when that section of the line was re-opened.

8 Left vacant on the abandoned GTP grade in 1917. This station was rehabilitated in 1927, when the Obed-Entrance (x-Dyke) section of the line was re-opened.

9 Demolished in derailment 1967.

13 This station was technically on the Edmonton Terminals Subdivision.

36 The former CNoR line between Peace River Jct. and Darson Jct. (near Magnolia) was abandoned in June 1936.

40 Abandoned on grade in 1917. Final dispositions unknown; likely sold and demolished.

41 There is a discrepancy in CNR records; one stating that a carbody (#6997) was placed here in 1914, while the GTP cost record indicates that a formal shelter costing $652 was erected here. A photograph in a local history clearly shows an FPS. Perhaps the carbody was a temporary station and there was a mix-up in record keeping.

42 Abandoned on grade in 1917. Relocated to CNR Mile 15.3 Brule Subdivision in 1923, used as residence by the CNR pumpman for the new water tank erected here. Relocated to Galloway (#3) in 1940. Sold to the Town of Edson in 1976 and relocated to Centennial Park on the eastern outskirts of the community. Converted into museum. The station's signboards read "Edson."

43 Abandoned on grade 1928, relocated to nearby GTP station grounds by 1934. Used by CNR for storage.

44 Abandoned on grade in 1917. Turned over to Department of the Interior (Parks) circa 1923.

45 Abandoned on site in 1917. Converted into section house.

46 Abandoned when the rehabilitated GTP line reopened 1 November 1924. It remained vacant until World War II when Lucerne was used as a Japanese internment camp, and the station was used as a bunkhouse for internees. The depot was finally razed by the Parks Department in the mid-1950s.

48 Constructed by the Mountain Park Collieries.

51 This station was left vacant on the abandoned grade in 1917. It was turned over to the Parks Department in 1924. The station is extant, but is gradually being pushed over by the constantly shifting sand dunes.

52 Abandoned on site in 1921; final disposition unknown.

53 Abandoned on site in 1921; turned over to Parks Department in 1923, for use as a base for Park fire rangers.

62 Dayson, Carrot Creek–CNoR, Fulstow, Horner, Scriven and Tollerton Ab. These stations were abandoned on grade in 1917. The following year, the CNoR apparently stripped all re-usable millwork (windows, doors, interior fittings, etc.) from these buildings. A local history makes reference to Carrot Creek–CNoR and Fulstow as being sold about 1923. It is likely that all of these stations were sold and removed at the same time.

64 This FPS was set up as a stores building for the Sleeping & Dining Car Department.

65 This was a temporary station set up during construction of the CN Tower (#4), on the site of the former station (#2).

66 The station facilities were located in the basement of this 26-floor office tower. VIA Rail Canada took over passenger operations in the building in 1978. In 1998, these premises were vacated in favour of a new VIA station built in north-western Edmonton.

67 The GTP depot was relocated from the abandoned grade to the CNoR station grounds by 1918.

68 Abandoned on site in 1917, sold in 1930.

73 CNR building records are somewhat unclear regarding this station. One record clearly shows that Pedley had a 'Design A' (Type E) station, but another also notes it as Plan 100-47, with stucco and rehabilitation in 1927. It is likely that the original GTP station burned down, and that this building was relocated from Dalehurst–CNoR, then abandoned in 1928.

74 Luscar is actually on the Luscar Spur 5.2 miles from its junction with the Mountain Park Subdivision at Leyland.

BRITISH COLUMBIA DISTRICT
Kamloops Division

ALBREDA SUBDIVISION
(continued)

Milepost	Locality	Proposed/Former Name	Type	Plan	Built	Notes
17.6	Yellowhead #2, BC		CSS-C	100-47	—	
21.8	Lucerne–GTP		Type E	100-152	1912	Note 1
28.0	Fitzwilliam	x-Alpland	Type E	100-152	1913	Note 1
[30.9]	Grant Brook–CNoR		CSS-C	100-98	1915	
31.8	Grant Brook–GTP		Type E	100-152	1913	Note 1
[38.1]	Rainbow–GTP		Type E	100-152	1913	Note 1
37.7	Rainbow–CNoR		CSS-C	100-98	1915	
43.8	Redpass Jct. #1		Type E	100-152	—	Note 1
43.8	Redpass Jct. #2		SPEC.	Trailer	1977	
45.6	Resplendent–CNoR		CSS-C	100-98	1915	
	Foster	x-Mt. Robson–CNoR	CSS-C	100-98	1915	1st location
54.4	Mt. Robson–CNoR #1-A		FPS	100-41	1922	2nd location
54.4	Mt. Robson–CNoR #1-B		PORT		1922	3rd location
65.4	Jackman		CSS-C	100-98	1915	
73.2	Swift Creek		CSS-C	100-98	1915	
74.4	Valemount	x-Cranberry	CSS-C	100-98	—	
83.3	Canoe River		CSS-C	100-98	1915	
91.6	Albreda–CNoR		CSS-C	100-98	1915	
97.0	Clemina		CSS-C	100-98	1915	
106.3	Lempriere		CSS-C	100-98	1915	
114.2	Pyramid		CSS-C	100-98	1915	
122.5	Thunder River		CSS-C	100-98	1915	
132.4	Blue River		2nd	100-82	1915	

ASHCROFT SUBDIVISION
Kamloops Jct., BC to Boston Bar, BC—125.6 miles

Milepost	Locality	Proposed/Former Name	Type	Plan	Built	Notes
1.0	Halston	x-Mytton	SPEC.	100-87	1916	
7.8	Tranquille		CSS-C	100-98	1916	
13.7	Frederick					
20.8	Copper Creek		CSS-C	100-98	1916	
25.8	Savona		CSS-C	100-98	1915	
32.6	Walhachin		CSS-C	100-98	1915	
36.4	Anglesey		FPS	100-41	1917	
41.0	McAbee		CSS-C	100-98	1915	
48.9	Ashcroft		3rd	100-64	1915	
58.6	Basque		CSS-C	100-98	1915	
65.5	Minnibariet					
69.2	Martel		FPS	100-41	1917	
74.8	Spences Bridge #1		3rd	100-64	1915	
74.8	Spences Bridge #2		FPS	100-41	1922	Temporary
74.8	Spences Bridge #3		3rd	100-72	1923	
79.2	Skoonka					
83.1	Seddell		CSS-C	100-98	1915	
89.9	Shushten	x-Shusten				
97.6	Lytton		3rd	100-64	1915	
98.5	Mile 98.5		FPS	100-41	1916	
104.2	Cisco		FPS	100-41	1917	
110.2	Falls Creek		CSS-C	100-98	1915	
114.8	Inkitsaph #1		SHLT		1917	
114.8	Inkitsaph #2		FPS	100-41B	1929	
125.6	Boston Bar		2nd	100-82	1915	

CLEARWATER SUBDIVISION
Blue River, BC to Kamloops Jct., BC—139.4 miles

Milepost	Locality	Proposed/Former Name	Type	Plan	Built	Notes
4.1	Trout Creek					
8.1	Wolfenden		CSS-C	100-98	1915	
13.6	Messiter		CSS-C	100-98	1915	
18.8	Cottonwood Flats		FPS	100-41		
24.8	Avola #1		CSS-C	100-98	1915	
24.8	Avola #2		FPS			
30.0	Wire Cache		FPS	100-41	—	
37.4	McMurphy		CSS-C	100-98	1915	
47.2	Irvine #1		CSS-C	100-98	1915	
47.2	Irvine #2		FPS	100-290	1926	
53.0	Vavenby		CSS-C	100-98	1915	
61.9	Birch Island		CSS-C	100-98	1915	
68.5	Clearwater #1		FPS	100-41	1918	
68.5	Clearwater #2		SPEC.	1920-1	1961	
74.2	Blackpool		CSS-C	100-98	1915	
82.9	Boulder		CSS-C	100-98	1915	
85.7	Little Fort	x-Mt. Olie	3rd	100-64	1916	
91.3	Chu Chua		3rd	100-64	1915	
98.4	Chinook Cove		CSS-C	100-98	1915	
104.2	Barriere #1		CSS-C	100-98	1916	
104.2	Barriere #2		FPS	100-334	1954	
107.3	Louis Creek		CSS-C	100-98	1915	
116.4	McLure		CSS-C	100-98	1915	
120.2	Ramage		FPS	100-41B	1927	

BRITISH COLUMBIA DISTRICT
Kamloops Division

CLEARWATER SUBDIVISION
(continued)

Milepost	Locality	Proposed/Former Name	Type	Plan	Built	Notes
123.7	Vinsulla	x-Hefferley/ xx-Heffley 1st	CSS-C	100-98	1915	
128.9	Heffley	Heffley 2nd site	FPS	100-35	—	
129.3	Mileage 129.3		FPS	100-41	1916	
132.2	Rayleigh	x-St. Paul	CSS-C	100-98	1916	
139.4	Kamloops Jct.		2nd	100-81	1915	

LUMBY SUBDIVISION
near Vernon, BC to Lumby, BC—14.5 miles

Milepost	Locality	Proposed/Former Name	Type	Plan	Built	Notes
3.6	Coldstream Ranch		FPS			
4.1	Coldstream		FPS	100-41B	1926	
7.8	Lavington					
14.5	Lumby #1		FPS	100-41B	1926	
14.5	Lumby #2		FPS	100-333	1951	

OKANAGAN SUBDIVISION
Kamloops Jct., BC to Kelowna, BC—118.9 miles

Milepost	Locality	Proposed/Former Name	Type	Plan	Built	Notes
2.0	Kamloops #1	North of river	STA		1913	Temporary, Note 49
2.8	Kamloops #2	South of river	STA		1921	Temporary
2.8	Kamloops #3-A	South of river	SPEC.	100-210	1927	
2.8	Kamloops #3-B	South of river	FPS	100-41B	1927	Note 50
3.5	CPR Jct.	Joint with CPR to Campbell Creek Jct.				
14.6	Campbell Creek Jct.	x-Bostock Jct.	STA	110-189	1940	SH
26.5	Duck Meadow	x-Ducks Meadow	FPS	100-41B	1927	
30.9	Monte Lake		FPS	100-41B	1927	
37.8	Westwold	x-West Wold	FPS	100-41B	1927	
47.3	Falkland		CN3rd	100-197	1926	
52.4	Sweetsbridge		FPS	100-41B	1926	
61.6	O'Keefe		FPS	100-41B	1926	
70.8	Armstrong Jct.	Joint with CPR				
85.4	Vernon	Joint with CPR	CPR Station			
99.2	Oyama		FPS	100-41B	1926	
105.9	Winfield		FPS	100-41B	1926	
109.5	Postill	x-Hood	FPS	100-41B	1926	
113.0	Rutland #1-A		FPS	100-41B	1926	
113.0	Rutland #1-B		FPS	100-41B	—	
118.9	Kelowna	Joint with CPR	SPEC.	100-214	1926	

YALE SUBDIVISION
Boston Bar, BC to Vancouver BC—131.8 miles

Milepost	Locality	Proposed/Former Name	Type	Plan	Built	Notes
7.4	Gorge	x-Hellsgate	CSS-SH	110-12	1916	Note 2
12.7	Chapmans		CSS-C	100-98	1916	
18.3	Stout					
26.7	Yale		CSS-C	100-98	1916	
31.7	Squeah		CSS-SH	110-12	1916	Note 2
36.0	Trafalgar					
40.2	Hope		2nd	100-84	1916	
44.1	Floods		FPS			
48.0	St. Elmo		FPS	100-41	1915	
49.8	Laidlaw		CSS-C	100-98	1916	
54.1	Cheam View		CSS-C	100-98	1915	
60.9	Popkum		FPS	100-41	1917	
65.3	Rosedale		3rd	100-64	1915	
68.4	Smithvale		FPS	100-41	1922	
71.8	Chilliwack		2nd	100-83	1915	
74.0	Arnold		FPS	100-41	1915	
77.2	Cannor		SHLT		1927	
83.1	Cox	x-Sumas	FPS	100-41	1915	
87.5	Matsqui		3rd	100-64	1915	
92.5	Mt. Lehman		FPS	100-41	1916	
98.0	Glen Valley		FPS	100-41	1915	
103.2	Langley	x-Fort Langley	3rd	100-64	1915	Museum-2
108.2	Westlang	x-Latimer Road/ xx-Port Kells	FPS		1921	
110.3	Tynehead		FPS	CB	1925	
114.8	Port Mann		2nd	100-83	1915	Note 70
117.5	Gyproc	x-Brownsville/ xx-Liverpool	Joint with GN			Note 70
120.1	North Westminster	x-Sapperton	Joint with GN			Note 70
131.8	Vancouver #1	Joint with GN	STA		1916	Temporary, Note 69
131.8	Vancouver #2		SPEC.	100-224	1917	Note 70

BRITISH COLUMBIA DISTRICT
Smithers Division

BULKLEY SUBDIVISION
Smithers, BC to Pacific, BC—107.1 miles

Milepost	Locality	Proposed/Former Name	Type	Plan	Built	Notes
3.4	Lake Kathlyn		Type F	100-151	1917	
9.4	Evelyn		Type E	100-152	1913	
15.4	Doughty #1		Type E	100-152	1913	
15.4	Doughty #2		FPS	GTP-FT	1950	
21.9	Moricetown		Type E	100-152	1913	
27.3	Seaton		Type E	100-152	1913	
31.9	Beament #1		Type E	100-152	1913	
31.9	Beamont #2		FPS	GTP-FT	1949	
39.3	Bulkley Canyon #1	x-Giles	Type E	100-152	1913	
39.3	Bulkley Canyon #2		FPS	GTP-FT		
45.9	New Hazelton #1		Type E	100-152	1913	
45.9	New Hazelton #2		PORT		1980	
49.6	Hazelton		Type E	100-152	1913	
56.9	Carnaby		Type E	100-152	1913	
62.0	Skeena Crossing #1		FPS-1A	CB	1917	
62.0	Skeena Crossing #2		FPS		1943	
63.8	Nash		Type E	100-152	1912	
68.4	Andimaul #1		Type E	100-152	1912	
68.4	Andimaul #2		FPS	GTP-FT	1951	
73.0	Kitwanga		Type E	100-152	1912	
80.6	Woodcock		Type E	100-152	1912	
86.1	Cedarvale #1		Type E	100-152	1912	
86.1	Cedarvale #2		FPS	100-41B	1931	
100.9	Doreen	later Grand Trunk	Type E	100-152	1913	
107.1	Pacific #1		SPEC.	100-155	1913	
107.1	Pacific #2		SPEC.	100-277	1935	

FRASER SUBDIVISION
McBride, BC to Prince George, BC—146.1 miles

Milepost	Locality	Proposed/Former Name	Type	Plan	Built	Notes
5.4	Lamming Mills		FPS			
6.9	Craibenn		FPS			
13.1	Legrand	x-Fleet	Type E	100-152	1914	
21.5	Rider	x-Knole	Type E	100-152	1914	
27.8	Goat River #1	x-Rooney/ xx-Brundell	Type E	100-152	1914	
27.8	Goat River #2		FPS	110-254		x-SMBH
33.9	Crescent Spur #1	x-Leboe	FPS			
33.9	Crescent Spur #2		FPS			
33.9	Crescent Spur #3		FPS			
36.3	Loos #1	x-Crescent Island	Type E	100-152	1914	
36.3	Loos #2		FPS	100-41		
45.0	Urling #1		Type E	100-152	1914	
45.0	Urling #2		FPS			
52.0	Kidd #1		Type E	100-152	1914	
52.0	Kidd #2		FPS	GTP-FT	1953	
57.8	Bend #1		Type E	100-152	1914	
57.8	Bend #2		FPS			
65.6	Guilford #1		Type E	100-152	1914	
65.6	Guilford #2		FPS	GTP-FT	1950	
69.5	Penny #1-A		FPS			x-ST
69.5	Penny #1-B		FPS	110-101		x-SMBH
69.5	Penny #2		Type E	100-152		
75.0	Lindup #1		Type E	100-152	1914	
75.0	Lindup #2		FPS	110-101		x-SMBH
79.4	Longworth		Type E	100-152	1914	
87.4	Hutton		Type E	100-152	1914	
90.6	Sinclair Mills		FPS	110-217		x-SMBH
92.3	Dewey		Type E	100-152	1914	
100.2	Hansard		Type E	100-152	1914	
104.0	Aleza Lake #1		Type E	100-152	1914	
108.8	Aleza Lake #2		STA			
115.3	Newlands #1		Type E	100-152	1914	
115.3	Newlands #2		FPS	GTP-FT	1949	
122.4	Giscome		Type E	100-152	1914	
127.0	Willow River #1		Type E	100-152	1914	
127.0	Willow River #2		FPS			
136.4	Shelley #1		Type E	100-152	1914	
136.4	Shelley #2		FPS	GTP-FT		
136.4	Shelley #3		STA			
140.8	Foreman #1		Type E	100-152	1914	
140.8	Foreman #2		FPS	GTP-FT	1948	
146.1	Prince George #1		STA		1913	
146.1	Prince George #2		SPEC.	100-136	1922	
146.1	Prince George #3		SPEC.		1971	

KITIMAT SUBDIVISION
Terrace, BC to Kitimat, BC—38.5 miles

Milepost	Locality	Proposed/Former Name	Type	Plan	Built	Notes
38.5	Kitimat		SPEC.	100-356	1955	

BRITISH COLUMBIA DISTRICT
Smithers Division

NECHAKO SUBDIVISION
(Prince George, BC to Endako, BC—115.5 miles)

Milepost	Locality	Proposed/Former Name	Type	Plan	Built	Notes
5.2	Otway		Type E	100-152	1915	
8.9	Miworth #1		Type E	100-152	1915	
8.9	Miworth #2		FPS	GTP-FT	1948	
13.9	Chilako #1		Type E	100-152	1914	
13.9	Chilako #2		FPS	GTP-FT	1952	
20.0	Bednesti		Type E	100-152	1914	
28.0	Nichol #1		Type E	100-152	1914	
28.0	Nichol #2		FPS-1B	100-162	1918	
32.4	Isle Pierre #1		Type E	100-152	1914	
32.4	Isle Pierre #2		FPS	100-41		
38.7	Hutchison		Type E	100-152	1914	
44.8	Wedgwood #1		Type E	100-152	1915	
44.8	Wedgwood #2		FPS	GTP-FT	1949	
50.1	Finmoore #1	x-Stuart	Type E	100-152	1914	
50.1	Finmoore #2		FPS	CB		
56.8	Hulatt		Type E	100-152	1915	
63.2	Sinkut #1	x-Tsinkut	Type E	100-152	1914	
63.2	Sinkut #2		FPS	GTP-FT	1948	
69.4	Vanderhoof #1		Type E	100-152	1914	
69.4	Vanderhoof #2		3rd	100-72	1924	
69.4	Vanderhoof #3		SPEC.	100-345	1960	
76.2	McCall		Type E	100-152	1915	
82.7	Engen		Type E	100-152	1915	
87.9	Marten Lake #1		Type E	100-152	1915	
87.9	Marten Lake #2		FPS	GTP-FT	1950	
94.3	Fort Fraser #1		FPS-1B	100-162	1916	
94.3	Fort Fraser #2		3rd	100-72	1923	
94.3	Fort Fraser #3		FPS	100-41B		
101.7	Encombe #1	x-Midlake	Type E	100-152	1914	
101.7	Encombe #2		FPS	GTP-FT	1950	
103.8	Lejac #1	x-Revsa	SHLT			x-PH
103.8	Lejac #2		FPS	100-41B	1945	
107.7	Fraser Lake		Type E	100-152	1914	
115.5	Endako #1		STA		1914	Temporary
115.5	Endako #2		SPEC.	100-143	1922	Similar to 100-142
115.5	Endako #3		TOS	Trailer	1970	
115.5	Endako #4		SPEC.		1985	Comb. Sta/ EMBH

SKEENA SUBDIVISION
Pacific, BC to Prince Rupert, BC—119.4 miles

Milepost	Locality	Proposed/Former Name	Type	Plan	Built	Notes
5.5	Pitman #1		Type E	100-152	1912	
5.5	Pitman #2		FPS	GTP-FT	1947	
12.2	Usk #1		Type E	100-152	1912	
12.2	Usk #2		FPS			
19.1	Kitselas	x-Vanarsdol	Type E	100-152	1911	
24.8	Terrace #1		Type E	100-152	1911	
24.8	Terrace #2		SPEC.	100-391	1960	
34.4	Amsbury		Type E	100-152	1911	
42.5	Shames		Type E	100-152	1912	
49.5	Exstew		Type E	100-152	1911	
61.3	Salvus #1		Type E	100-152	1912	
61.3	Salvus #2		CN3rd	100-256	1928	Variant
72.6	Kwinitsa		Type E	100-152	1911	Museum-2
86.6	Skeena	x-Skeena City	Type E	100-152	1912	
92.8	Tyee		Type E	100-152	1911	
95.8	Haysport		PORT	110-101		SMBH

NOTES:

1. These depots were left vacant on the abandoned GTP grade in 1917. Rainbow-GTP was relocated to Redpass in 1917 and Yellowhead burned down about 1918. The stations at Fitzwilliam, Grant Brook and Lucerne–GTP, BC were rehabilitated in 1924, when that section of the line was re-opened.

2. This was a conventional section house apparently used as station. It does not appear as if these buildings had bracket-supported awnings or formal waiting rooms as did earlier combination station-and-section-house designs such as Plan 110-10.

49. The temporary station for the Canadian Northern and the Northern Construction Company (involved in building the railway line) was situated north of the South Thompson River.

50. For trainmen's equipment.

69. The Great Northern Railway station on Pender Street was used by the CNoR commencing October 1915, until temporary passenger accommodations were built. These were apparently abandoned once the new depot on Main Street opened in 1917.

70. This station was technically on the Vancouver Terminals Subdivision.

BRITISH COLUMBIA DISTRICT
Smithers Division

SKEENA SUBDIVISION
(continued)

Milepost	Locality	Proposed/Former Name	Type	Plan	Built	Notes
102.7	Sockeye #1		Type E	100-152	1911	
102.7	Sockeye #2		FPS			x-ST
108.2	Inverness Cannery		FPS			x-ST
108.7	Phelan		Type E	100-152	1911	
114.0	Kaien		FPS			x-ST
119.4	Prince Rupert #1		SPEC.	140-210	1907	Temporary, Note 56
119.4	Prince Rupert #1		SPEC.	100-135	1922	

TELKWA SUBDIVISION
(Endako, BC to Smithers, BC—125.2 miles)

Milepost	Locality	Proposed/Former Name	Type	Plan	Built	Notes
6.2	Savory		Type E	100-152	1915	
14.8	Priestly		Type E	100-152	1915	
20.8	Sheraton #1		Type E	100-152	1915	
20.8	Sheraton #2		FPS	GTP-FT	1948	
27.1	Tintagel		Type E	100-152	1915	
35.0	Burns Lake #1		Type E	100-152	1914	
35.0	Burns Lake #2		SPEC.	100-332	1952	
40.3	Decker Lake		Type E	100-152	1915	
45.7	Palling #1		Type E	100-152	1914	
45.7	Palling #2		FPS	GTP-FT	1950	
51.7	Rose Lake		Type E	100-152	1915	
58.9	Forestdale #1		Type E	100-152	1915	
58.9	Forestdale #2		FPS	GTP-FT	1948	
67.1	Topley		Type E	100-152	1914	
72.9	Perow		Type E	100-152	1914	
80.1	Knockholt #1		Type E	100-152	1914	
80.1	Knockholt #2		FPS	GTP-FT	1951	
85.1	Houston #1		Type E	100-152	1914	
85.1	Houston #2		Type G	100-168	1920	
85.1	Houston #3		STA			
91.4	Barrett #1		Type E	100-152	1914	
91.4	Barrett #2		FPS	GTP-FT	1951	
98.8	Walcott #1		Type E	100-152	1913	
98.8	Walcott #2		FPS			
107.1	Quick		FPS-1B	100-162		
112.7	Hubert #1		Type E	100-152	1914	
112.7	Hubert #2		FPS	GTP-FT	1949	
116.0	Telkwa #1		FPS-1B	100-162	1914	
116.0	Telkwa #2		Type G	100-168	1922	
116.0	Telkwa #3		STA			Trailer
116.0	Telkwa #4		STA			STA/EMBH
119.4	Tatlow		Type E	100-152	1914	
125.2	Smithers #1		STA		1915	Temporary, Note 58
125.2	Smithers #2		SPEC.	100-166	1919	Museum-1

TETE JAUNE SUBDIVISION
Redpass Jct., BC to McBride, BC—63.6 miles

Milepost	Locality	Proposed/Former Name	Type	Plan	Built	Notes
1.8	Selwyn	x-Resplendent–GTP	Type E	100-152	1912	
8.2	Alpland #1	x-Mt. Robson–GTP	Type E	100-152	1913	
8.2	Alpland #2		FPS		1922	
10.0	Emperor		SHLT		1926	Open Shelter
14.3	Swiftwater		Type E	100-152	1913	
17.8	Rearguard #1	x-Albreda–GTP	Type E	100-152	1913	
17.8	Rearguard #2		SHLT		1949	
25.1	Tete Jaune		Type E	100-152	1912	
30.0	Shere		Type E	100-152	1913	
37.4	Croydon #1		Type E	100-152	1913	
37.4	Croydon #2		FPS	GTP-FT	1954	

BRITISH COLUMBIA DISTRICT
Vancouver Terminals Division

TETE JAUNE SUBDIVISION
(continued)

Milepost	Locality	Proposed/Former Name	Type	Plan	Built	Notes
43.6	Dunster		Type E	100-152	1913	Museum-2
51.2	Raush Valley #1		Type E	100-152	1913	
51.2	Raush Valley #2		FPS			
56.9	Eddy #1		Type E	100-152	1913	
56.9	Eddy #2		FPS	110-101		x-SMBH
63.6	McBride #1		SPEC.	100-156	1913	
63.6	McBride #2		STA		1918	Temporary
63.6	McBride #3		SPEC.	100-167	1919	

COWICHAN SUBDIVISION
Victoria, BC to Kissinger, BC—95.3 miles

Milepost	Locality	Proposed/Former Name	Type	Plan	Built	Notes
0.0	Victoria–Point Ellice		SPEC.			
—	Victoria–Alpha Street		SPEC.		1917	
8.1	Colwood		FPS	100-41	<1924	
10.6	Glen Lake		SHLT		<1924	
14.8	Metchosin		FPS	100-41	<1924	
18.2	Rocky Point Siding		FPS		<1924	
24.5	Sassenos	x-McNeil	FPS		<1924	
26.5	Milnes Landing		FPS		<1924	
34.1	Leechtown		FPS		<1924	
35.5	Kapoor					
36.4	Sooke Lake		SHLT		1920	
42.0	Lakend					
46.8	Shawnigan Lake					
51.9	Kinsol					
58.0	Deerholme		FPS	100-41	1921	
63.7	Camscot					
66.7	Culchillum		FPS	100-41B		
69.2	Chanlog					
72.9	Lake Cowichan	x-Cowichan Lake	FPS	100-41B		
82.9	Youbou		FPS	100-41B		
90.4	Hawes					
95.3	Kissinger		SHLT		1929	

PATRICIA BAY SUBDIVISION
near Victoria-Alpha Street, BC to Patricia Bay, BC—15.2 miles

Milepost	Locality	Proposed/Former Name	Type	Plan	Built	Notes
1.7	Sydney					
	Mt. Douglas					
4.8	Cordova	x-Cordova Bay				
	Elk Lake					
8.6	Dooley		FPS	100-41	1917	
9.0	Brynmoor					
10.8	Saanichton					
	Scott					
	Bazan					
	Sidney					
15.2	Patricia Bay #1-A		FPS	100-41	1916	
15.2	Patricia Bay #1-B		FPS	100-41	1916	
15.2	Patricia Bay #1-C		FPS	100-41	1916	

NOTES:

56 The Prince Rupert Inn was the first of what was supposed to be a string of cross-country hostelries designed by Francis Mawson Rattenbury for the GTP. As it turned out, it was the only Rattenbury-designed hotel built by the company. The Inn was opened in 1907 and it was subsequently acquired by the Operating Department and converted into an ad hoc station. Associated costs: purchase $9,419, annex $21,303, remodeling $1,540 and temporary baggage room $346.

58 Replaced in 1919, converted into B&B shop in 1921.

ROSTER III

CNR Stations in Western Canada, Listed by Type

This roster provides as much information as possible about the various Canadian National depot designs built in western Canada. Although the data presented are incomplete in some cases, and many depots may have undergone some unidentified changes, the authors believe that the information presented will be adequate for the reader to formulate reasonable generalizations.

Roster III is arranged as follows:

CANADIAN NORTHERN RAILWAY[1]
__[2] **Class Station**
built to Plan 100-___[3]

PROVINCE

Station Name	Blt.	Cost	Alterations	Disp.	Notes
Western Depot[4]	1914[5]	$2250[6]	EXT/S/EL[7] 1918/22/37/56	s-1967[8]	Note15[9]

1. Administration responsible for the design of the depot.
2. Class or Type of Station.
3. Plan number used by CNR to identify this station design. All CNR station plans use the prefix "100-".
4. Station Name as given in railway employee operating timetables.
5. Year built—indicates the nominal year in which a station building was constructed. For further details pertaining to these construction dates, refer to the introductory notes in Roster II, page 101.
6. Cost—Costs are based on a number of railway records: original cost, estimated cost, or insurance-replacement costs. All three sources are used but preference is given to original cost, when available. But even these costs are not necessarily representative since items such as furnishings, signaling equipment, platform construction, etc. are sometimes included or omitted from the recorded costs.
7. Improvements—Letter(s) in this column correspond to the following key:

    RENOV   Alterations, renovations or repairs—records are not usually specific as to nature of work involved.
    CF   New concrete foundation
    CPF   New cedar pile foundation.
    EXT   Addition built onto original building.
    EL   Electrical service installed; electric lighting.
    F   Foundations upgraded. Either the existing wood foundation was rebuilt, or a new concrete foundation was installed.
    G   Gas heating installed
    I   Insulation added. Usually installed into walls, sometimes in the attic as well.
    PL   Indoor plumbing installed—records are not usually specific, but usually involved the installation of public washrooms.
    rl to   "—" indicates that the depot was moved to another site, either as a station or another railway building. If converted to another use it is noted:

    CO   Converted to coal shed
    FT   Converted to freight shed
    OB   Converted to office.
    SMBH   Converted to bunkhouse
    SH   Converted to section house
    ST   Converted to section tool house

    rl on site indicates that the building was shifted within the station grounds. Refer to Disposition for the year the relocation occurred.
    S   Stucco applied to exterior walls. Walers were not always installed.
    x-   relocated from the location shown, in the year noted.

    For electrical and plumbing, complete installations were not made in every case. The date following the improvement is the year in which it was carried out. In the event that a given improvement was made but the date is not known, the corresponding letter(s) is shown, with the year shown as "??".

8. Disposition—current dispositions correspond to the following key:

    d-   Demolished. As noted on railway records and/or field notes. This indicates that the building has been destroyed on site by the railway or its agent/contractor. Also refer to "s-" (sold).
    f-   Fire. Building destroyed by fire. This was also a common method of demolition used by the railway company or its agents/contractors. If it has been determined that the building was razed by fire on purpose, it is considered as "demolished."
    rl-   Relocated. Building relocated in the year indicated. Refer to the entry in Roster III to determine details of where it was relocated.
    rm-   Removed. Used when no official disposition has been determined, but field notes indicate that the building is no longer on railway property.

rp- Replaced. Existing building destroyed, but the cause could not be determined, or superseded by new construction. Year of replacement is noted. Refer to "**Notes**" to determine any subsequent disposition (i.e. retained by the railway company and converted to other uses, etc.).

rt- Retired. Railway designation indicating that ownership of the building has passed from the company and was thus deleted from records in the year noted. Building may have been "sold" or "demolished," but this was not noted on records consulted. The building was not necessarily removed from its site in the year retired.

s- Sold. Sold by the railway to either related corporate interests or private individuals/companies. Removal of the building from the site is usually a condition of sale. Buildings were generally moved by the purchaser to new locations close to the original site, where they were usually converted into private dwellings or farm buildings. The purchaser sometimes demolished the building in situ for salvage of building materials, but for the purposes of this roster these are not considered as "demolished."

Although every attempt has been made to keep the disposition data current, entries left blank do not necessarily indicate that the station remains on the property. Where known, "**EXTANT**" is shown in this column. Dispositions shown with an asterisk (*) are cross-referenced to the *Canadian Railway Station Guide* (Bruce Ballantyne—Editor, The Bytown Railway Society Inc., 1998), which provides directions to off-site stations.

9. Notes—further pertinent data. These notes are found in the box at the bottom right of each page spread.

Where plan numbers were not available, and photographs either could not be found or were inconclusive, the authors have used their judgments in classifying these depots. Classifications made on this basis are flagged as "**Probable**" in the "**Notes**" column. The depots in this category are classified on the basis of date built, dimensional data or other information that suggests that they were similar to other buildings of a particular group.

The listings at the end of this Roster provide details for station buildings that the authors could not identify. Additional details such as footprint dimensions are given in the "**Notes**" column.

CNoR SHELTERS
Plan 100-95—CNoR Standard Passenger Shelter

ALBERTA

Station Name	Blt.	Cost	Alterations	Disp.	Notes
Blackfoot #1-A	1908	4350		rm-	
Legal #1	1912		rp-1917, used as ST	s-1960	
Oliver	1912		EXT 1915	rm-1960	
Ranfurly #1-B	1909	$300		rp-1922	

MANITOBA

Station Name	Blt.	Cost	Alterations	Disp.	Notes
Babcock	1909			s-1957	
Enterprise	1909	$200		s-1959	
Findlay Crossing	1905			rm-	
Golden Stream	1906	$150	Conv. to ST in 1960		
Hartney Crossing	1905		I 1943	s-1975	
Hazeldean	1914	$215		s-1959	
Louise	1904	$250		s-1960	
Munroe	1909	$250		rm-	
Overstone				s-	

MINNESOTA

Station Name	Blt.	Cost	Alterations	Disp.	Notes
Peary	1917	$421		rt-1962	Probable

SASKATCHEWAN

Station Name	Blt.	Cost	Alterations	Disp.	Notes
Eldersley #1				rp-1922	
Haultain	1908	$160	rl-McBride, BC as ST	rl-1960	
Laura #1	1908			rp-1911	
Murphy's #1	By14			rp-1929	
Waseca #1	1905			rp-1911	

CNoR Miscellaneous Shelters

Station Name	Blt.	Cost	Alterations	Disp.	Notes
Minburn #1, Ab	1908		Ext 1909	rm-	Plan 170-8 FT
Valley River, Mb	1897				

CNoR FREIGHT & PASSENGER SHELTERS
Plan 100-96—CNoR Standard Freight & Passenger Shelter

ALBERTA

Station Name	Blt.	Cost	Alterations	Disp.	Notes
Royal Park	1909			rm-1960	
Spruce Grove–CNoR #1	1907			f-1914	

MANITOBA

Station Name	Blt.	Cost	Alterations	Disp.	Notes
Amaranth	1909		RENOV-1 1939/ Added bay window	s-1975	
Deerwood	1908	$475		s-1975	
Grande Clairiere #1	1908	$350	Conv. to SMBH 1919	gb-1969	Probable

CNoR FREIGHT & PASSENGER SHELTERS
Plan 100-96—CNoR Standard Freight & Passenger Shelter

MANITOBA

Station Name	Blt.	Cost	Alterations	Disp.	Notes
Hobson	1909	$481	rl-Rignold as ST	rl-1960	Probable
Ladysmith	1905	$350		s-1960	
Learys	1908	$250		s-1959	
Longburn	1906	$350	rl-Plumas as ST	rl-1960	
Mayfeld	1909	$350		s-1960	
Menzie	1909	$480	rl-Erickson as ST	rl-1960	
Methven Jct.	1909	$175		s-1959	
Ninette #1-B	1917		secondhand?	rm-	Probable/ Express Shed
Orrville	1910	$350	Conv. to ST 1960	rm-	
Pratt	1906	$310	I 1946		
Silverton #1				rp-1922	
Springhill	1910	$400		s-1960	
Vista	1909	$350	EL/rl-Rackham as ST	rl-1961	
Youill	1907	$481		s-1961	Probable

MINNESOTA

Station Name	Blt.	Cost	Alterations	Disp.	Notes
Ash Lake #2	———	$446	x-Ericsburg #1 1917	rt-1962	Probable
Ericsburg #1	1910		rl-Ash Lake #2	rl-1917	Probable

MANITOBA

Station Name	Blt.	Cost	Alterations	Disp.	Notes
Bethany #1				rp-1927	
Edwin	1909	$298		rt-1967	

SASKATCHEWAN

Station Name	Blt.	Cost	Alterations	Disp.	Notes
Aberfeldy	1909	$250	rl-Kitscoty, Ab as ST	rl-1960	
Brada	1909	$350		rm-1960	
Carmel #1	1908	$481	Conv. to SMBH 1911	s-1956	
Clarkboro	1909			rt-1959	
Clark's Crossing #1	1910			rp-1946	
Davis	1910	$481	rl-Prince Albert–CNoR as ??		
Dixon	1908	$481	Conv. to SMBH 1917	rt-1960	
Findlater #1	1909			rp-1911	
Kindersley #2	1910		Conv. to SMBH 1910	rm-	Variant/Temp.
Kylemore #1	1909			rp-1917	
Naisberry	1906	$481		s-1960	
Paswegin #1	1908			rp-1918	
Prairie River #1	1908			f-1919?	Probable
Prudhomme #1				rp-1910	
Rama #1-A	1909	$480	EL 1956	rp-1960	
Tiny	1909	$750		gb-1970	
Waldheim #1	1909			rp-1912	Probable

CNoR FREIGHT & PASSENGER SHELTERS
Plan 100-41—CNoR Standard Freight & Passenger Shelter

ALBERTA

Station Name	Blt.	Cost	Alterations	Disp.	Notes
Alness				rm-1959	
Ancona				d-1964	Probable
Ankerton	—		x-Fairmount, Sk #1 1918	rm-1960	
Armena	1915	$481		d-1961	
Ashmont #1	1921	$970	Conv. to SMBH 1929	s-1971	
Baintree	1915	$481		s-1963	
Barlow	1915			rm-	
Bellis #1	1919		rl-Edmonton for Hotel Dept.	rl-1923	
Benton #1	1913	$480	rl-Lanfine as SMBH	rl-1919	
Beynon	1915	$480	rl on site/EL 1921/	s-1961	
Blackfoot #1-B	1911		Added to west end of #1-A 1911	rm-	
Blue Ridge	1922	$1000		s-1966	
Bonar	1913	$481		f-1956	
Borradaile	1911			s-1960	
Brazeau #1-B	—		x-Hardene, Sk 1950/ rl-Edberg as ST	rl-1953	Baggage Shed
Briggs	1919	$481		rm-1959	
Burbank	1915	$481	rl-Calahoo #2	rl-1959	
Calahoo #2	—		x-Burbank 1959	s-1966	
Cannel				rm-1960	
Carolside	1920	$900		s-1969	
Cherhill	1916	$481		s-1965	
Claysmore	1911	4481		s-19?? *	
Clover Bar #2	—	$600	x-Vilna #1-EXT 1924	rm-	
Codner	1920			rm-1960	
Demay	—	$1000	x-Whitecourt #1-B 1922	s-1967	
Dinosaur	1921	$500	rl-Viewpoint as SMBH	rl-1932	Note 25
Dobson #1	1913			rp-1924	
Duagh	1921			rm-1960	
Dunshalt	1922	$1000		rm-1960	
Edmonton #1B	1914			d-1930s	Notes 13, 64
Edmonton–Calder Yard	—		x-Mikado, Sk #1 1919	rm-	TOS, Note 13
Edwand	1919	$800		d-1990s	
Entwistle–CNoR #1	1914			rp-1915	
Evansburg–CNoR #1	1916		rl-Evansburg–GTP as ?	rl-1924	
Excel #1	1913		rl-Oberlin	rl-1917	
Fenn	1916	$481		s-1963*	
Ferrier				rm-1959	Probable
Foothills Sub Mile 48.5	—	$1200	x-Sterco 1953	s-1962	
Galloway #2			x-Rochfort Bridge #1 1930/ rl-Mountain Park #1-B	rl-1940	
Gartly	1913			rm-	
Gibbons #1	1919			rp-1927	
Glenevis	1916	$481		s-1966	
Green Court	—	$1200	x-Mayerthorpe #1 1929	d-1969	
Gunn	—	$481	x-Legal #2 1917	s-1966	
Halliday	—	$900	x-Pollockville #1 1920	rm-1949	
Hilliard	1917		EL 1954	rm-1961	
Horburg	1918	$900		rm-1959	
Inland	1922	$1200		rm-1960	
Janet	1916			f-1930	
Joffre	1916	$480		f-1961	
Kerensky	1919	$900		rm-1960	
Kiron	—	$481	x-Stanmore #1 1918	rm-1960	
Lake Isle #1	1916	$481		f-1923	
Lanfine #1				rp-1918	
Leahurst	1918	$500		s-1960	
Legal #2	1917	$480	rl-Gunn	rl-1917	
Lisburn	1917	$481		rm-1961	
Lloydminster #1-B	1917			rm-	Express Shed
Looma	1915	$481		s-1967	
Macleod Jct.	—		x-Merid, Sk 1918	rm-	
Marlboro–GTP #2	—		x-Riverbend 19??	rm-	
Mayerthorpe #1	1922	$650	rl-Green Court	rl-1929	
Meanook	1915	$448		s-1967*	
Mercoal	—	$1000	x-Michichi #1 1924	s-1964	
Michichi #1	1913		rl-Mercoal	rl-1924	
Nestow	1914	$481		s-1963*	
New Sarepta	1915	$481		s-1974	
Norfolk	1915		EXT 1920	rm-1960	
Oberlin	—		x-Excel #1 1917	s-	
Owlseye	1921		rl on site 1940	s-1979	
Pollockville #1	1920	$900	rl-Halliday	rl-1920	
Prevo				rm-1959	
Redland #1	1915			rp-1921	
Redwater #1	1920	$1000	Used as FT after 1950	rm-	

ALBERTA (cont.)

Station Name	Blt.	Cost	Alterations	Disp.	Notes
Riverbend	1912		rl-Marlboro–GTP #2	rl-	
Rochfort Bridge #1	1922		rl-Galloway #2	rl-1930	
Rosalind	—	$480	x-Wayne #1 1918/ EL 19??	rt-1967	
Rose Lynn	1922	$1200		s-1962	
Rosebud #1	1913			rp-1919	
Rosedale #1	1913		rl-Drumheller as switchmen's	rl-	
Rowley #1	1915		Conv. into SMBH	rp-1922	
Saunders	1918	$800		rm-1959	
Scotfield	1913	$481		s-1969	
Scotford	1911			rm-1960	
Spedden	1919	$900	EXT/EL 1938/53	d-	
Stanmore #1	1913		rl-Kiron	rl-1918	
Sterco	1922	$1200	rl-Mileage 48.5 Foothills Sub	rl-1953	
Taplow	1920		rl-Eyre, Sk as ST	rl-1950	
Troon				rm-	Probable
Vilna #1	1919	$600	rl-Clover Bar #2	rl-1924	
Vimy #1	1914			rp-1952	
Volmer	1913	$481		a-1947	Note 5
Wardlow	1921	$1200		rm-	
Warspite #1	1919			f-1950	
Waskatenau #1	1920	$1000	rl-Edmonton (B&B stores stock)	rl-1928	
Watts	1913	$481		s-1960*	
Wayne #1	1913		rl-Rosalind	rl-1918	
Whitecourt #1-A	1922	$1000	rl-Demay	rl-1922	
Whitecourt #1-B	1922		rl-Watrous, Sk as yard office	rl-1922	
Withrow				rm-1960	Probable

BRITISH COLUMBIA

Station Name	Blt.	Cost	Alterations	Disp.	Notes
Angelsey	1917			rt-1963	
Arnold	1915	$480		rm-1960	
Ashcroft Sub Mile 98.5	1916			rm-	Plan 100-35
Cisco	1917			rm-1960	
Clearwater #1	1918	$400		rp-1961	
Clearwater Sub Mile 129.3	1916		rl-Heffley–2nd site	rl-	Plan 100-35
Cottonwood Flats				rm-	Probable
Cox	1915	$481		rm-1959	
Deerholme	1921	$800			
Dooley	1917			rm-	
Glen Valley	1915	$480		rm-1960	
Heffley	—		x-Mileage 129.3 Clearwater Sub	rm-1960	Plan 100-35
Isle Pierre #2	—		x-Indi, Sk 1960		
Loos #2	—	$1188	x-Crocus, Mb 1958/ rl-Aleza Lake	rl-1966	
Martel	1917	$350		rm-	
Mt. Lehman	1916	$480		rm-1960	
Mt. Robson #1-A	1922	$696		rm-	2nd location
Patricia Bay #1-A	1916	$800	rl-Metchosin	rl-1921	
Patricia Bay #1-B	1916	$800	rl-Cowichan Lake	rl-1925	
Patricia Bay #1-C	1916	$800	rl-Youbou	rl-1926	
Popkum	1917	$350		rm-1960	
St. Elmo	1915			rm-	
Smithvale	1922	$500		rm-	
Spences Bridge #2	1922		rl-Wire Cache	rl-1923	Temporary
Wire Cache	—	$800	x-Spences Bridge #2 1923	rm-1960	

MANITOBA

Station Name	Blt.	Cost	Alterations	Disp.	Notes
Adelpha	1916	$470	rl-Hartney as ST	rl-1960	

NOTES:
5 The line between St. Albert and Morinville, Ab was abandoned effective 1 September 1947.
13 This station was technically on the Edmonton Terminals Subdivision.
25 A train-order station was set up at this junction by late 1921. The former scale house from Drumheller was joined to a Standard FPS north of the junction switch. The shelter building was converted into living quarters and the scale house into a telegraph office, complete with order-board. This arrangement lasted until May 1927, after which all operating was handled out of the nearby Munson depot. The train-order station was removed, replaced by a register booth.
64 This FPS was set up as a stores building for the Sleeping & Dining Car Department.

CNoR FREIGHT & PASSENGER SHELTERS
Plan 100-41—CNoR Standard Freight & Passenger Shelter

MANITOBA

Station Name	Blt.	Cost	Alterations	Disp.	Notes
Albert	1918	$570	rl-St. James as ST	rl-1963	
Agar	1911	$475	Conv. to ST	rm-	
Argue	1910	$475	rl-Elgin as ST	rl-1960	Probable
Argyle	1912	$475	rl-St. James as ST	rl-1959	
Arizona #2	—	$650	x-Hodgson 1915	rm-	
Ashdown	1912	$400	rl-Ray, Mn as ST	rl-1960	
Ashern #1	1914	$481	rl-Holmfield #2-B	rl-1918	
Ashville	1912	$450	rl-Cowan #2	rl-1966	
Balsam Bay	1915	$481			
Barrows #2	1923	$500	rl-Dauphin as gardener's store	rl-1923	
Bedford #1	1915	4481	rl-South Jct. #2	rl-1952	
Belair	—	$481	x-Parkmount 1940		
Benard	1912	$470	rl-Newton as ST	rl-	
Bield	1912	$450		d-1970	
Birch Bay	1918	$514	rl-Wanless	rl-1960	
Birch River #1	1911		Renov/l 1924/42/ rl-Rama, Sk #1-B	rl-1948	
Birdtail	1915	$360	rl-Rossburn as ST	rl-1960	
Bloom	—	$1200	x-Emerson		
Broad Valley	1915	$470			
Brumlie	1914	$470	rl-Elphinstone as ST	rl-1960	
Butler	1910	$400		s-1966	
Caliento	1913	$650	rl-Ridgeville as ST	rl-1960	
Calrin	1912	$470	rl-Searle as ST	rl-1960	
Camper	1913		Conv. to ST 1960		
Cartier	1919			s-1960	
Cawdor	—	$950	x-Dropmore #1 1921/Conv. to ST 1960		
Chatfield	1915	$412			
Colby	1916	$470	rl-McCreary as ST	rl-1960	
Cordova	1912	$500	rl-Portage la Prairie as ST	rl-1959	
Cormorant	—	$1251	x-Dufresne 1960	EXTANT*	
Cowan #2	—		x-Ashville 1966		
Crocus	1922		rl-Loos, BC #2	rl-1959	
Curtis	1911	$481	Conv. to ST 1960		
Dacotah	1917	$450	rl-Portage Jct. as ST	rl-1960	
Deepdale #1	1915			rp-1922	
Deerhorn	1915	$475	EXT 19??/ Conv. into ST 1960		
Dropmore #1			rl-Cawdor	rl-1921	
Dufresne	1913	$481	rl-Cormorant	rl-1960	
East Selkirk	1915	$481			
Elliotts	1912	$400	rl-Wawanesa as ST	rl-1960	
Erickson	1911		rl-Rackham	rl-1923	
Erinview	1912	$475	rl-Portage Jct.	rl-1960	
Fairview	1912	$475	Conv. to ST 1960		
Faulkner	1916	$475	rl-Steep Rock as ST	rl-1960	
Fork River #3	—	$487	x-Sturdee 1959/ rl-Pine River as SMBH	rl-1970	
Fortier #2	1923	$1200	rl-Carman as ST	rl-1959	
Fredenstahl	1910	$650	rl-Emerson as ST	rl-1958	
Fulton	1916	$480	rl-Somerset as ST	rl-1958	
Garland	1911	$533	Conv. to ST	EXTANT*	
Gateside	1912	$470	rl-Worby	rl-1951	
Glenforsa	1910	$480	rl-Portage la Prairie as ST	rl-1958	
Glenlea	1916	$480		s-1959	
Gonor	1915	$481	rl-East Selkirk as ST	rl-1960	
Gordon	1910	$481	Conv. to ST 1960		
Grande Clariere #2	1919	$804		f-1951	Probable
Grande Clariere #3	—		x-Tremaine 1951	rm-	
Hallboro #3	—	$475	x-Osprey 1948/ rl-Mulvihill #3	rl-1949	Temporary
Harcus	1922	$900	rl-Portage la Prairie as ST	rl-1959	
Herchmer Sub Mile 498.5	—		x-Mennon, Sk 1960/ rl-Dauphin as SMBH	rl-	
Hilbre	1916	$475	Conv. to ST 1960		
Hillside Beach	—	$490	x-Calley 1921	rm-	
Hodgson #1			rl-Arizona #2	rl-1915	
Holmfield #2-B	—	$481	x-Ashern #1 1918	s-1960	
Howden	1910	$481	rl-Rossburn Jct.	rl-1927	
Hummerston	1913	$475	rl-Portage la Prairie as ST	rl-1960	
Indian Springs	1911		Conv. into ST 1960	gb-1969	
Jordan	1917	$480	rl-Deerwood as ST	rl-1960	
Kane #1	1916	$470		f-1947	
Kane #2	—	$481	x-St. Charles 1947/Conv. to ST 1960		
Katrime	1919	$480		s-1971	
Lakeland	1915	$475	Conv. to ST 1960		
Lavina	1913	$470	rl-Rivers as ST	rl-1960	
Lelant	1916	$470	rl-St. James as ST	rl-1959	
Libau	1915	$470	EL 1951	rm-1975	
Makaroff #1-A	1912	$400	l 1949	s-1965	
Martinville	1912	$400	Conv. into SMBH 1960		
Meharry #1	1911			rp-1924	
Menisino	1910	$650	rl-Piney as ST	rl-1960*	
Merle	1910	$475		gb-1969	
Millwater	—		x-Hassan, Sk 1960		
Moore	1910	$401	rl-Transcona #2-B	rl-1952	
Moosehorn #1		$481	rl-Woodroyd	rl-1918	
Mountain Side	1916	$470	rl-Fairlight as ST	rl-1960	
Muir	1911	$350	EXT 1921	rt-1969	
Mulvihill #3	—	$475	x-Hallboro #3 1949/ Conv. to ST 1960	gb 1969	
Narcisse	1915	$470			
Navin	1910	$481	rl-Fort Frances as CO	rl-1960	
Newton	1911	$481	rl-West Tower as ST		rl-1960
Ochre River #1-B		$470		gb-1969	Express Shed
Ogilvie #2	—		x-Sandy Lake #1 1921	rl-1966	Probable
Osprey	1911	$475	rl-Hallboro #3	rl-1948	
Parkmount	1917	$470	rl-Belair	rl-1940	
Pawistik	—		x-Wampum 1960		
Petrel	1912	$475	Conv. into ST 1960		
Poplarfield	1915	$470		s-1970	
Powell	1919	$700	rl-Barrows as ST	rl-1961	
Rackham	—		x-Erickson #1 1923/ rl-Oakburn as ST	rl-1960	
Reids	1911	$475		gb-1965	
Renwer	1912	$480		s-19??*	
Riding Mountain	1910	$481	Conv. into ST 1960		
Rossburn Jct.	—	$481	x-Howden 1927/ rl-Cranberry Portage	rl-1958	
Rufford	1912	$500	rl-Clanwilliam as ST	rl-1960	
St. Charles	1917	$481	rl-Kane #2	rl-194	Note 34
St. Martin	1914	$500	EL 1951/ rl-Winnipeg Yard as ?	rl-1966	
Sandilands	1916	$481	rl-Jones, On #2	rl-1964	
Sandridge	1916	$470	rl-Inwood as ST	rl-1960	
Sandy Lake #1			rl-Ogilvie	rl-1921	Probable
Scanterbury	1915	$481		gb-1969	
Sclater	1911	$616			
Semple	1918	$481	rl-Fort Rouge as ?	rl-1960	
Sevick	1923	$882		gb-1970	
Shevlin	1911	$460		rm-	
Shortdale	1911	$450		s-1974	
South Jct. #2	—		x-Bedford #1 1952	s-1961	
Steep Rock Jct.	1920	$470	rl-Woodlands as ST	rl-1961	
Stephenfield	1911	$485	rl-Roseisle as ST	rl-1960	
Sundown	1910	$494	Conv. to ST 1960	s-1970	
Timberton #2	1918	$450		s-1964	
Tolstoi	1910	$471		EXTANT*	
Transcona #2-B	—		x-Moore 1952/ rl-Fort Rouge as ST	rl-1962	Note 34
Tremaine	1915	$500	rl-Grande Clariere #3	rl-1951	
Ukraina	1913	$451	EXT 1920		
Union Point	1915			gb-1969	
Villette	1911	$475	Conv. into ST 1960	rm-	
Wampum	1913	$550	rl-Pawistik	rl-1960	
Wanless	—	$514	x-Birch Bay 1960		
West Transcona	1913	$481	EL	gb-1969	
Willow Range	1912	$470	rl-Arona as ST	rl-1960	
Woodroyd	—	$475	x-Moosehorn #1 1918/ rl-Transcona as ST	rl-1960	
Worby	—	$470	x-Gateside 1951	s-1965	
Wyntonville	1914	$470	rl-Shilo as ST	rl-1960	

MINNESOTA

Station Name	Blt.	Cost	Alterations	Disp.	Notes
Cusson #2	—		rl-Falls Jct. #2	rl-1965	
Falls Jct. #2	—	$700	x-Cusson #2 1965		
Haley	1911	$430		rt-1962	
Nopeming	1913	$646		rt-1962	
Simar	1918	$439		rt-1962	
Twig	1918	$439		rt-1962	
Whiteface	1921	$715		rt-1962	

ONTARIO

Station Name	Blt.	Cost	Alterations	Disp.	Notes
Banning #2	—	$480	x-Hume 1959/ rl-Umfreville #3	rl-1964	
Collins #2	—		x-Rocky Inlet 1967		
Conmee	1923	$1000	l 1941/rl-McIntosh #2	rl-1964	

CNoR FREIGHT & PASSENGER SHELTERS
Plan 100-41—CNoR Standard Freight & Passenger Shelter

ONTARIO

Station Name	Blt.	Cost	Alterations	Disp.	Notes
Farrington #1	1911	$511	RENOV 1945	f-1954	
Hume	1914	$480	rl-Banning #2	rl-1959	
Jones #2	—		x-Sandilands, Mb 1964		
McIntosh #2	—		x-Conmee 1964		
Rocky Inlet	1911	$600	rl-Collins #2	rl-1967	Probable
Twin City	1912		rl-West Fort as ST	rl-1942	
Umfreville #3	—	$480	x-Banning #2 1964		

SASKATCHEWAN

Station Name	Blt.	Cost	Alterations	Disp.	Notes
Abbott	1923	$1200		s-1962	
Adams	—	$480	x-St. Boswells #1 1923/ rl-Fort Qu'Appelle as ST	rl-1960	
Amsterdam	1915	$800	Conv. to SMBH 1973	rm-	
Anerley #1	1913	$481	rl-Snipe Lake as SMBH	rl-1930	
Antar	1913	$480	rl-Moose Jaw Jct. as ST	rl-1949	
Ardill #1	1913			rp-1923	
Arma	—	$900	x-Canwood #1 1920	rt-1960	
Arran #1	1911	$481	rl-Mistatim #1-A	rl-1919	
Bannock #2	—	$481	x-Sturgis #1 1919	rp-1954	
Barbour	1916	$481	rl-Canora as ST	rl-1960	Not Moved?
Barvas	1915	$481	rl-Atimeg Lake, Mb as ST	rl-1959	
Beadle #1	By12		rl-Carlton	rl-1916	
Beechy #1	1921			rp-1923	
Bienfait #1	1913			rp-1915	Probable
Birling	1911			rm-	
Bodmin	—	$481	x-Dunblane #1 1917	s-1963*	
Brancepeth #1			EXT 1921	rp-1935	
Bratton	1912	$481	rl-Nutana as ST	rl-1960	
Bredin	1922	$1200		rm-	
Bresaylor #2	1923	$356	1 1937	rm-1960	
Brisbin	—		x-Debden #1 1918/ rl-Brock as ST	rl-1960*	Museum-2
Browning #1	1912	$470	Conv. to SMBH 1926	rm-	
Bryant	1912	$480		s-1960*	
Buckland	1914	4481		rm-	
Calder #1	1912			rp-1914	
Calley	1915		rl-Hillside Beach, Mb	rl-1960	
Canwood #1			rl-Arma	rl-1920	
Carlton	—	$481	x-Beadle #1 1916	s-1963	
Ceepee	1911	$481		rt-1960	
Chambers	1912	$481	rl-Nutana as ST	rl-1960	
Clair	1912		x-Tiny-EXT/1 1923/37	s-1979	
Claybank	1913	4480		rm-	
Cleeves	1922	$1000	rl-Turtleford as ST	rl-1966	
Clouston	1914	$481		s-1961	
Coppen	1923	$480	rl-Bateman as ST	rl-1960	
Cote	1912	$400		gb-1970	
Cowper	1912	$500	rl-Kipling as ST	rl-1960	
Crutwell #1	1912	$481		f-1947	
Cullen	1916	$480		s-1960	
D'Arcy #1	1915		rl-Kinhop	rl-1916	
Daylesford	1921	$990		s-1966*	
Debden #1	1914		rl-Brisbin	rl-1918	Museum-2
Donovan #1	1913	$480	rl-Strong	rl-1918	
Donwell	1913	$351		s-1985	
Doonside	1911	$575		rm-	
Dreghorn	1912	$470	rl-Jameson as ST/ rl-Montmartre	rl-1960/64	
Dudley	1922		rl-Saskatoon as office	rl-	
Dunblane #1			rl-Bodmin	rl-1917	
Eldred	1911	$481		s-1963	
Erwood #2	1918	$523	EL 1955	rm-	
Ettington #1	1913			rp-1914	
Fairmount #1	By14		rl-Ankerton, Ab	rl-1918	
Fenton #2	1914		rl-Mileage 15.4 St. Brieux Sub as SMBH	rl-1942	
Galilee	1916	$480	rl-Avonlea as ST	rl-1960	
Grasswood	—		x-Parkside #1 1916/ rl-McBride, BC as ST	rl-1960	Note 21
Greenan	1915	$481		s-1969	
Hamlin	1914	$481		s-1974	
Hamton #1	1913			rp-1924	
Hardene	1920		rl-Brazeau, Ab #1-B	rl-1950	
Hardy #1	1913			rp-1918	
Hassan	1915	$800	rl-Millwater, Mb	rl-1960	
Hazel Dell	1921	$1200		s-1974*	
Hearne #1	1913			rp-1917	
Hepburn #1		$800	EXT 1922/ Conv. to SMBH 1930	rt-1953	
Highgate	1919	$470		s-1960*	

CNoR FREIGHT & PASSENGER SHELTERS
Plan 100-41—CNoR Standard Freight & Passenger Shelter

SASKATCHEWAN

Station Name	Blt.	Cost	Alterations	Disp.	Notes
Holbein	1915	$481		s-1974	
Hyas #1	1912			rp-1937	
Inchkeith	1911	$475		s-1969	
Indi	1915	$480	rl on site/ rl-Isle Pierre, BC #2	rl-1960	
Juniper	1913	$800	rl-Dunblane as ST	rl-1960	
Kegworth #1	1911	$379		rp-1926	Probable
Kendal #1	1916	$481		gb-1969	
Kessock	1915	$481		gb-1969	
Ketchen	1920	$1200		rm-	
Kilwinning	1913	$481		s-1964	
Kingsford	1917	$480	rl-Estevan as ST	rl-1960	
Kinhop	—		x-D'Arcy #1 1916/ rl-Tessier as ST	rl-1960	
Krydor #1	1913			rp-1917	
Kuroki #2	1917		I/EL 1940/53	s-19??*	
Kylemore #2	—	$1000	x-Weldon #1 1917	s-1965*	
Leckford	1911	$481		s-1963	
Lilac	1917			s-1967	
Lintlaw #1				rp-1920	
Lipsett	1915	$481		s-1961	
Mair	1910	$470		s-1963	
Mennon	1913	$481	rl Mileage 498.5 Herchmer Sub, Mb	rl-1960	
Merid #1	1910		rl-Macleod Jct., Ab	rl-1918	
Mikado #1			rl-Edmonton- Calder Yard, Ab as TOS	rl-1919	
Mistatim #1-A	—	$481	x-Arran 1919/EXT 1945	rm-	
Moreland	1913	$480		s-1962	
Nut Mountain #1	1922	$600	rl-Sturgis as ST	rl-1947	
Okla	1922	$1100		s-1974*	
Palmer #1	1913			rp-1917	
Parkside #1	1912	$480	rl-Grasswood	rl-1916	
Parry #1	1913			rp-1916	Probable
Paswegin #2	1918	$1000		rm-	
Pathlow #1	1915			rm-1922	
Peesane #2	1911	$1000	EXT 1926	s-1964	
Peterson #2	—	$350	x-Ridgedale #1 1933	s-1963	
Pinkham #1	By14			rp-1915	
Polwarth	1915	$481		s-1961	
Prince #1	1914		rl-Richard as SMBH	rl-1928	
Pym	1915		rl-Rosetown as SMBH	rl-1960*	
Rama #1-B	—		x-Birch River #1 1948	rm-	Add to #1-A
Redberry	1913	$481		s-1963	
Richard #1	1913			rp-1916	Probable
Ridgedale #1	1922	$350		rl-1933	Note 6
Ritchie	1916	$470		s-1960	
Roddick	1916	$481		s-1960	
Roscoe #2	1918	$514	Conv. into SMBH 1960		
Runnymede #1			rl-Mileage 81.5 Togo Sub	rl-1919	
Ryerson	1912	$470	rl-Parkman as ST	rl-1963	
St. Boswells #1	1923		rl-Adams	rl-1923	
St. Brieux #1	1915			rp-1920	
Souris Valley	1913		rl-Woodley #2	rl-1947	
Spring Valley #1	1913			rp-1916	
Spruce Lake	1922	$1200	EL 1951	rt-1964	
Strehlow	1914	$480		rm-	
Strong	—	$480	x-Donovan #1 1918	rl-1960	Note 19
Sturdee	1915	$481	rl-Fork River, Mb #2	rl-1959	
Sturgis #1	By14	$481	rl-Bannock #2	rl-1919	
Surbiton	1913	$481	rl-Conquest as ST	rl-1960*	
Tadmore	1915	$500		EXTANT*	
Tichfield #1	1918			rp-1949	
Tilney #1	1913			rm-1922	
Togo Sub Mile 81.5	—		x-Runnymede #1 1919	rm-	
Tonkin	1916	$481	rl-Shellmouth, Mb as ST	rl-1961	

NOTES:

6 The sources regarding the disposition of this station are contradictory. One says that the structure was cut in half, one portion being shipped to Birch Hills and the other to Star City, for use as section bunkhouses. Another source indicates that, in 1933, this building was relocated to Peterson as a section bunkhouse.

19 The sources regarding the disposition of this station are contradictory. One states that it was relocated to McBride, BC, the other says it was moved to Redpass Jct., BC.

21 The sources regarding the disposition of this station are contradictory. One record indicates that both buildings were moved to Redpass Jct., BC while another source states that they were both relocated to McBride, BC.

34 This station was technically on the Winnipeg Terminals Subdivision.

CNoR FREIGHT & PASSENGER SHELTERS
Plans 100-41—CNoR Standard Freight & Passenger Shelter

SASKATCHEWAN

Station Name	Blt.	Cost	Alterations	Disp.	Notes
Tullis	1921	$900		s-1974*	
Valparaiso #1	1916			rp-1920	
Vanscoy #1	By11			rp-1912	
Weldon #1	By 12	$1000	rl-Kylemore #2	rl-1917	
Whittome	1923	$1000		s-1961	
Wimmer	1910			s-1976	
Woodley #2	—		x-Souris Valley 1947	rm-	
Wordsworth #1	1912	$500		rm-1929	

CNoR PORTABLE STATIONS
Plan 100-24—CNoR Standard Portable Station

ALBERTA

Station Name	Blt.	Cost	Alterations	Disp.	Notes
Ranfurly #1-A	1907	$386		rp-1922	

MANITOBA

Station Name	Blt.	Cost	Alterations	Disp.	Notes
Agnew #1					Probable
Clarkleigh	1911	$475	rl-Oak Point as ST	rl-1960	
Durban #1			rl-Prairie River, Sk #2	rl-1919	
Endcliffe	1910		rl-Shellmouth as ST	rl-1962	
Glenora	1908	$650		f-1959	
Grahamdale	1913	$475	rl-Ashern as ST	rl-1961	
Moline	1912	$400		s-1960	
Oak Bluff	1910	$1125		s-1960	
Pleasant Point	1910	$350		s-1960	
Timberton #1	1909		Conv. to dwelling 1918		

SASKATCHEWAN

Station Name	Blt.	Cost	Alterations	Disp.	Notes
Bresaylor #1	1908			rp-1923	
Crooked River #1-A	1907			rm-	
Dalzell	1911	$470		s-1962	
Dummer #1	1913			rp-1916	
Fenton #1	1907	$350	Conv. ST 1914	s-1974	
Prairie River #2	—	$481	x-Durban, Mb #1 1919/ Conv. To SMBH 1920		
Veregin #1	1908			rp-1911	

Plan 110-73A—CNoR Standard Portable Station (Based on Bunkhouse Plan)

ALBERTA

Station Name	Blt.	Cost	Alterations	Disp.	Notes
Barlow Jct.	1921			rm-	Reverse Plan
Coalspur #1-B	1923			gb-1964	
Nightingale	1922			rm-	
Rosedale #3	—		x-Wayne #2-B	rm-	
Sibbald #1	1913	$1200	rl-Drumheller as yard office	rl-1919	
Wayne #2-B	1919		rl-Rosedale #3	rm-	

MANITOBA

Station Name	Blt.	Cost	Alterations	Disp.	Notes
Grand Marais	1921	$1000		gb-1969	

SASKATCHEWAN

Station Name	Blt.	Cost	Alterations	Disp.	Notes
Eatonia #1	1922		rl-Richlea as ST	rl-1924	
Hawker	1914		rl-Delisle as SMBH	rl-1960*	
Kelvington #1	1922		rl-Moseley	rl-1922	
Moseley	—		x-Kelvington #1 1922	s-1974	
St. Walburg	1921		rl-Edmonton, Ab as ?	rl-1923	
Willow Bunch #1-A	1926	$1200	Conv. to SMBH 1927/ rl-Estevan	rl-1945	

CNoR COMBINATION STATION & SECTION HOUSES
Plan 100-16—Standard Combination Station & Section House (CSS-NPR)

MANITOBA

Station Name	Blt.	Cost	Alterations	Disp.	Notes
Altamont #1	1899	$2800	I 1938	s-1962	
Belmont #1-A	1889		EXT (see Entry under Plan 100-3)		
Miami	1889	$2800	EXT/I 19??/38	s-19??*	Reverse, Museum-1
Wawanesa	1889	$4000	EXT-S/I 1928/40	s-1977*	
White Plains	1891	$2000	I-S/EL 1936/51	s-1956	Probable

Plan 100-100—Standard Combination Station & Section House (CSS-CPR)

SASKATCHEWAN

Station Name	Blt.	Cost	Alterations	Disp.	Notes
Bethune	1890	$3000	S/I/EL 1928/40/53	s-1978*	Note 71
Chamberlain	1890	$3000	RENOV/S/I/EL 1917/28/40/55	d-1977	Note 71
Craik	1890	$4000	EXT-S/I/PI 1927/39/64	d-	Note 71
Duck Lake	1891	$4000	S/PL 1929/64	s-1982	Note 71
Dundurn	1892	$4369	S/EXT/PL 1927/45/64	s-1978	Note 71

CNoR COMBINATION STATION & SECTION HOUSES
Plan 100-100—CNoR Standard Combination Station & Section House (CSS-CPR)

SASKATCHEWAN

Station Name	Blt.	Cost	Alterations	Disp.	Notes
Kenaston	1890	$3000	S/I 1927/41	s-1980	Note 71
Lumsden #1	1890		EXT 1904	f-1908	Note 71
MacDowall	1891	$2963	S/EL 1929/56	s-1977	Note 71
Osler	1892	$2000	S 1929	s-1966	Note 71
Prince Albert–CNoR #1	1890		Conv. into FT 1906	rm-	Notes 28, 71
Saskatoon–CNoR #1	1891		EXT 1905	rp-1910	Notes 4, 71

Plan 100-63—CNoR Standard Combination Station & Section House (Type A)

MANITOBA

Station Name	Blt.	Cost	Alterations	Disp.	Notes
Cowan #1	1899	$1800	CPF-I/EL 1938/53	f-1965	
Dauphin #1	1897		Part conv. into yard office	d-1923?	
Ethelbert	1898	$5000	I 1938	s-19??*	
Fork River #1	1899			rp-1920	
Glencairn		$2400	I/S 1939/41	s-1965	Probable
Glenella #1	1897			rp-1913	
Grandview	1900	$4900	S/I 1928/37	rm-	
Laurier	1899	$2400	S/I/I 1929/37/45	rm-	
Ochre River #1-A	1899	$2400	S/I 1929/37	s-	
Plumas	1896	$2400	S/I/I 1929/38/43	rm-	
Sifton	1897	$5000	EXT/CPF-I 1919/38	s-1968	
Swan River	1899	$6500	EXT/EXT/EL/I/PL 1914/18/27/35/58	rm-	
Winnipegosis	1897	$5200	RENOV/I/S/RENOV 1918/23/38/40	s-19??*	

Plan 100-99—CNoR Standard Combination Station & Section House (Type B)

Station Name	Blt.	Cost	Alterations	Disp.	Notes
Baden, Mb	1901	$1800	I 1954	s-1970	
Barrows #1, Mb	1908			rt-1923	
Bowsman, Mb	1900	$3500	EXT/EXT/EXT/S 1909/10/25/??	s-1982*	Museum-2
Erwood #1, Sk	1901			rp-1918	
Gilbert Plains, Mb	1900		EXT/I-S 1914/37	s-1973*	
Minitonas, Mb	1899	$2000	RENOV/RENOV 19??/46	rm-	
Novra, Mb	1901	$1800	I/I/EL 1951/54/55	s-1970*	
Pine River #1, Mb	1907	$3500	I-S 1935	f-1962	
Westgate, Mb	1901	$1800	I 1954	rm-1970	
Woodridge, Mb	1902	$1200	I-S/EL 1937/55	s-1984	

Plans 100-47 & 100-98—CNoR Standard Combination Station & Section House (Type C)
(Plan 100-98 was the designation for this design in British Columbia)

ALBERTA

Station Name	Blt.	Cost	Alterations	Disp.	Notes
Bilby #1	1913	$2390		s-1959	
Bliss	1914	$2390		s-1932*	
Brule #1	1914	$2390	EXT/S 1922/42	f-1952	
Calahoo #1	1913	$2390		d-1959	
Carrot Creek–CNoR	1915	$2390		s-1923	Note 62
Chip Lake #1	1913	$2390	I-S 1942	d-1951	
Colinton	1913	$3200	EXT/CPF-I/S/EL 1939/40/45/??	rm-	
Dalehurst–CNoR	1915	$2390	rl-Pedley?	rl-1927	Note 73
Darwell	1913			s-1936	Note 36
Dayson	1913	$2390		rm-	Note 62
Decoigne	1914	$2400	I 19??/rl-Yellowhead, BC #2	rl-1944	
Entrance–CNoR	1914	$2390		s-1932*	
Forestburg	1916	$2390	CPF-I/S/EL-PL 1940/42/??	s-	
Fulstow	1914	$2390		s-1923	Note 62
Galahad	1916	$2390	CPF-I/S/EL 1940/42/??	rm-	
Galloway #3	—		x-SH, Mileage 15.3 Brule Sub 1940	s-1975*	Note 42, Museum-2
Heisler	1916	$2390	I-S/EL 1942/??	rm-1971	
Henry House–CNoR	1914	$2067		s-	Note 44
Horner	1914	$2390		rm-	Note 62
Kelsey #1	1916			rm-	
Lobstick	1913	$2390		s-1936*	
Magnolia	1913	$2400		s-1936	Note 36
Marlboro	1914	$2067	rl-Mileage15.3 Brule Sub as SH	rl-1940	Note 41
Miette	1914	$2390	CPF-I/S/EL 1940/42/60	d-1969	
Obed–CNoR	1914	$2390	rl-Obed-GTP, CPF-I/S 1940/42	rl-	Note 43
Pedley #2	—		x-Dalehurst–CNoR? EXT-R-S 1927	d-1961	Note 73
Perryvale	1913	$2400	S/EL/PL 1945/56/??	s-19??*	
Rochester	1913	$2390	I-S/EL 1937/56	d-1969	

CNoR COMBINATION STATION & SECTION HOUSES
Plans 100-47 & 100-98—CNoR Standard Combination Station & Section House (Type C)

ALBERTA

Station Name	Blt.	Cost	Alterations	Disp.	Notes
Scriven	1915	$2390		rm-	Note 62
Snaring	1915	$2390	CPF/I/S 1939/40/43	d-1969	
Sundance	1914	$2067		rm-	Note 40
Tawatinaw	1913	$2390	I-S/EL 937/56	s-19??*	
Villeneuve	1913	$2390	I-S/EL-PL 1937/53	s-1974	

BRITISH COLUMBIA

Station Name	Blt.	Cost	Alterations	Disp.	Notes
Albreda–CNoR	1915		I 1934	rm-	
Avola #1	1915	$2390	I-S/EL 1935/56	s-1976*	
Barriere #1	1916			f-1953	
Basque	1915	$2500		d-1973	
Birch Island	1915	$2390	I-S 1935	d-	
Blackpool	1915	$2390	I-S 1936	rm-	
Boulder	1915			rt-1963	
Canoe River	1915	$1800		rm-	
Chapmans	1915			d-	
Cheam View	1915	$2000		rm-1960	
Chinook Cove	1915			s-1942	
Clemina	1915	$2500	I 1937	rm-	
Copper Creek	1916	$2700	I-S 1936	rm-1960	
Falls Creek	1915	$2500	I-S 1936	rm-	
Grant Brook–CNoR	1915	$2390	rl-Redpass Jct. I 1937	rl-1924	
Irvine #1	1915			f-1925	
Jackman	1915	$2700	I/rl on site 1936/49	d-1965	
Laidlaw	1916			rm-1960	
Lempriere	1915	$2700	I 1937	d-1973	
Louis Creek	1915	$2390		rm-	
McAbee	1915			rm-	
McLure	1915	$2390	I-S/EL 1935/59	d-1974	
McMurphy	1915		I-S 1936	rm-	
Messiter	1915		I-S 1936	rm-	
Mt. Robson–CNoR	1915			d-1922	later Foster
Pyramid	1915	$2700		d-1963	
Rainbow–CNoR	1915	$2390	I 1937	d-1963	
Rayleigh	1916	$2390	I-S 1936	rm-	
Resplendent–CNoR	1915	$2390	rl-Redpass Jct. as dwelling	rl-1938	
Savona	1915	$2500	I-S/EL 1935/55	d-1980	
Seddell	1915	$2500		rm-	
Swift Creek	1915	$2700	rl-Valemount	rl-1927	
Thunder River	1915	$2500		d-1963	
Tranquille	1916	$2500	I-S 1936	d-1973	
Valemount	—	$2700	x-Swift Creek 1927/ EXT/EL/PL	s-19??*	Museum-2
Vavenby	1915	$2700	I-S/EL-PL 1936/64	d-1980	
Vinsulla	1915	$2390	S 1945	d-	
Walhachin	1915	$2500	I-S 1936	d-1973	
Wolfenden	1915	$2390	I-S 1936	d-1966	
Yale	1916			s-1973	
Yellowhead #2	—		x-Decoigne, Ab 1944	rt-1963	

NPR Combination Station & Section House (NPR-SH)
MANITOBA

Station Name	Blt.	Cost	Alterations	Disp.	Notes
Portage Jct. #1	1891	$1800		d-1949	Notes 34, 38

Plan 110-10—CNoR Standard Combination Station & Section House (CNoR-SH)
BRITISH COLUMBIA

Station Name	Blt.	Cost	Alterations	Disp.	Notes
Gorge	1916			rm-	Note 2
Pitquah	1915		I-S 1940		
Squeah				rm-	Note 2

SASKATCHEWAN

Station Name	Blt.	Cost	Alterations	Disp.	Notes
Bannock #1	1909			rp-1919	
Carmel #2	1911	$1320	Conv. to SH/S/I/EL 1917/26/50/51	s-1973	
Dana #1	1905	$1320	S 1926/rl-Bruno as SH	rl-1934/s-1966	
Greenbush #1	1902	$1000	Conv. to SH by 1915	s-19??*	
Kuroki #1	1905		Conv. to SH 1917	s-1970	
Peesane #1	1903	$1000	Conv. to SH 1911		Note 61

CNoR COMBINATION STATIONS
CNoR 5th Class Stations
Plan 100-17—CNoR Standard 5th Class Station

Station Name	Blt.	Cost	Alterations	Disp.	Notes
Birnie, Mb	1904	$1500		s-1963	
Graceton #1, Mn	1907			rp-1919	
Orr #1, Mn			EXT 1924	rp-1921	
Spruce Grove– CNoR #2, Ab	1914			rt-1923	

CNoR 4th Class Stations
Various Plans—NPR Standard 4th Class Station (NPR-4th)
MANITOBA

Station Name	Blt.	Cost	Alterations	Disp.	Notes
Baldur	1890	$1500	EXT/EXT/EXT/EL 1893/ 1919/26/51	s-1975*	Plan 100-26, Museum-2
Beaver	1900	$1500	I-S/EL 1937/52	s-1965*	Plan 100-26
Dunrea	1898				
Elgin #1-A	1898		EXT (see Entry under Plan 100-3)		
Fairfax					
Hartney	1898	$930		s-1975* Sim. to Plan 100-26, Hip roof	
Hilton		$1175		s-1961	Probable
Minto #1-A	1898		EXT (see Entry under Plan 100-3)		Plan 100-13
Ninette #1-A	1898				
Rignold	1901	$1500	I-S 1937	s-1960	Probable
Rosebank	1897	$1200	I 1938	s-1962	
Rounthwaite		$1175		s-1960	Probable
Somerset #1-A	1889		EXT (see Entry under Plan 100-3)	rb-1927	Plan 100-13
Underhill					Probable

Plan 100-12—CNoR Standard Stations (Kashabowie Type)
ONTARIO

Station Name	Blt.	Cost	Alterations	Disp.	Notes
Banning #1	1901	$1800	I 1946	s-1959	
Glenwater	1901	$1600	I-S 1941	s-1968	
Kashabowie	1901	$1600	EXT-I-S 1941		
Kawene	1901	$1200	S 1940	s-1961	
Laseine	1901		I/S 1941/43	s-1964	
Mabella	1901	$1600	I-S 1941	s-1959	
Mine Centre #1				rp-1941	Note 30
Mokomon	1901	$1600	I-S 1940		
Quetico	1901	$1200	I-S 1954		

NOTES:

2   This was a conventional section house apparently used as station. It does not appear as if these buildings had bracket-supported awnings or formal waiting rooms as did earlier combination station-and-section-house designs such as Plan 110-10.

4   This station was technically on the Saskatoon Terminals Subdivision.

28 It appears that the apartment-office-waiting room portion of this building was converted into a section house, while the freight shed was relocated next to the new station (#2) and used as a baggage-express shed.

30 The disposition of the first depot could not be established. It may have burned down and been replaced by a 4th Class structure.

34 This station was technically on the Winnipeg Terminals Subdivision.

36 The former CNoR line between Peace River Jct. and Darson Jct. (near Magnolia) was abandoned in June 1936.

38 Standard NP section house with a bay window on the trackside.

40 Abandoned on grade in 1917. Final dispositions unknown; likely sold and demolished.

41 There is a discrepancy in CNR records; one stating that a carbody (#6997) was placed here in 1914, while the GTP cost record indicates that a formal shelter costing $652 was erected here. A photograph in a local history clearly shows an FPS. Perhaps the carbody was a temporary station and there was a mix-up in record keeping.

42 Abandoned on grade in 1917. Relocated to CNR Mile 15.3 Brule Subdivision in 1923, used as residence by the CNR pumpman for the new water tank erected here. Relocated to Galloway (#3) in 1940. Sold to the Town of Edson in 1976 and relocated to Centennial Park on the eastern outskirts of the community. Converted into museum. The station's signboards read "Edson."

43 Abandoned on grade 1928, relocated to nearby GTP station grounds by 1934. Used by CNR for storage.

44 Abandoned on grade in 1917. Turned over to Department of the Interior (Parks) circa 1923.

61 Reference to the station name Midway was found on Plan 110-10. Other stations listed on this drawing suggest that Midway was situated on the east end of the Tisdale Subdivision. Since Peesane is the approximate mid-point between Hudson Bay Jct. and Melfort, it may have formerly been known as Midway.

62 Dayson, Carrot Creek–CNoR, Fulstow, Horner, Scriven and Tollerton, Ab. These stations were abandoned on grade in 1917. The following year, the CNoR apparently stripped all re-usable millwork (windows, doors, interior fittings, etc.) from these buildings. A local history makes reference to Carrot Creek–CNoR and Fulstow as being sold about 1923. It is likely that all of these stations were sold and removed at the same time.

71 This station was built by the Canadian Pacific Railway that operated the Qu'Appelle Long Lake and Saskatchewan Railway until 1906, when the line was acquired by the Canadian Northern Railway.

73 CNR building records are somewhat unclear regarding the this station. One record clearly shows that Pedley had a 'Design A' (Type E) station, but another also notes it as Plan 100-47, with stucco and rehabilitation in 1927. It is likely that the original GTP station burned down, and that this building was relocated from Dalehurst–CNoR, then abandoned in 1928.

CNoR 4th Class Stations
Plan 100-31—CNoR Standard 4th Class Station

ALBERTA

Station Name	Blt.	Cost	Alterations	Disp.	Notes
Donalda #2	—	$1350	x-Vandura, Sk 1992	EXTANT*	Note 23, Museum-1
Edmonton–EY&P at Ross Grade	1902		rl- CNoR Edmonton yard	rl-1906	Plan 100-6, Notes 10, 13
North Edmonton	1910		EXT/PL 1942/48	d-1983	Note 13
St. Albert #2	1909		EXT/I-S/EL-G 1921/37/53	s-1971*	Plan 100-6, Museum-2

MANITOBA

Station Name	Blt.	Cost	Alterations	Disp.	Notes
Badger	1909	$1200	I/S 1938/40	s-1963	
Cardinal	1911	$1096	EXT/I 1920/38	d-1963	
Greenway	1910	$1000	EXT 1918	s-1965	
Holmfield #2-A	1909	$1580	I 1943	s-1960	
Lorette	1909	$1200	I 1938	s-1960	
Mafeking	1909	$796	EXT/EXT/S-I/EL 1919/28/36/55	rm-	
Myrtle #2	1911	$1000	I 1938	s-1964	
Rossendale	1910	$1600	EXT/I-S 1919/37	s-1967	
Vassar	1907	$3200	CPF-EXT/I-S 1918/37	s-1970*	

MINNESOTA

Station Name	Blt.	Cost	Alterations	Disp.	Notes
Pitt	1909	$1000	I 1947	s-1962	
Rainier #1	1908		EXT	rp-1916	
Ray #1	1911		EXT 1917	rp-1921	
Swift	1909	$1200	CPF-I 1942	d-1964	
Williams	1909	$2500	EXT/EXT/I 1916/25/39	s-1982	

ONTARIO

Station Name	Blt.	Cost	Alterations	Disp.	Notes
Crozier	1910	$1100		gb-1970	
Devlin	1910	$1100	I-S 1943	s-1976	

SASKATCHEWAN

Station Name	Blt.	Cost	Alterations	Disp.	Notes
Aylesbury	1910	$1200	EXT/S/I/EL 1918/28/39/53	s-1977	
Candiac	1913	$2800	S 1924	s-1976*	
Disley	1914	$2025	S/EL 1928/53	rm-1975	
Englefeld	1912		EXT/S/I 1919/??/40	d-	
Findlater #2	1911	$2025	EXT/S 1917/28	s-1966*	
Kendal #2	1913	$1200	S 1924	s-1977*	
Laura #2	1911		EXT/I-S 1918/35	s-	
Margo #1	1911	$1061	I/S 1919/37	f-1952	
Muenster	1908		EXT/I/S 1919/40/43	s-19??*	
Prudhomme #2	1910	$1200	EXT/I-S 1919/36	d-1981	
Vandura	1909	$1950	I 1943/rl-Donalda, Ab #2	rl-1992	Note 23
Waseca #2	1911	$1200	EXT/I-S/EL 1919/36/??	d-1982	

Plan 100-68—CNoR Standard 4th Class Station

ALBERTA

Station Name	Blt.	Cost	Alterations	Disp.	Notes
Bissell #2	1922	$4220	I-S 1935	d-1963	
Cessford	1920			rm-	
Coronado #1	1921	$4200	Part rl-Gibbons as SH 1939	s-1971*	Note 14
Entwistle–CNoR #2	1915	$1800	rl-Onoway as SH	rl-1923*	
Legal #3	1917	$2050	CF-I/S/EL 1940/45/??	s-1960*	
Minburn #2	1914		S 1922	s-1982*	
Rosedale #2	1919	$4000	EXT/I-S/E? 1926/44/??	rm-	
Sangudo #2	1918	$4500	I-S/EL 1937/??	rm-	
Stanmore #2	1917	$2025		s-1963*	
Steveville	1921			See Note	Note 55
Sunnynook	1920	$2500	EL 1955	rm-	
Warden #1	1915	$2025		f-1919	
Wayne #2-A	1918	$2025	EXT/EL 1922/??	rm-	

MANITOBA

Station Name	Blt.	Cost	Alterations	Disp.	Notes
Alonsa	1922	$4220	I 1942	rm-	
Ashern #2	1918	$3024	I/S 1937/41	s-1977*	
Barrows #3	1923	$4200	I 1939	rm-	
Dropmore #2	1921	$5800	I-S/EL 1937/53	rm-	
Graysville #2	1920	$4500	I 1939	s-1961*	
Gypsumville #2	1916	$3000	I/I 1938/47	rm-	
Hallboro #4	—	$7400	x-Mulvihill #2 1949	rm-	
Hodgson #2	1920	$1500	EXT/I/EL 1935/38/51	s-1975	
Langruth	1916	42120	I/EL 1946/51	s-1966	
Marchand #2	1920	$6000	I/S 1938/40	s-1968*	
Moosehorn #2	1918	$3075	I/S 1938/41	s-19??*	Museum-2
Mulvihill #2	1920	$4500	rl-Hallboro #4	rl-1948	
Notre Dame de Lourdes	1921	$4500	EXT 1946	s-19??*	
Ste. Rose #1	1916	$4200	Cov. SH/S/I/I 1931/32/46/60		
Steep Rock	1916	$2500	EXT 1936	EXTANT*	
Vita #2	1923	$4721	CF	s-1964*	

CNoR COMBINATION STATIONS
Plan 100-68—CNoR Standard 4th Class Station

MINNESOTA

Station Name	Blt.	Cost	Alterations	Disp.	Notes
Angora #2	1921		ALT/I 1939/47	rt-1963	Plan 100-144
Gheen #2	1921	$3196	ALT/I 1939/47		Plan 100-145
Graceton #2	1919	$3000	I 1939	s-1962	

ONTARIO

Station Name	Blt.	Cost	Alterations	Disp.	Notes
Bear Pass #2	1920	$4107		d-1946	
Flanders	1916	$11200	I-S 1941	s-1978	
Huronian #1	1918	$3500	I 1943	d-1960	
Sleemans #2	1924	$44200	I-S 1943	gb-1974	

SASKATCHEWAN

Station Name	Blt.	Cost	Alterations	Disp.	Notes
Ardill #2	1923	$4220	I-S 1937	s-1968	
Bateman	1923	$4000	I-S/EL 1937/54	s-1977	
Beadle #2	1916	$2500	I-S/EL 1935/54	s-1966*	
Beechy #2	1923	$4500	I-S 1937	rm-	
Birsay	1920	$4500	I-S 1937	d-1986	
Brooksby	1923	$4000	I/S 1943/44	s-19??*	
Browning #3	1923	$3420	I/I/EL 1938/41/54	s-1966*	
Canwood #2	1916	$2025	I-S 1942	s-1983	
Carmel #3	1917	$1600	I-S 1936	s-1976	
D'Arcy #2	1916	$2000	EXT/I-S/EL 1922/35/56	s-1968	
Debden #2	1918	$2250	I-S/EL 1942/	d-1983	
Demaine	1922	$4500	I-S 1937	s-1969*	
Dummer #2	1916	$2025	I-S/EL 1936/57	s-1974	
Eldersley #2	1922	$4220	I-S/EL 1937/52	d-1981	
Eyre	1920	$5500	I 1937	s-1964	
Fairmount #2	1917			s-1960	
Hamton #2	1924	$4000	I/S 1938/39/rl-Rama #2	rl-1960	
Hardy #2	1918	$2000	S/EL 1929/55	s-1976	
Hearne #2	1917	$2025	I-S/EL 1936/56	s-1975	
Krydor #2	1917	$2025	EXT/I-S/EL 1940/42/53	s-1982*	
Laporte	1920	$4200	I/EL 1937/??	s-19??*	
Lintlaw #2	1920		I/EXT 1942/47	s-19??*	
Maryfield #2	—	$7400	x-Hallboro, Mb #4 1961	s-1984*	
Pinkham #2	1915	$3500	EXT/I-S 1920/36	s-1967	
Rama #2	—		x-Hamton #2 1960	s-1982*	
Runnymede #2	1923	$4200	I/EL 1937/53	s-1971*	
St. Boswells #2	1923	$5000	I-S 1937	s-1966	
St. Walburg #2	1922	$4000	EXT/PL 19??/64	s-1982*	Museum-1
Spring Valley #2	1916	$2025	I-S/EL 1937/56	d-	
Tilney #2	1922	$4000	I-S 1936	s-1960*	
Valparaiso #2	1920	$4000	EXT/I-S 1939/37	s-1967	

Miscellaneous CNoR Designs (Equivalent to 4th Class)

Station Name	Blt.	Cost	Alterations	Disp.	Notes
Halston, BC	1916	$3000	S 1940	rm-	Plan 100-87
Stanley, On	1900			rm-	Note 75

CNoR 3rd Class Stations
Plan 100-3—CNoR Standard 3rd Class Station

ALBERTA

Station Name	Blt.	Cost	Alterations	Disp.	Notes
Chipman	1907		EXT/CPF-S 1921/22	d-1978	
Innisfree #1	1906		EXT/CPF-S 1919/22	rm-	
Islay #1	1906		S 1928	f-1945	
Lamont	1907		EXT/EXT/CPF-S 1910/18/22	d-1978	
Lavoy	1906		S/EL	rm-	
Mannville	1906	$2963	EXT/EXT/CPF-S/PL 1911/19/22/58	f-1974	
Morinville	1906	$2963	EXT/S/EL 1914/45/??	f-1960s	
Mundare	1906		EXT/RENOV/S 1910/18/??	d-1978	
Stony Plains–CNoR	1907	$3000	Conv. to dwelling 1923	d-1934	Reverse, Note 57
Vegreville #1-A	1905		EXT/EXT 1907/14	rp-1930	

MANITOBA

Station Name	Blt.	Cost	Alterations	Disp.	Notes
Arizona #1	1905			f-1915	
Belmont #1-B	1907	$3000	EXT/I 1906/38	s-1975	Reverse, Plan 100-23, Add to Sta #1-A
Eden	1903	$2963	I-S 1935	s-1967	
Elgin #1-B	1904	$1830	I 1940	s-1978	Plan 100-20
Elphinstone	1904	$3000		s-1975	
Gardenton	1905	$1700	I 1946	rm-1964	
Grosse Isle	1904	$2200	I/S 1937/41	s-1974	
Helston	1901	$3000	I/EL 1941/51	s-1963	
Homewood	1901	$2200	I 1943	s-1966	
La Brouquierie	1905	$2963	I/S/EL 1938/40/??	s-19??*	
Lake Francis #1	1904	$2200	EL 1953	s-1966*	
Lavenham	1905	$2450	I-S/EL 1937/54	s-1967*	
Lena	1904	42200	I/EL 1943/51	a-1961	

CNoR COMBINATION STATIONS
Plan 100-3—CNoR Standard 3rd Class Station

MANITOBA

Station Name	Blt.	Cost	Alterations	Disp.	Notes
Lowe Farm	1905	$1331	I 1938	s-1971	
Makinak #2	1903	$2750	I-S 1938	s-1977	
Margaret		$2200	S/I 1928/40	s-1961	
Marieapolis	1906			s-1979*	
Minto #1-B	1906	$3183	EXT/I 19??/38	s-1973	Plan 100-14, Add to Sta #1-A
Neelin	1904	$2200	I 1943	rm-1970	
Oakville		$2250	EXT/S 1929/32	s-1976	
Piney	1905	$3150	I/I/EL 1938/46/51	s-1966*	
Ridgeville	1906	$3150	EXT/I 1926/40	s-1966	
Roblin	1906	$3480	EXT/EL-S/PL 1912/29/60	s-1996*	
Roseisle	1903	$2500	I 1939	s-1971	
Rossburn	1907	$3000	I/CPF/PL 1938/66/68	s-1980*	
St. Jean Baptiste	1902	$2500	I 1938	s-1975*	Reverse
St. Laurent	1904	$2400	I/ 1937/41	s-1966*	
Sanford	1901	$2400	I/EXT/I 1938/39/40	s-1968	
Somerset #1-B	1903	$6500	rl on site-EXT/I 1927/41	s-1981*	Plan 100-15, Add to Sta #1-A
Sperling	1901	$2400	EXT/I 1929/43	s-1967*	
Wakopa	1904	$2750	I/CPF/EL 1943/??/51	s-1961	
Woodlands	1904	$2200	I/EL 1947/52	rt-1970	

MINNESOTA

Station Name	Blt.	Cost	Alterations	Disp.	Notes
Roosevelt	1904	$2500	EXT/I/I 1914/41/45		

ONTARIO

Station Name	Blt.	Cost	Alterations	Disp.	Notes
Barwick #1	1904	$2963	I-S 1943	s-1969	
Emo	1901	$4272	RENOV/I-S 1923/41		
Pinewood	1901	$3299	EXT/I-s 1919/43	s-19??*	
Stratton	1903	$2800	I-S 1943	s-1975*	

SASKATCHEWAN

Station Name	Blt.	Cost	Alterations	Disp.	Notes
Aberdeen	1905	$5024	EXT/EXT/I-S/PL/E 1909/14/36/66/??	rm-	
Birch Hills	1905	$2963	EXT/S 1921/28	s-1981	
Borden	1907	$4033	EXT/I-S 1911/36	d-1983	
Bruno	1904	$3083	EXT/EXT/I-S 1910/25/36	rm-	
Buchanan	1904		EXT/S/I 1911/29/40	s-1982	
Canora	1904	$5000	EXT/EXT/I-S/PL 1907/19/41/55	s-1997*	Museum-1
Dalmeny	1907	$2963	I-S 1936	d-1981	
Delisle	1908		EXT/I-S/PL 1910/35/??	s-	
Delmas	1905	$2963	EXT/S/EL 19??/27/??	d-1982	
Fielding	1907	$3083	I-S 1936	s-1963	
Invermay	1904		S/EL/PL	s-19??*	
Kinistino	1905	$2963	EXT/S/PL 1916/28/60	s-1981*	
Langham	1905	$2963	EXT/I-S 1909/36	s-1982*	
Lashburn	1907	$3000	EXT/EXT/I-S/EL 1910/22/36/??	d-1982	
Lumsden #2	1908	$4050	S 1928	s-1977*	Plan 100-30, Museum-2
Maidstone	1905	$2963	I-S/EL 1936/??	s-1989*	Museum-2
Marshall	1905	$3000	I-S/EL 1936/??	d-1982	
Paynton	1905	$2963	EXT/S/EL 1910/24/??	d-1982	
Quill Lake	1904	$5040	EXT/RENOV-S/I/PL 1910/28/39/64	s-1980	
Radisson	1905	$8300	EXT/EXT/I-S/PL 1908/18/36/64	d-1982	
Ruddell	1905	$3083	I-S 1936	s-1973	
Star City	1904	$2963	EXT/I-S/PL 1916/37/64	s-1978	
Tisdale #1	1904	$2963	EXT/EXT/PL 1911/16/54	rm-1966	
Togo	1907	$2600	EXT/I/PL 1927/38/69	rm-	
Vonda	1905	$2963	EXT/I-S 1910/36	s-1982	
Wadena	1904		EXT/EXT/S/I/PI 1909/12/28/39/62	s-1991*	
Warman #1	1905	$5025	EXT/rl on site-REHAB-I-S 1907/43	s-1980*	x-Langham Sub
Watson	1905		EXT/RENOV/S/I/PL 1909/24/28/39/62	s-1983	

Plan 100-18—Special Station (3rd Class Type)

Station Name	Blt.	Cost	Alterations	Disp.	Notes
Humboldt, Sk	1905	$5268	EXT/S/EL-EXT-PL/EXT 1911/??/36/49	EXTANT*	
Kamsack #1, Sk	1904	$5266	CF-EXT/I-S 1919/35	rp-1968	

Plan 100-19—Special Station (3rd Class Type)

Station Name	Blt.	Cost	Alterations	Disp.	Notes
Battleford–CNoR, Sk	1907	$4215	S/EL 1929/??	s-1978*	
Ft. Saskatchewan, Ab	1905		EXT/CPF-S 1911/22	s-1987*	
Lloydminster #1-A, Ab	1906	$5014	EXT/I-S/EXT/EL/G 1920/36/40/?/	d-1991	

CNoR COMBINATION STATIONS
Plan 100-19—Special Station (3rd Class Type)

SASKATCHEWAN

Station Name	Blt.	Cost	Alterations	Disp.	Notes
Melfort, Sk	1904	$5772	EXT/EXT/I-S/EXT/PL 1915/20/37/40/??	d-1987	
Virden, Mb	1907	$4000	I-S 1937	s-1976*	

Plan 100-29—CNoR Standard 3rd Class Station
(Plan 100-64 was the designation for this design in British Columbia)

ALBERTA

Station Name	Blt.	Cost	Alterations	Disp.	Notes
Alix–CNoR	1912		rl-Alix–GTP	rl-1927	Note 59
Alix–GTP #2	—		x-Alix–CNoR 1927	d-1975	Note 59
Ardenode #1	1913	$2963	I-S/EL 1944/53	d-1972	
Bretona	1913	$2950	I-S/EL 1937/53	d-1974	
Camrose–CNoR	1911	$5020	EXT/I-S/EL-G-PL 1924/37/57	s-1991*	Museum-2
Cereal	1913	$3965	EXT/I-S EL 1920/36/50	s-19??*	
Chinook	1913	$3300	EXT/I-S/EL 1920/36/??	d-1975	
Clyde	1912	$3700	I-S/EL 1937/??	s-1976*	
Delia	1913	$3000	EXT/I-S/i/PL 1919/39/49/57	s-	
Dodds	1910		I-S/EL 1937/??	s-1963*	
Donalda #1	1911	$3000	I-S 1937	d-1984	
Drumheller #1	1912		EXT/EXT/S/PL-EL-G 1917/28/?/	d-1971	
Eckville	1912	$3000	S/EL 1945/??	rm-	
Edberg	1910	$3000	I-S/EL 1937/??	s-1983	
Elspeth	1913	$3000	I 1950	rt-1965	
Haight	1910	$2963	I-S/EL 1937/55	rt-1963	
Hay Lakes #1	1913	$2963		f-1924	
Haynes #1	1913	$2963	EL 1950	s-1963	
Kitscoty	1911	$2963	CPF-S/G/PL/EL 1928/53/57/??	d-1979	
Lac Ste. Anne	1912	$2963		s-1936	Note 36
Leslieville	1912	$3000	S/EL 1945/??	rm-	
Lyalta	1913	$2963	I-S 1944	rm-	
Meeting Creek	1913	$3000	I-S/EL 1937/??	EXTANT*	Museum-1
Morrin	1912	$2963	I-S/EL-EXR-PL 1942/57	s-1984	
Munson	1912	$2963	EXT/EXT/S/EL 1918/26/42/??	s-1975	
Nevis	1912	$3000	I/EL 1950/53	s-1962	
Onoway	1913	$2963	I-S/EL/G 1937/??/??	s-	
Oyen	1913	$3000	EXT/I-S/EL/PL 1917/35/??/56	rm-	
Prentiss	1912	$3000	I 1950	rm-	
Red Willow	1910	$3000	I-S/EL 1937/??	d-1984	
Richdale	1913	$3000	I-S 1942	s-1963	
Rockyford	1913	$2963	EXT/I-S/I/PI 1920/42/46/56	d-1979	

NOTES:

10 This 4th Class station, erected at the foot of Ross grade, was relocated in 1906 to the CNoR yard in Edmonton. It was used as Petty Stores until replaced in 1916. Final disposition is unknown, but it was likely demolished in 1916.

13 This station was technically on the Edmonton Terminals Subdivision.

14 Portion converted into section house; the freight shed was converted into FPS #2 in 1939.

23 Following inauguration of tourist passenger service on portions of the former CNR Stettler Subdivision in 1990, the Village of Donalda approached the Canadian Northern Society to acquire a station. The Society obtained an early design Canadian Northern 4th Class Station (Plan 100-31) from Vandura, Saskatchewan. It was moved onto the site of the original depot, extensively refurbished and opened in 1992 as an interpretive display in conjunction with the excursion trains that stopped here. The rail line serving Donalda was abandoned in 1997.

36 The former CNoR line between Peace River Jct. and Darson Jct. (near Magnolia) was abandoned in June 1936.

55 The track laid to this point in 1921 was abandoned in 1927. It could not be established whether this depot was ever built.

57 This depot was left on site in 1923. It was occupied by the local CNR operator as a dwelling until it was demolished in 1934.

59 Following trackage changes on the Brazeau Subdivision, this station was abandoned on site in 1922. The west end of the Endiang Subdivision was subsequently extended to include a portion of the Brazeau Subdivision. This depot was relocated to the GTP station grounds in 1927.

75 This station was constructed at the junction of the Ontario and Rainy River section and the "old" Port Arthur, Duluth & Western Railway. A photograph in THUNDER BAY TO GUNFLINT by Elinor Barr (Thunder Bay Historical Society, 1999), page 107, shows a 1½-storey wood-frame structure unlike anything else constructed by the CNoR.

CNoR COMBINATION STATIONS
Plan 100-29—CNoR Standard 3rd Class Station

ALBERTA

Station Name	Blt.	Cost	Alterations	Disp.	Notes
Round Hill	1910	$3000	I-S/EL-G 1937/??	s-1968	
Rumsey	1912	$3000	I/S/EL 1938/39/??	d-1984	
Scollard	1911	$3000	I/S/EL 1938/39/56	s-1964	
Sylvan Lake	1912	$3000		s-1976	
Viewpoint	1910	$3000	I-S/EL 1937/54	s-1962	
Yelger	1910	$2963		s-1930	
Youngstown	1913	$2963	EXT/I-S/EL 1922/35/??	d-1975	

BRITISH COLUMBIA

Station Name	Blt.	Cost	Alterations	Disp.	Notes
Ashcroft	1915	$3500	I-S 1935	d-1976	
Chu Chua	1915	$2963	I-S/CPF/EL 1935/41/56	d-1974	
Langley	1915	$2963		s-1983*	
Little Fort	1916		I-S 1936	d-1975	
Lytton	1915	$2500	EXT/I-S 1922/35	d-1980	
Matsqui	1915	$2963	EXT 1920	d-1985	
Rosedale	1915	$2963	EXT 1923	s-1961	
Spences Bridge #1	1915			rt-1924	

MANITOBA

Station Name	Blt.	Cost	Alterations	Disp.	Notes
Angusville	1908	$3000	S/I/I 1929/37/45	rm-	
Belleview	1915	$3000	CPF 1932	rm-	
Benito	1909		I/I/PL 1942/51/67	rm-	
Beulah	1911	$3050	S 1939	s-1976	
Brunkild	1909	$2396	I/I 1938/41	rt-1967	
Clanwilliam #2	1914	$3000		s-1975	
Cromer	1911	$3000	S/I/EL 1928/42/51	rt-1971	
Decker	1913	43050	I-S 1935	s-1961	
Glenella #2	1913	$2750	EXT/I/S/I 1919/39/41/45	s-1981	
Hallboro #2	1912	$3000	I-S 1936	f-1948	
Inwood	1912	$2400	I 1938	s-1975	
Isabella	1910	$3050	S 1929	s-1970	
Kelwood	1912	$2672	CPF/I-S 1931/35		
Kenville	1908	$3000	I-S 1941	rm-	
Lundar	1913	$2700	I/CPF/S 1937/40/41	s-1977*	
McConnell	1909	$3050	I-S 1935	s-1970*	Museum-2
McCreary #2	1912	$2700	I-S/I/PL 1936/45/66	EXTANT*	
Oakburn	1907	$3000		rm-	
Oak Point	1908	$2500	EXT/I/EL 1924/40/54		
Rapid City	1909	$3050	S/I 1929/39	rt-1971	
Russell	1908	$3000	I-S/PL 1937/59	rm-	
Scarth	1907	$3000	S 1932	rm-	
Shellmouth	1909	$3000	I-S/EL 1937/53	s-1979	
Swan Lake	1913	$2782		s-1976*	
Terence	1910	$3000	EXT/EL 1924/51	rm-	
The Pas #1	1908	$3000	EXT 1915/ Conv. into SH 1928	f-1973	

MINNESOTA

Station Name	Blt.	Cost	Alterations	Disp.	Notes
Cook #2	1914	$3990	I/I 1938/47		Variant, Plan 100-55
Melrude	1913	$3247	I 1947		

ONTARIO

Station Name	Blt.	Cost	Alterations	Disp.	Notes
La Vallee	1907	$3100	EXT/CPF 1922/43	s-1968	

SASKATCHEWAN

Station Name	Blt.	Cost	Alterations	Disp.	Notes
Alsask	1911	$2963	EXT/I-S/EL? 1915/35/?	d-1988	
Ardath	1912	$2963	EXT/S/I/EL 1921/28/41/53	rm-1964	
Avonlea	1912	$3000	EXT/EXT-RENOV/I-S 1916/17/36	s-1979*	Museum-1
Baildon	1912	$3000	I-S/EL 1936/53	s-1979*	Museum-2
Bayard	1913	$3000	I-S/EL 1937/57	s-	
Bengough	1912	$3500	S/I 1929/38	s-1977*	
Big River	1910	$3000	I-S/EXT/EL 1942/49/??	s-1981*	Museum-1
Bladworth	1908	$3000	EXT/S/I 19??/27/39	s-1976	
Blaine Lake	1912	$2963	I-S/PL 1942/64	s-1981*	
Blewett	1911	$3000	S/I 1929/42	s-1960*	
Briercrest	1912	$3000	I-S 1936	s-19??*	
Brock	1909		I-S 1935	s-19??*	Museum-2
Brooking	1913	$2675	S 1929	s-1964	
Carlsberg		$3000	S 1927	s-1949	
Carlyle	1909	$3050	EXT/I/PL 1916/50/58	s-19??*	Museum-2
Ceylon	1912	$2700	I-S/PL 1939/68	s-1976	
Chandler	1912	$3000	S/I 1929/42	s-1955*	
Colgate	1912	$3000	CF-RENOV/I-S 1923/39	s-1960*	
Condie	1911	$3000	S 1928	s-1959	
Conquest	1912	$2963	EXT-S/I/EL 1929/50/54	s-1980	
Davin	1912	$2800	S/PL 1924/55	f-1973	
Denholm #1	1912			rp-1936	

CNoR COMBINATION STATIONS
Plan 100-29—CNoR Standard 3rd Class Station

SASKATCHEWAN

Station Name	Blt.	Cost	Alterations	Disp.	Notes
Dinsmore	1913	$2963	S/PL/19??/64	d-	
Dunning	1912	$3000	S/I 1929/38	s-1958*	
Edam	1912	$2963	I-S/EL 1939/53	s-1982*	Museum-1
Elrose	1913	$2963	I-S/PL 1936/64	s-1977*	
Ettington #2	1914	$3000	I-S 1937	s-1965	
Fairlight	1907	$2200	S/rl on site 1928/49	s-	
Fiske	1910		S/EL 19??/56	s-1981	
Flaxcombe	1912	$3000	EXT/I-S/EL 1914/36/??	s-1975	
Forgan	1913	$2963	I-S 1936	s-1976*	
Forward	1912	$3000	I-S 1936	s-1963*	
Girvin #2	1910	$3000	I/S 1939/??	d-1977	
Glenavon	1911	$2395	I-S/PL 1936/66	s-1978*	
Goodwater	1911	$3000	S/EL 1929/52	s-1962*	
Gravelbourg	1913	$5000	I-S 1937	s-1977*	Plan 100-53
Hafford	1913	$2963	rl on site-EXT-S/EL/PL 1930/53/64	s-1983*	
Harris	1909		I-S 1935	s-1977*	
Hudson Bay	1911	$2500	S/EXT/PL 1930/47/62	EXTANT*	Plan 100-43
Jameson	1914	$2800	S/I 1924/38	s-1964*	
Kelso	1907	$3000	I-S/EL 1936/56	s-1982*	
Laird	1909	$2963	I/S 1943/44	f-1971	
Lampman	1910	$3000	EXT/S/I 1920/29/41	s-1983*	Note 76
Langbank	1911	$3000	S/I/EL/RENOV 1928/39/54/67	s-1976*	
Leask	1912	$2963	I-S/PL 1942/64	s-1982	
MacNutt	1910	$2963	I-S 1937	s-	
Macroroe	1912	$2963	EXT/S/I/EL 1921/28/38/54	s-1977	
Marcelin	1911	$2963	EXT/I/S 1927/38/42	s-1982	
Marengo	1911	$3000	S/EL 19??/57	d-1980	
Maymont	1908	$3913	EXT/I-S 1911/36	d-	
Mazenod	1913	$3000	EL 1953	d-1980	
McGee #2	1913		I-S 1935	rt-1964	
Meota	1910	$2963	S/EL 19??/51	s-1981	Reverse
Mervin	1914	$2963	S/EL	s-1980*	Note 63
Mitchellton	1913	$3000	EL 1955	s-1974	
Montmartre		$2800	S/I/PL 1924/40/60	s-1977*	
Mossbank	1913	$3000	rl on site/I-S 1931/37	d-1977	
Netherhill	1910		I-S 1935	s-1983	
Norquay	1911	$2200	I/S/EL 1938/41/58	s-1984*	
Odessa	1913	$2800	S 1924	s-1977	
Parkman	1913	$3100	I/EL 1940/52	s-	
Parry #2	1916	$3000	I-S/EL 1946/55	s-1975	
Pelly	1909	$2200	I/I 1942/50	s-1983*	Museum-2
Rhein	1911	$2250	I/S/EL 1938/39/??	s-19??*	
Richard #2	1916	$2963	I-S/EL 1942/53	s-1968	
Ridpath #1	1910			f-1925	
Rosetown	1909	$9000	EXT/EXT-S/PL 1911/30/64	d-1983	
Shellbrook	1910	$3000	EXT/I-S/PL 1918/39/59	s-1982*	Museum-1
Speers	1913	$2963	I-S/EL 1942/53	d-1983	
Stenen	1912	$2200	I-S 1936	rm-	
Stornoway	1913	$2766	I/S 1938/39	s-19??*	
Swanson	1912	$3000	EXT/S/I/EL 1921/28/41/54	rm-1966	
Tessier	1908		I-S 1935	s-19??*	
Truax	1912	$2300	I-S/EL 1936/55	s-1976*	
Turtleford	1914	$2963	I-S/PL 1939/64	s-1985*	Museum-2
Vanscoy #2	1912		I-S 1944	s-1977	
Vawn	1913	$2963	I-S/EL 1939/53	s-1981*	
Veregin #2	1911		S	s-1975	
Vibank	1913	$2620	S/I-S 1924/40	s-1978	
Waldheim #2	1912	$2963	I/S 1943/44	s-1984*	Museum-1
Willmar	1910	$3000	S 1929	s-1969*	
Wiseton	1913	$2963	I-S 1936	d-1980	
Wroxton	1913	$2962	I-S 1937	s-1983*	
Zealandia	1908		EXT/I-S 1912/35	s-1982	

CNoR COMBINATION STATIONS
Plans 100-72/-75—CNoR Standard 3rd Class Station

ALBERTA

Station Name	Blt.	Cost	Alterations	Disp.	Notes
Alliance	1916	$3683	CPF-I/S 1940/42	rm-	
Bellis #2	1923	$7500	S/EL	s-1978*	Museum-2
Benton #2	1918	$3500	I-S 1937	rm-	
Blackfoot #2	1922	$5186	S/EL/G 1946/??/??	rm-	
Brazeau #1-A	1914	$3000	S 1945	s-1962	Plan 100-75
Craigmyle #2	1916		S/I/EL 1942/48/??	rm-	
Evansburg–CNoR #2	1920		rl-Evansburg–GTP #2	rl-1922	
Evansburg–GTP #2	—		x-Evansburg– CNoR 32 1922/S	d-1984	

CNoR COMBINATION STATIONS
Plans 100-72/-75—CNoR Standard 3rd Class Station

ALBERTA

Station Name	Blt.	Cost	Alterations	Disp.	Notes
Excel #2	1917	$3000		rt-1963	
Lanfine #2	1918	$2800	I-S 1936	s-1961	
Michichi #2	1924	$7000	S/EL 1942/??	s-1975*	
Pollockville #2	1920	$5100	s-1969*		Museum-2
Radway	1919		I-S/EL 1936/??	f-1977	
Ranfurly #2	1922	$7500		rm-	
Redland #2	1921	$4000	I-S 1944	rm-1968	
Rosebud #2	1919	$6550	I-S/EL 1944/50	rm-1968	
Rowley #2	1922		I-S/EL 1939/??	EXTANT*	Museum-1
St. Paul	1921	$9500	S/EL-G-PL	d-	Plan 100-138
Sheerness	1920	$4000	I/EL 1938/59	d-1976	
Sibbald #2	1917	$3000	I-S/EL 1936/??	rm-	
Smoky Lake	1919	$4000	I-S/EL-EXT-PL 1936/57	s-1993*	Museum-2
Vilna #2	1922	$7500	I-S/EL-PL 1936/57	d-	
Warden #2	1919	$4000	I/S/EL 1938/42/57	s-1984	
Whitecourt #2	1922	$5000	EL-PL	rm-	

BRITISH COLUMBIA

Station Name	Blt.	Cost	Alterations	Disp.	Notes
Fort Fraser #2	1923	$7500	EL 1956	d-1971	
Spences Bridge #3	1923	$6900	I-S 1935	d-1975	
Vanderhoof #2	1924	$7500	EXT 1927	rp-1960	

MANITOBA

Station Name	Blt.	Cost	Alterations	Disp.	Notes
Cardale #2	1914	$3145	I/EXT-I 1939/43	s-1965	Plan 100-75
Deepdale #2	1922	$6075	CPF-I/S 1938/41	s-1973	
Deloraine #2	1915	$2700	I 1943	a-1961	
Durban #2	1919		I-S 1941	s-19??*	Plan 100-75
Elie–CNoR #2	1919	$7716	S/I 1936/40	s-19??*	
Erickson #2	1923	$7092	I 1948	s-19??*	
Eriksdale #2	1918	$4290	I/S 1937/41	rm-1974	
Fisher Branch	1915	$2930	I/EXT/EL 1938/39/??	s-1975*	
Fork River #2	1920		I-S 1936	s-1969	Plan 100-75
Sandy Lake #2	1921	$6865	I/RENOV 1940/67	s-19??*	
Silverton #2		$6176		s-1961	
Warren #2	1922	$6500	I/S 1939/41	s-1966	
Woodnorth #2	1916	$3600	S 1932	rt-1969	

MINNESOTA

Station Name	Blt.	Cost	Alterations	Disp.	Notes
Britt	1918	$2792		rt-1963	
Ericsburg #3	1923	$9808	I 1951	d-1964	
Harney #2	1918	$2856		s-1963	
Orr #2	1921	$7433	EXT/I 1936/47		
Ray #2	1921	$7777	EXT/I/I 1925/38/48	rt-1963	

ONTARIO

Station Name	Blt.	Cost	Alterations	Disp.	Notes
Kakabeka Falls #2	1915	$3220	I-S 1941		

SASKATCHEWAN

Station Name	Blt.	Cost	Alterations	Disp.	Notes
Arran #2	1919	$4500	S/I/RENOV 19??/42/46	s-1975*	
Beatty #2	1918	$4500	S/EL 1928/53	s-1981	
Bechard #2	1921	$3000	I 1938	d-1974	
Bienfait #2	1915	$3000	S/EXT-I/ 1929/39 rl on site/EXT/PL 1941/54/63	s-1984*	
Calder #2	1914	$3063	I-S 1937	s-1969	Plan 100-75
Donovan #2	1917	$2850	EXT/S/I 1921/28/57	s-1970	
Dunblane #2	1917	$2973	EXT-S/EL 1927/??	rm-	
Eston #1	1915	$2963	EXT/I-S 1918/36	s-1972	
Fonehill	1915	$2963	I/S/EL 1938/45/55	s-1969*	
Glidden	1918	$3000	S	s-1982	
Griffin #3	1921	$3000		s-1966	
Hodgeville	1922	$3000		s-1977	
Hughton	1914	42963	I-S/EL 1936/54	d-1978	Plan 100-75
Kelvington #2	1922	$6650	I/PL 1939/67	s-19??*	Plan 100-75, Museum-2
Lake Lenore	1921	$5000	I-S 1937	s-1986	
Lucky Lake	1923	$5550	EXT/I-S 1928/37	d-1986	
Madison	1917	$2963	I-S 1936	s-1978*	
Mantario	1920	$5100	I/EL 1927/52	d-1977	
Merid #2	1918	$3700	I-S/EL 1937/57	d-1975	
Mikado #2	1917		I/S 1938/41	s-1970	
Palmer #2	1917	$3000	rl on site/EL 1927/53	s-1974	
Parkside #2	1916	$2963	I-S 1942	s-1982*	
Pathlow	1922	$5000	I-S 1937	d-1982	
Plato	1915	$2963	S	s-1978*	
Prairie River #3	1920	$5000	I-S/EXT/EL 1937/38/56	s-1981*	Museum-1
Preeceville	1912	$3500	EXT/I/I/PL 1927/39/50/62	s-1978*	Plan 100-71
Richlea	1915	$2963		d-1978	
Ridgedale #2	1922	$5000	I/S 1943/44	d-1984	
St. Brieux #2	1920	$5000	I-S/EL/PL 1937/53/66	s-1981*	

CNoR COMBINATION STATIONS
Plans 100-72/-75—CNoR Standard 3rd Class Station

SASKATCHEWAN

Station Name	Blt.	Cost	Alterations	Disp.	Notes
St. Gregor #2	1914	$3000	I/E-EL 1939/41	s-1979	Plan 100-75
Snipe Lake	1917	$2963	I-S 1936	s-1966	
Sturgis #2	1918	$4000	EXT/I/PL 1927/39/67	s-1987*	Museum-2
Wartime	1915	$2963	I-S 1936	d-1978	
Weldon #2	1916	$2963	S/I 1928/50	s-1977	
Willowbrook	1916	$2963	I/S/EL 1938/45/58	s-19??*	
Winter #2	1922	$7500	I/S/EL 1934/??/56	s-19??*	Note 72

Miscellaneous NPR Designs (Equivalent to CNoR 3rd Class)

MANITOBA

Station Name	Blt.	Cost	Alterations	Disp.	Notes
Letellier #1	1894		EXT/EXT/I 1920/27/40	s-1966	Plan 100-116
Morris	1894	$3500	CF-S/I/PL 1924/38/58		
Oakland	1898	$2500	I/EL 1938/52	s-1960	
Roland #1	1900	$3000	I 1938	s-1977	
St. Agathe #1	1894	$2250	I/EL 199/51	f-1962	Plan 100-116
St. Norbert	1894	$2000	I 1939	s-1964	Plan 100-116

Miscellaneous CPR Designs (Equivalent to CNoR 3rd Class)

SASKATCHEWAN

Station Name	Blt.	Cost	Alterations	Disp.	Notes
Davidson #2	1905	$4350	EXT/S/PL 1923/27/62	d-1988	Plan 100-110 (CP#5), Notes 18, 71
East Prince Albert	1898			cl-1941	(Type BK-7), Note 71
Hague	1905	$3000	S/PL 1929/66	s-1982	Plan 100-110 (CP#5), Note 71
Hanley #2	1905	$4350	S/PL 1927/64	s-1980	Plan 100-110 (CP#5), Notes 20, 71
Maryfield				d-1961	Plan 100-86 (CP A-2)
Rosthern	1902	$4000	EXT/S/PL 1919/29/64	s-1982*	Plan 100-18 (Type BK-8), Note 71, Museum-2*

CNoR PASSENGER STATIONS
CNoR 2nd Class Stations
Various Plans—CNoR Early 2nd Class Stations

Station Name	Blt.	Cost	Alterations	Disp.	Notes
Baudette #1, Mn	1907			rp-1923	Plan 100-28
Carberry, Mb	1904	$5200	CF/I 1922/38	s-1966	Plan 100-21
Carman, Mb	1902	$3200	CF/I 1920/43	s-1972*	Plan 100-2
Gladstone #2, Mb	1901	$7500	CF/S 1918/29	s-1982*	Plan 100-5, Museum-2
Neepawa #1, Mb	1902	$11900	I/G 1938/60	s-1980*	Plan 100-8, Brick, Museum-1
Prince Albert–CNoR, Sk #3	1906	$13801	EXT/EXT 1916/20	d-1960s	Plan 100-25, Brick
Portage la Prairie–CNoR, Mb #2	1904	$20450		f-1960	Plan 100-45, Note 31
Rainy River, On #1	1901			rp-1918	Plan 100-1

Various Plans—CNoR Special Station (2nd Class Type)

Station Name	Blt.	Cost	Alterations	Disp.	Notes
Blue River, BC	1916	$9451	EXT/PL 1955/??	f-1989	Plan 100-82
Boston Bar, BC	1915	$9451	S/RENOV/EL-PL 1940/52/??/??	s-1980s*	Plan 100-82, Museum-2
Grand Beach, Mb	1916	$11145	I 1939	rm-	Plan 100-89
Kamloops Jct., BC	1915	$9451	EXT/EXT/I-S/EXT 1919/22/35/57	d-1985	Plan 100-81
Kipling, Sk	1908	$8274	CF/I-S/PL 1924/36/59	EXTANT*	Plan 100-22

NOTES:

18 The first depot was actually built by the Qu'Appelle Long Lake and Saskatchewan Railway at a station named Finsbury, located two miles south of present day Davidson, was abandoned in 1905. As this CSS-CPR (#1) was removed prior to the acquisition of the QLL&S by the CNoR in 1906, it is not listed here.

20 The original site of Hanley station grounds was about three miles north of its present location.

31 The CNoR and the joint GTP–Midland Railway of Manitoba (Great Northern) lines through Portage la Prairie were coordinated in 1923. Track connections between the two lines were made at either end of town. The GTP–MRM line was retained. The CNoR line was abandoned and pulled up. The CNoR's Portage station was retained on site and used by the railway for offices. The station gutted by fire in 1960, and subsequently demolished by the CNR.

63 CNR records classify this as Plan 100-29, but it incorporates all the features of Plan 100-72.

71 This station was built by the Canadian Pacific Railway that operated the Qu'Appelle Long Lake and Saskatchewan Railway until 1906, when the line was acquired by the Canadian Northern Railway.

72 CNR records classify this as Plan 100-197, but it incorporates all the features of Plan 100-72.

76 The second storey was removed, circa 1941, rendering it unrecognizable as a 3rd Class station.

CNoR PASSENGER STATIONS
Various Plans—CNoR Special Stations (2nd Class Type)

Station Name	Blt.	Cost	Alterations	Disp.	Notes
Lucerne–CNoR, BC	1915	$9451		a-1924	Plan 100-79, Note 46
North Battleford, Sk #1	1905			f-1908	Plan 100-22
North Battleford, Sk #2	1908	$17900	EXT 1912	d-1956	Plan 100-22
Port Mann, BC	1916	$3988	PL 1953	d-	Plan 100-83, Note 70
Vermilion, Ab	1906	$8354	S	s-1982*	Plan 100-22, Museum-2
Victoria Beach, Mb	1916	$6500		s-19??*	Plan 100-89
Yorkton–CNoR #2, Sk	1915	$5000	EL/I 1926/35	rt-1959	Plan 100-85

CNoR Special Station (2nd Class Type)

Station Name	Blt.	Cost	Alterations	Disp.	Notes
Chilliwack, BC	1915	$4988	PL 1943	f-1984	Plan 100-83
Estevan, Sk	1915	$4000	S/I 1929/43	s-1984*	Plan 100-83
Hope, BC	1916	$7250	EL 1938	s-1984*	Plan 100-84

Plan 100-39—CNoR Standard 2nd Class Station

Station Name	Blt.	Cost	Alterations	Disp.	Notes
Athabasca, Ab	1912	$8274	EL-G-PL	s-1973*	
Big Valley, Ab	1912	$8200	I/S/EL/PL 1938/42/52/56	EXTANT*	Museum-1
Hanna, Ab	1913	$8274	EXT/I-s/EL/PL 19??/37/53/??	EXTANT*	
Kindersley, Sk #3	1910		I-S/EXT 1935/48	s-1968	
Radville, Sk	1912	$8300	S/PL 1929/58	s-1984*	Museum-1
Stettler, Ab	1911		I-S/PL/EL-G 1937/44/	s-1979*	Museum-2
Tollerton, Ab	1913	$8274		s-1923?	Note 62

CNoR Special Stations
Plan 100-4—CNoR Special Station—St. Boniface Type

Station Name	Blt.	Cost	Alterations	Disp.	Notes
St. Boniface, Mb #1	1901	$4620	Conv. into FT 1914/ EXT 1922	s-1965	Notes 29, 34
Fort Frances, On #1	1901			rp-1913	Note 29

CNoR Special Stations—St. James Type

Station Name	Blt.	Cost	Alterations	Disp.	Notes
Alberta Beach, Ab	1917	$4000		s-1936*	Plan 100-90
Chestermere Lake, Ab	1913			f-1930s	Plan 100-51
Delta, Mb	1917			s-1940s	Plan 100-90, Note 24
Jasper Park, Ab	1915	$4730	Conv. into SH 1920	d-1974	Plan 100-80, Note 45
St. James, Mb	1910	$4000	EXT 1921	EXTANT*	Plan 100-40, Note 34

CNoR Special Stations—Featuring Standard CNoR Detailing

Station Name	Blt.	Cost	Alterations	Disp.	Notes
Edmonton #1-A, Ab	1906		Conv. into yard office 1927	d-1955	Plan 100-34, Note 13
Dauphin #2, Mb	1913	$38400		s-19??*	Plan 100-44
Port Arthur #2, On	1905	$43400	EXT 1920	EXTANT*	Plan 100-49
Saskatoon–CNoR #2, Sk	1910		EXT 1924	d-1939	Plan 100-33, Note 4
Virginia #2, Mn	1913	$31576	I 1946	EXTANT	Plan 100-46

CNoR Special Stations

ALBERTA

Station Name	Blt.	Cost	Alterations	Disp.	Notes
Calgary–CNoR #1	1914	$15300	Conv. into FT 1916	d-1923	Plan 100-56, Temporary
Calgary–CNoR #2	1916	$50000		s-1979*	Plan 100-91, Note 27
South Edmonton	1912	$26915		s-1954	Plan 100-50, Notes 11, 13

BRITISH COLUMBIA

Station Name	Blt.	Cost	Alterations	Disp.	Notes
Kamloops #1	1913			rp-1921	Temporary, Note 49
Kamloops #2	1921			rp-1927	Temp., 30x75
Vancouver #1	1916			rp-1917	Temporary, Note 69
Vancouver #2	1917	$782203		EXTANT*	Plan 100-224, Note 70
Victoria–Alpha St.			rl-Victoria–Point Ellice	rl-1919	Temporary

MANITOBA

Station Name	Blt.	Cost	Alterations	Disp.	Notes
Brandon #1	1890			rp-1911	NPR
Brandon #2	1911	$73368		d-	Plan 140-144
Emerson #1	1904?			f-1923	Plan 100-7, NPR?
Emerson Jct.	1900		EXT/S 1913/32	rm-1971	Plan 100-52, NPR

CNoR PASSENGER STATIONS
CNoR Special Stations

MANITOBA

Station Name	Blt.	Cost	Alterations	Disp.	Notes
St. Boniface #2	1914	$4620	Conv FT/EXP 1914/22	s-1965	Plan 100-54, Note 34
Sprague #2	1910	$6273	EXT/I-S 1915/37	s-1976	Plan 100-37
Winnipeg #1	1889	$80000	Conv. Immig. Shed 1926	d-1982	Plan 100-10, Notes 34, 37
Winnipeg–Union Station #2	1911	$1651239		EXTANT*	Plan UD15, Note 34

MINNESOTA

Station Name	Blt.	Cost	Alterations	Disp.	Notes
Rainier #2	1916	$7622	I/EXT/I 1939/41/51		Plan 100-92
Warroad #2	1914	$15000		s-1982	Plan 100-77
West Duluth	1912	$14310	I/I 1947/51	rt-	Plan 100-48

ONTARIO

Station Name	Blt.	Cost	Alterations	Disp.	Notes
Fort Frances #2	1913	$29500	EXT 1928	EXTANT*	Plan 100-42
Fort William	1918	$37940		EXTANT*	Plan 100-109
Rainy River #2	1918	$25500		s-1986*	Plan 100-120, Add to Sta #1
West Fort William			EXT 1918	rm-	STA

SASKATCHEWAN

Station Name	Blt.	Cost	Alterations	Disp.	Notes
Moose Jaw–CNoR #1	1913		EXT 1916	rp-1918	Plan 100-57, Temporary
Moose Jaw–CNoR #2	1918			rp-1919	Plan 100-123
Moose Jaw–CNoR #3	1919	$57500	EXT 1962	EXTANT*	Plan 100-124
Regina–Union Station	1912			EXTANT*	Plan 100-58, Note 16

GTP PASSENGER SHELTERS

ALBERTA

Station Name	Blt.	Cost	Alterations	Disp.	Notes
Cooking Lake #1-B	By15	$760		rm-	

GTP FREIGHT & PASSENGER SHELTERS
Plan 100-162B—GTP Standard Freight & Passenger Shelters

ALBERTA

Station Name	Blt.	Cost	Alterations	Disp.	Notes
Bremner	1913	$474		rm-	
Evansburg–GTP #1-A	1914	$652		rp-1922	Note 41
Heath	1913	$432		s-1961	
Kapasiwin	1918			rm-	
Lindbrook	1914	$490		s-1958*	
Ribstone #1	1914	$437	Conv. to SMBH 1920	rm-	
Ryley #1	1910			f-1913	
Seba Beach	1917	$520	EXT 1929/rl-Yates #2	rl-1941	
West Jct.	1913		rl-Edmonton-Calder Yard Car Dept.	rl-1917	Note 13
Yates #2		—	x-Seba Beach 1941	rm-	

BRITISH COLUMBIA

Station Name	Blt.	Cost	Alterations	Disp.	Notes
Fort Fraser #1	1916		Conv. SMBH 1923	rm-	Plan 100-162
Nichol #2	1918			d-1960	
Quick		—	x-Telkwa #1 1922	d-1963	
Telkwa #1	1914	$860	rl-Quick	rl-1922	

MANITOBA

Station Name	Blt.	Cost	Alterations	Disp.	Notes
Firdale	1909	$432	rl on site 1958		

SASKATCHEWAN

Station Name	Blt.	Cost	Alterations	Disp.	Notes
Driver	1920	$666		s-1962*	
Hoey #1	1914			rm-1922	
Mead #1	1908	$470	rl-Moose Jaw–CNoR as ST	rl-1958	
Palo	1917	$480		rm-1987*	
St. Louis	1914		rl on site/RENOV/I/EL 1929/30/43/50	s-1982	Probable
Vera	1914	$373		s-1963*	
Welby #1	1910	$351		rp-1946	Plan 100-173
Worcester #1	1917			rp-1939	
York Lake	1912	$427		gb-1969	

GTP PORTABLE STATIONS
Plan 110-101—GTP Standard Portable Station (Based on Bunkhouse Plan)

Station Name	Blt.	Cost	Alterations	Disp.	Notes
Burt, Sk			I 1928	rm-	Probable
Butze, Ab		—	x-Winter #1 1924	rm-	Part only
Evansburg–GTP #1-B, Ab	1918			rp-1922	
Haysport, BC		$1000		rm-	
Innes, Sk		$1200	x-Weyburn #1-A 1929	s-1966	
Moose Jaw–GTP, Sk	1914		rl-North Regina-GTP as SMBH	rl-1921	

GTP PORTABLE STATIONS
Plan 110-101—GTP Standard Portable Station (based on Bunkhouse Plan)

Station Name	Blt.	Cost	Alterations	Disp.	Notes
Weyburn #1-A, Sk	1914	$1200	rl-Innes	rl-1929	
Winter #1, Sk	1914	$419	Part rl-Butze, Ab	rl-1927	
Yonker #1, Sk				rp-1911	

Plan 100-154—GTP Standard 24 Ft.x60 Ft. Station (Type D)

ALBERTA

Station Name	Blt.	Cost	Alterations	Disp.	Notes
Chauvin	1909	$2861	EL	rm-	
Viking	1909	$3046	I-S/EL/G 1939/53/??	s-19??*	

MANITOBA

Station Name	Blt.	Cost	Alterations	Disp.	Notes
Gregg	1909	$3101	S	gb-1969	
Ingelow	1909	$3113	I-S 1942	s-1976	
Justice	1909	$2975	I-S 1942	gb-1969	
Pope #1	1909	$2973	I/S/EL 1938/??/55	s-1963	
St. Lazare	1909	$3051	S/I 1918/38	rm-	

SASKATCHEWAN

Station Name	Blt.	Cost	Alterations	Disp.	Notes
Allan	1909	$3181	S/RENOV 1924/68	s-1977*	
Atwater #1	1909	$3093	I-S/EL 1939/66	s-1966	
Bradwell #1	1909	$1893		f-1910	Probable
Cavell	1910	$2978	I-S 1939	s-1963	
Goodeve	1909	$2979	S/I/EL 1918/38/52	s-	
Kelliher	1909	$2986	S/I/PL 1921/38/66	s-1978	
Kinley	1909	$3021	S/I 1923/38	s-1964*	
Leney	1910	$3042	S/I 1923/38	s-1968	
Punnichy	1909	$3077	S/ rl on site?	s-1977	
Raymore #1	1907	$3049		f-1919	
Scott #1	1909	$3388		f-1935	
Semans	1909	$2995	I/PL 1939/63	s-1977*	
South Saskatoon #1	1909	$3240	Refer to Notes	rl-1927	Notes 3, 4
Unity	1909	$3041	EXT/I-S/EL 1912/39/53	s-1992*	
Venn #1	1907	$3149		f-1923	

GTP COMBINATION STATIONS
Plan 100-152—GTP Standard 'Design A' Station (Type E)

ALBERTA

Station Name	Blt.	Cost	Alterations	Disp.	Notes
Acheson #1	1911	$1825		d-1951	
Alix–GTP #1	1911	$2064	Conv. into SH 1927	rm-	Note 60
Ansell	1911	$2063	CPF-I/S 1940/42	s-1964	
Ardley	1911	$2050	I-S 1936	s-19??*	
Ardrossan	1910	$1698	S/EL 1920/??	s-1968*	
Bardo #1	1913	$1864		rp-	
Bashaw	1911	$2123	I/EL 1940/??	s-1977*	
Beiseker	1913	$2250	EXT/EL-I/PL 1930/50/58	d-1975	
Bickerdike	1911	$2127	S 1922	s-1966*	
Bircham	1912	$2250	EL-I-S 1944	s-	
Bissell #1	1910	$1766		f-1921	
Bruce	1910	$1967	S/I/EL-G 1920/34/??	s-1969	
Carrot Creek–GTP #1	1911	$2190		d-1951	
Carvel	1910	$1728	I-S/EL 1935/54	s-1967	
Clover Bar #1	1911	$1851		f-1920	
Coalspur #1-A	1913		rl on site-S 1930	d-1972	
Dalehurst–GTP	1911	$2160	S-RENOV 1927	d-1960	Note 8
Delacour	1913	$2250	I-S/EL 1935/50	d-1975	
Delburne	1912		S/EL-G-PL 1922/??	s-1976*	Museum-2
Deville #1-A	1910	$1802	I-S/EL/G 1939/57/??	s-1965	
Dinant	1912	$1842	S	s-1960*	
Dorenlee	1912	$2081	I-S/EL 1935/53	s-1967*	
Duffield	1911	42236	I/S/EL 1937/44/54	s-1962*	
Duhamel	1911	$2250	I-S/EL 1935/??	s-1963	
Edgerton	1911	$2276	S/I/EL 1920/34/??	s-1977*	Museum-2
Elnora	1911	$2000	S/EL 1922/??	d-1975	
Embarras	1912	$2250	I-S 1936	rm-	
Entrance–GTP	1911	$2027	I-RENOV-S 1927	d-1967	Note 8
Entwistle–GTP	1910	$1815	S/EL 1920/56	s-1968*	
Erith	1912	$2250	I-S 1936	rm-	
Fabyan #1	1910	$1850		f-1924	
Fallis	1910	$1918	I-S 1935	s-1968	
Ferintosh	1911	$2156	S/EL 1923/??	s-1976	
Foothills		$2750	x-Lovett 1937/EL	f-1961	
Gainford	1911	$1854	S/I/I/EL 1922/34/43/54	s-1963*	
Galloway #1	1911	$2076		f-1930	
Geikie	1912	$1783	I 1937	d-1959	
Greenshields	1911	$2284	I-S/EL 1935/39	s-1976	
Hargwen #1	1911	$2032		f-1919	
Hawes	1913	$2029		rt-1921	Note 52
Hawkins #1	1911	$2297	S 1929	d-1950	
Henry House–GTP	1911	$2165		f-1938	

GTP COMBINATION STATIONS
Plan 100-152—GTP Standard 'Design A' Station (Type E)

ALBERTA

Station Name	Blt.	Cost	Alterations	Disp.	Notes
Hinton	1912	$1959	I-RENOV-S/EL/PL 1927/56/59	EXTANT*	Note 8
Holden	1910	$1833	S/I/EL-G-PL 1920/34/57	rm-	
Huxley	1913	$1960	S 1922	d-1976	
Interlaken	1913	$2035	s-1923		Note 53
Irma	1910	$1917	S/PL/EL-G 1920/57/??	s-1973*	
Irricana	1911	$2300	EL	d-1975	
Jarrow	1910	$1837		rm-	
Junkins–GTP	1911	$1894	rl-Junkins-CNoR (later Wildwood)	rl-1918	Note 67
Keston	1913	$2250		s-1930	Note 68
Kingman	1910		I/S/EL 1937/42	s-1967	
Kinsella #1	1911	$2251	S/I/EL-G 1920/34/??	s-19??*	
Leaman	1911	$1745		d-1951	
Lousana #1	1912	$1922		rt-1959	

NOTES:

3. In 1927 the freight shed was converted into a dwelling for the coalman, while the balance of the depot was relocated to Nutana and converted into a section house.
4. This station was technically on the Saskatoon Terminals Subdivision.
8. Left vacant on the abandoned GTP grade in 1917. This station was rehabilitated in 1927, when the Obed–Entrance (x-Dyke) section of the line was re-opened.
11. This station was little used after operations commenced on the Bretona to Bretville Jct. cut-off in 1929. The building was sold in 1954 and demolished the following year. It was rumored that the boilers from this building were salvaged and re-used in the shopping complex erected on this site.
13. This station was technically on the Edmonton Terminals Subdivision.
16. With the Canadian Northern take-over of the Qu'Appelle Long Lake and Saskatchewan Railway in December 1906, it retained the joint station agreement between the CPR and QLL&S for use of the Regina depot and freight sheds. This station—the CPR's second depot at Regina—was replaced in 1912 by a "Union Station" built by the CPR for joint use and occupancy by the CNoR, then later the GTP, and subsequently the CNR. Only the 1912 station is included in the rosters. It is located on the CPR main line in downtown Regina on that company's Indian Head Subdivision. The station was subsequently acquired by VIA Rail Canada. It has since been sold, "restored" and redeveloped into a casino.
24. The Delta Subdivision was abandoned 1 March 1941. The Delta station was apparently sold in situ in 1941, being used as a fish warehouse until it burned down in the mid-1940s.
27. The St. Mary's Hall was constructed in 1894. The CNoR obtained an option on the property in 1911, but did not take over the building until 1914. Conversion into a railway depot was completed in 1916.
29. The CNoR classified this as a 2nd Class Station.
34. This station was technically on the Winnipeg Terminals Subdivision.
37. In 1889, the Northern Pacific & Manitoba Railway constructed this three-storey brick station-hotel on Water Avenue. The hotel portion of the complex was destroyed in a spectacular fire in February 1899. After the opening of the new Union depot in 1911, the old station was integrated into the Winnipeg Industrial Bureau and used as a convention hall. In 1926 it was converted into an immigration shed. During the Depression it was used as a hostel by the unemployed and homeless. The military took over the building during World War II, after which it again served as a shelter for the homeless. The third floor of the station was removed in 1954.
41. There is a discrepancy in CNR records; one stating that a carbody (#6997) was placed here in 1914, while the GTP cost record indicates that a formal shelter costing $652 was erected here. A photograph in a local history clearly shows an FPS. Perhaps the carbody was a temporary station and there was a mix-up in record keeping.
45. Abandoned on site in 1917. Converted into section house.
46. Abandoned when the rehabilitated GTP line reopened 1 November 1924. It remained vacant until World War II when Lucerne was used as a Japanese internment camp, and the station was used as a bunkhouse for internees. The depot was finally razed by the Parks Department in the mid-1950s.
49. The temporary station for the Canadian Northern and the Northern Construction Company (involved in building the railway line) was situated north of the South Thompson River.
52. Abandoned on site in 1921; final disposition unknown.
60. In 1927, after the former CNoR depot was moved to the Alix–GTP station grounds, the former GTP depot was converted into a section house.
62. Dayson, Carrot Creek–CNoR, Fulstow, Horner, Scriven and Tollerton, Ab. These stations were abandoned on grade in 1917. The following year, the CNoR apparently stripped all re-usable millwork (windows, doors, interior fittings, etc.) from these buildings. A local history makes reference to Carrot Creek–CNoR and Fulstow as being sold about 1923. It is likely that all of these stations were sold and removed at the same time.
67. The GTP depot was relocated from the abandoned grade to the CNoR station grounds by 1918.
68. Abandoned on site in 1917, sold in 1930.
69. The Great Northern Railway station, on Pender Street was used by the CNoR commencing October 1915, until temporary passenger accommodations were built. These were apparently abandoned once the new depot on Main Street opened in 1917.
70. This station was technically on the Vancouver Terminals Subdivision.

GTP COMBINATION STATIONS
Plan 100-152—GTP Standard 'Design A' Station (Type E)

ALBERTA

Station Name	Blt.	Cost	Alterations	Disp.	Notes
Lovett	1913		S 1922/rl-Foothills	rl-1937	
MacKay	1911	$2350	S 1920	s-1968*	
Marlboro–GTP #1	1911	$2060	S 1918	rm-	
McLeod River	1912	$2250	I-S 1936	s-1993*	Museum-2
Medicine Lodge #1	1911	$2028		d-1951	
New Norway	1911	$2250	I-S/EL-PL 1935/58	d-1975	
Niton	1911	$1863	I/CPF/S 1934/40/44	d-1967	
Obed–GTP	1911	$2028	S-RENOV 1927	d-1963	Note 8
Parkgate	1913	$2069		s-1924*	Note 51
Pedley #1	1913	$2044		f-?	Note 73
Peers	1911	$1758	S/I 1920/34	rm-	
Philips	1910	$1828		s-1960*	
Pocahontas	1912	$1854		rt-1921	Note 52
Poe	1911	$2291		s-1958	
Robb	1912	$2250	I-S 1936	f-	
Rosevear	1911	$2231	CPF-I/S 1940/42	rm-	
Ryley #2	1913	$1967	S/I/EL-G-PL 1920/34/57	s-1972	
Shonts	1911	$2277		rt-1960	
Spruce Grove–GTP	1910	$1647	S/EL	d-1972	
Stony Plain–GTP	1911	$1902	EXT/S/EXT/I/EL 1920/23/28/34/??	d-1967	
Styal	1911	$2308	I-S 1935	s-1970*	
Swalwell	1912		EXT/I-S/EL 1920/35/50/??	d-1975	
Three Hills #1	1912	$2700	Conv. into SH 1919	d-1975	
Torlea	1911	$2293		rm-1960	
Trochu #1	1912		S 1922	rp-1959	
Uncas	1911	$2270	I-S/EL-G 1939/??	s-1966	
Wabamun	1911	$1783	S/I/EL/PI 1920/34/54/??	s-1982	
Weald	1912	$2250	I-S 1936	rt-1963	
Wildwood			x-Junkins-GTP 1918/ S/I/PL 1918/22/34/59	d-	Note 67
Wolf Creek	1911	$2000	CPF/I/S 1940/41/42	rm-	
Yates #1	1913	$2200	I 1938	f-1940	

BRITISH COLUMBIA

Station Name	Blt.	Cost	Alterations	Disp.	Notes
Aleza Lake #1	1914	$1899	I-S 1936	s-1968*	
Alpland #1	1913	$2099	S 1924	f-1936	
Amsbury	1911	$2403	I-S 1937	d-1966	
Andimaul #1	1912	$2318		d-1951	
Barrett #1	1914	$2516		d-1951	
Beament #1	1913	$2283		d-1940	
Bednesti	1914	$2240	I-S 1936	d-1971	
Bend #1	1914	$1908	S/I 1928/38	d-1962	
Bulkley Canyon #1	1913	$2379		d-	
Burns Lake #1	1914	$2185	EXT/EXT 1921/30	rp-1951	
Carnaby	1913	$2452		rt-1959	
Cedarvale #1	1912	$2364		f-1930	
Chilako #1	1914	$2167		d-1952	
Croydon #1	1913	$1898	S 1927	d-1954	
Decker Lake	1915	$1908	I-S/EL 1935/53	rt-1958	
Dewey	1914	$1953	I-S 1936	d-1962	
Doreen	1913	$2317	I-S 1937	d-1971	
Doughty #1	1913	$2298		d-1950	
Dunster	1913	$1891	S 1927	s-19??*	Museum-2
Eddy #1	1913	$1932	S/I 1927/41	rp-1960	
Encombe #1	1914	$2334		d-1950	
Engen	1915	$2042	S/I/EL 1935/41/56	rm-	
Evelyn	1913	$2167	I-S/EL 1937/57		
Exstew	1911	$2434	I-S 1937	d-1966	
Finmoore #1	1914	$2434	I-S 1936	rp-	
Fitzwilliam	1913	$1850		gb-1942	Note 1
Foreman #1	1914	$2049		d-1948	
Forestdale #1	1915	$1921		d-1948	
Fraser Lake	1914	$2634		rm-	
Giscome	1914	$1911	EXT 1923	rm-	
Goat River #1	1914	$2034	S/I 1928/30	rm-	
Grant Brook–GTP	1913	$1962	I 1937	d-	Note 1
Guilford #1	1914	$1945		d-1950	
Hansard	1914	$1726		rm-	
Hazelton	1913	$2924	I-S 1937	d-1965	
Houston #1	1914	$2412		f-1920	
Hubert #1	1914	$2393		d-1949	
Hulatt	1915	$2208	I-S 1936	rm-	
Hutchison	1914	$2243	I-S 1936	rm-	
Hutton	1914	$1990	S 1932	d-1969	
Isle Pierre #1	1914	$2377		d-1958	
Kidd #1	1914	$2009	S 1928	d-1953	
Kitselas	1911	$2499	I-S 1937	d-1971	
Kitwanga	1912	$2374	I-S 1937	s-19??*	
Knockholt #1	1914	$2316		d-1951	

GTP COMBINATION STATIONS
Plan 100-152—GTP Standard 'Design A' Station (Type E)

BRITISH COLUMBIA

Station Name	Blt.	Cost	Alterations	Disp.	Notes
Kwinitsa	1911	$2494	I-S 1937	s-1985*	Museum-2
Legrand	1914	$1918	S/I 1928/40	rm-	
Lindup #1	1914	$2026	rl-Penny #3	rl-1947	
Longworth	1914	$1929	S/I 1928/38	d-1969	
Loos #1	1914	$1878		f-1959	
Lucerne–GTP	1912	$1843	RENOV/I 1924/34	d-1968	Note 1
Marten Lake #1	1915	$2078		d-1950	
McCall	1915	$2036		rm-	
Miworth #1	1915	$2324		d-1948	
Moricetown	1913	$2217	I 1940	rm-	
Nash	1912	$2357	I-S	d-1966	
New Hazelton #1	1913	$2452	I-S/EXT 1937/46	d-1980	
Newlands #1	1914	$2124		d-1949	
Nichol #1	1914			rp-1918	
Otway	1915	$2325	I-S/RENOV 1936/45	rt-1966	
Palling #1	1914	$2003		d-1950	
Penny #2			x-Lindup 1947/I 1951	s-1987*	Museum-2
Perow	1914	$2232	I-S 1936	rm-	
Phelan	1911	$2512	I-S 1937	d-1970	
Pitman #1	1912	$2404		d-1947	
Priestly	1915	$1833		rt-1967	
Rainbow–GTP	1913	$1800	rl-Redpass Jct.	rl-1917	Note 1
Raush Valley #1	1913	$2012	S/I 1927/41	s-1963	
Rearguard #1	1913	$2273	S 1927	f-1949	
Redpass Jct. #1			x-Rainbow–GTP 1917/ EXT/S/RENOV 1937	d-1977	Note 1
Rider	1914	$2964		d-1967	
Rose Lake	1915	$1910		rm-	
Salvus #1	1912	$2438		f-1928	
Savory	1915	$1883		rt-1969	
Seaton	1913	$2456		rm-	
Selwyn	1912	$1949	S 1924/rl-Redpass Jct. as dwelling	rl-1949	
Shames	1912	$2423		d-1966	
Shelley #1	1914	$1920		d-1969	
Sheraton #1	1915	$1914		d-1948	
Shere	1913	$2085	S 1927	rm-1960	
Sinkut #1	1914	$2379		d-1948	
Skeena	1912	$2432	I-S 1937	d-1966	
Sockeye #1	1911	$2433		rp-1947	
Swiftwater	1913	$2099	I-S 1936	d-1969	
Tatlow	1914	$2324		rt-1958	
Terrace #1	1911	$2439		rp-1960	
Tete Jaune	1912	$2182	S/EL 1927/??	d-1977	
Tintagel	1915	$1971	I-S 1935	d-1971	
Topley	1914	$2247		d-1971	
Tyee	1911	$2483	I-S 1937	rt-1963	
Urling #1	1914	$1946		rm-	
Usk #1	1912	$2345		rp-	
Vanderhoof #1	1914	$2248		f-1924	
Walcott #1	1913	$2302	I-S 1936	rt-1965	
Wedgwood #1	1915	$1960		d-1949	
Willow River #1	1914	$2107		d-1969	
Woodcock	1912	$2365	I-S 1937	d-1963	
Yellowhead #1	1912	$1865	f-1918?		Note 1

MANITOBA

Station Name	Blt.	Cost	Alterations	Disp.	Notes
Beaudry	1911	$2236	S/I 19??/46	s-1962	
Cabot	1911	$2191	S/I 19??/45	s-1960	
Caye	1911	$2112	S/EL/I 1923/55/57	s-1965	
Exira	1911	$2286	S/I 1934/41	gb-1969	
Fortier #1	1911	$2110		rp-1923	
Gervais #1	1911	$2111		rp-1937	
Harte	1911	$2294	S/EL 19??/54	gb-1969	
Knox	1911	$2181	I-S 1939	f-1943	
Miniota	1912	$2508	I/S/EL 1938/??/53	s-1962	
Myra	1911	$2275		f-1931	
Norman	1911	$2253	I/S 1936/??	s-1960	
North Elie	1911	$2090	S/I 19??/45	s-1963	
Oakner	1911	$2264	I/S 1934/??	s-1971	
Pacific Jct. #1	1911	$2091		f-1927	
Quadra	1911	$2291	I/S/EL 1939/??/51	s-1966	
Searle	1911	$2100	S/I/EL 1918/40/57	s-1962	

ONTARIO

Station Name	Blt.	Cost	Alterations	Disp.	Notes
Alcona	1911	$2250	I-S 1941	s-1960	
Baird	1912			a-1925	Note 32
Crest	1912			a-1925	Note 32
Dona	1912			a-1925	Note 32
Ellis	1912	$1690	CPF-I 1940	s-1964	

GTP COMBINATION STATIONS
Plan 100-152—GTP Standard 'Design A' Station (Type E)

ONTARIO

Station Name	Blt.	Cost	Alterations	Disp.	Notes
Flett	1911	$2500	CPF-I-S/I 1942/51	s-1960	
Graham	1910	$2250	RENOV/I 1946/53	d-1980	
Griff	1911	$2500	I/I 1942/51	s-1961	
Horne	1911	$2500	I	s-1961	
James	1910	$1690	CPF-I 1943	s-1961	
Jones #1	1911			s-1963*	
Kelly	1911	$1690	CPF-I/I 1943/51	s-1962	
Larson	1911	$1690		rm-	
Linko	1910	$1690	I 1942	s-1960	
Mack	1911	$1690		rm-	
Oscar #1	1910		RENOV-I/I 1944/48	f-1949	
Petry #1	1910			rt-1943	
Quorn #1	1910		CPF-I 1945	f-1947	
Raith	1910	$1415		s-1960	
Reba	1911	$2500	RENOV/I 1945/51	s-1961	
Ritchan #1	1912	$1690	I-S 1937	rm-	
Snowden	1911	$2500	CPF-I 1942	d-1979	
Sunstrum	1912	$1690	I-S 1937	rm-	
Tannin	1910	$2500	RENOV-I/S 1941/45	d-1964	
Umfreville #1	1910	$2500		rp-1927	
Unaka	1911	$2500	S 1945	f-1963	
Valora #1	1911	$2500		f-1925	
Watcomb	1910	$2500	I/S 1940/45	s-1964	
Westfort	1912	$1912	rl on site- RENOV-S-Pl 1931	s-1962	
White	1912	$1690	I-S 1935	d-1968	
Yonde	1911	$2500	CPF-I/S 1942/45	s-1961	
Zarn	1910	$2500	I/S 1940/45	s-1961	

SASKATCHEWAN

Station Name	Blt.	Cost	Alterations	Disp.	Notes
Ancrum #1	1912			rp-1920	
Archydal	1913	$2250	S/I 1923/38	s-1963	
Argo	1913	$2011	I 1938	s-1961*	Museum-2
Artland	1911	$2311	S/I/EL 1920/37/57	s-1978	
Asquith #1	By15	$2265		f-1918	
Ava	1913	$2113	I/S 1938/45	s-1960*	
Bangor	1913	$2251	S/EL 1927/53	s-1969	
Beaufield #1	1913			f-1956	
Benson	1913	$1975	S/I 1921/37	s-1978	
Birmingham	1911	$2260	I-S 1938	s-1963	
Bradwell #2	1910	$2250	I-S 1934	d-1980	
Bremen	1911	$2250	S 1927	s-1966	
Brewer	1910	$1551	I 1938	s-1959	
Burdick	1913	$2250	S/I 1923/39	s-1963	
Burgis #1	1911	$1900		d-1950	
Cana #1	1911	$2238	S/I/EL 1918/38/53	s-1964	
Cando	1913	$1921	S/EL 19??/57	s-1980	
Cedoux	1912	$2085	S/EL 1923/40/56	s-1980	
Clavet	1911	$2251	S/I/EL 1923/34/56	s-1974	
Coleville	1913	$2250	S/EL 1923/54	d-1987	
Colfax #1	1913	$2027	S 1923	f-1929	
Colmer	1911	$1689	S/I 1923/41	s-1964	
Cudworth #1	1911	$2098		f-1925	
Cutknife	1913	$1818	I 1943	s-1960	
Dacer #1	1913			rp-1941	
Darmody	1914	$2250	S/I 1921/39	s-1964*	Reverse
Dodsland #1	1913		S	f-1948	
Domremy #1	1915			rp-1919	
Duff	1913	$2089	S 1921	s-1975*	Museum-2
Duro	1911	$2293	I-S 1935	s-1958	
Ebenezer	1911	$1900	I/EL 1938/53	rt-1970	
Edenwold	1911	$2087	S/EXT 1921/28	s-1974	
Edgeley	1911	$2090	S/I 1921/41	s-1977	
Elcott	1912			f-1919	
Estlin	1912	$2086	S/I/EL 1923/38/52	d-1977	
Farley	1911	$2298	S 1924	s-1946	
Fenwood	1911	$2243	I-S 1934	s-	
Finnie	1910	$1712	A/I/EL 1923/41/54	s-1960*	
Fort Qu'Appelle	1911	$1800	S/EXT/I/PL 1921/25/38/53	s-1984*	
Frobisher	1913	$1989	S/I/RENOV/EL 1923/37/43/54	f-1970	
Gallivan	1913	$1764	I/EL 1943/56	s-1963*	
Gerald	1911	$2277	S/I/EL 1918/34/53	d-	
Gillespie	1910	$1848	S/EL 1923/54	s-1966	
Gorlitz	1913	$2344	I/EL 1938/52	s-1964	
Grandora	1911	$2255	S/I/EL 1924/38/57	s-19??*	
Gray	1914	$1885	A/I/EL 1921/37/53	s-1977	
Grayburn	1914	$2250	S/I 1922/38	s-1966	
Griffin #1	1913			f-1920	

GTP COMBINATION STATIONS
Plan 100-152—GTP Standard 'Design A' Station (Type E)

SASKATCHEWAN

Station Name	Blt.	Cost	Alterations	Disp.	Notes
Hawoods #1	1911	$2285		f-1920	
Hoosier	1913	$1919	I-S/EL 1938/??	d-1975	
Hubbard	1911	$2254	S/I/EL 1918/34/53	rm-1966	
Huntoon #1	1913	$2048	S 1923?	s-1965	
Ibstone	1913	$2250	I 1958	s-1968	
Ituna	1911	$2276	I-S 1934	f-1962	
Jasmin	1911	$2269	S 1927	s-1967	
Juniata	1911	$2298	S/I 1924/38	s-1959	
Keystown	1913	$2177	S/I/EL 1923/38/56	s-1970	
Lake Valley #1	1914	$2250	I-S/EL 1937/54	s-1969	
Landis	1911	$2287	S/I/EL 1919/37/??	d-1981	
Lebret	1911	$2250	S/I 1923/39	s-1976*	
Leross	1911	$2258	S/I 1922/38	s-1969*	
Lestock	1911	$2311	S/I 1922/34	d-1980	
Lett	1913	$2000	S/I 19??/40	s-1963*	
Lewvan	1912	$2142	S/I/EL 1921/39/54	d-1977	
Loverna	1913	$1989	EXT/S 19??/23	d-1981	
Mawer #1	1913		S 1921	f-1924	
Meacham	1911	$2031	S/EL 1927/54	s-1982*	
Mehan #1	1911	$1900		s-1959	
Millerdale	1913	$2141	I/S 1938/45	s-1962*	
Minard	1913	$2007	S/I/I 1923/38/41	s-1963	
Muscow	1911	$2250	S/I 1923/41	s-1966	
Neely	1911	$2250	S 1927	s-1964	
Oban #1	1911	$2171		d-1958	
Openshaw	1913	$1944	S/I 1923/37	s-1963	
Otthon	1911	$2500	S/I/EL 1921/38/56	s-1969*	
Prongua	1913	$2250	I/EL 1943/56	s-1962	
Quinton #1	1911	$2282		f-1918	
Reford	1911	$1787		d-1958	
Riceton	1912	$2087	S/I/EL 1921/37/53	d-1958	
Rowatt	1912	$2150	S/I 1922/39	s-1975	
Ruthilda	1913	$2222	S/I/EL 1922/38/54	s-1981	
Sidmar	1913	$2250	S/I 1923/37	s-1960	
Smiley	1913	$2053	I/S 1938/39	d-1981	
Springwater	1913	$2250	S/I/EL 1923/38/56	rm-	
Spy Hill #1	1910	$2111	S/I/EL 1934/39/53	f-1960	
Steelman	1913	$1999	S/I/EL 1923/38/57	rm-	
Stony Beach	1913	$2250	S/I/EL 1921/41/54	s-1974	
Tako	1911	$2285	I-S 1939	s-1969*	
Talmage	1913	$1973	S/I/EL 1921/37/52	s-1980	
Tate	1911	$2273	I-S 1934	s-1960*	
Totzke #1	1911	$2015	Conv. into SH 1927	rm-	
Undora	1911	$2250	I 1938	s-1960	
Victoria Plains	1911	$2103	S 1923	s-1959	
Wakaw #1	1911			rp-1919	
Waldron	1910	$1897	I-S/EL 1934/53	s-1969	
Xena	1911	$2339	S/I 1924/40	s-1965*	
Yarbo #1	1911	$2301		rp-1934	
Yonker #2	1911	$2297	S/I 1922/38	s-1962	
Young	1911	$2252	I-S 1934	f-1962	
Zehner #1	1911	$2044		f-1920	
Zelma	1911	42266	S/I 1918/34	s-1969	
Zeneta #1	1911	$2255	Conv. into SH 1928	d-1960	

Plan 100-151—Standard NTR 'Design A' Station (Type F)

ALBERTA

Station Name	Blt.	Cost	Alterations	Disp.	Notes
Grainger #2	1919	$3593		rt-1927	
Hubalta	1913	$1902	I-S 1935	d-1970s	
Three Hills #2	1919	$8024	S/EL-PL 19??/57	s-19**	Museum-2

NOTES:

1 These depots were left vacant on the abandoned GTP grade in 1917. Rainbow–GTP was relocated to Redpass in 1917 and Yellowhead burned down about 1918. The stations at Fitzwilliam, Grant Brook and Lucerne–GTP, BC were rehabilitated in 1924, when that section of the line was re-opened.

8 Left vacant on the abandoned GTP grade in 1917. This station was rehabilitated in 1927, when the Obed–Entrance (x-Dyke) section of the line was re-opened.

32 The 26-mile section between Conmee and Fort William was abandoned in 1925. The final disposition of this station could not be established.

51 This station was left vacant on the abandoned grade in 1917. It was turned over to the Parks Department in 1923. The station is extant, but is gradually being pushed over by the constantly shifting sand dunes.

52 Abandoned on site in 1921; final disposition unknown.

67 The GTP depot was relocated from the abandoned grade to the CNoR station grounds by 1918.

73 CNR building records are somewhat unclear regarding this station. One record clearly shows that Pedley had a 'Design A' (Type E) station, but another also notes it as Plan 100-47, with stucco and rehabilitation in 1927. It is likely that the original GTP station burned down, and that this building was relocated from Dalehurst–CNoR, then abandoned in 1928.

GTP COMBINATION STATIONS
Plan 100-151—Standard NTR 'Design A' Station (Type F)

BRITISH COLUMBIA

Station Name	Blt.	Cost	Alterations	Disp.	Notes
Lake Kathlyn	1917			rm-	

ONTARIO

Station Name	Blt.	Cost	Alterations	Disp.	Notes
Allanwater	1911	$1690	I-S 1941	s-1962	
Amesdale	1911		I-S 1937	s-1965	
Cameo	1911	$1690	I-S 1941	d-1955	
Collins #1	1911	$1690	I-S 1941	s-1967	
Fowler	1912	$1690	I-S 1940	s-1970	
Ghost River	1912	$1690	S 1940	s-1961*	
Harvey	1911	$1690	I-S 1940	s-1967	
Jacobs	1911	$1690	I 1953	s-1961	
Kawa	1911	$1690	I 1953	s-1961	
Ogaki	1911	$1690	I-S 1941	d-1962	
Onaping	1911	$1690		s-1962	
Pascopee	1911	$1690	I-S 1941	s-1962	
Robinson	1912	$1690	I-S 1940	d-1967	
Rosnel	1912	$1690	I-S 1940	s-1967	
Savant Lake	1912	$1690	I/I-S/EL 1934/40/57	s-	
Staunton	1912	$1690	I-S 1940	s-1962	
Ycliff #1	1912	$1690	S 1940	s-1964	

SASKATCHEWAN

Station Name	Blt.	Cost	Alterations	Disp.	Notes
Asquith #2	1918	$3615	S/I 1923/34	s-1969	
Central Butte #2	1919	$2250	S/PL 1928/64	d-1977	
Dewar Lake #2	1920	$5423	I/S 1938/39	d-1975	
Duperow #2	1919	$4502	I/S/EL 1938/45/57	rm-	
Lawson #2	1919	$2300	I 1939	d-1977	
Mead #2	1917			d-1967	
Quinton #2	1918	$2250	S/EL	s-1976	
Red Deer Hill	1918	$4000	S/I 1927/43	s-1974	
Riverhurst	1917	$2412	I-S/RENOV/PL 1937/57/66	s-1976	

Plan 100-168—GTP Standard "New Design A" Station (Type G)

ALBERTA

Station Name	Blt.	Cost	Alterations	Disp.	Notes
Hargwen #2	1920	$7267		d-1967	Note 9
Ribstone #2	1920	$6500	EL 1952	d-1970	

BRITISH COLUMBIA

Station Name	Blt.	Cost	Alterations	Disp.	Notes
Houston #2	1920	$2811		rm-	
Telkwa #2	1922	$7253	EL	d-1980	

SASKATCHEWAN

Station Name	Blt.	Cost	Alterations	Disp.	Notes
Avonhurst #2	1920	$6200		s-19??*	
Carruthers	1920	$5517		d-1962	
Domremy #2	1919	$5000		s-	
Gilroy #2	1919	$6200		s-1968	
Hoey #2	1920	$5000		d-1982	
Lorlie #2	1920	$3000		s-1969	
Raymore #3	1921	$6985	EL/PL 19??/66	d-1982	
Venn #2	1924	$5026	I 1934	d-	
Wakaw #2	1919	$2050	PL 1964	s-1983*	

Plan 100-179—NTR Standard No. 1 Station

Station Name	Blt.	Cost	Alterations	Disp.	Notes
Elma, Mb	1910	$2300	S/I/I 1930/34/40		
Redditt #1, On	1910		Conv. to SH/I-S 1912/36	s-1968	
Nokomis, Sk	1908	$5214	S/I 1927/34	s-19??	Plan 100-160, Museum-2
Transcona #1, Mb	1912	$5000	Conv. to Yard Office/S 1929/48	EXTANT*	

Plan 100-180—NTR Standard No. 2 Station

MANITOBA

Station Name	Blt.	Cost	Alterations	Disp.	Notes
Dugald	1910	$2963	S 1930	s-1964	
Vivian	1910	$4100	I-S 1935	s-1967	

ONTARIO

Station Name	Blt.	Cost	Alterations	Disp.	Notes
Hudson	1911		I-S 1934		
McIntosh #1	1910		I-S/EL 1936/195?	s-1964	
Millidge	1910		I-S 1937	s-1963	
Minaki	1910		I/EXT-S 1934/39	s-19??*	
Niddrie	1910		I-S 1937	d-1961	
Superior Jct. #1	1910	$4500	I/S 1934/37	d-1963	
Webster #1	1910				

Plan 100-181—NTR Standard No. 3 Station

MANITOBA

Station Name	Blt.	Cost	Alterations	Disp.	Notes
Anola	1910	$2963	I-S/EL-I 1935/53	s-1961*	
Decimal	1910	$3000	I-S/EXT 1935/39	s-1965	
Hazell	1910			rm-	
Hoctor	1910	$2250	I-S 1935	s-1960	
Lewis	1910	$2500	I-S/I/EL 1935/53/55	s-1964	

ONTARIO

Station Name	Blt.	Cost	Alterations	Disp.	Notes
Farlane	1910		I-S 1936	EXTANT*	
Malachi	1910		S 1930	EXTANT*	
Pelican	1910		I-S 1937	s-1965	
Quibell	1910		EXT/I-S/EL 1918/38/52	EXTANT*	

Miscellaneous GTP Combination Stations

Station Name	Blt.	Cost	Alterations	Disp.	Notes
Cooking Lake #1-A, Ab	1910	$1026		rm-	Plan 100-153
Mountain Park #2, Ab	1920	$3100	RENOV	d-1950s	Note 48
Uno #1, Mb	1907			f-1909	Plan 100-153
Uno #2, Mb	1910	$894	I/EL/EXT 1938/52/53	s-1966*	Plan 100-153

GTP PASSENGER STATIONS
Plan 100-155—GTP Standard No. 2 Terminal Station

Station Name	Blt.	Cost	Alterations	Disp.	Notes
Biggar, Sk	1909	$9119	S/EXT/I 1926/27/39	EXTANT*	
Jasper #1, Ab	1912	$6314		f-1924	Plan 100-159
Pacific #1, BC	1913	$14978		f-1935	Plan 100-159
Wainwright #1, Ab	1909	$9209		f-1928	
Watrous, Sk	1909	$9000	EXT/PL/S 1919/23/24	d-1986	

Plan 100-157—GTP Standard 'Design E' Station

Station Name	Blt.	Cost	Alterations	Disp.	Notes
Balcarres #1, Sk	1910		S 1923	f-1931	
Battleford–GTP, Sk	1912	$1950	Conv. into SH 1926	s-1969*	
Camrose–GTP, Ab	1910			d-1924	Note 12
Mirror, Ab	1911	$2300	I-S/EL 1944/??	f-1975	
South Canora, Sk	1911	$1900	I-S 1938	s-1962	
Tofield, Ab	1911	$4400	I-S/PL/EL-G 1939/58/??	rm-	
Yorkton–GTP, Sk	1910	$7250	I-S 1935	s-	

Plans 100-158/-163—GTP Standard 'Design D' Station

Station Name	Blt.	Cost	Alterations	Disp.	Notes
Armstrong #1, On	1912			f-1926	
Edson, Ab	1910	$21811	I/S/EL/PL/G 1937/38/??/??/??	d-1976	Plan 100-163
Redditt #2, On	1912		I-S 1936	d-1978	

GTP Special Stations

ALBERTA

Station Name	Blt.	Cost	Alterations	Disp.	Notes
Calgary–GTP	1914	$5580	rl on site 1914	d-	Temporary

BRITISH COLUMBIA

Station Name	Blt.	Cost	Alterations	Disp.	Notes
Endako #1	1914	$1190		s-1923	Temporary
McBride #1	1913	$44046		f-1918	Plan 100-156
McBride #2	1918			rp-1919	Temporary
McBride #3	1919	$14225		EXTANT*	Plan 100-167, Museum-1
Prince George #1	1913	$5232		rp-1922	Temporary
Prince Rupert #1	1907	$29886		rp-1922	Plan 140-210, Temp., Note 56
Smithers #1	1915	$1772		rp-1919	Temporary, Note 58
Smithers #2	1919	$11496		EXTANT*	Plan 100-166, Museum-1

MANITOBA

Station Name	Blt.	Cost	Alterations	Disp.	Notes
Portage la Prairie–GTP	1908	$22650		EXTANT*	Plan 100-175
Rivers #1	1909	$20950		f-1917	
Rivers #2	1917	$10750	I 1934	EXTANT*	Plan 100-169
West Winnipeg	1908	$3390	I 1940	s-1968	Plan 100-177

ONTARIO

Station Name	Blt.	Cost	Alterations	Disp.	Notes
Sioux Lookout	1911	$14900	EXT/I-S 1923/37	EXTANT*	Plan 100-195

SASKATCHEWAN

Station Name	Blt.	Cost	Alterations	Disp.	Notes
Melville	1908	$23444	S-1924	EXTANT*	Plan 100-156
Northgate	1914	$5699	S 1923	s-1983	Plan 100-164
Prince Albert–GTP	1917	$12500		d-1957	Plan 100-171
Regina–GTP	1914	$7526	Conv. into dwelling 1924	s-1946	Plan 110-131, Notes 22, 39

CNR FREIGHT & PASSENGER SHELTERS
Plan 100-41B—CNR Standard Freight & Passenger Shelter

ALBERTA

Station Name	Blt.	Cost	Alterations	Disp.	Notes
Alexo	1924	$1097		rm-1959	
Anatole	1927	$1200	rl-Smiley as ST	rl-1960	
Anshaw	1929	$1380	rl-Ashmont as ST	rl-1960	
Armistice	1927	$1200		gb-1959	

CNR FREIGHT & PASSENGER SHELTERS
Plan 100-41B—CNR Standard Freight & Passenger Shelter

ALBERTA

Station Name	Blt.	Cost	Alterations	Disp.	Notes
Arneson	1927	$1200	rl-Fairmount, Sk #3	rl-1960	
Ballenden	1932			rm-	
Boscombe	1929	$1380		s-1963	
Cadomin #1-B	1923	$1200	EXT 1937	rm-	
Calthorpe	1926	$1200	rl-Coleville, Sk as ST	rl-1960	
Deville #1-B	——	$1380	x-Weinsburg, Mb 1951/	rl-1958	
			rl-Redwater as operator's dwelling		
Dobson #2	1924	$1208	rl-Richdale as FT	rl-	
Dowling	1926	$1200		rm-	
Eduoardville	1927	$1200		gb-1959	
Esther	1926	$1200		s-1968	
Franchere	1929	$1380		s-1964	
Garden Plain	1930			rm-	
Glendon #1	1929	$1380	EL	f-1957	
Hackett	1927	$1200		rm-	
Hawkins #2	1950		rl-Edmonton–	rl-1960	
			Calder Yard as ST		
Hay Lakes #2	——		x-Edmonton	rl-1925	Temporary (B&B stock?) 1924/rl-Edmonton-Calder Yard as ?
Heinsburg #1	1930	$1580		rp-1950	
Le Goff	1930			gb-1959	
Leo	1927	$1200		s-1960*	
Lindbergh	1930	$1580		gb-1959	
Little Gem	1926	$1200	rl-Dodsland as ST	rl-1960	
Magnolia Bridge #2	1926	$1000		s-	
Mallaig	1929	$1380	EXT-EL 1947	rm-	
Middle Creek	1930	$1580		rm-	
Naco	1927	$1200	rl-Loverna, Sk as ST	rl-1960	
New Brigden #1	1926			rp-1927	
Sabine	1927			rm-	
Scapa	1926	$1200		s-1962*	
Sedalia #1	1926	$1200	rl-Loverna, Sk as SMBH	rl-1930	
Spondin	1930			rm-	
Therien	1929	$1380	EXT-EL 1947	rm-	Note 78
Whatcheer	1930			rm-	

BRITISH COLUMBIA

Station Name	Blt.	Cost	Alterations	Disp.	Notes
Cedarvale #2	1931				Probable
Coldstream	1926	$1200		rm-	
Colwood	By 24		rl-Culchillum	rl-1938	Plan 100-41?
Culchillum	——		x-Colwood 1938		Plan 100-41?
Duck Meadow	1927	$1200		rm-1961	
Fort Fraser #3	——		secondhand?		
Inkitsaph #2	1929	$1000		rm-1960	
Kamloops #3-B	1927	$1500		rm-	Note 50
Lake Cowichan	——	$800	x-Patricia Bay B 1925		Probable
Lejac #2	1945	$1310			
Lumby #1	1926	$1200	rl on site 1942	rm-	
Metchosin	——	$1000	x-Patricia Bay A 1916/	rl-1963	Plan 100-41?
			rl-Crescent Spur		
Milnes Landing	By24			rt-1959	Plan 100-41?
Monte Lake	1927	$1200		rm-	
O'Keefe	1926	$1200		rt-1963	
Oyama	1926	$1200	rl-to ???	rl-1965	
Postill	1926	$1200	rl-Rutland #1-B	rl-1963	
Ramage	1927		rl-Kamloops Jct. as EMBH	rl-1943	
Rutland #1-A	1926	$1200		rt-1963	
Rutland #1-B	——	$1200	x-Postill 1963		
Sweetsbridge	1926	$1200		rm-1960	
Westwold	1926	$1200		rm-	
Winfield	1926	$1200	rl-to ???	rl-1965	
Youbou	——	$800	x-Patricia Bay C 1926		Plan 100-41?

MANITOBA

Station Name	Blt.	Cost	Alterations	Disp.	Notes
Agnew #2	1923	$1200		f-1951	
Beaconia #2	1927	$1200	EL 1953		
Bellsite	1929	$1200			
Brainerd	1935	$1200			
Brandon Jct.	1929	$950	Conv. to ST 1960	s-19??*	
Carrick #2	1934	$947		s-	
Chisel Lake #1-A		$1300	x-Fitzmaurice 1960	EXTANT*	
Chisel Lake #1-B	——	$1200	x-Lepine, Sk 1961	EXTANT*	
Deer		$1200	x-Winnipeg Tmls 1925/	rl-1959	
			rl-St. James as ST		
Fairford #2	1943	$2395	rl-Lake Francis #2	rl-1964	
Giroux #3	1944	$1250	rl-Maon #2	rl-1946	Temporary
Ilford	1927	$1250		EXTANT*	
Lake Francis #2			x-Fairford #2 1964		

CNR FREIGHT & PASSENGER SHELTERS
Plan 100-41B—CNR Standard Freight & Passenger Shelter

MANITOBA

Station Name	Blt.	Cost	Alterations	Disp.	Notes
Magnet	1926	$1200		s-1972	
Makaroff #1-B	1923	$1200			
Manlius	1929?		Conv. into ST		
Maon #2	——		x-Giroux #3 1944/	rl-1960	
			rl-Scarth as ST		
Maples	1910	$475	rl-Virden as ST	rl-1960	
Meharry #2	1924	$1000		rm-1960	
Mentmore	1943	$1548	rl-Brandon as ST	rl-1960	
Methley	1926	$1200	rl-Rorketon as ST	rl-1960	
Myra #2	1931	$1200	rl-N. Regina, Sk as ST	rl-1959	
National Mills #2	——	$4168	x-Tall Pines, Sk 1960	s-1971	
Silver Plains #2	1943	$1400			
Stead	1927	$1200			
Valpoy	1926	$1200	rl-Ste. Rose as ST	rl-1960	

ONTARIO

Station Name	Blt.	Cost	Alterations	Disp.	Notes
Elizabeth	1924		RENOV 1968		
Sapawe	1950	$1931		s-1969	

SASKATCHEWAN

Station Name	Blt.	Cost	Alterations	Disp.	Notes
Akosane	1930	$1500	rl-Armit #2	rl-1960	
Alticane	1929	$1375		s-1974	
Amiens	1930	$1200	rl-Richard as SMBH	rl-1966*	
Armit #2	——	$1419	x-Akosane 1960	s-1970	
Bapaume	1930	$1200		s-1976	
Bazentin	1930	$1200		d-1960	
Beaverdale	1929	$1380		s-1960	
Belbutte	1930	$1200		s-1974	
Bemersyde	1925	$1200	rl-Corning as ST	rl-1966	
Bertwell	1930	$1500	rl-Canora as ST	rl-1964	
Bjorkdale #1	1930	$1300	EXT 1944	f-1948	
Bolney	1929	$1250		s-1974	
Bournemouth	1928	$1200		rt-1960	
Brancepeth #3	——		x-Crutwell #2 1960	s-19??*	
Cameo	1929	$1200	rl-Nutana as ST	rl-1962	
Carpenter	1931	$1200		rm-	
Carragana	1930	$1300	EL 1954	d-1982	
Chelan	1930	$1300	EL 1954	s-1981	
Claggett	1931	$1200		rm-1960	
Clashmoor	1930	$1480	rl-Prairie River as ST	rl-1966	
Cleardale	1928	$1200	rl-Ceylon as SMBH	rl-1960	
Clemenceau	1930	$1500	rl on site 1939	rm-	
Crutwell #2	1947	$1191	rl-Brancepeth #3	rl-1960	
Cuthbert	1927	$1200		s-19??*	
Dankin	1923	$1000		rm-1960	
Deer Creek	1929	$1300	rl-North Battleford as ST	rl-1959	
Dillabough	1930	$1300		s-1973	
Endeavour #1-A	1930	$1300	rl-Chemong as SH	rl-1949	

NOTES:

9   Demolished in derailment 1967.

12 The GTP line though Camrose was abandoned in 1923. The disposition of this station is unknown, but it is believed to have been sold shortly after abandonment.

22 This station was technically on the Regina Terminals Subdivision.

39 This temporary station—opened at 16th and Albert streets in 1912—was a recycled residence, renovated to provide a waiting room and ticket and administrative offices. The station facilities were consolidated in 1920 with those of the CNoR and CPR, at the Union Depot. The GTP's Regina station was subsequently closed. In 1924 it was converted into a residence for the CNR Divisional Superintendent. The building was later sold and used as a boys' home. It survived until at least 1961.

48 Constructed by the Mountain Park Collieries.

50 For trainmen's equipment.

56 The Prince Rupert Inn was the first of what was supposed to be a string of cross-country hostelries designed by Francis Mawson Rattenbury for the GTP. As it turned out, it was the only Rattenbury-designed hotel built by the company. The Inn was opened in 1907 and it was subsequently acquired by the Operating Department and converted into an ad hoc station. Associated costs: purchase $9,419, annex $21,303, remodeling $1,540 and temporary baggage room $346.

58 Replaced in 1919, relocated and converted into B&B shop in 1921.

78 The extension made in 1947 was comprised of the CPR Portable Station (CPR Plan H-14-38) purchased by the CNR and relocated from Sancroft, Alberta (built 1930). It was added onto the east end of the existing shelter. A door was cut into the end walls of the adjoining buildings. A bay window was installed on the trackside of the former CPR portion, which was the Agent's office and apartment. A carbody was moved next to the depot as a freight shed. The original section was removed (burned?) in 1976.

CNR FREIGHT & PASSENGER SHELTERS
Plan 100-41B—CNR Standard Freight & Passenger Shelter

SASKATCHEWAN

Station Name	Blt.	Cost	Alterations	Disp.	Notes
Eskbank #2	1928	$1000	rl-Valley Lake #2	rl-1967	Probable
Ethelton	1931	$1200	EL 1953	rm-	
Euclid	1927	$1200	rl-Darmody as ST	rl-1960	
Fairholme	1928	$1200		s-1968	
Fairmount #3	——	$1200	x-Arneson, Ab 1960	rm-	
Fitzmaurice	1929	$1380	rl-Chisel Lake, Mb #1-A	rl-1960	
Glenbush	1928	$1200	EL 1959	s-1980	
Grainland	1927	$1200		s-1966	
Grassdale	1928	$1200	rl-Baildon as ST	rl-1960	
Gye	1926	$1200	rl-Forward as ST	rl-1960	
Handsworth	1925	$1200		s-1974*	
Harptree	1926	$1200		rm-	
Hartwell	1928	$1200		rt-1960	
Hawkeye	1930	$1200		s-1963	
Hinchcliffe	1930	$1300	rl-Wanless, Mb as ST	rl-1964*	
Iffley	1931	$1200		s-1961	
Inglenook	1929	$1375	rl-Eston as ST	rl-1960*	
Isham	1927	$1400		s-19??*	
Keatley	1929	$1375		s-1974*	
Kegworth #2	1926	$1220	rl-Peebles as ST	rl-1966*	
Lady Lake	1930	$1300	Added bay window	s-19??*	
Lake Valley #2	——	$1000	x-Eskbank #2 1967	rm-	Probable
Lepine	1931	$1200	rl-Chisel Lake, Mb #1-B	rl-1961	
Livelong	1928	$1200		s-1974	
Longacre	1926	$1200		s-1966	
McCallum Jct.	1926		rl-N. Regina–GTP as ST	rl-1967	
McMichael	1931	$1200	rl-Unity as ST	rl-1959*	
Mildred	1930	$1200		s-1974	
Mont Nebo	1930	$1200		s-1974	
Moose Range #1-A	1931			s-1962	
Mullingar	1929	$1375		s-19??*	
New Osgoode	1930	$1480		s-1963	
Ordale	1930	$1200		rm-	
Paddockwood	1925	$1200	rl-Prince Albert–CNoR as ST	rl-1966	
Pattee	1923	$1000	rl-Lake Valley #2	rl-1959	
Peebles	1927	$1000		s-1969	
Porcupine Plain #1	1930	$1300	EXT 1945	s-1959*	
Rak	1931	$1200		rm-	
Ridpath #2	1925		rl-Fiske as ST	rl-1960	
Robinhood	1928	$1200		ss-1968	
Roncott	1926	$1200	rl-Brooking as ST	rl-1960	
Sandgren	1929	$1375	rl-Glidden as ST	rl-1960	
Sandwith	1931	$1200		s-1976	
Scentgrass	1931	$1200		s-1961	
Scottsburgh	1925	$1200	rl-Neidpath as ST	rl-1960	
Service	1924	$1000	rl-Steelman as ST/rl-Frobisher	rl-1960*	
Smales	1923	$1000		s-1963*	
Smuts	1931	$1200		d-1981	
Steen	1930	$1300		rt-1960	
Tallman	1929	$1500	s-1967		
Tall Pines	1930	$1300	rl-National Mills, Mb	rl-1960	
Tarnapol	1931	$1200		rm-	
Tyner	1927	$1200		rm-	
Usherville	1930	$1300		rm-	
Veillardville	1929	$1500		s-1967	
Verendrye	1929	$1375	rl-Kindersley as ST	rl-1960	
White Star	1925	$1200		s-1963*	
Willow Bunch #1-B	1926	$1200		rp-1927	
Witley	1927	$1200	rl-Elrose as ST	rl-1960	
Zenon Park #1	1930	$1480		rp-1960	

Plan 100-41C—CNR Standard Freight & Passenger Shelter (Unlined)

ALBERTA

Station Name	Blt.	Cost	Alterations	Disp.	Notes
Bodo	1932	$600		f-1977	

SASKATCHEWAN

Station Name	Blt.	Cost	Alterations	Disp.	Notes
Aylsham #1	1932	$600	rl-Wakaw as FT/Rutan #1-B	rl-1949/50	
Cactus Lake	1932	$600		s-1975*	
Calderbank	1932		rl-Gouldtown as ST/back to Calderbank	rl-1960/63	
Carlea	1932	$600		rm-	
Carrot River #1	1932	$600	EXT 1942	s-1972	Note 7
Cosine	1932	$600		s-1971*	
Donegal	1931	$600		rm-	
End Lake	1931	$600		rm-	
Glen Kerr	1930			rm-	
Gouldtown	1930			s-1966	

CNR FREIGHT & PASSENGER SHELTERS
Plan 41C—CNR Standard Freight & Passenger Shelter (Unlined)

SASKATCHEWAN

Station Name	Blt.	Cost	Alterations	Disp.	Notes
Halvorgate	1932	$500		s-1966	
Hearts Hill	1933	4600		rm-	
Main Centre	1932	$600		s-1966	
Nicklen #1	1930			rp-1938	
Reward	1932	$600		rm-	
Salvador	1931	$500		s-1964	
Sunny Glen	1931	$600		rm-	
Teakle	1930			rm-	

Later CNR Standard Freight & Passenger Shelter (Superceding Plan 100-41B)

Station Name	Blt.	Cost	Alterations	Disp.	Notes
Barriere #2, BC	1954	$2907		s-1979	Plan 100-334
Brule #2, Ab	1953		rl-Stony Plain as ST	rl-1960	Plan 100-320
Lumby #2, BC	1951				Plan 100-333
Tichfield #2, Sk	1949	$2056	rl-MacRorie as ST	rl-1966	Plan 100-320
Vimy #2, Ab	1952			s-1967	Plan 100-334

Plan 100-290—CNR Portable Freight & Passenger Shelter

BRITISH COLUMBIA

Station Name	Blt.	Cost	Alterations	Disp.	Notes
Irvine #2	1926	$400		d-1963	Probable

MANITOBA

Station Name	Blt.	Cost	Alterations	Disp.	Notes
Atikameg Lake	1928	$850			
Bedford #2	1952			gb-1965	
Christie	1939	$500	rl-Letellier as SMBH	rl-1960	
Craig Siding	1936	$400	rl-Savant Lake	rl-1960	
Middlebro #2	1939	$350	rl-Quibell, On	rl-1964	
Portage Jct. #2	1949	$1000		rm-	Probable, Note 34
South Jct. #1	1937	$600		f-1952	

ONTARIO

Station Name	Blt.	Cost	Alterations	Disp.	Notes
Glenorchy #2	1943	$950		d-1978	
Oscar #2	1949	$1120	Conv. into SMBH	EXTANT*	
Ottermere	1937	$450	EXT		
Petry #2	1943	$867		EXTANT*	
Ritchan #2	1937		rl-Sioux Lookout as ST	rl-1960	
Superior Jct. #2	——	$450	x-Sioux Lookout 1969?		

Plan 100-318—CNR Freight & Passenger Shelter Converted From Type E Station

ALBERTA

Station Name	Blt.	Cost	Alterations	Disp.	Notes
Acheson #2	1951			d-1961	
Carrot Creek–GTP #2	1951			s-	
Medicine Lodge #2	1951			rm-	

BRITISH COLUMBIA

Station Name	Blt.	Cost	Alterations	Disp.	Notes
Andimaul #2	1951	$1015		rm-	
Barrett #2	1951			d-	
Beament #2	1949			d-1960	
Bulkley Canyon #2				d-1960	
Chilako #2	1952			d-	
Croydon #2	1954			s-19??*	
Doughty #2	1950			d-1960	
Encombe #2	1950	$808		d-1960	
Foreman #2	1948	$800	rl-Shelley #2	rl-1963	
Forestdale #2	1948	$800		d-	
Guilford #2	1950	$1945		d-1968	
Hubert #2	1949	$1191		d-1960	
Kidd #2	1953	$800		rm-	
Knockholt #2	1951			d-1961	
Marten Lake #2	1950	$547		d-1960	
Miworth #2	1948	$800		d-1960	
Newlands #2	1949	$804		d-	
Palling #2	1950	$863		d-1959	
Pitman #2	1947	$800		d-	
Shelley #2	——	$800	x-Foreman #2 1963	d-1969	
Sheraton #2	1948	$800		d-1960	
Sinkut #2	1948	$800		rm-	
Wedgwood #2	1949	$787		d-	

Miscellaneous—CNR Freight & Passenger Shelters Converted From Stations

Station Name	Blt.	Cost	Alterations	Disp.	Notes
Chip Lake #2, Ab	1951			d-1970	x-CSS-C
Coronado #2, Ab	1939			rt-1960	Plan 100-286, Note 14

CNR FREIGHT & PASSENGER SHELTERS
CNR Stations or Shelters Converted From Bunkhouses

ALBERTA

Station Name	Blt.	Cost	Alterations	Disp.	Notes
Camrose Sub Mile 2.2	1952				Plan 110-258
East Edmonton		$2104	x-Bissell SMBH 1954	rm-1980s	Plan 110-159
Glendon #2			x-??? (secondhand) SMBH 1958	rm-	
Granada		$1000	x-Edmonton SMBH 1930	s-1960	
Haynes #2			x-SMBH Elspeth 1963	rm-	
Innisfree #2				EXTANT	
Kinsella #2			x-??? (secondhand) SMBH	rm-	
Mannville #2			x-Yale, BC SMBH 1974	EXTANT*	
North Jct.			x-Cavell, Sk SMBH 1941	s-1961	Plan 110-101
Redwater #2	1952			d-1987	Plan 110-259, Note 15

BRITISH COLUMBIA

Station Name	Blt.	Cost	Alterations	Disp.	Notes
Eddy #2		$960	x-Lindup #2 1960	rm-	Plan 110-101
Goat River #2		$1542	x-Cheam View SMBH 1953	EXTANT*	Plan 110-254
Lindup #2		$960	x-Penny #1-B 1947/rl-Eddy #2	rl-1960	Plan 110-101
Penny #1-B			Conv. from SMBH 1928/rl-Lindup #2	rl-1947	Plan 110-101
Raush Valley #2			x-??? (secondhand?) SMBH 1963	rm-	
Sinclair Mills			x-Terrace, SMBH		Plan 110-217
Usk #2			x-??? (secondhand) SMBH		

MANITOBA

Station Name	Blt.	Cost	Alterations	Disp.	Notes
Bird #1	1927	$1200			Plan 110-148
Gervais #2		$1174	x-Rivers SMBH 1937		Plan 110-101
Pine River #2		$5058	x-Parlee SMBH 1962		Plan 110-296
Pit Siding #1-A		$1500			
Sherridon #1-B	1928	$1200			Plan 110-148
Thicket Portage #1-A			x-Lipsett SMBH 1961		
Thicket Portage #1-B			x-N. Battleford SMBH 1961	EXTANT*	
Turnberry	1938			gb-1970	
Wekusko				EXTANT*	

ONTARIO

Station Name	Blt.	Cost	Alterations	Disp.	Notes
Mine Centre #3-B				rp-1971	Plan 110-159
Mine Centre #4		$2592	x-Graham SMBH 1971		Plan 110-237
Webster #2			x-Atikokan SMBH 1942/rl-Ycliff #2	rl-1964	Plan 110-42
Webster #3		$1300	x-?? SMBH	s-1971	Plan 110-159
Ycliff #2			x-Webster #2 1964		Plan 110-42

SASKATCHEWAN

Station Name	Blt.	Cost	Alterations	Disp.	Notes
Crooked River #1-B		$1400	x-Ordale SMBH 1933/EXT 1943	rm-	Plan 110-159
Dumble		$481	x-??? (secondhand) SMBH/rl-Clarks Crossing as SMBH	rl-1946	Plan 110-42
Eastview #2		$1000	x-Weyburn SMBH 1929	s-19??*	
Endeavour #1-B		$1588	x-Bertwell, Mb SMBH 1938/rl-Dauphin as SMBH	s-19??*	Plan 110-159
Eston #2			x-??? (secondhand) SMBH	rm-1990	Plan 110-159
Frankslake #2			x-??? (secondhand) SMBH 1947	s-1963	
Mistatim #1-B			x-??? (secondhand) SMBH	rm-	
North Saskatoon #3			x-??? (secondhand) SMBH 1960s		Note 4
Saskatoon–Loop Jct.		$877	x-Dundurn SMBH 1943/Conv. to SH	rm-1965	Plan 110-73, Note 4

CNR Stations or Shelters Converted From Other Railway Buildings

ALBERTA

Station Name	Blt.	Cost	Alterations	Disp.	Notes
Drumheller #2	1915		EXT/EXT/EXT 1918/20/29	d-	Plan 170-2, x-FT, Note 26
Magnolia Bridge #1		$110	x-??? (secondhand) ST	rp-1926	Plan 110-117
Red Deer #2	1961			EXTANT*	Plan 170-154, x-FT

BRITISH COLUMBIA

Station Name	Blt.	Cost	Alterations	Disp.	Notes
Campbell Creek	1940			rm-	Plan 110-189 SH
Inverness Cannery			x-??? (secondhand) ST		FPS 10x12
Kaien			x-??? (secondhand) ST		FPS 10x12

CNR FREIGHT & PASSENGER SHELTERS
CNR Stations or Shelters Converted From Other Railway Buildings

BRITISH COLUMBIA

Station Name	Blt.	Cost	Alterations	Disp.	Notes
Lejac #1			x-New Hazelton PH 1923	rp-1945	SHLT
Penny #1-A			x-Miworth ST 1927	rp-1947	FPS
Sockeye #2		$175	x-Skeena ST 1947	d-1970	FPS

MANITOBA

Station Name	Blt.	Cost	Alterations	Disp.	Notes
Altamont #2			x-Transcona CO 1962	s-	SHLT 12x18
Minto #2			x-N. Elie ST 1973		SHLT
Ophir			x-Wade ST 1960	EXTANT*	SHLT 10x20, Plan 110-116
Pope #2			x-ST Norman 1953		

SASKATCHEWAN

Station Name	Blt.	Cost	Alterations	Disp.	Notes
Ancrum #2		$300	x-Mileage 6.5 Cudworth Sub PH 1920	rt-1960	Plan 150-52
Beaufield #2		$525	x-Mileage 38.7 Dodsland Sub PH 1957	s-1987	
Brett		$350	x-Smuts ST 1933	s-1962	Plan 110-153
Cazalet		$360	x-Neola PH 1932	s-1960	Plan 150-53
Ens		$250	x-??? (secondhand) ST	s-1962	Plan 110-153
Huntoon #2			x-Huntoon ST 1965	rm-	Plan 110-117
Mansur #2		$300	x-Talmage PH 1947	s-1963	
Neola #1		$360	x-Ituna 1924 PH/rl-Cazalet	rl-1932	Plan 150-53
Rutan		$106	EXT part x-Aylsham ST 1950	rt-1959	Plan 110-117
Senator		$100	x-??? (secondhand) ST 1930	rm-	

CNR PORTABLE STATIONS
Plan 100-132—CNR Standard Portable Station

Station Name	Blt.	Cost	Alterations	Disp.	Notes
Meskanaw, Sk	1931	$1000	EL 1952	s-19??*	
Quorn #2, On	1947		Secondhand?	rm-	Hip roof?
Somme, Sk	1930	$1300	EL 1954	rt-1966	
Weekes, Sk	1930	$1300	EL/RENOV 1954/??	s-1982*	Reverse Plan
Yellow Creek, Sk	1931	$1200	EL 1955	rm-19??*	

Plan 100-221—CNR Portable Station

Station Name	Blt.	Cost	Alterations	Disp.	Notes
Pine Falls, Mb	1926	$1200	rl on site/Conv. into ST 1947/60		

Plan 100-323—CNR Portable Station

Station Name	Blt.	Cost	Alterations	Disp.	Notes
Bjorkdale #3, Sk	1948	$3337	Add SMBH/EL 19??/54	s-1982*	

CNR COMBINATION STATIONS
Plan 100-184—CNR Standard 3rd Class Station

Station Name	Blt.	Cost	Alterations	Disp.	Notes
Glaslyn, Sk	1928	$9500	PL 1966	s-1981*	Museum-1
Kathyrn #2, Ab	1928	$10000		s-1962	
Medstead, Sk	1928	$9500		d-1982	
Rabbit Lake, Sk	1928	$9500	EL 1955	s-1981*	Museum-1
Waskatenau #2, Ab	1928	$10000	I-EL/PL 1938/58	d-	
Zeneta #2, Sk	1928		EL 1953	d-1960	

Plan 100-197—CNR Standard 3rd Class Station

Station Name	Blt.	Cost	Alterations	Disp.	Notes
Byemoor, Ab	1927	$7200	EL 1953	rm-	
Corning, Sk	1925	$6500	I/EL 19??/54	rm-	
Cudworth #2, Sk	1925	$7800		s-19??*	Museum-1
Hay Lakes #3, Ab	1925	$7000	I-S/PL 1942/58	d-	
Henribourg, Sk	1925	$8050		s-1976	
Falkland, BC	1926	$8500		rm-	
Mawer #2, Sk	1924			s-1975	
Neidpath, Sk	1925	$8500	I-S/EL 1945/5?	s-	
New Brigden #2, Ab	1927	$7500		rm-	
Rorketon, Mb	1926	$7650	I/EL 1945/5		Variant
South Elbow, Sk	1927	$5500	S 1945	s-1963*	

Plan 100-250—CNR Standard 3rd Class Station

Station Name	Blt.	Cost	Alterations	Disp.	Notes
Arborfield, Sk	1930	$10700		s-1982*	
Ashmont #2, Ab	1929	$10500	EL 1953	d-	

NOTES:
4 This station was technically on the Saskatoon Terminals Subdivision.
7 Converted into section tool house in 1947. Converted into enginemen's bunkhouse in 1967.
14 Portion converted into section house; the freight shed was converted into FPS #2 in 1939.
15 Constructed from two second-hand section bunkhouses.
26 Following the demolition of the station at Drumheller, the nearby freight shed office was occupied by the agent and used as the ad hoc station.
34 This station was technically on the Winnipeg Terminals Subdivision.

Roster III: CNR Stations in Western Canada, Listed by Type

CNR COMBINATION STATIONS
Plan 100-250—CNR Standard 3rd Class Station

Station Name	Blt.	Cost	Alterations	Disp.	Notes
Colfax #2, Sk	1930	$11000		s-1971	
Jedburgh, Sk	1929	$10500	EL 1953	s-1979*	
Mayfair, Sk	1929	$11000	EL 1956	f-1972	
Murphys #2, Sk	1929			rm-	
Spiritwood, Sk	1930	$11600	E/PL 19??/64	s-1982	
Taft #2, Mn	1929	$12624			
Wordsworth, Sk	1929	$11300	EL 1954	s-	

Plan 100-253—CNR Standard 3rd Class Station

Station Name	Blt.	Cost	Alterations	Disp.	Notes
Alvena, Sk	1931	$10500		s-1980*	
Balcarres #2, Sk	1932	$13700	EL	s-1976	
Bonnyville, Ab	1929	$10500	El-G-PL 1956	d-	
Frenchman Butte, Sk	1929	$10450	EL 1956	s-1978*	Museum-1
Hatherleigh, Sk	1931	$11000		EXTANT*	
Hyas #2, Sk	1937	$10560		rm-	
Paradise Hill, Sk	1929	$10500	EL 1951	d-1982	
Parkerview, Sk	1929	$10500		s-1969*	
Reserve, Sk	1930	$11500		s-1986*	Museum-2
Reynaud, Sk	1931	$10500	EL 1952	d-1962	
Ste. Rose #2, Mb	1930	$11825			
Scott #2, Sk	1935	$9000		s-1980	
Shell Lake, Sk	1930	$11600	EL 1952	s-1982*	

Miscellaneous CNR 3rd Class Stations

Station Name	Blt.	Cost	Alterations	Disp.	Notes
Acadia Valley, Ab	1927	$8700		d-	Plan 100-227
Cranberry Portage, Mb	1929	$26660		EXTANT*	Plan 100-251
Eatonia #2, Sk	1924	$10155	I/EL-PL 1950/??	s-1975*	Plan 100-199, Museum-1
Elk Point, Ab	1927	$7400	EL-PL 1958	s-1972	Plan 100-227
Endiang, Ab	1927	$7200	EL 1953	d-	Plan 100-227
Hemaruka, Ab	1927	$7200	EL 1957	d-1969	Plan 100-227
Lacadena, Sk	1927	$7150	EL 1952	s-1982	Plan 100-227
Red Deer #1, Ab	1923	$8500	EL-PL 1956	s-1961	Plan 100-148
Salvus #2, BC	1928	$5200		d-1966	Plan 100-256
Wabowden, Mb	1930	$33186	EL	EXTANT*	Plan 100-251
White Bear, Sk	1927	$7150	EL 1954		Plan 100-227
Willow Bunch #2, Sk	1927	$8000	I 1938	s-1976	Plan 100-216

Miscellaneous CNR Standard 4th Class Stations

Station Name	Blt.	Cost	Alterations	Disp.	Notes
Anerley #2, Sk	1930	$8000	EL 1954	d-1983	Plan 100-252
Bethany #2, Mb	1927	$7500		gb-1969*	Plan 100-220
Denholm #2, Sk	1936	$8500		s-1981	Plan 100-279
Fabyan #3, Ab	1925	$4300	EL 1952	s-1964	Plan 100-207
Gibbons #2, Ab	1927	$7000	S/EL-G 1946/??	d-1981	Plan 100-186
Hepburn #2, Sk	1930	$8000		d-	Plan 100-252
Mayerthorpe, Ab	1928	$6500			Plan 100-220
Prince #2, Sk	1928	$6500	I-S 1939	s-1967*	Plan 100-220
Rochfort Bridge #2, Ab	1930	$7570	PL 1959	s-1971	Plan 100-252
Sedalia #2, Ab	1930	$8500	EL 1957	rm-	Plan 100-252
Totzke #2, Sk	1927	$7000			Plan 100-220

CNR Standard #4A Stations

Station Name	Blt.	Cost	Alterations	Disp.	Notes
Aylesham #2, Sk	1949	$21541	EL	s-	Plan 100-313
Birch River #2, Mb	1948	$10501	EXT 1949	rm-	Plan 100-310
Carrot River #2, Sk	1947	$24759	PL 1963	d-1983	Plan 100-309
Dodsland #2, Sk	1948	$20906		d-1981	Plan 100-315
Endeavour #2, Sk	1948	$10406	EL 1953	s-19??*	Plan 100-310
Giroux #4, Mb	1946				Plan 100-305
Heinsburg #2, Ab	1950	$18555		s-1982*	Plan 100-310
Leyland #2, Ab	1951	$18143		EXTANT*	Plan 100-310
Nut Mountain #2, Sk	1945	$19517		s-1970	Plan 100-305
Porcupine Plain #2, Sk	1953			f-1959	Plan 100-310
Red Lake Rd. #2, On	1947	$17354		EXTANT*	Plan 100-317
Warspite #3, Ab	1950	$17892	EL	s-1967*	Plan 100-310

Plan 100-328—CNR Standard #4B Stations

Station Name	Blt.	Cost	Alterations	Disp.	Notes
Islay #3, Ab	1952	$16615		s-1981	
Margo #3, Sk	1953	$16917		s-19??*	

Miscellaneous CNR Combination Stations—Pre World War II

Station Name	Blt.	Cost	Alterations	Disp.	Notes
Brancepeth #2, Sk	1935	$2850	rl-Zenon Park #2	rl-1960	Plan 100-280
Endako #2, BC	1922	$7000	EXT 1946	rm-	Plan 100-143, Sim. to 100-142
Umfreville #2, On	1927	$4800	S/I 1945/56	s-1964	Plan 100-218
Valora #2, On	1926	$4800	S/I 1945/53		Plan 100-218
Zehner #2, Sk	1921	$4000	EL 1956	s-1975*	Plan 100-142, Sim. to 100-143
Zenon Park #2, Sk	——		x-Brancepeth #2 1960	s-19??*	Plan 100-280

CNR COMBINATION STATIONS
Miscellaneous CNR Combination Stations—Post World War II

Station Name	Blt.	Cost	Alterations	Disp.	Notes
Burns Lake #2, BC	1952	$73000		EXTANT*	Plan 100-332
Clearwater #2, BC	1961			EXTANT*	Plan 1920-1
Grand Centre, Ab	1958	$30326		d-1990s	Plan 100-373
Kitimat, BC	1955	$92142		EXTANT*	Plan 100-356
Lynn Lake, Mb	1966	$35000		EXTANT*	Plan 100-393
Porcupine Plain #3, Sk	1959	$24140	PL 1972	s-1982*	Plan 100-366
Terrace #2, BC	1960				Plan 100-391
Thompson, Mb	1960	$67467	EXT 1969	EXTANT*	Plan 100-382
Trochu #2, Ab	1959	$20865		s-19??*	Plan 100-365
Vanderhoof #3, BC	1960				Plan 100-345
Yarbo #3, Sk	1960	$22300		EXTANT*	Plan 100-392

CNR PASSENGER STATIONS
Pre-World War II

ALBERTA

Station Name	Blt.	Cost	Alterations	Disp.	Notes
Edmonton #2	1927		Ext 1948	d-1965	Plan 100-219, Note 13
Jasper #2	1925	$7000		d-1925	Plan 100-206, Temporary
Jasper #3	1925	$130000	RENOV	EXTANT*	Plan 100-205
Vegreville #2	1930	$46000		s-1990s*	Plan 100-255
Wainwright #3	1930	$70000		s-1990*	Plan 100-249, Museum-1

BRITISH COLUMBIA

Station Name	Blt.	Cost	Alterations	Disp.	Notes
Kamloops #3-A	1927	$48000		EXTANT*	Plan 100-210
Kelowna	1926	$36860		EXTANT*	Plan 100-214
Pacific #2	1935			d-1959	Plan 100-277
Prince George #2	1922	$47156	EXT 1943	d-1971	Plan 100-136
Prince Rupert #2	1922	$66750	EXT 1944	EXTANT*	Plan 100-135
Victoria–Point Ellice	——		½ Conv. into lumber shed 1949	rm-	

MANITOBA

Station Name	Blt.	Cost	Alterations	Disp.	Notes
Brandon North	1941	$3400		rm-	Plan 100-294
Churchill	1930	$52000	EXT 1944	EXTANT*	Plan 100-271
Emerson #2	1923		I/RENOV 1940/70	s-1988*	Plan 100-191
Flin Flon	1934	$22300	RENOV 1947	s-19??*	Plan 100-275, Museum-1
Gillam	1930	$44848		EXTANT*	Plan 100-244
Giroux #2	1923		I/S 1934/40	f-1944	Plan 100-190
Ste. Anne #2	1920	$8000	I-S/PL 1937/68	s-19??*	Plan 100-133
The Pas #2	1928	$79925		EXTANT*	Plan 100-189

MINNESOTA

Station Name	Blt.	Cost	Alterations	Disp.	Notes
Baudette #2	1923	$25000	I 1942		Plan 100-192

ONTARIO

Station Name	Blt.	Cost	Alterations	Disp.	Notes
Armstrong #2	1927			EXTANT*	
Atikokan #2	1923	$9995	I/EXT 1947/49	EXTANT*	Plan 100-193, Note 35

SASKATCHEWAN

Station Name	Blt.	Cost	Alterations	Disp.	Notes
Saskatoon–CNoR #3	1939	$381081		d-1969	Plan 100-288, Notes 4, 54
Weyburn #2	1928	$30000	S/EL/PL 19??/??/53	s-1969	Plan 100-238

Post-World War II

ALBERTA

Station Name	Blt.	Cost	Alterations	Disp.	Notes
Edmonton #3	1965			d-1966	Notes 13, 65, Temporary
Edmonton #4	1966			EXTANT*	Notes 13, 66
Whitecourt #3	1973			EXTANT*	

BRITISH COLUMBIA

Station Name	Blt.	Cost	Alterations	Disp.	Notes
Endako #4	1985			EXTANT*	Comb. Sta/EMBH
Prince George #3	1971			EXTANT*	

MANITOBA

Station Name	Blt.	Cost	Alterations	Disp.	Notes
Sherridon #2	1953			EXTANT*	Plan 140-234
Shiloh–2nd site	1942	$30664	S-1943	s-1975	Plan 100-299

SASKATCHEWAN

Station Name	Blt.	Cost	Alterations	Disp.	Notes
Kamsack #2	1968	$21335		EXTANT*	Plan 100-399
North Battleford #3	1955	$205751		EXTANT*	Plan 100-330
Prince Albert–CNoR #4	1960	$223908		EXTANT*	Plan 100-385
Saskatoon-CNR	1964	$253574		EXTANT*	Plan 100-419, Notes 4, 54

CNR PASSENGER STATIONS
Post-World War II

ALBERTA

Station Name	Blt.	Cost	Alterations	Disp.	Notes
Spy Hill #2	—	$12000	EI-S 1953	s-1980	Plan 100-187, Note 47
Tisdale #2	1964	23164		EXTANT*	Plan 100-412
Touchwood	1943	$3400	EL 1952	s-1965	Plan 100-298
Welby #2	1946	$2790	EL 1958	s-1969	Plan 100-307
Yorkton–GTP #2	1964			EXTANT*	Plan 100-210

CARBODY SHELTERS/STATIONS
(Partial listing only)

ALBERTA

Station Name	Blt.	Cost	Alterations	Disp.	Notes
Beaver River				rm-	
Berks	1914	$200		rm-	Note 40
Cadomin #1-A	1923		rl-Luscar	rl-1923	
Errington		$200		rm-1924	
Heatburg	1927			rm-1951	
Islay #2	—	$700	x-Edmonton–Calder Yard 1945	rp-1952	Temporary
Lake Isle #2	1923			s-1936	Note 36
Luscar	—		x-Cadomin #1 1923	rm-	Note 74
Phoenix				rt-1959	
Robinsons #1	1921			rp-1940	
Robinsons #2	1940	$250		rm-	
Solomon				rm-	
Wainwright #2	1929			rp-1930	Temporary

BRITISH COLUMBIA

Station Name	Blt.	Cost	Alterations	Disp.	Notes
Finmoore #2				rm-	
Skeena Crossing #1	1917			rp-	
Tynehead	1925			rm-	

MANITOBA

Station Name	Blt.	Cost	Alterations	Disp.	Notes
Athapap	1939	$100		EXTANT*	
Channing	1929		rl-Gilbert Plains as ST	rl-1965	
Coatstone	1928	$300	rl-Minto as ST	rl-1960	
Dipples	1919	$300	rl-Roland as ST	rl-1958	
Dugas	1925	$400	rl-N. Elie	rl-1958	
Ekhart	1916	$310		s-1959	
Embury					
Horton	1920	$200		a-1961	
Huddleston				rm-	Probable
Lobbville	1929	$360	rl-Muir as ST	rl-1960	
Marius	1949	$480	rl-Amaranth as ST	rl-1960	
Oak Point Sub Mile 144.1	1949			gb 1969	
Myrtle #3	—			s-1975	
National Mills #1	1943	$60	Conv. into ST 1960		
Norwood	1927	$200	Conv. into SMBH 1960		
Pacific Jct. #2	1927	$400		f-1947	
Paulson #2	1926	$350	Conv. into ST 1959/ rl-Dauphin	rl-1966	
Pit Siding #1-B	1959				
Rea				rm-	
Reeve #1	1928	$160	rl-Homewood	rl-1946	
Reeve #2	1947	$450		rt-1967	
Roland #2	—		x-Hodgson EMBH 1965	s-1975	
Ste. Agathe #2	—		x-Winnipeg–Symington Yard 1962	rm-	
Simonhouse			x-Chemong, Sk 1949		
Tenby #1	1911			s-1966	Listed as 100-41
Townline	1915	$300	Conv. into ST	rl-1959	
Treat	1936	$250		s-1960	
Wassewa	1920	$325	rl-Cromer as ST	rl-1960	

ONTARIO

Station Name	Blt.	Cost	Alterations	Disp.	Notes
Allanwater Sub Mile 53.9	1925			d-1970	
Clarkdon	1946	$100		d-1965	
Farrington #2	—	$350	x-Mabella 1955	s-1961	
Hematite	1906			d-1960	
Mine Centre #2	1941	$300		rp-1955	
Mine Centre #3-A	—	$400	x-Kawene FT 1955	s-1971*	
Nickel Lake	1939	$400		s-1960	
Olcott	1950		x-Oscar SMBH 1950/ xx-Quorn 1947	d-1958	
Olive	1942			d-1961	
Red Lake Road #1	1946	$200	I/EL 1947/52	d-1959	
Wells Camp	1950	$200		s-1964	

SASKATCHEWAN

Station Name	Blt.	Cost	Alterations	Disp.	Notes
Aquadell	1930			s-1967*	

CARBODY SHELTERS/STATIONS

SASKATCHEWAN

Station Name	Blt.	Cost	Alterations	Disp.	Notes
Avonhurst #1	1914			rp-1920	
Bechard #1	1917			rm-1921	
Bjorkdale #2	1948	$600	Conv. into agent's dwelling 1948	rt-1961	Temporary
Burgis #2	1950	$410		s-1961	
Cavalier	1927	$150	rl-Saskatoon into B&B stores	rl-1962	
Central Butte #1				rp-1919	
Clarks Crossing #2	—	$100	x-N. Saskatoon #2 1946	s-1961	
Dacer #2	1941			rm-1960	
Dana #2	1934	$450		s-1967	x-CO
Denny	1939	$100		s-1960*	
Dulwich	1929	$100		s-1961	
Elswick	1937	$100		gb-1969	
Erinferry		450		gb-1950	
Eskbank #1	1919			rp-1928	
Frankslake	1916		Conv. into FT 1947	rp-	
Greenbush #2	—	$800	x-St. Walburg SMBH 1942	rt-1959	
Greene	1914	$90		rt-1960	
Kettlehut	1931			s-1960	
Kindersley #1	1910			rp-1910	Temporary
Lawson #1	1914			rp-1919	Probable
Lorlie #1	1915			rm-1920	
Mansur #1				rp-1947	
Margo #2	—	$600	x-Quill Lake SMBH 1952	s-1982	CB x2, Temporary
McKim	1927	$500		s-1969	
Nicklen #2	1938	$610		s-1961*	
North Saskatoon #2	1933	$100	rl-Clarks Crossing #2	rl-1946	Note 4
Otosquen #1-A	1944		rl on site 1944	d-1971	
Otosquen #1-B	1953			rm-	
Peterson #1	1916	$90		rp-1933	
Prinham	1939	$450		rt-1959	
Raymore #2	1919	$600		rp-1921	Temporary
Red Pheasant #1				rp-1950	Probable
Red Pheasant #2	1950	$350		s-1963	
Roscoe #1				rp-1918	
Rowletta #2	1940	$100		d-1972	
Salter	1914			s-1960	
Smoking Tent	1950			gb-1970	
Souris River		$300		s-1960	
Tatsfield	By20		EXT 1932	s-1963	Probable
Thunder Creek	1931			s-1960*	
Weyburn #1-B		$300	rl-Stony Beach as ??	rl-1929	
Woodley #1			rl-Lampman as SMBH	rl-1947	
Worcester #2	1939	$100		s-1960	

UNIDENTIFIED STATIONS/SHELTERS
A listing of station buildings which are one-of-a-kind or for which there is limited information

ALBERTA

Station Name	Blt.	Cost	Alterations	Disp.	Notes
Abilene	1928	$500		s-19??*	SHLT 11x27, Museum-2
Ardenode #2				rm-	FPS

NOTES:

4 This station was technically on the Saskatoon Terminals Subdivision.

13 This station was technically on the Edmonton Terminals Subdivision.

35 The second storey was removed in 1947.

36 The former CNoR line between Peace River Jct. and Darson Jct. (near Magnolia) was abandoned in June 1936.

40 Abandoned on grade in 1917. Final dispositions unknown; likely sold and demolished.

47 This was originally constructed as a telegraph repeater station in 1928. It was converted into a section house in 1951, and then into a station after the original depot was razed by fire in 1960.

54 In 1964, a new passenger station was established near the northwestern outskirts of the city in Chappell Yards. The former downtown station building was used by CNR as an office building until 1969. Once it was vacated, the building was razed and the site was re-developed.

65 This was a temporary station set up during construction of the CN Tower (#4), on the site of the former station (#2).

66 The station facilities were located in the basement of this 26-floor office tower. VIA Rail Canada took over passenger operations in the building in 1978. In 1998, these premises were vacated in favor of a new VIA station built in northwestern Edmonton.

74 Luscar is actually on the Luscar Spur 5.2 miles from its junction with the Mountain Park Subdivision at Leyland.

UNIDENTIFIED STATIONS/SHELTERS

ALBERTA

Station Name	Blt.	Cost	Alterations	Disp.	Notes
Ardmore	1939	$598		rm-	FPS 8x36
Bardo #2				rm-1959	FPS
Battle	1918	$150		rm-	SHLT 10x12
Bilby #2	1959			d-1968	SHLT 12x16
Bretville Jct.		$740	x-?? (secondhand) 1928	rm-	PORT, Note 13
Conrich				rm-	SHLT
Drinnan				rm-	FPS
Fort Kent	1934	$350		rm-	SHLT
Grainger #1				rp-1919	SHLT
Grainger #3	1928			s-1962	STA 16x30, Temporary
Kathyrn #1				rp-1928	SHLT
Kelsey #2				s-1962	FPS
Leyland #1	1921	$1200	Ext 1937	rp-1951	STA, Note 48
Lousana #2			x-Ardenode 1959	rm-	FPS 10x16
Peace River Jct.	1916			rm-	PORT
Peavey	1945	$500		s-1963	SHLT 10x20, Museum-2
Twining				rt-1960	SHLT
Vegreville #1-B	1920			rm-	FPS, Express Shed
Warspite #2			x-Edmonton–Calder Yard Loco FM 1948	rl-1950	FPS, Temporary

BRITISH COLUMBIA

Station Name	Blt.	Cost	Alterations	Disp.	Notes
Aleza Lake #2					STA
Alpland #2	1922			rm-	FPS 10x32
Avola #2					FPS
Cannor	1927	$630		rm-1944	SHLT 10x18
Coldstream Ranch			rl-Lumby as FT	rl-1941	FPS
Craibenn		$500	rl-Lamming Mills	rl-1945	FPS
Crescent Spur #1			x-Finmoore 1946	rm-	FPS 9x16
Crescent Spur #2			x-Metchosin 1963	rp-	FPS 10x32
Crescent Spur #3					FPS
Emperor	1926	$350		d-1960	Open Shelter 12x25
Endako #3	1970			rp-1985	Trailer
Floods				rm-1944	FPS
Glen Lake	By24			rm-1944	SHLT
Houston #3				EXTANT*	STA
Inkitsaph #1	1917			d-1929	SHLT 11x17
Kissinger	1929				SHLT 9x18
Lamming Mills		$500	x-Craibenn 1945	d-	FPS
Leechtown	By24				FPS
Mt. Robson–CNoR #1-B	1922	$580		rm-1940s	PORT
New Hazelton #2	1980			EXTANT*	PORT
Rearguard #2	1949			rm-1960	SHLT
Redpass Jct. #2	1977			rm-	Trailer
Rocky Point Siding	By24				FPS
Sassenos	By24				FPS
Shelley #3					STA
Skeena Crossing #2	1943				FPS
Sooke Lake	1920	$300			Open Shelter 6x10
Telkwa #3				EXTANT*	STA
Walcott #2			rl-Prince George Stores Dept.	rl-1960	FPS
Westlang	1921		rl-Vancouver as office	rl-1943	FPS 9x25
Willow River #2			x-Decker Lake 1969		FPS

MANITOBA

Station Name	Blt.	Cost	Alterations	Disp.	Notes
Bird #2	1961	$1200	(secondhand?)		FPS, x-SMBH?
Brereton Lake			x-Minaki Sub M57.4 1940/Conv ST 1966		FPS 12x20
Diamond	1904				SHLT 10x14
Letellier #2			x-St. James 1966		FPS
Maon #1	1910	$300		f-1944	SHLT 10x12
Minaki Sub Mileage 57.4	1926	$700	rl-Brereton Lake	rl-1940	FPS 12x20
Neepawa #2	1980			rm-	PORT
Oak Point Sub Mileage 4.2	1977				SHLT 8x17, Plan 100-434, Note 34
Paddington	1911	$100		d-1958	TOS, Note 34
Sherridon #1A	1928	$1400	11939		STA 11x40, Temporary
Tenby #2			x-??? (secondhand) 1966		SHLT 10x12
Transcona #2-A	1929	#3060	EL/PL 1953/58		SHLT 13x39, Plan 100-258, Note 34

UNIDENTIFIED STATIONS/SHELTERS

MANITOBA

Station Name	Blt.	Cost	Alterations	Disp.	Notes
Winnipeg–Pembina Subway		$1145	x-??? (secondhand) 1950	EXTANT*	FPS 10x32, Note 34
Winnitoba		$600	x-North Pines, On 1934	EXTANT*	FPS 10x24, Plan CGR1

MINNESOTA

Station Name	Blt.	Cost	Alterations	Disp.	Notes
Arbutus #2		$429	x-Ericsburg 1924	rt-1962	SHLT 11x17
Central Lakes	1909	$710			STA 12x42
Ericsburg #2	1917		rl-Arbutus #2	rl-1924	SHLT 11x17

ONTARIO

Station Name	Blt.	Cost	Alterations	Disp.	Notes
Barwick #2		$518	x-Bear Pass 1968	s-1983	FPS
Crilly	1926	$100	Rebuilt 1943	s-1968	SHLT
Fort Frances Sub Mileage 68.1	1945			f-1962	FPS
Neebing #1	1923	$200		d-1971	SHLT
Neebing #2	1977				SHLT, Plan 100-433
North Pines		$600	rl-Winnitoba, Mb	rl-1934	FPS 10x24, Plan CGR1
Wade #1-A	1920				SHLT
Wade #1-B	1926	$850			SHLT 14x58, Plan 100-201

SASKATCHEWAN

Station Name	Blt.	Cost	Alterations	Disp.	Notes
Armit, Sk #1	1943			gb-1960	FPS
Atwater #2			x-??? (secondhand) 1965		SHLT 10x12
Bannock #3	1954				FPS
Beatty #1				rp-1918	FPS
Browning #2	1917			rp-1923	SHLT 10x30
Chappell				rm-1965	TOS, Note 4
Chemong	By20			rm-	SHLT
Crystal Beach	1927	$2000		s-1952*	Open Shelter 20x40
Dewar Lake #1	By15			rp-1920	FPS
Duperow #1	1915			rp-1919	FPS, Temp.
Eastview #1	1915			rm-	FPS
Frederick	1922			rm-	FPS
Gilroy #1	By15			rp-1919	FPS, Temp.
Griffin #2	1921			rp-1921	FPS, Temp.
Hawoods #2	1920	$600	rl-Clavet as ST	rl-1960	FPS 10x32, 100-41?
Mattes	1920	$980		s-1962	FPS 10x20
McGee #1				rp-1913	FPS, 100-41?
Mehan #2	1959			s-	PORT
Moose Range #1-B		$610	x-Ballast Pit Shack 19??	s-1962	FPS
Neola #2	1930			rm-	FPS
Newcross	1929		rl-South Saskatoon #2	rl-1933	TOS, Note 4
North Regina–CNoR	1911			rm-1912	FPS, Note 17
North Regina–GTP				rm-	TOS 16x32, Note 22
North Saskatoon #1	By 14			gb-1916	FPS, Note 4
Nutana	1905			s-1964	TOS 14x14, Note 4
Oban #2				s-1980	FPS
Prince Albert–	1905			rp-1906	FPS, Temp.
Richmond				rm-	STA
Rowletta #1	1916			rp-1940	FPS, Temp.
St. Gregor #1				rp-1914	FPS, 100-96?
Saskatoon–Lorne Avenue	1951	$2450		s-1965	TOS, Plan 110-250
South Saskatoon #2			x-Newcross 1933	rm-	TOS, Note 4
Speddington	1946			rt-1961	FPS
Mileage 34.4 Turnberry Sub	By20			rm-	SHLT
Wallisville	1913			rm-1960	FPS
Warman #2	1970s			EXTANT*	Trailer
Yarbo #2	1934	$500		s-1960	SHLT
Yorkton–CNoR #1			Conv. to office bldg. 1916	rp-	FPS

NOTES:
4 This station was technically on the Saskatoon Terminals Subdivision.
13 This station was technically on the Edmonton Terminals Subdivision.
17 The CNoR constructed a temporary station adjacent to its Regina divisional yards in 1911. No description of this structure has been found. It was likely removed after the downtown CPR–CNoR Union station opened in 1912.
22 This station was technically on the Regina Terminals Subdivision.
34 This station was technically on the Winnipeg Terminals Subdivision.
48 Constructed by the Mountain Park Collieries.

ROSTER IV

Summary of Stations Constructed, by Type

CANADIAN NORTHERN RAILWAY

		Rlwy. Plan #	Alta.	B.C.	Man.	Ont.	Sask.	Minn.	TOTAL
Passenger Shelters									
		100-95	4	0	9	0	5	1	19
Miscellaneous			1	0	1	0	0	0	2
		Total	5	0	10	0	5	1	21
Freight and Passenger Shelters									
		100-96	2	0	17	0	17	3	39
		100-41	83	21	110	5	119	5	343
		Total	85	21	127	5	136	8	382
Portable Stations									
		100-24	1	0	10	0	5	0	16
Bunkhouse Type		110-73A	5	0	1	0	5	0	11
		Total	6	0	11	0	10	0	27
Combination Station-and-Section-Houses									
NPR Type		100-16	0	0	5	0	0	0	5
CPR Type		100-100	0	0	0	0	11	0	11
Type A		100-63	0	0	13	0	0	0	13
Type B		100-99	0	0	9	0	1	0	10
Type C		100-47/-98	31	39	0	0	0	0	70
NPR-SH			0	0	1	0	0	0	1
CNoR–SH		110-10	0	2	0	0	6	0	8
		Total	31	41	28	0	18	0	118
Combination Stations									
	5th Class	100-17	1	0	1	0	0	2	4
		Total	1	0	1	0	0	2	4
NP Type	4th Class		0	0	13	0	0	0	13
Kashabowie Type		100-12	0	0	0	9	0	0	9
	4th Class	100-31	3	0	9	2	12	5	31
	4th Class	100-68	13	0	13	4	30	3	63
CNoR Equivalent to	4th Class		0	1	0	1	0	0	2
		Total	16	1	35	16	42	8	118
	3rd Class	100-3	9	0	32	4	28	1	74
Special	3rd Class	100-18	0	0	0	0	2	0	2
Special	3rd Class	100-19	2	0	1	0	2	0	5
	3rd Class	100-29/-64	38	8	26	1	84	2	159
	3rd Class	100-72/-75	23	3	13	1	36	5	81
NPR Equivalent to	3rd Class		0	0	6	0	0	0	6
CPR Equivalent to	3rd Class		0	0	0	0	6	0	6
		Total	72	11	78	6	158	8	333
		Total	89	12	114	22	200	18	455
Passenger Stations									
Early Versions	2nd Class		0	0	5	1	1	1	8
Various Designs	2nd Class		1	5	2	0	4	0	12
Special Design	2nd Class	100-83/-84	0	2	0	0	1	0	3
Standard	2nd Class	100-39	5	0	0	0	2	0	7
		Total	6	7	7	1	8	1	30
St. Boniface Type		100-4	0	0	1	1	0	0	2
St. James Type			3	0	2	0	0	0	5
		Total	3	0	3	1	0	0	7
Special Designs	CNoR Detailing		1	0	1	1	1	1	5
Special Designs			3	5	9	4	4	3	28
		Total	4	5	10	5	5	4	33
		Total	13	12	20	7	13	5	70
	Total CNoR Stations		229	86	310	34	382	32	1073

GRAND TRUNK PACIFIC RAILWAY

		Rlwy. Plan #	Alta.	B.C.	Man.	Ont.	Sask.	Minn.	TOTAL
Passenger Shelters									
Miscellaneous			1	0	0	0	0	0	1
	Total		1	0	0	0	0	0	1
Freight and Passenger Shelters									
		100-162B/-173	9	2	1	0	9	0	21
	Total		9	2	1	0	9	0	21
Portable Stations									
Bunkhouse Type		110-101	1	1	0	0	5	0	7
	Total		1	1	0	0	5	0	7
Combination Stations									
Type D	24Ft.x60Ft.	100-154	3	0	5	0	14	0	22
Type E	'Design A'	100-152	84	96	16	32	102	0	330
Type F	NTR 'A'	100-151	3	1	0	17	9	0	30
Type G	New 'A'	100-168	2	2	0	0	9	0	13
	NTR No. 1	100-179	0	0	2	1	1	0	4
	NTR No. 2	100-180	0	0	2	7	0	0	9
	NTR No. 3	100-181	0	0	4	5	0	0	9
Miscellaneous			2	1	2	0	0	0	5
	Total		94	100	31	62	135	0	422
Passenger Stations									
	No. 2 Terminal	100-155/-159	2	1	0	2	0	0	5
	'Design E'	100-157	3	0	0	0	4	0	7
	'Design D'	100-158/-163	1	0	0	2	0	0	3
	Special Designs		1	8	4	1	4	0	18
	Total		7	9	4	5	8	0	33
	Total GTP Stations		112	112	36	76	148	0	484

CANADIAN NATIONAL RAILWAYS

		Rlwy. Plan #	Alta.	B.C.	Man.	Ont.	Sask.	Minn.	TOTAL
Freight and Passenger Shelters									
		100-41B	34	18	20	2	84	0	158
		100-41C	2	0	0	0	17	0	19
Later Types			2	2	0	0	1	0	5
		100-290	0	1	7	6	0	0	14
x-Type 'E'		100-318	3	22	0	0	0	0	25
x-Depots			2	0	0	0	0	0	2
x-SMBH			9	5	9	4	9	0	36
x-Other Buildings			3	6	2	1	10	0	22
	Total		55	54	38	13	121	0	281
Portable Stations									
Bunkhouse Type		100-132, et al	0	0	1	1	5	0	7
	Total		0	0	1	1	5	0	7
Combination Stations									
	3rd Class	100-184	2	0	0	0	4	0	6
	3rd Class	100-197	3	1	1	0	6	0	11
	3rd Class	100-250	1	0	0	0	7	1	9
	3rd Class	100-253	1	0	1	0	11	0	13
Miscellaneous			1	1	2	0	2	0	6
	Total		8	2	4	0	30	1	45
	4th Class		3	0	0	0	3	0	6
	4A		3	0	1	1	6	0	11
	4B		1	0	0	0	1	0	2
	Total		7	0	1	1	10	0	19
Miscellaneous Pre-War			0	1	0	2	2	0	5
Miscellaneous Post-War			2	2	2	0	2	0	8
	Total		2	3	2	2	4	0	13
Passenger Stations									
Miscellaneous Pre-War			5	5	8	2	2	1	23
Miscellaneous Post-War			3	2	2	0	8	0	15
	Total		8	7	10	2	10	1	38
	Total CNR Stations		65	64	51	18	140	1	339
Carbodies			12	3	28	11	43	0	97
Unidentified/Miscellaneous			21	31	14	8	37	0	111
	TOTAL STATIONS		439	296	439	138	759	33	2104

Note: based on the original location of the station only (no relocations); includes "Variants" and "Probables".

Selected Plans

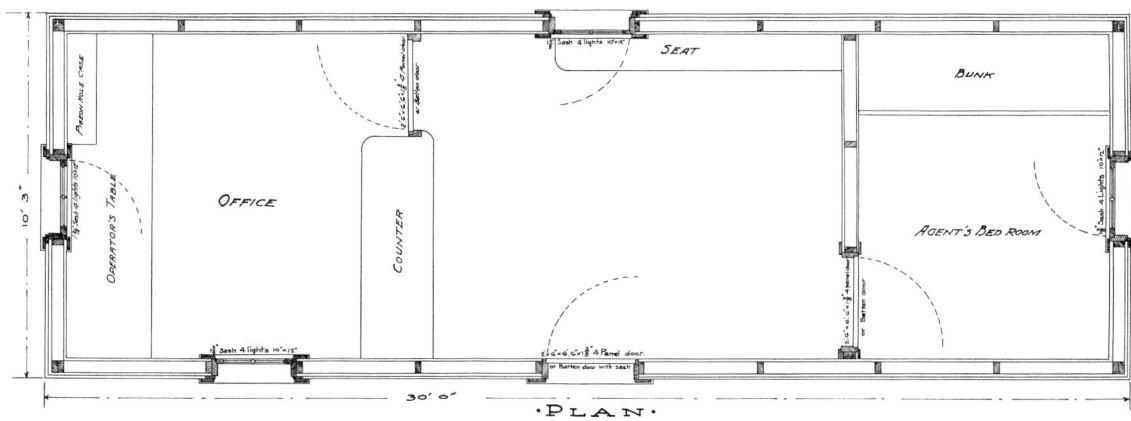

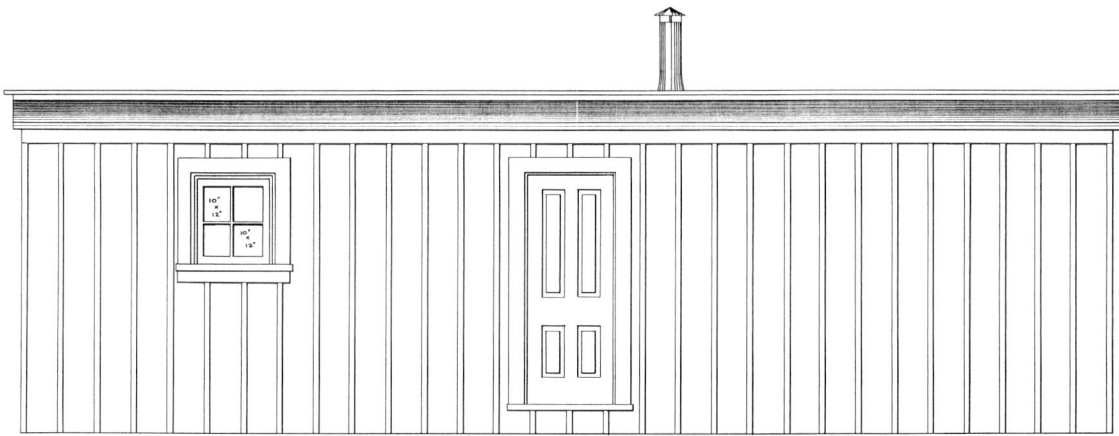

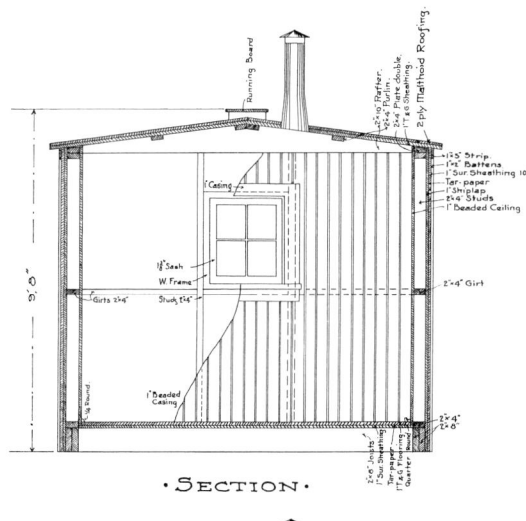

Canadian Northern Railway

Standard Portable Depot

April 18, 1906
CNoR Plan 100-24

Scale=3/16 inch to one foot

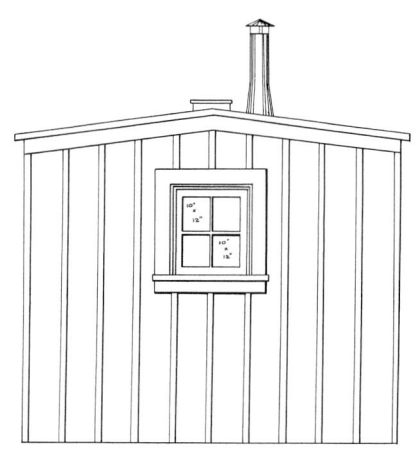

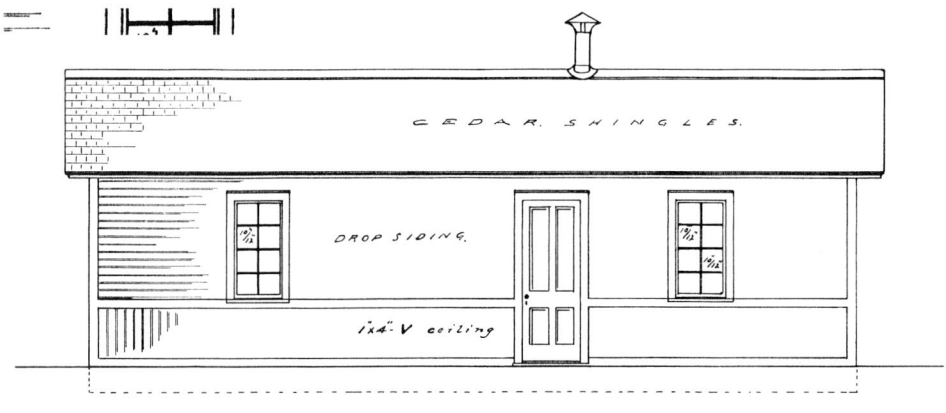

GRAND TRUNK PACIFIC RAILWAY

Standard Portable Station

July 18, 1907
Plan 100-172

Scale = 1/8 inch to one foot
Detail drawings not to scale

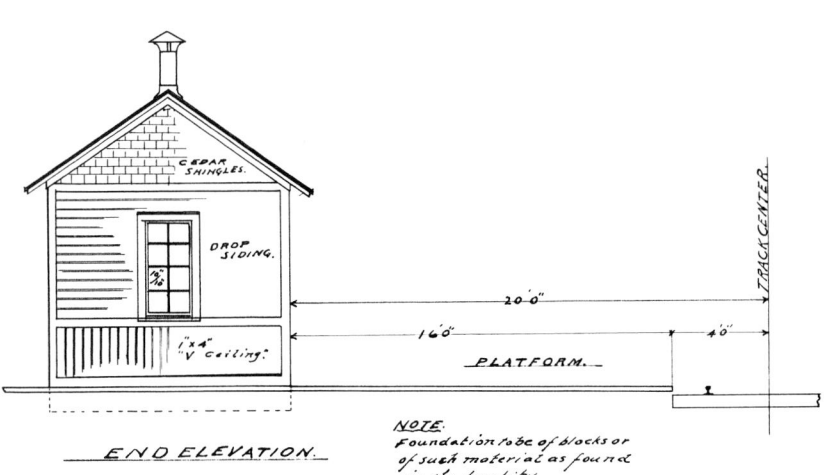

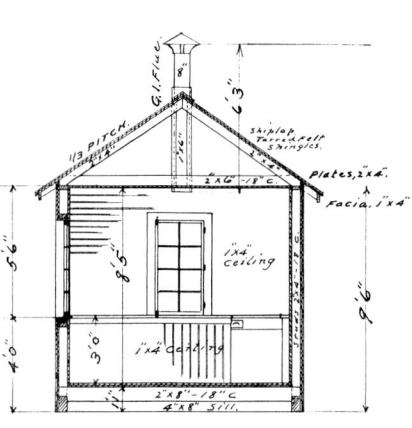

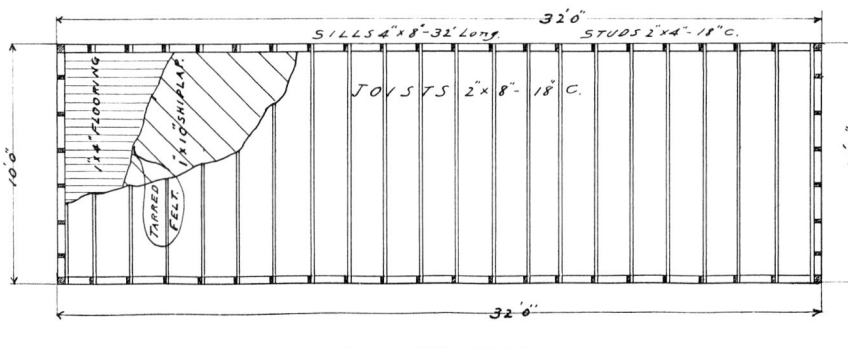

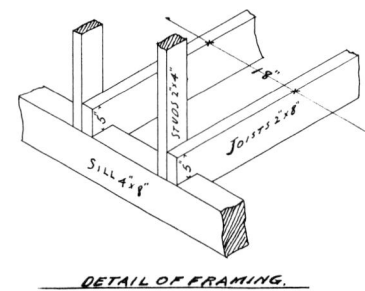

Canadian National Railways
Standard Portable Station
October 1921—Plan 100-132
Scale = 1/8 inch to one foot
Section C-C scale = 1/3 inch to one foot

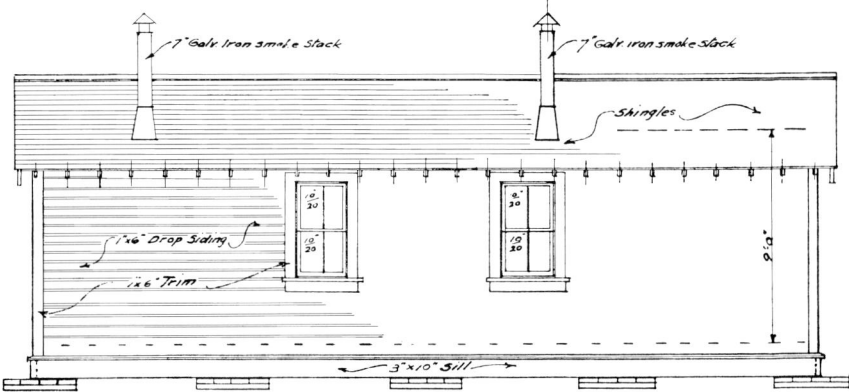
REAR ELEVATION

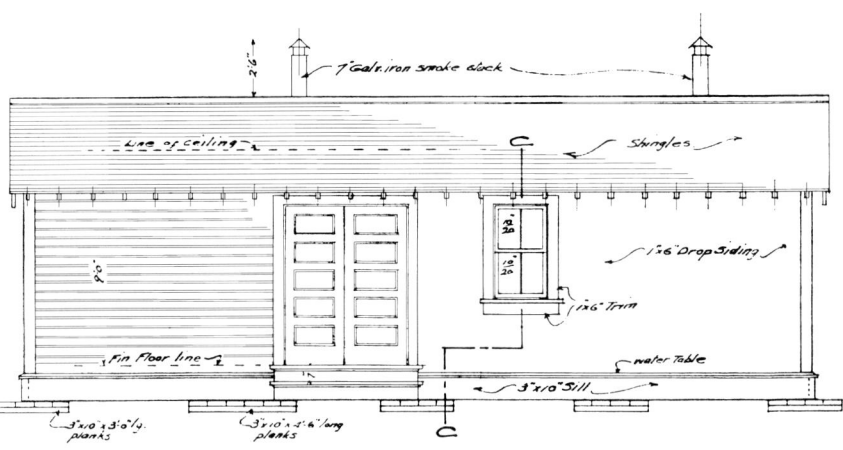
FRONT ELEVATION

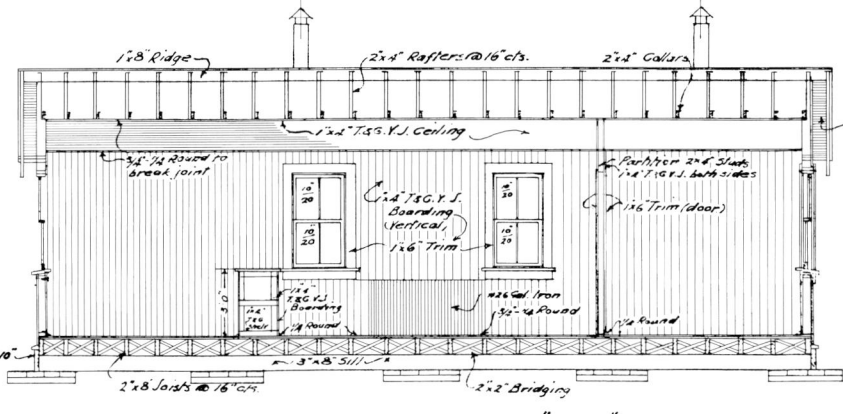
LONGITUDINAL SECTION "B-B"

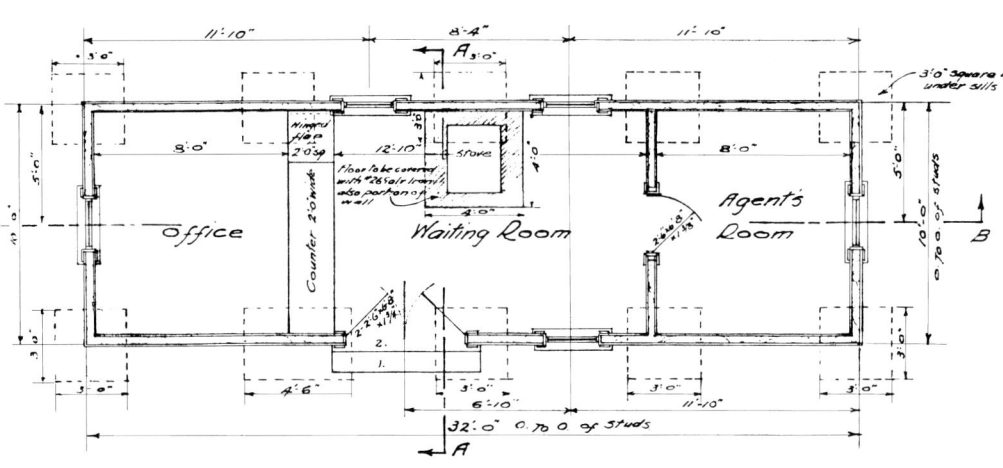
FLOOR PLAN

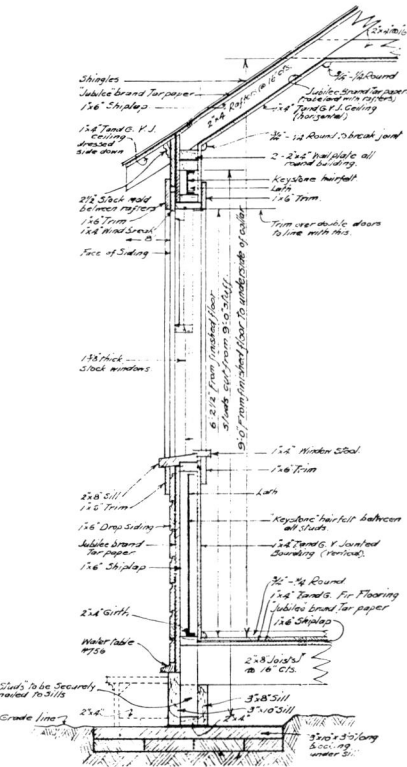
SECTION "C-C"

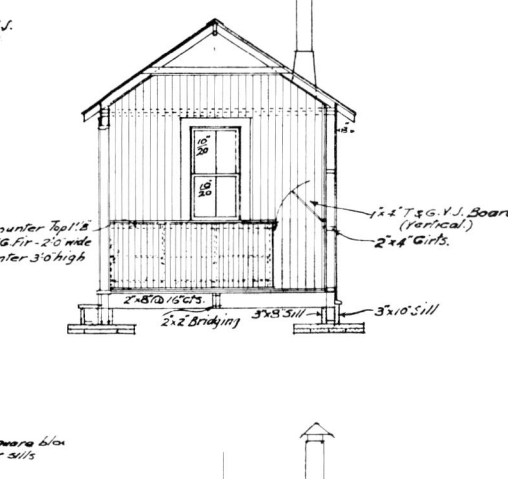
END ELEVATION

Selected Plans

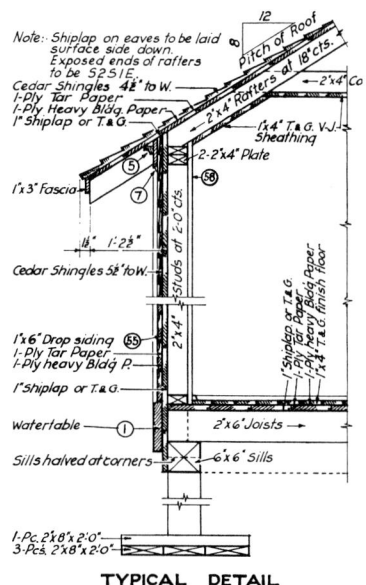
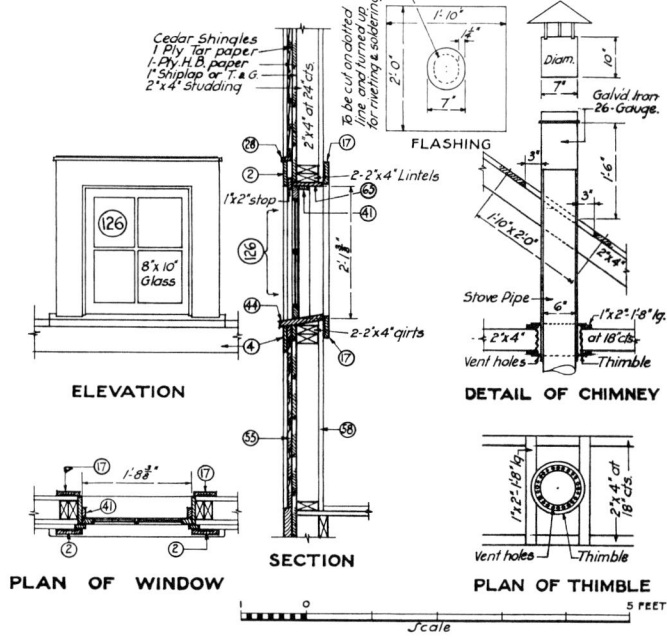
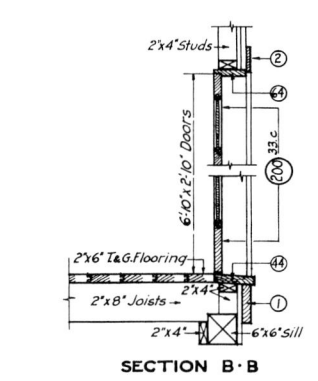
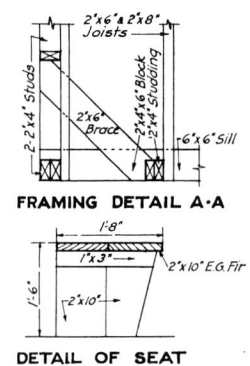
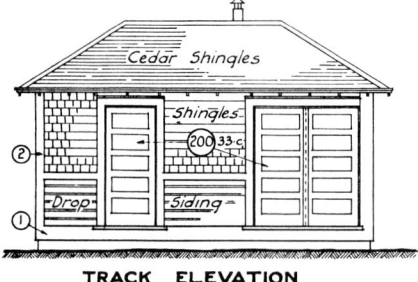
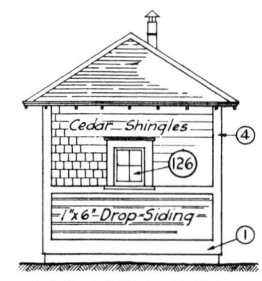
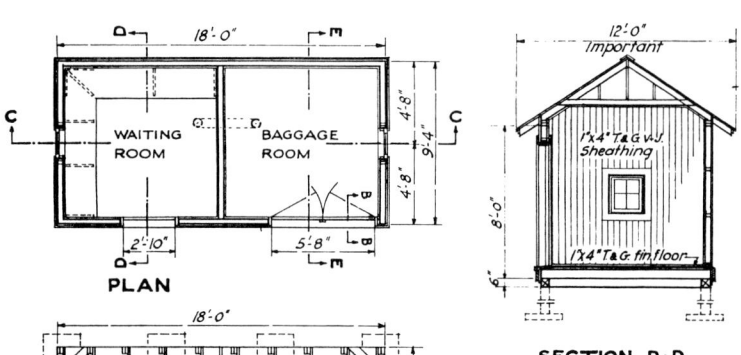

CANADIAN NATIONAL RAILWAYS

Standard Small Portable Station

May 28, 1925
Plan 100-290

Scale = 3/32 inch to one foot
Details scale = 1/3 inch to one foot
Location plan = 1/24 inch to one foot

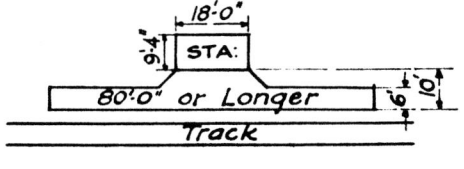
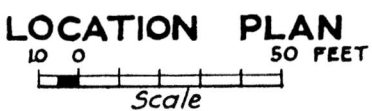
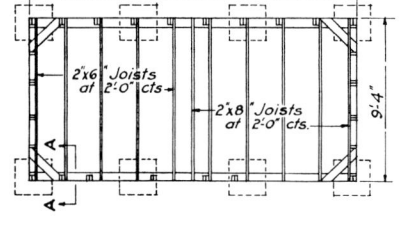
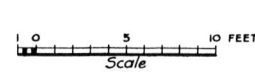

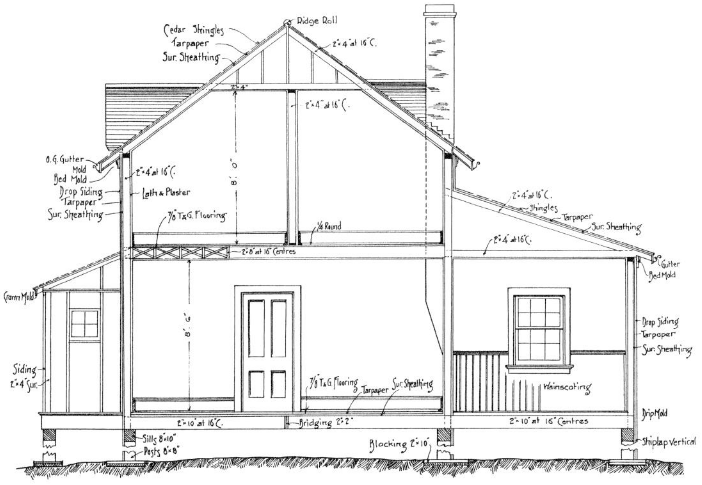

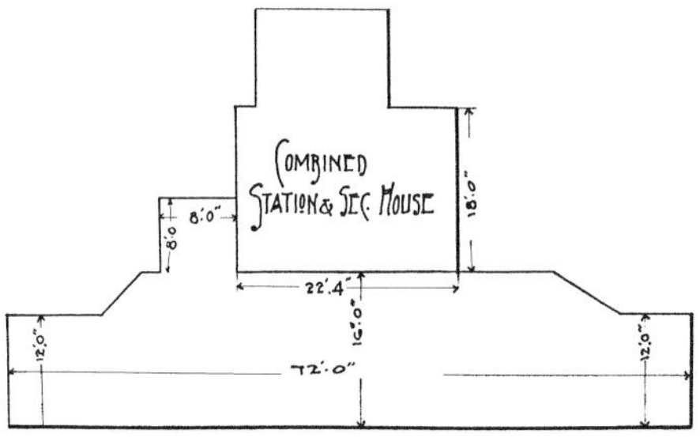

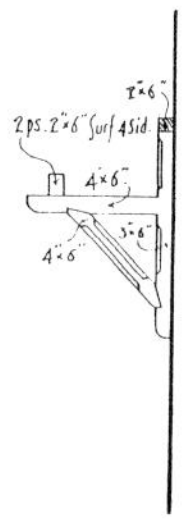

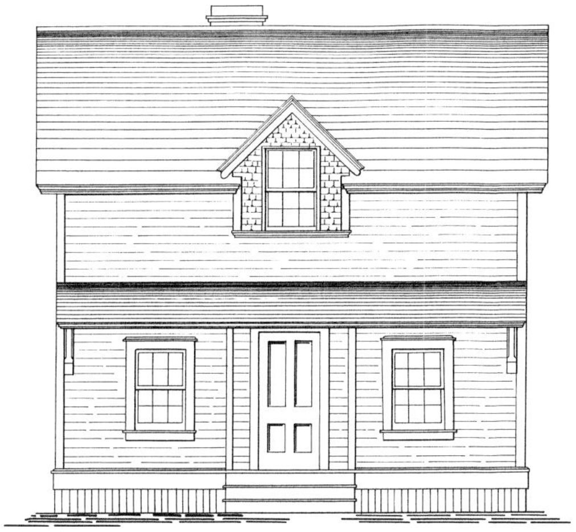

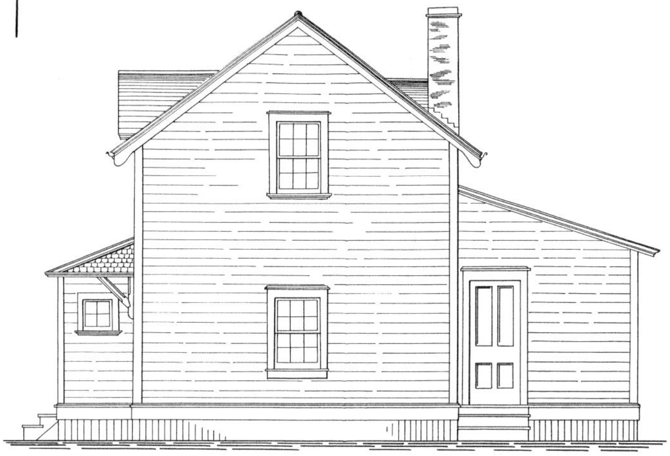

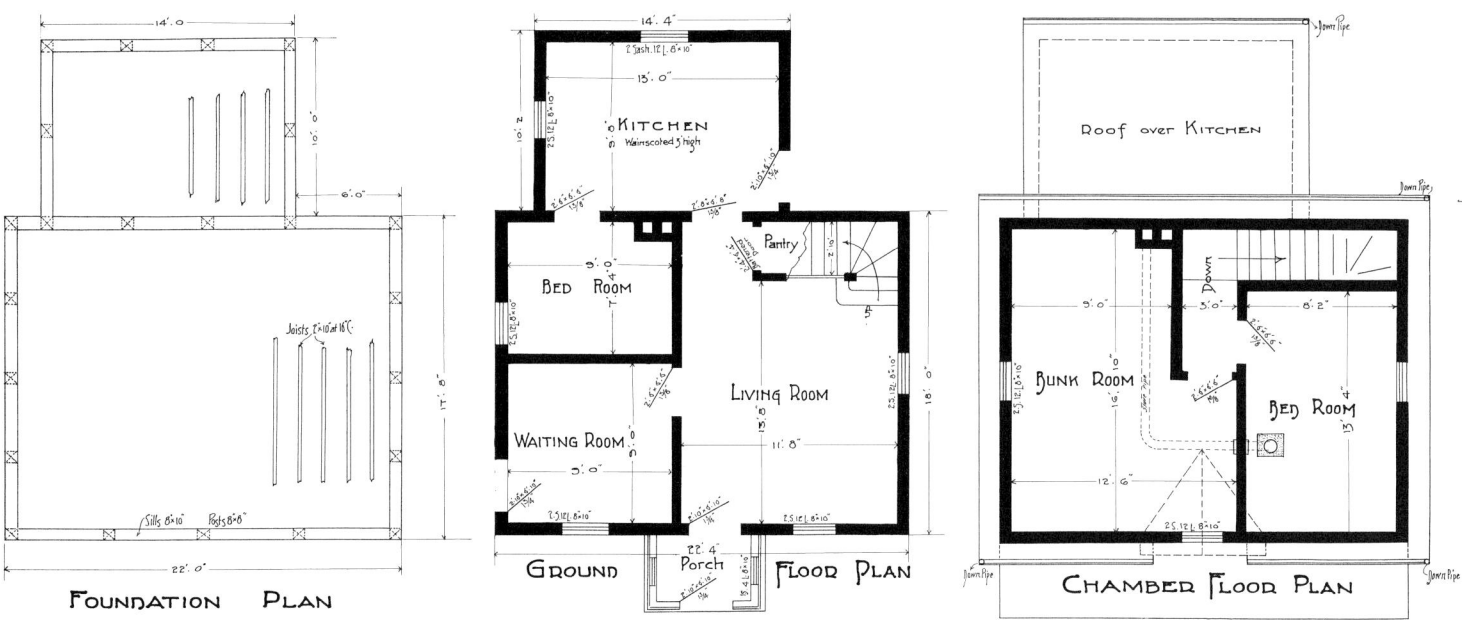

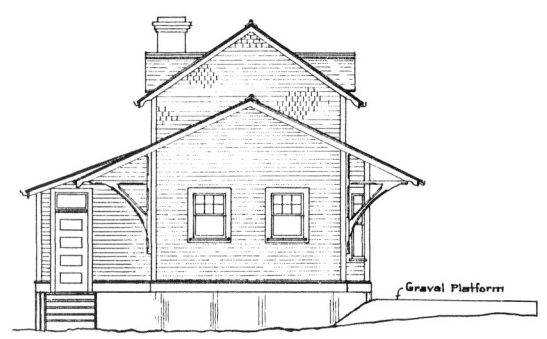

END ELEVATION.

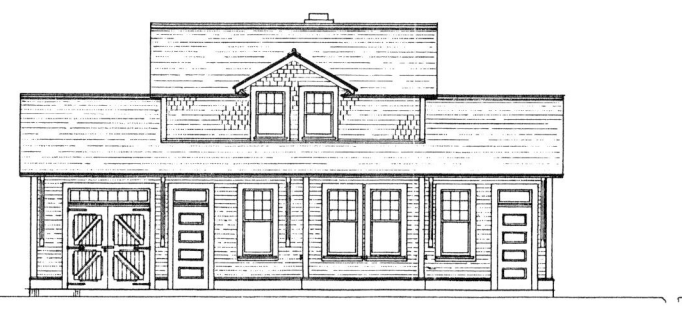

FRONT ELEVATION.

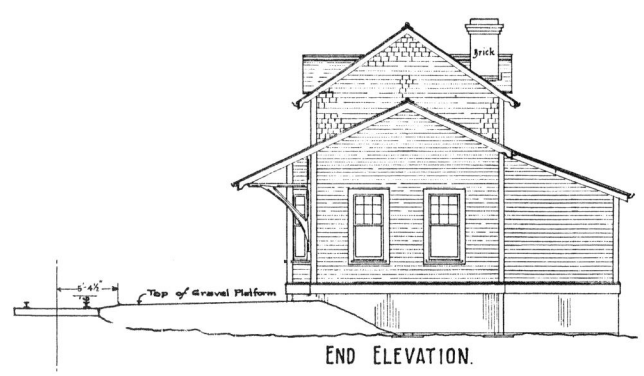

END ELEVATION.

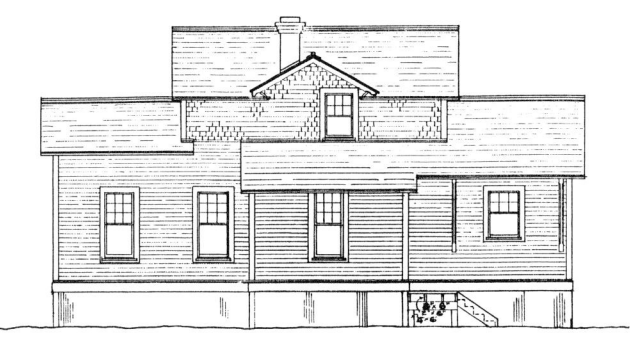

REAR ELEVATION.

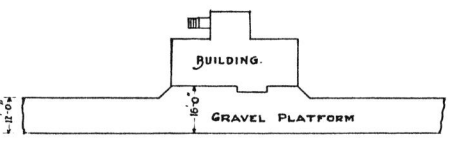

PLAN OF PLATFORM.

Canadian Northern Railway

Combined Station & Section House

April 4, 1923
CNR Plan 100-47 & 100-98

Scale = 1/16 inch to one foot
Platform scale = 1/64 inch to one foot

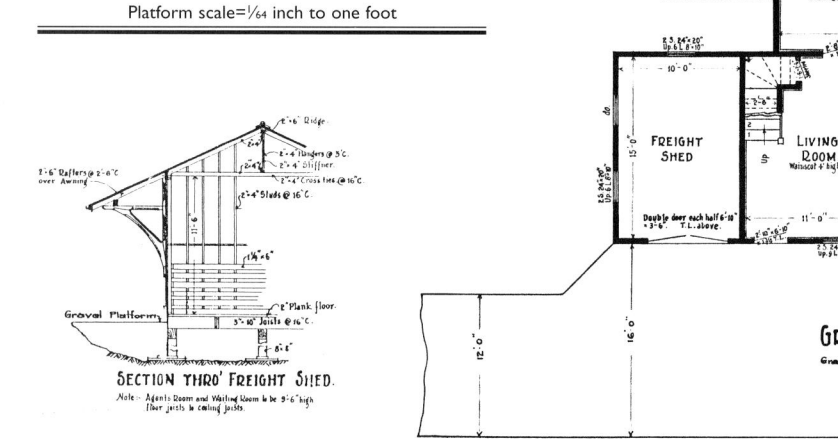

SECTION THRO' FREIGHT SHED.

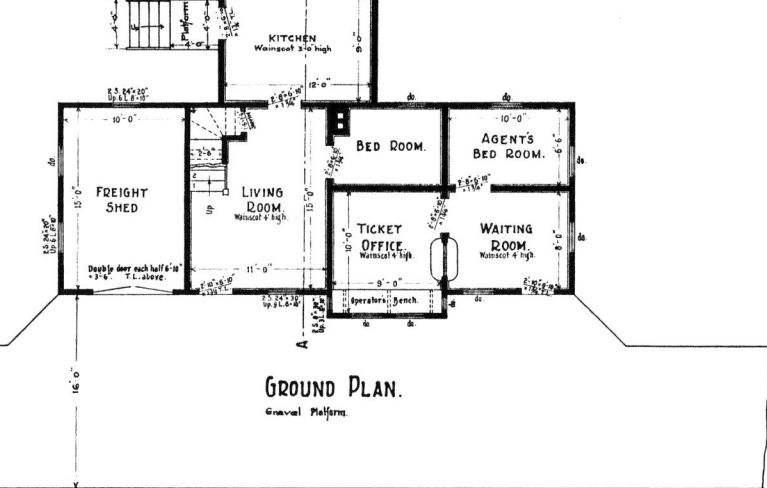

GROUND PLAN.

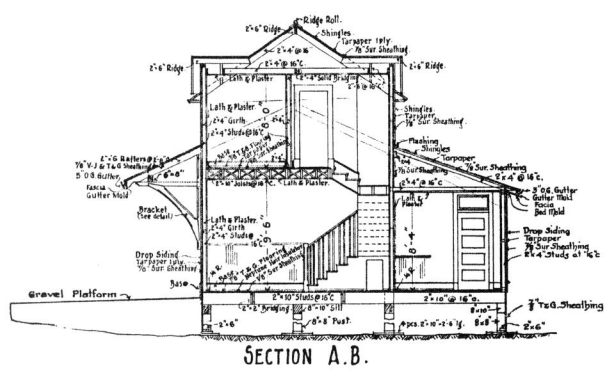

SECTION A.B.

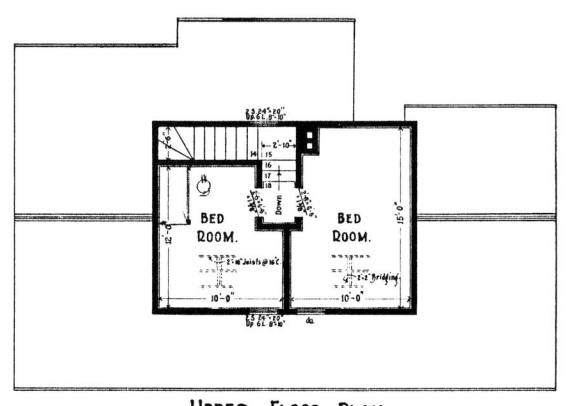

UPPER FLOOR PLAN.

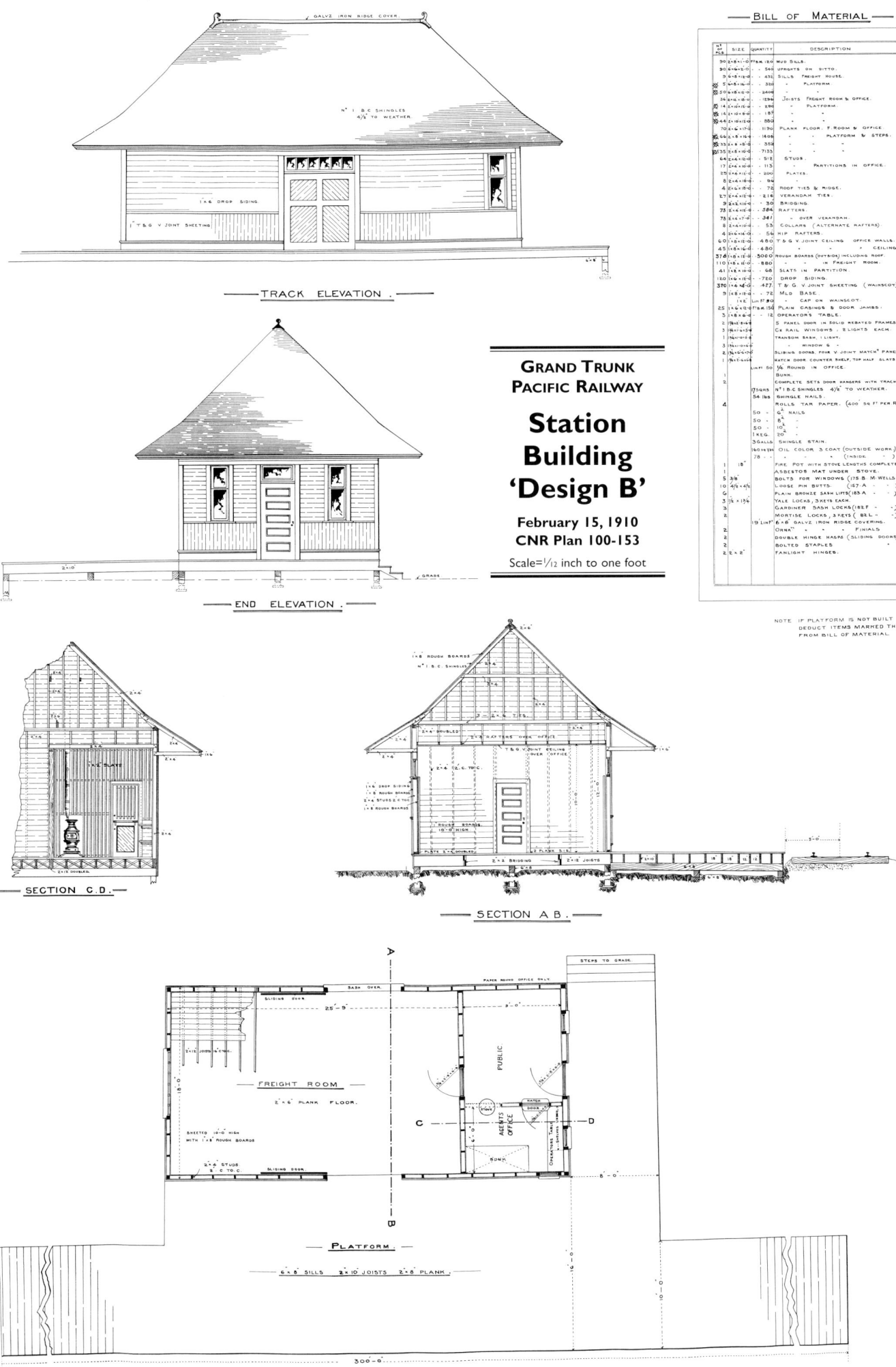

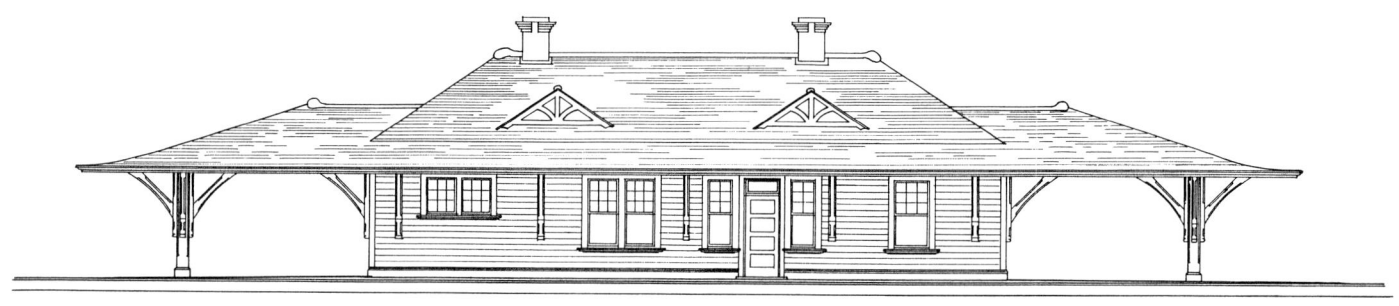

REAR ELEVATION

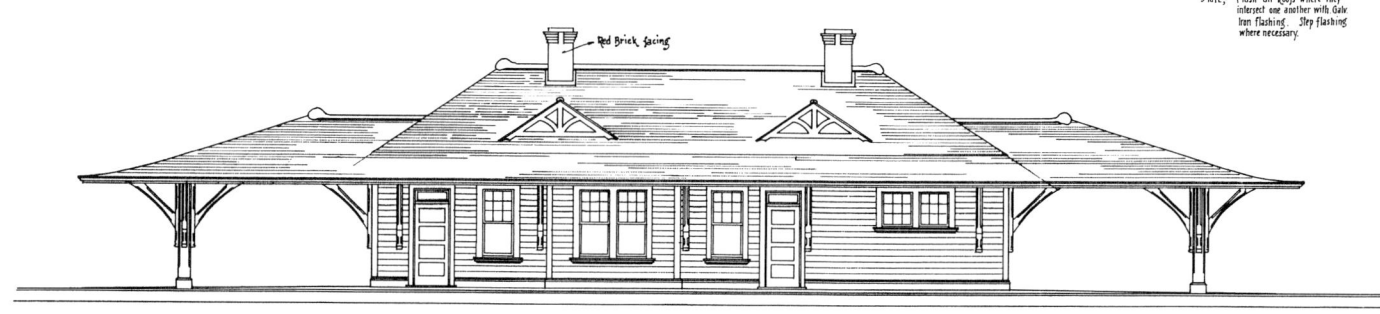

TRACK ELEVATION

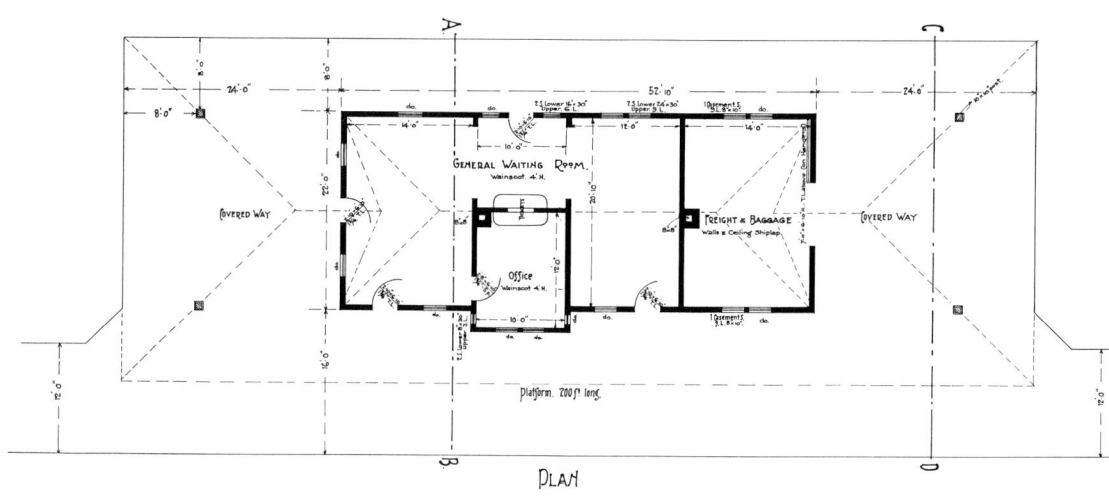

PLAN

CANADIAN NORTHERN RAILWAY

Station Building to be erected at Westside, Manitoba

August 2, 1910
CNR Plan 100-40

Scale=1/16 inch to one foot
Floor plan scale=3/64 inch to one foot

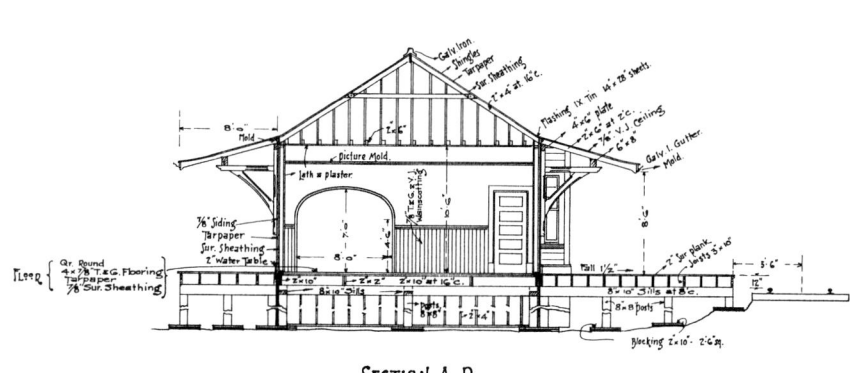

SECTION A.B.

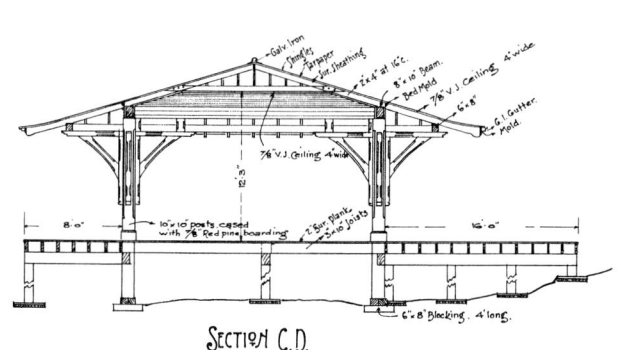

SECTION C.D.

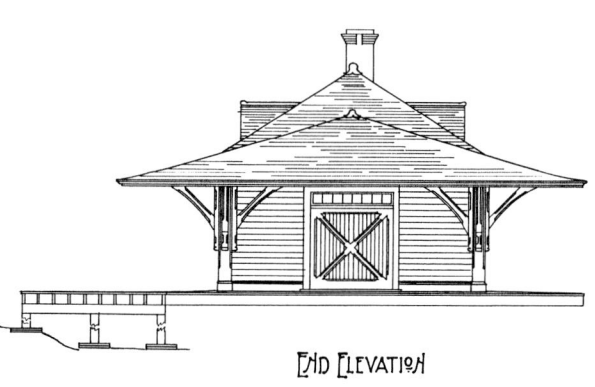

END ELEVATION

END ELEVATION

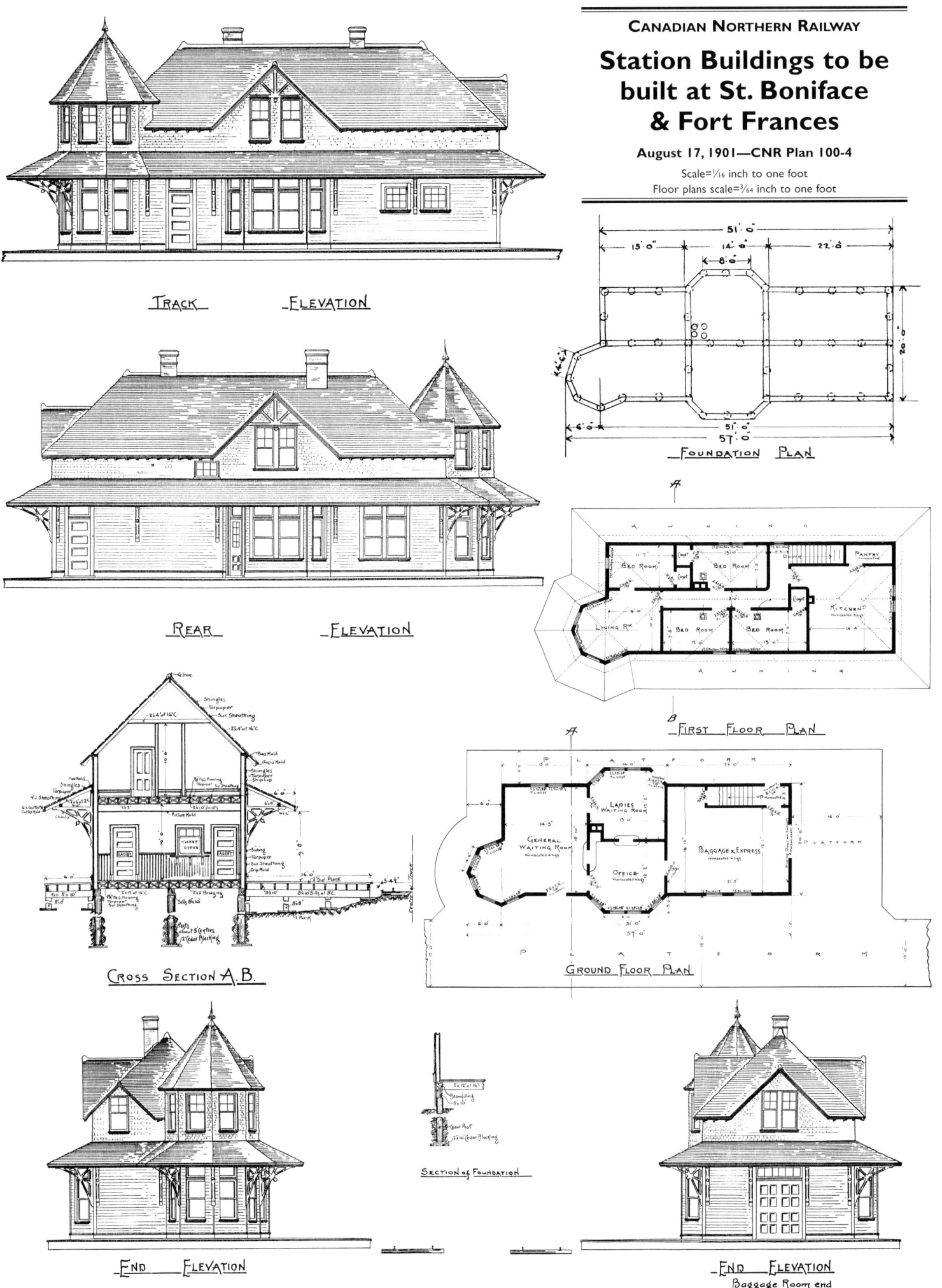

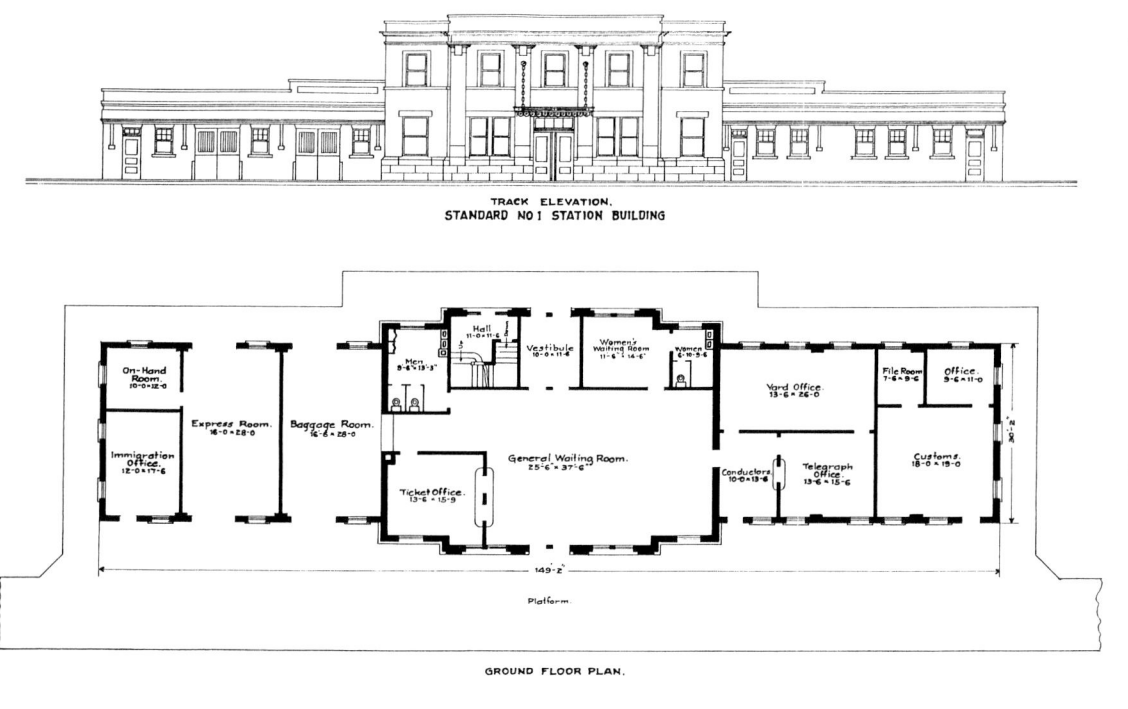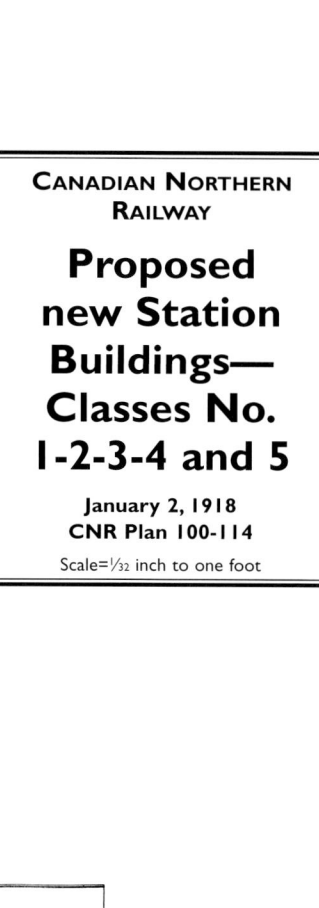

Canadian Northern Railway

Proposed new Station Buildings— Classes No. 1-2-3-4 and 5

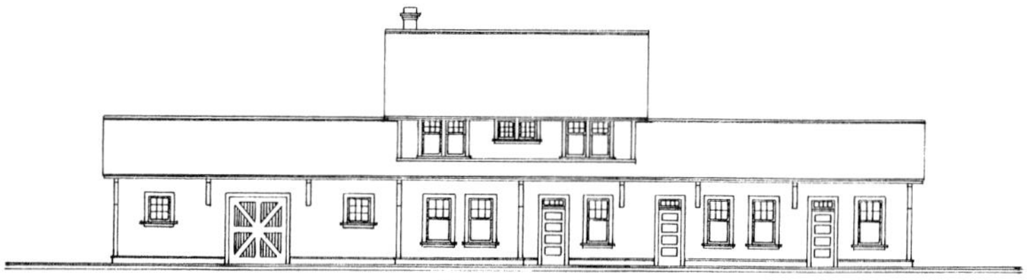

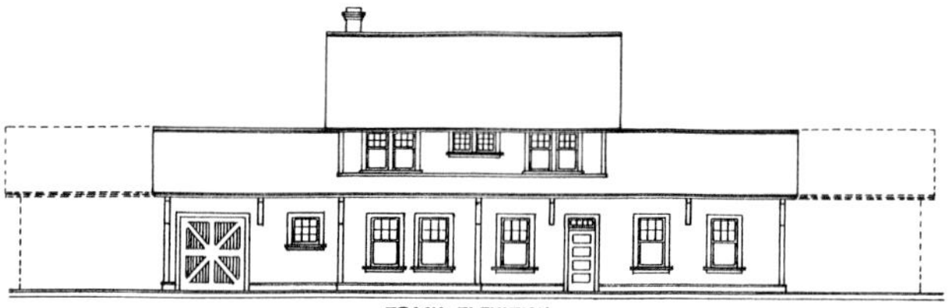

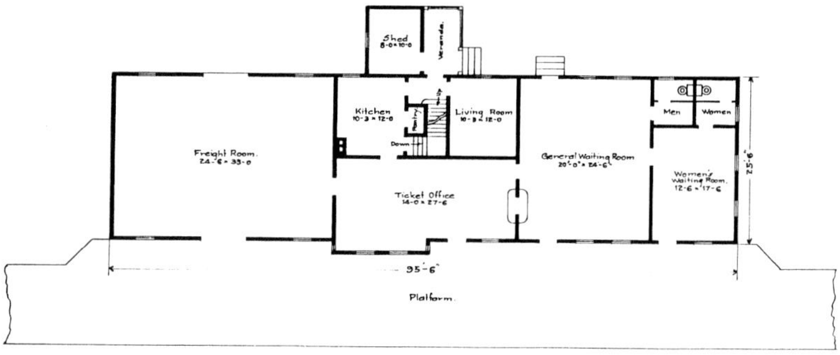

January 2, 1918
CNR Plan 100-114

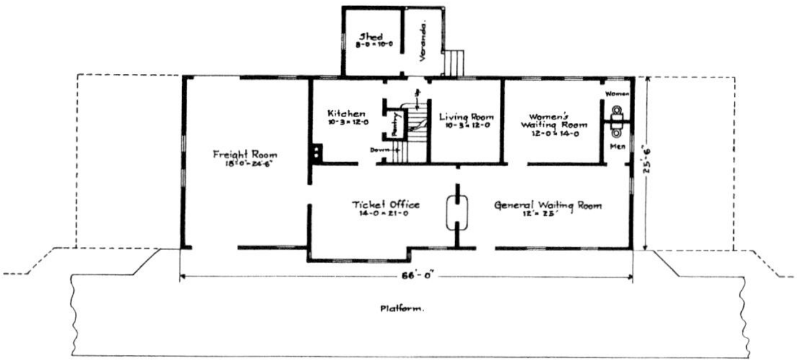

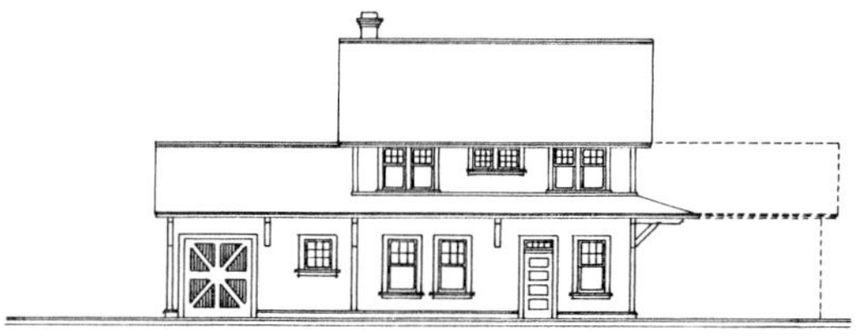

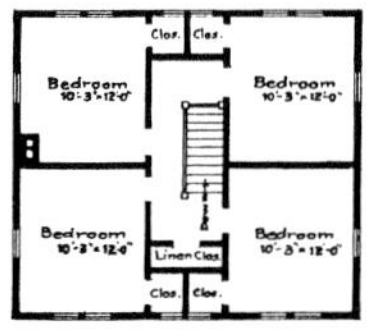

Scale = 1/32 inch to one foot

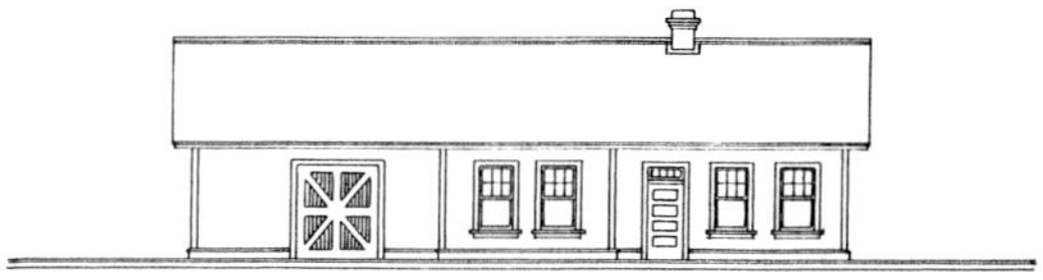

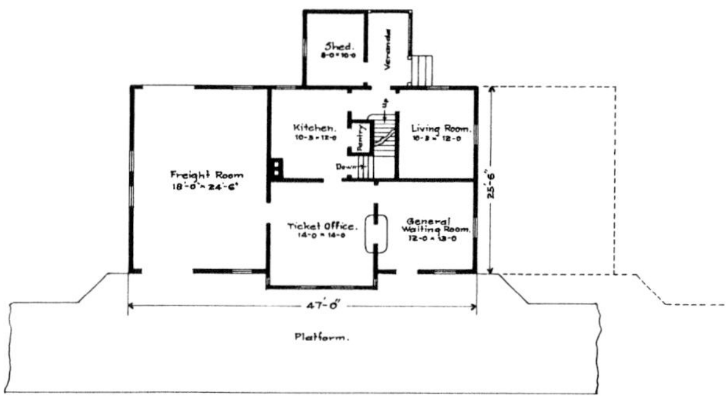

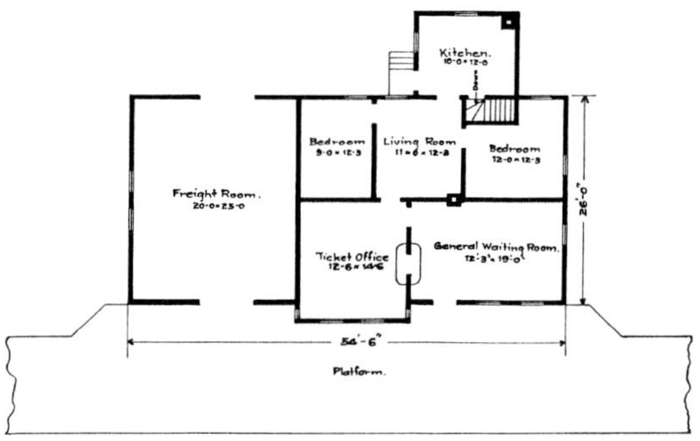

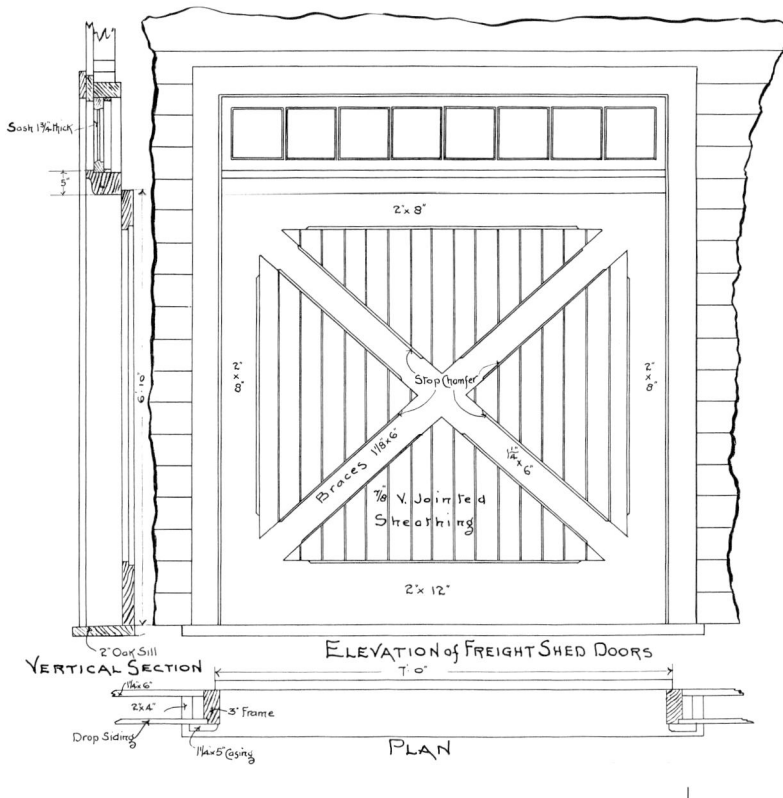

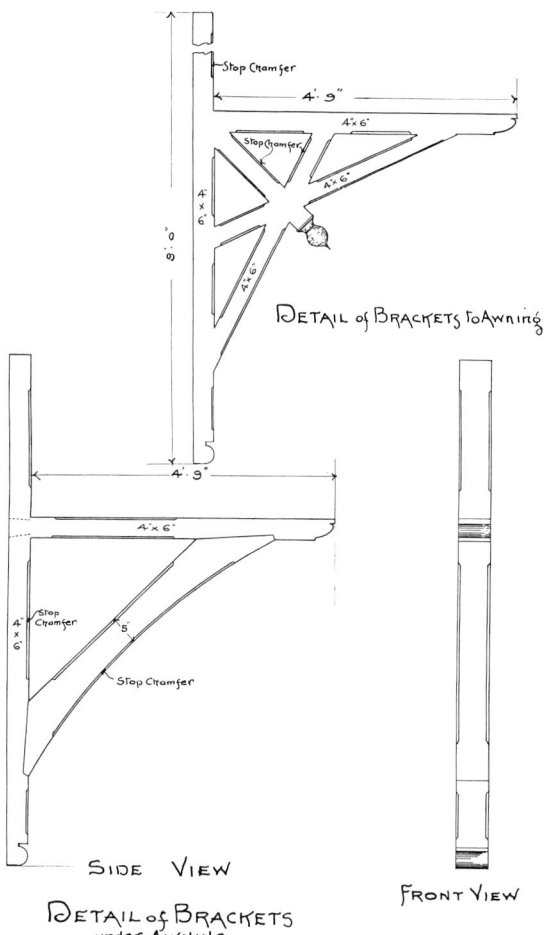

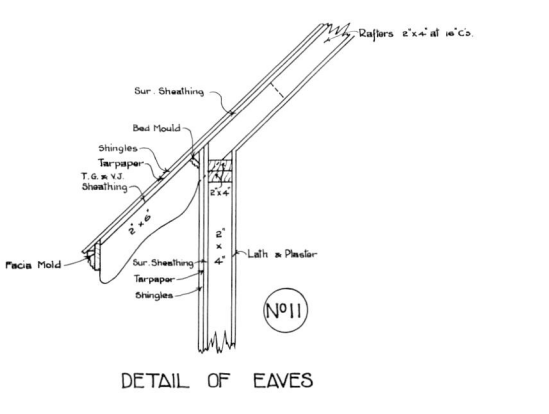

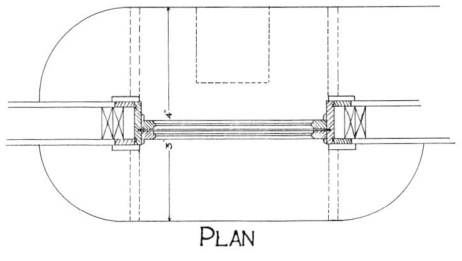

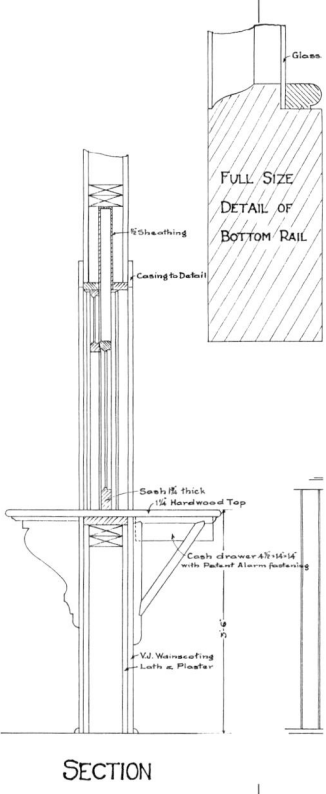

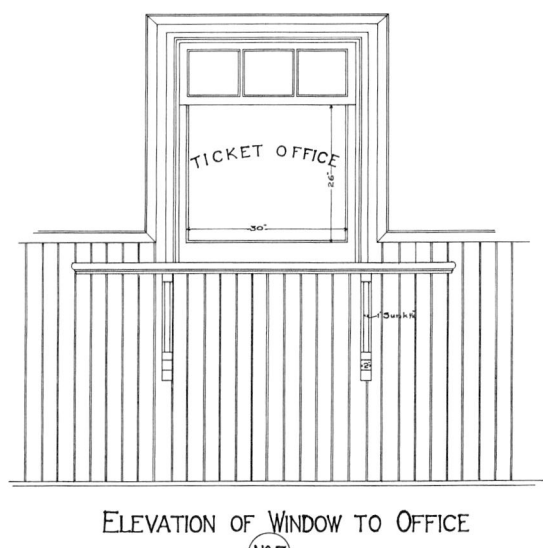

Canadian Northern Railway

Details for Station Buildings

September 1901
December 1912 &
October 28, 1913
CNR Plan 100-9

Original drawing scale=1 inch to one foot, reproduced at ⅓ original size

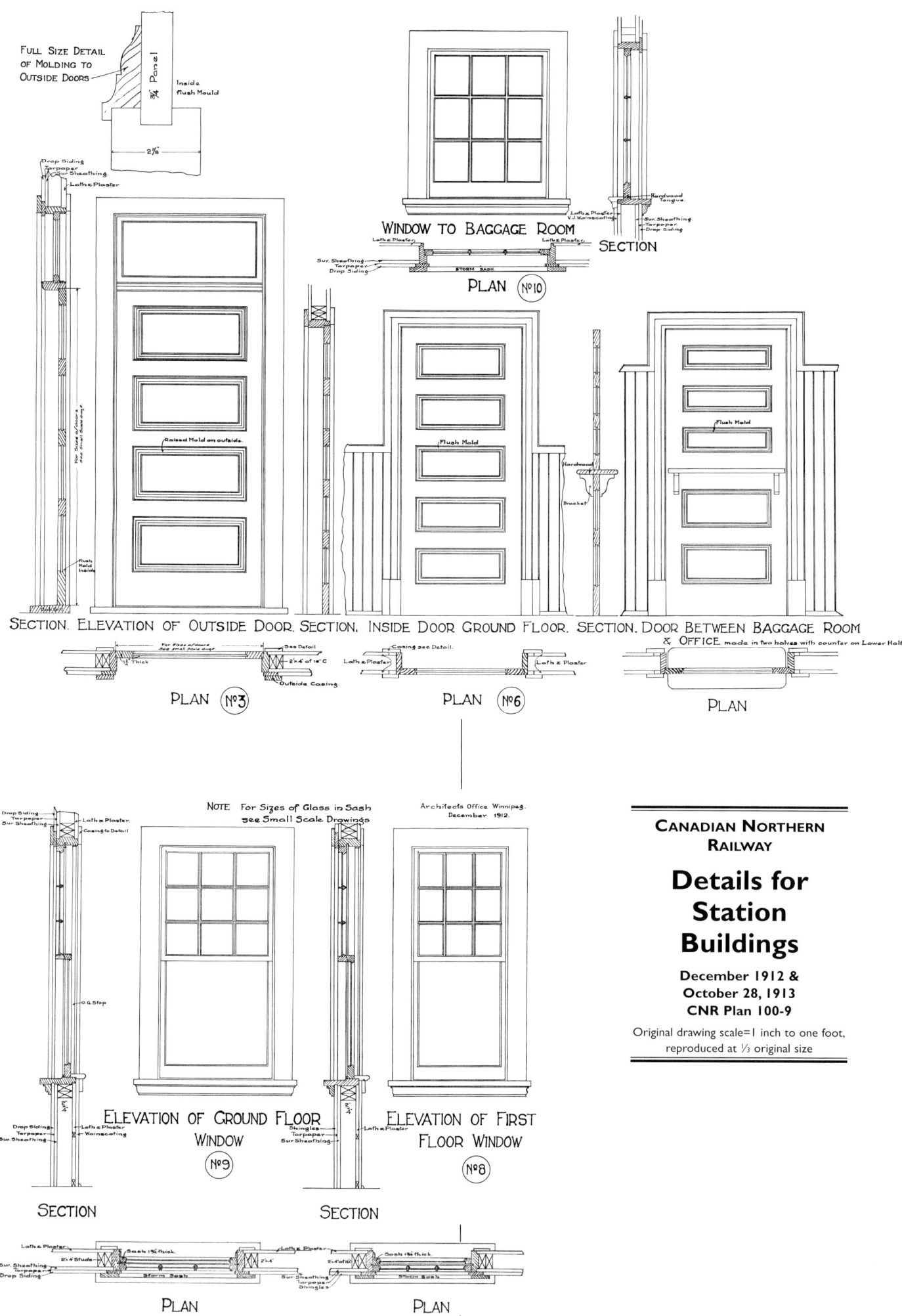

Index

Amaranth, Man. (CNoR) 21
Ashern, Man. (CNoR) 26

Barlow Jct., Alta. (CNoR) 19
Barriere, BC #2 (CNR) 20
Bellis, Alta. 50
Big Valley, Alta. (CNoR) 38
Bjorkdale, Sask (CNR) 21
Brandon North, Man. (CNR) 60
Briercrest, Sask. (CNoR) 28

Calgary, Alta. #1 (CNoR) 18
Calgary, Alta. (GTP) 19
Carman, Man. (CNoR) 6
Cooking Lake, Alta. (GTP) 26

Deerholme, BC (CNR) 56
Delburne, Alta. (GTP) 29
Dugald, Man. (NTR) 31
Duperow, Sask. #2 (GTP) 31

Edmonton, Alta. #4 (CNR) 61
Edson, Alta. (CNR) 41
Elie, Man. (GTP) 46
Elma, Man. (NTR) 52
Entrance, Alta. (CNoR) 22
Erickson, Man. (CNoR) 58
Eriksdale, Man. (CNoR) 32

Fabyan, Alta. #2 (CNR) 33
Falkland, BC (CNR) 34
Fort Frances, Ont. #1 & #2 (CNoR) 36

Gladstone, Man. (CNoR) 59
Grosse Isle, Man. (CNoR) 51
Gypsumville, Man. (CNoR) 55

Harte, Man. (GTP) 30
Hartney, Man. (NP) 24
Hodgson, Man. (CNoR) 51
Hope, BC (CNR) 38
Hyas, Sask. (CNR) 57

Janet, Alta. (CNoR) 15
Jasper, Alta. (CNoR) 37
Jasper, Alta. #3 (CNR) 42

Kelowna, BC (CNR) 43
Kelwood, Man. (CNoR) 53
Kitimat, BC (CNR) 54
Kwinitsa, BC (GTP) 160

Lebret, Sask. (GTP) 54

Miami, Man. (NP) 25
Minitonas, Man. (CNoR) 55
Minto, Man. (NP/CNoR) 27
Moose Jaw, Sask. (GTP) (proposed) 42
Mount Robson, BC (CNR) 16

Neepawa, Man. (CNoR) 56
New Hazelton, BC (GTP) 30
Ninette, Man. (NP) 24
Nipigon, Ont. (CNoR) 33
North Battleford, Sask. #3 (CNR) 45
North Edmonton, Alta. (CNoR) 59
Notre Dame de Lourdes, Man. (CNoR) 62

Ochre River, Man. (CNoR) 53

Pollockville, Alta. (CNoR) 49
Porcupine Plain, Sask. (CNR) 57
Prairie River, Sask. #1 (CNoR) 15
Prince Albert, Sask. #2 (CNoR) 36
Prince Albert, Sask. (GTP) 43

Quinton, Sask #1 (GTP) 13

Rabbit Lake, Sask. (CNR) 52
Rausch Valley, BC (GTP) 23
Roosevelt, Minn. (CNoR) 27
Rorketon, Man. (CNR) 34

Ste. Rose, Man. (CNR) 35
Saskatoon, Sask. #2 (CNoR) 44
Saskatoon, Sask. #3 (CNR) 45
Scott, Sask. #1 (GTP) 28
Semans, Sask. (GTP) 6
Shellmouth, Man. (CNoR) 1, 64
Sioux Lookout, Ont. (NTR) 61
Smithers, BC (GTP) 41
Smoky Lake, Alta. (CNoR) 32, 46
Stratton, Ont. (CNoR) 13
Swan River, Man. (CNoR) 22

Telkwa, BC #1 (GTP) 16
Turtleford, Sask (CNoR) 5

Underhill, Man. (CNoR) 8
Unity, Sask. (GTP) 58

Valley River, Man. (CNoR) 14
Vermillion, Alta. (CNoR) 49
Vilna, Alta. (CNoR) 10
Virginia, Minn. (DW&P) 44

Wadena, Sask. (CNoR) 49
Wainwright, Alta. #1 (GTP) 39
Waskatenau, Alta. #2 (CNR) 35
Wawanesa, Man. (NP) 25
Wiseton, Sask. (CNoR) 62
Wolf Creek, Alta. (GTP) 14
Wroxton, Sask. (CNoR) 62

Yonker, Sask. (GTP) 17

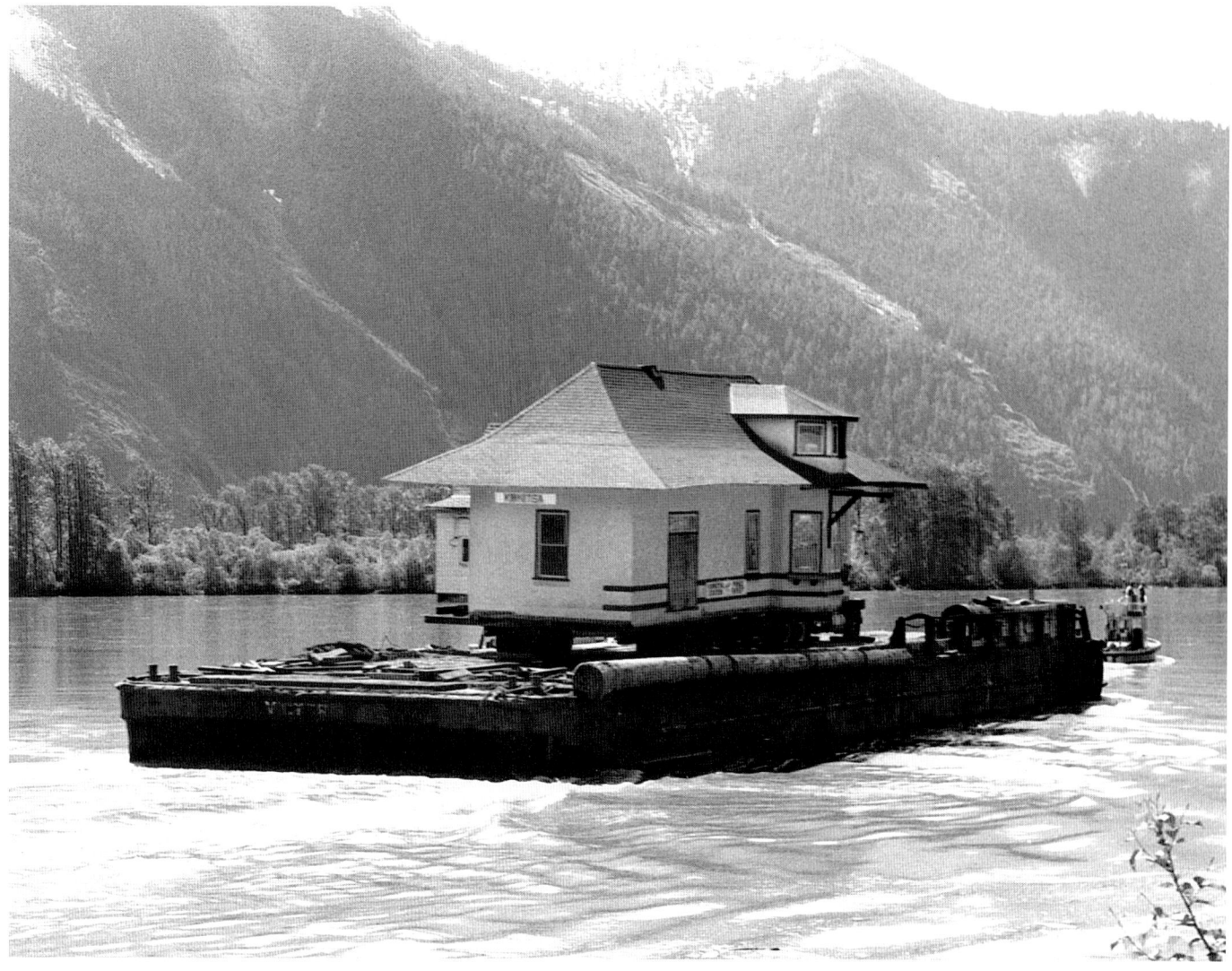

GTP Kwinitsa, British Columbia (CN Photo), July 1, 1985

On July 1, 1985, the Kwinitsa, BC Type E station was relocated to Prince Rupert. Since the building was too wide to be transported the entire distance by road or rail, it was loaded onto a truck, taken onto a barge waiting on the Kwinitsa River, thence floated down the Skeena River, reaching its new home in a few hours. At Prince Rupert it was set up on a temporary foundation near the shore and opened as a museum. The foundations became unstable, so in 1996 the depot was relocated farther up the bank.

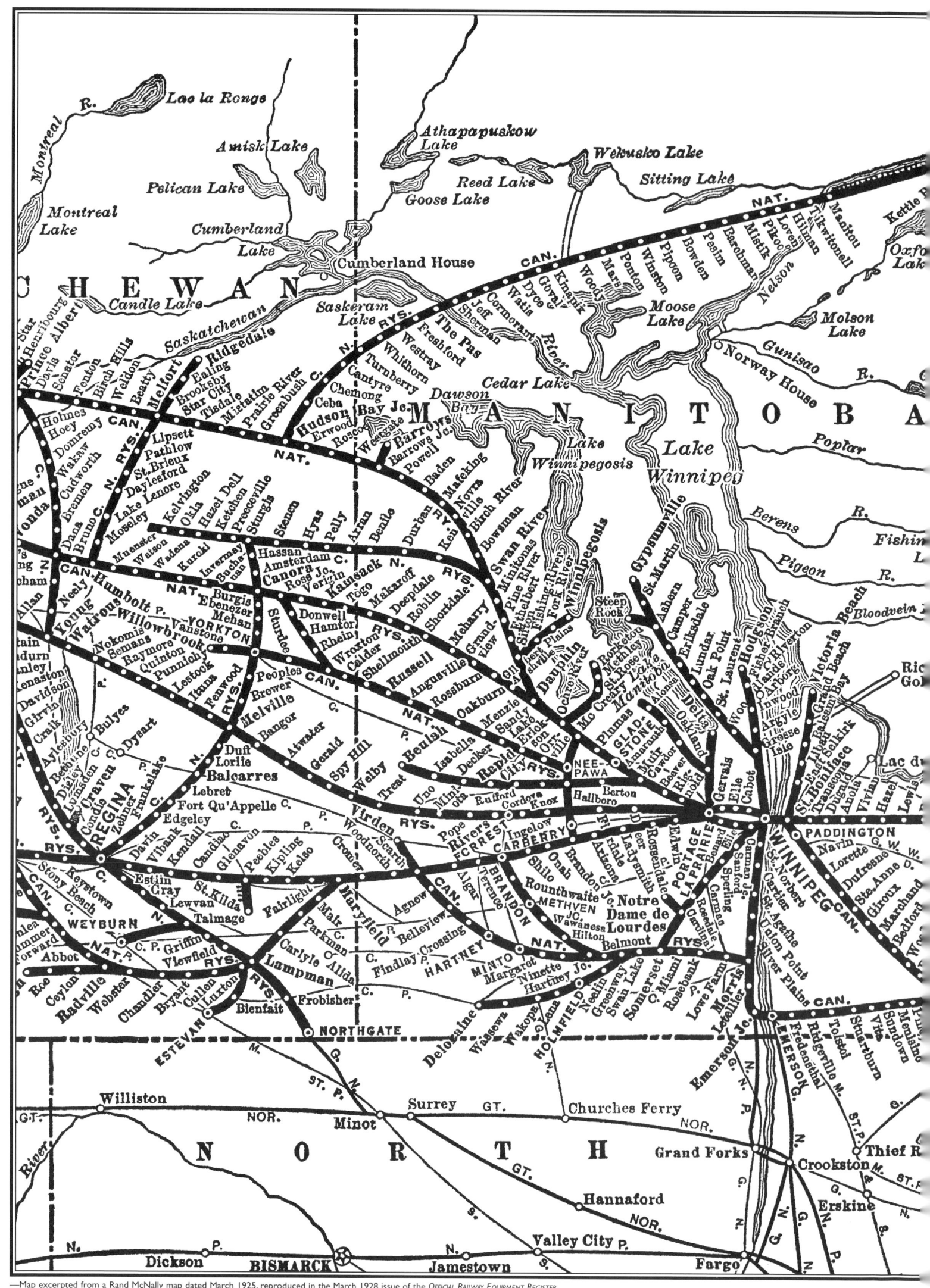

—Map excerpted from a Rand McNally map dated March 1925, reproduced in the March 1928 issue of the *Official Railway Equipment Register*